David Thompson's Narrative of His Explorations in Western America

THE PUBLICATIONS OF
THE CHAMPLAIN
SOCIETY

XII

THE
PUBLICATIONS OF
THE CHAMPLAIN
SOCIETY

DAVID THOMPSON'S
NARRATIVE

TORONTO
THE CHAMPLAIN SOCIETY

DAVID THOMPSON'S
NARRATIVE
OF HIS EXPLORATIONS IN
WESTERN AMERICA
1784-1812

EDITED BY

J. B. TYRRELL

TORONTO
THE CHAMPLAIN SOCIETY
1916

CONTENTS

CONTENTS

CONTENTS

LIST OF ILLUSTRATIONS

LIST OF MAPS AND PLANS

xiii

PREFACE

THE account here published of the explorations of David Thompson in the western parts of Canada and the United States was written by Thompson himself when he was about seventy years old and still in the full possession of all his faculties, but after the active part of his life-work was completed and when he had retired to Montreal in the hope of enjoying his remaining years in quietude. While he was writing this history of the portion of his life in which he undoubtedly took the most interest, he kept his note-books before him, and with their assistance he retraced the scenes through which he had passed in the days of his youth and strength. He tells his story with an accuracy that has rarely been equalled in the case of an old man who is recounting the experiences of his younger days. I have carefully compared his narrative with his note-books, written by him from day to day as he travelled through the country, and in comparatively few instances were discrepancies found; where these occur they are indicated in the notes at the bottom of the pages.

Part II of the Narrative covers in detail the years 1807 to 1812, which were spent as a partner in the North-West Company in the provinces of Alberta and British Columbia, and the states of Montana, Idaho, and Washington, while Part I is a more general account of his life while in the employ of the Hudson's Bay and North-West Companies between the years 1784 and 1807, in the country from Lake Superior and Hudson Bay westward to the Rocky Mountains. It must be clearly understood, however, that this narrative tells but a small part of the work accomplished by Thompson during those twenty-eight years, being confined to a general account of his travels and of the people and things encountered by him.   But Thompson, besides being an excellent traveller, was an exceedingly accurate and methodical surveyor, and his original note-books are largely occupied with mathematical records of his surveys and of the astronomical observations by which he filled out and checked those surveys.   At the same time they include extensive meteorological data and partial vocabularies of many of the Indian tribes among whom he dwelt.

The main features of his geographical work are recorded on the large map reproduced with this volume, but the minor topographic details, with which his note-books are overflowing, can only be appreciated by reference to the note-books themselves.   In the Itinerary, which I have included as a second part of the Introduction in this volume, a bald statement of the journeys and surveys accomplished by Thompson has been given in detail year by year, without any attempt at recording the incidents of his journeys.   A thorough understanding of this Itinerary will make his own account more interesting and intelligible.

The reader will quickly see that Thompson was a man of great natural ability and strong moral character.   His school education had ceased when he was only fourteen years of age, but he had been taught to spell and write, for his early handwriting is beautifully distinct and regular, and his spelling is remarkably good for the time and circumstances in which he lived.   In character he was bold and fearless of consequences, and therefore he early assumed the leadership among his associates.   This was shown when the traders and clerks in the Hudson's Bay Company, under the jurisdiction of York Factory, were smarting under the obloquy heaped on them by Joseph Colen, their Chief, and were afraid to protest against such treatment until Thompson arrived from the interior to lead them, although he was probably the youngest among them.

He was constantly occupied, either mentally or physically. Inactivity was utterly repugnant to him, but his activity was always directed to some definite and useful purpose. He worked hard to perform his duty as he saw it, and when it was accomplished he gave the product of his work freely to others, for there was no trace of self-seeking or vainglory in his nature.

The second part of Thompson's great life-work was performed when, as Astronomer to the International Boundary Commission under the Treaty of Ghent, he surveyed the boundary line between British North America (Canada) and the United States from St. Regis, Quebec, where the 45th parallel of latitude strikes the St. Lawrence river, to the north-west angle of the Lake of the Woods. This task was accomplished between 1816 and 1826, and is not dealt with in this volume.

The Narrative is here printed just as it was written by Thompson himself, except that for the convenience of the reader the liberty has been taken of altering the punctuation slightly and of introducing some capital letters. In the manuscript as received by me, several of the chapters of Part I had been written twice in somewhat different form, and in each case the one that appeared to have most merit has been printed. However, only one set of Contents was prepared by Thompson for these chapters, and in the case of Chapter XX it has been necessary to use the contents of the chapter that has not been printed for the one that has been printed.

This narrative remained in Thompson's hands until his death in 1857, after which it passed to one of his sons, who sold it to the late Mr. Charles Lindsey of Toronto. Mr. Lindsey intended to edit it, and made a partial use of it in preparing an account of the " Extent of Country which the

North-West Company occupied " in his *Investigation of the Unsettled Boundaries of Ontario* (pp. 225-45), but he found himself constantly hampered by a want of personal knowledge of the country described, and finally he decided not to proceed with the publication of the book.

My interest in Thompson's work began in 1883 and the following years, when, as a Geologist on the staff of the Geological Survey of Canada, I was travelling in or near the Rocky Mountains, and was making maps on which to record my geological investigations. In conducting these surveys the number of places with names of unknown origin, and the accuracy of the main features of the maps then in use, greatly impressed me. In searching for the sources of this geographical information the late Mr. Andrew Russell, Assistant Commissioner of Crown Lands for the province of Ontario, advised me of the existence of Thompson's map and note-books in the possession of the Crown Lands Department of the province of Ontario. After making such examination of these note-books as was then possible, at which time, however, I was unable to find Volume XI, which contains many of the notes of his surveys west of the Rocky Mountains, and especially of his journeys to the mouth of the Columbia river, I published a *Brief Narrative of the Journeys of David Thompson* in the Proceedings of the Canadian Institute, Toronto, 3rd section, vol. vi, 1887-88, pp. 135-60.

After the publication of this paper, Mr. Charles Lindsey wrote to me and told me of the existence of the Narrative here published, and very kindly offered to allow me to inspect it. Some years later I purchased it from him. Shortly after purchasing it, I removed to Dawson in the Yukon Territory, and it was not until my return to Toronto in 1906 that it was possible for me to undertake seriously the study of this journal which had been lying untouched for nearly ten years.

Between the years 1883 and 1898, while engaged on the

staff of the Geological Survey of Canada, it fell to my lot to
carry on explorations in canoes, on horseback, or on foot, over
many of the routes which had been surveyed and explored
by David Thompson a century before, to survey the rivers
that he had surveyed, to measure the portages on which he
had walked, to cross the plains and mountains on the trails
which he had travelled, to camp on his old camping grounds,
and to take astronomical observations on the same places
where he had taken them. Everywhere his work was found
to be of the very highest order, considering the means and
facilities at his disposal, and as my knowledge of his achieve-
ments widened, my admiration for this fur-trading geographer
increased, and in order to show my appreciation of the
splendid work which he did I decided to offer this narrative
to the public. My original intention was to abbreviate, and
partly rewrite it, in the hope of being able to reduce it to
somewhat more popular form, and with that object in view
my wife assisted me until it was almost ready for the printer.
Just at this time, however, the Council of the Champlain
Society learned of its existence, and offered to publish it in
its original form, and also to take the burden of reading and
revising proofs, preparing index, etc., off my hands. This
offer was accepted, and the present volume, with its wealth of
new information about Western America, is issued with the
hope that it may assist in confirming David Thompson in
his rightful place as one of the greatest geographers of the
world.

There is no portrait of Thompson in existence, but Mrs.
Shaw, his daughter, once handed me an old print of John
Bunyan, saying that the picture was as good a likeness of her
father as if it had actually been taken of him.

There is not even a monument marking the last resting-
place of this great geographer. It is not creditable to
Canadians, proud as we are of our country and its limitless
natural possibilities, that this pioneer who did so much

without remuneration to render the country known to us and others should remain neglected. The least that we could do as a token of our respect for the man and his work would be to erect a statue to him in some prominent place in the capital of the Dominion.

In the notes and Introduction, in spelling the names of Indian tribes, I have followed the *Handbook of the Indians of Canada*, issued by the Commission of Conservation of the Government of Canada, and in regard to geographic names of natural features I have followed the decision of the Geographic Board of Canada, but in speaking of places occupied by Thompson, and not since known by any other name, I have used the spelling which he adopted. This will account for such apparent discrepancies as Kootanae House, the Kutenai Indians, and Kootenay river.

I wish to express my deep indebtedness to Sir Edmund Walker, who has given his careful attention to every detail in connection with the preparation of the book for the press, and to Mr. W. S. Wallace, one of the editors of the publications of the Champlain Society, who has faithfully carried out its engagements to me in correcting proofs, preparing the index, and assisting in the revision of the manuscript of the Introduction and notes.

While engaged in the preparation of the notes the government of the province of Ontario, and Dr. Alexander Fraser, the Provincial Archivist, kindly loaned me Thompson's original note-books, so that I have been able to examine them carefully in such spare time as has been at my disposal.

In compiling the notes on the country west of the mountains I have been especially fortunate in securing the assistance of Mr. T. C. Elliott, of Walla Walla, Washington, U.S.A., who is intimately acquainted with the early history of the north-western states and especially of the Columbia valley. He was kind enough to visit me in Toronto, where we had the pleasure of reading over Thompson's original note-books together. His notes throughout are signed with his initials, T. C. E.

Mr. E. A. Preble, of the Biological Survey Department of Agriculture, Washington, D.C., U.S.A., has very kindly added notes on the animals and plants mentioned by Thompson, thus greatly adding to the scientific value of the book. His notes are signed with his initials, E. A. P.

I am also indebted to Mr. James White, Deputy Head of the Commission of Conservation for Canada, of Ottawa, for assistance, advice and notes, and also for permission to publish Thompson's large map from a tracing which he had had made, for it was found quite impossible to reproduce the old faded yellow original by any mechanical process.

I also desire to thank Miss Shaw, Thompson's granddaughter, Miss Elsie Day, Messrs. G. R. Ray, A. C. McNab, J. Meyers, and others for kind assistance in supplying information about Thompson or the country through which he travelled.

J. B. TYRRELL.

TORONTO,
April 19, 1915.

INTRODUCTION

DAVID THOMPSON, the author of this hitherto unpublished manuscript, was born in the parish of St. John the Evangelist, Westminster, England, on April 30, 1770, and was baptized on May 20 of the same year. The parish register gives the names of his parents as " David Thompson and Ann his wife," though it gives no information as to their antecedents or the time or place of their marriage. On subsequent pages of the register, however, it is recorded that another son, named John, was born to David Thompson and Ann his wife on January 25, 1772, and was baptized on February 16 of the same year. The next and last record that has been discovered about the family is of the death of David Thompson, doubtless the father, on February 28, 1772. Opposite his name no burial fee is entered, a fact which shows that he was buried at the expense of the parish. Mrs. Shaw, one of Thompson's daughters, informed the writer that her father's brother John, who was a sea captain, had once visited her father in Montreal. She also said that her grandparents came from Wales, and that their family name was originally Ap-Thomas, but that it had been changed to Thompson on going to London. In this connection, it is interesting to notice that late in life the speech of David Thompson the younger was remarked by an observer to betray his Welsh origin.[1]

On April 29, 1777, when just seven years of age, David Thompson entered the Grey Coat School, Westminster. This

---

[1] J. J. Bigsby, *The Shoe and Canoe*, London, 1850, vol. i. p. 113.

interesting old school [1] is now, and has been since its re-
organisation by the Endowed Schools Commission in 1873, a
charity school for girls. It may still be seen by the visitor,
some five minutes' walk from Westminster Abbey : an old
red house, built in the Elizabethan manner, covered at the
back with grape-vine and Virginia creeper, and surrounded
by a large garden and playground. But in 1777 it was a
school devoted to the education of poor boys : its "principall
designe" was "to educate poor children in the principles of
piety and virtue, and thereby lay a foundation for a sober
and Christian life." The early training which David
Thompson received within the walls of this school coloured
his whole career, and marked him off in later life from the
dissolute traders and *voyageurs* among whom his lot was cast.

Some years ago the opportunity of visiting this school
presented itself, and Miss Day, the head mistress, kindly
allowed me the privilege of inspecting the old minute-book
of the meetings of the Board of Governors of the school, in
which are to be found the following entries relating to David
Thompson. Under the date of Tuesday, April 29, 1777, his
admission to the school is recorded :

"Abram Acworth, Esq. was this day pleased to present David
Thompson to be admitted into this Hosp[l] on y[e] Foundation and y[e]
Governors present being satisfy with y[e] said child's settlement. Ord[d]
that he be admitted on bringing in the usual necessaries."

Over six years later, at a quarterly meeting of the Board held
on Tuesday, December 30, 1783, the name of David Thompson
reappears in the minutes :

"The Master also reports that application was made by the Secretary belonging to the Hudson's Bay Company, to know, if this Charity
could furnish them with 4 boys against the month of May next, for
their settlements in America. The Master, by order of the Treas[r]

---

[1] For an account of the school, see a paper entitled *An Old Westminster
Endowment*, by Miss Elsie Day, in the *Journal of Education*, September,
1885.

wrote a letter informing the Governor and Directors that there were
but two boys that had been taught navigation in the school, which
two boys they desire may be qualified for them, viz : Samuel John
McPherson and David Thompson."

Samuel John McPherson was evidently averse to being sent
away to America, for he " elop^d from this Hospital on the
7th Jan^y " following, and as he did not return he was ex-
pelled ; but David Thompson accepted the fate for which
the Governors of the school had destined him. In the
minutes of the quarterly meeting of the Board of Governors
of the school, held on Tuesday, June 29, 1784, his apprentice-
ship to the Hudson's Bay Company is recorded :

" David Thompson bound to the Secretary of the Hudson's Bay Company for seven years & paid.	On the 20th May David Thompson, a mathematical Boy belonging to the Hosp^l was bound to the Hudson's Bay Company & the Trea^r then paid Mr Thos. Hutchins, Corresponding Secretary to the said Company, the sum of five pounds for taking the said Boy appren^ce for seven years."	5 ———

David Thompson was thus a pupil in the Grey Coat
School for seven years (1777–84). During this time his
mathematical master was one Thomas Adams, of whom
nothing further is known, and the sort of teaching which the
poor child received may be judged from the following list of
books, many of them then nearly a hundred years old, from
which he was taught :

Wallis, *Mechanics*	. published	1655
Wallis, *A Treatise of Algebra* . . .	„	1685
Thesaurus Geographicus	„	1695
Leybourn, *Dialling*	„	1682
Leybourn, *Mathematical Institutions* . .	„	1704
Gordon, *Geography Anatomized* . . .	„	1716
Atkinson, *Epitome of the Art of Navigation* .	„	1711
Newton, *An Idea of Geography* . . .	„	1708
Barlow, *A Survey of the Tide* . . .	„	1717

From such books as these, David Thompson received the preparation for his life-work in surveying the northern forests and plains of America.

David Thompson sailed from London in May, 1784, in the Hudson's Bay Company's ship *Prince Rupert*, and arrived at Churchill in the beginning of September. Here he took up his quarters in the new trading establishment that had just been built on the site which is still occupied by the trading store of the Hudson's Bay Company ; for Fort Prince of Wales, the great stone fort five miles away at the mouth of the river, had been taken and burned by the French two years before. He spent the winter of 1784–85 under Samuel Hearne, the traveller who, fifteen years before, had started from Churchill on foot with a few Indians to discover and explore a "mine" of copper near the Coppermine river, and incidentally to set at rest the question of the existence or non-existence of a practicable passage for ships around the north coast of America from Europe to Asia. Although he does not appear to have been imbued with any admiration for Hearne's character—for Thompson was a very devout man, and Hearne an unbeliever—the intimate knowledge gained of Hearne's journeyings must have been more or less of an inspiration to him throughout his after life.

After the arrival of the annual ship at Churchill in 1785, Thompson was sent to York Factory, the journey being accomplished on foot, along with two Indians, on the low shore of Hudson Bay. This was his first experience of travel in the North-West, and evidently the memory of it remained clear and distinct in his mind. A growing boy, fifteen years old, set down on the inhospitable shore of Hudson Bay in the autumn of the year, without provisions, and with instructions to walk to another fur-trading station a hundred and fifty miles away, was not likely to forget the journey.

York Factory, like Fort Prince of Wales, had been taken and burned by the French in 1782, and as, unlike Fort Prince of Wales, it was built entirely of wood, the burning had completely destroyed it. When the fort was destroyed, Humphrey Marten, the officer in charge for the Hudson's Bay Company, had been carried away prisoner by the French, but in the following year, that is in 1783, he had returned and rebuilt a trading house on the site of the one that had been burned, half a mile below the position on which York Factory stands to-day. By this time Marten had been in charge of York Factory, or some other trading post of the Hudson's Bay Company, for twenty-four years, and had become so rough and overbearing that life under him must have been anything but agreeable. Edward Umfreville, who spent seven years as a clerk under him before the destruction of York Factory, says that he used to beat the Indians most cruelly, and thus drive them away burning with revenge. He was respected neither by the Indians, nor " by those who were so unfortunate as to serve under him. His disposition was vindictive and unsociable to the last degree. English, as well as Indians, felt the weight of his oppressive temper, which diffused its corroding effect to every object. Domestic happiness was a stranger to his table, and his messmates lived a most unhappy life, under the rod of this unrelenting taskmaster." [1]

Thompson arrived at York about September 13, and the two Indians were rewarded for the care that they had taken of him on the journey by a present of three gallons of brandy and four pounds of tobacco. He now settled down at York for a year, his principal companions, besides Marten, being Joseph Colen, John Ballenden, Alfred Robinson, and John Jennings. The accounts for the year are in his neat handwriting. Besides doing clerical work, he assisted in the trading store, and at the same time was an indefatigable hunter, and thus materially assisted in supplying his companions with geese, ducks, and such other game as abounded in the vicinity.

[1] Edward Umfreville, *The Present State of Hudson's Bay*, London, 1790, pp. 91-2.

As shown in the Servants' Accounts, his purchases from the Company for the year amounted to £6, 12s. 9d., but in contrast with most of the other accounts, none of this was for brandy.

The year 1786 was a time of commotion among the employees of the Hudson's Bay Company on the shore of the Bay. Humphrey Marten had been recalled to England, and Joseph Colen was appointed as Resident Chief at York in his place. William Tomison, a Scotchman from Ronaldshay, had been "Chief Inland" for some years, and had resigned, but on Colen's accession to command at York had withdrawn his resignation and had decided to go back to the Saskatchewan, with Robert Longmore[1] as principal lieutenant. Malcolm Ross, who was afterwards closely associated with Thompson, was being sent up the Churchill river from Churchill to endeavour to open up a direct route from that post to Cumberland House on the Saskatchewan river. At the same time more trading posts were being established on the Saskatchewan river by the brigades from York itself, in order to compete with the Canadian traders. The establishment of these posts had been delayed first by the epidemic of smallpox in 1781, and then by the destruction of Forts York and Churchill (or Prince of Wales) in 1782.

On July 21, 1786, after having remained a year at York, Thompson was fitted out with a trunk, a handkerchief, shoes, shirts, a gun, powder, and a tin pot or cup, and the next day he, with forty-six other "Englishmen" in charge of Robert Longmore, started inland up the Hayes river to establish more trading posts on the Saskatchewan river, above Hudson's

---

[1] Robert Longmore was a trader in the employ of the Hudson's Bay Company for many years. He was in charge of the brigade of canoes with which Thompson first went inland in 1786, and afterwards in 1799 was Master at Swan River, with a salary of £70 a year. Samuel Hearne wrote of him in 1786, "He possesses a very essential qualification, which is, that of being universally beloved by the natives. To add to this, his long residence in those parts [the Saskatchewan country], together with an invariable attention to the Company's interests, must long since have made him a competent judge of their affairs in that quarter."

House, which appears to have been the most remote post of the Hudson's Bay Company occupied at that time. Tomison remained behind at York Factory till August 30, when, with two young men, Hugh Folster and Magnus Tate, and one Indian, he followed the brigade with its loaded canoes to the Saskatchewan. The party ascended the North Saskatchewan river to a point on its northern bank, forty-two miles above Battleford and twelve miles north of the present station of Birling on the Canadian Northern Railway, where they cleared the ground and built a trading post composed of one or more log houses, probably surrounded by a wooden stockade. When completed, they dignified this collection of huts with the name of Manchester House.

Edward Umfreville, who had once been employed by the Hudson's Bay Company as a clerk or writer at York Factory, but who was now in the employ of the North-West Company, had been occupying a similar trading store for the past three years at a point forty miles farther up the river, but as far as we know there were no white men beyond him, and it was not until three years later that Peter Pangman, one of the partners of the North-West Company, ascended the Saskatchewan as far as Rocky Mountain House, so that young Thompson had now reached almost to the very limit of the country with which civilised men were familiar on the Saskatchewan at that time. Far to the north and north-west there were a couple of trading posts on the Churchill and Athabaska rivers in charge of such men as Alexander Mackenzie and Peter Pond, but to the south and west was a great unknown wilderness inhabited only by the native Indians.

It was a time of strenuous opposition in the fur trade between the English traders from Hudson Bay and the Scotch traders with French employees from Montreal, and some of these latter evidently came and settled near Manchester House, for Thompson makes incidental mention in his journal

of these traders who were opposed to his employers. The
Company was working hard to secure furs wherever they
might be found, and the Blackfeet and Piegan Indians who
roamed over the plains to the south brought quite a few
wolf skins to the traders, and with care it was hoped they
might be taught to catch beaver and some of the other more
valuable fur-bearing animals. It was therefore necessary to
send some one out among these Indians to gain their friendship and to secure their trade, and Thompson and six others
were chosen for the enterprise. The party travelled south-
westward to the Bow river, probably to somewhere in the
vicinity of the present city of Calgary, where there was a
large camp of Piegan. Here, after sending some of his men
back to Manchester House, he settled down for the greater
part of the winter in the tent of an old Chief named Saukamappee, and the friendship of this chief, though it did not
always prevent trouble, stood him in good stead many times
in his after life. Some of the stories and traditions of the
Indians which he obtained at the time form an interesting
part of the present book.

This was Thompson's first introduction to the great
plains, and as he went to them so young, being then only
seventeen years old, he evidently got a thorough, sympathetic
conception of the natural untainted life and habits of the
western Indians who wandered over them.

Some time during the following winter or spring he
returned to the trading post on the Saskatchewan river,
and later he descended the river for about one hundred and
twenty-five miles to an older trading post called Hudson's
House, which had been built by Tomison some years before.
This post was situated a short distance above the present city
of Prince Albert, three or four miles below a place now known
as ' Yellow Banks,' on the edge of a forest of spruce and pine.
The Blackfoot tribes of the plains would hardly be likely to
come to a place so far east and so completely surrounded by

forest as this was, so that the Indians whom he would meet here would probably be Cree and Assiniboin.

The only thing we know about him during the following summer is that in some way he had the misfortune to break his right leg; and through improper setting, or for some other reason, this accident caused him considerable discomfort for some years.

Towards the end of summer, he again continued down the river, on this occasion as far as Cumberland House on Pine Island lake, a post that had been built by Samuel Hearne, his former master at Fort Churchill, fifteen years before, with the object of intercepting the Indians who were coming down with their furs from the Athabaska and Churchill river regions, and of preventing them, if possible, from disposing of these furs to the Frobishers and the other traders who came west from Montreal.

He was at this time nineteen years old. It is evident that he had always been interested in surveying and in observing and recording natural phenomena, so when he had settled down for the winter he began to keep a careful meteorological journal in which were noted the readings of the thermometer three or four times a day, the direction and force of the wind, and general remarks on the climate. During this same winter he took also a series of astronomical observations, six being meridian altitudes of the sun for latitude, and thirty-five lunar distances for longitude. The results of the observations place Cumberland House in north latitude 53° 56′ 44″, and west longitude 102° 13′, a position almost identical with that which it occupies to-day on the latest official maps. When one considers the nautical almanacs that were available at that time, this result is quite astonishing and puts to shame much even of the good observing of the present day. At that time there were very few other points on this whole continent of America whose positions on the earth's surface were as accurately known as this remote trading post on the Saskatchewan river. On the maps of Canada its position has been changed many times, but the latest surveys have brought it back to the place to which it was assigned by this young astronomer one hundred and twenty-five years ago.

Such was the beginning of his long career of geodetic surveying which was to make him the greatest practical land geographer that the world has produced. Very few men have had the opportunity of exploring the half of a great new continent, and no one else has ever seized the opportunity as David Thompson did. For many thousands of miles, in pursuit of my work when engaged as a geologist on the staff of the Geological Survey of Canada between the years 1883 and 1898, it was my good fortune to travel over the same routes that he had travelled a century before, and to take observations on the sun and stars on the very spots where he had observed; and while my instruments may have been better than his, his surveys and observations were invariably found to have an accuracy that left little or nothing to be desired.[1]

In the following spring, after having determined by astronomical observations the position of his winter home, he started with the fur brigade for York Factory and made a survey of the Saskatchewan and Hayes rivers to that place, a distance of seven hundred and fifty miles.

Later on in the summer, he again returned to Cumberland House, and spent the winter with Philip Turnor, a surveyor in the employ of the Hudson's Bay Company. With this man as a tutor, and doubtless with the thought of some of the difficulties in the work of the previous winter in his mind, he devoted himself heart and soul to the study of practical astronomy and surveying.

In the following spring he again descended to York, while

[1] In a letter dated 1817, Thompson states that a large ten-inch brass sextant of Dolland's, reading to the 15″, had been his constant companion for twenty-eight years. He evidently obtained it about this time.

his friend and teacher, Philip Turnor, started north-westward by Frog Portage to Lake Athabaska.

After having thus spent four years in the Saskatchewan country, he left it for a while, and remained for a year at York Factory, where his time was largely occupied in taking a long series of astronomical observations for latitude and longitude, the results of which correctly placed the position of the factory half a degree west of the location previously determined by Turnor.

During the spring of 1788, the mouth of the Hayes river, on the west bank of which York Factory was situated, became blocked with broken ice, which caused the water to rise behind it and flood the adjoining land. The water rose several feet in the dwelling-house and did a large amount of damage to the buildings and stores. In order to prevent a recurrence of such a calamity, Colen moved the fort upstream about half a mile to its present position, on a spot of higher and drier ground. The process of moving occupied several years, and was not completed until 1793, so that doubtless Thompson, among other duties, assisted in building the Factory in its present position.

South-west of York Factory, and at no great distance from it, is the country called by Thompson the Muskrat country. It is situated on some of the western tributaries of Nelson river that flow into that stream at Split lake, and in a general way lies between the Churchill river to the north and the Saskatchewan river to the south. Curiously enough this region, though so near York Factory and so rich in fur-bearing animals, had been occupied exclusively by the traders of the North-West Company from Montreal. Even as early as 1780 Samuel Hearne wrote from Churchill with regard to these traders and others acting under instructions from Peter Pond on Athabaska river, "The Canadians have found means to intercept some of my best Northern Leaders. However, I still live in hopes of getting a few [furs] from that quarter."

In 1792 Colen and his associates on the Council of the Hudson's Bay Company at York decided to make an effort to wrest the trade of this country from the Canadians, and accordingly they sent William Cook, Malcolm Ross, and David Thompson to establish trading posts in the district. With his appointment to a fur-trading post in the Muskrat country, Thompson was thus placed in the front of the firing line in a struggle in which his adversaries were not only the Canadian traders of the North-West Company, who were the natural antagonists of the Hudson's Bay Company, but also the traders of his own Company under the jurisdiction of Churchill and not of York Factory; for Churchill and York, though both trading posts of the Hudson's Bay Company, sent their reports in to the head office at London independently, and the rivalry between them was such that it became occasionally necessary for the Board of Directors to intervene.

In order to understand the conditions by which Thompson was surrounded, it will be necessary to review briefly the condition of the fur trade at York and Churchill at that time. The traders from Montreal, who afterwards united into the North-West Company, travelling in canoes through Lakes Superior and Winnipeg, reached the upper portion of the Churchill river in 1776, and built a house on the Athabaska river, a short distance above Lake Athabaska, in 1778, from which place they extended their trading posts westward up Peace river and northward down the Mackenzie river. Churchill and York, the trading posts of the Hudson's Bay Company on Hudson Bay, immediately felt the effect of this invasion of the "Canadians," for the Indians had always brought their furs to the posts on the Bay to trade for such articles as they wanted, and now they were able to dispose of them inland. Consequently, in 1774, the Hudson's Bay Company's men went inland and built Cumberland House on the Saskatchewan river, and two years later they went farther up the same river and built Hudson's House, from which place an outpost appears to have been established still farther up the Saskatchewan at the Elbow. Here both the employees of the Hudson's Bay Company and the Canadians appear to have lived in the winter of 1779–80 ; and here, in the spring of 1780, Cole, one of the Canadian traders, was killed in a quarrel with the Indians, and all the other traders, no matter what Company they were serving, were obliged to flee down the river for safety. Immediately afterwards smallpox ravaged the country, swept away great numbers of the Indians, and disheartened the survivors. After the smallpox epidemic had abated, York and Churchill Factories were destroyed by the French, and all the furs contained in them were confiscated. These disasters paralyzed the energies of the Hudson's Bay Company for a time, and it was not until 1786 that the party under William Tomison, of which Thompson was a member, ascended the Saskatchewan river past Cumberland House and built Manchester House 425 miles above it.

About the same time it had occurred to some one that it should be possible to reach the Saskatchewan river more easily from Churchill than from York by a direct route up the Churchill river, and accordingly in the same year in which Thompson left for the Saskatchewan, Malcolm Ross, who had already been at Cumberland, was sent from York on July 27, 1786, to Churchill, with instructions to go up the Churchill river to Cumberland House.

In regard to this expedition, Samuel Hearne, then in charge of Churchill, wrote to Joseph Colen at York as follows, under date of August 6, 1786 :

"Malcolm Ross's experience in the interior parts of the country will, I hope, render him perfect master of the business he is going about. Since Malcolm's arrival here five canoes of Nelson Indians came to the Factory, two of which have been prevailed upon to carry him and his companions to Cumberland House, where they will be ready to prosecute the remainder of the Company's orders in the spring."

As will be seen later, Hearne himself had no confidence in the successful issue of this expedition from a commercial point of view.

The following summer Malcolm Ross had evidently returned to York, for in a letter to Samuel Hearne, dated York Factory, July 19, 1787, Joseph Colen wrote :

"Malcolm Ross tells me he had many difficulties to encounter before he reached Cumberland House from Churchill, the water so shoal as to prevent the navigation of small canoes."

In answer Hearne wrote :

"I am sorry to hear of the difficulties Malcolm Ross had to encounter with, tho' from my own knowledge no less could be expected ; this river a little distance from here is inaccessible for anything much larger than a light canoe."

In the following year, 1788, Colen sent Robert Longmore from York to Churchill to prosecute the discoveries from Churchill inland. His party did not succeed in opening a trade route to the Saskatchewan river, but it did succeed in establishing, or arranging for the establishment of, trading posts at several places up the Churchill river.

In 1789 the Board of Directors of the Hudson's Bay Company in London sent Philip Turnor from London to Lake Athabaska in order to find out its exact location, and after his return they kept instructing Colen and his associates on the Council at York to send Ross and Thompson to that country, but Colen seems to have taken a very perfunctory interest in the enterprise, and to have been much more interested in competing with the Company's men from Churchill for the trade of the country near the headwaters of the Burntwood and Grass rivers in what Thompson calls the Muskrat country.

In 1792 Ross and Thompson, instead of being sent to Lake Athabaska, were, as stated above, despatched up the Nelson river to winter at Sipiwesk lake. In the following spring

Thompson alone, without any assistance from York, endeavoured to explore a new route to the Athabaska country by Reindeer lake, but being unable to obtain Indian canoemen was obliged to turn back and return to York.

Later in the year 1793, he left York and, accompanied by Malcolm Ross, went up to Cumberland House on the Saskatchewan river, and after remaining there three days continued on to Buckingham House, where he spent the winter of 1793–94. With regard to this journey the directors in London wrote that they would expect much good to follow the expedition of Ross and Thompson to the Athabaska country, and also that the arrangements made by which William Cook was to return in winter from Split lake, where he was in charge, and accompany Ross and Thompson to the Athabaska country, met with their "full approbation." At the same time they wrote, expressing the hope that George Charles, who had gone up the Churchill river from Fort Churchill, would "restore a considerable part of the long lost trade to Churchill."

But William Cook remained at Split lake all winter, and while it is possible that Colen intended that Thompson should proceed from Cumberland House to Lake Athabaska instead of going to Buckingham House, there is no notice of any such intention in Thompson's journals, and it is impossible to avoid the conclusion that Colen was guilty of duplicity, and that while he had no interest in the exploration of the more remote interior parts of the country, he endeavoured to put the blame for his want of enterprise on other shoulders. This opinion is strengthened by a statement in a letter from the Board of Directors in London to the Council at York, dated May 30, 1795, with reference to Peter Fidler, who was Thompson's fellow surveyor in the Hudson's Bay Company, though at a much lower salary. It is as follows :

"We observe that Mr. P. Fidler has been kept at the Factory for two seasons past, but for the future we direct him to proceed inland on discoveries."

When Thompson arrived at York Factory from the Saskat-chewan river in the summer of 1794, Colen and his associates at York wrote to England as follows :

"Notwithstanding the steps pursued last fall to ensure the success of the Athapascow Expedition, we are sorry to remark it was again set aside at Cumberland House this Spring. As these transactions happened many hundred miles distance from us, and with much secrecy, we cannot from our own knowledge inform your honours the real cause, and it is from letter and hearsay we form our judgment. It, however, appears surprising, for when Mr. Colen accompanied the men and boats up Hill River, with trading goods, many volunteers offered their service for the Athapascow Expedition, and said they were ready to have gone from Cumberland House with Messrs. Ross and Thompson, but Mr. Tomison refusing to pass his word for the advance of wages promised by the Honourable Committee it of course stopt the Expedition in question and the considerable loss of your honours. Indeed we find this business involved in mystery, and as are many other transactions inland. . . . We have already remarked on the overthrow of the Athapascow Expedition this season. The repeated disappointments so much disheartened Mr. Ross determined him to return to England had not Mr. Thompson prevailed on him to pursue some other track into the Athapascow country, for they declare it will be impossible to carry it on from Cumberland as the Honourable Company's affairs at present stand, as every obstacle is thrown in the way to prevent its success. In order to suppress similar obstructions Mr. Ross took men and one canoe cargo of goods with him from Cumberland House and built a house to the northward near to a station occupied by a Mr. Thompson, a Canadian Proprietor whose success of late years in collecting of furs has been great. Mr. David Thompson has been fitted out with men and three canoe cargoes from this place to supply Mr. Ross by proceeding up Nelson River track."

It would thus appear that Ross had become thoroughly disgusted with the obstructions put in the way of an expedition into the Athabaska country either at York or by those in charge on the Saskatchewan river, and had decided to go to England, doubtless in order to be able to appeal directly to the Board of Directors, but that Thompson had urged him to consent to remain in the country until they had definitely found out whether the route by Reindeer lake was feasible as a trade route or not. But Ross's heart was not in this work of discovery, and he would furnish no assistance for the exploration of a new route when he believed that the old one followed by the North-Westers was good enough.

It is difficult to understand some of the statements made in the letter cited above. It is evident, however, that it was Colen's avowed intention that Ross and Thompson should proceed from Cumberland House to the Athabaska country by the route which had been travelled by the traders of the North-West Company for a number of years, and by Philip Turnor of the Hudson's Bay Company in 1791, but that he claimed that this had been frustrated by Tomison, the Chief at Cumberland in charge of the inland trade, or by the insubordination of the canoemen, and that Thompson was sent up the Saskatchewan river instead.

In their answer to this letter, written in May, 1795, the directors in London show their sympathy for David Thompson by saying, "We are perfectly satisfied with the conduct of Messrs. David Thompson, Ross, and others," and by requesting that Thompson should be advised of their approbation. They wrote also, "Obstacles are again, we perceive, thrown in the way of the Athapascow Expedition, but we trust all difficulties which occur and impede the Company's success will soon be removed."

That Colen believed that he had shelved the Athabaska question for a time is shown by the fact that he sent Ross, Thompson, Cook, Tate, and Sinclair back into the Muskrat country to oppose two Canadian traders named Robert Thompson and McKay who had been cutting into the York Factory trade for some years past. That winter Robert Thompson, who had been for many years on the Churchill and Nelson rivers, was killed in a quarrel with some Indians.

David Thompson spent the winter of 1794–95 at Reed lake.

and in July, 1795, paid his last visit to York Factory. He had been making surveys wherever he went, so that the amount of geographical information that he had collected was very large, but there had been no attempt on the part of the Company to help him push westward to the Athabaska country. Nevertheless Colen and his Council at York wrote to London as follows : " The steps pursued last season in the exploring a new track towards the Athabasca country we hope will meet your Honour's approbation." In return the directors demanded to see the maps of the country which had been explored.

But the end of this truculent quibbling was at hand. Ross and Thompson left York for the Nelson river on July 18, 1795, and the Council wrote to London with reference to Athabaska exploration that " Messrs. Ross and Thompson were despatched from the factory with men in four large canoes loaded with trading goods last July, and we hope to give a good account of their success next season " ; but they added a sentence which shows they were thinking only of the trade in the Muskrat country itself, " Should the track up Seal River be found nearer and a better road, the whole of that track will be surrendered up to Churchill."

Ross and Thompson went directly to Fairford House and Duck Portage respectively, where they built trading stores and spent the following winter, being obliged to compete on the one hand with traders from Canada and on the other with traders in the employ of the Hudson's Bay Company from Churchill.

The following summer, 1796, Ross went down to York alone, while Thompson made a final and in this case successful attempt to push north-westward through Deer and Wollaston lakes to Lake Athabaska.

But how different was the outfit and assistance supplied him from what he had a right to expect, considering the anxiety shown by the directors of the Company in the success of his expedition. Instead of a proper supply of men, canoes, and trading goods, he was obliged to engage two previously untried Indians who knew nothing of such work; no canoe was to be had, so that it was necessary for him to go into the woods, collect birch bark, and make one; all he had was a fish net and a small quantity of ammunition, except the compass and sextant, which were his own private property. So provided, he started out on a long exploring expedition into a new country. The account of this expedition is given in his own words on pages 133–53, so that we need not repeat it here.

On his return from Lake Athabaska he built a trading post on the west side of Reindeer lake, where he was later joined by Malcolm Ross, his old companion, who brought with him fresh supplies, but at the same time he brought also an order from Joseph Colen, the Resident Chief at York, instructing him to stop surveying. Such an order, which he must have felt to be contrary to the earnest wishes of the directors of the Company, after the great personal exertions and sacrifices which he had made to carry out those wishes, cut him to the heart. Nevertheless the two men settled down quietly to the routine of trade, and spent together what proved to be one of the coldest winters ever known in western Canada.

As his term of service had expired, Thompson now decided to leave the service of the Hudson's Bay Company. On Tuesday, May 23, 1797, he therefore left the little cabin on Reindeer lake which had been his home during the winter, and with it the service of the Hudson's Bay Company. "This day," runs the entry in his journal, "left the service of the Hudson's Bay Company, and entered that of the Company of the Merchants from Canada. May God Almighty prosper me."

Thompson had been with the Hudson's Bay Company for thirteen years. During these years he had travelled in all about nine thousand miles, and of this distance he had made careful surveys, checked by numerous astronomical observations, of three thousand five hundred miles. He had also correctly determined by multiple observations for latitude and longitude, the positions of eight widely separated places in the interior of the continent, and of one (York Factory) on Hudson Bay, so that his surveys extended between known positions. In addition to his surveying work he had taken and recorded regular observations on the climate and general natural phenomena.

The following letter, written after he reached the trading post of the North-West Company, shows how keenly he felt the opposition which Colen had shown to his surveying work.

"DEERS RIVER, *June* 1, 1797.

" MR. COLEN.

"SIR :—I take this opportunity of returning you my most respectful thanks for your loan of two guineas to my mother. I have enclosed a bill to you for the above amount.

"My friends belonging to York inform me that you are very desirous to find out who was the author of those letters that were wrote to H. B. Co. and militated against you 1795. I will give you that satisfaction. When I came down that year the other gentlemen were waiting my arrival in order to assist them in drawing up their grievances; as you were then absent I accepted the office with some hesitation, but as the letters were to be delivered to you on your landing at York for your inspection, and that you might have time to answer them, I considered you in a manner as present.—Those letters were drawn up by me, assisted by my friend Dr. Thomas, and not one half of the evils complained of were enumerated.

" You told Mr. Ross that when in England you were endeavouring to serve those, who behind your back were trying to cut your throat.— Before you went to England I had always a Letter and Books from the Co., since that neither the one nor the other, and I have been put the whole winter to the greatest inconvenience for want of a Nautical Almanac.

" Many of us acknowledge with readiness that you have some good qualities, and I had once the greatest respect for you ; I have some yet, but . . . it is not my wish to say those things which I know you do not wish to hear. How is it, Sir, that everyone who has once wished you well should turn to be indifferent to you, and even some to hate you, altho' they are constant in their other friendships,—there must be a defect somewhere.

"The fact is, that from your peculiar manner of conduct, you are also one of those unfortunate men who will have many an acquaintance, but never never a real friend.—Your humble Servant,

"D. THOMPSON."

But if the Hudson's Bay Company did not need Thompson's services as a surveyor, the North-West Company, which was controlled by men with much larger and more progressive ideas, was anxious to obtain some accurate knowledge of the extent and character of the country in which it was carrying on its business. When he left the little trading post of the Hudson's Bay Company on the west shore of Reindeer lake and walked down to the nearest post of the North-Westers, about seventy-five miles farther south, Thompson felt sure of a welcome from the Canadians. After staying at Fraser's House for about ten days, he proceeded to Grand Portage on Lake Superior. On the way he met some of the members of the North-West Company, among them Roderick Mackenzie, a cousin of Sir Alexander Mackenzie, and the author of *The History of the Fur Trade* which forms the Introduction to Alexander Mackenzie's *Voyages*, and Simon Fraser, who afterwards descended the Fraser river. These men were henceforward to be his associates.

For the last three years during which Thompson had been in the employ of the Hudson's Bay Company he had been receiving £60 a year, which was probably the largest salary paid to any employee of his age at the time, but it is not known on what terms he was engaged by the North-West Company. His first work, however, was to consist of one continuous surveying trip unhampered by any necessity for looking after trade returns. His instructions were (1) to determine the position of the 49th parallel of latitude, which

by the Treaty of 1792, had been decided on as the boundary
line between the United States and British North America;
(2) to visit the villages of the Mandan Indians on the Missouri river; (3) to search for fossil bones of large animals;
(4) to determine the positions of the trading posts of the
North-West Company.

Starting from Grand Portage on Lake Superior, he turned
back into the western country by the ordinary trade route
down the Rainy and Winnipeg rivers and through Lakes
Winnipeg and Winnipegosis to Swan and Assiniboine rivers,
and down this latter stream to the mouth of the Souris river,
which he reached about the beginning of winter. From
there he struck southward across the plains to the Mandan
villages on the Missouri, back again to the Assiniboine, down
that river, up the Red river and across the head waters of
the Mississippi river to the site of the present city of
Duluth, and then around the south shore to Lake Superior
to Sault Ste. Marie and back by the north shore to Grand
Portage, where he arrived early in June, having been about
ten months accomplishing his journey. Since he had left
Grand Portage in the previous year, he had covered a total
of four thousand miles of survey through previously un-
surveyed territory, a record that has rarely been equalled.

The partners of the North-West Company seem to have
been very well satisfied with the work so far done by him, but
he was an able and experienced fur-trader as well as a surveyor,
and the North-West Company was a commercial concern
and needed furs, therefore they apparently decided not to
continue to employ Thompson exclusively at survey work,
but to engage him at his old business of trading for furs, with
the privilege of making surveys at the same time. This
arrangement was satisfactory to Thompson, and about the
middle of July he started west again, this time for Lake La
Biche at the headwaters of one of the branches of the
Athabaska river, where he spent the following winter.

In the summer of 1799 he extended his surveys to the Athabaska river and some of its tributaries, and from Methy Portage, which is on the canoe route to Lake Athabaska, he started on his way down the Churchill river to Grand Portage. At Isle à la Crosse he stopped for a few days, and on June 10 married Charlotte Small, a half-breed girl fourteen years of age. A memorandum in an old Bible belonging to Mrs. Shaw, one of his daughters, states that Charlotte Small was born at Isle à la Crosse on September 1, 1785. It is highly probable that she was a daughter of Patrick Small, who was one of the earliest traders on the Churchill river.[1]

After the wedding, Thompson went eastward to Grand Portage, probably taking his bride with him. To this place drawing-paper had been sent from Montreal for his maps, and with the precious paper in his possession he accompanied John McDonald of Garth, back to Fort George on the Saskatchewan, which was situated close to Buckingham House of the Hudson's Bay Company, his old home of the winter of 1793-4, where he wintered and drew his maps.[2]

On March 25 he was again on the move, for he then crossed to the south side of the Saskatchewan, and started overland for Fort Augustus, travelling along the north side

[1] Patrick Small was a native of Glengarry, and a nephew of Major-General Small of the 42nd Highlanders. In 1786-7 he was in charge of the post at Isle à la Crosse for the North-West Company. In 1790 he was one of the partners in the North-West Company, owning two shares, or a one-tenth interest in it. He was a Roman Catholic in religion, and had married a Chippewa woman in the west. There was also another and younger man named Patrick Small in the employ of the North-West and Hudson's Bay Companies, probably a brother of Mrs. Thompson; he married a daughter of James Hughes, by whom he had nine children, and he died in 1846 at Carlton. His wife died in Manitoba, and lies buried in the St. Boniface cemetery.

[2] In the list of partners and employees of the North-West Company for this year, published by Masson in the "Reminiscences of Roderick Mackenzie," David Thompson's name appears as an employee assigned to "Upper Fort des Prairie and Rocky Mountains" with a salary of 1200 G.P. Currency, which was the same salary that was then being paid to Simon Fraser, Alexander McKay, Hugh McGillis, and James Hughes. G.P. undoubtedly stands for Grand Portage, but I have been unable to learn what was the unit of value.

of the " Chain of Lakes " north of the Vermilion river, near
the north line of Township 54. On March 28 he reached
Fort Augustus, and on the 31st he left it for Rocky Mountain
House, which had been built the previous autumn. He
travelled southward to the east of Bear's Hills, across two
branches of Battle river, down the Wolf's trail, and westward
across Wolf Creek (Blind Man river), to a crossing of Clearwater river, two miles above its mouth, and arrived at Rocky
Mountain House on April 7, crossing the river on the ice,
which was still strong.

The old house of the North-West Company was on the
north bank of the Saskatchewan on a beautiful wide level flat
a mile and a quarter above the mouth of the Clearwater
river. After the union of the companies it continued to be
occupied for many years. It was strongly fortified on account
of the possible hostility of the Blackfeet who traded there,
and the ruins of these old fortifications were still standing
when I visited the place in 1886.

From here he had intended to cross southward to the
Red Deer river and descend it in a boat, but having been
lamed in some way, he sent four men, Chauvette, La Gassi,
Clement, and Jacco Cardinal, on this journey. As he records
the fact that they started from Rocky Mountain House, and
that a boat had been built for them beforehand, and as some
of them at all events are afterwards mentioned in his journal,
it seems probable that these men successfully descended the
Red Deer and South Saskatchewan rivers, being probably
the first white men to accomplish this journey.

The next two years were spent by Thompson at Rocky
Mountain House or in its vicinity, and in exploring the
country to the west of it as far as the foot of the Rocky
Mountains from the Bow river northward to the Saskatchewan. Then he moved to the Peace river, and made his
headquarters at the trading post at the Forks, which had been
built by Alexander Mackenzie in 1792, when preparing to

make his journey westward to the Pacific. While there he made a survey up the river to the last post occupied by the traders, and when leaving the country he descended and surveyed the river to its mouth in Lake Athabaska. After leaving Peace river, he went back into the Muskrat country, where he had previously spent four years while in the employ of the Hudson's Bay Company. Through the inattention and carelessness of some of the partners of the North-West Company, and through the greater efficiency in management shown by the Hudson's Bay Company, the trade of this district had been allowed to fall largely into the hands of the latter Company.

In previous years, while working under the jurisdiction of York Factory, Thompson had had to contend against the traders from Churchill, as well as against the Canadian traders of the North-West Company. On this occasion the Hudson's Bay traders from York had withdrawn, and had left the field to those from Churchill who were now under the control of Thompson's old schoolmate, George Charles. At the same time there was also a third interest struggling for the trade in the X Y Company of Montreal.

Thompson brought with him three canoes loaded with trading supplies, which he distributed among five different trading posts from Cranberry lake on the south to Indian lake on the north. He himself went almost directly to Nelson House on the Churchill river, where George Charles, governor of the Churchill district, now had his headquarters, and from there he went a little farther down the river to a place called Musquawegan (or Bear's Backbone), where he built a house and spent the winter. That summer Charles had made a prisoner of Louis Dupleix of the North-West Company for stealing furs from the Hudson's Bay Company and had sent him to Churchill, where he was to be tried. But neither this incident, nor the hard conditions of the fur trade, served to cause any serious disagreement between old friends.

d

During the winter they extended to each other various civilities, including the loan of books, and when Thompson was leaving Churchill river in the spring of 1805, everything that he did not need to take with him was left in the care of Charles in the Hudson's Bay Company's store at Nelson House. The two men had done their utmost to outwit each other in trade for the benefit of their respective companies, but at the same time they had remained neighbours and friends.

After rounding up the furs from Indian lake, Musquawegan, and Nelson House, which he calls "the old post," he started for Cumberland with all hands, picking up the furs from the post on Cranberry lake as he passed it. At Cumberland House, where he was welcomed by Hamilton, then in charge, he baled his furs and sent them down to Kaministikwia with Morrin and Carter, while he spent the summer visiting his posts at Reindeer lake and river and at Cranberry lake.

In the autumn, with a new and larger supply of goods, he started back into the same country. On the way he dismantled the post on Cranberry lake, and passing the old post in Reed lake, where he and Malcolm Ross had spent a winter together, he decided on a place to build a house near where an old house had stood about twenty years before, for here fish were said to be most plentiful, and it was on fish that he was obliged to rely almost entirely for food. He sent Connelly on to Indian lake, Joseph Plante to Old Fort (Nelson House), and François Morrin to Pukkatowagan (Setting) lake, while he himself, surrounded by his family, spent the winter at the house which he had just built on the shore of Reed lake.

The following spring, when all the men came in from his three outposts, the returns were found to be small, and it was probably with considerable relief that he handed over the charge of the district to a partner named Wills and started eastward for Kaministikwia.

On November 5, 1804, the North-West and X Y Companies had discontinued their expensive struggle for the furs caught by the Indians and agreed to unite their forces, and David Thompson's name appears among the list of the partners as having signed the agreement by attorney. As a consequence of the strength thus gained by union, the North-West Company decided to extend its trade into the country west of the Rocky Mountains which is now covered by the province of British Columbia and the states of Idaho, Washington, Oregon, and the western portion of Montana.

In 1805 Simon Fraser was sent up the Peace river to establish posts at its head-waters and around the sources of the Fraser river, in the country subsequently known as New Caledonia, and in the following year Thompson was sent up the Saskatchewan river to his old home at Rocky Mountain House, to be ready to cross the mountains the following year. An attempt to trade with the Indians west of the Rocky Mountains made from this place in 1801 had been futile, but renewed efforts were now determined on. On the previous occasion Duncan McGillivray, who was stationed at Rocky Mountain House, was probably Thompson's superior in the Company, and controlled the policy of exploration pursued from the uppermost trading post on the Saskatchewan river, but now Thompson himself was in charge and was to lead the trading parties through the mountains.

During the winter great preparations were made for an expedition westward, and John McDonald of Garth, who was in charge at Fort de l'Isle on the Saskatchewan river, came up to Rocky Mountain House twice to assist in the arrangements, on one occasion in February going to the mountains himself. Quesnel and Finan McDonald, who were Thompson's assistants, also went to the mountains and freighted up some goods in advance. But everything was done quietly, for the employees of the Hudson's Bay Company under a trader named J. P. Prudens were living in an adjoining house, and were watching all their movements.

Having spent the winter of 1806-7 at Rocky Mountain House, Thompson pushed westward, accompanied by his wife and family, to the Columbia river, through what has since been called the Howse Pass, though Joseph Howse, who was a clerk in the employ of the Hudson's Bay Company, did not travel over it until it had been beaten by Thompson for two years. For three years he travelled backwards and forwards across the mountains through this pass, during which time he was engaged in establishing numerous trading posts on the Columbia river and its tributaries, in making surveys of every mile travelled, and in taking astronomical observations to supplement these surveys and to determine the positions of the houses which he occupied.

While Thompson was thus extending the fur-trade of the North-West Company into the country west of the Rocky Mountains, his old employers had not forgotten him, and the reports of his explorations were anxiously listened to by the Governors of the Hudson's Bay Company in their board-room in London. In the spring of 1808, the Governors wrote to the Council at York Factory asking how far west Thompson had succeeded in going, and John McNab and his colleagues on the Council sent answer that he had wintered across the mountains the previous year.

That winter McNab and his Council determined, if possible, to see just how far Thompson had gone, and consequently in 1809 they sent Joseph Howse, a writer in their employ, in default of some one better trained in exploratory work, to go west to the Rocky Mountains and discover where Thompson was going every year. After a short journey into the mountains Howse returned with his report.

In 1810 Howse again went west, this time prepared with a plentiful supply of trading goods, and ascending to the head-waters of the Saskatchewan river, along the route followed by Thompson in previous years, he crossed the divide and reached the Columbia river, which he ascended to its head, and thence made his way to the Flathead river north of Flathead lake, where he spent the winter of 1810-11, not far from the site of the present town of Kalispell in Montana.

But one winter of such trading, near the battle-ground of the Piegan and Flathead Indians, was enough, and in the spring of 1811 Howse and all the employees of the Hudson's Bay Company abandoned the Columbia valley to their rivals of the North-West Company, and did not enter it again until after the union of the two companies in 1821.

In going up the Saskatchewan river, Thompson had been obliged to pass through the country of the Piegan Indians, who were constantly at war with the Kutenai Indians on the west side of the mountains, and naturally the Piegan objected to a trade which supplied their enemies with knives, spears, guns, powder, bullets, and many other articles which made them much more formidable in battle than they had been before. Even Thompson's friendship with them could not outweigh their objections to this trade, and they warned him that he must stop taking supplies to their enemies, or they would be obliged to kill him and all his party.

In 1810 they intercepted Thompson's brigade in the mountains and forced the men to fly for their lives back down the river. But the Piegan were Indians of the plains and not of the woods, and Thompson, who knew them thoroughly, decided to outwit them for all time by establishing a route so far to the north that they would not be able to reach or interfere with it. He therefore descended the Saskatchewan for a short distance to the site of an abandoned house which had been known as " Boggy Hall." The season was already late, for there had been just time enough to cross the mountains by the usual route, and the Indians had caused him a great deal of delay, but in spite of the terrors of a journey over these mountains by an unknown pass so late in the year

that it would probably extend into the heart of winter, he
started with a train of pack-horses north-westward through
the forest to the head of the Athabaska river, and, after
overcoming tremendous difficulties and enduring extreme
privations, he reached the Columbia river at the mouth of
the Canoe river, at a place now known as the Big Bend, on
January 26, 1811. It has often been stated that Thompson
was sent on a rush journey to the mouth of the Columbia
river to forestall the employees of the Pacific Fur Company
in building a trading post there, but in his journals there is
no intimation whatever that such was his errand. He was
perfectly well aware that the Pacific Fur Company was making
elaborate preparations to establish trading posts on the
Columbia river, but for several years he and his people had
occupied advantageous positions on that river and its tributaries, and he felt that he was able to hold the trade. He
was extending the fur trade of the North-West Company
among the Indians west of the mountains, and was searching
out and surveying the best routes by which those Indians
could be reached and by which the furs obtained from them
could be transported to Montreal, and he travelled deliber-
ately and carefully with that object always in view. At the
same time he remembered how the North-West Company
had been turned out of Minnesota by the agents of the
American government, and he determined to avoid a similar
contingency here by publicly claiming for Great Britain the
country in which his posts were situated.

In the spring of 1811 he ascended the Columbia river as
usual and descended the Kootenay river to his old trading
posts, travelled by canoe and on horseback among these posts,
and then returned to the Columbia river, which he reached
at Ilthkoyape or Kettle Falls. From this place he descended
the stream to Fort Astoria at its mouth, where he landed on
July 15, 1811, and where he found Duncan McDougall,
an old partner of his, in charge for the Pacific Fur Company.

After spending a few days at Astoria with McDougall, he started back up the Columbia river to the mouth of Snake river. After travelling backwards and forwards among his trading posts until the autumn, he again reached Ilthkoyape Falls. Here he built a canoe and ascended the river through Arrow lakes, past the present site of Revelstoke, and up through the Dalles des Morts, whose treacherous rapids and whirlpools have been fatal to so many boatmen, to the Big Bend, or Boat Encampment, and thus completed the survey of the river from its source to its mouth. Portions of this river have never been resurveyed since that time, so that Thompson's surveys still appear on every map of the Columbia river that is published.

Thompson had now been more than twenty-eight years in northern and western America, and his survey of the Columbia had completed his preparations for the making of the map of north-western America toward which he had been working during these years. The winter of 1811–12 he spent on Clark's Fork and its tributaries, with headquarters at Saleesh House, and in the spring of 1812 he recrossed the mountains and set off down the Athabaska and Churchill rivers for Montreal. He arrived in Montreal late in the summer, after a long and arduous journey and a narrow escape from the Americans, between whom and Great Britain war had just been declared; and never again did he visit the scenes of his western exploits. At this point the narrative which is here presented concludes.

Thompson took up his residence at Terrebonne, in the province of Quebec, and immediately enlisted as an ensign in the 2nd Battalion under Lieutenant-Colonel Roderick Mackenzie, with his old companion Simon Fraser as one of his fellow officers. He spent the two years 1813–14 in preparing his map of western Canada for the North-West Company, on a scale of about fifteen miles to an inch, from the observations and surveys that he had made during the previous twenty-three years. This map, which is in the possession of the Government of the Province of Ontario, and is reproduced on a somewhat reduced scale in the present volume, is entitled :

"Map of the North West Territory of the Province of Canada, 1792–1812, embracing region between Latitudes 45 and 56, and Longitudes 84 and 124.
"Map made for the North West Company in 1813–1814."

It is interesting to note that it is almost on the same scale as the great international map of the world which is now being prepared under the auspices of the governments of the various civilized countries.

On February 10, 1814, he was registered in Terrebonne as a land surveyor. From 1816 to 1826 he was engaged in surveying and defining the boundary line, on the part of Great Britain, between Canada and the United States. He was employed in 1817 in the St. Lawrence, and thence proceeding westward around the shores of the Great Lakes he reached the north-west angle of the Lake of the Woods in 1825. In 1834 he surveyed Lake St. Francis on the St. Lawrence river ; in 1837 he made a survey of the canoe route from Lake Huron to the Ottawa river ; and a few years later he made a survey of Lake St. Peter.

The last years of his life were spent by Thompson first at Williamstown, Glengarry county, Ontario, and afterwards in Longueuil, opposite Montreal. In Williamstown, he bought the property of the Rev. John Bethune, the father of the former Bishop of Toronto ; and for a time he was in comfortable, if not indeed wealthy, circumstances. But towards the end of his life he fell on evil days. A mortgage which he held on the Presbyterian church in Williamstown, the congregation proved unable to pay ; and Thompson deeded to them the church and the grounds.[1]   He set up his

---

[1] This statement depends upon the authority of one of David Thompson's daughters, Mrs. W. R. Scott.

THOMPSON'S HOUSE AT WILLIAMSTOWN, GLENGARRY CO., ONTARIO

Now owned by Farquhar Robertson, Esq.

sons[1] in business, and they failed; and in paying off their debts, he impoverished himself. When he removed to Longueuil, he was still able to make a comfortable living, until his eyesight failed him. His position then became pathetic. He was so poor that he had to sell his instruments and even to pawn his coat to procure food for himself and his family. In one of his note-books, he writes: " Borrowed 2s. 6d. from a friend. Thank God for this relief." And in another place he tells

---

[1] Thompson had seven sons and six daughters. In the family Bible there are inscribed in Thompson's own handwriting the following entries :

" David Thompson, born in the Westminster Parish of St. John, April 30th, 1770.

" Charlotte Small, wife of David Thompson, born September 1st, 1785, at Isle à la Crosse, married to David Thompson, June 10th, 1799.

" Fanny Thompson, born June 10th, 1801. Rocky Mountain House.

" Samuel Thompson, born March 5th, 1804. Peace River Forks.

" Emma Thompson, born March, 1806. Reed Lake House.

" John Thompson, born August 25th, 1808. Boggy Hall, Saskatchewan.

" Joshua Thompson, born March 28th, 1811. Fort Augustus.

" Henry Thompson, born July 30th, 1813. Terrebonne Village.

" John Thompson, deceased January 11th, 1814, at 7 A.M. in the Village of Terrebonne, buried in Montreal the 12th inst. No. 353. Aged 5 years and near 5 months, a beautiful, promising boy.

" Emma Thompson, deceased Feb. 22nd, 1814, at 7.25 P.M. Aged 7 years and near 11 months. Buried close touching her brother in Montreal. No 353. An amiable, innocent girl, too good for this world.

" Charlotte Thompson, born 7th July, 1815, at 11¼ A.M. Village of Terrebonne.

" Elizabeth Thompson, born 25th April, 1817, at 8 P.M., at the Village of Williamstown, River Raisin, Glengarry.

" William Thompson, born 9th November, 1819, at the Village of Williamstown, River Raisin, Glengarry.

" Thomas Thompson, born July 10th, 1822, at 4 P.M. Williamstown, Glengarry, Up. Canada.

" George Thompson, born 13th July, 1 A.M., 1824, Williamstown, Glengarry, Up. Canada, died August 27th, 10½ A.M. Buried August 28th, 1824. Aged 7 weeks.

" Mary Thompson, born April 2, 1827, at Williamstown, 12 P.M. Glengarry, Up. Canada.

" Eliza Thompson, born March 4, 1829, at Williamstown, baptized by the Rev. John Mackenzie, April 12, 1829.

" Henry Thompson, died 23 October, 1855, aged 42, buried in Mount Royal Cemetery, Montreal."

of trying to sell to a gentleman his maps of Lake Superior and his sketches of the Rocky Mountains. " He would not purchase, but loaned me $5.00. A good relief, for I had been a week without a penny."

Thompson died at Longueuil, on February 10, 1857, at the ripe old age of nearly eighty-seven years. His wife survived him by only three months ; she died on May 7 of the same year; and they both lie buried in Mount Royal cemetery in Montreal, without mark or monument to show their resting-place.

David Thompson was a man of somewhat singular appearance. " He was plainly dressed, quiet and observant," wrote the naturalist of the International Boundary Commission with regard to his first meeting him in the year 1817.[1] " His figure was short and compact, and his black hair was worn long all round, and cut square, as if by one stroke of the shears, just above the eyebrows. His complexion was of the gardener's ruddy brown, while the expression of deeply furrowed features was friendly and intelligent, but his cut-short nose gave him an odd look. . . . I might have spared this description of Mr. David Thompson by saying he greatly resembled Curran, the Irish orator." Dr. Bigsby conceived a great admiration for his colleague. " Never mind his Bunyan-like face and cropped hair ; he has a very powerful mind, and a singular faculty of picture-making. He can create a wilderness and people it with warring savages, or climb the Rocky Mountains with you in a snow storm, so clearly and palpably, that only shut your eyes and you hear the crack of the rifle, or feel the snow-flakes on your cheeks as he talks."

One of Thompson's most striking characteristics was his piety, the fruit of his early years in the Grey Coat School in Westminster. The " thank Good Providence," with which he so frequently concludes the account of his expeditions,

[1] J. J. Bigsby, *The Shoe and Canoe*, vol. i. pp. 113-14.

was no mere formula, but the sincere thanksgiving of a devout man. "Our astronomer, Mr. Thompson," wrote Dr. Bigsby,[1] "was a firm churchman; while most of our men were Roman Catholics. Many a time have I seen these uneducated Canadians most attentively and thankfully listen, as they sat upon some bank of shingle, to Mr. Thompson, while he read to them, in most extraordinarily pronounced French, three chapters out of the Old Testament, and as many out of the New, adding such explanations as seemed to him suitable." Thompson's piety was not of an obtrusive sort, but there were few white men in the West in those early days who bore so consistently as he did the white flower of a blameless life.

Typical of him was his attitude towards the trading of spirituous liquors to the Indians. He was a strong opponent of the liquor traffic; and while he was in charge of the western posts no alcoholic liquors were allowed to be taken to them. The years in which Thompson was in the West were perhaps the period in which this debasing trade was at its worst. Rival companies were vying with each other for the furs; and cheap spirits were regarded by the traders as the most profitable sort of barter. Such, however, was not Thompson's view. He believed that the use of intoxicating liquor in trade was a short-sighted policy; and he gives in his own words an amusing account of how he prevented the trade from spreading during his time beyond the Rockies.

"I was obliged," he says in his account of the expedition of 1808, "to take two kegs of alcohol, overruled by my Partners (Messrs Donᵈ McTavish and Jo McDonald [of] Gart[h]) for I had made it a law to myself, that no alcohol should pass the Mountains in my company, and thus be clear of the sad sight of drunkeness, and its many evils: but these gentlemen insisted upon alcohol being the most profitable article that could be taken for the indian trade. In this I knew they had mis-calculated; accordingly when we came to the defiles of the Mountains

---

[1] J. J. Bigsby, *The Shoe and Canoe*, vol. ii. pp. 205-6.

I placed the two Kegs of Alcohol on a vicious horse ; and by noon the Kegs were empty, and in pieces, the Horse rubbing his load against the Rocks to get rid of it ; I wrote to my partners what I had done ; and that I would do the same to every Keg of Alcohol, and for the next six years I had charge of the furr trade on the west side of the Mountains, no further attempt was made to introduce spirituous Liquors."

Thus for a few years at least Thompson kept the curse of alcoholism from debasing the Indians of southern British Columbia, Washington, and Idaho.

It is difficult for us at this time to appreciate to its full extent the work which Thompson did for the furtherance of geographical knowledge on the continent of North America. It is necessary to go back a little and to review briefly what was known of the geography of western Canada at the time when Thompson landed on the shore of Hudson Bay. An idea may be obtained of the geographical knowledge that was prevalent in the latter half of the eighteenth century by reference to page xxv, where the books which were used in the Grey Coat School at the time are enumerated. It is true that geographical knowledge and progress were just beginning to pervade the thoughts of the educated people throughout the world, but exploration, led by Captain James Cook and a few others, was being largely confined to the ocean rather than to the land. Moreover, the settlements in eastern America had carried with them a knowledge of the geography of the country westward as far as Lake Superior and the valley of the Mississippi, but beyond these parts the country was still entirely in the hands of the native Indians. Away to the north, a mining fever had induced the Hudson's Bay Company to send a man inland from Hudson Bay to investigate the report of an enormous copper deposit in the vicinity of the Coppermine river, and this man, Samuel Hearne, had made a sketch of the route which he followed.

In 1784, the year in which Thompson reached Hudson Bay, the great map of the world accompanying the account

of Cook's third voyage was published, and in that map, part
of which is reproduced in this volume, it will be seen that
almost the whole of north-western America, with the exception of that portion sketched by Hearne in his journey to the
Coppermine river, is left blank. This map represents the
very latest information in the possession of the British Government and people, and, in fact, in the possession of the whole
civilized world, at that time.

Thompson had thus a large part of a new continent ready
for his work, and he must have recognised that rough sketches,
such as had undoubtedly been made by some of his companions in the fur trade, were of little permanent value, and
that to make such a map as would be a credit to him and an
advantage to geographers in the world at large, he must first
carefully determine the positions of some of the principal
places or natural objects in the country. In fact, he recognised the true importance of a great trigonometrical survey
of the country, with some places carefully located by observations for latitude and longitude, and then with connecting
surveys made in such ways as were possible to him between
those places. Thus, from the very first, he laid his plans for
a map of the country carefully and well.

In the prosecution of the fur trade Thompson travelled
more than 50,000 miles in canoes, on horseback, and on foot
through what was then an unmapped country, and no matter
what the difficulties or dangers of the journeys might be, he
never neglected his surveys. While a good deal of this distance was made up of trips over ground that he might have
been over before, advantage was always taken to make re-
surveys and check the correctness or accuracy of previous
work. He always continued to occupy his spare time in the
winter, when he was not travelling, in taking observations and
determining with great care the positions of any places at
which he might be stopping.

He obtained a thorough knowledge of the topography of

the whole of the country which he was able to visit. The
lengths of the rivers, the heights of the mountains, the extent
of the plains, were all alike investigated, and the results were
recorded by him. All the explorers who preceded him, and
most of those who followed him, were content to survey
individual lines of travel and to be able to place these lines
in approximately their correct positions on a map, but
Thompson's ambition was to accomplish much greater results
than these, namely, to determine and delineate the physical
features of the whole of north-western America. Alexander
Mackenzie and Simon Fraser, two of the early explorers whose
work has received public recognition, devoted all their time
and energy during their exploring trips to the one object of
successfully accomplishing their explorations and surveys, and
after these explorations were completed they turned to other
work; but Thompson was not a spasmodic explorer; with him
surveying was his chief pleasure and life-work. During only
one year, when on his journey to the Mandan Indian villages
and to the head waters of the Mississippi river, was he able
to devote his whole time to surveying and exploring work.
During the rest of his life in the West he was merely taking
advantage of the positions in which he might be situated.
His business was the trading in furs, but he was in the middle
of unknown country, surrounded on all sides by pristine
wilderness waiting to be surveyed. In the intervals of his
trade, he was exploring, surveying, and depicting by regular
methods on the map, the features of the country in which
he was living, so that ever afterwards anyone else would be
able to form an intelligent idea of it. The excellence and
greatness of his work is accounted for largely by this systematic
continuation of surveys, practically without a break, for
twenty-three years.

His surveys were not merely rough sketches sufficient to
give some idea of the general character of the country, but
were careful traverses made by a master in the art, short

courses being taken with a magnetic compass, the variation of which was constantly determined, distances being carefully estimated by the time taken to travel them, and the whole checked by numerous astronomical observations for latitude and longitude.

His astronomical observations were made with the greatest care, his latitudes being taken from the sun or any star or planet which was conveniently situated at the time, while his longitudes were usually determined by one or more observations for lunar distances. Geographers will readily appreciate the excellence of this work by a glance at the following table of longitudes chosen at random from the large number recorded by him between the years 1789 and 1812.

Place.	Thompson's Longitude.	Longitude by latest Surveys.
York Factory	92° 29′ 20″	92° 27′
Cumberland House . . .	102° 13′	102° 16′
Kootanae House . . .	115° 51′ 40″	116° 00′
Rocky Mountain House . .	114° 52′	114° 57′
Fort Augustus	113° 11′	113° 2′
Buckingham House . . .	110° 41′	110° 45′
Peace River Forks . . .	117° 13′ 14″	117° 23′
McDonnell's House . . .	99° 27′ 15″	99° 37′
Saleesh House	115° 22′ 51″	115° 15′
Spokane House . . .	117° 27′	117° 33′

A reduced copy of the great map which he drew is published at the end of the present volume, and by comparing it with the Cook map opposite page lx some little idea may be gained of the magnitude of the work which Thompson, almost single-handed, accomplished in the intervals of time that he was able to spare from his work as a fur trader.

It may seem strange that a man who has done such magnificent work as was accomplished by this great geographer should have received so little recognition. But recognition is, or should be, founded on knowledge, and his geographical work has remained almost unknown. The first and perhaps

the chief reason which has contributed to the general ignorance of Thompson's work was the remarkable modesty and
single-mindedness of the man himself. Self-abasement had
doubtless been taught to him in the Grey Coat School, and
his lonely life in the West had emphasized this side of his
character. He never talked much, or boasted of his own
exploits, and his writing was confined almost entirely to his
note-books, in which he entered with perfect regularity the
details of his surveys and the incidents of trade.

It is true that in his later years, when the competence
which he had accumulated in the West had disappeared, and
when he was scarcely able to get enough work to do to enable
him to provide food for his family, he wrote the account of
his life in the West which is here given ; but it was not
published.[1]

He was an excellent story teller, but very retiring, and the
fact that his wife was a native of the West and, like other
natives, perhaps shy and diffident, doubtless kept him from
participating in the social life of Montreal. He was hardly
the sort of man who was likely to be in his element among
the rollicking, heavy-drinking North-Westers who made
Beaver Hall Club in Montreal their headquarters.

Moreover, during the time when he was in the employ
of the Hudson's Bay Company, his note-books and maps
were turned over to the Company, and by them passed on to
Arrowsmith, the mapmaker, in London, who incorporated
them in the maps of British North America, and for this
information Arrowsmith gave the Hudson's Bay Company
credit, but nothing was said of Thompson, the man who had
made the surveys. Therefore, his work was entirely unknown
to anyone outside of the Hudson's Bay Company at that time ;

[1] Thompson's daughter, Mrs. Shaw, is authority for the statement that
Washington Irving endeavoured to obtain the manuscript, but that the terms or
conditions which he offered, chiefly as regards acknowledgment, were not
satisfactory, and Thompson would not give it to him.

and as to the Hudson's Bay Company's records themselves, they are even yet practically closed to investigators.

After he had joined the North-West Company, he continued to hand over his sketches and the records of his surveys to his associates, and when his great map was finally completed it was taken by them and hung on the walls of their board-room in Fort William, where scarcely anyone but the traders themselves was likely to see it. The information contained in it was sent to Arrowsmith as before, but we look in vain on any of his maps for recognition of Thompson or his work. That some people of influence at the time recognised his ability is certain, or this poor boy from a charity school in London, who had educated himself as a surveyor on the plains and mountains of the West, would not have been appointed as astronomer for the British Government to run the boundary line between the United States and British North America. But the record of that survey was made on maps and not in books. The people who study maps are few compared to those who read books, and consequently, often great maps may remain in manuscript unpublished when even trivial books are published with profit and read with enthusiasm.

In addition to the reasons for non-recognition inherent in the man himself, the fur trade of the country, which was its only tangible asset at that time, became centred in the hands of two great Companies, and after the union of these Companies in 1821, in the Hudson's Bay Company alone, which became a virtual monopoly with headquarters in London. Private enterprise was stifled, and the people of Canada, and in fact of the whole of North America, lost touch with a country in which they had no commercial interest and in the trade of which they were not allowed to participate. Thus, while thrilling accounts of adventure in north-western America, such as Irving's *Astoria*, or Ross's *Fur Hunters of the Far West*, might be read with interest, regardless of location, accounts

e

of work done to promote a fuller knowledge of the country were disregarded.

After Thompson left north-western Canada, the inspiration for surveying that country died completely out, except where it was connected with the exploration of the northern shore of the continent of America, and the determination of the possibility of a water passage from Europe to Asia to the north of it; and when in 1857, forty-five years after the termination of Thompson's work, the Government of Canada began to look westward and wanted a map of western Canada, the very best that it could do was to republish Thompson's map of 1813, without, however, giving him credit for it, except by a small note in one corner; and to this day some parts of the maps of Canada published by the Canadian Government, the railway companies, and others, are taken from Thompson's map.

Thompson's maps and note-books are a lasting monument to the work he accomplished for north-western America, and while this monument has remained in obscurity up to the present, the people, both of the east and west, will eventually recognize its grandeur, and will do homage to the memory of the man who designed and constructed it.

DAVID THOMPSON'S ITINERARY IN
NORTH-WESTERN AMERICA, 1785-1812

1785-1789

FOR the first five years after Thompson landed on the shores of
Hudson Bay, he spent his time chiefly at Churchill and York Factories,
and on the Saskatchewan river; and during this period he appears to
have travelled about two thousand miles, though he had not yet begun
to make surveys of any of the routes which he followed. In 1785 he
made the journey from Churchill to York Factory along the shores of
Hudson Bay; in 1786 he ascended the Hayes and Saskatchewan rivers
from York Factory past Cumberland and Hudson Houses to Manchester
House. From there he made a journey south-westward across the
great plains to a camp of the Piegan on the banks of Bow river, where
he spent a winter (1787–88 ?), returning to Manchester House in the
following year. About 1788 he seems to have returned to Hudson's
House; and from Hudson's House he travelled in 1789 to Cumberland
House, in Pine Island lake, one of the expansions of the Saskatchewan
river. It was here, in the winter of 1789–90, that he began his life-
work as a surveyor by taking a large number of astronomical observations.
By these observations he determined the exact position of Cumberland
House on the surface of the globe, so that no matter how hastily his
surveys of the surrounding country might be made, he had that as a
definite fixed position to which to refer.

1790

In the spring of 1790 he was ordered to accompany the fur brigade
to York Factory; and on June 9 he left Cumberland House, and
began the survey from there down the Saskatchewan river to its
mouth, which was reached on June 15. Thence he proceeded along
the north shore of Great Lake (Lake Winnipeg) through Playgreen
(Buscuscoggan) lake, and from there by the regular water route

through Holy (Oxford) lake, Trout river, Knee and Swampy lakes, and Hayes river to York Factory. After staying a while at York Factory he returned to Cumberland House, doubtless by the same route (for he did not make another survey), and wintered there.

1791

In the summer of 1791 he again descended to York Factory, and here he spent the following year.

1792

On September 5, 1792, he left York Factory with two canoes, descended Hayes river, rounded the point in Hudson Bay, and ascended the Nelson river, making a survey of the route as he went. On September 28 he reached Split lake, and on September 30 the "Saskatchewan River."[1] A little farther up stream William Cook with one of the canoes turned up Grass river to Chatham House on Wintering lake, but Thompson with the other canoe kept on up the main stream, and on October 8 arrived at a rocky point on the west side of Sipiwesk lake, where he built a trading post.[2] During the winter he took no less than twenty-eight lunar observations for longitude. However, this proved to be a poor place for either fish or game, and on several occasions he was obliged to go to Chatham House, which was only about thirty miles away, and seek provisions from his friend William Cook.

1793

In the following spring, when the river was clear of ice, he started from Seepaywisk House, and descended to the lower end of the lake,

[1] In applying the name "Saskatchewan River" to that portion of the Nelson river above Split river, Thompson was doubtless following the usage of the natives and employees of the Hudson's Bay Company of that time. There is ground for believing that the name Saskatchewan was originally applied to that portion of the Nelson river which flows from Lake Winnipeg to Split lake, rather than to the great river above Lake Winnipeg to which the name is now applied.
[2] The place where "Seepaywisk House" appears to have stood is now covered with a grove of poplars, with a forest of spruce in the background. Two rocky points project into the lake and form a snug little harbour for small boats. Looking towards the south-west, Sipiwesk lake, dotted with dark green islands, extends away to the distant horizon.

carried over Cross Portage, surveyed Susquagemow (Landing) lake,[1] carried over Thicket Portage, and entered Chatham (Wintering) lake, where, on a long point extending northward into the lake, the Company had a post. After three days spent here he resumed his journey, first across the rest of Wintering lake, then over two portages, two-thirds of a mile and a mile and a quarter long respectively, to McKay's (Paint) lake, now known as Manuminan or (Red) Paint lake, and thence across into Pipe lake and up Weepiskow (Burntwood) river, and through Wuskwatim and Burntwood lakes.   From Burntwood river he carried his canoe across Duck Portage into Missinipi (Churchill) river, which he ascended for thirty-three miles, intending to proceed to Reindeer lake. He was, however, unable to find the Indians whom he expected to meet, and in latitude 55° 25′ 20″ N., longitude 102° 10′ 49″ W., he turned back and made his way down the Burntwood and Nelson rivers to York Factory, where he arrived on July 21. During this journey he had discovered, and determined the positions of, three settlements of the Canadian traders, kept respectively by McKay, Baldwin, and White (Wabiscow), and he had found a route which was short and easy compared to that used by the Canadian traders by which to bring in supplies to oppose them.   His journal contains minute descriptions of all parts of this route, with the lengths and positions of the portages, how to approach or depart from them with canoes, how and where the rapids should be run, and so forth.

After stopping a few weeks at the headquarters of the Hudson's Bay Company on the shore of Hudson Bay, the energetic young surveyor set off once more. By the Hayes river route he ascended again to the Saskatchewan river, and arrived on October 5 at his old home at Cumberland House.   On the 8th he left Cumberland House, and continued the ascent of the Saskatchewan.   On the 15th he reached the Forks, where he turned up the south branch, and after three days' travel he reached South Branch House,[2] situated somewhere

---

[1] The Cree name for this lake is Suskiskwegimew Sakahigan, translated as Where-the-Sturgeon-put-their-heads-against-the-Rock lake. This is the lake called by Jéremie, who was in charge of Fort Bourbon in 1714, Anisquaoui-gamou, although the meaning given by him for the Indian word is incorrect.

[2] It does not appear when this trading post was founded, but it was visited by Thompson on October 18, 1793. On June 24, 1794, according to the journal of Peter Fidler, who was at York Factory at the time, it was plundered and burnt by the Fall Indians who had plundered Manchester House the previous autumn. There were nine people in the fort at the time. Of these,

near Gardepui's Crossing, east of Duck lake. Here he took horses, and reached Manchester House, his former home on the North Saskatchewan, on October 28, and Buckingham House on October 31, the latter situated on the north side of the North Saskatchewan, in latitude 53° 52' 7″ N. In the immediate vicinity was a new post of the North-West Company, called Fort George, which had been built by Angus Shaw the previous year, and which was then in charge of Angus Shaw and John McDonald of Garth.

While Thompson travelled on horseback, the boats with their cargoes continued up the stream, but unfortunately the winter set in early that year, and they were caught in the ice near the site of the present town of Battleford, and were obliged to transport the goods on horseback the rest of the way to Buckingham House.

From Buckingham House Thompson rode out to the Beaver hills, near where Fort Augustus was afterwards built, and returned to Buckingham House on November 29. Here he spent the winter, keeping, as usual, a meteorological register, taking observations for longitude and latitude, and working out his former traverses by latitude and departure.

1794

On May 16, 1794, he started down stream to York Factory. The river from Buckingham House to the Forks had not yet been surveyed, therefore he surveyed that portion of it, and continued on making a resurvey of the rest of the river. Manchester House was passed on the evening of May 18, and on May 22 he reached what he calls the Lower Crossing, a place which his observation for

three men, Magnus Annel, Hugh Brough, and William Fea, one woman and two children were murdered ; two young women were carried away as slaves ; and one man named Vandereil escaped by concealing himself in an old cellar, and reached York Factory with the news of the massacre on August 11. The North-West Company had a post about one thousand yards away, which the Indians attacked, but from which they were beaten off with a loss of fourteen killed and wounded. After this, however, the post was abandoned, and the men went down the river to some place on the Saskatchewan below the Forks. Later, in 1804, the post was rebuilt at a place six miles above its former site, after the abandonment of Chesterfield House, which was at the Forks of the Red Deer and Bow rivers still farther up the same river. Daniel Harmon was at this post for the North-West Company in 1805, and Joseph Howse for the Hudson's Bay Company in 1806-7. Peter Fidler puts it in latitude 52° 53′ N., which would be near Gardepui's Crossing.

latitude places in Section 18, Tp. 46, Range 3, west of the Third
Principle Meridian, near the village of Silver Grove. From here
William Tomison, who was probably now in charge of this brigade of
canoes, rode over to South Branch House. Two places of the name
of Hudson's House were then passed, the lower of the two being
Tomison's old home.[1]   On May 27 the mouth of the South Branch
was reached, and next day Thompson seems to have passed the site of
Fort à la Corne, which was not occupied at that time, without noticing
it; for the first place he mentions is Isaac's House, 38' of longitude
east of the Forks, which would place it somewhere in Range 17 west
of the Second Meridian.   Nine and three-quarter miles below it was
the Canadian post at the "Nepoin," kept by Porter and McLeod.
Still lower down the river was "Hungry Hall," where Ross and
Thoburn had lived in 1792–93, doubtless at Tobin Rapids, which is
about fourteen miles above Sturgeon river.[2]

On June 2 he arrived at Cumberland House.   But instead of
returning to the Saskatchewan by Tearing river, and proceeding
thence by the regular route through Lake Winnipeg to York Factory,
he turned north-eastward through his old trading ground, and paddled
through Namew or Sturgeon lake, up Goose river to Goose lake,
and thence into Athapapuskow lake.   On the east side of this
lake he left the waters which flow southward to the Saskatchewan,
and crossed Cranberry Portage, a level portage of two thousand six
hundred and seventy-five paces, which, when visited by the writer
in the fall of 1896, was beautifully dry throughout its length.   From

---

[1] These two houses, referred to respectively as Upper and Lower Hudson's
House, are shown by Thompson's survey to have been situated on the north-
west bank of the river about fifteen miles apart.   The upper post was established by Philip Turnor for the Hudson's Bay Company, about 1776, as an
outpost from Cumberland House, and was then the uppermost settlement on the
Saskatchewan river.   In the Introduction to Captain Cook's *Third Voyage*,
it is stated, apparently on Turnor's authority, to have been in latitude 53° 0'
32" N.   This agrees closely with Thompson's survey, and places it in
Section 32, Tp. 46, Range 3, west of the Third Meridian, about four miles
north of Silver Grove, Saskatchewan.   Lower Hudson's House, which was
built at a later date, apparently by Tomison, was situated fifteen miles
farther down the river three or four miles below a place now known as Yellow
Banks, opposite the mouth of Steep Creek.   Here Thompson had spent the
winter of 1788–89.

[2] Alexander Henry, ascending this river in 1808, speaks of "an old establishment, abandoned many years ago," just above " Grand " (Tobin) Rapids.

the portage he crossed Cranberry lake, descended the Elbow river to Ithenootosequan or Elbow lake, and thence went on down Grass river, between barren, rocky hills, to Reed lake. Here he left Ross to build a trading post, and himself continued down Crooked and File rivers to Burntwood lake, noting on the way two places which had been occupied respectively by the traders from Churchill and by Robert Thompson during the previous winter. Thence he followed his route of the previous spring down the Burntwood and Nelson rivers to York Factory. He arrived at the latter place on July 5, and remained there twenty-one days. Then he turned back, and travelling up Nelson and Grass rivers, reached Reed Lake House on Reed lake on September 2. Here, in the midst of an excellent country for fish, game, and fur-bearing animals, he spent the winter of 1794–95, and during the intervals of an active fur trade, he took forty-six lunar distance observations for longitude.

1795

This year, in company with Malcolm Ross, Thompson arrived at York Factory on July 5 with three large and two small canoes. On July 18, he and Ross left York Factory and ascended the Nelson river. On September 6, they arrived at Duck Portage at the west end of Sisipuk lake, which is one of the expansions of the Churchill river. Here they decided to divide the goods they had brought for trade, Ross going on with two large canoes and one small canoe to a point a mile below the mouth of Reindeer river, where he built a house named by him Fairford House. Thompson with four men built a trading post on the south side of Duck Portage. His observations place it in latitude 55° 40′ 30″ N., and longitude 102° 7′ 37″ W., a position practically identical with that which it occupies on the most recent maps. He had hardly got his house built when a Canadian arrived with six Indians in a large canoe, and built a house thirty yards to the eastward.

1796

On January 12, 1796, George Charles with five men from Churchill called with the ostensible object of seeing if it were possible to collect some debts that were owed to them by the Indians, and when Charles departed two days later for Three Point lake he left three men behind for the winter. Thus Thompson had not only to compete with the

Canadians from Montreal, but he had also to compete in trade with other employees of the Hudson's Bay Company from Churchill, who were not under the authority of the Council at York. The remainder of the winter seems to have been rather uneventful, broken only by visits from employees of the Company from Reed lake, Fairford House, and Three Point lake.

In the spring Thompson first made a survey eastward to the mouth of the Kississing river. Then, after returning to Duck Portage House, he ascended and surveyed the Churchill river to Fairford House, a mile below the mouth of Reindeer river. Here he obtained, with difficulty, two Indian canoemen, and on June 10 started to make a survey northward through Reindeer and Wollaston lakes, and down Black river to the east end of Lake Athabaska; but the account of this survey need not be repeated here, as it will be found in full in Thompson's own words on pages 133–53. That autumn Thompson returned to Reindeer lake, and spent the winter of 1796–97 with Malcolm Ross at a post which he called Bedford House, on the west side of that lake.

<h2 style="text-align:center">1797</h2>

On May 28, 1797, having decided to sever his connection with the Hudson's Bay Company, Thompson arrived on foot at the house of Alexander Fraser, at the head of the Reindeer river,[1] and took employment with the North-West Company. On June 7, after having been hospitably entertained by the North-West Company's agent, he set out for Cumberland House, and reached it on June 23. After a stay of four days here, he set out once more, reached Lake Winnipeg on June 28, and travelling by way of Winnipeg river, arrived at Grand Portage, Lake Superior, on July 22, having as usual made a survey of his route.

On August 9 he set out from Grand Portage on one of his most remarkable journeys. In company with Hugh McGillis, he descended Rainy river, passing a fort half a mile below the Falls on the 21st, and went on through Rainy lake and Lake of the Woods. From this lake he descended Winnipeg river, and on September 1 he reached

[1] No sign of this old trading post could be found when I passed through the lake in 1894; but Thompson states that it was in latitude 56° 20′ 22″ N., which would place it on Big Island a little north of the present outpost of the Hudson's Bay Company, or on the mainland opposite this island.

Lake Winnipeg. He crossed this lake, ascended the Dauphin river, crossed Lake Manito (Manitoba), and reached Lake Winnipegosis by way of the Meadow Portage. On September 17, being camped a mile and a half north of the Little Dauphin (Mossy) river, the party received provisions from Fort Dauphin, on or near Dauphin lake.[1] They then proceeded northward up the west shore of Lake

---

[1] Fort Dauphin was one of the oldest trading posts in the North-West. Its position was changed from time to time, although it was always in the good hunting ground in the vicinity of Dauphin lake. It was first built on the Mossy river in the autumn of 1741, by Pierre, one of the sons of the Sieur de la Vérendrye, who had travelled northward from Fort la Reine (Portage la Prairie), across Prairie Portage into Lake Manitoba, and thence by Lake Winnipegosis into Mossy river. Bougainville states that it was eighty leagues from La Reine on the river Minanghenachequeké, which is the present Indian name for Mossy river. Harmon, in his *Journal*, p. 52, speaks of "the establishment at the entrance of the River Dauphin, which falls into the west end of this [Winnepegosis] lake. At that place a French missionary resided before the British obtained possession of Canada. He remained there but a short time." In 1889, I found the cellars and ruins of an old trading post on the east bank of the Mossy river, three-quarters of a mile above its mouth, on a narrow strip of grassy land between the forest and the river. The site was probably built upon several times; but possibly the first house erected here was that of Pierre de la Vérendrye. Peter Pond, who appears to have been the first Englishman to occupy a fort of this name after the place was abandoned by the French, gives the location of the post occupied by him in 1775, at the north-west angle of Lake Dauphin. (See Peter Pond's map of 1790, Can. Arch. Report, 1890, p. 53.) But I could find no trace of the existence of a house at that place.

When Thompson was at the mouth of Mossy river in 1797, Fort Dauphin was evidently a supply depot for provisions. The post was not then, however, at the mouth of Mossy river, for it took four days for the canoes to go from Meadow Portage to the mouth of Mossy river, a distance of thirteen miles, thence to the trading post, and back to the mouth of the river. Thompson was never on Lake Dauphin, but his map shows it as lying east and west, and the post of the North-West Company appears on a stream flowing into the lake on its southern side. The lake lies north-west and south-east, and the south-western sides of all these lakes were commonly spoken of by travellers as their southern sides, the error being in large part accounted for by the considerable variation of the magnetic needle. The largest stream flowing into the south-west side of the lake is Valley river; and in all probability the house visited by Thompson's men in 1797 must be identified with the remains of an old post on the south side of Valley river a few miles above its mouth, and about two miles in a straight line back from the lake.

Ruins of another trading post of a later date, belonging to the Hudson's Bay Company, exist in the poplar forest on the west side of the lake eight

Winnipegosis. On September 19, McGillis left to go up the Red Deer river, whereas Thompson stopped at the mouth of Shoal river. He ascended this river, passed through Swan lake, and ascended Swan river for four miles and three-quarters to Swan River House, on the north bank of the stream, in latitude 52° 24′ 5″ N.[1]

Horses were then in common use in the Swan river valley, and after resting a day at the post, Thompson and Cuthbert Grant borrowed two horses from Thomas Swain of the Hudson's Bay Company, and started up the valley on a trail which ran for most of the distance along the north side of the river. On the second day they crossed to the south side of Swan river, and rode six miles to a house kept by one Belleau in a "hummock of pines" on the bank of Snake Creek, almost on the present line of the Second Principal Meridian, and about six miles north of Fort Pelly. From here he turned southward, and continued his survey past the post of the Hudson's Bay Company at the Elbow of the Assiniboine river to the house of Cuthbert Grant, which was situated in Tp. 28, Range 31, south-west of the present village of Runnymede on the Canadian Northern Railway.[2] Here he remained till October 14, when he returned to Belleau's House on Snake Creek, in order, if possible, to obtain guides to take him up the Swan river, across the watershed to Red Deer river, and thence around to the head waters of the Assiniboine river. From this date to November 28 his journal was lost, but he states, "I surveyed the Stone Indian [Assiniboine] River upward, and its sources, and the Red Deer River and its sources, and

miles south of the mouth of Valley river. Alexander Murray is said to have traded here in the late seventies. The ruins of yet another house of the Hudson's Bay Company, which was only used as a winter post for a short time in the seventies, is to be seen at the south-east angle of the lake.

[1] As Harmon, who arrived here three years later, points out in his *Journal*, this post is twelve miles up the river from its mouth; and this is where it is placed on J. B. Tyrrell's map of North-Western Manitoba (1891), published by the Geological Survey of Canada. The house was in a grove of poplar; and half a mile farther west was the Dog Knoll, where the men used to move the stores in times of flood. A couple of miles higher up the river, and twenty-five paces back of it on the north side, where the banks are fifteen feet high, is the position of a post of the Hudson's Bay Company.

[2] In 1890 the remains of an old establishment were to be seen in the south-west quarter, Section 14, Tp. 28, R. 31, west of the First Meridian, five hundred paces east of the bank of the river, and fifty paces from the foot of the side of the valley, at the mouth of a dry ravine.

from thence returned to the house of Mr. Cuthbert Grant, at the
Brooks, on the Stone Indian River." He gives in his journal, however, traverses worked out by latitude and departure which show his
course to have been from Belleau's House to the Upper House on Red
Deer river, in latitude 52° 47′ 44″ N.[1] From here he turned south-
westward, and continued his survey to the "Upper House on Stone
Indian River," afterwards known as Alexandria, where Daniel Harmon
spent the years 1800-1805.[2] From Alexandria he travelled down the
river to the Elbow, and thence to Cuthbert Grant's House. From
there he continued southward to Thorburn's House on the Qu' Appelle
river, a few miles above its mouth, in latitude 50° 28′ 57″ N., and
thence to McDonnell's House a mile and a half above the mouth of
the Souris river.

The winter had by this time set in, when travelling on the open
plains was unpleasant and dangerous, but Thompson was anxious to
find out the exact positions of those Indian villages on the Missouri
where the people lived by the cultivation of corn as well as by hunting
the buffalo. With this object in view, and with the hope also that
some of these Indians might be induced to establish a regular trade
with the North-West Company, he set out from McDonnell's (Assiniboine) House, on November 28, with nine men, a few horses, and
thirty dogs, and started south-westward across the plain. On December 7 he reached Old Ash House on the Souris river, "settled
two years ago and abandoned the following spring" ; and here, having
been unable to procure a guide for the rest of the journey, he was
himself compelled to assume the lead. By way of Turtle Mountain,
he struck across the plains until he again reached the Souris river,

---

[1] Thompson's map shows this house to have been on the north bank of the
Red Deer river. It was probably opposite the mouth of the Etoimami river,
between three and four miles south of Hudson Bay Junction on the Canadian
Northern Railway, where the ruins of two old houses were to be seen in 1889.
This post is probably the one referred to as Fort La Biche on Pond's map of
1790, though there it is wrongly placed on the Swan river. It was doubtless
one of the oldest trading posts south of the Saskatchewan river and west of
the Manitoba lakes ; the only other posts designated on this map being Fort
Dauphin on Lake Dauphin, and Fort Epinette on the Assiniboine river.

[2] See Harmon's *Journal*, p. 59. Thompson's map places this post on the
west side of the Assiniboine river in latitude 51° 46′ 58″ N., which would place
it in Section 27, Tp. 32, R. 3, west of the Second Meridian. Peter Fidler had
spent the winter of 1795-96 in an adjoining house belonging to the Hudson's
Bay Company, which was called by him Charlton House.

which he followed up to its "bight"; thence he crossed the plains, a distance of thirty-seven miles, to the Missouri river, reaching it on December 29 at a point six miles above the upper of the Mandan villages. At these villages, which were five in number, he remained until January 10, trying to induce the Indians to come north to trade, but with very little success, as they were afraid of the Sioux. While here, he wrote down a vocabulary of the Mandan language, containing about three hundred and seventy-five words.

1798

He left the Mandan villages on January 10, 1798, but being delayed by severe storms, did not reach the Souris river until January 24, and he did not arrive at McDonnell's House at the mouth of Souris river until February 3. The account of this journey is given in his own words on pages 209–42. At Souris River Post he remained until February 26, making up his notes and plans, and preparing himself for a longer trip, this time on foot, to connect the waters of the Red and Mississippi rivers, and thence onward to Lake Superior, a trip which his companions ridiculed as being impossible to accomplish before the advent of summer. On February 26, however, he started out on foot with a dog team, and followed the course of the Assiniboine eastward to its mouth, making as usual a survey of his route; and passing on his way Pine Fort and Poplar House, both of which had been abandoned, and some houses a little below the Meadow Portage to Lake Manitoba. On March 7 he reached the Forks of the Assiniboine and Red rivers, the site of the present city of Winnipeg, though no mention is made of any habitation there at that time. Travelling on the ice, he turned up the latter stream, and on the second day reached Chaboillez's old house of the North-West Company, a quarter of a mile up Rat Creek above its mouth, in latitude 49° 33′ 58″ N., a few miles west of Niverville, on the Emerson branch of the Canadian Pacific Railway.

On March 14 he crossed the boundary line into the United States, and reached the house of Charles Chaboillez at the mouth of Summerberry or Pembina river, in latitude 48° 58′ 29″ N., on the site of the present town of Pembina in North Dakota. After a week spent here, he proceeded up Red river, passing the house of the North-West Company kept by a trader named Roy, at the mouth of Salt river, and then ascended Red Lake river to the mouth of Clear river, where there was a North-West Company's house kept by Baptiste Cadotte, in latitude 47° 54′ 21″ N., close to the present site of Red Lake Falls. He reached this house on March 24, and at once endeavoured to proceed eastward on foot, but was obliged to return and wait for the breaking up of the ice, as "the snow thawing made the open country like a lake of open water." On April 9 he made a fresh start from Cadotte's House, this time in a canoe with three men. He ascended Clear river for six days, carried across to Red Lake river, and ascended Red Lake river to Red lake, which he reached at a point in latitude 47° 58′ 15″ N.

The lake was still covered with ice, but after waiting for three days he was able to force his canoe southward for two miles between the ice and the shore to an old house which had been occupied by Cadotte the previous winter. Here, farther progress by water being impossible, he built a sled, and putting the canoe and all the baggage of the party on it, he harnessed himself and men in front of it, and hauled it for fifteen miles across the ice of the lake to a portage six miles in length, which was crossed the following day to a small brook; after which he wound his way through small lakes and brooks, and walked over short portages till, on April 27, he arrived at Turtle lake, from which flows "Turtle Brook." This lake was pronounced by Thompson to be the source of the Mississippi. A generation later it was discovered that the Mississippi took its rise in Itasca lake, a few miles farther south. But the two lakes are so near together that it may be said that to this indefatigable, but hitherto almost unknown, geographer belongs the virtual credit of discovering the head-waters of this great river.

From Turtle lake Thompson descended Turtle Brook to Red Cedar (Cass) lake, on which there was a North-West Company's house, kept by John Sayer, which he places in latitude 47° 27′ 56″ N. and longitude 95° W. He remained here from April 29 to May 3; then he again embarked and struck across to the Mississippi river, down which he travelled through "Winnipegoos" (Winnibigoshish) lake to the mouth of Sand Lake river. Here he left the main stream of the Mississippi, and turned up Sand Lake river to Sand lake (Sandy lake in Aitkin county), on which was a house belonging to the North-West Company, a mile and a quarter east from the head of the river, in latitude 46° 46′ 39″ N. From this house he crossed the lake to the mouth of Savannah Brook, which he followed up to the Savannah Carrying Place, a deep bog four miles across. He crossed this portage to a small creek that flows into the St. Louis river, and descended the latter stream to Fond du Lac House, in latitude 46° 44′ 2″ N., three miles up the river from Lake Superior. He reached this post on May 10, two months and eighteen days after leaving the mouth of the Souris river. From here he surveyed the south shore of. Lake Superior; and on May 20 he arrived at the Falls of Ste. Marie. On June 1 he left Sault Ste. Marie in a light canoe with eleven men, in company with Messrs. Mackenzie, McLeod, and Stuart, and reached Grand Portage on June 7. The time was a busy one at this the central post of the North-West Company, and in his journal Thompson gives a very interesting account of the men who were almost daily arriving from, and departing for, many widely separated posts throughout the west.

On July 14 he started once more for the interior with the English (Churchill) river brigade, and after passing Fort Charlotte, Rainy Lake House, and Rat Portage, he arrived at "Winnipeg House,"[1] at the mouth of the Winnipeg river, on July 31. Having travelled along the east shore of Lake Winnipeg, he reached the mouth of the Saskatchewan on August 9, and on August 18 Cumberland House, where Peter Fidler was in charge at the English (Hudson's Bay Company) House, and Primo was in charge of the post of the North-West Company. On August 19 he left here, his destination being Lake La Biche, or Red Deer lake. Ascending the Sturgeon-weir river, and passing through Amisk lake, he reached Missinipi (Churchill) river by way of the Frog Portage on August 24, ascended Churchill river to the mouth of the Rapid river where there was a house occupied at the time by "Roy, a Canadian, all alone," and up this stream to Lake La Ronge, on which was the site of an old post where Simon Fraser had wintered in 1795-96. He then returned to Churchill river, and a mile above the mouth of Rapid river found a house on the north bank which the men of the Hudson's Bay Company had recently abandoned. He continued to ascend the

---

[1] This house, called also Fort Alexander and Bas de la Rivière, is said by Roderick Mackenzie to have been established in 1792 by Toussaint Lesieur a few miles below and opposite the old French Fort Maurepas. Gabriel Franchère, who passed the place in 1814, wrote: "This trading post had more the air of a large and well-cultivated farm, than a fur traders' factory; a neat and elegant mansion, built on a slight eminence, and surrounded with barns, stables, storehouses, &c., and by fields of barley, peas, oats, and potatoes." The site is still occupied by the Hudson's Bay Company.

river to Isle à la Crosse lake. On September 6 he reached the "new fort of the North-West Company's"[1] at the southern end of the lake, in latitude 56° 26′ 15″ N., three-quarters of a mile north-east of the old settlement which had been visited by Turnor several years before.

Here he left goods for Alexander McKay, who was in charge of the post, and on September 8 he began the ascent of Beaver river, and continued south to the trading post on Green lake, in latitude 54° 17′ 9″ N., on the east side of the lake, near its north end. At Green Lake House he left his canoes to proceed up Beaver river, while he himself took horses and struck across the country a little south of west to Fort George, on the Saskatchewan river, close to the Hudson's Bay Company's post at Buckingham House, where he had wintered in 1793–94. After a delay of three or four days at this place, he turned north-westward to Beaver river, which he reached at the mouth of Moose Creek in latitude 54° 22′ 14″ N., whence with great difficulty he ascended Beaver river and Red Deer Brook to Red Deer lake (Lake La Biche), where he built a house[2] in latitude 54° 46′ 32″ N. At this house he remained for the winter, trading with the Indians and taking astronomical observations.

1799

Some time between the middle and end of March 1799, he left Lake La Biche for Fort Augustus, which at this time was situated on the north bank of the North Saskatchewan river, a mile and a half above the mouth of Sturgeon river, within the present settlement of Fort Saskatchewan. This post he places in latitude 53° 44′ 52″ N. and longitude 113° 11′ W., a mile east of its true position. It had been built four or five years before in order to secure the trade with the Blackfeet. After staying here about two weeks, he set out on April 19, with three horses and five men, and travelling north-westward, reached the Pembina river on the evening of the 21st, in latitude

[1] The position now occupied by the Hudson's Bay Company post of Isle à la Crosse is at the bottom of a little bay opening eastward near the south end of the lake. A little farther north is the site of a former post of the Hudson's Bay Company; and two other sites, one of which is said to have been occupied by the North-West Company, are on the point still farther north. On Thompson's map the post of the North-West Company is marked on the point north of the arm of the lake which stretches westward, toward Buffalo lake; but its exact position is not known.

[2] A post had previously been built by Angus Shaw on this lake in 1789.

54° 15′ 4″ N., near where it crosses the Fifth Meridian. Here a canoe had been built for him; so, sending back the horses, he started down the river, and reached its mouth on Athabaska river on April 25. He surveyed this stream down to the mouth of Lesser Slave Lake river; then he turned into this stream, and surveyed it up to Lesser Slave lake; and having returned thence, he continued down the Athabaska river to the new post at the mouth of the Clearwater, where Fort McMurray now stands. On May 10, after remaining at this post for a few days, he continued his survey, this time up the "Methy Portage" (Clearwater) river, crossed the Methy Portage, and descended the Churchill river through Buffalo lake to Isle à la Crosse lake, which he reached on May 20. Thence he proceeded direct to Grand Portage. From Grand Portage he accompanied John McDonald of Garth westward up the Saskatchewan river to Fort George, which was found to be in a ruinous condition; and here he spent the winter.

1800

In the spring of 1800 Thompson made an expedition on horseback from Fort George to Fort Augustus, and thence to Rocky Mountain House. On May 5 he embarked at Rocky Mountain House on the North Saskatchewan river, and made a survey of it to "The Elbow." On May 7 he "found the English [Hudson's Bay Company] encamped for building" at the mouth of a creek flowing in from the right, which he calls Sturgeon Creek (Buck Lake Creek), and on the same evening he reached White Mud House, where a clerk named Hughes was in charge for the North-West Company. This post was situated on the north bank in Section 30, Tp. 51, Range 2, west of the Fifth Meridian. On May 9 he reached Fort Augustus, and on May 12 Fort George, having passed a few miles above it what he designates as "Isle of Scotland, North-West Company, 1800 and 1801," apparently the island now known as Fort island, in Section 12, Tp. 55, R. 8, west of the Fourth Meridian.

On May 18 he again left Fort George, and on May 20 passed Umfreville's old house, in Section 4, Tp. 53, R. 25, west of the Third Meridian, where this trader had spent the winters of 1784–8. On May 21 he passed Island House, a mile and a half above the mouth of Birch Brook, near Manchester House of the Hudson's Bay Company; and on May 22, Turtle River House, a mile and a half below the mouth of Turtle Brook, evidently in Section 4, Tp. 46, R. 18, west

f

of the Third Meridian. Alexander Henry the younger describes this
house as situated on a low bottom on the south side of the river. On
May 28 Thompson camped at the Forks, and on June 7 he arrived at
the mouth of the Saskatchewan. His note-books give no further record
of his proceedings that summer, but a summary in his own handwriting
states that he continued east to Grand Portage, and returned to Rocky
Mountain House. He adds that "Mr. Duncan McGillivray came
and wintered also, to prepare to cross the mountains."

From Rocky Mountain House Thompson set out on horseback,
with five men and three pack-horses, on October 5. He travelled
up the Clearwater river, and over to the Red Deer river, which he
ascended till he reached the mouth of William Creek, a small brook
in latitude 51° 41' 41" N., longitude 114° 56' 40" W. There, in a
camp of Piegan Indians, he remained for a few days, and from there he
rode twenty-two miles west to the foot of the mountains to meet a band
of Kutenai, consisting of twenty-six men and seven women, who had
crossed the mountain in the hope of being able to reach his trading
post. He returned at once with them, in order to encourage them to
proceed, for the Piegan did their utmost to hinder and annoy them.
When they were ready to return to their own country west of the
mountains, he sent La Gassi and Le Blanc along to spend the following
winter with them. The route which they took, in order to avoid the
Piegan, was up the north side of the Saskatchewan river. These
two men, La Gassi and Le Blanc, were therefore in all probability the
first white men to cross the mountains at the head of the Saskatchewan
to the upper waters of the Columbia river.

On November 17, accompanied by Duncan McGillivray, and
attended by four men, he set out on horseback along the trail up
Clearwater river, crossed Red Deer river, and reached Bow river at
a point opposite to where the town of Calgary now stands, in latitude
51° 2' 56" N., longitude 113° 59' W. From here he surveyed the
north-east side of the river down to a short distance below the bend,
where he crossed it and went on to the Spitchee or Highwood river,
which he reached two miles above its mouth. From here he turned
a little west of south, and reached a camp of the Pikenows, or Piegan,
in latitude 50° 35' 30" N., probably on Tongue Flag Creek. After
stopping here for a short time in order to establish friendly relations
with these Indians, he turned north-westward and again reached Bow
river at a point which he places in latitude 51° 13' 57" N., longitude
114° 48' 22" W., a short distance above the mouth of Ghost river.

From here he followed the Bow river upwards, on its south bank for three miles, and then fording the stream he followed the trail on its north bank to the steep cliffs of the mountains near where the town of Exshaw is now situated.[1] Thence he returned to his old camp on the Bow river, and, crossing the stream, struck northward to Rocky Mountain House, which he reached on December 3.

During the same year Duncan McGillivray made a traverse westward from Rocky Mountain House, at first up the north side of the North Saskatchewan river for eight miles, thence across country to Brazeau river and up it to Brazeau lake, three miles beyond which he "proceeded to cross the Chain of Mountains that separates the sources of the North Branch (Brazeau) and the Athabaska River." Continuing still farther westward, he travelled four miles down a stream flowing towards the west into Athabaska river, from which point he returned to Rocky Mountain House. His traverse is carefully laid down in Thompson's note-book.

1801

During the winter of 1800–1801, Thompson remained at Rocky Mountain House, trading with the Indians, working out old observations and taking new ones, although the last record to be found for the winter is dated March 18.

In June Thompson made "a journey into the Rocky Mountains by land," which is to be found in his note-books worked out by latitude and departure. Accompanied by Hughes and seven men and an Indian guide, he followed the Saskatchewan up to a point twenty-eight miles above Rocky Mountain House, measured in a straight line. Here he left the main river and struck southward up the valley of Sheep river to its source in one of the eastern ranges of the Rocky Mountains. At this point it was found impossible to take the

---

[1] Near this point, McGillivray killed and preserved a mountain sheep, which about three years later formed the basis of three names—*Ovis canadensis* Shaw, *Ovis cervina* Desmarest, and " belier de montagne " of Geoffroy (later latinized as *Ovis montana* by Cuvier). Although wild sheep had long been known to inhabit North America, this specimen was the first to reach the hands of systematic naturalists. Curiously enough, the two names first mentioned were published so nearly at the same time that the question of priority has been the subject even within the past few years of considerable controversy. Though the evidence is not absolutely conclusive, the name *canadensis* seems best entitled to recognition. The important matter in the present connection, however, is the locality from which the type came. [E. A. P.]

horses further; and, as the guide knew of no other pass, the party returned to the Saskatchewan river. An effort was made to ascend the stream in a canoe; but the river was in flood, and it proved impossible to stem the current. The attempt to cross the mountains was therefore abandoned for the time; and the party returned to Rocky Mountain House, where they arrived on June 30.

The remainder of the summer and the following winter were spent at Rocky Mountain House; but in August and September Thompson made a trip to Fort Augustus and back on horseback.

1802

In May, 1802, he again descended the Saskatchewan river, and continued on to Lake Superior, this time to the mouth of the Kaministikwia river at Fort William, to which place the headquarters of the North-West Company had been moved the previous year. From Fort William he returned westward to Lesser Slave lake, though by what route does not appear from his journals. Probably he ascended the Saskatchewan, and crossed overland from Fort Augustus to Athabaska river, as he had done in 1799. Between October 21 and November 9 he ascended from the mouth of Lesser Slave Lake river to the house on the west side of Lesser Slave lake, which he places in latitude 55° 32' 36" N., on or near the site of the present trading post of the Hudson's Bay Company. Thence he continued northward to a post which he speaks of as the "Forks of the Peace River,"[1] a name which still survives in a slightly changed form as Peace River Landing. He places this post five miles above the mouth of Smoky river, in latitude 56° 8' 17" N., and longitude 117° 13' 14" W.; at that time the variation of the magnetic needle was 23½° East.

1803

The year 1803 Thompson spent almost wholly at Peace River Forks. From January 18 to June 5 he kept a meteorological journal at this post, jotting down at the same time many interesting notes. On June 5 he notices the arrival of a canoe of the X Y Company, who put up one hundred yards farther up the stream, "where they are going to build." From June 5 to June 24 he

---

[1] This post had been built by Alexander Mackenzie ten years before, when he was on his journey from Lake Athabaska to the Pacific ocean.

was hunting in the vicinity; but on June 25 the meteorological journal was resumed, and kept up regularly to December 11. Between this date and December 29, Thompson made a trip with dogs to Lesser Slave lake and back.

1804

On February 29 he set off up the river on foot, with a team of dogs to carry his provisions and baggage, and reached "Rocky Mountain House,"[1] the most westerly post of the North-West Company at that time, on March 6. This post he places in latitude 56° 12′ 54″ N., longitude 120° 38′ W. After remaining here for two days, he once more turned eastward, and retraced his steps down the river, and arrived at Peace River Forks on March 13.

On March 15, probably accompanied by his wife and two children, he started on the long journey to Fort William. He travelled down the river on the ice to Horse Shoe House, in latitude 57° 8′ N.; here he remained from March 20 to April 30, until the ice should break and clear out of the river; then he continued his journey down the river by canoe. On May 2 he passed a post of the North-West Company, which he calls Fort Vermilion, though it was considerably higher up the river than the present Fort Vermilion of the Hudson's Bay Company. Below it the following places are recorded by him in succession : " Old Fort du Tremble " ; " Fort Liard, N. W. Co., Mr. Fraser " (not far from the site of the present Fort Vermilion); " Fort, Mr. Wintzel, N. W. Co." (five miles below the lower portion of Vermilion Falls); and " Grand Marais, N. W. Co., now deserted." On May 12, in company with a trader named Wentzel, he arrived at Athabaska House, on the north shore of Lake Athabaska, in latitude 58° 42′ 50″ N., on the site of the present Fort Chipewyan.[2] Here he remained for three days ; then he continued his survey across Lake Athabaska and up Athabaska river. On May 17 he passed Peter Pond's old

[1] This post must not be confounded with Rocky Mountain House on the Saskatchewan river, which was Thompson's home for so many winters.

[2] The old fort which had been built by Roderick Mackenzie in 1788, where Philip Turnor spent the winter of 1791-92, was on the south side of Lake Athabaska in latitude 58° 38′ N., longitude 110° 26¼′ W., about twenty-five miles east of Fort Chipewyan, on the point marked Old Fort Point on J. B. Tyrrell's map of Lake Athabaska. It was from this post that Alexander Mackenzie started, in 1789 and 1792, on his journeys of discovery down the Mackenzie river to the Arctic ocean, and up the Peace river and westward to the Pacific

trading post on the bank of the river, where Pond, the first white trader who had ventured so far west and north as this river, had wintered in 1778–9; and on May 19 he reached the trading post at the mouth of the Clearwater river. From here he proceeded along the route he had already surveyed, up Clearwater river, across the Methy Portage, down the Churchill river to Frog Portage, and thence by Cumberland House to Fort William.

After a short stay at headquarters, he turned back toward the west. This time he travelled up the Kaministikwia river to Dog lake, through this lake, and up the Dog river, and across to Lac des Mille Lacs, where the North-West Company had a post to the right of two islands in latitude 48° 48′ 27″ N., and thence westward to Lake La Croix and Rainy lake, and thence onward by the usual route to Cumberland House, where he arrived on September 8.

From Cumberland House he now turned aside to spend the winter on his old trading ground in what he calls the "Muskrat Country." On September 10 he struck off northward through Sturgeon, Goose, and Athapapuskow lakes to Cranberry Portage, which he crossed into Cranberry lake. At the narrows in this lake he left men to build a trading post. He himself continued on to Reed lake, ascended Little Swan river, and portaged into File lake, whence he descended File river into Burntwood lake, and continued on to Missinipi (Churchill) river, down which he travelled for a short distance to an old fort (Nelson House), which he reached on October 1. After making arrangements to provision this post, he continued on down the river, and arrived at Musquawegan (Bear's Backbone) Post on October 6, in latitude 56° 13′ 7″ N., longitude 100° 25′ 50″ W. The exact location of this post has never been determined, except as it is shown on Thompson's map, for no white man is known to have visited this place since his time. Here Thompson remained until the following spring, with his old schoolmate, George Charles, opposing him in the interest of the Hudson's Bay Company.

---

ocean. When Thompson passed it in 1804, it seems to have been abandoned, as the North-West Company had moved the post over to the present site of Fort Chipewyan at the west end of the lake some years before. The Hudson's Bay Company's trading post at this lake was first built by Peter Fidler in 1802, and was called Nottingham House, after the North-Westers had already been in occupation of the country for twenty-four years. Fidler occupied the post until 1806, when he abandoned it, as he had had no success in trading with the Indians.

On May 27 and 28, 1805, he made a journey to the post at the south end of (South) Indian lake and Churchill river, which he places in latitude 56° 48′ 20″ N. This place is about two hundred and fifty miles from Fort Churchill on Hudson Bay, and is the most north-easterly point reached by Thompson while in the service of the North-West Company. On June 1 he left Musquawegan, and travelled upstream to the Forks of the Missinipi (Churchill), which he reached on June 4, and thence he proceeded by Burntwood Portage, File river, and Cranberry Portage to Cumberland House, where he arrived on June 17. Here he learned for the first time that the North-West and X Y Companies had united, by an agreement signed on November 5, 1804. He left Cumberland House on June 23, and returned to the fort on Cranberry lake, where he arrived on June 27, and remained until July 25. On this date he set out for Reindeer lake. He carried over the Cranberry portage, passed through Athapapuskow lake and river, crossed Goose lake, and descended Goose river to Sturgeon-weir river, up which he turned to Beaver lake. Thence he followed the regular route to Trade (Frog) Portage, descended the Churchill river, and ascended Reindeer river to Reindeer lake, where he arrived on August 4. Here he left Benjamin Frobisher to build a house close to the old houses, and he himself returned to Cumberland House, where he arrived on August 24. On August 12 he met Peter Fidler, of the Hudson's Bay Company, going to Lake Athabaska, but for some reason these old companions passed each other without speaking. On September 10 he again started north to Cranberry Portage, and thence to Reed lake, where he had wintered in 1794–95, while in the service of the Hudson's Bay Company. Here he built a house some distance east of the old one which he had occupied eleven years before, and remained for the winter quietly trading furs and taking astronomical observations.

After Thompson completed his surveys of this "Muskrat Country," no further information was obtained about it for nearly a century, and when, in 1896, I travelled through it, the only map of any service which was available was that drawn by David Thompson in 1813 from surveys made at this time.

1806

On June 10, 1806, he left this post in the Muskrat country never to return to it, and returned to Cumberland House, where he arrived on June 14. Thence he proceeded at once to Fort William. Here he received instructions to attempt once more to open trade relations with the Indians west of the Rocky Mountains, and he at once returned by way of Cumberland House, where Harmon met him on September 11, to his old home at Rocky Mountain House, where he arrived on October 29.* Here he remained trading with the Indians throughout the following winter, and preparing for his journey across the mountains in the following spring.

1807

On May 10, accompanied by his wife and family, Thompson started from Rocky Mountain House to cross the mountains. Finan McDonald took a canoe with provisions up the Saskatchewan river, while Thompson himself travelled on horseback on the north side of the river. On June 3 they reached Kootenay Plain, a wide, open flat on the north side of the river within the mountains, in latitude 56° 2' 6" N.; and on June 6 they reached the Forks. They then turned up the south branch of the stream; but after ascending it for three miles were obliged to stop, as they could take the canoes no further. They remained here till June 25, when they started across the mountains, packing all their supplies with them on horses. At 1 P.M. on June 25 they reached the height of land in latitude 51° 48' 27" N.[1] Thence they descended along the banks of a mountain torrent (Blaeberry river) to "Kootanie" (Columbia) river, which they reached on June 30, in latitude 51° 25' 14" N., longitude 116° 52' 45" W., a mile or two north-west of Moberly station on the Canadian Pacific Railway. Jaco Finlay had been across the mountains to this place the year before, and had built a canoe and left it in what he sup-

---

[1] The pass by which Thompson here crossed the mountains is now known as Howse Pass, although Joseph Howse, a clerk of the Hudson's Bay Company, did not begin to use the pass until 1809, two years after Thompson had made his first trip over it. The eastern portion of the pass below the mouth of Whirlpool River was examined by Dr. Hector in 1859, and described by him in *The Journals, Detailed Reports, and Observations relative to the Exploration by Captain Palliser*, London, 1863, pp. 122-130.

posed to be a safe place for Thompson's use when he should arrive, but it was found to have been so badly broken in the meantime as to be now utterly useless. He camped here, near the mouth of the Blaeberry, and the members of the party for several days devoted themselves to repacking their stuff and building canoes. On July 12, having placed all the trading goods in canoes, they set out and ascended (not descended) the Columbia river, and reached Lower Columbia lake (now Lake Windermere) on July 18. At the south end of this lake Thompson began to build in latitude 50° 31′ 24″ N.; but finding the place unsuitable, he moved on July 29 down the river to about a mile from the lake, and built "Kootanae House" on the west side of the Columbia river, in latitude 50° 32′ 15″ N., longitude 115° 51′ 40″ W., variation 24½° East. Here he remained for the rest of the year, trading with the Kutenai Indians, and taking meteorological and astronomical observations. With the chief of the Flatbow Indians for a guide he made a trip for a few days down the banks of the Kootenay river. He also carefully measured the heights of some of the neighbouring mountains, from a measured base of 6,920 feet. Mount Nelson, to the west of the fort, he found to be 7,223 feet above the surface of the lake, which would give it a height of 9,900 feet above the sea—a height 100 feet lower than that given on Dr. Dawson's map of 1885.

1808

On April 20, 1808, Thompson set out with canoes toward the south, and the next day reached the portage to the "Flat Bow" or "McGillivray's" (Kootenay) river, which he calls "McGillivray's Portage." From here he descended the "Flat Bow" (Kootenay) river in a canoe, making a careful survey with a compass, checked by latitudes. On April 24 he passed the mouth of the "Torrent" (St. Mary's) river, and on April 27 he reached the mouth of the "Fine Meadow" (Tobacco) river in Montana. On May 6 he reached the Kootenay Falls, and portaged past them, and two days later he reached a camp of Flatheads and Kutenai in latitude 48° 42′ 52″ N., longitude 116° W., at or near Bonner's Ferry in Idaho. Having induced these Indians to promise to trade with him, he again set off on May 13, and on the next day reached Flat Bow or Kootenay lake at Kootenay Landing. From here he returned up the river to the camp of the Flatheads, whence he took horses and travelled in a north-easterly direction up "McDonald's" (Moyie, or

Choecoos, or Grand Quête) river along the line of the Canadian
Pacific Railway ; and on May 18 he reached McGillivray's (Kootenay)
river, about Fort Steele. He crossed the river, followed up the bank
across Wild Horse Creek and "Lussier" (Sheep) river, and reached
Kootanae House on June 5. From here, taking his family with him, he
continued northward down the Columbia to the mouth of the Blaeberry river, from which place he crossed the mountains with the furs
obtained during the year, and reached Kootenay Plain on June 22.
On this journey he and his party were obliged to kill and eat several
of their horses, as they were unable to obtain other provisions.

At Kootenay Plain, Thompson embarked in a canoe, and descended
the Saskatchewan. At Boggy Hall, he left his family ; but he himself
continued down the river as fast as possible, and on to Rainy lake.
On his way he notes some places of interest in his note-books. The
first is Muskako Fort, four and a half hours below Wolf Brook,
doubtless at the bend in the river in Tp. 30, R. 6, west of the Fifth
Meridian, where "North-West Company" is marked on his large
map. "Old Island Fort," three hours and a half above Fort George,
is the "Isle of Scotland" of his journey of 1800. Fort George was
probably unoccupied at that time, having been abandoned in favour of
Fort Vermilion,[1] to which place the headquarters of the district had
been removed. Two days were spent at Fort Vermilion ; then on
July 3 the journey was resumed. On July 4, Thompson passed
"burnt Fort de l'Isle," his Island House of 1800 ; "the Crossing
Place," probably near Fort Carlton ; "Fort de Milieu," probably the
same as his Upper Hudson House of 1794. Three hours and a half
after passing the Forks, he reached Fort St. Louis, near the site of the
present Fort à la Corne. Three-quarters of an hour later he passed
the site of Fort à la Corne, about four miles down the river, at the
extreme north-east corner of the Hudson's Bay Company's reserve,
on the site of the old French Fort des Prairies.[2] On August 2,

[1] Fort Vermilion was situated, says Alexander Henry the younger, in
latitude 53° 51′ 7″ N., on the north side of the Saskatchewan river, "in a long
flat bottom of meadow directly opposite the Vermilion River." This post was
occupied by Alexander Henry the younger from 1808 to 1810, when it was
abandoned in favour of White Earth Fort. But before long it was again
occupied, for in 1814 Gabriel Franchère "found at this post some ninety
persons, men, women, and children" (Franchère's *Narrative*, p. 319).

[2] There has been a good deal of confusion as to the position of these two
posts, arising doubtless from the interchange of names. The exact position
of Fort St. Louis of the North-West Company, which Alexander Henry states

Thompson reached his destination at Rainy Lake House; and two days later he set out on his return journey westward. On August 18, about Wicked Point, on the west shore of Lake Winnipeg, he was joined by Alexander Henry, with canoes from Red River on the way to Fort Vermilion. The two parties reached Cumberland House on August 26; and on September 13 and 14 they reached Fort Vermilion, Henry a day in advance of Thompson. On September 16, Thompson's canoes left for up the river; while he himself left the next day on horseback, and arrived on September 23 at Fort Augustus. On October 3 he arrived at Boggy Hall, where he probably rejoined his family. Here, sending on the canoes, he took men and horses, and set out for the height of land. On October 9 he passed old Rocky Mountain House, and continued on up the river until October 17, when sharp frosts prevented the canoes being brought any further. Having therefore camped for a few days to rearrange the packs, he set out with the pack-horses on October 22, passed the Kootenay Plain on the 24th, and crossed the height of land on the 27th. On October 31 he once more reached the Columbia river. From here he sent the horses southward through the woods, while he ascended the river in a boat as far as a hoard that had been built beside the river the year before, in latitude 50° 53′ 34″ N., apparently not far from the mouth of Spillimacheen river. From here he sent Finan McDonald southward with the canoes, to establish a fort and

was abandoned in 1805, is not quite certain, but it was probably close to the present store of the Hudson's Bay Company. The old French fort was at a bend several miles farther down the river, about the north-east corner of the Hudson's Bay reserve. In 1896, the old trails and marks where the stockades had been were distinctly traceable. The fort would appear to have been built first by Legardeur de St. Pierre in 1753; and it was occupied by six men when visited by Anthony Hendry of the Hudson's Bay Company in May, 1755. In August, 1772, the place was visited by Mathew Cocking, another employee of the Hudson's Bay Company, and it was then found to be occupied by an Indian camp. But in the winter of 1776, when the place was visited by Alexander Henry the elder, it was in charge of James Finlay, who had a fort with an area of about an acre enclosed in a stockade, and from fifty to eighty men for its defence. After the abandonment of Fort St. Louis by the North-West Company in 1805, the location seems to have been unoccupied until about 1846, when the Hudson's Bay Company rebuilt on the site of the old French fort. In 1887, when in charge of Philip Turner, the grandson of either Philip or John Turnor, it was moved three miles up the river to its present position. Dr. Elliott Coues, in his *New Light on the Earlier History of the Greater Northwest*, New York, 1897, puts the positions of both these posts too far up the river.

winter at the falls on the Kootenay river; while he himself went
on horseback to the old Kootanae House, where he arrived on
November 10, and where he spent the winter trading with the
Kutenai Indians. James McMillan was his assistant, and Jaco Finlay
was hunting in the vicinity.

1809

After the winter's trade at Kootanae House was finished, on
April 17, 1809, Thompson removed a short distance down the river,
and camped till the 27th. He then descended the Columbia river in
a canoe, the horses being at the same time driven through the woods
to the Mountain Portage, and crossed the mountains to the Saskatchewan. At the Kootenay Plain, at which he arrived on June 18,
a canoe was built, and loaded with some of the furs which he had
obtained during the winter. In it he descended the river to Fort
Augustus,[1] where he arrived on June 24, and was welcomed by his
old friend James Hughes. On June 27, two canoes were sent eastward with his furs, but he himself remained at the fort until July 18.
On this date, having sent canoes up the Saskatchewan four days
before him, he set off on horseback towards the mountains. Near
the mouth of Wolf Creek, he caught up to and joined the canoes,
and sent back the horses as they had come. Travelling up the river,
he reached Kootenay Plain on August 3. Here he remained for a
few days, arranging the packs for the journey across the mountains,
and on August 8 he started westward on horseback. Next day he
met Joseph Howse, a clerk of the Hudson's Bay Company, who had
left Fort Edmonton on July 18 on an exploring trip, returning again
to the east. On August 11 he crossed the height of land, and two
days later he reached the Columbia. He ascended this river as far as
McGillivray's Portage, which he reached on August 20; then he
descended the Kootenay river, and on August 29 he reached the
Great Road of the Flatheads, where he had come to the large camp
of these Indians in the spring of 1808, near Bonner's Ferry.

Having obtained horses from the Indians, he set out toward the
south on September 6, and reached Pend d'Oreille lake on September 8;
and the next day he arrived at the mouth of Clark's Fork, where

[1] This was new Fort Augustus on the site of the present city of Edmonton.
The old fort twenty miles farther down the river had been destroyed by the
Blackfeet in 1807.

it empties into the lake.   Here he found a large camp of Flatheads and other Indians.   On September 10 he found a spot on a peninsula on the east side of this lake, a mile and a half from the mouth of the river, in latitude 48° 11′ 30″ N., where he built a house, which he called Kullyspell House.   Here he remained for about two weeks, to see that building operations were being pushed on as rapidly as possible.   On September 27 he rode around the north side of the lake, and down the river flowing from it to latitude 48° 51′ N., and returned on October 6.   On October 11 he set off again on horseback, and travelled about sixty miles in a south-easterly direction up the Saleesh river, called on his map the Nemissoolatakoo river (Clark's Fork).   Turning aside from this river near Thompson's Prairie, he travelled first north-east and then north-west, till he reached the Kootenay river above the falls, where he met his clerk, McMillan, bringing the canoes loaded with trading goods that had been left behind him on the Columbia river. Here, sending the horses ahead of him, he embarked in one of the canoes, descended to the Flathead Road, crossed over to Pend d'Oreille lake, and arrived at Kullyspell House on October 30.

On November 2 he set off again on horseback up the river, and a week later reached a point in latitude 47° 34′ 35″ N., near the present station of Woodlin on the Northern Pacific Railway, where he built a house which he called Saleesh House.   The position of this house is well described on page 418.

1810

In the spring of 1810 he made several expeditions in the vicinity of Saleesh House.   On February 23 he started out on horseback with Mousseau, Lussier, Boulard, and two Indians to look for birch bark for canoes.   They travelled up the river for fifty miles, examining the woods closely as they went, until they reached the great camp of the Salish Indians, which was situated on the Flathead river, twenty miles above its mouth, in latitude 47° 21′ 14″ N., and arrived back at Saleesh House on March 6.   From March 8 to March 14 he made another journey to the Salish camp, and in this case he returned down the river in a canoe which he had had built at the camp.   And from March 17 to March 25 he made a third journey to the same camp, returning in this case also down the river in a canoe, while his horses were sent in loaded with furs.   On both trips down the river he made a careful survey of it.

After his return he engaged Jaco Finlay in his old capacity as clerk and interpreter.

On April 6 he sent off Mousseau, Beaulieu, and several others with ten packs of furs to Pend d'Oreille lake.

On April 19 he left Saleesh House and embarked in canoes down the Saleesh river, and on the evening of Saturday the 21st he arrived at Kullyspell House, where Finan McDonald had spent the winter. Before leaving he sent McDonald up to Saleesh House to spend the summer.

While at Kullyspell House he decided to make a further investigation of the Pend d'Oreille river down to its junction with the Columbia, in order to determine definitely whether it and the Columbia could be used as a trade route to the east or not. Accordingly, on April 24 he embarked in a canoe, crossed the lake and descended the river to latitude 48° 51' N., twenty-two miles from its mouth, but as it proved to be quite unnavigable he decided to return eastward up the Kootenay river as before. Returning he reached Kullyspell House on May 1.

On May 9 he left Kullyspell House for the Kootenay river, and on the 17th, accompanied by McMillan, he started up that river with his brigade of canoes. He reached McGillivray's Portage on June 6, and thence descended the Columbia as far as Mountain Portage, where he arrived on June 16. He then crossed to the Saskatchewan, and arrived at the Forks in the mountains on June 19, having left the men to follow him with the pack-horses. Here he embarked in a canoe, and proceeded down stream. On his way he passed the ruins of old Fort Augustus; and on the next day he reached White Earth House,[1] where Alexander Henry was in charge for the North-West Company, and a trader named Henry Hallett for the Hudson's Bay Company. This house appears to have been at the mouth of White Earth river, a short distance below the present site of Victoria. On July 4 he reached Cumberland House, and on July 22 Rainy Lake House.

After loading four canoes with goods to trade, he again turned westward, and on September 6 reached White Earth House on the Saskatchewan. On September 11, having sent his four canoes on ahead of him, he started on horseback for Fort Augustus, where he seems to have left his family for the winter. Thence he rode up the valley of

[1] According to Henry, Thompson had his family with him when he passed this house.

the Saskatchewan to the foot of the mountains, but as his canoes had been intercepted and turned back by the Piegan, he was obliged to return down the river, and find a new trail to the Columbia river by Athabaska Pass at the head-waters of the Athabaska river.

Collecting his men, horses, and supplies at a point on the banks of the Saskatchewan river about sixty miles below Rocky Mountain House, where the North-West Company had had a trading post for a couple of years, which they named Boggy Hall, he started westward through the woods on an old footpath that had been used by the Assiniboin Indians when going to their hunting grounds. Taking a north-westerly course he reached the Athabaska river at the mouth of a brook in about latitude 53° 38′ N., a few miles below where the Grand Trunk Pacific Railway now reaches it. The next day he crossed the river and continued up along its bank to Brulé lake, to an island on which was a deserted cabin previously built by some half-breed or Indian hunters. As there was no food here for his horses, he moved northward for five miles to a more favourable spot where he camped and made snow-shoes and sleds for his journey across the mountains.

On December 29 he set out with sleds and dogs, and also with four horses to help them for a short distance.

1811

On January 6 he left the four horses somewhere about the mouth of the Miette river, near where Yellowhead Pass turns off to the west. He then crossed the height of land by Athabaska Pass which was afterwards used for many years by the Hudson's Bay Company as their main line of travel from the Great Plains to the valley of the Columbia river. Thence he descended Wood river to the Columbia at the mouth of Canoe river. He reached it on January 18, and continued up the Columbia, hauling the sleds, for twelve miles. Here some of his men mutinied, and he was obliged to return to the Canoe river, where he remained for the winter.

Having constructed a clinker-built canoe of cedar boards hewn from trees in the surrounding forest, and sewed after the manner of a birch canoe, as he had no nails with which to fasten it, he embarked on the Columbia river on April 17.

Instead of descending, he ascended the river, which was new to him as far as Blaeberry Creek, overcoming natural obstacles as he met

them, and on May 14 he reached McGillivray's Portage at the head
of Upper Columbia lake. Thence he descended the Kootenay
river to its south-eastern bend, and having here obtained horses,
crossed to Saleesh House on Clark's Fork, in Montana. Having built
a canoe, he descended Clark's Fork, passed through Pend d'Oreille
lake, and continued down the river to the site of the present town
of Cusick in Washington. From here he travelled, with the aid of
thirteen horses, to Spokane House, ten miles north-west of the
present city of Spokane, where Finan McDonald was living at the
time. This trading post is stated by Thompson to have been situated
on the east bank of Spokane river, a mile above the mouth of Little
Spokane river. From Spokane House a ride of three days brought
him to Ilthkoyape (Kettle) Falls on the Columbia river. After some
difficulty in obtaining cedar boards with which to build a canoe, he set
out down the river on July 3, and on July 15, at 1 P.M., he landed at
Fort Astoria, the newly built trading post of the Pacific Fur Company
at the mouth of the Columbia river.

After spending a few days with McDougall, the trader in charge
at Astoria, Thompson started back up the Columbia. On July 28
he reached the Cascades, which he had difficulty in passing on account
of the hostility of the Indians. On August 5 he reached the mouth
of Shawpatin (Snake) river, up which he struggled with the canoe
for "56" miles till, on August 8, he, reached the southern end of the
road leading to the Spokane river, in latitude 46° 36′ 13″ N. Here he
laid up the canoe, and rode overland to Spokane House. Thence he
rode to Ilthkoyape Falls, and, having built a canoe there, ascended the
Columbia river to Canoe river, thus completing the survey of the
whole river from its source to its mouth.

As there is lacking in Thompson's manuscript a description of his
voyage up this part of the Columbia, and as it is important to complete
his record of the survey of the river, the following diary has been com-
piled from Thompson's note-books :

September 2.—Thompson's party left Ilthkoyape Falls at 1 P.M.,
accompanied by eight canoes of Indians, and paddled upstream against
a strong current until 5.20 P.M., when they put up for the night.

September 3.—The party embarked at 5.30 A.M. Shortly before
noon they reached, in latitude 48° 52′ N., a portage on the east bank
1,100 yards long. All afternoon they paddled against a strong current,
and at night they camped five miles below the mouth of Pend d'Oreille
river.

September 4.—They embarked at 5.50 A.M., and ascended a swift current all day. They crossed the international boundary line, passed the mouth of Pend d'Oreille river and the site of the present town of Trail, and at 6.10 P.M. pitched camp at the mouth of Murphy Creek. On the right the country was becoming rapidly more rocky.

September 5.—They embarked at 5.50 A.M., and about noon reached the mouth of the Kootenay river. Here the Indians who had been accompanying them, left them. They camped for the night near the site of the town of Castlegar.

September 6.—They set off at 5.40 A.M., and travelled up the river till 3.15 P.M., when they camped for the night near the site of the present village of Deer Park. The hills now came down close to the river, those to the west being thickly covered with forest, but those to the east being rather bare and rocky. Tracks of reindeer and the black-tailed chevreuil were plentiful, but they hunted without success.

September 7.—They set off at 6 A.M., and travelled northward over Lower Arrow lake against a head wind and high waves, and camped at 6.30 P.M. on the shores of the lake in latitude 49° 44′ N., about three miles south of Edgewood.

September 8.—They set off at 5.38 A.M., passed through the Lower Arrow lake, and camped on the bank of the river between the two Arrow lakes, about the mouth of Mosquito Creek. "The lake we have passed has always current in the middle and very often from side to side. The last half has a ledge of low wood and land with fine shore on both sides; the middle steep, ugly rocks; and the lower end rocks and good shore by turns."

September 9.—They set off at 5.40 A.M., and soon entered Upper Arrow lake. Through this lake they pushed on northward, and camped somewhere near the site of the hotel at Halcyon Hot Springs.

September 10.—They set off at 5.15 A.M., and early in the day reached Arrowhead at the north end of the lake. Here they entered the river, and, encountering a heavy current, were often obliged to pole their canoe, or haul it against the stream with a line. Though much delayed by rain, they travelled till 6 P.M.

September 11.—They embarked at 5.35 A.M., and ascended the stream until 5 P.M., when they camped in latitude 51° 2′ 13″ N. at the place to which Finan McDonald had ascended the river in a canoe a few weeks before. This was about two miles above the present town of Revelstoke, and one mile below the Little Dalles.

September 12.—They set off at 6 A.M., and ascended the stream until 5.15 P.M., when they camped for the night in latitude 51° 11′ N. "From early morning the Dalles very bad, all the rest is very strong current and rapids. Came up with the line."

September 13.—They set off at 6.45 A.M., and camped at 5.30 P.M. in latitude 51° 22′ 30″ N.

g

September 14.—They set off at 7.15 A.M. At noon they were in latitude 51° 30′ N., two miles below the Dalles des Morts. In the afternoon they ascended the Dalles des Morts, which were destined to be the graveyard of the Columbia river in the early days of the western fur-trade; and the following is Thompson's survey and description of these rapids: "N. 78 W. ⅓ [mile] N. 50 W. 1/8, N. 36 W. 2/3, W. 1/8, N. 35 W. ⅓, all bad, N. 50 W. 1/8, N. 36 W. 2/3. Strong rapid current, lined on the left, good to run, W. 1/8 strong rapid, discharged all the heavy pieces and for 250 yards carried, lined up the canoe on the left, having crossed—N. 30 W. ½ m. Beginning of Co. A fall and rush of water. Discharged all for 150 yds. and lined up, quite light, very dangerous to line down. The rest of Co. strong Rapid Current. Lined the whole up loaded. On the right end of Course a large rock between which and the shore lined and handed. Here the canoes going down ought to bring up N. 40 W. ⅔, N. 10 E. 1/6, Strong Rapid, Course N. 30 W. ½, N. 45 W. ⅔, N. 35 W. ½, N. 50 W. ½, N. 60 W. ½, N. 50 W. ½. Crossed over in middle of Course and camped at 5.50 P.M. Sight a large bold mountain on the right. Still much snow on them. The river is very strong Current. I suppose loaded canoes must line down much of the Dalles."

September 15.—They set off at 5.15 A.M., and ascended a rapid current, with dangerous rocky points all day. They camped for the night on the bank of the stream in latitude 51° 45′ N.

September 16.—They set off at 10 A.M., and first ascended a long strong rapid, after which the current became more moderate.

September 17.—They set off at 6.30 A.M., and travelled till 6.30 P.M. up a constant rapid stream to camp in latitude 52° 31′ N.

September 18.—They embarked at 7.15 A.M., and about noon reached Thompson's old hut at the mouth of the Canoe river. They had hoped to find some of their associates of the North-West Company from across the mountains waiting for them here with trading supplies, but in this they were disappointed. Leaving behind them a message written in the Iroquois language, they set off up the Canoe river, which was the route they expected their friends to use in coming from the Athabaska river.

Thompson ascended Canoe river for forty-eight miles, then returned to its mouth. Part of the trading goods for the next year having been brought across the mountains, he sent them down the river to Ilthkoyape Falls; while he himself crossed the mountains to Henry's House, and returned with the rest of the goods to the falls. Thence he walked to Spokane House, where he obtained horses, and returned to the Columbia for the goods left at the canoe.

THE DALLES OF THE COLUMBIA RIVER IN FLOOD, AS WHEN THOMPSON PASSED IN 1811.
NEW CANAL IN THE FOREGROUND

He then rode southward to Spokane House, up the Spokane river for twenty-five miles above the house, and northward to Pend d'Oreille river at a point twelve miles below Pend d'Oreille lake, after which he followed the trail along the north bank of this river upwards to Saleesh House, where he arrived on November 19. It seems to have been deserted, though Finan McDonald was trading with the Indians in the vicinity. After rebuilding the house, he made a trip on horseback up the south branch for thirty miles, but finding no place more suitable for a trading post than the one he was occupying, he returned.

1812

On February 15 he left Saleesh House with Finan McDonald, Michel, and ten men in two canoes to go to the Salish Indians to trade provisions. They went up to the Salish camp which was then pitched on Flathead river, four miles below the mouth of Jocko Creek. From here, on February 25, 26, and 27, he rode up the bank of Flathead river to Jocko Creek, up that creek, and over a defile to the summit of what is now known as Jumbo Hill in the city of Missoula, Montana, near the banks of Hell Gate river, which he called " Courter's Branch." Here he spent several hours making a sketch of the surrounding country, and tracing out the route by which Lewis and Clark had travelled through it, after which he returned as quickly as possible to the Salish camp. On March 1 he rode northward from the Salish camp as far as the south end of Flathead lake, and returned to camp the same day. The next day he, with his whole party, started back for Saleesh House, where letters had just arrived from John McDonald of Garth, who was spending the winter at Kootanae House.

On March 13 he left Saleesh House, and embarking in his canoe started on his voyage to the east. Four days later he encamped at the north end of the Skeetshoo road where he had reached the river in the previous autumn. After a delay of four days McTavish met him with horses and men, and took him south to Spokane House. Pushing on from there he reached a place eight miles east of Ilthkoyape Falls where he found cedar and some birch bark suitable for building canoes. Here he stayed hard at work building canoes from March 31 to April 21, on which latter date McTavish and McMillan arrived with all the furs from Spokane House.

All was now ready, and on April 22 he bade good-bye to Ilthkoyape Falls and, accompanied by McTavish, started with his brigade of six canoès for Fort William. He reached the mouth of Canoe river on May 5. On May 6 he set out on foot from the Boat Encampment at the mouth of Canoe river on the journey which was to take him back at last to civilization. Travelling eastward by Athabaska Pass, he crossed the height of land on May 8, and on May 11 reached the house of William Henry on the Athabaska river, in latitude 52° 55′ 16″ N. On May 13 he started down the river in a canoe. On May 20 he reached the mouth of Lesser Slave river, up which he pushed to the house at its head ; having returned thence, he continued down the Athabaska to the Red Deer or La Biche river, which he reached on May 25. He turned up this stream, and reached Red Deer lake, or Lake La Biche, on May 27. Having crossed the portage from this lake, he descended the Beaver river to Isle à la Crosse, and continuing down Churchill river, reached Cumberland House on June 18. Thence he continued eastward along the ordinary trade route through Lake Winnipeg and up the Winnipeg and Rainy rivers to Lake Superior. On August 12 he left Fort William, the western head-quarters of the North-West Company, and continuing eastward, re-surveyed the north shore of Lake Superior as far as Sault Ste. Marie, which he reached on August 24. Thence he continued along the north shore of Lake Huron, up the French river and down the Ottawa river, and arrived at Terrebonne, north of Montreal. Here he took up his residence ; and although in the course of his survey of the boundary line between the United States and Canada he travelled as far west as the Lake of the Woods, he never returned to his old fields of labour in the far West, or revisited any of his early homes on the banks of the Saskatchewan or Columbia rivers.

PART I

A

DAVID THOMPSON'S NARRATIVE

CHAPTER I

JOIN HUDSON'S BAY COMPANY

*Leave London on Hudson's Bay Company's Ship—Arrive at
Stromness—Early education—Set sail for Hudson's Bay—
Fort Prince of Wales—M' Samuel Hearne—Life at
Churchill—Tame Polar Bear at the Factory—Musketoes,
Sand Flies, and Midgeuks—Companions at the Factory—
Arrival of George Charles—Means of obtaining a Surveyor
by Hudson's Bay Company.*

IN the month of May 1784 at the Port of London, I
embarked in the ship Prince Rupert belonging to the
Hudson's Bay Company, as apprentice and clerk to
the said company, bound for Churchill Factory, on the west
side of the bay.   None of the Officers or Men had their stock
of liquor on board from the high price of those articles.   On
the third morning at dawn of day, we perceived a dutch
lugger about half a mile from us.   A boat was directly lowered,
and the gunner a tall handsome young man, stepped into her
with four men, they were soon on board of the lugger, a
case of gin was produced, a glass tasted ; approved, the
dutchman was in a hurry, as he said a Revenue Cutter was
cruising near hand, and he must luff off ; a Guinea was paid,
the case locked, put into the boat, and was soon placed in

the steerage cabin of our ship. The case was of half inch boards tacked together, and daubed red, on opening it there were nine square bottles of common glass, each was full with the corks cut close to the neck of the bottle, except one with a long cork, the one which the gunner had tasted, it was taken out a glass handed round and each praised it; but the carpenter who was an old cruiser wished to taste some of the other bottles, a cork was drawn, a glass filled, the colour had a fine look, it was tasted, spit out and declared to be sea water, all the others were found to be the same.

The gunner who had thus paid a guinea for three half pints of gin, the contents of the bottle, got into a fighting humour, but to no purpose, the dutchman was luffing off in fine style. The next morning about sun rise, the hills of Scotland lying blue in the western horizon, to the east of us about two miles, we saw a boat with six men coming from the deep sea fishing. The wind was light, and they soon came alongside. They were fine manly hardy looking men, they were sitting up to their knees in fish, for the boat was full of the various kinds they had caught; Our Captain bought some fine halibut and skate fish from them, for which they would not take money, but old rope in exchange to make fettels for their creels, these words I did not understand until the Boatswain, who was a Scotchman told me it was to make rope handles to their baskets and buckets. Our captain pleased with his bargain, told me to give them a hat full of biscuit. Umbrella's were not in those days, but our broad brimmed hats served for both purposes. Pleased with the ruddy looks of them, I filled my hat as full as it could hold, and had to carry it by the edges of the brim. As I passed by the Captain I heard him give me a hearty curse, and saying I'll never send him for biscuit again; but the boat's crew were so pleased they told me to hand down a bucket, which they filled with fresh caught herrings, a great relief from salt meat.

On the sixth day about nine PM. we anchored in the harbour of Stromness, where the three ships bound for Hudsons Bay had to wait for final instructions and sailing orders, as there were no telegraphs in those [days] we were delayed three weeks. Until this Voyage I had passed my life near to Westminster Abbey, the last seven year in the grey coat school on royal foundation. This school was formerly something of a Monastery and belonged to Westminster Abbey from which it was taken at the suppression of the monastic order, but not finally settled until the reign of Queen Anne. It is still held of the Dean and Chapter of the Abbey by the Tenure of paying a peper corn to the said Dean and Chapter on a certain day, which the Governors annually pay.

During the year our holidays at different times were about eighteen to twenty days, the greatest part of which I spent in this venerable Abbey and it's cloisters, reading the monumental inscriptions and [as] often as possible [in] Henry the seventh chapel. My strolls were to London Bridge, Chelsea, and Vauxhall and S' James's Park. Books in those days were scarce and dear and most of the scholars got the loan of such books as his parents could lend him. Those which pleased us most were the Tales of the Genii, the Persian, and Arabian Tales, with Robinson Crusoe and Gullivers Travels : these gave us many subjects for discussion and how each would behave on various occasions.

With such an account of the several regions of the Earth and on such credible authority, I conceived myself to have knowledge to say something of any place I might come to, and the blue hills of Scotland were so distant as to leave to imagination to paint them as she pleased. When I woke in the morning and went upon deck, I could not help staring to see if [what] was before me was reality for I had never read of such a place. And at length exclaimed I see no trees, to which a Sailor answered No no, people here do not spoil their clothes by climbing up trees. One of the first objects that drew my attention were several kelp kilns for burning sea weed into a kind of potash. The sea weeds were collected by a number of Men and Women their legs appeared red and swelled. The sea weeds were collected into baskets, the rope handles of which were passed round their breasts, each helped up the load for one another, and as they carried it over rough rocky shore left by the ebb tide to the kilns, the sea water streamed down their backs.

The smoke of the fires of these kilns was as black as that of a coal fire. One day our Captain had invited the other captains and some gentlemen from the Island to dine with him, a little before the time the wind changed, and the smoke of five of the kilns came direct on our ship turning day into night, the Boatswain was ordered to go and make them put out their kilns, which they refused to do ; upon which he threatened to send cannon balls among them to smash their kilns, but the sturdy fellows replied, You may as well take our lives as our means, we will not put them out. Finding threats would not do, he enquired how much they gained a day : they said, when the kilns burn well they gained tenpence ; upon which he gave to each one shilling ; the kilns were then soon put out, the smoke cleared away and we again saw daylight. I could not help comparing this hard, wet labour for tenpence a day where not even a whistle was heard, with the merry songs of the ploughboys in England.

This place was to me a new world, nothing reminded me of Westminster Abbey, and my strolls to Vauxhall, Spring Gardens and other places, where all was beauty to the eye, and verdure to the feet ; here all was rock with very little soil, everywhere loose stones that hurt my feet ; not a tree to be seen. I sadly missed the old Oaks, under whose shade I sat, and played. I could not conceive by what means the people lived ; they appeared comfortable, and their low dark houses, with a peat fire, the smoke of which escaped by a small hole, contained all they required.

They carried on a considerable contraband trade with Holland; which from the very high duties on Liquors and other articles gave them a profitable trade. None of the officers and crews of the three Ships had provided themselves with liquors for the voyage, as they knew these things could be procured here cheaper and better than in London. One afternoon, taking a walk with one of the petty officers, we entered a low dark house. It was three or four minutes before we could perceive the gudeman, who in his homespun blue coat was sitting alone by his turf fire; my companion enquired how times went, and if he had an anker keg of comfort for a cold voyage; he said of late the Revenue Cutters had been very active, and stocks low; but he could accommodate him. The price was soon settled, and the gin found a place in the ship. And thus it will always be with high duties. The Kirk was on the shore of the Harbor, the Minister was the Reverend Mr. Falkner, a gentleman remarkable for a fine powerful voice and using plain language adapted to the education of his flock, he appeared to be much respected. Altho' many of his congregation came several miles over a rough country, yet his Kirk of a Sunday was filled; every man woman and child came with their blue stockings and thick soled shoes neatly folded under their arms. Sitting down on the stones near the church they were put on their feet, and thus [they] entered the Kirk; on coming out the shoes and stockings were taken off, folded and placed under the arms and thus [they] returned home: their behaviour was remarkably good, grave yet cheerfull with respect for each other, and kind attention to the women and children. In those days there was no Telegraph; it took three weeks to send letters to London and receive an answer for sailing orders. We now held our course over the western ocean; and near the islands of America saw several icebergs, and

Hudson's Straits were so full of ice, as to require the time of near a month to pass them; this being effected the three ships separated, one for Albany and Moose Factories, another for York Factory, and the third for Churchill Factory at which last place we arrived in the beginning of September 1784.

Hudson's Bay, including Jame's Bay, may be said to be an inland sea, connected to the Atlantic Ocean by Hudson's Straits: it is in the form of a Horse Shoe; and in Latitude extends from 52 degrees to 60 degrees north, and from 70 degrees to 95 degrees west of Greenwich in the northern part; and covers an area of about 192,770 square statute miles.[1] On it's west side it receives Seal, Churchill, the Kissiskatchewan,[2] Hayes, Severn, Albany, and Moose Rivers; on the east side Ruperts and several other Rivers, the names of which are unknown as they come from barren, desolate, countries. From Seal River leading south to Churchill River, about thirty six miles, the country is of granite rock, along the Bay shore of which is a narrow strip of marsh land, apparently the alluvial of Seal River. The granitic rocks which bounds the sea coast from far to the northward have their southern termination at Churchill River; in Latitude 58°. 47′ North Longitude 94°. 3′ West, then forms a retiring line from the sea shore; for 150 miles to the Kissiskatchewan River, up which the first granite is found at the distance of one hundred and thirty five miles, being the borders of the most eastern Lakes; and this distance appears to be wholly alluvial; and to be of much the same width all along the Bay side:

[1] Hudson Bay extends from latitude 51° 10′ N. at the south end of James Bay to latitude 64° N. and from longitude 77° 30′ E. to 94° 30′ E., and has a total area of about 500,000 square miles.

[2] It is interesting to note that Thompson constantly speaks of the Nelson river as the Kissiskatchewan river, though I am unable to learn that this name was used for it by the Indians. Among the Cree Indians who live on its banks, the Nelson river is called Powinigow or Powininigow, which probably means " the Rapid Strangers' river."

these alluvials especially of the Kissiskatchewan and Hayes's
Rivers have high steep banks of earth and gravel intermixed,
from ten to forty feet; the gravel and small stones are all
rounded by the action of water; the Rivers passing through
this alluvial have a very rapid current with several Falls.
Churchill River where it enters the Sea, is an noble stream
of about one and a half mile in width; on the south side ,it
is bounded by a low point of rock and sand; on the north
side by a low neck of sand with rock appearing through it;
at the extremity of which the Point is about an acre in width,
on which was erected about the year 1745 a regular, well
constructed Fort of Granite:[1] having about thirty cannon of
six to eighteen pound shot. There was no approach to it but
by the narrow isthmus of sand. The water was too shoal for
three fourths of a mile to the middle of the River for Ships,
and this was the only place a ship could come to. (It was at
this Fort that Mr Wales the Astronomer observed the Transit
of Venus over the Sun in 1769).[2] In the war with the United
States, and with France; in the year 1782 the celebrated
Navigator De la Peyrouse[3] was sent from France, with one
Ship of seventy four Guns, and two Frigates to take and
destroy the Forts of the Hudson's Bay Company. In the
month of August these vessels anchored in the Bay, about

[1] For a description and plan of Fort Prince of Wales, which is here
referred to, and an account of its capture by Admiral de la Pérouse, see
Samuel Hearne's *Journey*, edited by J. B. Tyrrell, The Champlain Society,
Toronto, 1911, pp. 6, 7, 21-2.

[2] William Wales was one of the ablest astronomers and mathema-
ticians of his day. With Joseph Dymond he spent a year at Churchill
between August 9, 1768, and September 7, 1769, for the purpose of observing the transit of Venus over the sun on June 3, 1769. His obser-
vatory was situated on the top of the wall of the south-east bastion of
Fort Prince of Wales, within the parapet.

[3] Admiral de la Pérouse was not only one of the most famous admirals
of the French Navy, but he was also one of France's greatest geographers.
After destroying Forts York and Churchill on Hudson Bay in 1782, he started
on a voyage round the world, and was last heard from in 1788 from Botany
Bay.

four miles north of the Fort; and the next day sent a boat
well manned, to sound the River; at this time the Fort was
under the command of the well known traveller Mr Samuel
Hearne;[1] who had been in the naval service. He allowed the
french Boat to sound the River to their satisfaction; without
firing a single shot at them; from this conduct Admiral De
la Peyrouse judged what kind of a Commander of the Fort
he had to contend with; accordingly next day, on the narrow
isthmus of sand and rock of a full mile in length which leads to
the Fort, he landed four hundred men, who marched direct
on the Fort with only small arms. The men in the Fort
begged of Mr Hearne to allow them to mow down the
French Troops with the heavy guns loaded with grape shot,
which he absolutely refused; and as they approached he
ordered the gates to be opened, and went out to meet them,
and surrendered at discretion; all the goods, stores, with
a large quantity of valuable Furrs fell into their hands. The
Fort was destroyed and burnt; but the stone walls of the
Fort were of such solid masonry [that] the fire scarcely injured
them. The french Commander declared, that had his sounding Boat been fired at, he would not have thought of attacking
such a strong Fort so late in the season, when there was not
time for a regular siege. Mr Hearne was received with cold
politeness, and looked upon with contempt by the french
Officers. (Note. Mr Samuel Hearne was a handsome man
of six feet in height, of a ruddy complexion and remarkably
well made, enjoying good health; as soon as the Hudson's
Bay Company could do without his services they dismissed
him for cowardice. Under him I served my first year. It
was customary of a Sunday for a Sermon to be read to the
Men, which was done in his room, the only comfortable one

---

[1] Samuel Hearne sailed from Churchill for England in the ship *Sea
Horse* in August, 1787, and died in England in November, 1792, at the
age of forty-seven. A sketch of his life and character will be found in
Samuel Hearne's *Journey*, edited by J. B. Tyrrell, pp. 1–23.

in the Factory ; one Sunday, after the service, Mr Jefferson [1]
the reader and myself staid a few minutes on orders, he then
took Voltaire's Dictionary, and said to us, here is my belief,
and I have no other. In the Autumn of 1785 he returned
to England, became a member of the Bucks Club and in two
years was buried :) The present Factory [2] is about five miles
above the Fort, in a small Bay formed by a ledge of rocks
which closes on the river about five hundred yards below the
Factory, above which for seven miles is an extensive marsh
to the lower rapids of the River. The Factory is supplied
once a year with goods and provisions, by a Ship which
arrives on the last days of August, or early in September, and
in about ten days is ready for her homeward voyage ; the
severity of the climate requiring all possible dispatch. The
cold weather now comes rapidly on, but as there was no
Thermometer, we could only judge of the intensity of the
cold by our sensations, and it's action on the land and water.
On the fifteenth day of November this great and deep River
was frozen over from side to side, and although the Spring
tides of New and full Moon rose ten to twelve feet above
the ordinary level, no impression was made on the ice, it kept
firm, and it was the middle of June the following year when
the ice broke up and gave us the pleasant sight of water.
About the middle of October the Marshes and Swamps are
frozen over, and the Snow lies on the ground ; for about
two months the Factory yard, enclosed by stockades of twelve
feet in height, was kept clear of snow, but in the latter end
of December a north east snow storm of three days con-
tinuance drifted the snow to the height of the stockades and

[1] Jefferson was second in command at Churchill during the latter part
of Samuel Hearne's régime ; and after Hearne's departure he was for a
year or two in command of the post.

[2] Churchill Factory is still situated in the place where it was when
Thompson lived in it in 1785. For a description of it and its surroundings,
see J. B. Tyrrell, *Report on the Dubawnt, Kasan, and Ferguson Rivers*,
Ottawa, 1897, pp. 93-8.

over them, and filled the whole yard to the depth of six to
ten feet, which could not be cleared, and through which
avenues had to be cut and cleared of about four feet in width ;
and thus remained till late in April, when a gradual thaw
cleared the snow away. From the end of October to the
end of April every step we walk is in Snow Shoes. The
Natives walk with ease and activity, and also many of us :
but some find them a sad incumbrance, their feet become
sore and their ankles sprained ; with many a tumble in the
snow from which it is sometimes difficult to rise.   In the open
season in the months of July and August, Salmon[1] from two
to five pounds weight are plentiful ; two nets each of thirty
fathoms in length by five feet in height maintain the Factory
from three to four days in the week. This fish is not
found south of Churchill River. Peculiar to Churchill is a
large species of Hare,[2] it dwells among the rocks, it's nest is
better than other Hares, it's skin stronger, the fur long and
very soft, of a beautiful white ; twenty two were caught,
their skins sent to London and readily bought by the Barbers.
The country, soil, and climate in which we live, have always
a powerful effect upon the state of society, and the movements
and comforts of every individual, he must conform himself
to the circumstances under which he is placed, and as such
we lived and conducted ourselves in this extreme cold climate.
All our movements more, or less, were for self-preservation :
All the wood that could be collected for fuel, gave us only
one fire in the morning, and another in the evening.[3] The rest

[1] Probably some form of the wide-ranging *Salvelinus alpinus* (Linn.)
[E. A. P.]
[2] *Lepus arcticus canus* Preble. [E. A. P.]
[3] The house in which Thompson lived at Churchill in the winter of
1784–85 had doubtless been but recently built, for the old dwelling-house
at Fort Prince of Wales had been burned in 1782, and the employees of
the Hudson's Bay Company had only begun the construction of a new
trading post in the fall of 1783, when they had been allowed to go back
to Hudson Bay. In the hurry of building, Hearne and those with him

of the day, if bad weather, we had to walk in the guard room with our heavy coats of dressed Beaver ; but when the weather was tolerable we passed the day in shooting Grouse.[1] The interior of the walls of the House were covered with rime to the thickness of four inches, pieces of which often broke off, to prevent which we wetted the whole extent, and made it a coat of ice, after which it remained firm, and added to the warmth of the House, for the cold is so intense, that everything in a manner is shivered by it, continually the Rocks are split with a sound like the report of a gun. Everywhere the rocks are fractured from the well known effects of freezing water. This is very well for winter, but in the summer season the Rocks are also fractured ; although more than half of their surface is covered with Ponds and rills of water, I could not believe that water thawing could produce this effect ; but in the month of July I was sitting on a rock to shoot Curlews[2] as they passed, when a large rock not ten yards from me split, I went to it, the fracture was about an inch in width. In looking down it, about ten feet from the surface, was a bed of solid ice, the surface of which appeared damp as if beginning to thaw ; a few days after another large Rock split close to me, by the fracture, at the depth of about twenty feet was a bed of ice in the same state : these rocks are not isolated, they are part of an immense extent to the westward and northward, every where with innumerable fractures ; among these rocks are narrow vallies of rolled granite pebbles, now twenty to fifty feet above the level of the sea ; which was once the beach of the sea : has the land been elevated, or the sea retired ; who can tell what has passed in ancient times. By the early part of October all the birds of passage

appear to have neglected to lay in a sufficient supply of firewood for the winter. With well-built houses and plenty of fuel men can be as warm in winter at Churchill as in any other part of Canada.

[1] *Lagopus albus* (Gmelin), and *L. rupestris* (Gmelin), both described from Hudson Bay specimens. [E. A. P.]

[2] *Numenius borealis* (Forster), and *N. hudsonicus* Latham. [E. A. P.]

have left us for milder climes, and winter commences, the pools
of water are frozen over and ice [is] on the river side.   The
polar Bear[1] now makes his appearance, and prowls about until
the ice at the sea shore is extended to a considerable distance ;
when he leaves to prey on the Seal, his favourite food : during
his stay he is for plunder and every kind of mischief, but not
willing to fight for it.   Only one accident happened, it was
in November the snow about eighteen inches deep.   A she
Bear prowling about came near to one of the grouse hunters,
his gun snaped and in turning about to get away he fell, fortunately on his back, the Bear now came and hooked one of her
fore paws in one of his snow shoes, and dragged him along
for her cubs ; sadly frightened, after a short distance he recovered himself, pricked and primed his gun, and sent the
load of shot like a ball into her belly ; she fell with a growl,
and left him.   He lost no time in getting up, and running
away as fast as snow shoes would permit him.

The polar, or white, Bear, when taken young is easily
tamed ;   In the early part of July the whaling boat in chase
of the Beluga[2] came up with a she bear and her two cubs ;
the bear and one of her cubs were killed ; the other, a male,
was kept, brought to the factory and tamed.   At first he had
to be carefully protected from the dogs, but he soon increased
in size and strength to be a full match for them, and the
blows of his fore feet kept them at a distance.   This Bruin
continued to grow, and his many tricks made him a favourite,
especially with the sailors, who often wrestled with him, and
his growing strength gave them a cornish hug.   In the
severity of winter when spruce beer could not be kept from
freezing each mess of four men get a quart of molasses instead
of beer, of which Bruin was fond as well as grog, and
every Saturday used to accompany the men to the steward's
shed when the rations were served to them, the steward

[1] *Thalarctos maritimus* (Phipps).   [E. A. P.]
[2] *Delphinapterus catodon* (Linn.).   [E. A. P.]

always gave him some on one of his fore paws, which he licked into his mouth. On one of these days the steward and Bruin had quarreled and as punishment he got no molasses : he sat very quietly while the steward was putting all to rights, but seeing him ready to shut the door, made a dash at the hogshead of molasses, and thrusting his head and neck to the shoulders, into it, to the utter dismay of the steward, he carried off a large gallon on his shaggy hair ; he walked to the middle of the yard, sat down, and then first with one paw, then the other, brought the molasses into his mouth until he had cleaned all that part of his coat, all the time deliciously smacking his lips. Whatever quarrels the steward and the bear had afterwards, the latter always got his ration of molasses. On Saturday the sailors had an allowance of rum, and frequently bought some for the week, and on that night Bruin was sure to find his way into the guard room ; one night having tasted some grog, he came to a sailor with whom he was accustomed to wrestle, and who was drinking too freely, and was treated by him so liberally that he got drunk, knocked the sailor down and took possession of his bed ; at fisty cuffs he knew the bear would beat him and being determined to have his bed he shot the bear. This is the fate of almost every Bear that is tamed when grown to their strength. This animal affects a northern climate and is found only on the sea side, and the mouths of large rivers but not beyond the ascent of the tide, and keeping the line of the sea coasts appear more numerous than they really are. Some of the males grow to a large size, I have measured a skin when stretched to a frame to dry, ten and a half feet in length. The fore paw of one of them kept at Churchill weighed in the scales thirty two pounds, a decent paw to shake hands with, the claws are [sharp ?] but only about three inches in length, the flesh is so fat and oily that a considerable quantity is collected for the lamps, and other purposes. The skin is loose and when taken off appears capable of covering a much larger animal; he swims with ease and swiftness, and requires a good boat with four men to come up with him. Although the white bear is found along the coasts inhabited by the Esquimaux yet very few of the skins of this animal are traded from, or seen with, them. For the white bear though seldom he attacks a man, yet when attacked will fight hard for his life, and as he is, what the Indians call Seepnak (strong of life) he is very rarely killed by a single ball; much less with an arrow that cannot break a bone; hence they must be unwilling to attack him.

The Nahathaway Indians are all armed with guns, and are good shots, but they only attack this species of Bear when they are two together, and one after the other keep a steady fire on him, but a ball in the brain or heart is directly fatal.

The Esquimaux are a people with whom we are very little acquainted, although in a manner surrounding us, they live wholly on the sea coast, which they possess from the gulph of the St Lawrence, round the shores of Labrador to Hudsons Straits, these Straits and adjacent Islands, to Hudson's Bay, part of it's east shores; but on the west side of this Bay, only north of Churchill River, thence northward and westward to the Coppermine River; thence to the McKenzie and westward to Icy Cape, the east side of Behring's Strait. Along this immense line of sea coast they appear to have restricted themselves to the sea shores,[1] their Canoes give them free access to ascend the Rivers, yet they never do, every part they frequent is wholly destitute of growing Trees, their whole dependence for fuel and other purposes is on drift wood, of which, fortunately there is plenty. The whole is a

[1] In a general way, this statement that the Eskimo live exclusively on the sea coast is correct. Nevertheless, while exploring the Kazan river, which flows into Chesterfield Inlet, in 1894, I encountered a tribe of Eskimo who live on its banks and rarely visit the salt water. They subsist chiefly on the meat of the caribou, which they kill with their spears in great numbers, and from the skins of the caribou they make their clothing and the coverings for their kayaks or small canoes.

dreary, monotonous coast of Rock and Moss without Hills
or Mountains to the McKenzie River, thence westward the
Mountains are near the shore.

In the latter end of February and the months of
March and April, from the mouth of the River seaward for
several miles the Seals are numerous, and have many holes in
the ice through which they come up : how these holes are
made in the apparent solid ice, I never could divine ; to
look into them, they appear like so many wells of a round
form, with sides of smooth solid ice and their size seldom
large enough to admit two seals to pass together.

The Seals [1] do not come up on the ice before nine or ten
in the morning as the weather may be, and go down between
two and three in the afternoon ; they are always on the
watch, scarce a minute passes without some one lifting his
head, to see if any danger is near from the Bear or Man,
apparently their only enemies.   Three of us several times
made an attempt to kill one, or more ; but to no purpose,
however wounded they had always life enough to fall into
the ice hole and we lost them ; and I have not heard of any
Seal being killed on the spot by a Ball.   The Esquimaux
who live to the northward of us kill these animals for food
and clothing in a quiet and sure manner: the Hunter is
armed with a Lance headed with Bone or Iron, the latter
always preferred : the handle of which, sometimes is the
length of twenty yards (measured) made of pieces of drift
larch wood, neatly fitted to each other, bound together with
sinew, the handle is shortened, or lengthened, as occasion
may require.   The Esquimaux Hunter in the evening, when
the Seals are gone to the sea, examines their holes, the places
where they lie, and having selected the hole, best adapted to

[1] Three species of seal are common on the coast of Hudson Bay near
Fort Churchill : the Rough or Ringed Seal, *Phoca hispida* Schreber ;
the Common or Harbour Seal, *Phoca vitulina* Linn. ; and the Bearded
Seal, *Erignathus barbatus* (Erxleben).   [E. A. P.]

B

his purpose, early in the morning before the seals come up, goes to the ice hole he has selected, on the south side of which he places his Lance, the handle directed northward, the point of the Lance close to the hole, for the seals lie on the north side of the ice hole, and directing his Lance to the spot [where] the Seals have been lying, having firmly laid the helve of his lance, he retires to the end of it, and there hides himself behind some broken ice, which if he does not find to his purpose, he brings pieces of ice to make the shelter he requires.   Lying flat on his belly he awaits with patience the coming up of the Seals; the first Seal takes his place at the north edge of the hole, this is also the direction in which the Lance is laid; the other seals, two, or three more, are close on each side, or behind; if the Seal is not in the direct line of the Lance, which is sometimes the case, he gently twists the handle of the Lance until it is directly opposite to the heart of the Seal; still he waits with patience until the Seal appears asleep; when with all his skill and strength he drives the Lance across the hole (near three feet) into the body of the Seal, which, finding itself wounded, and trying to throw itself into the ice hole, which the handle of the lance prevents, only aids the wound; the hunter keeps the handle firm, and goes on hands and knees to near the hole, where he quietly waits the death of the seal; he then drags the seal from the hole, takes out his lance and carefully washes the blood from it.   When the hunter shows himself all the seals for some distance around dive into the ice holes, and do not come up for several minutes; this gives time to the Esquimaux to place his lance at another hole, and await the seals return, and thus he sometimes kills two of them in one day but this is not often, as the weather is frequently stormy and cloudy. The Esquimaux are of a square, plump make, few of them exceed five feet eight inches in height, the general stature is below this size, and the women are in proportion to the men, their features though broad are not unpleasing, with a tendency to ruddy, they appear cheerful and contented, they are supple active and strong; from the land, in the open season, they have berries, and a few rein-deer, but it is to the sea they look for their subsistence: the sea birds, the seal, morse, beluga, and the whale; living on these oily foods, they are supposed not to be clean, but the fact is, they are as cleanly as people living as they do, and without soap can be expected [to be], all their cooking utensils are in good order. In summer part of them dwell in tents made of the dressed skins of the reindeer, these are pitched on the gravel banks, and kept very neat, they make no fire in them to prevent [them] being soiled with smoke, which is made near the tent. The salmon and meat of the reindeer they cure by smoke of drift wood of which they have plenty. They are very industrious and ingenious, being for eight months of the year exposed to the glare of the snow, their eyes become weak; at the age of forty years almost every man has an impaired sight. The eyesight of the women is less injured at this age. They make neat goggles of wood with a narrow slit, which are placed on the eyes, to lessen the light. They all use Darts, Lances, Bows and Arrows, as weapons of defence, and for hunting; their Darts and Lances are made of drift Larch wood, headed with bone of the leg of the Rein Deer,[1] or a piece of iron, the latter preferred, and the length of the Dart is proportioned to it's intended use—for Birds, the Seal, the Beluga,[2] Whale[3] or the Morse;[4] to the Dart or Lance for the three latter, a large bladder made of sealskins, and blown full of air is attached by a strong line of neatly twisted sinew. This not only shews the place of the wounded animal but soon tires him, [so] that he becomes an easy prey, though sometimes with risque to the Hunter and Canoe. The Morse is

---

[1] *Rangifer arcticus* (Richardson). [E. A. P.]
[2] *Delphinapterus catodon* (Linn.). [E. A. P.]
[3] *Balæna mysticetus* (Linn.). [E. A. P.]
[4] The Walrus, *Odobænus rosmarus* (Linn.). [E. A. P.]

the animal most dreaded, and he is allowed to worry himself
to death before they approach him. Whale Bone is part of
their trade, but whether they procure it by attacking the
Whale as they do the Morse or it is the spoils of those thrown
ashore, is somewhat uncertain. They are dextrous in throwing the dart, although their Canoes allow only the motion of
the upper part of their bodies, and seldom miss a sea bird at
thirty yards distance. Their Bows and Arrows are employed
on the Rein Deer, Wolf and Fox, they draw the Arrow well
and sure, whatever they make displays a neatness and ingenuity
that would do honor to a first rate european workman if he
had no other tools than those poor people have. All along
the sea coast where the Esquimaux are found, there are no
standing woods of any kind, the whole country is rock and
moss, the drift wood is what they wholly depend on for
every purpose for which wood is required, and fortunately it
is plentiful; brought down by the rivers from the interior
countries, and thrown ashore by the waves and tides of the
sea; their country everywhere exhibits Rocks, Ponds, and
Moss, a hundred miles has not ground for a garden, even if
the climate allowed it; their cloathing is much the same
everywhere, made of Rein Deer leather and Seal skins, both
men and women wear boots, which come to the knee, the
foot is made of Morse skin, the upper part of seal skin with
the hair off, the whole so neatly sewed together as to be
perfectly water tight : these boots are much sought after by
the people of the Factories, to walk with in the marshes,
where our boots cannot stand the water. They are worth six
shillings pʳ pair, (at Quebec three dollars) and with care last
two years, of open seasons. Their kettles are made of black,
or dark grey marble, of various sizes, some will hold four to
six gallons, they are of an oblong form, shallow in proportion
to their size, this shape serves for fish as well as flesh, they do
not put them on the fire, the victuals in them is cooked by
means of hot stones to make the water boil, to keep it boiling

by the same means requires very little trouble; the kettles
are kept clean and in good order, polished both in the inside
and outside; they set a high value on them but prefer a
brass kettle, as lighter and more useful. Their canoes are
made of sealskins sewed together, and held to a proper shape
by gunwales, and ribs made of drift Larch, and sometimes
whalebones added; they are very sharp at both ends and no
wider in the middle than to admit a man; their length from
twelve to sixteen feet, they are decked with seal skins so as to
prevent any water getting into the canoe, the place to admit
the man is strengthened by a broad hoop of wood, to the upper
part of which is sewed a sealskin made to draw around the
man like a purse, this the Esquimaux tightens round his waist
so that only the upper part of the body is exposed to the
waves and weather; they urge along their canoes with great
swiftness, by a paddle having a blade at both ends; the handle
is in the middle. Early habit has rendered him expert in
balancing himself on the waves of the sea in these sharp canoes
called kaijack. I never saw a european who could balance
himself in these canoes for three minutes. Their weapons for
killing sea birds, seals &c. are placed on the deck of the canoe,
quite at hand, secured by small cords of sinew. For the
removal of their families they have canoes of about thirty
feet in length by six feet in breadth called oomiaks, made of
seal skin, the gunwales and ribs of larch wood, and whale-
bone; these are paddled by the women and steered by an
old man. Their Bows are made of the Larch found on the
beach, they are from $3\frac{1}{2}$ to five feet in length, made of three
pieces of wood of equal lengths, and morticed into each other,
at the back of each joint, or mortice, is a piece of Morse tooth
neatly made to fit the Bow, of nine inches long, a quarter of
an inch thick, on each side thinned to an edge : the back of
the Bow is a groove of half an inch in depth, leaving the sides
for an inch thick along the groove; this is filled with twisted,
or plaited sinew, running alternately from end to end of the

Bow, each layer secured by cross sinews. In undoing a large
Bow, about four hundred fathoms of this sinew line was
measured : their arrows are twenty eight to thirty inches
long headed with bone, or iron ; but being made of Larch,
for want of better wood, which occasions them to be too large
in proportion to their weight, and lessens their velocity ; yet
such is the strength of their Bows, they pierce a Rein Deer
at one hundred and twenty yards : almost all their weapons
are barbed. When the winter moderates sufficiently to allow
them to travel, they use a large sled made of two runners of
Larch, each runner is six to seven feet long, six to eight
inches deep, and four inches wide, each turning up at the
fore part, the runners are fastened together by bars of wood
let into the upper side of each runner, on these they lay,
and with cords, secure all their baggage, utensils, and provisions ; the men to the number of six, or eight, harness themselves to the sled and march from campment to campment in
quest of animals for food and clothing : the women carry
their children, and light things, and sometimes assist the men.
As soon as mild weather comes on, [so] that they can dwell
in tents, they willingly leave their earthy, or snow huts, and
live in tents made of the dressed leather of the Rein Deer,
which are pitched on clean gravel : they rarely allow a fire
to be made in them as it would soil the leather, but for all
purposes make a fire without. When they lie down at night,
they have their particular blankets made of Rein Deer or
Seal skins, beside which, a large coverlet made of the same
material extends all round each half of the tent and covers
everyone, generally there are two families to each tent.

In their conduct to each other they are sociable, friendly,
and of a cheerful temper. But we are not sufficiently
acquainted with their language to say much more ; in their
traffic with us they are honest and friendly. They are not of
the race of the north american Indians, but of european
descent. Nothing can oblige an Indian to work at anything

but stern necessity; whereas the Esquimaux is naturally industrious, very ingenious, fond of the comforts of life so far as they can attain them, always cheerful, and even gay; it is true that in the morning, when he is about to embark in his shell of a Canoe, to face the waves of the sea, and the powerful animals he has to contend with, for food and clothing for himself and family, he is for many minutes very serious, because he is a man of reflection, knows the dangers to which he.is exposed, but steps into his canoe, and bravely goes through the toil and dangers of the day.

The steady enemy of the Seal is the Polar Bear. How this awkward animal catches the watchful Seal, I could not imagine. The Esquimaux say, he prowls about examining the ice holes of the Seals and finding one close to high broken ice there hides himself, and when the Seals are basking in the Sun and half asleep, he springs upon them, seizes one, which he hugs to death, and as fast as possible, with his teeth cuts the back sinews of the neck, the Seal is then powerless and Bruin feasts on him at his leisure. Few Porpoises [1] are seen, but the Beluga, a small species of white Whale, are very numerous from the latter end of May to the beginning of September, their average length is about fifteen feet, and [they] are covered with fat from three to five inches in thickness, which yields an oil superior to that of the black whale. This Summer the Company had a Boat and six Men employed for the taking of the Beluga, the Boat was of light construction and painted white, which is the color of this fish, and as experience has proved the color best adapted to them as they often, in a manner, touch the Boat; while they avoid Boats of any other color, those taken were all struck with the Harpoon, and often held the Boat in play from three to five miles before they were killed by the Lance, towing the Boat

---

[1] *Phocæna phocæna* (Linn.) is common in Baffin's Bay and about the mouth of Hudson Strait, but apparently has not been detected on the west shore of Hudson Bay. [E. A. P.]

at the rate of five miles an hour; when struck they dive to
the bottom with such force as sometimes to strike the harpoon
out of them, and thus many escape; in some of those killed
I have seen the harpoon much bent. Their young are of a
blueish color, and in the month of July weigh about one
hundred and twenty pounds, they are struck with a strong
boat hook. The Beluga in chase of the Salmon sometimes
runs himself ashore, especially up large Brooks and Creeks.
If it is ebb tide he stands every chance of remaining and becoming the prey of Gulls and the Polar Bear. The produce
of this summers fishing, was three tuns of oil, which could
not pay the expenses. There is scarce a doubt but strong
Nets well anchored would take very many and be profitable
to the Company.[1]

After passing a long gloomy, and most .severe winter, it
will naturally be thought with what delight we enjoy the
Spring, and Summer; of the former we know nothing but
the melting of the snow and the ice becoming dangerous;
Summer such as it is, comes at once, and with it myriads of
tormenting Musketoes; the air is thick with them, there is
no cessation day nor night of suffering from them. Smoke
is no relief, they can stand more smoke than we can, and
smoke cannot be carried about with us. The narrow windows
were so crowded with them, they trod each other to death in
such numbers, we had to sweep them out twice a day; a
chance cold northeast gale of wind was a grateful relief, and
[we] were thankful for the cold weather that put an end to our
sufferings. The Musketoe Bill, when viewed through a good
microscope, is of a curious formation, composed of two distinct pieces; the upper is three sided, of a black color, and
sharp-pointed, under which is a round white tube, like clear

---

[1] For many years the White Whale or Beluga has been taken in some
numbers by means of a net stretched across the mouth of some natural
basin, which, being raised after entrance of a school, imprisons the animals
until the falling tide leaves them helpless. [E. A. P.]

glass, the mouth inverted inwards ; with the upper part the skin is perforated, it is then drawn back, and the clear tube applied to the wound, and the blood sucked through it into the body, till it is full ; thus their bite are two distinct operations, but so quickly done as to feel as only one ; different Persons feel them in a different manner ; some are swelled, even bloated, with intolerable itching ; others feel only the smart of the minute wounds ; Oil is the only remedy and that frequently applied ; the Natives rub themselves with Sturgeon Oil, which is found to be far more effective than any other oil. All animals suffer from them, almost to madness, even the well feathered Birds suffer about the eyes and neck. The cold nights of September are the first, and most steady relief. A question has often been asked to which no satisfactory answer has ever been given ; where, and how, do they pass the winter, for on their first appearance they are all full grown, and the young brood does not come forward until July. The opinion of the Natives, as well as many of ourselves, is, that they pass the winter at the bottom of ponds of water, for when these ponds are free of ice, they appear covered with gnats in a weak state ; and two, or three days after the Musketoes are on us in full force. This theory may do very well for the low countries, where except the bare rock, the whole surface may be said to be wet, and more, or less, covered with water, but will not do for the extensive high and dry Plains, where, when the warm season comes on, they start up in myriads a veritable full grown plague. We must conclude that wherever they find themselves when the frost sets in, there they shelter themselves from the winter, be the country wet or dry ; and this theory appears probable, for all those countries where they were in myriads, and which are now under cultivation by the plough, are in a manner clear of them, and also the Cities and Towns of Canada. But in America there always has been, and will be Woods, Swamps, and rough ground, not fit for the plough, but admirably adapted to produce Musketoes, and the Cows turned out to graze, when they return to be milked bring with them more than enough to plague the farmer. In September the Sand Fly, and Midgeuks, are numerous, the latter insinuates itself all over the body; the skin becomes heated with itching; these cease at sun set, but remain until the season becomes cold. October puts an end to all these plagues. It is a curious fact [that] the farther to the northward, the more, and more, numerous are all those flies, but their time is short.

While these insects are so numerous they are a terrour to every creature on dry lands if swamps may be so called, the dogs howl, roll themselves on the ground, or hide themselves in the water; the Fox seems always in a fighting humour; he barks, snaps on all sides, and however hungry and ready to go a birdsnesting, of which he is fond, is fairly driven to seek shelter in his hole. A sailor finding swearing of no use, tried what Tar could do, and covered his face with it, but the musketoes stuck to it in such numbers as to blind him, and the tickling of their wings were worse than their bites; in fact Oil is the only remedy. I was fortunate in passing my time in the company of three gentlemen the officers of the factory, Mr Jefferson the deputy governor, Mr Prince the captain of the Sloop, that annually traded with the Esquimaux to the northward, and Mr Hodges the Surgeon;[1] they had books which they freely lent to me, among them were several on history and on animated nature, these were what I paid most attention to as the most instructive. Writing paper there was none but what was in the hands of the Governor, and a few sheets among the officers. On my complaining that I should lose my writing for want of practice, Mr Hearne

[1] The Hudson's Bay Company was accustomed to keep a surgeon or doctor at each of its most important trading posts on Hudson Bay. As a rule these surgeons were young men who remained only a few years in the service.

employed me a few days on his manuscript entitled " A journey to the North,"[1] and at another time I copied an Invoice.

It had been the custom for many years, when the governors of the factory required a clerk, to send to the school in which I was educated to procure a Scholar who had a mathematical education to send out as Clerk, and, to save expenses, he was bound apprentice to them for seven years. To learn what ; for all I had seen in their service neither writing nor reading was required. and my only business was to amuse myself, in winter growling at the cold ; and in the open season shooting Gulls, Ducks, Plover and Curlews, and quarelling with Musketoes and Sand flies.

The Hudsons Bay Company annually send out three Ships to their Factories, which generally arrive at their respective ports in the latter end of August or the early part of September, and this year (1785) the Ship arrived as usual. When the Captain landed, I was surprised to see with him Mr John Charles,[2] a school fellow and of the same age as myself, whom

---

[1] This book was published ten years later, and three years after Hearne's death, under the editorship of Dr. John Douglas, Bishop of Salisbury, with the title *A Journey from Prince of Wales's Fort in Hudson's Bay to the Northern Ocean*, and was republished, with introduction and notes, by the Champlain Society in 1911. It describes Hearne's three journeys on foot from Fort Prince of Wales, at the mouth of the Churchill river, to the Coppermine river, in the years between 1769 and 1772.

[2] Thompson here refers to George Charles, who came to Churchill in 1785. George Charles was in training for the Company at the Grey Coat School at the time of Thompson's departure from it. In the minutes of the Grey Coat School under date of June 29, 1785, "The Master reports that there is but one boy in the School, viz. George Charles, who is under instruction for the service of the Hudson's Bay Company by order of the Treasurer at the desire and request of his uncle, Mr. John Allen, Coachmaker, of Petty France, Westminster." On May 20, 1785, young Charles, who was then about fifteen years of age, was bound to the Hudson's Bay Company, and the Grey Coat School paid the Company five pounds, and four pounds more " in lieu of instruments." George Charles remained at Churchill, or at the trading posts up the Churchill river, for a number of years, at least until the winter of 1805, but it does not appear that he ever

I had left to be bound out to a trade. I enquired of him what had made him change his mind, he informed me that shortly after my departure, from what he could learn some maps drawn by the fur traders of Canada had been seen by M[r] Dalrymple,[1] which showed the rivers and lakes for many hundred miles to the westward of Hudsons Bay. That he applied to the Company to send out a gentleman well qualified to survey the interior country, all which they promised to do, and have [a] gentleman fit for that purpose

made any surveys of the interior country. The work of making a survey as far west as Lake Athabaska was afterwards assigned to Philip Turnor. John Charles, with whose name Thompson appears to have confused George Charles, was a younger man who was born in the Parish of St. Margaret, Westminster, about the year 1785, and who entered the service of the Hudson's Bay Company about 1799. In 1815–16 he was at Nelson House on Churchill river, and in 1820 he was in charge of New Churchill district, with headquarters at Indian lake. In 1821, at the union of the Hudson's Bay and North-West Companies, he was a chief factor with residence at the same place. Later he was at Isle à la Crosse in charge of the English river district, and in 1833, when Sir George Back conducted an exploring expedition down the Great Fish river to the Arctic ocean, he was in charge of the Athabaska district. He retired from active service in the Company in 1842. R. M. Ballantyne, in his *Hudson's Bay*, Edinburgh, 1848, gives an interesting sketch of his appearance and character under the name of Carles.

[1] Alexander Dalrymple was Hydrographer to the Admiralty from 1795, when the post was created, until a few weeks before his death in 1808. He was born in Scotland on July 24, 1737, and when fifteen years of age went to India in the service of the East India Company. For twenty-eight years he remained in the East ; then he returned to England, and during the next ten years he published a number of books and papers, chiefly relating to geography and travel. Towards the end of this time he was appointed Hydrographer to the East India Company. He criticized Hearne's geographical work on his journey to the Coppermine river ; and he seems to have been largely instrumental in having Philip Turnor sent out to determine the extent and correct position of Lake Athabaska. It is difficult, however, to understand Thompson's reference to him in the text. It is hardly likely that any map drawn by the Canadian fur-traders had been seen by him before 1785. It is generally assumed that the map made by Peter Pond, in or about the year 1785, which showed Lake Athabaska much too far west and too near the Pacific ocean, is the one which incited Dalrymple to urge fuller surveys of that lake and its vicinity.

to go out with their ships next year ; they accordingly sent
to the School to have one ready. As he was the only one
of age, he was placed in the mathematical school, run quickly
over his studies, for which he had no wish to learn, for three
days, for a few minutes each day, taught to handle Hadley's
quadrant, and bring down the Sun to a chalk mark on the
wall [and] his education was complete, and pronounced fit for
the duties he had to perform ; he was very much disappointed
at all he saw, but he could not return. Hudson's Bay, is
certainly a country that Sinbad the Sailor never saw, as he
makes no mention of Musketoes.

CHAPTER II

LIFE AT A TRADING POST ON HUDSON'S BAY

*Orders to set out for York Factory—Packet Indians—Leave
Churchill—West shore of Hudson's Bay—Meet several
Polar Bears—Indian superstitions regarding Polar Bears—
Cross Nelson River and arrive at York Factory—Great
Marsh—Shooting wild Geese—Southward migration of Geese
—Orders of the Manito—Cranes and Bitterns—Life at
York Factory—Ship arrives and leaves—Winter sets in—
Hunting parties—Depart for Factory—Unwelcome visitor—
His death—Wrath of Indian Woman—Polar Bear in a
trap—Speckled Trout—Hares—White grouse or ptarmigan
—Feeding ground—Netting grouse—Feathers of grouse—
Pine Grouse—Pheasants—Snow Bunting—Tomtit—Cross
beak — Whiskeyjack — Raven—White Fox — Hawks and
Foxes—Snow blindness.*

EARLY in September the annual Ship arrived, and
orders were sent for me to proceed directly to York
Factory, a distance of one hundred and fifty miles
to the southward.[1] The Hudson's Bay Company had established a very useful line of communication between their
several Factories by means of what were called, Packet Indians,
these were each of two Indian men, who left each Factory
with letters to arrive at the next Factory about the expected
time of the arrival of the Ship at such Factory, and thus the
safe arrival of these annual Ships, and the state of the Factories

---

[1] Thompson was at this time fifteen years of age.

became known to each other, and assistance was given where required. The Boat from Churchill Factory crossed the River with the two Packet Indians and myself to Cape Churchill, and landed us without any Provisions, and only one blanket to cover me at night; for we had to carry everything: it was a very fine day; but unfortunately a gallon of very strong Grog was given to these Indians, who as usual, as soon as they landed, began drinking, and were soon drunk and the day lost; we slept on the ground each in his single blanket, the dew was heavy: Early in the morning we set off and continued our march to sunset, without breakfast or dinner; the Indians now shot one Goose [1] and three stock Ducks.[2] We came to something like a dry spot, and stopped for the night with plenty of drift wood for fuel; the three Ducks were soon picked, stuck on a stick to roast at the fire; meantime the Goose was picked, and put to roast. Each of us had a Duck, and the Goose among us three. Our march all day had been on the marshy beach of the Bay, which made it fatigueing; and directly after supper, each wrapped himself in his blanket and slept soundly on the ground: the banks of the Brooks were the only kind of dry ground. The incidents of every day were so much the same that I shall make one story of the whole: on the evening of the sixth day we arrived at Kisiskatchewan River, a bold, deep, stream of two miles in width; we put up on the bank of a Brook, where my companions had laid up a Canoe, but the wind blowing fresh we could not proceed. Our line of march had constantly been along the Bay side, at high water mark, always wet and muddy, tiresome walking and very dull; on the left hand was the sea, which when the tide was in appeared deep, but the Ebb retired to such a distance, that the Sea was not visible and showed an immense surface of Mud with innumerable boulders of rock, from one to five or seven tons

[1] Probably *Branta canadensis hutchinsi* (Rich.). [E. A. P.]
[2] Mallard, *Anas platyrhynchos* Linn. [E. A. P.]

weight, the greatest part were lodged at about half tide,
where the greatest part of the drift ice remains on the shore;
as Seal River, north of Churchill River, is the most southern
place where the shore is of Rock, the whole of these boulders
must have come with the ice from the northward of that
River, for south of it, and of Churchill River all is alluvial;
this evidently shows a strong set of the north sea into Hudson's
Bay on it's west side, returning by the east side into Hudson's
Straits; for these boulders are found on the west side shores
to the most southern part of the Bay. On our right hand
was an immense extent of alluvial in marsh, morass, and
numerous ponds of water, which furnished water to many
small Brooks; the woods, such as they are, were out of sight.
Every day we passed from twelve to fifteen Polar Bears,
lying on the marsh, a short distance from the shore, they were
from three to five together, their heads close to each other,
and their bodies lying as radii from a centre. I enquired of
the Indians if the Polar Bears always lay in that form, they
said, it was the common manner in which they lie. As we
passed them, one, or two would lift up their heads and look
at us, but never rose to molest us. The indian rule is to
walk past them with a steady step without seeming to notice
them. On the sixth day we had a deep Brook to cross, and
on the opposite side of the ford was a large Polar Bear feasting
on a Beluga, we boldly took the ford thinking the bear would
go away, but when [we were] about half way across, he lifted
his head, placed his fore paws on the Beluga, and uttering a
loud growl, showed to us such a sett of teeth as made us
turn up the stream, and for fifty yards wade up to our middle
before we could cross; during this time the Bear eyed us,
growling like a Mastiff Dog. During the time we were
waiting [for] the wind to calm, I had an opportunity of seeing
the Indian superstition on the Polar Bear; on one of these
days we noticed a Polar Bear prowling about in the ebb tide,
the Indians set off to kill it as the skin could be taken to the

Factory in the Canoe; when the Bear was shot, before they could skin him and cut off his head, the tide was coming in, which put them in danger, they left the skin to float ashore, and seizing the head, each man having hold of an ear, with their utmost speed in the mud brought the head to land, the tide was up to their knees when they reached the shore; on the first grass they laid down the head, with the nose to the sea, which they made red with ochre; then made a speech to the Manito of the Bears, that he would be kind to them as they had performed all his orders, had brought the head of the Bear ashore, and placed it with it's nose to the sea, begging him to make the skin float ashore, which, at the Factory would sell for three pints of Brandy; the Manito had no intention that they should get drunk, the skin did not float ashore and was lost. In the afternoon of the third day the wind calmed, the Indians told me at Noon that we had staid there too long, that they would now sing and calm the wind, for their song had great power; they sung for about half an hour; and then said to me, you see the wind is calming, such is the power of our song. I was hurt at their pretensions and replied; you see the Ducks, the Plover and other Birds, follow the ebb tide, they know the wind is calming without your song : if you possess such power why did you not sing on the first day of our being here. They gave no answer, it is a sad weakness of the human character, and [one] which is constantly found, more, or less, in the lower orders of thinly populated countries; they all possess, if we may credit them, some superhuman power. The Ebb tide had now retired about one and a half mile from us. Near sunset, each of us cut a bundle of small willows, and with the Canoe and paddles, carried them about a mile, when we laid the Canoe down, spread the willows on the mud, and laid down to await the return of the tide; as soon as it reached us, we got into the canoe, and proceeded up the Kisiskatchewan River for several miles, then crossed to the south shore and

c

landed at a path[1] of four miles in length through woods of small pines, on low, wet, marsh ground to York Factory, thank good Providence.[2]

I now return to the great marsh along which we travelled. The aquatic fowl in the seasons of spring and autumn are very numerous. They seem to confine themselves to a belt of these great marshes, of about two miles in width from the seashore, and this belt is mostly covered with small ponds; and the intervals have much short tender grass, which serves for food, the interior of the marsh has too much moss. Of these fowls the wild geese are the most numerous and the most valuable, and of these the grey goose,[3] of which there are four species, and the brent goose,[4] a lesser species of the gray goose, it's feathers are darker and it's cry different. Of the Snow Geese [5] there are three varieties, the least of which is of a blueish color,[6] they are all somewhat less than the gray geese, but of richer meat. It may be remarked that of wild fowl, the darker the feather, the lighter the color of the meat; and the whiter the feather, the darker the meat, as the Snow Goose and the Swan &c. The shooting of the wild Geese, (or as it is called, the hunt) is of great importance to the Factories not only for present fresh meat, but also [because it] forms a supply of Provisions for a great part of the winter; the gray geese are the first to arrive in the early

[1] This path or track is still used in crossing from the Nelson to the Hayes river at York Factory, but the land is so wet and boggy that it is always avoided when it is possible to go round the point of marsh between the two rivers in canoes.

[2] Thompson arrived at York Factory about September 15, and on that date the following entry was made in the books of the Company: "Gave as a gratuity to the two Indians, for the care they have taken of David Thompson,

"brandy	3 gals.	16 MB.
"tobacco	4 lbs.	4 MB."

[3] *Branta canadensis* (Linn.). [E. A. P.]
[4] Probably *Branta c. hutchinsi* (Richardson). [E. A. P.]
[5] *Chen h. nivalis* (Forster). [E. A. P.]
[6] Probably Blue Goose, *Chen cærulescens* (Linn.). [E. A. P.]

part of May; the Snow geese arrive about ten days after. About ten of the best shots of the men of the Factory, with several Indians, are now sent to the marshes to shoot them. For this purpose each man has always two guns, each makes what is called a Stand, this is composed of drift wood and pine branches, about three feet high, six feet in diameter, and half round in form, to shelter himself from the weather and the view of the geese; each Stand is about 120 yards from the other, or more, and forms a line on the usual passage of the geese, [which is] always near the sea shore; two, or three, parties are formed, as circumstances may direct; each hunter has about ten mock geese, which are sticks made and painted to resemble the head and neck of the gray goose, to which is added a piece of canvas for a body. They are placed about twenty yards from the Stands, with their beaks to windward : the position in which the geese feed. When the geese first arrive, they readily answer to the call of the Hunter. The Indians imitate them so well that they would alight among the mock geese, if the shots of the hunter did not prevent them. The geese are all shot on the wing; they are too shy, and the marsh too level, to be approached. Some good shots, in the spring hunt, kill from 70 to 90 geese, but the general average is from 40 to 50 geese p^r man, as the season may be. The Snow Goose is very unsteady on the wing, now high, now low, they are hard to hit, they seldom answer to our call, but the Indians imitate them well; for the spring, they answer the call, but do not notice it in autumn; for the table, the Snow Goose is the richest bird that flies. The feathers of the geese are taken care of and sent to London, where they command a ready sale. The feathers of four grey geese, and of five Snow geese weigh one pound. The duration of their stay depends much on the weather; a month at the most, and seldom less than three weeks. The flight of the geese is from daylight to about 8 AM. and from 5 PM. to dusk. By the end of May, or the

first week in June, the geese have all left us for their breeding
places, much farther to the northward. In the spring several
of the Geese are found with wild rice in their crops.[1] The
wild rice grows in abundance to the south westward; the
nearest place to York Factory are the small Lakes at the
mouth of the River Winipeg, distant about 420 miles. When
M[r] Wales was at Fort Churchill in 1769 to observe the
transit of Venus over the Sun,[2] from curiosity he several
times took angles of the swiftnes of the wild geese and found
that in a steady gale of wind, their flight before it was sixty
miles an hour. When shooting at them going before a gale
of wind, at the distance of 40 to 50 yards, the aim is taken
two or three inches before his beak. When going against the
wind, at the insertion of the neck. In the middle of July
several flocks of a very large species of grey goose arrived
from the southward, they have a deep harsh note, and are
called Gronkers, by others Barren Geese,[3] from its being supposed they never lay eggs. If so, how is this species propa-
gated, they very seldom alight in our marshes; but as they
fly low a few of them are shot. Their meat is like that of
the common gray goose. I do not remember seeing these
geese in autumn. In the spring all the geese, ducks and other
fowls come from the southward; in autumn they all come
from the northward. Their first arrival is in the early part
of September, and their stay about three weeks. They keep
arriving, night and day, and our solitary marshes become
covered with noisy, animated life. The same mode of shooting them, is now as in the spring, but they do not answer the
call so well, and the average number each man may kill is
from 25 to 30 geese for the season. The geese salted of the

---

[1] In 1895, while exploring the country east of Lake Winnipeg, I found
wild rice growing in some of the small streams as far north as latitude
53°, or only 350 miles south-west of York Factory.

[2] See note on p. 9.

[3] Probably barren individuals of the Canada Goose, _Branta cana-
densis_ (Linn.). [E. A. P.]

spring hunt, are better than those of autumn; they are fatter, and more firm, those salted in Autumn are only beginning to be fat, which, with young geese, in this state, make poor salted food. In autumn, the last three days of the geese appear to be wholly given in cleaning and adjusting every feather of every part, instead of feeding at pleasure everywhere; the Manito of the geese, ducks and other fowls had given his orders, they collect, and form flocks of, from 40 to 60, or more; and seem to have leaders; the Manito of the aquatic fowl has now given his orders for their departure to milder climates; his presence sees the setting in of winter, and the freezing of the ponds &c. The leaders of the flock have now a deep note. The order is given, and flock after flock, in innumerable numbers, rise. Their flight is of a regular form, making an angle of about 25 degrees; the two sides of the angle are unequal, that side next to the sea being more than twice the length of the side next to the land; where I have counted 30 geese on one side, the short side has only ten to twelve, and so in proportion; the point of the angle is a single goose, which leads the flock; when tired of opening the air, [it] falls into the rear of the short line, and the goose next on the long, or sea, line, takes his place, and thus in succession. Thus in two, or three days, these extensive marshes, swarming with noisy life, become silent, and wholly deserted; except when wounded, no instance has ever been known of geese, or ducks, being found in frozen ponds, or Lakes. The Swan is sometimes frozen in, and loses his life.

The different species of Geese on the east side of the [Rocky] Mountains pass the winter in the mild climate of the Floridas, the mouths of the Mississippe, and around the Gulph of Mexico, from these shores the wild Geese and Swans proceed to the northward as far as the Latitude of 67 to 69 north, where they have the benefit of the Sun's light and heat for the twenty four hours for incubation, and rarely breed under twenty hours of Sunlight. These wild birds proceed, through the pathless air, from where they winter to where they breed, a distance of about two thousand seven hundred miles, in a straight line; and from the place of breeding to the mouths of the Mississippe, and adjacent shores the same distance. The question arises, by what means do the wild geese make such long journeys with such precision of place; the wise, and learned, civilized man answers, by Instinct, but what is Instinct: a property of mind that has never been defined. The Indian believes the geese are directed by the Manito, who has the care of them. Which of the two is right.

The Frogs[1] now cease to croak; for they must also prepare for winter. A few Cranes[2] frequent these marshes, as also a few Bitterns.[3] They pass the whole of the open season in pairs, yet their eggs are never, or very rarely found, they are so well hid in the rushes of quagmires which cannot be approached. The Bittern arrives and departs in pairs mostly in the night, it is a bird of slow wing, easy to be killed. The Cranes arrive, and depart in flocks of thirty to fifty, their flight is an angle of full thirty degrees, both sides [of which] are nearly equal; I have never seen the leader quit his place. They are good eating, fleshy, but not fat. They make the best of broth: the ducks and lesser birds arrive and depart in flocks, but in no regular order.

The society and occupations of the Factories along the shores of Hudson's Bay are so much alike, that the description of one Factory may serve for all the others. I shall describe York Factory, being the principal Factory and in point of commerce worth all the other Factories.[4] The establishment

[1] *Rana cantabrigensis latiremis* Cope. [E. A. P.]
[2] *Grus canadensis* (Linn.). [E. A. P.]
[3] *Botaurus lentiginosus* (Montagu). [E. A. P.]
[4] York Factory is situated on the top of a cliff of clay thirty feet high, on the west bank of the Hayes river, five miles above its mouth. Opposite to it the water in the river is from ten to twenty feet in depth, quite

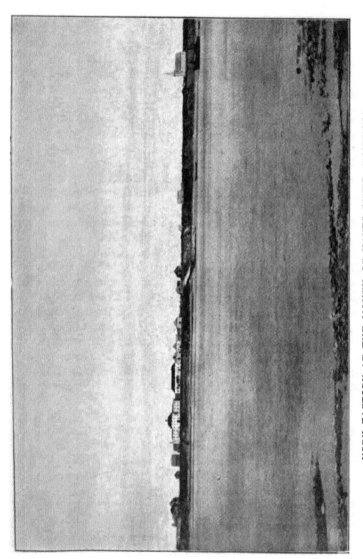

YORK FACTORY AT THE MOUTH OF HAYES RIVER, MANITOBA

was composed of a Resident, an Assistant, with one, or two clerks, a Steward and about forty men, over whom there was a foreman. The Ship for the Factory arrives generally about the latter end of August, sometimes later, this depends on their passage through Hudson's Straits, which in some years sufficiently deep for small ships or sloops of moderate draught, but at the mouth of the river are extensive flats over which it is difficult to pass, except at high tide, and over which the sea-going ships that bring the supplies from England to York Factory do not attempt to cross.

At the present time the Factory consists of a series of buildings arranged around a quadrangle, some of which are large stores or warehouses, while others are residences for the masters and employees engaged there. The present buildings, or more probably smaller ones which preceded them, were erected by Joseph Colen in 1789 and the following years, the central " depot " having been built some time in the early part of last century.

Old York Fort was situated about half a mile below the present fort on the same side of the river, and it was to this fort that Thompson came when he arrived from Churchill in 1785. Previous to that time it had been occupied by the English and French alternately for about a hundred years, until 1782, when it was taken by the French under Admiral de la Pérouse, and was burned to the ground, and the English inhabitants were carried captive to France.

In the following year it was rebuilt by the Hudson's Bay Company, and from that time was occupied for several years; but in the spring of 1788 the ground on which it stood was flooded to a depth of several feet, and Joseph Colen, who was in charge at the time, determined that he would move it to a higher situation. Accordingly, shortly afterwards, he commenced to build the fort on its present site, and by 1792 the moving was completed, and the men with their goods and supplies were all at the new fort.

Until the building of the Canadian Pacific Railway across the continent in 1885, the trading goods for the whole of the interior of the western country from Hudson Bay to the Rocky Mountains, and even beyond these mountains, were brought here from England, whence they were distributed by canoes or boats throughout the interior country, and the same boats which took the supplies into the country brought back to York Factory loads of furs which were carried to England and were disposed of in the markets of London.

Since the building of the Canadian Pacific Railway, over which trading goods and furs can be easily carried in and out of the country, the importance of York Factory as a centre of distribution has greatly decreased, until now it is merely a distributing point for a few small fur-trading stations within a radius of a few hundred miles that as yet have no easier and more rapid mode of access to the civilized world.

is sadly blocked up with ice; the Ship anchors in the mouth
of the River, about five miles below the Factory, the whole
attention of all hands is turned with unloading, and reloading
of the Ship; the time of doing which, depends on the weather,
and takes from ten to fifteen days. The ship having sailed
for London, this may be called the beginning of our year.
The regular occupations of the Factory now commence;
eight or ten of the best shots among us, among which are sure
to be the clerks, with the few indians that may be near, are
sent off to the marshes to shoot geese, ducks, cranes &c for
the present supply of the Factory, and to be salted for the
winter. Axes are put in order, Boats got ready with Provisions, and about twenty men sent up the River to the
nearest forests to cut down pine trees, branch them, lop off
the heads, and carry them on their shoulders to the great
wood pile, near the river bank; the trees are so small that a
man generally carries two, or three, to the wood pile.   When
the quantity required for fuel, is thus cut and piled, the wood
is taken by a large sledge drawn by the men to a bay of the
River, where rafts can be made and floated to the Factory,
which is completed in April, but not floated to the Factory
until June and July.   Accounts, Books, grouse shooting &c
employ the time of those at the Factory.   Winter soon sets
in; the geese hunters return, and out of them are formed two
parties of three or four men, each for grouse shooting, snareing hares &c.   Each party has a canvas tent, like a soldier's
bell tent with the top cut off to let the smoke out.   Fowling
pieces, ammunition, fish hooks and lines, steel traps and three
weeks of salted provisions, with our bedding of blankets &c
completes our equipment.   The shore ice of the River is
now frozen to the width of half a mile, or more; the current
of the River has much drift ice, it is time for the hunters to
be off, the boats are ready, and we are placed on the ice, with
four flat sleds, and a fine large Newfoundland Dog; the
Boats return and we are left to our exertions.   Our party

consisted of four men and an indian woman. We loaded the
sleds with the tent, our baggage and some provisions, leaving
the rest for another trip, each of us hauled about seventy
pounds and the fine dog 100 pounds weight. We proceeded
to a large Brook, called French Creek,[1] up which we went
about a mile to where the Pines of the forest were of some
size and clean growth; the tent poles were now cut, and
placed to form a circular area of about 12 to 14 feet diameter
and 12 feet in heighth; the door poles are the strongest,
about these poles we wrapped our tents, the fire place is in
the centre, and our beds of pine branches, with a Log next
to the fire. Our furniture [was] a three gallon brass kettle,
with a lesser one for water, two, or three tin dishes, spoons &c.
A Hoard is next made of Logs well notched into each·other
of about eight feet in length, six feet wide at the bottom,
five feet in height, and the top narrowed to two feet covered
with Logs to secure our provisions and game from the
carnivorous animals. Our occupations were angling of Trout,[2]
snareing of Hares,[3] shooting white Grouse,[4] trapping of
Martens,[5] Foxes[6] and Wolverines.[7] Our enemy the Polar Bear,
was prowling about, the sea not being sufficiently frozen to
allow him to catch Seals.

By the latter end of November we had procured sufficient
game to load three flat sleds, for the Factory, hauled by two of
us and our Dog. To arrive at the Factory took us the whole
of the day   The same evening Wm Budge, a fine handsome
man, John Mellam, and the indian woman were frying pork

[1] French Creek is below and on the opposite side of Hayes river from
York Factory, and is seven miles distant from it in a direct line. Its
Indian name is Notawatowi Sipi, meaning " The Creek-from-which-you-
fetch-the-people."
[2] *Cristivomer namaycush* (Walbaum). [E. A. P.]
[3] *Lepus americanus* Erxleben. [E. A. P.]
[4] Ptarmigan. *Lagopus albus* and *L. rupestris.* [E. A. P.]
[5] *Martes americana abieticola* (Preble). [E. A. P.]
[6] *Alopex lagopus innuitus* (Merriam). [E. A. P.]
[7] *Gulo luscus* (Linn.). [E. A. P.]

and grouse for supper, [when] the smell attracted a Polar
Bear, who marched to the Tent, and around it, his heavy
tread was heard, and no more cooking thought of. As usual
in the evening, the fowling pieces were being washed and
cleaned, and were then not fit for use, but there was a loaded
musquet. At length Bruin found the door, and thrust in his
head and neck, the Tent Poles prevented further entrance.
Budge climbed up the tent poles and left Mellam and his
indian woman to fight the Bear, the former snatched up the
Musket, it snapped ; seizing it by the muzzle he broke off the
stock on the head of the Bear, and then with hearty blows
applied the barrel and lock to his head ; the indian woman
caught up her axe on the other side of the door, and in like
manner struck Bruin on the head, such an incessant storm of
blows, [as] made him withdraw himself ; he went to the
Hoard and began to tear it in pieces, for the game ; a fowling
piece was quickly dried, loaded with two balls, and fired into
him, the wound was mortal, he went a few paces and fell,
with a dreadful growl. Budge now wanted to descend from
the smoky top of the Tent, but the Woman with her axe in
her hand (2½ lbs) heaped wood on the fire, and threatened to
brain him if he came down. He begged hard for his life, she
was determined, fortunately Mellam snatched the axe from
her, but she never forgave him, for the indian woman pardons
Man for everything but want of courage, this is her sole
support and protection, there are no laws to defend her.
The next morning on examining the head of the Bear, the
skin was much bruised and cut, but the bone had not a mark
on it. We had two steel traps of double springs, with strong
iron teeth, weighing each seventy pounds, and five feet in
length, for Wolves [1] and Wolverines : one of these was baited
with a Grouse, and placed on the ice at the mouth of the
brook, a Polar Bear took the bait, the iron teeth closed on his
head, he went about half [a] mile and then laid down ; the

---

[1] *Canis occidentalis* Richardson. [E. A. P.]

next morning we traced the Bear, he rose up, a curious looking figure with a trap of five feet across his nose, he went directly for the sea, and we respectfully followed; our guns had only small shot; when arrived at the edge of the ice, Bruin made a halt, and no doubt thought such a trap across his nose would be an impediment to swimming, and catching Seals, wisely determined to get rid of it, turning round and looking at us, he bent his head and the trap on the ice, and placing his heavy fore paws on each of the springs, he loosened himself from the trap, and looking at us with an air of contempt, dashed into the sea, and swam away. We got the trap, but his heavy paws had broken one of the springs and rendered the trap useless. The other hunting party about three miles to the eastward of us had also the visit of a Polar Bear; one evening from the smell of fried pork and grouse, he came to the tent, marched round, and round it, but found no entrance, his heavy tread warned the inmates to be on their guard. The bear reared himself up on the tent, he placed the claws of his fore paws through the canvas, the man opposite ready with his gun, guided by his paws, fired and mortally wounded him; but in falling the Bear brought down the tent and tent poles, under which, with the bear were three men and one woman, whom, the Bear in the agonies of death, sadly kicked about, until relieved by the man who had shot the Bear, the tent was drawn over his head, and he was free.

I must return to our occupations; of the speckled Trout[1] we caught about ten dozen of two to three pounds weight, through holes in the ice of the brook, they were readily caught with a common hook and line, baited with the heart of a Grouse; as the cold increased and the thickness of the ice, the Trout went to deeper water, where we could not find them. The Hares, when they go to feed, which is mostly in the night time, keep a regular path in the snow, across which a hedge is thrown of pine trees of close branches, but

---

[1] *Cristivomer namaycush* (Walbaum). [E. A. P.]

cut away at the path; a long pole is tied to a tree, in such a manner that the butt end shall overbalance the upper end and the weight of a hare; to this end the snare of brass wire is tied by a piece of strong twine, this end of the pole is tied to the tree laid across the path, by a slip knot, and the snare suspended at four inches above the snow. The Hare comes bounding along, enters the snare, the slip knot is undone, the top of the pole is free, the butt end by it's weight descends, and Puss is suspended by the snare about six to eight feet above the surface of the snow. This height is required to prevent them being taken by Foxes and Martens. The other Hares that follow this path, have for the night a free passage; but the next day the snare is reset, until no more can be caught; where the Hares are plenty, hedges of pine trees, with their branches extend 200 yards, or more, in length; on a fine Moonlight night the Hares move about freely, and from eighteen to twenty [are] caught in a night, but in bad weather, three, or four, or none; the average may be six to eight p^r night : of all furrs the furr of the hare is the warmest, we place pieces of it in our mittens, the skin is too thin for any other purpose. When the cold becomes very severe, we leave off snareing until February or March, as the Hares lie still.

There are two species of white Grouse, the Rock[1] and the Willow, the former is a lesser species with a black stripe round the upper eyelid, and feeds among the rocks. The willow Grouse[2] has a red stripe round the upper eyelid, is a finer bird than the rock grouse, and one fifth larger : they are both well feathered to the very toe nails ; all their feathers are double, lie close on each other, two in one quill, or socket, and appear as one feather ; the under side of the foot have hard, rough, elastic feathers like bristles. The white Grouse, in the very early part of winter, arrive in small flocks of ten to twenty, but as the winter advances and the cold increases,

[1] *Lagopus rupestris* (Gmelin). [E. A. P.]
[2] *Lagopus albus* (Gmelin). [E. A. P.]

they become more plentiful, and form flocks of fifty to one hundred; they live on the buds of the willows, which cover the ground between the sea shore and the pine forests; on the south side of Hayes's River, there is a strip of alluvial formed by a few bold Brooks of half, to one mile in width, and about ten miles in length, next to impassable in summer for marsh and water, where they feed; they are shot on the ground as they feed: at first each man may average ten grouse p^r day; but by the beginning of December they become numerous, and the average of each man may be about twenty p^r day. Each grouse weighs two pounds, forming a good load to walk with in snow shoes; and at length to carry to the tent; when the feathers are taken off, the bowels taken out, and in this state [they are] put into the hoard to freeze, and thus taken to the Factory; they now average one pound each, and the feathers of twenty grouse weigh one pound. At night the Grouse, each singly, burrows in the snow, and when the cold is intense, do the same in the middle of the day. However intense the cold, even to 85 degrees below the freezing point, I never knew any to perish with cold, when not wounded; the same of all other birds, kind Providence has admirably adapted them to the climate.

After the bitter cold of December and January is passed, they congregate in large flocks. Each man now bags from thirty to forty grouse p^r day, but as this is a Load too heavy to hunt with, part is buried in the Snow and only taken up when going to the Tent. The weather now allowing us to load our guns; for in the intense cold, the shot is no sooner fired than our hands are in our large mittens; we walk and pick up the bird, then get the powder in, and walk again, at length [put in] the shot, and the gun is loaded; it is needless to say, exposed to such bitter cold, with no shelter, we cannot fire many shots in a short day. Gloves are found to be worse than useless.

In the latter end of February, the month of March, and to the end of the season, the Grouse are netted, during which [time] not a shot is fired, except at Hawks :[1] They are a great plague to us, as the flocks were going before us, by short flights, a Hawk appearing, they dived down under the Snow, and for some time staid there.   For this purpose a large snow drift is chosen, level on the top, or made so, on which is placed a square net of strong twine of twenty feet each side, well tied to four strong poles, the front side is supported by two uprights, four feet in height ; to which is tied a strong line of about fifty feet in length, conducted to a bush of willows, the side poles being about four feet longer than the other, the back of the net is also lifted up about two feet above the snow, so as to leave room for the grouse to pass ; two, or three bags of fine gravel are brought, and laid under the centre of the net, mixed with willow buds taken out of the crops of the Grouse we have shot, these are gently dried over the fire to make them look like fresh buds : at first we have no great difficulty in starting and guiding the flocks towards the net, and so soon as we can bring them within view of the gravel and buds, they eagerly run to them, and crowd one on another, the man at the end of the line pulls away the two uprights, the net falls, we directly run and throw ourselves on the net, as the strong efforts of forty or fifty of these active birds might make an opening in the net. We have now to take the neck of each grouse between our teeth, and crack the neck bone, without breaking the skin, and drawing blood, which if done, the foxes destroy the part of the net on which is blood and around it, which sometimes happens to our vexation, and we have to mend the net. Although for the first few days we may net 120 Grouse p^r day, yet in about a fortnight they become so tame, they no longer form a large flock, and at length we are obliged to drive them before us like barn

---

[1] The Gyrfalcons, *Falco islandus* Brünnich, and *F. i. gyrfalco* Linn., and the Goshawk, are inveterate enemies of the ptarmigan. [E. A. P.]

door fowls, by eight or ten at a time, for every haul of the net, and thus in the course of a long day, we do not net more than forty to sixty grouse. In these months they have a pleasing cheerful call, in the early and latter parts of the day, of Kabow, Kabow, Kow á é. The hens have the same call, but in a low note. In bad weather the willow grouse shelters itself under the snow, but the Rock grouse run about, as if enjoying the Storm. During the winter whatever may be the number of the flock, and however near to each other, each burrows singly in the snow, their feathers are of a brilliant white, if possible whiter than the snow. In the months of March and April, part of the feathers, particularly about the neck, and the fore part of the body, change color to a glossy brown, or deep chocolate, upon a ground of brilliant white, very beautiful, and in this state are often stuffed and sent to London. No dove is more meek than the white grouse, I have often taken them from under the net, and provoked them all I could without injuring them, but all was submissive meekness. Rough beings as we were, sometimes of an evening we could not help enquiring why such an angelic bird should be doomed to be the prey of carnivorous animals and birds, the ways of Providence are unknown to us. They pair in May, and retire to the Pine Forests, make their nests on the ground, under the low spreading branches of the dwarf Pine, they lay from eleven to thirteen eggs, the young, from the shell, are very active and follow their dam. There is a third species called the Pine, or Swamp, grouse,[1] of dark brown feathers, it feeds on the leaves of the white pine, and it's flesh tastes of the pine on which it feeds ; it is found sitting on the branches of the tree, ten, or twelve, feet above the snow, or ground ; it is a stupid bird, a snare is tied to the end of a stick put round it's neck and pulled to the ground. It is only eaten for want of better ; they are not numerous, [are] solitary and never in

[1] Spruce Grouse, *Canachites canadensis* (Linn.). [E. A. P.]

flocks. A few Pheasants[1] are shot, they are something larger
than the white grouse, of fine dark plumage, but not to be
compared to the English Pheasant. Their habits are much
the same as the white grouse except [that] when they are
started, they fly to, and settle on the Trees, and not on the
snow, or ground. Late in Autumn and early in the Spring
the delicate Snow Bunting[2] appear in small flocks, they are
shot, and also taken by small nets, they are a delicacy for the
table. They fly from place to place, feed on the seeds of grass,
but do not stay more than three weeks each time. The
Tomtits[3] stay all winter, and feed on grass seeds. The handsome, little curious bird, the Cross Beak,[4] leave us late in
Autumn and arrive early in March. They are always in small
flocks, and their whole employment seems to be, cutting off
the cones of the Pines, which their cross beaks perform as
with a pair of scissors. The flock takes one tree, if large, at a
time and shower down the Cones like hail, I never saw them
feed on them : they remain and breed in the summer. At
all seasons the Butcher bird is with us, and called Whiskyjack,[5]
from the Indian name "Weeskaijohn." It is a noisy, familiar
bird, always close about the tents, and will alight at the very
doors, to pick up what is thrown out ; he lives by plunder,
and on berries, and what he cannot eat he hides ; it is easily
taken by a snare, and brought into the room, seems directly
quite at home ; when spirits is offered, it directly drinks, is
soon drunk and fastens itself anywhere till sober. A Hunter
marching through the forest may see a chance one, but if an
animal is killed, in a few minutes there are twenty of them.
They are a nuisance, picking and dirtying the meat, and
nothing frightens them which the hunter can hang up. When

[1] Sharp-tailed Grouse, *Pedioecetes phasianellus* (Linn.). [E. A. P.]
[2] *Plectrophenax nivalis* (Linn.). [E. A. P.]
[3] Probably Hudsonian Chickadee, *Penthestes hudsonicus* (Forster).
[E. A. P.]
[4] *Loxia curvirostra minor* (Brehm), and *L. leucoptera* Gmelin. [E. A. P.]
[5] Canada Jay, *Perisoreus canadensis* (Linn.). [E. A. P.]

the cold is intense, the feathers are ruffled out to twice it's
size ; all carnivorous birds appear, as it were, to loosen their
feathers, whereas the Grouse seem to tighten their feathers
around them. The Raven [1] is the same bird here, as over all
the world, stealing and plundering whatever he can, early
and late on the wing, and sometimes taken in the traps not
intended for him. In winter, when taken to shelter, he
ruffles his feathers, and chooses a snug place in the pines
exposed to the sun. The Indians do not like the Raven, as
in hunting he often follows them, and by cawing noise,
startles the animals, so as to make them look about, and be
on their guard ; when in their power he is sure to die. Other
Birds and Animals I shall notice when writing on the interior
countries, except the White Fox [2] which is found only along
the sea shore (and not in the interior) and near the mouths
of Rivers ; he is the least in size of all the Foxes, and the
least in value ; it's skin is worth only, about six to ten shillings ;
like all his species by nature a thief, following the Hunters
to pick up wounded birds, they are readily caught in traps
and killed by set guns. By a well laid line of traps and guns,
the produce of the early part of the winter is about six of
these Foxes p[r] night. With all their cunning they are a stupid
animal. On meeting one of them on the ice, I have often
made a trap of pieces of ice, baited it, while he was looking
at me, then retired some forty yards, he would then run to
the trap, look at me as if asking permission to take the bait,
run his head into the trap and be caught ; in this respect he
differs very much from all the other species. Speaking so
often of traps and set guns, I may as well describe them :
For a Marten, a throat log, of about 4 feet in length, of a
small pine is first laid on the snow, frequently some branches
under it to keep it from sinking in the snow, two stakes are
then driven, one on each side into the snow and moss near

[1] *Corvus corax principalis* Ridgway. [E. A. P.]
[2] *Alopex lagopus innuitus* (Merriam). [E. A. P.]

D

the middle; about eight inches from these, other two are driven, to form a doorway. The sides and back are also of small stakes; the neck log is about six feet in length, and passes thro' between the four stakes a few inches, the other end rests on some branches on the snow, a small stick of about six inches, on one end baited with the head of a grouse, the other end is half round, and rests on the throat log, on which a post of four inches in height is placed and supports the neck log, to give free entrance to the animal, the top of the trap, and above the neck log is well covered with pine branches to prevent any access to the bait; other logs are laid on the neck log for wait to detain the animal, which commonly is soon dead. These traps are made large, and strong, in proportion to the animal they are intended for. Set guns and steel traps are well known to the civilized world.

The month of April, from the thawing of the snow, and the grouse leaving to make their nests, obliges us to give up the winter hunting, and we return to the Factory to pass a dull time until the arrival of the geese, for which we get ready. In our Tents we had a comfortable fire, and the chances of the day in shooting, trapping and netting, with a few hearty curses on the hawks and foxes for the grouse they took from us, at which they were very clever, frequently keeping near us, though out of shot, and as soon as we killed a bird, before we could load the gun, one, or the other, would pounce on a grouse and carry it off: We had sometimes the satisfaction of seeing these two rogues worry each other; the Hawks [1] were mostly of the short wing and could not carry much, and a grouse weighing about two pounds, at about two or three hundred yards they had to alight and tear out the bowels, their favourite food, the fox was upon them, and made them take another flight. Sometimes the fox seized the bird, in this case the hawk was continually attacking him with blows of his claws on his neck, near to his head, the

---

[1] Probably the Goshawk, *Astur atricapillus* (Wilson). [E. A. P.]

fox sprang at the hawk, to no purpose, and the moment he put down his head to seize the bird, the hawk again struck him, and thus the fox made his meal. The long winged hawks carry a grouse with ease to the Trees, where they are secure from the foxes. The summer months pass away without regret, the myriads of tormenting flies allow no respite, and we see the cold months advance with something like pleasure, for we can now enjoy a book, or a walk. October and November produce their ice and snow, the Rivers freeze over and form a solid bridge to cross where we please, our winter clothing is ready, and gloomy December is on us. The cold increases continually, with very little relaxation, the snow is now as dry as dust, about two feet in depth, it adheres to nothing, we may throw a gun into it and take it up as free of snow, as if in the air, and no snow adheres to our Snow Shoes. The Aurora Borealis is seen only to the northward, sometimes with a tremulous motion, but seldom bright ; halos of the sun also appear. The month of January comes, and continues with intense cold ; from the density of the air, the halos, or mock suns, at times appear as bright as the real Sun ; but when in this state, betokens bad weather. The halos of the Moon are also very pleasing.

A curious formation now takes place called Rime, of extreme thinness, adhering to the trees, willows and everything it can fasten on, it's beautiful, clear, spangles forming flowers of every shape, of a most brilliant appearance, and the sun shining on them makes them too dazzling to the sight. The lower the ground, the larger is the leaf, and the flower ; this brilliant Rime can only be formed in calm clear weather and a gale of wind sweeps away all this magic scenery, to be reformed on calm days ; it appears to be formed of frozen dew. The actual quantity of snow on the ground is not more than 2½ feet in depth in the woods, clear of drift, very light and dry ; almost every fall of snow is attended with a gale of NE. wind. The falling snow with the moveable snow on the ground, causes a drift and darkness in which the traveller is bewildered, and sometimes perishes.   The months of February and March have many pleasant clear days, the gaudy, spangled Rime is most brilliant, and requires a strong eye to look upon it.   The climate is more moderate, there are a few fine days, the sun is bright with a little warmth, the snow lower, but does not thaw.   In the months of March and April, the Snow too often causes snow blindness, of a most painful nature.   As I never had it, I can only describe the sensations of my companions.   Accustomed to march in all weathers, I had acquired a power over my eyelids to open, or contract them as circumstances required, and to admit only the requisite quantity of light to guide me, and thus [I] prevented the painful effects of snow blindness.   In the case of those affected the blue eye suffers first and most, the gray eye next, and the black eye the least; but none are exempt from snow blindness; the sensations of my companions, and others, were all the same; they all complained of their eyes, being, as it were, full of burning sand; I have seen hardy men crying like children, after a hard march of four months in winter.   Three men and myself made for a trading post in the latter part of March.   They all became snow blind, and for the last four days I had to lead them with a string tied to my belt, and [they] were so completely blind that when they wished to drink of the little pools of melted snow, I had to put their hands in the water.   They could not sleep at night. On arriving at the trading Post, they were soon relieved by the application of the steam of boiling water as hot as they could bear it, this is the indian mode of cure, and the only efficient cure yet known, but all complained of weakness of sight for several months after.   Black crape is sometimes used to protect the eyes from the dazzling light of the snow, but the Hunter cannot long make use of it, the chase demands the whole power of his eyesight.   When thirsty a mouthful of snow wets the mouth but does not relieve thirst; the water of snow melted by the sun has a good taste, but snow melted in a kettle over a fire, has a smoky taste, until made to boil for a few minutes, this takes away the smoky taste, and snow being put in, makes good water.

Of the native Indians along the shore of Hudson's Bay I wish to say as little as possible. The Company has the Bay in full possession, and can enforce the strictest temperance of spirituous liquors, by their orders to their chief Factors, but the ships at the same time bringing out several hundred gallons of vile spirits called Eng. Brandy,[1] no such morality is thought of. No matter what service the Indian performs, or does he come to trade his furrs, strong grog is given to him, and sometimes for two or three days Men and Women are all drunk, and become the most degraded of human beings.[2]

[1] In 1785 the Hudson's Bay Company imported to York Factory, over and above what it had imported to Churchill and Moose Factories, 2,028 gallons of brandy. In 1794, under Colen's régime, the importation of brandy to the same place rose to 7,900 gallons. In addition to this, the Company operated a small distillery at York Factory at the same time.

[2] In Thompson's note-books some pages are taken up by what he calls "Index of his Journals as Extended," in which he gives the contents of a number of pages which were not in the original manuscript as I obtained it, and of which I have been able to find no trace among any of his papers. It is possible that the pages were never written, though he may have outlined their contents. These pages come in at this point in his Journal, and the following is the extension of the index as he gives it :

"27ᵃ· The fur trade H. B. only 2 inland houses.
"27ᵇ· Embark as Clerk to Mr. Mitchell Oman. Tracking.
"27ᶜ· Description of route to the Great Rapid & C. Place.
"27ᵈ· Description of route to Cumberland House.
"27ᵉ· Description of route to the Houses for Winter.
"27ᶠ· Cleared ground & builded a house.
"27ᵍ· Character of our neighbours.
"27ʰ· Advantages of the Canada Fur traders.
"27ⁱ· Bow River trade in furs & provisions.
"27ᵏ· Mr. Hudson, his character.
"27ˡ· Cumberland Lake.
"27ᵐ· Up the river to Buckingham House. Outfit to trade.
"27ⁿ· Barter, trade, &c.
"27ᵒ· Eagle catching on conical knolls.
"27ᵖ· Journey to the one Pine. Cut down for one third.
"27ᵠ· March on. Animals very scarce.

CHAPTER III

MUSK RAT COUNTRY[1]

Musk Rat country—Boundaries—Frozen soil—Forest—White Birch — Rind of White Birch — Berries — Misaskutum Berry — Fish — Pike — Trout — White Fish — Carp — Sturgeon—Swan—Marten—Accident while trapping Marten —Nature of Marten—Wolverine—Pranks of Wolverine.

HAVING described what is peculiar to the wild shores of Hudson's Bay, I now turn to the interior country, and include a space from Hudson's Bay of about three hundred miles in width, known to the Fur Traders by the name of the Musk Rat country. The geology of this country is quite distinct from the countries westward, it is composed of granitic and other silicious Rocks; from the parallel of 54 or 55 degrees north, this rocky region extends northward to the extremity of the continent, and is about 400 miles in width; to the southward of the above line, this region extends southward to the coasts of Labrador; every where it's character is much the same, almost everywhere rock covered with moss, the spots of tolerable soil are neither large, nor frequent, containing very many Lakes, the Streams from which find their way to the large Rivers. This Region is bounded on the west by the great chain of Lakes, the principal of which are Lake Superior, the Rainy Lake, the Lake of the Woods, Winepeg, the Cedar, and chain of Lakes north-

[1] The country here designated the Muskrat country is a portion of the great Archaean protaxis or hinterland of Canada which is only now being opened to settlement. The Hudson Bay Railway, which is now being built, will run through it from The Pas on the Saskatchewan river to the mouth of the Nelson river.

ward to the Athabasca and great Slave Lakes. The northern parts are either destitute of Woods, or they are low and small; especially about Hudson's Bay where the ground is always frozen; even in the month of August, in the woods, on taking away the moss, the ground is thawed at most, for two inches in depth: M[r] Joseph Colen,[1] the Resident at York Factory, on having a Cellar dug for a new building, found the earth frozen to the depth of five and a half feet, below which it was not frozen. All the Trees on this frozen soil have no tap roots; their roots spread on the ground, the fibres of the roots interlace with each other for mutual support; and although around Hudson's Bay there is a wide belt of earth of about one hundred miles in width, apparently of ancient alluvial from the rounded gravel in the banks of the Rivers, yet it is mostly all a cold wet soil, the surface covered with wet moss, ponds, marsh and dwarf trees. The only dry places are the banks of the Brooks, Rivulets and Lakes. The rocky region close westward of this coarse alluvial already noticed, in very many places, especially around it's Lakes, and their intervals, have fine Forests of Pines, Firs, Aspins, Poplar, white and grey Birch, Alder and Willow; all these grow in abundance, which makes all this region of rock and Lake appear a dense forest, but the surface of the Lakes cover full two fifths, or more, of the whole extent. The most usefull trees are the White Birch,[2] the Larch,[3] and the Aspin.[4]

[1] Joseph Colen was one of the clerks at York Factory under Humphrey Marten when Thompson arrived there in 1785. On the departure of Marten for England in 1786, Colen succeeded him as Resident in charge of the fort, and remained in charge until his own recall in 1798. During these twelve years, he seems to have handled the fur-trade of the Company in a fairly capable manner, but he was often at cross-purposes with the Resident in charge of the Churchill district, and he did not get along well with William Tomison, who was in charge of the Saskatchewan trade, and who received his supplies from York. After Colen's recall, Tomison was made President of the Council at York.

[2] *Betula papyrifera* Marsh. [E. A. P.]
[3] *Larix laricina* (Du Roi). [E. A. P.]
[4] *Populus tremuloides* Michx. [E. A. P.]

The White Birch, besides it's bark, which is good for tanning
leather, has also a Rind which covers the bark, of which
Canoes are made; this Rind is thick in proportion to the
intense cold of winter where the tree grows, in high Latitudes,
it is one fourth of an inch thick, and wherever the winter
is very cold. On the west side of the Mountains where the
winters are very mild, the Rind is too thin to be of any use;
it thus appears to be a protection to the tree against the frost.
The Wood of the Birch tree is used for making Sledges and
Sleds, Axe helves and whatever requires strength and neatness, as the frames of Snow Shoes, but does not bear exposure
to wet weather. The Rind is very useful to the natives and
traders for making Canoes, Dishes, coverings for canoes, and
for Tents and Lodges in the open Seasons. The White
Birch is seldom more than four feet in circumference, but to
the branches of which the head is formed, carries this girth
with little diminution; it can be raised from the bark only
in mild weather, in hot weather it freely comes away, and a
well grown tree will give from fifteen to thirty feet of Birch
Rind; it requires a practised Man to raise it without injuring
it. The rind is never renewed, and the bark not having the
shelter of the rinds becomes full of cracks, and the tree decays.
In the spring of the year incisions in the tree yield a sap,
which is boiled to a well tasted syrup. The grey birch[1]
grows among the Rocks, it [is] a dwarf tree, crooked, knotty,
and full of branches; it's wood is stronger than the white
birch; it's rind too thin to be of use, it has many tatters
hanging to it, which are much used for quickly lighting a
fire. The Larch is well known, a strong elastic wood, and
make the best of Sleds. The poplar[2] and aspin,[3] make the best
of fire wood for a tent, [as] the wood does not sparkle, and
the smoke is mild; the smoke of no other woods should be

[1] Probably *Betula glandulosa* Michx. [E. A. P.]
[2] *Populus balsamifera* Linn. [E. A. P.]
[3] *P. tremuloides.* [E. A. P.]

used for drying meat and fish. The smoke of these woods preserves both and gives an agreeable taste ; in places, there are fine forests of aspins of six inches to one foot diameter, and thirty to forty feet without branches. The White and Red Firs grow on a sandy soil, they are of dwarf growth, and full of knots and branches. There are four species of the Pine,[1] besides the Cypress ;[2] the white Spruce[3] is noted for it's fine spreading branches, which form the beds of the traveller and the hunter ; In the frozen clime of Hudson's Bay, only half of this tree can be used, the north east side being very brittle, and can hardly be called wood. The other Pines are mostly found in the interior, they thrive most near Lakes and Rivers, and in favorable places are of six feet girth, and forty to fifty feet in height.

By the Natives the saplings of these serve for tent poles, laths and timbers for canoes, by the traders, the same purposes, and building of Houses. Of Berries there are twenty species all known in europe but one. They are, the dry[4] and swamp Cranberry,[5] the Crow[6] and Black Berries, two kinds of Raspberries ;[7] the Strawberry ;[8] two kinds of Cherry's,[9] both are small. White and Red Currants ;[10] the black Currant,[11] a mild purgative ; two kinds of Gooseberries,[12] two of Hipberries ;[13] the Juniper berry ;[14] the Eye berry :[15] the Bear Berry ;[16]

[1] The only true pine is *Pinus divaricata* (Ait.). [E. A. P.]
[2] Probably White Cedar, *Thuja occidentalis* Linn. [E. A. P.]
[3] *Picea canadensis* (Mill.). [E. A. P.]
[4] Probably *Vaccinium vitisidaa.* [E. A. P.]
[5] Probably *Oxycoccus oxycoccus* (Linn.). [E. A. P.]
[6] *Empetrum nigrum* Linn. [E. A. P.]
[7] *Rubus strigosus* Michx., and *R. chamæmorus* Linn. [E. A. P.]
[8] *Fragaria canadensis* (Michx.). [E. A. P.]
[9] *Prunus virginiana* Linn., and *P. pennsylvanica* Linn. [E. A. P.]
[10] Red Currant, *Ribes rubrum* Linn. [E. A. P.]
[11] *Ribes hudsonianum* Richardson. [E. A. P.]
[12] Northern Gooseberry, *Ribes oxyacanthoides* Linn. [E. A. P.]
[13] Wild Rose, *Rosa acicularis* Lindl. [E. A. P.]
[14] Probably *Juniperus sabina* Linn. [E. A. P.]
[15] *Rubus arcticus* Linn. [E. A. P.]
[16] *Arctostaphylos uva-ursi* (Linn.). [E. A. P.]

this has a low spreading plant which lies flat on the ground, it has it's use in medicine; the Natives collect and dry the leaves, wherever it can be procured; it is mixed with tobacco for smoking, giving to the smoke a mild, agreeable flavour. A berry of an agreeable acid called the Summer berry,[1] it ripens late in Autumn, the Shrub of this berry has a large pith, takes a good polish and is used for Pipe Stems; and the Misaskutum berry,[2] perhaps peculiar to north america; the berry grows abundantly on willow like shrubs, is of the color of deep blue, or black; the size of a full grown green pea, very sweet and nourishing, the favorite food of small birds, and the Bears. They are very wholesome, and may safely be eaten as long as the appetite continues; they are much sought after by the Natives, they collect and dry them in quantities for future use; and mixed with Pimmecan, becomes a rich and agreeable food. The wood is of a fine size for arrows, and where this can be got, no other is employed; it is weighty, pliant, and non-elastic. As this berry is preceded by a beautiful flower, and the berry is as rich as any currant from Smyrna and keeps as well, it ought to be cultivated in Canada, and in England.

The Rivers and Lakes have Pike,[3] (the water wolf.) He preys on every fish he can master, even on his own species; he seises his prey by the middle of the back, and keeps his hold until it is dead: when he swallows it. It catches readily at any bait, even a bit of red rag. It is a bold active fish, and in summer is often found with a mouse in it's stomach. It's jaws are strong, set with sharp teeth, somewhat curved, it is of all sizes from one to fifteen pounds; it is seldom found in company with the Trout,[4] which last appears to be

[1] *Viburnum opulus* Linn. [E. A. P.]
[2] *Amelanchier alnifolia* Nutt. This is the Saskatoon or Service Berry. [E. A. P.]
[3] *Esox lucius* Linn. [E. A. P.]
[4] *Cristivomer namaycush* (Walb.). [E. A. P.]

the master fish, for where they are found in the same Lake, the Pike are confined to the shallow bays. The Trout to attain to a large size, they require to be in extensive deep Lakes. In this region they are from one to twenty pounds. They are as rich as meat. The white fish[1] is well known, their quality and size depends much on the depths of the Lakes. In shoal Lakes they are generally poor, and in deep Lakes fat and large, they are almost the sole subsistence of the Traders and their men in the winter, and part of the summer : they are caught in nets of five to six inches mesh, fifty fathoms in length, and five to six feet in depth ; which are set and anchored by stones in three to five fathoms water, if possible on sandy, or fine gravel, bottom. They weigh from two to ten pounds. They are a delicate fish, the net ought not to stand more than two nights, then [it ought to be] taken up and washed in hot water, dried and mended : Some of the Lakes have only a fall fishery and another in the spring, in this case the fish are frozen, and lose part of their good taste. Fish do not bear keeping, the maxim is ; " from the hook or the net directly into the kettle " of boiling water. Those who live wholly on fish, without any sauce, and frequently without salt, know how to cook fish in their best state, for sauces make a fish taste well, which otherwise would not be eatable. There are two species of Carp, the red[2] and grey ;[3] the former is a tolerable fish ; the latter is so full of small bones, only the head and shoulders are eaten. They spawn in the spring, on the small Rapids, are in shoals, the prey of the Eagle, the Bear, and other animals. The Sturgeon[4] to be good must be caught in muddy Lakes, he is the fresh water hog, fond of being in shoal alluvials ; in such lakes it is a rich fish ; but in clear water not so good ; they weigh from ten to fifty pounds.

[1] Several species of *Coregonus*.   [E. A. P.]
[2] *Catostomus catostomus* (Forster).   [E. A. P.]
[3] *Moxostoma lesueuri* (Richardson).   [E. A. P.]
[4] *Acipenser rubicundus* Le Sueur.   [E. A. P.]

The Pickerel,[1] the Perch[2] and Methy[3] are all common; these are all the varieties of fish found in this region worth notice.

With the Spring a variety of small birds arrive, they breed and remain during the summer, and depart for the southward in Autumn, they are all known to Europe. The Whippoorwill[4] arrives in the month of March. In the afternoon and evening as well as the morning, he flits from tree to tree about ten feet above the snow, with it's head downwards, repeats it's cry of Whip poor will for two, or three minutes, and then flies to another tree; only one species is known. The natives regard it as a peculiar bird and never hurt it. In some summers the flocks of Pigeons[5] are numerous, and make sad havoc of the Straw and Raspberries, in other summers they are very few. The Rooks[6] arrive in the latter end of April. The Natives regard the time of their arrival as the sure sign that winter has passed away, and the mild weather set in. The British population in Canada call them Crows, which latter bird is not known in North America. Two species of Eagle visit us, the large brown Eagle[7] is seen in March, and gives it's name to the Moon of this month; it is merely a visitor, soars high, seldom alights, and then shows itself a most majestic bird; it is sometimes shot, as the Natives set a high value on its plumage, and respect it as the master of all other birds; from the tip of one wing to the tip of the other wing, it has been measured nine feet; it's talons are long, very curved and strong, and it strikes with great

[1] Probably *Stizostedion vitreum* (Mitchill), the Wall-eyed Pike or Pikeperch. [E. A. P.]

[2] The Yellow Perch, *Perca flavescens* (Mitchill), is probably found in the southern part of the region. [E. A. P.]

[3] *Lota maculosa* (Le Sueur). [E. A. P.]

[4] I am unable to decide what bird is meant; perhaps some small owl, but certainly not the Whip-poor-will. [E. A. P.]

[5] *Ectopistes migratorius* (Linn.). [E. A. P.]

[6] The American Crow, *Corvus brachyrhynchos* Brehm. [E. A. P.]

[7] *Aquila chrysaëtos* (Linn.). [E. A. P.]

force; it is supposed capable of carrying off a bird equal to it's own weight, which is ten to twelve pounds, some have weighed fourteen pounds; yet the great Eagle of the Plains is larger than these. The Gray Goose[1] is accounted a very swift bird on the wing, at a distance we perceived a flock of these geese pursued by an Eagle. The latter did not seem to gain much on the former, they passed about one hundred yards from us (out of shot), the Eagle was then close to them, and going a short distance further, it came up to the third goose from the rear, and with one of it's claws, drove it's talons thro' the back of the goose close behind the wings, it fell as if shot, the Eagle stooped to take it, we ran and frightened it away; and it kept on its flight after the other geese; we picked up the goose, quite dead, the claws had perforated through the back bone over the heart. As they passed us, we remarked, the Eagle gained fast on the geese.

The Hawks in like manner strike the birds they prey on; The Natives say the Eagle readily carries off Ducks and Hares, but the gray goose is too heavy for him, but he soon tears it to pieces with his sharp crooked beak; the Fox will contend with the Hawks for the birds they kill in the great Marshes and plains, but never with the Eagle. The wolf tries for the prey of the latter, and is sure to be beaten.

The other species of Eagle is the White Headed,[2] from the head and upper part of the neck being covered with white feathers which lie close on each other, it is called the bald-headed Eagle. I believe it to be peculiar to North America, the color of the rest of the neck, and of the body, is all the shades of a deep brown, with tinges of dark yellow. It lives mostly on fish, without any objection to a chance hare or duck. They are generally found in pairs, and build their nest in the branches of a poplar, close to the banks of a Lake, or River; like the other species they lay only two, or three

[1] *Branta canadensis* (Linn.). [E. A. P.]
[2] *Haliæetus leucocephalus alascanus* Townsend. [E. A. P.]

eggs, and rears it's young with great care : as it is, comparatively, slow of flight, although it's wings extend seven to
eight feet, it hovers over the surface of the water, [looking]
for some fish of a weight that it can take out of the water,
and carry off to it's nest. That it is successful the old, and
young eagles, attest by their fatness ; the inside fat is
purgative, and when they feed on trout, highly so : their
flesh is eaten by the Natives, as being more fat and juicy,
and [they] prefer them to Grouse. They seize their prey by
the back, between the fins, and if weighty, make for the
shore ; and there with their beak cut off the head of the
fish, and thus take it to the nest. It sometimes strikes a fish
too weighty for it, in this case the fish carries the Eagle under
water where it loosens it's claws, and comes to the surface,
its feathers all wet. It floats well, but as it cannot swim, is
drifted to the shore by the wind or current, and must wait
for it's feathers to dry, before it can take flight.

There are five species of Hawk, three pass the winter.
They prey on everything they can master. There are four
species of the owl, one of them is very small. Two of the
others are large, one of these is called the great White Owl ;[1]
it weighs from ten to twelve pounds : the other is the noted
Horned Owl,[2] so named from it's having on each side of the
head, stiff, erect, feathers in shape and size, like the ears of
the White Fox ; it is a fine looking, grave bird, with large
lustrous eyes, and in the dark sees remarkably well, and preys
wholly in the night. They are easily tamed, I have often
kept one during the winter; it lived chiefly on mice, which
it never attempts to swallow until it is sure it is dead, of this
it judges by the animal ceasing to move; perched on it's
stand, and a live mouse presented to it, with its formidable
talons, it seized the mouse by the loins, and instantly carried
it to its mouth, and crushed the head of the mouse; still

[1] *Nyctea nyctea* (Linn.). [E. A. P.]
[2] *Bubo virginianus subarcticus* Hoy. [E. A. P.]

holding it in one of it's claws, it watched till all motion ceased and then head foremost swallowed the mouse: often while the owl was watching the cessation of motion, with the end of a small willow, I have touched the head of the mouse, which instantly received another crush in it's beak, and thus [it] continued till it was weary, when losening it's claws, it seized the mouse by the head; by giving motion to the body, it crushed it, and have thus vexed it until the body was in a pulp, yet the skin whole; by leaving the Mouse quiet for about half a minute, it was swallowed; from seve[ral] experiments I concluded that to carnivorous birds, the death of its prey is only known by the cessation of motion: like all other birds that swallow their prey whole, the hair, if an animal, or the feathers if a bird, are by some process in the stomach, rolled into hard, small, round balls, and ejected from the mouth with a slight force. The meat of the Owl is good and well tasted to hunters. The aquatic birds are more numerous, and in great variety: but they pass to the southward as the cold weather comes on. They arrive in the month of May, and leave us by the middle, or latter end of October, as the season may be. There are two species of Swan, the largest[1] weighs about twenty four pounds, the lesser[2] about fifteen, when fat. They lay from seven to nine eggs. When shot, twelve eggs have been counted in them; but nine is the greatest number I have found in a nest, and also of the number they rear; when fat they are good eating, but when poor the flesh is hard and dry. They are a shy bird, and their nests not often found: they frequent the lesser Lakes; and seldom approach the shores. The Natives often shoot them in the night; for this purpose, fir wood, split into laths, to burn freely, is made into small parcels, one of which is placed in an old kettle, or one made of wood, placed on a strong, short, stick, to keep it two, or

[1] Trumpeter Swan, *Olor buccinator* (Richardson). [E. A. P.]
[2] Whistling Swan, *Olor columbianus* (Ord). [E. A. P.]

three feet above the Canoe. When it is quite dark, two Indians embark, one steers the Canoe quietly, and steadily, towards the Swans, (they keep near each other;) the other is in the bow of the Canoe, with his gun, and the torch wood; which is lighted and soon in full blaze, and is kept in this state by the man in the bow; as soon as the Swans perceive the fire, they commence, and continue their call of Koke, Koke. They appear aware of danger, but are fascinated by the fire, they keep calling and swimming half round, and back in the same place, gazing on the fire; until the Canoe is within about thirty yards, when the bow man, by the light of the fire, levels his gun, and shoots the Swan nearest to him; if he has two guns the other Swan is shot as he rises on his flight. Another mode by which the Swan is enticed within shot, is, the Indian lies down in some long grass rushes, or willows near the edge of the Lake, with a piece of very white birch rind in his hand, or fastened to a short stick; this is made to show like a Swan, and the call made; then drawn back; then again shown; thus it attracts the Swans who gently approach, to within shot; this requires great patience, perhaps three, or four hours. It is more successful with a single Swan, than with a pair, or more. The several species of Geese I have already noticed: but very few breed in this region, and those only of the Gray Geese,[1] they lay from eleven to thirteen Eggs; which they will defend against the Fox and the Mink to no purpose, the Eggs are sure to be eaten and perhaps one of the geese.

There is a great variety of Ducks, some of them lay fifteen eggs. The young are reared with great care, in a heavy shower of rain the young are all under their parents wings; one variety builds in hollow trees, which it enters by a hole in the side of the tree; and is named the Wood Duck.[2] Two

---

[1] *Branta canadensis* (Linn.). [E. A. P.]
[2] The reference is probably to the American Goldeneye, *Clangula c. americana* Bonap. [E. A. P.]

E

species of Crane[1] pass the open season, they make their nests among quagmire rushes, which cannot be approached; they have about nine young, which are hidden until they are fully half grown.   The Bittern[2] is found among the rushes, reeds, and tall grass of the marshes. It does not weigh more than three, or four, pounds, and holding it's long neck and bill erect it gives a hollow note, as loud almost as an Ox. And keeping itself hid, those not acquainted with it, are at a loss to know what animal it can be; it takes it's name from having on each breast a narrow stripe about two inches in length, of rough, raised, yellow skin, which is very bitter, and must be taken off, otherwise, this well tasted bird is too bitter to be eaten. Like the Crane, it lives on Roots, frogs and small lizards. Of the Plover, there are a few species, they are not plenty, the Boys kill them with their arrows. The water is the element of the Loon,[3] on the land he is unable to walk, his legs being placed too far backwards, nor from the ground can he raise his flight, and is quite helpless; but in the water, of all birds he is the most completely at home. He swims swiftly and dives well, going under water apparently with the same ease, as on the surface; he has the power of placing his body at any depth, and when harassed in a small lake, places his body under water to be secure from the shot, leaving only his neck and head exposed and this he sinks to the head; in any of these positions he remains at pleasure; he prefers acting thus on the defensive, than flying away, for being very short winged, he has to go some thirty yards near the surface before he can raise his flight, and is so steady on the wing, that he is accounted a dead shot: the Loon is very destructive among the small fish, yet seldom fat: it lays only three eggs, when boiled, the inside appears streaked

[1] Brown Crane, *Grus canadensis* (Linn.); and Whooping Crane, *Grus americana* (Linn.). [E. A. P.]

[2] *Botaurus lentiginosus* (Montagu). [E. A. P.]

[3] *Gavia immer* (Brünn.). [E. A. P.]

black and yellow, and [they] are so ill tasted they cannot be
eaten, it's flesh is also bad. When on discovery to the northward, one evening on camping we found a Loons nest; the
eggs were taken, but were found not to be eatable: two
Lads lay down near the nest, in the night the pair of Loons
came, and missing their eggs, fell upon the Lads, screeching
and screaming, and beating them with their wings; the Lads
thought themselves attacked by enemies, and roared out for
help; two of us threw off our blankets and seized our guns,
the Loons seeing this returned to the Lake, we were at a loss
what to think or do, the Lads were frightened out of their
wits; in a few minutes we heard the wild call of the Loons;
the Indian said it was the Loons, in revenge for the loss of
their eggs; and giving them his hearty curse of "death be
to you," told us there was no danger, and the Loons left us
quiet for the rest of the night. The Pelican [1] is represented
as a solitary bird, it may be so in other countries; but not in
this region. They are always in pairs, or in flocks of five to
twenty. This is the largest fishing bird in the country, it is
occasionally shot, or knocked on the head for it's feathers and
pouch; the color is a dirty white, the wings extend about
seven and a half feet; it's height is about thirty to thirty
four inches, of which the bill, which is straight, measures
about fourteen inches, it is capacious, and under the bill and
upper part of the throat is a pouch that will hold a full
quart of water. This bird when measured from the end of
the tail to the point of the beak is about five feet in length;
it's tail feathers are used for arrows, and the pouch, when
cleaned and dried, is used to keep tobacco and Bear's weed
for smoking; The Pelican is very destructive among small
fish to a pound in weight. It has a wide throat, and after
filling it's stomach, also fills it's pouch, which becomes much
distended, and half putrid, is, fish by fish, emptied into the

---

[1] White Pelican, *Pelecanus erythrorhynchos* Gmel. [E. A. P.]

throat. Such is it's fishing habits in the morning, and the same in the afternoon; they frequent the Rapids of small Streams, and when thus gorged sit close to each other in a line. In this state they are unable to fly, and when our voyage in canoes leads us among them, before they can rise, they have to disgorge the putrid fish in their pouches, the smell of which is so very bad, that we hurry past as fast as possible; the Black Bears,[1] who frequent the same Rapids, never injure them; these birds are so impure, they are the bye word of the Natives and the Traders. There are two species of Cormorant,[2] both of them very expert in fishing, their flesh and Eggs are almost as bad as those of the Loon; There are also several species of the Merganser, or fishing Ducks,[3] altho' they live on fish, yet both their flesh and eggs are eatable, when no better can be got: The three species of Gulls[4] conclude the list of birds that live on fish; they are all good to eat, their eggs are good as those of a Duck, especially the largest kind which is the size of a teal duck; their young cannot fly until they are full grown, and as all the species are too light to dive, become an easy prey to the Eagle, the Hawk, and to Man: On some of the Islets in the Lakes, they breed in such numbers that the Native Women collect as many as their blankets can hold.

All the Animals of this Region are known to the civilized world, I shall therefore only give those traits of them which naturalists do not, or have not noticed in their discriptions. There are two species of the Mouse, the common,[5] and the

[1] *Ursus americanus* Pallas. [E. A. P.]

[2] But one species, *Phalacrocorax auritus* (Lesson). [E. A. P.]

[3] Common Merganser, *Mergus americanus* Cass.; Red-breasted Merganser, *Mergus serrator* Linn.; and Hooded Merganser, *Lophodytes cucullatus* (Linn.). [E. A. P.]

[4] The three most likely to be referred to are the Herring Gull, *Larus argentatus* Pontoppidan; Ring-billed Gull, *Larus delawarensis* Ord; and the Common Tern, *Sterna hirundo* Linn. [E. A. P.]

[5] White-footed Mouse, *Peromyscus maniculatus borealis* Mearns. [E. A. P.]

field Mouse[1] with a short tail; they appear to be numerous, and build a House where we will, as soon as it is inhabited they make their appearance; but the country is clear of the plague of the Norway Rat,[2] which, although he comes from England, part owner of the cargo, as yet has not travelled beyond the Factories at the sea side. The Ermine,[3] this active little animal is an Ermine only in winter, in summer of a light brown color, he is most indefatigable after mice and small birds, and in the season, a plunderer of eggs; wherever we build, some of them soon make their burrows, and sometimes become too familiar. Having in June purchased from a Native about three dozen of Gull eggs, I put them in a room, up stairs, a plain flight of about eight feet. The Ermine soon found them, and having made a meal of one egg, was determined to carry the rest to his burrow for his young; I watched to see how he would take the eggs down stairs; holding an egg between his throat and two fore paws, he came to the head of the stairs; there he made a long stop, at a loss how to get the egg down without breaking it, his resolution was taken, and holding fast to the egg dropped down to the next stair on his neck and back; and thus to the floor, and carried it to his nest: he returned and brought two more eggs in the same manner; while he was gone for the fourth, I took the three eggs away; laying down the egg he brought, he looked all around for the others, standing on his hind legs and chattering, he was evidently in a fighting humour; at length he set off and brought another, these two I took away, and he arrived with the sixth egg, which I allowed him to keep; he was too fatigued to go for another. The next morning he returned, but the eggs were in a basket out of his reach, he knew where they were but could not get

---

[1] Meadow Mouse, *Microtus pennsylvanicus drummondi* (Aud. and Bach.). [E. A. P.]

[2] *Epimys norvegicus* Erxleben. [E. A. P.]

[3] *Mustela cicognani* Bonap. [E. A. P.]

at them, and after chattering awhile, had to look for other prey. In winter we take the Ermine in small traps for the skin, which is valued to ornament dresses.

There are two separate species of Squirrel, the common[1] and the flying Squirrel,[2] the former burrows under the roots of large Pines, from which he has several outlets, [so] that when the Marten, or the Fox dig for him, he has a safe egress, and escapes up the tree with surprising agility, where he is safe. The flying Squirrel is about one fifth larger, and of the same color, it's name arises from a hairy membrane, which on each side extends from the fore to the hind leg : and which it extends when leaping from tree to tree ; this latter builds it's nest in the trees ; they both feed on the cones of the Pine, using only those in a dry state ; they are numerous ; their elegant forms, agile movements, and chatterings, very much relieve the silence of the Pine Forests. The haunts of the Marten[3] are confined to the extensive forests of Pine, especially the thickest parts, they are of the size of a large cat, but of a more compact and stronger make ; the color brown, the deeper color the more valuable, some few approach to a black color ; two he, or three she Martens, in trade are of the value of one Beaver. They are always on the hunt of mice, squirrels and birds : They are caught in traps, already described ; and as their skins are valuable, and their flesh good, they are trapped by the Natives and the Men of the Factories : the best bait for them is the head of a Grouse with the feathers on ; or the head of a hare ; even the leg of a hare is preferred to a bait of frozen meat, which he seldom takes. Among the Natives the snareing of hares, and trapping of Martens are the business of the Women, and become their property for trade. The White Men sometimes make ranges of Marten Traps for the length of forty or fifty

---

[1] Spruce Squirrel, *Sciurus hudsonicus* Erxleben. [E. A. P.]

[2] *Sciuropterus sabrinus* (Shaw). [E. A. P.]

[3] *Martes americana abieticola* (Preble). [E. A. P.]

miles, at about six to eight traps p^r mile : in this case the Trapper makes a hut of Pine Branches about every ten miles, which length of traps is as much as he can manage in a day ; the trapping is most successful in the month of November and early part of December : and the months of February and March, after which the skin soon becomes out of season. At each hut the Trapper ought to leave a stock of fire wood sufficient for the next night he passes there, as he frequently does not arrive until the daylight is gone, and cutting wood in the night is dangerous. An old acquaintance who had a long range of traps, had neglected to leave fire wood at the hut at the end of the range, arriving late in the evening had to cut fire wood for the night, with all his caution a twig caught the axe and made the blow descend on his foot, which was cut from the little toe, to near the instep ; he felt the blood gushing, but finished cutting the wood required ; having put everything in order, he took off his shoe and the two blanket socks, tore up a spare shirt, and bound up the wound, using for salve a piece of tallow ; he was six days journey from the Factory and alone ; the next morning, having mended his shoe and socks he got them on, but how to march forward was the difficulty ; a hut with firewood at the end of every ten miles along the range was some encouragement ; having tied his blankets and little baggage on the flat sled which every Trapper has, with pain he tied his foot to the snow shoe, then tied a string to the bar of the snowshoe, the other end in his hand, thus set off alone, to perform a winter journey of about one hundred and twenty miles, hauling a sled, and with one hand lifting his wounded foot. the Snow Shoe was steady and soft on the snow ; the first mile made him stop several times, and shook his resolution ; but continuing his foot became less painful and could easily be borne ; he had so much of the spirit of the Trapper in him that he could not pass a trap in which a Marten was caught without taking it out, although it added to the weight he was hauling : In the evening he arrived at the first hut, put every thing in order, lighted his fire, and sat down, and as he told me, [was] more proud of the fortitude of the day, than of any day of his life ; he slept well, his foot did not swell ; and the next morning, with some pain [he] renewed his journey to the second hut ; and thus to the fifth hut. During these days he had the trapping path to walk on, which was soft and steady ; he had now about sixty miles to go without a path ; he had now to hang up the Martens and everything he could do without, boil the bark of the Larch Tree which lies close to the wood, beat it to a soft poultice and lay it on the wound ; his sled was now light and his hand regular in lifting his foot and snow shoe ; in five days he arrived at the Factory having suffered much each evening in getting firewood : during all this time of travelling his foot was not in the least swelled ; when at the Factory he thought he would be at his ease, but this was not the case, his foot became swollen, with considerable pain, and for a month he had to make use of a crutch.

I have often tried to tame the Marten, but could never trust him beyond his chain : to one which I kept some time, I brought a small hawk slightly wounded, and placed it near him, he seemed willing to get away ; and did not like it ; two days after I winged a middle sized owl, and brought it to him, he appeared afraid of it, and would willingly have run away, but did not dare to cease watching it. Shortly after I found a Hare in one of the snares just taken. I brought it alive to near the Marten, he became much agitated, the skin of his head distorted to a ferocious aspect, he chattered, sprung to the Hare, as if with mortal hatred ; this appeared to me strangely unaccountable, all this state of excitement against a weak animal it's common prey. Walking quickly through the Forest to visit the snares and traps, I have several times been amused with the Marten trying to steal the Hare, suspended by a snare from a pole ; the Marten is very active, but the soft snow does not allow him to spring more than his own height above the surface; the Hare is suspended full five feet above the surface; determined to get the Hare, he finds the pole to which the Hare is hanging, and running along the pole, when near the small end, his weight over balances the other end, and the Marten is precipitated into the snow with the hare, before he recovers, the pole has risen with the Hare out of his reach; he would stand on his hind feet, chatter at the hare with vexation; return to the Pole, to try to get the hare, to be again plunged in the snow; how long he would have continued, I do not know, the cold did not allow me to remain long; seeing me, he ran away.

The Lynx[1] may be regarded as a very large cat, readily climbs trees, and preys on Mice, Hares, Squirrels and Birds, it's habits are those of a Cat: it is a shy animal; it's skin is not much worth, the skin being thin and weak; the Natives take this animal in a trap, in which is a wisp of grass rolled round some Castorum and the oil stones of the Beaver,[2] against this he rubs his head, displaces the stick which suspends the trap, and he is caught; by the same means he is caught in a snare; while rubbing his head he purrs like a cat. The flesh is white and good, and makes a good roast.

His fine large lustrous eyes have been noticed by naturalists, and other writers, they are certainly beautiful, but better adapted to the twilight, than the glare of the sunshine. I am inclined to think that the habits of the Fox are better known in Europe than to us, for in populous countries it requires all his wits and wiles to preserve his life. The Wolverene,[3] is an animal unknown to other parts of the world, and we would willingly dispense with his being round here. It is a strong, well made, powerful animal; his legs short,

[1] *Lynx canadensis* Kerr. [E. A. P.]
[2] *Castor canadensis* Kuhl. [E. A. P.]
[3] *Gulo luscus* (Linn.). [E. A. P.]

armed with long sharp claws, he climbs trees with ease and nothing is safe that he can get at; by nature a plunderer, and mischievous, he is the plague of the country.

A party of six men were sent to square timber for the Factory, and as usual left their heavy axes where they were working, when they went to the tent for the night. One morning the six axes were not to be found, and as they knew there was no person within many miles of them they were utterly at a loss what to think or do. They were all from the very north of Scotland, and staunch believers in ghosts, fairies and such like folk, except one; at length one of them who thought himself wiser than the rest, addressed his unbelieving companion, "Now Jamie, you infidel, this comes of your laughing at ghosts and fairies, I told you that they would make us suffer for it, here now all our axes are gone and if a ghost has not taken them, what has?" Jamie was sadly puzzled what to say, for the axes were gone; fortunately the Indian lad who was tenting with them, to supply them with grouse came to them; they told him all their axes were taken away, upon looking about he perceived the footmarks of a Wolverene, and told them who the thief was, which they could not believe until tracking the Wolverene, he found one of the axes hid under the snow : in like manner three more were found, the others were carried to some distance and took two hours to find them, they were all hidden separately, and to secure their axes they had to shoulder them every evening to their tent. During the winter hunt, the feathers of the birds are the property of the hunters ; and those of the white Grouse sell for six pence a pound to the Officer's of the ship, we gave our share to Robert Tennant, whom we called Old Scot. He had collected the feathers of about 300 grouse in a canvas bag, and to take it to the Factory, tied it on the Dog's sled, but some snow having fallen in the night, the hauling was heavy ; and after going a short distance the bag of feathers had to be left,

which was suspended to the branch of a tree; On our return
we were surprized to see feathers on the snow, on coming to
the tree on which we had hung the bag we found a wolverene
had cut it down, torn the bag to pieces, and scattered the
feathers so as hardly to leave two together. He was too
knowing for a trap but [was] killed by a set Gun. In trapping
of Martens, ranges of traps sometimes extend forty miles, or
more. An old trapper always begins with a Wolverene trap,
and at the end of every twenty traps makes one for the
Wolverene, this is a work of some labor, as the trap must be
strongly made and well loaded, for this strong animal, his
weight is about that of an english Mastiff, but more firmly
made; his skin is thick, the hair coarse, of a dark brown color,
value about ten shillings, but to encourage the natives to
kill it, [it] is valued at two beavers, being four times it's real
value.

Of the three species of Wolf,[1] only one is found in this
stony region that I have described, and this species appears
peculiar to this region; it is the largest of them, and by way
of convenience is called the Wood, or Forest Wolf, as it is
not found elsewhere; it's form and color [is] much the same
as the others, of a dark grey, the hair, though not coarse,
cannot be called soft and fine, it is in plenty, and with the
skin makes warm clothing. It is a solitary animal. Two are
seldom seen together except when in chase of some animal
of the Deer species. Fortunately they are not numerous,
they are very rarely caught in a trap, but redily take the
bait of a set Gun, and [are] killed. The cased skin of one of
these Wolves, came with ease over a man of six feet, two
inches in height dressed in his winter clothing, and was ten
inches above his head, yet powerful and active as he is, he
is not known to attack mankind, except in a rare case of something like canine madness, and his bite does not produce
hydrophobia. At least it never has been so among the

[1] *Canis occidentalis* Richardson. [E. A. P.]

Natives, and the dogs bitten by him, only suffer the pain of the bite. Foxes have sometimes this canine madness or something like it, but hydrophobia is wholly unknown. Two of these Wolves are a full match of either the Moose,[1] or Rein Deer,[2] the only two species found in this region. When they start one of these Deer, they are left far behind, but the Deer must stop to feed, they then come up to, and again start the Deer, and thus continue until the animal, harrassed for want of food and rest becomes weak and turns to bay in this state ready to defend itself with it's powerful feet. The wolves cautiously approach, one going close in front to threaten an attack, yet keeping out of the reach of it's fore feet. The other wolf goes behind, keeping a little on one side to be out of the direct stroke of the hind feet ; and watching, gives a sharp bite to cut the back sinew of one of the hind legs, this brings on a smart stroke of the hind legs of the Deer, but the wolf is on one side, and repeats his bites until the back sinew is cut, the Deer can now no longer defend itself, the back sinew of the other hind leg is soon cut, the Deer falls down and becomes the easy prey of the Wolves ; the tongue and the bowels are the first to be devoured. From the teeth of the old Wolves being sharp pointed, it does not appear they knaw the bones, but only clean them of the flesh, and in this state we find the bones. The Deer in summer sometimes takes to the water, but this only prolongs his life for a few hours. They are very destructive to the young deer ; and their loud howlings in the night make the Deer start from their beds and run to a greater distance. When wounded, he will defend himself, but tries to get away, and dies as hard as he lived. There is something in the erect form of man, while he shows no fear, that awes every animal.

The animals described in this Stony Region are few in proportion to the extent of country, the Natives with all their

---

[1] *Alces americanus* (Clinton). [E. A. P.]
[2] *Rangifer sylvestris* (Richardson). [E. A. P.]

address can only collect furrs sufficient to purchase the
necessaries of life; and part of their clothing is of leather in
summer, very disagreeable in rainy weather, and the avidity
with which the furr bearing animals is sought, almost
threatens their extinction; the birds of passage may be as
numerous as ever, comparatively only a very few can be
killed as they pass, and the Natives acknowledge, that with all
their endeavours they can barely subsist by the chase, even
when making use of all the animals they catch for food.

CHAPTER IV

NAHATHAWAY INDIANS

Nahathaway Language — Appearance — Dress — Manners — Traditions—Immortality of the Soul—Keeche Keeche Manito—Manitos—Ghosts—Pah kok—Sun and Moon— Names of Moons of each month—Earth—Forest—Manitos— Metchee Manito—Dog Feasts—Weesarkejauk—The story of the Deluge—Rainbow—The conjurer Isepesawan dances —Poowaggan—Resentful dispositions—Early Marriages— Duties of Wife—Duties of Husband—Superstitions of hunter —Marriages—Polygamy—Children—Metis—Ingenuity of Indians—Wishes—Sleds—Dogs—Moving of Indians— Arrangement of Tents.

HAVING passed six years [1] in different parts of this Region, exploring and surveying it, I may be allowed to know something of the natives, as well as the productions of the country. It's inhabitants are two distinct races of Indians ; North of the latitude of fifty six degrees, the country is occupied by a people who call themselves " Dinnie," by the Hudson Bay Traders " Northern Indians " and by their southern neighbours " Cheepawyans " whom I shall notice hereafter. Southward of the above latitude the country is in the possession of the Nahathaway

[1] The six years so spent were as follows, the first four being with the Hudson's Bay Company, and the last two with the North-West Company : 1792–93, at Sipiwesk lake ; 1794–95, at Reed lake ; 1795–96, at Duck Portage ; 1796–97, at Reindeer lake ; 1804–05, at Musquawegan ; 1805–06, at Reed lake.

Indians[1] their native name (Note. These people by the French Canadians, who are all without the least education, in their jargon call them " Krees " a name which none of the Indians can pronounce; this name appears to be taken from " Keethisteno " so called by one of their tribes and which the french pronounce " Kristeno," and by contraction Krees (R, rough, cannot be pronounced by any Native) these people are separated into many tribes or extended families, under different names, but all speaking dialects of the same language, which extends over this stony region, and along the Atlantic coasts southward to the Delaware River in the United States, (the language of the Delaware Indians being a dialect of the parent Nahathaway) and by the Saskatchewan River westward, to the Rocky Mountains. The Nathaway, as it is spoken by the southern tribes is softened and made more sonorous, the frequent th of the parent tongue is changed to the letter y as Neether (me) into Neeyer, Keether (thou) into Keeyer, Weether (him) into Weeyer, and as it proceeds southward [it] becomes almost a different language. It is easy of pronunciation, and is readily acquired by the white people for the purposes of trade, and common conversation.

The appearance of these people depends much on the climate and ease of subsistence. Around Hudson's Bay and near the sea coasts, where the climate is very severe, and

[1] Nahathaway is one of several variants of the name applied by the Cree Indians to themselves, and is that form of the name which is commonly used by the Cree who live in the country around Isle à la Crosse and the upper waters of the Churchill river. Among the Cree of the Saskatchewan river and the Great Plains the *th* sound is eliminated and the word is pronounced *Nihiaway*. Kristeno, the name by which this great tribe was usually known to the early traders, and of which the word Cree is a corruption, was the name which the Chippewa applied to them, and as the white people came in contact with, and learned to speak the language of, the Chippewa first, they naturally adopted the Chippewa name. The Cree are one of the most important tribes of the Algonquin family. They are naturally inhabitants of the forest. Their range was from the Rocky Mountains eastward north of the Great Plains, and thence north of Lake Winnipeg to the southern shore of Hudson Bay.

game scarce, they are seldom above the middle size, of spare make, the features round, or slightly oval, hair black, strong and lank; eyes black and of full size, cheek bones rather high, mouth and teeth good, the chin round; the countenance grave yet with a tendency to cheerful, the mild countenances of the women make many, while young, appear lovely; but like the labouring classes the softness of youth soon passes away. In the interior where the climate is not so severe, and hunting more successful, the Men attain to the stature of six feet; well proportioned, the face more oval, and the features good, giving them a manly appearance; the complexion is of a light olive, and their colour much the same as a native of the south of Spain; the skin soft and smooth. They bear cold and exposure to the weather better than we do and the natural heat of their bodies is greater than ours, probably from living wholly on animal food. They can bear great fatigue but not hard labor, they would rather walk six hours over rough ground than work one hour with the pick axe and spade, and the labor they perform, is mostly in an erect posture as working with the ice chissel piercing holes through the ice or through a beaver house, and naturally they are not industrious; they do not work from choice, but necessity; yet the industrious of both sexes are praised and admired; the civilized man has many things to tempt him to an active life, the Indian has none, and is happy sitting still, and smoking his pipe.

The dress of the Men is simply of one or two loose coats of coarse broad cloth, or molton, a piece of the same sewed to form a rude kind of stockings to half way up the thigh, a blanket by way of a cloak; the shoes are of well dressed Moose, or Rein Deer skin, and from it's pliancy enables them to run with safety, they have no covering for the head in summer, except the skin of the spotted northern Diver; but in winter, they wrap a piece of Otter, or Beaver skin with the furr on, round their heads, still leaving the crown of the head bare, from which they suffer no inconvenience. The dress of the women is of 1½ yards of broad cloth sewed like a sack, open at both ends, one end is tied over the shoulders, the middle belted round the waist, the lower part like a petticoat, covers to the ankles, and gives them a decent appearance. The sleeves covers the arms and shoulders, and are separate from the body dress. The rest is much the same as the men. For a head dress they have a foot of broad cloth sewed at one end, ornamented with beads and gartering, this end is on the head, the loose parts are over the shoulders, and is well adapted to defend the head and neck from the cold and snow. The women seldom disfigure their faces with paint, and are not over fond of ornaments. Most of the men are tattoed, on some part of their bodies, arms &c. Some of the Women have a small circle on each cheek.

The natives in their manners are mild and decent, treat each other with kindness and respect, and very rarely interrupt each other in conversation ; after a long separation the nearest relations meet each other with the same seeming indifference, as if they had constantly lived in the same tent, but they have not the less affection for each other, for they hold all show of joy, or sorrow to be unmanly ; on the death of a relation, or friend, the women accompany their tears for the dead with piercing shrieks, but the men sorrow in silence, and when the sad pang of recollection becomes too strong to be borne, retire into the forest to give free vent to their grief. Those acts that pass between man and man for generous charity and kind compassion in civilized society, are no more than what is every day practised by these Savages ; as acts of common duty ; is any one unsuccessful in the chase, has he lost his little all by some accident, he is sure to be relieved by the others to the utmost of their power, in sickness they carefully attend each other to the latest breath decently . . . the dead . . .[1]

---

[1] The bottom of the page of manuscript has here been torn off.

F

Of all the several distinct Tribes of Natives on the east side of the mountains, the Nahathaway Indians appear to deserve the most consideration; under different names the great families of this race occupy a great extent of country, and however separated and unknown to each other, they have the same opinions on religion, on morals, and their customs and manners differ very little. They are the only Natives that have some remains of ancient times from tradition. In the following account I have carefully avoided as their national opinions all they have learned from white men, and my knowledge was collected from old men, whom with my own age extend backwards to upwards of one hundred years ago, and I must remark, that what [ever] other people may write as the creed of these natives, I have always found it very difficult to learn their real opinion on what may be termed religious subjects. Asking them questions on this head, is to no purpose, they will give the answer best adapted to avoid other questions, and please the enquirer. My knowledge has been gained when living and travelling with them and in times of distress and danger in their prayers to invisible powers, and their view of a future state of themselves and others, and like most of mankind, those in youth and in the prime of life think only of the present but declining manhood, and escapes from danger turn their thoughts on futurity.

After a weary day's march we sat by a log fire, the bright Moon, with thousands of sparkling stars passing before us, we could not help enquiring who lived in those bright mansions; for I frequently conversed with them as one of themselves; the brilliancy of the planets always attracted their attention, and when their nature was explained to them, they concluded them to be the abodes of the spirits of those who had led a good life.

A Missionary has never been among them, and my knowledge of their language has not enabled me to do more than teach the unity of God, and a future state of rewards and punishments; hell fire they do not believe, for they do not think it possible that any thing can resist the continued action of fire: It is doubtful if their language in its present simple state can clearly express the doctrines of Christianity in their full force. They believe in the self existence of the Keeche Keeche Manito (The Great, Great Spirit) they appear to derive their belief from tradition, and [believe] that the visible world, with all it's inhabitants must have been made by some powerful being: but have not the same idea of his constant omnipresence, omniscience and omnipotence that we have, but [think] that he is so when he pleases, he is the master of life, and all things are at his disposal; he is always kind to the human race, and hates to see the blood of mankind on the ground, and sends heavy rain to wash it away. He leaves the human race to their own conduct, but has placed all other living creatures under the care of Manitos (or inferior Angels) all of whom are responsible to Him; but all this belief is obscure and confused, especially on the Manitos, the guardians and guides of every genus of Birds and Beasts; each Manito has a separate command and care, as one has the Bison, another the Deer; and thus the whole animal creation is divided amongst them. On this account the Indians, as much as possible, neither say, nor do anything to offend them, and the religious hunter, at the death of each animal, says, or does, something, as thanks to the Manito of the species for being permitted to kill it. At the death of a Moose Deer, the hunter in a low voice, cries "wut, wut, wut"; cuts a narrow stripe of skin from off the throat, and hangs it up to the Manito. The bones of the head of a Bear are thrown into the water, and thus of other animals; if this acknowledgment was not made the Manito would drive away the animals from the hunter, although the Indians often doubt their power or existence yet like other invisible beings they are more feared than loved. They believe in ghosts but as very rarely seen, and those only of wicked men, or women; when this belief takes place, their opinion is, that the spirit of the wicked person being in a miserable state comes back to the body and round where he used to hunt; to get rid of such a hateful visitor, they burn the body to ashes and the ghost then no longer haunts them. The dark Pine Forests have spirits, but there is only one of them which they dread, it is the Pah kok, a tall hateful spirit, he frequents the depths of the Forest; his howlings are heard in the storm, he delights to add to its terrors, it is a misfortune to hear him, something ill will happen to the person, but when he approaches a Tent and howls, he announces the death of one of the inmates; of all beings he is the most hateful and the most dreaded. The Sun and Moon are accounted Divinities and though they do not worship them, [they] always speak of them with great reverence. They appear to think [of] the Stars only as a great number of luminous points perhaps also divinities, and mention them with respect; they have names for the brightest stars, as Serius, Orion and others, and by them learn the change of the seasons, as the rising of Orion for winter, and the setting of the Pleiades for summer. The Earth is also a divinity, and is alive, but [they] cannot define what kind of life it is, but say, if it was not alive it could not give and continue life to other things and to animated creatures.

The Forests, the ledges and hills of Rock, the Lakes and Rivers have all something of the Manito about them, especially the Falls in the Rivers, and those to which the fish come to spawn. The Indians when the season is over, frequently place their spears at the Manito stone at the Fall, as an offering to the Spirit of the Fall, for the fish they have caught. These stones are rare, and sought after by the natives to place at the edge of a water fall; they are of the shape of a Cobler's lap stone, but much larger, and polished by the wash of the water. The "Metchee Manito," or Evil Spirit, they believe to be evil, delighting in making men miserable, and bringing misfortune and sickness on them, and if he had the power would wholly destroy them; he is not the tempter, his whole power is for mischief to, and harrassing of, them, to avert all which they use many ceremonies, and other sacrifices, which consists of such things as they can spare, and sometimes a dog is painted and killed; whatever is given to him is laid on the ground, frequently at the foot of a pine tree. They believe in the immortality of the soul, and that death is only a change of existence which takes place directly after death. The good find themselves in a happy country, where they rejoin their friends and relations, the Sun is always bright, and the animals plenty; and most of them carry this belief so far, that they believe whatever creatures the great Spirit has made must continue to exist somewhere, and under some form; But this fine belief is dark and uncertain; when danger was certain, and it was doubtful if we saw the day, or if we saw it, whether we should live through it, and a future state appeared close to them, their minds wavered, they wished to believe what they felt to be uncertain, all that I could do was to show the immortality of the soul, as necessary to the reward of the good and punishment of the wicked but all this was the talk of man with man. It wanted the sure and sacred promise of the Heavenly Redeemer of mankind, who brought life and immortality to light.

There is an important being, with whom the Natives appear better acquainted with than the other, whom they call "Weesarkejauk" (the Flatterer) he is the hero of all their stories always promising them some good, or inciting them to some pleasure, and always deceiving them. They have some tradition of the Deluge, as may be seen from the following account related by the old men. After the Great Spirit made mankind, and all the animals, he told Weesarkejauk to take care of them and teach them how to live, and not to eat of bad roots; that would hurt and kill them; but he did not mind the Great Spirit; became careless and incited them to pleasure, mankind and the animals all did as they pleased, quarelled and shed much blood, with which the Great Spirit was displeased ; he threatened Weesarkejauk that if he did not keep the ground clean he would take everything from him and make him miserable but he did not believe the Great Spirit and in a short time became more careless ; and the quarrels of Men, and the animals made the ground red with blood, and so far from taking care of them he incited them to do and live badly ; this made the Great Spirit very angry and he told Weesarkejauk that he would take every thing from him, and wash the ground clean ; but still he did not believe ; until the Rivers and Lakes rose very high and over flowed the ground for it was always raining ; and the Keeche Gahme (the Sea) came on the land, and every man and animal were drowned, except one Otter, one Beaver and one Musk Rat. Weesarkejauk tried to stop the sea, but it was too strong for him, and he sat on the water crying for his loss, the Otter, the Beaver and the Musk Rat rested their heads on one of his thighs.

When the rain ceased and the sea went away, he took courage, but did not dare to speak to the Great Spirit. After musing a long time upon his sad condition he thought if he could get a bit of the old ground he could make a little island of it, for he has the power of extending, but not creating anything ; and as he had not the power of diving under the water, and did not know the depth to the old ground he was at a loss what to do. Some say the Great Spirit took pity on him, and gave him the power to renovate everything, provided he made use of the old materials, all of which lay buried under the water to an unknown depth. In this sad state, as he sat floating on the water he told the three animals that they must starve unless he could get a bit of the old ground from under the water of which he would make a fine Island for them, then addressing himself to the Otter, and praising him for his courage, strength and activity and pro-

mising him plenty of fish to eat, he persuaded the Otter to
dive, and bring up a bit of earth; the Otter came up without
having reached the ground : by praises, he got the Otter to
make two more attempts, but without success, and [he] was so
much exhausted he could do no more. Weesarkejauk called
him a coward of a weak heart, and [said] that the Beaver
would put him to shame : then, speaking to the Beaver, praised
his strength and wisdom and promised to make him a good
house for winter, and telling him to dive straight down, the
Beaver made two attempts without success, and came up so
tired that Weesarkejauk had to let him repose a long time,
then promising him a wife if he brought up a bit of earth,
told him to try a third time; to obtain a wife, he boldly
went down and staid so long, that he came up almost lifeless.
Weesarkejauk was now very sad, for what the active Otter
and strong Beaver could not do, he had little hopes the Musk
Rat could do; but this was his only resource : He now praised
the musk rat and promised him plenty of roots to eat, with
rushes and earth to make himself a house; the Otter and the
Beaver he said were fools, and lost themselves, and he would
find the ground, if he went straight down. Thus encouraged
he dived, and came up, but brought nothing; after reposing,
he went down a second time, and staid a long time, on coming
up Weesarkejauk examined his fore paws and found they had
the smell of earth, and showing this to the Musk Rat, promised
to make him a Wife, who should give him a great many
children, and become more numerous than any other animal,
and telling him to have a strong heart; and go direct down,
the Musk Rat went down the third time and staid so long
that Weesarkejauk feared he was drowned. At length seeing
some bubbles come up, he put down his long arm and brought
up the Musk Rat, almost dead, but to his great joy with a
piece of earth between his fore paws and his breast, this he
seized, and in a short time extended it to a little island, on
which they all reposed. Some say Weesarkejauk procured a

bit of wood, from which he made the Trees, and from bones, he made the animals; but the greater number deny this, and say, the Great Spirit made the rivers take the water to the Keeche gahma of bad water (the salt sea) and then renovated Mankind, the Animals, and the Trees; in proof of which, the Great Spirit deprived him of all authority over Mankind and the animals, and he has since had only the power to flatter and deceive. It has been already noticed that this visionary being is the hero of many stories, which the women relate to amuse away the evenings. They are all founded upon the tricks he plays upon, and the mischief he leads the animals into, by flattering and deceiving them, especially the Wolf and the Fox. But the recital of the best of these stories would be tameness itself to the splendid Language and gorgeous scenery of the tales of the oriental nations.

The Nahathaway Indians have also another tradition relative to the Deluge to which no fable is attached. In the latter end of May 1806, at the Rocky Mountain House,[1] (where I passed the summer) the Rain continued the very unusual space of full three weeks, the Brooks and the River became swollen, and could not be forded, each stream became a torrent, and [there was] much water on the ground: A band of these Indians were at the house, waiting [for] the Rain to cease and the streams to lower, before they could proceed to hunting; all was anxiety, they smoked and made speaches to the Great Spirit for the Rain to cease, and at length became alarmed at the quantity of water on the

[1] The Rocky Mountain House here referred to was situated on the north bank of the North Saskatchewan river, in latitude 52° 21′ 30″ N., longitude 114° 57′ W., a mile and a quarter above the mouth of Clearwater river, on a beautiful level prairie in a wide bend of the river. It was built by the North-Westers in the autumn of 1799; and it was Thompson's home during the winters of 1800–01, 1801–02, 1806–07. The trading post which the Hudson's Bay Company afterwards built near it was called Acton House.

RUINS OF ROCKY MOUNTAIN HOUSE ON THE BANKS OF THE SASKATCHEWAN RIVER, ALBERTA

(*Photograph: J. B. Tyrrell, 1886*)

ground; at length the rain ceased, I was standing at the door watching the breaking up of the clouds, when of a sudden the Indians gave a loud shout, and called out "Oh, there is the mark of life, we shall yet live." On looking to the east-ward there was one of the widest and most splendid Rainbows I ever beheld; and joy was now in every face. The name of the Rainbow is Peeshim Cappeah (Sun lines). I had now been twenty two years among them, and never before heard the name of the Mark of Life given to the rainbow (Peemah tisoo nan oo Chegun) nor have I ever heard it since; upon enquiring of the old Men why they kept this name secret from me, they gave me the usual reply, You white men always laugh and treat with contempt what we have heard and learned from our fathers, and why should we expose our-selves to be laughed at; I replied I have never done so, our books also call the Rainbow the mark of life; what the white sometimes despise you for, is your one day, making prayers to the Good Spirit for all you want; and another shutting yourselves up, making speeches with ceremonies and offer-ings to the Evil Spirit; it is for the worship of the Evil Spirit that we despise you, you fear him because he is wicked, and the more you worship him, the more power he will have over you; worship the Good Spirit only and the bad spirit will have no power over you. Ah, said they; he is strong, we fear for ourselves, our wives and our children. Christianity alone can eradicate these sad superstitions, and who will teach them. Where the Natives are in villages, or even where they occasionally assemble together for two, or three months; a Missionary may do some good, but the Natives who in a hard country live by hunting, scattered by three, or four families over a wide extent of forest, are beyond the labors of a Missionary; yet the influence of the white people have done much to lessen the worship and offerings to the Evil Spirit. From the french Canadians they cannot add to their morality, and the dreadful oaths and curses they make use of,

shocks an Indian. The Indian, altho' naturally grave is fond
of cheerful amusements, and listening to stories, especially of
a wonderful cast; and [is] fond of news, which he listens to
with attention, and his common discourse is easy and cheerful.
Like the rest of mankind, he is anxious to know something
of futurity, and [where] he shall take up his wintering ground.

For to acquire this important knowledge, they have re-
course to Dreams and other superstitions; and a few of their
best conjurers sometimes take a bold method of imposing
upon themselves and others. One of my best acquaintances,
named "Isepesawan," was the most relied on by the Natives,
to inquire into futurity by conjuring; he was a good hunter,
fluent in speech, had a fine manly voice; and very early
every morning took his rattle, and beating time with it, made
a fluent speech of about twenty minutes to the Great Spirit
and the Spirits of the forests, for health to all of them and
success in hunting, and to give to his Poowoggin where to
find the Deer, and to be always kind to them, and to give
them straight Dreams, that they may live straight. The
time chosen was a fine afternoon, in the open season;
"Isepesawan" was the actor. After taking the sweating
bath; he had four long slender poles brought of about sixteen
feet in length; these were fixed in the ground to form a
square of full three feet: At five feet above the ground four
cross pieces were tied firmly; and about full three feet above
these, other four pieces were strongly tied across the upright
poles; all this, at the bottom and top, with the sides were
closely covered with the dressed leather skins of Deer; leaving
one side loose for a door. This being done, fine sinew line
was brought; with this, the thumb was tied to the fore finger
in two places, the fingers to each other in the same manner;
both hands being then tied they were brought together palm
to palm and tied together at the wrist; then the arms tied
close above the elbows. The Legs were tied together close
above the ancles, and above the knees; sometimes the toes

are tied together in the same manner as the hands; a few yards of leather line is tied round his body and arms; a strong line is passed under the knees, and round the back of the neck, which draws the knees to a sitting posture. A large Moose leather skin, or a Bison Robe, is wrapped around him, and several yards of leather line bind the Robe or leather skin close around him; in this helpless state two men lift and place him in the conjuring box in a sitting posture, with his rattle on his right side. All is now suspense, the Men, Women, and Children keep strict silence; In about fifteen or twenty minutes; the whole of the cords, wrapped together are thrown out, and instantly the Rattle and the Song are heard, the conjuring box violently shaken, as if the conjurer was actually possessed; sometimes the Song ceases, and a speech is heard of ambiguous predictions of what is to happen. In half an hours time, he appears exhausted, leaves the leather box and retires to his tent, the perspiration running down him, smokes his pipe, and goes to sleep.

The above is acted on a piece of clear ground; I sometimes thought there must be some collusion, and the apparent fast knots, were really slip knots; but the more I became convinced the whole was a neat piece of jugglery. On one of these occasions, five Scotchmen were with me on some business we had with the Natives; we found the above Indian preparing his conjuring box: of course our business could not be done till this was over. When my men perceived the conjurer about being tied, they said, if they had the tying of him, he would never get loose, this I told to the Indians, who readily agreed the Scotchmen should tie him: which they did in the usual way, and placed him in the conjuring box; quite sure he could not get loose: In about fifteen minutes, to their utter astonishment, all the cords were thrown out in a bundle, the Rattle, and the Song [was heard] in full force, and the conjuring box shaken, as if going to pieces; my men were at a loss what to think, or say. the

Natives smiled at their incredulity; at length they consoled themselves by saying, the Devil himself had untied him, and set him loose.

I found many of the Men, especially those who had been much in company with white men, to be all half infidels, but the Women kept them in order; for they fear the Manito's; All their dances have a religious tendency, they are not, as with us, dances of mere pleasure, of the joyous countenance: they are grave, each dancer considers it is a religious rite for some purpose; their motions are slow and graceful; yet I have sometimes seen occasional dances of a gay character; I was at their Tents on business, when the Women came and told me they wanted Beads and Ribbons, to which I replied I wanted Marten Skins; early the next morning, five young women set off to make Marten Traps; and did not return until the evening. They were rallyed by their husbands and brothers; who proposed they should dance to the Manito of the Martens, to this they willingly consented, it was a fine, calm, moonlight night, the young men came with the Rattle and Tambour, about nine women formed the dance, to which they sung with their fine voices, and lively they danced hand in hand in a half circle for a long hour; it is now many years ago, yet I remember this gay hour.

Every man believes or wishes to believe that he has a familiar being who takes care of him, and warns him of danger, and other matters which otherwise he could not know; this imaginary being he calls his Poowoggan; upon conversing with them on the Being on whom they relied; it appeared to me to be no other than the powers of his own mind when somewhat excited by danger or difficulty, especially as they suppose their dreams to be caused by him, " Ne poo war tin " (I have dreamed); too often a troubled dream from a heavy supper; but at times they know how to dream for their own interest or convenience; and when one of them told me he had been dreaming it was for what he wished to have, or to do, for some favor, or as some excuse for not performing his promises, for so far as their interests are concerned they do not want policy.

When injured they are resentful, but not more than the lower classes of europeans. They frequently pass over injuries, and are always appeased with a present, unless blood has been shed, in this case however they may seem to forgive, they defer revenge to a more convenient opportunity ; courage is not accounted an essential to the men, any more than chastity to the women, though both are sometimes found in a high degree. The greatest praise that one Indian can give to another, is, that he is a man of steady humane disposition, and a fortunate hunter, and the praise of the women is to be active and good humoured ; their marriages are without noise or ceremony. Nothing is requisite but the consent of the parties, and Parents : the riches of a man consists solely in his ability as a Hunter, and the portion of the woman is good health, and a willingness to relieve her husband from all domestic duties. Although the young men appear not to be passionate lovers, they seldom fail of being good husbands, and when contrariety of disposition prevails, so that they cannot live peaceably together, they separate with as little ceremony as they came together, and both parties are free to attach themselves to whom they will, without any stain on their characters ; but if they have lived so long together so as to have children, one, or both, are severely blamed. Polygamy is allowed, and each may have as many wives as he can maintain, but few indulge themselves in this liberty, yet some have even three ; this is seldom a matter of choice, it is frequently from the death of a friend who has left his wife, sister, or daughter to him, for every woman must have a husband. The children are brought up with great care and tenderness. They are very seldom corrected, the constant company and admonition of the old people is their only education, whom they soon learn to imitate in gravity as far as youth will permit; they very early and readily betake themselves to fishing and hunting, from both men and women impressing on their minds, that the man truly miserable is he, who is dependent on another for his subsistence. They have no genius for mechanics, their domestic utensils are all rude, their snow shoes and canoes show ingenuity which necessity has forced on them, the state of every thing with them rises no higher than absolute necessity, and in all probability their ancestors some hundred years ago, were equal to the present generation in the arts of life.

CHAPTER V

DEER

Hunting—Moose—Rein Deer—Hedges for trapping Rein Deer —Vast herds of Rein Deer—Mahthee Mooswah.

THE Natives of this Stoney Region subsist wholly by the chase and by fishing, the country produces no vegetables but berries on which they can live. The term "hunting" they apply only to the Moose and Rein Deer, and the Bear; they look for, and find the Beaver, they kill with the Gun, and by traps the Otter and other animals. Hunting is divided into what may be termed "tracking" and "tracing." Tracking an animal is by following it's footsteps, as the Rein Deer and the Bear and other beasts; tracing, is following the marks of feeding, rubbing itself on the ground, and against trees, and lying down : which is for the Moose Deer, and for other animals on rocks and hard grounds. My remarks are from the Natives who are intimately acquainted with them, and make them their peculiar study. The first in order is the Moose Deer,[1] the pride of the forest, and the largest of all the Deer, [it] is too well known to need a description. It is not numerous in proportion to the extent of country, but may even be said to be scarce. It is of a most watchful nature; it's long, large, capacious ears enables it to catch and discriminate, every sound; his sagacity for self preservation is almost incredible; it feeds in wide circles, one within the other, and then lies down to ruminate near the centre; so that in tracking of it, the

---

[1] *Alces americanus* (Clinton). [E. A. P.]

unwary, or unskillful, hunter is sure to come to windward of, and start it; when, in about two hours, by his long trot, he is at the distance of thirty or forty miles, from where it started; when chased it can trot, (it's favorite pace) about twenty five to thirty miles an hour; and when forced to a gallop, rather loses, than gains ground. In calm weather it feeds among the Pines, Aspins and Willows; the buds, and tender branches of the two latter are it's food: but in a gale of wind he retires among the close growth of Aspins, Alders and Willows on low ground still observing the same circular manner of feeding and lying down. If not molested it travels no farther than to find it's food, and is strongly attached to it's first haunts, and after being harrassed it frequently returns to it's usual feeding places. The flesh of a Moose in good condition, contains more nourishment than that of any other Deer; five pounds of this meat being held to be equal in nourishment to seven pounds of any other meat even of the Bison, but for this, it must be killed where it is quietly feeding; when run by Men, Dogs, or Wolves for any distance, it's flesh is alltogether changed, becomes weak and watery and when boiled; the juices separates from the meat like small globules of blood, and does not make broth; the change is so great, one can hardly be persuaded it is the meat of a Moose Deer. The nose of the Moose, which is very large and soft, is accounted a great delicacy. It is very rich meat. The bones of it's legs are very hard and several things are made of them. His skin makes the best of leather. It is the noblest animal of the Forest, and the richest prize the Hunter can take. In the rutting season the Bucks become very fierce, and in their encounters sometimes interlock their large palmated horns so strongly that they cannot extricate them, and both die on the spot, and [this is a thing] which happens too often: three of us tried to unlock the horns of two Moose which had died in this manner, but could not do it, although they had been a year in this state, and we had to use the axe.

In the latter end of September [1804] we had to build a trading house at Musquawegun Lake,[1] an Indian named Huggemowequan came to hunt for us, and on looking about thought the ground good for Moose, and told us to make no noise; he was told no noise would be made except the falling of the trees, this he said the Moose did not mind; when he returned, he told us he had seen the place a Doe Moose had been feeding in the beginning of May; in two days more he had unravelled her feeding places to the beginning of September. One evening he remarked to us, that he had been so near to her that he could proceed no nearer, unless it blew a gale of wind, when this took place he set off early, and shot the Moose Deer. This took place in the very early part of October.

This piece of hunting the Indians regarded as the work of a matchless hunter beyond all praise. The Natives are very dextrous in cutting up, and separating the joints, of a Deer, which in the open season has to be carried by them to the tent, or if near the water, to a canoe; this is heavy work; but if the distance is too great, the meat is split and dried by smoke, in which no resinous wood must be used; this reduces the meat to less than one third of its weight. In winter this is not required, as the flat sleds are brought to the Deer, and the meat with all that is useful is hauled on the Snow to the tent. The Moose Deer, have rarely more than one Fawn at a birth, it's numbers are decreasing for, from it's settled habits a skillful hunter is sure to find, and wound, or kill this Deer, and it is much sought for, for food, for clothing and for Tents. The bones of the head of a Moose must be put into the water or covered with earth or snow.

I have already described the Stony Region as extending from the most northern part of this continent, bounded, on the east by the sea, southward to Labrador and Nova Scotia, on the west by the chain of great Lakes: this great extent

---

[1] Musquawegan (which means Bear's Backbone) was situated on the Churchill river. Thompson spent here the winter of 1804-05.

may properly be called the country of the Rein Deer, an animal too well known to need description ; and this Region is peculiar to the Rein Deer, on this continent it is found no where else. The Natives have well named it "Marthee Teek" the "ugly deer," and from its migratory habits, the Wandering Deer.[1] It's form and way of life, though admirably adapted to the rude countries and severe climates it inhabits, yet when compared with the graceful Antelope, it may be called not handsome. Their sight appears not good, and the eye dull, and has nothing of the brilliancy of the eyes of other deer. When examining anything that appears doubtful, it extends it's neck and head in an awkward manner, and cautiously approaches until it is sure what the object is. It's large, broad, hard, hoofs make it very sure footed, and quite safe, and swift on swamps, rocks, or smooth ice. It's meat is good, but has something of a peculiar taste ; the fat

[1] The Reindeer here referred to belong to a form of caribou provisionally described by Richardson under the name *Cervus tarandus* var. B. *sylvestris.* These caribou spend the winter chiefly in the region now under consideration and migrate in spring eastward to the shore of Hudson Bay, about 150 miles south-east of York Factory, and return in autumn. In former years these animals were very numerous, but they have been subjected to such slaughter during their semi-annual migrations that their numbers are now much reduced, though they are still sometimes found in good-sized herds. Richardson's name has been revived recently on the basis of specimens examined from Upper Nelson river, and east of Lake Winnipeg (see Hollister, *Smithsonian Misc. Coll.*, vol. 56, no. 5, p. 4, 1912). These specimens are of the Woodland Caribou type, and when compared with specimens from eastern Canada show differences of subspecific rank. Their identity with the animals referred to by Richardson is still open to some question, as specimens actually from the Hayes river herds were not available for comparison. The inhabitants of the region consider the animals which cross Hayes river to be identical with the Barren Ground Caribou, *Rangifer arcticus* (Richardson). Mr. J. B. Tyrrell informs me that they are similar to the latter species in size, and not noticeably different in any way when observed at a little distance, but that they are certainly different from the larger Woodland Caribou of the same general region. It is important therefore that a series of specimens be secured which will permit comparison of this form both with the Barren Ground species and with the larger Woodland Caribou. [E. A. P.]

is somewhat like that of mutton; the Tongue in richness
and delicacy far exceeds any other deer, and is even superior
to the tongue of the Bison. It's strong form and broad hoofs
enables it to swim with ease and swiftness; they boldly cross
the largest Rivers and even Bays and Straits of the sea; but
in doing this, their want of clear eye sight leads them too far
from land, and [they] are lost. When few in number, and
scattered, they are cautious and timid; but when in large
herds, quite the reverse and are ready to trample down all
before them.

At York Factory, in the early part of the open season,
the Rein Deer are sometimes numerous; when they are so,
commencing about four miles above the Factory, strong
hedges of small pine trees, clear of their branches, are made,
near to, and running parallel with, the bank of the River;
at intervals of about fifteen yards door ways are made in which
is placed a snare of strong line, in which, the Deer in attempting to pass, entangles itself; when thus caught, it is sometimes
strangled, but more frequently found alive; and ready to
defend itself; the men, who every morning visit the hedge,
are each armed with a spear of ten to twelve feet; and must
take care that the deer is at the length of his line and carefully avoid the stroke of his fore feet, with which he is very
active, and defends itself. The meat at this season is
always poor and what is salted is barely eatable; it is only
in Autumn and the early part of winter that they are in good
condition.

In the latter end of the month of May 1792, the ice had
broken up. Mr Cooke[1] and myself in a canoe proceeded
about twenty miles up the River to shoot the Rein Deer, as

[1] William Cook was a native of London, England, and was engaged
in the service of the Hudson's Bay Company for a number of years at the
end of the eighteenth and the beginning of the nineteenth century. In
1799–1800 he was rated as a trader with a salary of £60 a year, and in
1801–02 his salary was £80 a year. He was engaged chiefly at York Factory
and up the Nelson river.

they crossed the River; we passed two days, in which time
we had killed ten deer. On the third morning the weather
cold and uncomfortable, we were sitting by our fire, when we
heard a noise as of distant thunder, and somewhat alarmed,
put our four guns, and blankets into the canoe, and sat
quietly in it; waiting what it could be; with surprise we
heard the sound increasing and rushing towards us, but we
were not long in suspense. About forty yards below us, a
vast herd of Rein Deer, of about one hundred yards of front,
rushing through the woods, headlong descended the steep
bank and swam across the river; in the same manner ascended
the opposite bank, and continued full speed through the
woods; we waited to see this vast herd pass, expecting to
see it followed by a number of wolves; but not one appeared,
and in this manner the herd continued to pass the whole
day to near sunset, when a cessation took place. On each
hand were small herds of ten to twenty deer, all rushing
forward with the same speed. The great herd were so
closely packed together that not one more, if dropped among
them, could find a place. The next day, a while after sun
rise, the same sound and rushing noise was heard, and a deer
herd of the same front, with the same headlong haste came
down the bank and crossed the river, and continued to about
two in the afternoon, attended by small herds on either side,
after which small herds passed, but not with the same speed,
and by sun set finally ceased. When we returned to the
Factory and related what we had seen, they could hardly
believe us, and had we not by chance been up the river,
nothing would have been known of the passage of this great
herd : for the weather, for a long fortnight after the breaking
up of the ice is very precarious and uncomfor[t]able. Some
time after, conversing with some of the Natives on this herd
of Rein Deer they said that large herds do sometimes pass in
the spring, they [had] often seen their roads, but had seldom
seen the herds. The Factory next southward, [in] the direc-

tion of the Deer was that of Severn River,[1] about 250 miles distant, they knew nothing of this herd and through the summer had no more than usual. At York Factory it was otherwise, the Deer were more numerous than usual, but only near the sea side. We attempted to estimate the number of Deer that passed in this great herd but the Natives pointed out their method, which was thought the best; this was to allow the Deer a full hour and a half (by the Sun) in the morning to feed, and the same before sunset; this would give ten full hours of running, of what we thought twenty miles an hour, which they reduced to twelve miles, observing that large herds appear to run faster than they really do. By this means they extended the herd of the first day to one hundred and twenty miles in length and the herd of the second day to half as much more, making the whole length of the herd to be one hundred and eighty miles in length; by one hundred yards in breadth. The Natives do not understand high numbers, but they readily comprehend space, though they cannot define it by miles and acres; and their Clock is the path of the Sun. By the above space, allowing to each deer, ten feet by eight feet; an area of eighty square feet; the number of Rein Deer that passed was 3,564,000, an immense number; without including the many small herds. Thus what we learn by numbers, we learn by space. Then applying themselves to me, they said, You that look at the Stars tell us the cause of the regular march of this herd of Deer. I replied, "Instinct." What do you mean by that word. It's meaning is "the free and voluntary actions of an animal for it's self preservation." Oh Oh, then you think this herd

---

[1] The factory or trading post near the mouth of the Severn river was established by the Hudson's Bay Company sometime about the middle of the eighteenth century to secure the trade of the Indians, whose hunting-grounds were on the Severn river and its tributaries. The post is situated 240 miles south-eastward along the shore of Hudson Bay from York Factory on the west bank of the Severn river, six miles above its mouth, and is still annually supplied from York Factory.

of Deer rushed forward over deep swamps, in which some perished, the others ran over them; down steep banks to break their necks; swam across large Rivers, where the strong drowned the weak; went a long way through woods where they had nothing to eat, merely to take care of themselves. You white people, you look like wise men, and talk like fools. The Deer feeds quietly, and lays down when left to itself. Do you not perceive this great herd was under the direct order of their Manito and that he was with them, he had gathered them together, made them take a regular line, and drove them on to where they are to go : "And where is that place. We don't know. But when he gets them there, they will disperse, none of them will ever come back; and I had to give up my doctrine of Instinct, to that of their Manito. I have sometimes thought Instinct, to be a word invented by the learned to cover their ignorance of the ways and doings of animals for their self preservation; it is a learned word and shuts up all the reasoning powers.

On this stony region, there is another species of Deer, which I take to be a nondescript; by the Nahathaway Indians it is called "Mahthee Mooswah," (the ugly Moose)[1] it is found only on a small extent of country mostly about the Hatchet Lake,[2] in Latitude . . . and Longitude . . . This deer seems to be a link between the Moose and the Rein Deer; it is about twice the weight of the latter; and has the habits of the former; it's horns are palmated somewhat like those of a Moose, and it's colour is much the same; it feeds on buds and the tender branches of Willows and Aspins, and also on moss. In all my wanderings I have

---

[1] Evidently some form of the Woodland Caribou, but if recognizable, not known to science. No specimens from this region appear to have been examined by naturalists. The animals are said to be much larger than the Barren Ground Caribou, *Rangifer arcticus* (Rich.). [E. A. P.]

[2] Hatchet lake is a small rectangular body of clear water lying on the Stone river in latitude 58° 45' N. and longitude 103 45' W. Its greatest length is twelve miles, and its greatest width seven miles.

seen only two alive, and but a glimpse of them, they bounded
off with the trot of the Moose; and two that were killed by
the Hunters; one of them was entirely cut up, the other
had only the bowels taken out; this I wished to measure,
but I saw the Hunters eyed with superstition what I wished
to do, and desisted, and turned the matter off by enquiring
how many of their skins make a comfortable Tent, they told
me ten to twelve. They keep their haunts like the Moose,
and when started return to them, but [I] could not learn
whether they fed in rude circles, like the Moose; Their
meat is almost as good as that of the Moose, and far better
than that of the Rein Deer; When each of us was roasting
a small piece at the fire, one of the Hunters said to me, We
did not like to see you measure the Deer, for fear their Manito
would be angry, he is soon displeased, and does not like his
Deer to be killed, and has not many of them.

The reason that this species of deer is so very little known
is, it's haunts is on the verge of the barren lands, far to the
eastward of the route of the Traders, and the country produces but very few furrs.

CHAPTER VI

LIFE AMONG THE NAHATHAWAYS

Instruments—Observations—Indian superstition—Ability of the Indian to travel—Journey down the Winipeg River—Character of the French Canadians—Reed Lake—Indian character—Small pox—Amount of game—Trading Posts—their position and food—White Fish—Nets—Beaver—Bears — Trees—Canoes — Will o' the Wisp — Climate—December—Tapahpahtum Conjuring for wind—A Gale—Indian logic—Wiskahoo—Apistawahshish—Cannibalism.

IT may now [be well to] say something of myself, and of the character the Natives and the french Canadians entertained of me, they were almost my only companions. My instruments for practical astronomy, were a brass Sextant of ten inches radius, an achromatic Telescope of high power for observing the Satellites of Jupiter and other phenomena, one of the same construction for common use, Parallel glasses and quicksilver horizon for double Altitudes; Compass, Thermometer, and other requisite instruments, which I was in the constant practice of using in clear weather for observations on the Sun, Moon, Planets and Stars; to determine the positions of the Rivers, Lakes, Mountains and other parts of the country I surveyed from Hudson Bay to the Pacific Ocean. Both Canadians and Indians often inquired of me why I observed the Sun, and sometimes the Moon, in the day time, and passed whole nights with my instruments looking at the Moon and Stars. I told them it was to determine the distance and direction from the place I observed to other places; neither the Canadians nor the Indians believed me; for both argued that if what I said was truth, I ought to look to the ground, and over it; and not to the Stars. Their opinions were, that I was looking into futurity and seeing every body, and what they were doing; how to raise the wind; but did not believe I could calm it, this they argued from seeing me obliged to wait the calming of the wind on the great Lakes, to which the Indians added that I knew where the Deer were, and other superstitious opinions. During my life I have always been careful not to pretend to any knowledge of futurity, and [said] that I knew nothing beyond the present hour; neither argument, nor ridicule had any effect, and I had to leave them to their own opinions and yet inadvertingly on my part, several things happened to confirm their opinions One fine evening in February two Indians came to the house to trade; the Moon rose bright and clear with the planet Jupiter a few degrees on it's east side; and the Canadians as usual predicted that Indians would come to trade in the direction of this star. To show them the folly of such predictions, I told them the same bright star, the next night, would be as far from the Moon on it's west side; this of course took place from the Moon's motion in her orbit; and is the common occurence of almost every month, and yet all parties were persuaded I had done it by some occult power to falsify the predictions of the canadians. Mankind are fond of the marvelous, it seems to heighten their character by relating they have seen such things. I had always admired the tact of the Indian in being able to guide himself through the darkest pine forests to exactly the place he intended to go, his keen, constant attention on every thing; the removal of the smallest stone, the bent or broken twig; a slight mark on the ground, all spoke plain language to him. I was anxious to acquire this knowledge, and often being in company with them, sometimes for several months, I paid attention to what they pointed out to me, and became

almost equal to some of them; which became of great use
to me : The North West Company[1] of Furr Traders, from
their Depot in Lake Superior sent off Brigades of Canoes
loaded with about three Tons weight of Merchandise, Provisions and Baggage; those for the most distant trading
Posts are sent off first; with an allowance of two days time
between each Brigade to prevent incumbrances on the
Carrying Places; I was in my first year in the third Brigade
of six Canoes each and having nothing to do but sketch off
my survey and make Observations, I was noticing how far
we gained, or lost ground on the Brigade before us, by the
fires they made, and other marks, as we were equally manned
with five men to each canoe : In order to prevent the winter
coming on us, before we reached our distant winter quarters
the Men had to work very hard from daylight to sunset, or
later, and at night slept on the ground, constantly worried
by Musketoes; and had no time to look about them; I
found we gained very little on them; at the end of fifteen
days we had to arrive at Lake Winipeg, (that is the Sea Lake
from it's size) and for more than two days it had been blowing

[1] The North-West Company was first formed in 1783, when a number
of English fur-traders trading from Montreal, realizing that competition
was proving ruinous to them and to the Canadian fur-trade, united their
forces. The chief figures in the new company were Peter Pond, Peter
Pangman, Benjamin and Joseph Frobisher, and Simon McTavish. Those
traders who were not included in this company formed a rival organization
under the name of Gregory, McLeod, and Company. After three or four
years of competition, these two companies were amalgamated in 1787
under the title of the North-West Company. The amalgamated company
operated throughout the west until 1798, when several of the partners,
among them Alexander Mackenzie, broke away from their former associates, and formed an independent company, officially styled Forsyth,
Richardson, and Company, but popularly known as the X Y Company.
For the next six years these two companies, composed of men who had
been old associates, and who had been trained in the same school, waged
a severe commercial war with each other; but in 1804 they decided to
reunite their interests in one company, which retained the name of the
North-West Company. In 1821 the North-West Company was merged in
the Hudson's Bay Company.

a north west gale, which did not allow the Brigade before us
to proceed; and I told the Guide, that early the next morning
we should see them; these Guides have charge of conducting
the march and are all proud of coming up to the canoes
ahead of them, and by dawn of day we entered the Lake
now calm, and as the day came on us, saw the Brigade that
were before us, only one Mile ahead of us. The Guide and
the men shouted with joy, and when we came up to them
told them of my wonderful predictions, and that I had
pointed out every place they had slept at, and all by looking
at the Stars; one party seemed delighted in being credulous,
the other in exageration; such are ignorant men, who never
give themselves a moments reflection. The fact is Jean
Baptiste will not think, he is not paid for it; when he has a
minute's respite he smokes his pipe, his constant companion
and all goes well; he will go through hardships, but requires
a belly full, at least once a day, good Tobacco to smoke, a
warm Blanket, and a kind Master who will take his share of
hard times and be the first in danger. Naval and Military
Men are not fit to command them in distant countries, neither
do they place confidence in one of themselves as a leader;
they always prefer an Englishman, but they ought always to
be kept in constant employment however light it may be.

Having passed eight winters in different parts of this
Stony Region, and as many open Seasons in discovering part
of it's many Rivers and Lakes, and surveying them; and as
the productions, the mode and manner of subsistence is
everywhere the same; to prevent repetition I shall confine
myself to a central position, for the phenomena of the
climate, and every thing else worth attention; This place is
[called] the Reed Lake[1] (Peepeequoonuskoo Sakahagan) by

[1] The trading post at this lake was built in 1794 by Thompson for the
Hudson's Bay Company; and in it he spent the following winter. Later,
he spent the winter of 1805–06 not far from the same place while trading
for the North-West Company. The lake, which has an area of 85 square
miles, is situated in the forest area north of the Saskatchewan river, and

the Natives. It is a sheet of water about forty miles in length,
by three to five miles in width; the land all around it,
sometimes showing cliffs, but in most places rising gently to
about the height of one hundred feet, everywhere having fine
forests of Birch Aspins and several kinds of Pine: the Trading
House in Latitude 54° 40' N. Longitude 101° 30' west of
Greenwich. The Thermometer was made by Dolland and
divided to 102 degrees below Zero. This section of the
Stony Region is called the Musk Rat Country and contains
an area of about 22,360 square miles, of which, full two fifths
of this surface is Rivers and Lakes, having phenomena distinct
from the dry, elevated, distant, interior countries. The
Natives are Nahathaway Indians, whose fathers from time
beyond any tradition, have hunted in these Lands; in conversing with them on their origin, they appear never to have
turned their minds to this subject; and [think] that mankind
and the animals are in a constant state of succession; and
the time of their great grandfathers is the extent of their
actual knowledge of times past; their tradition of the
Deluge and of the Rainbow I have already mentioned; yet
their stories all refer to times when Men were much taller
and stronger than at present, the animals more numerous,
and many could converse with mankind, particularly, the
Bear, Beaver, Lynx and Fox. Writers on the North American
Indians always write as comparing them, with themselves
who are all men of education, and of course [the Indians]
lose by comparison; this is not fair; let them be compared
with those who are uneducated in Europe, yet even in this
comparison the Indian has the disadvantage in not having
the light of Christianity. Of course his moral character has
not the firmness of christian morality, but in practice he is

just at the foot of a low escarpment of limestone which rises to the south
of it. Except on the south side the rock underlying the surrounding
country is granite, but overlying the granite in many places is a moderate
thickness of good clay soil.

fully equal to those of his class in Europe; living without law, they are a law to themselves. The Indian is said to be a creature of apathy, when he appears to be so, he is in an assumed character to conceal what is passing in his mind; as he has nothing of the almost infinite diversity of things which interest and amuse the civilised man; his passions, desires and affections are strong, however appeared subdued, and engage the whole man; the law of retaliation, which is fully allowed, makes the life of man respected; and in general he abhors the sheding of blood, and should sad necessity compel him to it, which is sometimes the case, he is held to be an unfortunate man; but he who has committed wilful murder is held in abhorrence, as one with whom the life of no person is in safety, and possessed with an evil spirit. When Hudson Bay was discovered, and the first trading settlement made, the Natives were far more numerous than at present.

In the year 1782, the small pox[1] from Canada extended to them, and more than one half of them died; since which although they have no enemies, their country very healthy, yet their numbers increase very slowly. The Musk Rat country, of which I have given the area, may have ninety two families, each of seven souls, giving to each family an area of two hundred and forty eight square miles of hunting grounds; or thirty five square miles to each soul, a very thin population. A recent writer (Ballantyne)[2] talks of myriads

[1] The exact date when smallpox first spread among the Indians throughout the North-West is not quite certain; but it would appear that it was sometime during 1781, and that it disappeared, or at least greatly decreased in virulence, in 1782. A full account of the havoc played among the Indians by this dread disease will be found in Thompson's own words on pages 321–25.

[2] It was about the time when Thompson was writing his memoirs that R. M. Ballantyne began to publish his interesting stories of life among the fur-traders of the Hudson's Bay Company in western Canada. Ballantyne was then a young man, and Thompson was getting very old; and it is possible that the exuberance of spirit shown by the former may have grated on the mature judgment of the older man. Game was then, and is yet, fairly abundant throughout many parts of what Thompson calls

of wild animals ; such writers talk at random, they have never counted, nor calculated ; the animals are by no means numerous, and only in sufficient numbers to give a tolerable subsistence to the Natives, who are too often obliged to live on very little food, and sometimes all but perish with hunger. Very few Beaver are to be found, the Bears are not many and all the furr bearing animals an Indian can kill can scarcely furnish himself and family with the bare necessaries of life. A strange Idea prevails among these Natives, and also of all the Indians to the Rocky Mountains, though unknown to each other, that when they were numerous, before they were destroyed by the Small Pox all the animals of every species were also very numerous and more so in comparison of the number of Natives than at present ; and this was confirmed to me by old Scotchmen in the service of the Hudson's Bay Company, and by the Canadians from Canada ; the knowledge of the latter extended over all the interior countries, yet no disorder was known among the animals ; the fact was certain, and nothing they knew of could account for it ; it might justly be supposed the destruction of Mankind would allow the animals to increase, even to become formidable to the few Natives who survived, but neither the Bison, the Deer, nor the carnivorous animals increased, and as I have already remarked, are no more than sufficient for the subsistence of the Natives and Traders. The trading Houses over the whole country are situated on the banks of lakes, of at least twenty miles in length by two or three miles in width ; and as much larger as may be, as it is only large and deep Lakes that have Fish sufficient to maintain the Trader and his Men, for the Indians at best can only afford a Deer now and then.

Some Lakes give only what is called a Fall Fishery. This

the Muskrat country, but the hunter's life is everywhere a precarious one, for the wild animals may move quickly from place to place and the natives, who need to obtain food daily in order to live, may not be able to follow them or to find them quickly enough to avert starvation.

fishery commences in October and lasts to about Christmas ;
the fish caught are white fish[1] and pike.[2] Whatever is not
required for the day is frozen and laid by in a hoard ; and
with all care is seldom more than enough for the winter
and a fish once frozen loses it's good taste unless kept in that
state until it is thrown into the kettle of boiling water. Fish
thawed and then boiled are never good ; We who pass the
winter on fish, and sometimes also the summer, are the best
judges, for we have nothing with them, neither butter nor
sauces ; and too often not a grain of salt. The best Lakes
are those that have a steady fishery ; and according to the
number and length of the Nets give a certain number of
White Fish ; throughout the winter. The deep Lakes that
have sandy, pebbly beaches, with bottoms of the same may
be depended on for a steady fishery The Fish on which the
Traders place dependance are the White Fish, in such Lakes
as I have last described. It is a rich well tasted, nourishing
food ; but in shoal muddy Lakes it is poor and not well
tasted ; and when a new trading House is built which is
almost every year, every one is anxious to know the quality
of the fish it contains for whatever it is they have no other
for the winter. These fish vary very much in size and weight,
from two to thirteen pounds and each great Lake appears to
have a sort peculiar to itself, it is preyed upon by the Pike
and Trout ; and also the white headed, or bald, Eagle. The
seine is seldom used, it is too heavy and expensive, and useless
in winter. The set Net is that which is in constant use ;
those best made are of holland twine, with a five and a half
inch mesh but this mesh must be adapted to the size of the
fish and ranges from three to seven inches ; the best length is
fifty fathoms, the back lines, on which the net is extended and
fastened are of small cord ; every thing must be neat and
fine : Instead of Corks and Leads, small stones are tied to
the bottom line with twine at every two fathoms, opposite

[1] *Coregonus.* [E. A. P.]   [2] *Esox lucius* Linn. [E. A. P.]

to each on the upper line, a float of light pine, or cedar wood is tied which keeps the net distended; both in summer and winter the best depth for nets, is three to five fathom water; in shoal water the fish are not so good. In winter the nets being sheltered by the ice, the fishery is more steady, not being disturbed by gales of wind. In some Lakes in Spring and Autumn there are an abundance of grey[1] and red Carp;[2] the former have so very many small bones that only the head and a piece behind it are eaten; but the red Carp are a good fish though weak food. The daily allowance of a Man is eight pounds of fish, which is held to be equal to five pounds of meat; almost the only change through the year are hares and grouse, very dry eating; a few Martens,[3] a chance Beaver,[4] Lynx[5] and Porcupine.[6] Vegetables would be acceptable but [are] not worth the trouble and risk of raising, and almost every small trading house is deserted during the summer, or only two men [are] left to take care of the place; every person with very few exceptions, enjoys good health, and we neither had, nor required a medical Man. Formerly the Beavers were very numerous, the many Lakes and Rivers gave them ample space; and the poor Indian had then only a pointed stick shaped and hardened in the fire, a stone Hatchet, Spear and Arrow heads of the same; thus armed he was weak against the sagacious Beaver, who, on the banks of a Lake, made itself a house of a foot thick, or more; composed of earth and small flat stones, crossed and bound together with pieces of wood; upon which no impression could be made but by fire. But when the arrival of the White People had changed all their weapons from stone to iron and steel, and added the fatal Gun, every animal fell before the Indian;

[1] *Moxostoma lesueuri* (Richardson). [E. A. P.]
[2] *Catostomus catostomus* (Forster). [E. A. P.]
[3] *Martes a. abieticola* (Preble). [E. A. P.]
[4] *Castor canadensis* Kuhl. [E. A. P.]
[5] *Lynx canadensis* Kerr. [E. A. P.]
[6] *Erethizon dorsatum* (Linn.). [E. A. P.]

the Bear was no longer dreaded, and the Beaver became a desirable animal for food and clothing, and the furr a valuable article of trade; and as the Beaver is a stationary animal, it could be attacked at any convenient time in all seasons, and thus their numbers soon became reduced.

The old Indians, when speaking of their ancestors, wonder how they could live as the Beaver was wiser, and the Bear stronger, than them, and confess, that if they were deprived of the Gun, they could not live by the Bow and Arrow, and must soon perish. The Beaver skin is the standard by which other Furrs are traded; and London prices have very little influence on this value of barter, which is more a matter of expedience and convenience to the Trader and the Native, than of real value. The only Bears of this country, are the small black Bear,[1] with a chance Yellow Bear, this latter has a fine furr and trades for three Beavers in barter, when full grown. The Black Bear is common and according to size passes for one or two Beavers, the young are often tamed by the Natives, and are harmless and playful, until near full grown, when they become troublesome, and are killed, or sent into the woods; while they can procure roots and berries, they look for nothing else. But in the Spring, when they leave their winter dens, they can get neither the one, nor the other, prowl about, and go to the Rapids where the Carp are spawning; here Bruin lives in plenty; but not content with what it can eat, amuses itself with tossing ashore ten times more than it can devour, each stroke of it's fore paw sending a fish eight or ten yards according to it's size; the fish thus thrown ashore attract the Eagle and the Raven;[2] the sight of these birds flying about, leads the Indian to the place, and Bruin loses his life and his skin. The meat of the Bear feeding on roots and berries becomes

[1] *Ursus americanus* Pallas. The so-called Yellow Bear is merely a colour phase of the Black Bear. [E. A. P.]

[2] *Corvus corax principalis* Ridgway. [E. A. P.]

H

very fat and good, and in this condition it enters it's den for the winter; at the end of which the meat is still good, and has some fat, but the very first meal of fish the taste of the meat is changed for the worse, and soon becomes disagreeable. When a Mahmees Dog, in the winter season has discovered a den, and the Natives go to kill the Bear, on uncovering the top of the den, Bruin is found roused out of it's dormant state, and sitting ready to defend itself; the eldest man now makes a speech to it; reproaching the Bear and all it's race with being the old enemies of Man, killing the children and women, when it was large and strong; but now, since the Manito has made him, small and weak to what he was before, he has all the will, though not the power to be as bad as ever, that he is treacherous and cannot be trusted, that although he has sense he makes bad use of it, and must therefore be killed; parts of the speech have many repetitions to impress it's truth on the Bear, who all the time is grinning and growling, willing to fight, but more willing to escape, until the axe descends on it's head, or [it] is shot; the latter more frequently, as the den is often under the roots of fallen trees, and protected by the branches of the roots.

When a Bear thus killed was hauled out of it's den, I enquired of the Indian who made the speech, whether he really thought the Bear understood him. He replied, " how can you doubt it, did you not see how ashamed I made him, and how he held down his head;" " He might well hold down his head, when you were flourishing a heavy axe over it, with which you killed him." On this animal they have several superstitions, and he acts a prominent part in many of their tales. All the other furr bearing animals have been already noticed. On the western parts of this region the Forests have trees of a finer and larger growth, and now contain two kinds of Birch, the white [1] and the red; [2] one of

---

[1] *Betula papyrifera* Marsh. [E. A. P.]
[2] Probably *Betula alaskana* Sargent. [E. A. P.]

Poplar[1] and one of Aspin,[2] one kind of Larch,[3] two of Fir;[4] four of Pine;[5] with Alders and Willows. Of these the White Birch is the most valuable, and contributes more than all the others to the necessaries and comforts of life. Of the Birch their Bows, Axe helves and Spear handles are made, and several other things; in the Spring the sap, when boiled down, yields a weak molasses: but the most useful part is the Rind, which is peculiar to this tree; the bark is of a redish color, and good for tanning: this bark is covered with a Rind, it's growth in a horizontal, or longitudinal, direction; while that of the Tree, and it's bark are vertical; in my travels I have noticed, that the thickness of the Rind depends on the climate; the colder the climate the thicker the Birch Rind; on the west side of the Mountains where the winter is very mild, the White Birch is a noble large Tree, but the Rind too thin to be useful for Canoes. In this region, few white Birch exceed thirty inches in girth; but in general the Rind is excellent for all purposes and is from two eights to three eights in thickness; it is all marked with what is called cores on the outside of the rind, of about an inch in length; and narrow, when these go through the rind, it makes it useless for canoes. When the Natives see a Birch tree with deep cores, they say it has been severely flogged by Weesaukejauk (the Flatterer) for by their tradition, when the Trees were renovated after the deluge, Weesaukejauk commanded them all to appear before him, which order they all obeyed but the Birch Tree; which for disobedience he flogged, of which the cores are the marks. The best time for raising the rind off the Birch Tree is the early part of the summer; the tree being smooth is difficult to ascend, and

[1] *Populus balsamifera* Linn. [E. A. P.]
[2] *Populus tremuloides* Michx. [E. A. P.]
[3] *Larix laricina* (Du Roi). [E. A. P.]
[4] *Abies balsamea* (Linn.). [E. A. P.]
[5] *Pinus divaricata* (Ait.). Thompson evidently had in mind other species found farther west. [E. A. P.]

for this purpose the Native ties a strong leather cord to the great toes of his feet, leaving a space between them of about one foot, and having a strong square headed knife, very sharp at the point, in his belt, he ascends the tree to as high as the Rind is good, then raising a small strip from around the tree, in a straight line downwards cuts quite through the rind, which readily leaves the bark, and while the sap is rising comes off so freely that two persons with light poles keep it to the tree until it can be carefully taken down; it is then warmed and it's circular form made flat, laid on the ground, and kept so, by light logs of wood; and thus [it] becomes fit for use. The common length from one tree is from nine to fifteen feet, with a breadth of twenty four to thirty inches, very few trees yield a greater breadth, in this climate. As the Birch Rind is impervious to water; Canoes are made of it of all sizes to thirty feet in length, by four to five feet in breadth on the middle bar; this large size is made use of by the Traders, for the conveyance of furrs and goods, and is so light, it is carried by two men, when turned up. On shore, it affords good shelter to the Men, against Rain and the night. The canoes of the Natives are from ten to sixteen feet in length, and breadth in proportion, during the open season, they are almost constantly in them; hunting; removing from place to place, the Rivers and numerous Lakes giving free access through the whole country. Their dishes and domestic utensils are mostly of Birch Rind, which are made of various sizes, and pack up with [each] other and being light, with a smooth, firm, surface are easily kept clean. This Rind is inflamable, and makes bright torches. For coverings to their tents and lodges, the Rind is sewed together so as to take the form required; and being water proof, make a light comfortable tent in all weathers, and when the rain is over, the Natives can directly remove; whereas a leather tent when soaked with rain, requires a day's time and fire to dry it. Unfortunately the cold of winter renders it brittle and liable to accidents; and it must be warmed before it can be rolled up for removal; and the same to unroll it. The red Birch has a tougher wood, and in this respect is preferred to the White, but it's rind is thin, and as it grows among rocks, very often is small, crooked and knotty. The Fir is resinous, and makes good flambeaux's for spearing fish at night. The Larch is in request for making flat Sleds, used by the Natives for the removal of their goods and provisions in winter, it sparkles too much to be used for fire wood, and all the Pine woods are more or less the same for fuel. The Firs and resinous Pines when wholly decayed, become fine sand, without any vegetable mould, but all the trees and willows, not of the pine genus, enrich the soil by the decay of the leaves and the wood; The Larch is leafless all winter, and other Pines shed their leaves in summer, yet they also become sand, and do not profit the soil. The great expanse of Lake surface in this region, causes phenomena, that are peculiar to such a surface; In the winter season, every calm clear night, especially in the early part; there are innumerable very small luminous, meteoric points, which are visible for the twinkling of an eye, and disappear. When they are more numerous and brighter than usual, they fore-tell a gale of wind. On one occasion, five of us had to leave our new built winter house, as the fishery could not maintain us, and try to get another trading house where the fish were more plentifull; On coming to the Susquagemow Lake,[1] of about thirty miles in length, by three to five miles in width; it was so slightly frozen over we did not think proper to cross

---

[1] Suskwagemow or Sturgeon lake, now known as Landing lake, lies a short distance north-west of Nelson river, from which it is reached by a portage known as Cross Portage, one and a half miles in length. The water from it flows northward through the Grass river, which flows into the Nelson river a short distance above Split lake. The Hudson Bay Railway is at present being constructed down the valley of this stream. The incident here referred to probably occurred in the autumn of 1792.

it, but [preferred to] wait until the ice became stronger. This was in November, roaming about for hares and grouse; I found a fine River of about thirty yards in width that entered the Lake through a marsh; about half a mile up which, was a Beaver House, with a few yards of open water, kept from freezing over by the Beaver. The Moon was full and rose beautifully over the east end of the Lake; While the water can be kept open, in the early part of the night the Beaver swim about; and Andrew Davy, a tall young scotchman and myself took our guns and lay down near the Beaver House to shoot the Beaver as they swam about; a Beaver came near to Andrew, his gun snapped, the Beaver gave a smart stroke on the water with his broad tail, as if to bid us good night, and plunged into his house; although there was no more hope for that night, being hungry, we continued to watch until about eleven O'clock; As we were about to rise, a brilliant light [rose] over the east end of the Lake, its greatest length; it was a Meteor of a globular form, and appeared larger than the Moon, which was then high; it seemed to come direct towards us, lowering as it came; when within three hundred yards of us, it struck the River ice, with a sound like a mass of jelly, was dashed into in- numerable luminous pieces and instantly expired. Andrew would have run away but he had no time to do so; curiosity chained me to the spot. We got up, went to our fire, found nothing to eat, and lay down. As the ice of the River was covered with about one sixth of an inch of frozen snow, just enough to show our footsteps, the next morning we went to see what marks this meteor had made on the ice, but could not discover that a single particle was marked, or re- moved; it's form appeared globular, and from its size must have had some weight; it had no tail, and no luminous sparks came from it until dashed to pieces. The Meteors that have been seen in Europe, have all appeared to be of a fiery nature, some have exploded with a loud noise, and stones have descended from them. Two, or three nights afterwards, I was, as usual roaming about to find some game, about six in the evening, from the east end of the lake, coming in the same direction, I saw a Meteor, which appeared larger but not so bright as the first; I was near the Beaver house, but walking in a large grove of fine Aspins, the Meteor entered the wood about eight feet above the ground, as it struck the trees, pieces flew from it, and went out; as it passed close by me striking the trees with the sound of a mass of jelly, I noticed them; although it must have lost much of it's size from the many trees it struck, it went out of my sight, a large mass. The Aspins have on their bark a whitish substance like flour, after dry weather; the next day I examined the Aspins struck by the Meteor, but even this fine flour on the bark was not marked; I was at a loss what to think of it, it's stroke gave sound, and therefore must have substance. These two Meteors were, perhaps, compressed bodies of phosphoric air; but without the least heat, for had there been any, the second Meteor passed so near to me I must have felt it.

I have already described the brilliant Rime which covers the Willows and Shrubs along the shores of Hudson's Bay, this is readily accounted for, by the evaporation from the sea; but the inland Lake shores have it equally brilliant, though not in such abundance; and [it] also proceeds from the evaporation from the Lakes though frozen over, and the open rapids, and half frozen swamps have it in abundance, the Lake shores less, until swept away by a gale of wind, to be reformed in calm weather. It is well known that water frozen into ice, the latter has a greater bulk than the quantity of water frozen; and however solid the ice appears, it is actually porous: When the lakes are frozen over and there is from three to four inches in thickness, the vapours through it, form plots of ice flowers, which are composed of thin shining leaves of ice round a centre, and have a brilliant appearance;

they are of all sizes, some so small as to be called snow pearl. The clearest ice have the plots of small flowers, that which is opaque has the largest flowers; when the Sun shines, the leaves are slightly tinged with the colours of the Rainbow, have fine gaudy appearance, but [are] too bright for the eye to bear any time; the first fall of snow covers them to be seen no more.

What is called Mirage is common on all these Lakes, but frequently [is] simply an elevation of the woods and shores that bound the horizon; yet at times draw attention to the change of scenery it exhibits, and on these Lakes has often kept me watching it for many minutes; and [I] would have stayed longer if the cold had permitted: The first and most changeable Mirage is seen in the latter part of February and the month of March, the weather clear, the wind calm, or light; the Thermometer from ten above to twelve degrees below zero, the time about ten in the morning. On one occasion, going to an Isle where I had two traps for Foxes, when about one mile distant, the ice between me and the Isle appeared of a concave form, which, if I entered, I should slide into it's hollow, sensible of the illusion, it had the power to perplex me. I found my snow shoes, on a level, and advanced slowly, as afraid to slide into it; in about ten minutes this mirage ceased, the ice became [distinct] and showed a level surface, and with confidence I walked to my traps, in one of which I found a red Fox;[1] this sort of Mirage is not frequent. That most common elevates and depresses objects, and sometimes makes them appear to change places: In the latter end of February at the Reed Lake, at it's west end, a Mirage took place in one of it's boldest forms; About three miles from me was the extreme shore of the Bay; the Lake was near three miles in width, in which was a steep Isle of rock, and another of tall Pines; on the other side a bold

---

[1] *Vulpes fulva* (Desmarest).   [E. A. P.]

Point of steep rock. The Mirage began slowly to elevate all objects, then gently to lower them, until the Isles, and the Point appeared like black spots on the ice, and no higher than it's surface; the above bold Bay Shore, was a dark black curved line on the ice; in the time of three minutes, they all arose to their former height, and became elevated to twice their height, beyond the Bay, the rising grounds, distant eight miles, with all their woods appeared, and remained somewhat steady for a few minutes; the Isles and Point again disappeared; the Bay Shore with the distant Forests, came rolling forward, with an undulating motion, as if in a dance, the distant Forests became so near to me I could see their branches, then with the same motion retired to half distance; the Bay shore could not be distinguished, it was blended with the distant land; thus advancing and retiring with different elevations for about fifteen minutes, when the distant Forests vanished, the Isles took their place and the Lake shores their form; the whole wild scenery was a powerful illusion, too fleeting and changeful for any pencil. This was one of the clearest and most distinct Mirages I had ever seen. There can be no doubt it is the effect of a cause which, perhaps, was waves of the atmosphere loaded with vapours, though not perceptible to the eye, between the beholder and the objects on which the mirage acts, with the Sun in a certain position, when the objects were seen on the ridge of the wave, it gave them their elevation; when in the hollow of the wave, their greatest depression; and viewed obliquely to the direction of the wave, the objects appeared to change places. There may be a better theory to account for the Mirage.

While the Mirage is in full action, the scenery is so clear and vivid, the illusion so strong, as to perplex the Hunter and the Traveller; it appears more like the power of magic, than the play of nature.

When enquiring of the Natives what they thought of it,

they said it was Manito Korso; the work of a Manito; and with this argument they account for every thing that is uncommon.

Although the climate and country of which I am writing is far better than that of Hudson's Bay, yet the climate is severe in Winter the Thermometer often from thirty to forty degrees below Zero. The month of December is the coldest; the long absence of the Sun gives full effect to the action of the cold; the Snow increases in depth, it may be said to fall as dry as dust; the ice rapidly increases in thickness, and the steady cold of the rest of winter adds but little to that of the end of this month; but it's contraction by intense cold, causes the ice to rend in many places with a loud rumbling noise, and through these rents, water is often thrown out, and flows over part of the ice, making bad walking. This month has very variable weather, sometimes a calm of several days, then Gales of wind with light snow, which from it's lightness is driven about like dust. This dull month of long nights we wish to pass away; the country affords no tallow for candles; nor fish oil for lamps; the light of the fire is what we have to work and read by. Christmas when it comes finds us glad to see it and pass; we have nothing to welcome it with. In one of the calms of this month Tapahpahtum, a good hunter came to us for some provisions and fish hooks, he said his three wives and his children had had very little to eat for nearly a whole Moon adding you may be sure that we suffer hunger when I come to beg fish, and get hooks for my women to angle with. He took away about thirty pounds of fish, which he had to carry about twenty miles to his tent. I felt for him, for nothing but sad necessity can compel a Nahathaway hunter to carry away fish, and angle for them, this is too mean for a hunter; meat he carries with pleasure, but fish is degradation. The calm still continued; and two days after Tapapahtum came in the evening; he looked somewhat wild; he was a powerful man of strong passions; as usual I gave him a bit of Tobacco, he sat down and smoked, inhaling the smoke as if he would have drawn the tobacco through the pipe stem; then saying, now I have smoked, I may speak; I do not come to you for fish, I hope never to disgrace myself again; I now come for a wind which you must give me; in the mood he was in to argue with him was of no use, and I said, why did you not bring one of your women with you, she would have taken some fish to the tent; " My women are too weak, they snare a hare, or two every day, barely enough to keep them alive. I am come for a wind which you must give me "; " You know as well as I do that the Great Spirit alone is master of the Winds; you must apply to him, and not to me "; " Ah, that is always your way of talking to us, when you will not hear us, then you talk to us of the Great Spirit. I want a Wind, I must have it, now think on it, and dream, how I am to get it." I lent him an old Bison Robe to sleep on; which was all we could spare. The next day was calm; he sat on the floor in a despondent mood, at times smoking his pipe; and saying to me, " Be kind to me, be kind to me, give me a Wind that we may live." I told him the Good Spirit alone could cause the wind to blow, and my French Canadians were as foolish as the poor Indian; saying to one another, it would be a good thing, and well done, if he got a wind; we should get meat to eat. The night was very fine and clear, I passed most of it observing the Moon and Stars as usual; the small meteors were very numerous, which indicated a Gale of Wind; the morning rose fine, and before the appearance of the Sun, tho' calm with us, the tops of the tall Pines were waving, all foretelling a heavy gale, which usually follows a long calm; all this was plain to every one; Very early Tapahpahtum said; Be kind and give me a strong wind; vexed with him, I told him to go, and take care that the trees did not fall upon him; he shouted " I have got it "; sprang from the floor, snatched his gun, whipt on his Snow

Shoes, and dashed away at five miles an hour; the gale from
North East came on as usual with snow and high drift, and
lasted three days; for the two first days we could not visit
the nets, which sometimes happens; the third day the drift
ceased, but the nets had been too long in the water without
being washed, and we had to take them up. On this gale of
wind, a common occurence, I learnt my men were more
strangely foolish than the Indians; something better than
two months after this gale, I sent three of the men with
letters to an other trading house and to bring some articles
I wanted; here these men related how I had raised a storm
of wind for the Indian, but had made it so strong that for
two days they got no fish from the nets, adding, they thought
I would take better care another time. In these distant
solitudes, Men's minds seem to partake of the wildness of
the country they live in. Four days after Tapahpahtum
with one of his women came, he had killed three Moose Deer,
of which he gave us one, for which I paid him; He was now
in his calm senses: and I reasoned with him on the folly of
looking to any one, to get what the Good Spirit alone could
give, and that it made us all liable to his anger. He said I
believe it, I know it, I spent the autumn and the early part
of the winter working on Beaver Houses, it is hard work,
and only gives meat while we are working; When the Snow
was well on the ground I left off to hunt Moose Deer, but
the winds were weak, and unsteady; my women had to
snare hares, my little boy, with his Bow killed a few grouse,
which kept us alive until the long Calm came. I waited a
little, then in the evening I took my Rattle and tambour
and sung to the Great Spirit and the Manito of the Winds;
the next morning I did the same, and took out of my medicine
bag, sweet smelling herbs and laid them on a small fire to
the Manito. I smoked and sung to him for a wind, but he
shut his ears and would not listen to me: for three days I
did the same; but he kept his ears shut. I became afraid

that he was angry with me; I left my tent and came to you, my head was not right; what you gave me was a relief for my women and children, I again sung, but the wind did not blow, he would not hear me, my heart was sore, and I came to you, in hopes that you had power over the winds; for we all believe the Great Spirit speaks to you in the night, when you are looking at the Moon and Stars, and tells you of what we know nothing. It seems a natural weakness of the human mind when in distress, to hope from others, equally helpless, when we have lost confidence in ourselves. Wiskahoo was naturally a cheerful, good natured, careless man, but hard times had changed him. He was a good Beaver worker and trapper, but an indifferent Moose Hunter, now and then killed one by chance, he had been twice so reduced by hunger, as to be twice on the point of eating one of his children to save the others, when he was fortunately found and relieved by the other Natives; these sufferings had, at times, unhinged his mind, and made him dread being alone, he had for about a month, been working Beaver, and had now joined Tapap- pahtum; and their Tents were together; he came to trade, and brought some meat the other had sent. It is usual when the Natives come to trade to give them a pint of grog; a liquor which I always used very sparingly; it was a bad custom, but could not be broken off: Wiskahoo as soon as he got it, and while drinking of it, used to say in a thoughtful mood " Nee weet to go " " I must be a Man eater." This word seemed to imply " I am possessed of an evil spirit to eat human flesh "; " Wee tee go " is the evil Spirit, that devours humankind. When he had said this a few times, one of the Men used to tie him slightly, and he soon became quiet; these sad thoughts at times came upon him, from the dreadful distress he had suffered; and at times took him in his tent, when he always allowed himself to be tied during this sad mood, which did not last long.

Three years afterwards this sad mood came upon him so

often, that the Natives got alarmed. They shot him, and burnt his body to ashes, to prevent his ghost remaining in this world. Apistawahshish (the Dwarf) was of low stature, but strongly made and very active, a good Beaver worker, and a second rate hunter of Moose deer; he was careful and industrious; When the leaves of the trees had fallen, and winter was coming on, he had parted from the others to work Beaver; at first he was successful; but the third house he attacked, the beaver had worked many stones into it, [so] that he broke his ice chissel and blunted one of his axes useless; the other was all they had to cut fire wood; the edges of the Lakes were frozen over and canoes could not be used. Distressing times came, and they were reduced to use as food the youngest child to save the others. They were so weak they could barely get a little wood for the fire; sitting in sorrow and despair looking at the child next to lose it's life, a Rein Deer came and stood a few yards from the tent door; he shot it and [it] became the means of saving them, and recovering their strength; and for the winter he was a fortunate hunter. Both himself, his family, and the Natives believed that this Deer was sent by the Manito in pity to himself and family; he kept the skin, which I saw.

The Indians did not hold him culpable, they felt they were all liable to the same sad affliction; and the Manito sending him a Deer, showed a mark of favor. As the strong affections of an Indian is centered in his children, for they may be said to be all he has to depend upon, they believe the dreadful distressed state of mind which necessity forces on them to take the life of one of their children to preserve the others, leaves such sad indelible impressions that the parents are never again the same [as] they were before, and are liable to aberrations of mind. It is only on this Region and the Lakes westward to near the great plains, where there are Horses, that the Natives are subject to this distress of hunger, their Dogs are starved and do them very little good. If the country contained but half the Deer and other animals some writers speak of, the Natives would not suffer as they do. Notwithstanding the hardships the Natives sometimes suffer, they are strongly attached to the country of Rivers, Lakes, and Forests.

CHAPTER VII

CHEPAWYANS

Dinnae or Chepawyans—Origin of Name—Character—Hard lot of Women—Religion—Tradition as to Creation of Mankind—Morals—Migration.

HITHERTO my remarks have been on that portion of the great Stoney Region hunted on by the Nahathaway Indians; the northern portion of this region, interior and north of Hudson's Bay to far westward is hunted upon, and claimed by a distinct race of Indians, whom, however dispersed, claim their origen and country to be, from Churchill River[1] at it's sortie into the sea; and since the building of the Stone Fort, they call the place by the name of the Stone House.[2] Their Native name, by which they distinguish themselves, is "Dinnae," to some hunting on a particular tract of country, an adjective is added. " Tza Dinnae ": Beaver Dinnae. Their southern neighbours, the Nahathaway's call them " Chepawyans " (pointed skins), from the form in which they dry the Beaver skins. By the Hudson's Bay traders [they are called] " Northern Indians."

---

[1] The Churchill river is known to the Chipewyan Indians as the Tzan-dézé or Metal river, possibly on account of the quantity of iron and copper derived by them from a ship called *Enhiorningen*, which was left there by Jens Munck, after he had wintered in the harbour in the winter of 1619–20, when all but two of his men died of scurvy.

[2] Fort Prince of Wales. For an account of this " Stone Fort," see Samuel Hearne, *A Journey from Prince of Wales's Fort in Hudson's Bay to the Northern Ocean*, edited by J. B. Tyrrell, pp. 21–2.

Their physiognomy is of an oval form, the skull convex, the chin pointed, the cheek bones raised, the nose prominent and sharp, the eyes black and small, forehead high, mouth and teeth good, hair black, long and lank, and of the men coarse. The countenance, though not handsome is manly; [they are] tall in stature, of spare make, but capable of great fatigue; they are a peaceable people, abhoring blood shed; The Nahathaways look on them with a sort of contempt, being themselves too much inclined to war, they consider the Hunter to be naturally a Warrior; The Dinnae themselves give some occasion for this, in imitating what ceremonies they learn from them; yet treating their women like slaves, a conduct which the Nahathaways detest; When quarrelling the Dinnae never resort to Arms but settle the affair by wrestling, pulling hair, and twisting each other's necks. Although to their neighbours they are open to ridicule, yet not so to the white people, who encourage their peaceable habits, and themselves justly remark that a fine country, and plenty to eat, may encourage people to go to war on each other; but the fatigue they go through in hunting make them glad to rest at night. Although they often suffer hunger, yet the steady frugality they strictly observe, never allows distress to come on their families. Their country has very large, and many lesser Lakes. When the land is scarce of Deer, or long calms come on, they take to the Lakes to angle Trout or Pike at which they are very expert, and although they use our hooks; for large fish prefer their own, which are of bone, and a fish caught with their bone hook does not get loose, as sometimes happens to our hooks : Whether fish or meat, whatever is not required is carefully put by for next meal. They carefully collect every article that can be of use to them; and when they remove, which they very often do, from place to place the women are very heavily loaded; the men with little else than their gun and their fishing tackle, even a girl of eight

years will have her share to carry; while the Boys have some
trifle, or only their Bows and Arrows. This hard usage
makes women scarce among them, and by the time a girl is
twelve years of age, she is given as a Wife to a man of twice
her age, for the young men cannot readily obtain a wife,
and on this account Polygamy is rare among them. The
hardships the Women suffer, induces them, too often to let
the female infants die, as soon as born; and [they] look upon
it as an act of kindness to them. And when any of us spoke
to a woman who had thus acted; the common answer was:
"She wished her mother had done the same to herself."
Upon reasoning with the Men, on the severe laborious life of
the women, and the early deaths it occasioned; and that it
was a disgrace to them; and how very different the Nahathaways treated their women; they always intimated, they
were an inferior order of mankind, made for the use of the
Men; the Nahathaways were a different people from, and
they were not guided by, them; and I found they were too
often regarded as the property of the strongest Man; until
they have one or more children; I have been alone with them
for months, and always found them a kind good people, but
their treatment of the Women always made me regard them
as an unmanly race of Men. Whether in distress, or in
plenty, or in whatever state they may be I never saw any
act of a religious tendency; they make no feasts, have no
dances, nor thanksgivings; they appear to think every thing
depends on their own abilities and industry, and have no
belief in the greater part of the religious opinions of the
Nahathaways; from the regular migrations of the water fowl
and the rein deer, they infer something of a Manito takes
care of them, but neither does, nor can, prevent their killing
them; they believe in a future state, and that it is much the
same as in this life; they appear to have no high ideas of it,
but somewhat better than the present; they dread death as
a great evil, but meet it with calmness and fortitude; the

wife of the deceased must mourn his loss for a year, her hair
which is cut off and placed beside him when dead, is now
allowed to grow, and she may become a Wife, but there is
no restraint on the Men at the death of their wives; they
take a wife as soon as they can, and seldom allow a Widow
woman to pass a year of mourning: They do not bury their
dead, but leave them to be devoured; this they might easily
prevent by covering them with wood, or stones: which is
sometimes done, and sometimes the dead is placed on a
scaffold, but these instances are very rare; Some of them
have an ancient tradition that a Great Spirit descended on a
rock, took a Dog, tore it to small pieces and scattered it, that
these pieces each become a Man, or a Woman, and that these
Men and Women are their original parents, from whom they
have all come; and thus the Dog is their common origin;
On this account they have very few dogs; frequently several
tents have not a Dog among them; and they abhor the
Dog Feasts of the Nahathaway's and of the French Canadians;
the latter regard a fat dog as a luxury, equal to a fat pig:
Their morals are as good as can be expected, they exact
chastity from their wives and seem to practise it themselves;
they are strictly honest; and detest a thief; and are as charit-
able and humane to those in want, as circumstances will allow
them. When the martial Tribes [1] by right of conquest over
the Snake Indians, took possession of the Great Plains the
Nahathaways occupied the lands thus left; and from the
rigorous clime of sixty one degrees north, went southward to
fifty six degrees north; the Dinnae, or Chepawyans, in like

---

[1] The martial tribes here spoken of are probably the Blackfeet, Bloods,
and Piegan, though I do not know of any evidence to show that they ever
occupied the wooded country north of the Saskatchewan river as here
indicated by Thompson. The Chipewyans, however, have continued to
move southward even in historic times, for about the time Thompson
first reached Churchill they occupied the Barren Lands west of Hudson
Bay as far north as Chesterfield Inlet, while at the present time they have
retired southward to the edge of the woods, and their old haunts along the
Kazan river are occupied by Eskimo.

manner occupied the country down to the last named Latitude, and westward by the Peace River to the Rocky Mountains ; and have thus quietly extended themselves from the arctic regions to their present boundary, and will continue to press to the southward as far as the Nahathaways will permit.

CHAPTER VIII

TRIP TO LAKE ATHABASCA

Receive permission to explore the unknown country to the North-westward—Fairford House—Want of Men—Two Chepa-wyan Companions—The start—Rein Deer River—Rein Deer Lake—Trading Post—Manito Lake—Two Outlets—Character of Shores of Manito Lake—Black River—Hatchet Lake—Manito Falls—Second Black Falls—Atha-basca Lake—Hardships of the trip—Wreck—Destitute condition—Safe at last—Reach Fairford House.

HAVING now given a sketch of the people among whom I am about to travel; I have to return back a few years from my wintering place in Reed Lake, where I brought together that part of the Great Stony Region, and now enter on the northern part of this Region hunted on by the Natives I have described.

Having requested permission of Mr Joseph Colen, the Resident at York Factory, to explore the country north westward from the junction of the Rein Deer's River with the Missinippe (Great Waters) to the east end of the Atha-basca Lake a country then wholly unknown,[1] I proceeded to Fairford House,[2] for we must give titles to our Log Huts,

---

[1] The journey here described had a larger significance than that here given to it by Thompson, for it was part of a scheme which he had been urging on the Hudson's Bay Company for some years to push westward and participate with the North-West Company in the trade of the Mac-kenzie river valley. See Introduction, pp. xxxiv.-xxxix.

[2] Fairford House was situated on the bank of the Churchill (or Mis-sinipi) river, a mile below the mouth of Reindeer (or Deer) river, in latitude 53° 33′ 28″ N., longitude 103° 12′ W. It was built by Malcolm Ross in 1795, but seems to have been abandoned in 1796 in favour of

where Mʳ Malcolm Ross[1] had wintered, but not a single man
could be spared from the trade in furrs to accompany me,
and with great difficulty the Hudson's Bay Company then
procured Men to keep up the few interior Trading Houses
they then had; for the War which raged between England
and France drained the Orkney Islands of all the Men, that
were fit for the Navy, or the Army; and only those refused
were obtained for the furr trade: There is always a Canoe
with three steady men and a native woman waiting the
arrival of the annual Ship from England to carry the Letters
and Instructions of the Company to the interior country
trading houses; but very few men came out with her for the
trade, and those few were only five feet five inches and under;
a Mʳ James Spence was in charge of the Canoe, and his Indian

Bedford House on the west side of Reindeer lake. It was doubtless
named after the village of Fairford in Gloucestershire, though on whose
account is not known.

[1] Malcolm Ross was a Scotsman who had entered the service of the
Hudson's Bay Company, and had been among those first sent inland to
the Saskatchewan valley. After the Hudson's Bay Company had been
sending parties and supplies inland from York Factory for a number of
years it became anxious to learn if a route could be opened up from
Churchill directly up the Churchill river to its central trading post at
Cumberland House, and in 1786 Ross was sent from Churchill to try
to discover such a route. He succeeded in accomplishing the journey,
probably by the Little Churchill river, Split lake, and Grass river, but
reported that it was an exceedingly difficult one of no commercial value.
The following year he returned to York, and, when a couple of years later
the Company wished to send Philip Turnor westward as far as Lake
Athabaska to make a survey of that lake and determine its position,
Ross was sent with him to look after his supplies. From that time onward Ross's great object appears to have been to induce the Hudson's
Bay Company to go into the Athabaska country and establish trading
posts there, but in this he was not successful. In 1798 he visited England,
probably with the object of urging on the directors of the Company
more active measures for securing the Athabaska trade, and the following
year he returned to the western country, but shortly after his arrival in
Hudson Bay he died at Churchill. It was not until three years after his
death, in 1802, that Peter Fidler was able to establish the first trading
post of the Hudson's Bay Company on Lake Athabaska, on the site of the
present Fort Chipewyan.

wife looking steadily at the Men, and then at her husband;
at length said, James have you not always told me, that the
people in your country are as numerous as the leaves on the
trees, how can you speak such a falsehood, do not we all see
plainly that the very last of them is come, if there were any
more would these dwarfs have come here. This appeared a
home truth, and James Spence had to be silent. Finding
that I could have no white man to accompany me somewhat
damped my ardor, but my curiosity to see unknown countries
prevailed, and a few Chepawyans happening to be there;
and had traded their few furrs I engaged two young men of
them to accompany me; both of them had hunted for two
winters over the country we were to explore, but had never
been on the Rivers and Lakes in summer. Their only practice
in canoes had been, on a calm day to watch for the Deer
taking refuge in the Lakes from the flies, and for Otters and
Fowls, which gave them no experience of the currents and
rapids of Rivers; yet such as they were, I was obliged to
take them; they were both unmarried young men; One of
them named Kozdaw,[1] was of a powerful, active, make; gay,
thoughtless, and ready for every kind of service: would
climb the trees, and brave the Eagles in their nests: yet
under all this wildness was a kind and faithful heart. The
other from his hard name, which I could not pronounce, I
named Paddy, he was of a slender form, thoughtful, of a mild
disposition; As nothing whatever was ready for us, we had
to go into the Forests for all the materials to make a Canoe;
of seventeen feet in length by thirty inches on the middle bar.

This House though well situated for trade; had but a
poor fishery with three Nets, each of fifty fathoms in length,
we could barely maintain ourselves, the fish caught were
White Fish, Pike and Carp, with a few Pickerel, none of

---

[1] When I surveyed the Black river in the summer of 1892, I gave the
name of this Indian companion of Thompson to one of the smaller lakes
on the stream.

them very good. Fairford House is in Latitude 55°. 33'. 28"
North, and Longitude 103°. 9'. 52" West of Greenwich, on
the banks of the Missinippe (Great Waters)[1] so called from
the spreading of it's waters. It's southern head is the Beaver
River from the Beaver Lake not far from the east foot of the
Mountains, which, on entering the chain of Lakes, and the
land of Rocks, spreads into very irregular forms of Lakes,
which at distances are crossed by Dams of rock, and by
channels falls into the same rude Lakes, to within one hundred
miles of Churchill Factory, having for this last distance, the
regular form of a River with many Rapids and Falls to within
about ten miles of the sea where it meets the tide waters.
The whole of the above distance from the valley of the chain
of Lakes to the sea, is a poor country for Deer and the furr
bearing animals ; and also for fish ; There are some very
good fisheries, but they are in the deep Lakes of this Region
wholly independent of the Missinippe, though the Streams
from them are discharged into it.

Early on the tenth day of June 1796 we were ready, our
outfit consisted of one fowling gun ; forty balls, five pounds of
shot, three flints and five pounds of powder, one Net of
thirty fathoms ; one small Axe, a small Tent of grey cotton ;
with a few trifles to trade provisions, as beads, brass rings
and awls, of which we had little hopes ; our chief dependence
next to good Providence, was on our Net and Gun.

The sortie of the Rein Deer's River ;[2] which is the great

[1] Thompson constantly used the name Missinipi for the river now
known throughout most of its length as the Churchill, though the longest
of its upper branches is still known as Beaver river. In 1798 he surveyed
this river to its source near Lake La Biche (or Red Deer lake), where he
built a trading post and spent the winter.

[2] Reindeer river is a beautiful clear stream draining the waters of
Reindeer lake southward into the Churchill river. At the confluence
the waters of the two streams are very distinct, that of Reindeer
river being beautifully clear and white in contrast to the dark brownish
water of the Churchill river. The river has a length of seventy miles,
in which distance it is obstructed by four rapids over rocky barriers of
granite.

northern branch of Churchill River is about one mile above
Fairford House; and up this stream we proceeded in a north
direction for sixty four miles to the Rein Deer's Lake;
Lat^{de} 56.20.22 Long^{de} 103.18.47. The River is a fine deep
stream, of about three hundred yards in width, having five
falls and the same number of Carrying Places; the Falls
have a descent of four to fourteen feet, with only one rapid.
It's current is moderate from one to two miles p^r hour, and
forms several small Lakes. The banks are of sloping high
rocks, with several sandy bays; the woods of small Birch,
Aspin, and Pines, growing on the rocks with very little soil;
in many places none whatever: the Trees supported each
other by the roots being interlaced in the same manner as
the Trees are supported on the frozen lands of Hudson's
Bay which never thaw; and both are kept moist in summer by
being covered with wet moss.

The Natives are frequently very careless in putting out
the fires they make, and a high wind kindles it among the
Pines always ready to catch fire; and [they] burn until stopped
by some large swamp or lake; which makes many miles of
the country appear very unsightly, and destroys many animals
and birds especially the grouse, who do not appear to know
how to save themselves, but all this devastation is nothing
to the Indian, his country is large.

We proceeded along the west side of the Lake, in a direction of due North, for one hundred and eight miles to a Point
of tolerable good Pines, the best we had seen, and on which,
late in Autumn we built a trading House. Latitude 57.23.N.
Longitude 102.59 W.

The whole distance we have passed has a rocky barren
appearance; the woods small and stunted; in several places
the fire had passed. In the above distance the Paint River
falls in, a considerable stream from the westward; and also
a few Brooks. The water is clear and deep, and the Lake
is studded with Islands of rock, and dwarf Pines cover them.

We proceeded up the Rivulet which we found shoal, with many rapids, and soon led us to Ponds and Brooks, with several Carrying Places, which connected them together for fifty miles, the last of which placed us on the banks of the Manito Lake. Latitude 57.47.38 N. Longitude 103.17.12 W. The whole of this route can be passed in the open season only by small Canoes ; the country as usual poor and rocky ; Hitherto we had not met with a single Native, and our Gun and Net gave us but short allowance ; This Route is practised by the Natives to avoid the great length of the Rein Deer's and Manito Lakes, and the crossing of the great Bays of these Lakes, which would be dangerous to their small Canoes. This great Lake is called Manito [1] (supernatural) from it's sending out two Rivers, each in a different direction ; from it's east side a bold Stream runs southward and enters the Rein Deers Lake on it's east side ; and from the west side of the Manito Lake, it sends out the Black River, which runs westward into the east end of the Athabasca Lake ; which is perhaps without a parallel in the world. Some have argued that such a Lake must soon be drained of its water ; they forget that it is the quantity of water that runs off, that drains a Lake ; and were the two Rivers that now flow in opposite directions made to be one River in a single direction, the effect on the Lake would be the same Add to this, the head of a River flowing out of a Lake is a kind of a Dam, and can only operate on the Lake in proportion to the depth to the bottom ; which in general is several hundred feet

---

[1] On the present maps of Canada it is Wollaston lake. Thompson is quite correct in his statement that this lake has two outlets, which are of about equal size, one of which flows to the Mackenzie river and the other to the Churchill. The former he descended to Lake Athabaska, while the latter I surveyed in part in 1894 and named the Cochrane river. The lake has an area of 900 square miles, and its water, like that of Reindeer lake, is very clear and pure, as there is no soluble rock or mud on its shores. The pines here spoken of, and in fact throughout this narrative, are spruce, either black or white. Throughout all the northern country spruce trees are still spoken of as pines.

below this bottom of the head of the River; and were the River to drain the Lake to this level, the River would cease to flow but the Lake would still contain a great body of water.

The last fifty miles had been over a low rocky, swampy country, and tormented with myriads of Musketoes; we were now on the banks of the Manito Lake, all around which, as far as the eye could see, were bold shores, the land rising several hundred feet in bold swells, all crowned with Forests of Pines; in the Lake were several fine Isles of a rude conical form, equally well clothed with Woods. I was highly pleased with this grand scenery; but soon found the apparent fine forests to be an illusion, they were only dwarf Pines growing on the rocks; and held together by their roots being twisted with each other. On our route, seeing a fine Isle, which appeared a perfect cone of about sixty feet in height, apparently remarkably well wooded to the very top of the cone; I went to it, my companions saying it was lost time; on landing, we walked through the apparent fine forest, with our heads clear above all the trees, the tallest only came to our chins; While we were thus amusing ourselves, the Wind arose and detained us until near sunset. To while away the time, we amused ourselves with undoing the roots of these shrub Pines for about twenty feet on each side; when the whole slid down the steep rock into the Lake, making a floating Isle of an area of four hundred feet; and so well the fibres of the roots were bound together, that when it came to where the waves were running high, it held together, not a piece separated and thus [it] drifted out of our sight. We set loose a second islet of about the same area; then a third, and a fourth islet, all floated away in the same manner: On the Isle, the roots of these small pines were covered with a compact moss of a yellow color, about two inches thick.

The mould on the rock under these pines, was very black and rich, but so scant, that had the area of four hundred feet been clean swept, it would not have filled a bushel measure.

perhaps the produce of centuries. This Isle was a steep cone, the sixteen hundred square feet we uncovered, showed the rock to be as smooth as a file, and no where rougher than a rasp; and had it been bare it would have been difficult of ascent; it was about two miles from other land; then how came these pines to grow upon it; they bare no cones, nor seeds and no birds feed on them; These wild northern countries produce questions, difficult to answer.

After coasting the west side of this Lake for Eighty miles we put up on the evening of the twenty third of June at the head of the Black River; which flows out of this Lake and finally discharges itself into the east end of the Athabasca Lake, which I found to be in Latitude 50°. 27'. 55" North; and in Longitude 103°. 27'. 1" West of Greenwich Variation 15° East. What I afterwards learned of the Indians on the geography of the Manito Lake confirmed my opinions of it; By their information this Lake is of very great extent; the eighty miles we coasted they counted as nothing; they say that none of them has seen its northern extent, and of the east side, except the southern part. The deep, long rolling waves in a gale of wind, equal to any I have seen in Lake Superior, showed a very deep Lake and that the roll of the waves came from a great distance.

It was always my intention to have fully surveyed this and the Rein Deer's Lake, but the sad misfortune which happened in the lower part of the Black River, made me thankfull to save our lives. That these countries are unknown, even to the natives, can excite no surprise; their canoes are small and when loaded with their Wives, Children, and Baggage, are only fit for calm water, which is seldom seen on these Lakes; The east side of these two Lakes, have a range of full six hundred miles, on which there are no Woods,[1]

---

[1] This would appear to refer to the Barren Grounds, some distance to the north of Reindeer and Manitou lakes, rather than the country to the east of them, for this latter country is within the forest area, and

all is Rock and Moss; on these barren lands, in the open season the Rein Deer are numerous; they have food in abundance, and the constant cold nights puts down the flies.

The Natives, when they hunt on the North East parts of the Rein Deer's Lake, cannot stay long; the Moss, when dry, makes a tolerable fire; but in wet weather, which often happens, it holds the rain like a sponge, and cannot be made to burn; this want of fire often obliges them to eat the meat raw, and also the fish; the latter I have seen them by choice; especially the pike, and a Trout is no sooner caught than the eyes are scooped out and swallowed whole, as most delicious morsels.

Whatever Deer they may kill, they cannot dry the meat; and as soon as they have eaten plentifully and procured as many skins as they can carry, they leave these lands of Moss, for those of Woods where they can have a comfortable fire, and get poles of pine wood to pitch their Tents for shelter.

The Natives told me, when enquiring of the country to the eastward of the Manito Lake; that two of them had been two day's journey direct eastward of the Lake, and saw nothing of woods, but everywhere rock and moss, with small Lakes, in which the Ducks were taking care of their young, and no other animal than a few herds of Rein Deer, and Musk Oxen;[1] and it seems such is all the country between these great Lakes and Churchill River Factory and far to the northward. The Rein Deer's Lake[2] contains an area of 18,400

though the trees are mostly small, they are there in greater or less abundance. The east shore of Reindeer lake, along which I travelled in 1894, was found to be all fairly well wooded.

[1] *Ovibos moschatus* (Zimmerman). [E. A. P.]

[2] Reindeer lake is one of the most picturesque of the many large lakes of northern Canada, with its shores of low rounded hills of granite, and its many rocky islands rising out of clear green water. It has an area of 2,400 square miles, a greatest length of 140 miles, and a greatest width of 35 miles, but on account of the irregularity of its shore line, and the great number of islands in it, no large part of the lake can be seen from any one place. The water is remarkably pure, an analysis made some years ago showing it to be one of the purest lake waters in the world.

square miles : and the Manito Lake has an area of not less than about 30,000 square miles : From the head of the Black River to Churchill Factory is 339 statute miles, including the width of the Manito Lake, which may be reckoned at eighty miles, or more. It is a pity the Hudsons Bay Company do not have these countries explored; by their charter they hold these extensive countries to the exclusion of all other persons.

By civilised men, especially those of the United States, who have a mortal antipathy to the North American Indian; or, as he is now called the, " Red Man " ; it is confidently predicted, that the Red Man, must soon cease to exist, and give place to the White Man ; this is true of all the lands formerly possessed by the Red Man, that the White Man has thought it worth his while to seize by fraud or force; but the Stony Region is an immense extent of country, on which the White Man cannot live ; except by hunting, which he will not submit to. Here then is an immense tract of country which the Supreme Being, the Lord of the whole Earth, has given to the Deer, and other wild animals ; and to the Red Man forever, here, as his fathers of many centuries past have done, he may roam, free as the wind ; but this wandering life, and the poverty of the country, prevents the labors of the Missionary to teach them the sacred truths of Christianity.

On the 25th day of June we descended the Black River[1]

---

[1] Black or Stone river flows westward from Wollaston lake into the east end of Lake Athabaska, at first through quiet pools, then over rocky granite ridges, and afterwards over a bed of rough boulders and pebbles of sandstone, where the water sometimes contracts into a narrow swift stream and then spreads out and almost loses itself among the stones. Such is its character until it flows into Black lake, but below Black lake it tumbles in two wild cascades with a combined height of 300 feet to the level of Lake Athabaska. Past these two falls the Indians from time immemorial have had well beaten paths or portages, respectively two and three and a half miles in length. As yet comparatively few white men have travelled this river, the list as far as known being as follows : David Thompson (1796) ; Peter Fidler (1807 ?) ; A. S. Cochrane (1881) ; J. B. Tyrrell (1892 and 1893).

for nine miles to the Hatchet Lake.[1]   The River flows between
two hills, in a valley with coarse grass on each side ; it is about
twenty yards in width, and five feet in depth, and moderate
current.   The Hatchet Lake, has an area of about three
hundred square miles, the banks rise to about three hundred
feet apparently well wooded with Pines, but very few are
above twenty feet in height, and full of branches.   The whole
is a wretched country of solitude, which is broken only by
the large Gull and the Loons.   The first twelve miles of the
River have several strong rapids and two carrying places, one
of 204, the other of 298 yards.   By observations the Latitude was 58°.44'.35" Longitude 103°.56'.28" West near
the north end of the Black Lake,[2] which is a small Lake.

The River had now increased it's water by the addition
of the Porcupine and Trout Rivers, and several Brooks ; it
had also a greater descent ; In it's course of One hundred
and fifty three miles from the above place of observation in
the Black Lake, it meets with, and forms, many small Lakes ;
and collects their waters to form a Stream of about one, to
two, hundred yards in width : it's bottom is sand and pebbles,
or rude stones and small rocks, smoothed by the water ; on
a bed of Limestone, which is the rock of the country ; its
course is sinuous, from the many hills it meets, and runs
round in it's passage ; it's current is strong, with many
rapids, some of them one mile in length : it has four falls.
Three of these are about half way down the River ; the fourth
fall is the end of a series of rapids, cutting through a high
hill ; at length the banks become perpendicular, and the
river falls eight feet, the carrying place is six hundred yards
in length.   For half a mile further the current is very swift ;
it is then for one hundred and eighteen yards, compressed in

[1] Hatchet lake, probably so called by Thompson himself, is a small
lake on the Black river with an area of about 60 square miles.
[2] This is a very small expansion of the Stone or Black river, which is
now known as Kosdaw lake.

a narrow channel of rock of only twelve yards in width. At the end of this channel a bold perpendicular sided point of limestone rock projects at right angles to the course of the river, against which the rapid current rushes and appears driven back with such force that the whole river seems as if turned up from it's bottom. It boils, foams and every drop is white; part of the water is driven down a precipice of twenty feet descent; the greater part rushes through the point of rock and disappears for two hundred yards; then issues out in boiling whirlpools. The dashing of the water against the rocks, the deep roar of the torrent, the hollow sound of the fall, with the surrounding high, dark frowning hills form a scenery grand and awful, and it is well named the Manito Fall. While the Nahathaways possessed the country, they made offerings to it, and thought it the residence of a Manito; they have retired to milder climates; and the Chepawyans have taken their place who make no offerings to anything; but my companions were so awe struck, that the one gave a ring, and the other a bit of tobacco. They had heard of this Fall, but never saw it before.

The second Black Lake [1] is a fine sheet of water it's length about thirty miles in a west direction, it's breadth one to six miles; in the east end there are five small isles and a large Island near the north shore. The north side of the Lake is a high hill, in some places abrupt cliffs of rock; the south side

---

[1] This lake, which is still known as Black lake, lies at the junction of the Stone river from the east, the Cree river from the south, and the Chipman river from the north. It has a greatest length of 41 miles, a greatest width of 9 miles, a total area of 200 square miles, and an elevation of 1000 feet above the sea. Its name seems to have been given to it by David Thompson, probably on account of the dark hills of Norite which form its north-western shore. By the Chipewyan Indians of Lake Athabaska it is called Dess-da-tara-tua, or, "The Mouths of Three Rivers Lake," alluding to the mouths of Cree, Stone, and Chipman rivers, which empty into it. Its northern shore is steep and rocky, being composed of granite or similar rocks, while its southern shore is low and sandy, and a great sand plain stretches away to the south of it.

is more pleasing, it's fine sandy beaches, the banks with small
Aspins and Birch in full leaf; the ground firm and dry,
covered with Bear's Berries,[1] the leaf of which is mixed with
tobacco for smoking, the interior rising by easy ascents, and
apparently well wooded formed a pleasing landscape to us,
who had so long been accustomed to rude scenery; it is the
only place which had an appearance of being fit for cultivation; but it was appearance only; the woods were small,
even the Pines rarely rose to the height of twenty feet; and
the soil was too sandy. The area of this Lake may be about
one hundred and twenty miles. This Lake appears to be the
principal haunts of the species of Deer which I have already
described; and which I believe to be yet a nondescript.

The Nahathaways, who pay great attention to distinguish
every species of Beast and Bird from each, do not class them
with the Rein Deer, and call them Mahthe Moosewah.[2] (the
Ugly Moose). This is the only Lake in which I have seen
them, and the Natives say they are not numerous, and are
confined to this Lake and its environs; A civilized man may
never travel this way again; there is nothing to tempt him;
a rude barren country that has neither provisions nor furrs,
and there are no woods of which he could build a warm hut;
and at best his fuel, of which a large quantity is required,
could be only of small poles, which would burn away, almost
as fast as he could cut them. In the winter the Natives do
not frequent these countries but hunt to the westward.

On the North side, the Black River rushes through a
low mountain in a long cataract, on the south side is a carrying
place of 5560 yards of open woods, the ground level and sandy.
from hence we went three miles to a heavy Fall in several
precipices of full forty feet. The carrying place is one mile
in length, the banks high and steep, and the path bad from
much fallen wood, and rocky ground, at the end of which

---

[1] *Arctostaphylos uva-ursi* (Linn.). [E. A. P.]
[2] Probably a large form of Woodland Caribou. See note, p. 102.

K

we had to descend a high steep bank of loose earth and gravel : one fourth of a mile lower was another fall, and carrying place of half a mile, we then proceeded eight miles to a long heavy rapid, six miles farther the Black River enters the east end of the Athabasca Lake,[1] the end of our journey in Latitude 50°. 16′. 22″ N. Longitude 105°. 26′ West on the 2nd of July. This great Lake had been surveyed by Mr Philip Turnor[2] in 1791. He had marked and lopped a pine tree at which we passed the night. From the Manito to the

[1] Lake Athabaska is a long and comparatively narrow sheet of water, extending westward from the mouth of Black river to where the Athabaska-Mackenzie river drains the country towards the north. It lies in the bottom of a great valley excavated along the line of contact of the Archæan granites, etc., to the north, and the undisturbed Athabaska sandstone to the south. On its south side is a great sandy plain, rising at its east end to a height of 500 feet above the lake, and gradually sloping westward towards the Athabaska-Mackenzie valley. It has a greatest length of 195 miles, a greatest width of 35 miles, a shore line of 425 miles, an area of 2,850 square miles, and an altitude of 690 feet above the sea.

[2] Comparatively little is as yet known of Philip Turnor. The first published reference to him that I can find is where Henry Roberts, in giving the authorities for his map (Cook's *Third Voyage*, Introduction, p. lxxi), refers to " the discoveries from York to Cumberland and Hudson House (this last is the most western settlement belonging to the Company), extending to Lake Winnipeg, from the draft of Mr. Philip Turner, corrected by astronomical observations." " The Albany and Moose Rivers to Gloucester House and to Lake Abbitibbe and Superior," says Roberts, " are also drawn from a map of Mr. Turner's, adjusted by observations for the longitudes." From Roberts's map, it appears that Turnor had gone inland from York Factory by the Nelson and Grass rivers, and had returned by Lake Winnipeg and the Hayes river route, or vice versa, for these are the only routes indicated. Neither the Churchill river nor the Nelson river between Split lake and Lake Winnipeg is shown on this map. These journeys inland were probably first made in company with Samuel Hearne, when, in 1774, he went from York Factory, and established Cumberland House on Pine Island lake, an enlargement of the Saskatchewan river.

In 1776, according to Thompson, Turnor ascended the Saskatchewan river from Cumberland House, and built Hudson House, on the North Saskatchewan river, a short distance above the present site of Prince Albert.

In 1779 Turnor was at Severn Factory, under Matthew Cocking ; and on September 28 of that year he left there in the sloop *Severn*, of which

Athabasca Lake, by the course of the Black River, and it's
Lakes is 162 miles, of varied country, but the further westward the better.   And the bold, high, sloping, woody hills of
the Athabasca Lake had something soft and pleasing.   This
journey was attended with much danger, toil and suffering,
for my guide knew nothing of the river, it's rapids and falls,
haveing merely crossed it in places in hunting.   We were
always naked below the belt, on account of the rapids, from
the rocks, shoals, and other obstructions we had to hand them,
that is, we were in the water, with our hands grasping the

John Turnor, his brother, was master, and arrived at Moose Factory on
October 21.
    On December 15, he left Moose for Albany, where he remained with
Thomas Hutchins throughout the winter and until the following September.
During this time he probably made his survey of the Albany river up to
Gloucester House on Washi lake, and probably also of the Kenogami and
Kabinakagami rivers, which form together a southern branch of the
Albany river, to "Capoonacaumistic" (Kabinakagami) lake and Lake
Superior.   On December 19, 1780, E. Jarvis, then in charge at Moose, sent
him back to Albany for some trading supplies.   He returned on January 12,
1781, having made on the way a survey of the intervening portion of the
coast of Hudson Bay.   On May 11, he set out on a trip by canoe up the
Moose and Missinaibi rivers, past Wappiscoggamy House (Old Brunswick
House) to Missinaibi lake and thence to Lake Superior at Michipicoten
Harbour.   On July 13, he was again back at Moose.
    In the summer of 1782 he made a survey of Lake Abitibi.   After
completing this survey, he was appointed to take charge of Brunswick
House on the Missinaibi river; and it is recorded that in 1783 he was
too ill to descend the river to Moose Factory, and was consequently unable
to attend the meeting of the Council there.   For several years after this,
he remained at Brunswick House; then he descended to Moose Factory,
where he assumed the position of second in charge.
    On September 9, 1787, he sailed for England in the sloop *Beaver*.   He
appears to have returned to York Factory in 1789, and from there to have
proceeded to Cumberland House.   In this journey he was accompanied
by Peter Fidler, then a young man of twenty years of age, while David
Thompson came down from the west to join them.   Turnor probably
spent the next two winters at Cumberland House.   During this time he
taught David Thompson and Peter Fidler the principles of geography
and the methods of surveying, and so laid the foundation of the knowledge of much of the geography of north-western America.
    In the spring of 1791, Turnor, accompanied by Malcolm Ross, left
Cumberland House for Lake Athabaska.   On June 1, at Buffalo lake,

canoe, and leading it down the rapids.   The bed of the river is of rough or round loose stones, and gravel, our bare feet became so sore that we descended several rough rapids at great risque of our lives.   On the 25ᵗʰ June we came to three tents of Chepawyan Indians of five families ; they were clean, comfortable, and everything in good order.   As usual, they received us in a hospitable manner, we put up for the night, and staid next day until past Noon to refresh ourselves and I obtained an observation for Latitude.   They were hunting and living on the large species of Deer, the Mahthe Moose, the meat was fat and good, they told me the habits of this species are utterly different from the common wandering Rein Deer, it's meat far superior, and in size nearly twice that of the common Deer, their eyesight much better, and the hunting of them almost as difficult as that of the Moose Deer, of which there are none in these parts.

On our return, about half way up the black river, we came to one of the falls, with a strong rapid both above and below it, we had a carrying place of 200 yards, we then attempted the strong current above the fall, they were to track the canoe up by a line, walking on shore, while I steered it, when they had proceeded about eighty yards, they came to a

he met Alexander Mackenzie going to England to study astronomy and geology, in order that he might be better prepared to make a proper survey of the route which he intended to explore from Lake Athabaska to the Pacific ocean.   Alexander Mackenzie gave Turnor a letter to his cousin, Roderick Mackenzie, at Lake Athabaska, asking him to show Turnor the fullest hospitality ; but had he appreciated fully the character of the man whom he had thus casually met in a canoe on the Churchill river, he might possibly have turned back, and studied under him.   Turnor made a survey of Lake Athabaska, and doubtless also of the route from Cumberland House to it.   The winter of 1791–92 he spent with Roderick Mackenzie at Fort Chipewyan ; and the following year he apparently returned to England.

As late as 1795 he was in communication with the directors of the Hudson's Bay Company in London, but that is the last that has been learned of him.

Whatever else may become known of him, Turnor's greatest distinction will always be that he was Thompson's tutor.

Birch Tree, growing at the edge of the water, and there stood and disputed between themselves on which side of the tree the tracking line should pass. I called to them to go on, they could not hear me for the noise of the fall, I then waved my hand for them to proceed, meanwhile the current was drifting me out, and having only one hand to guide the canoe, the Indians standing still, the canoe took a sheer across the current, to prevent the canoe upsetting, I waved my hand to them to let go the line and leave me to my fate, which they obeyed. I sprang to the bow of the canoe took out my clasp knife, cut the line from the canoe and put the knife in my pocket, by this time I was on the head of the fall, all I could do was to place the canoe to go down bow foremost, in an instant the canoe was precipitated down the fall (twelve feet), and buried under the waves, I was struck out of the canoe, and when I arose among the waves, the canoe came on me and buried [me] beneath it, to raise myself I struck my feet against the rough bottom and came up close to the canoe which I grasped, and being now on shoal water, I was able to conduct the canoe to the shore. My two companions ran down the beach to my assistance; nothing remained in the canoe but an axe, a small tent of grey cotton, and my gun: also a pewter basin. When the canoe was hauled on shore I had to lay down on the rocks, wounded, bruised, and exhausted by my exertions. The Indians went down along the shore, and in half an hours time returned with my box, lined with cork, containing my Sextant and a few instruments, and papers of the survey Maps &c. and our three paddles. We had no time to lose, my all was my shirt and a thin linen vest, my companions were in the same condition, we divided the small tent into three pieces to wrap round ourselves, as a defence against the flies in the day, and something to keep us from the cold at night, for the nights are always cold. On rising from my rocky bed, I perceived much blood at my left foot, on looking at it, I found the flesh of my foot, from the heel to near the toes torn away, this was done when I struck my feet against the rough bottom to rise above the waves of the fall of water. A bit of my share of the tent bound the wound, and thus barefooted I had to walk over the carrying places with their rude stones and banks. The Indians went to the woods and procured Gum of the Pines to repair the canoe, when they returned, the question was how to make a fire, we had neither steel, nor flint, I pointed to the gun from which we took the flint. I then produced my pocket knife with it's steel blade, if I had drawn a ghost out of my pocket it would not more have surprized them, they whispered to each other, how avaricious a white man must be, who rushing on death takes care of his little knife, this was often related to other Indians who all made the same remark. I said to them if I had not saved my little knife how could we make a fire, you fools go to the Birch Trees and get some touchwood, which they soon brought, a fire was made, we repaired our canoe, and carried all above the Fall and the rapid, they carried the canoe, my share was the gun, axe, and pewter basin; and Sextant Box. Late in the evening we made a fire and warmed ourselves. It was now our destitute condition stared us in the face, a long journey through a barren country, without provisions, or the means of obtaining any, almost naked, and suffering from the weather, all before us was very dark, but I had hopes that the Supreme Being through our great Redeemer to whom I made my short prayers morning and evening would find some way to preserve us; on the second day, in the afternoon we came on a small lake of the river, and in a grassy bay we saw two large Gulls hovering, this lead us to think they were taking care of their young, we went, and found three young gulls, which we put in the canoe, it may here be remarked, the Gull cannot dive, he is too light; these gulls gave us but a little meat. They had not four ounces of meat on them. It appeared to sharpen hunger.

The next day as we proceeded, I remembered an Eagles Nest on the banks of a small Lake before us. I enquired of my companions if the young eagles could fly, they said, they are now large but cannot yet fly, why do you enquire, I said, do you not remember the Eagle's Nest on a Lake before us, we shall be there by mid day, and get the young eagles for supper, accordingly we came on the Lake and went to the Eagles Nest, it was about sixteen feet from the ground, in the spreading branches of a Birch tree, the old ones were absent, but Kozdaw was barely at the nest before they arrived, and Paddy and myself, with shouts and pelting them with stones, with difficulty prevented the Eagles [1] from attacking Kozdaw, he soon threw the two young eagles down to us, they placed themselves on their backs, and with beak and claws fought for their lives, when apparently dead, Kozdaw incautiously laid hold of one of them, who immediately struck the claws of one foot deep into his arm above the wrist. So firm were the claws in his arm, I had to cut off the leg at the first joint above the claws, even then when we took out a claw, it closed in again, and we had to put bits of wood under each claw until we got the whole out.

We continued our journey to the evening, when as usual we put ashore, and made a fire, on opening the young eagles their insides appeared a mass of yellow fat, which we collected, and with the meat, divided into three equal portions : Paddy and myself eat only the inside fat, reserving the meat for next day, but we noticed Kozdaw, roasting the meat ; and oiling himself with the fat : in the night we were both awakened by a violent dysentry from the effects of the eagles fat, Kozdaw now told us that such was always the effects of the inside fat of the fishing Eagle (the bald headed) and also of most birds of prey that live on fish, Paddy bitterly reproached him for allowing us to eat it, we had to march all day in this state, in the evening, I filled the pewter basin

[1] *Haliæetus l. alascanus* Townsend. [E. A. P.]

with Labrador Tea,[1] and by means of hot stones made a strong infusion, drank it as hot as I could, which very much relieved me. Paddy did the same with like effect. We continued our voyage day after day, subsisting on berries, mostly the crowberry, which grows on the ground; and is not nutritious. To the sixteenth of July; both Paddy and myself were now like skeletons, the effects of hunger, and dysentry from cold nights, and so weak, that we thought it useless to go any further but die where we were. Kozdaw now burst out into tears, upon which we told him that he was yet strong, as he had not suffered from disease. He replied, if both of you die, I am sure to be killed, for everyone will believe that I have killed you both, the white men will revenge your death on me, and the Indians will do the same for him; I told him to get some thin white birch rind, and I would give him a writing, which he did, with charcoal I wrote a short account of our situation, which I gave him, upon which he said now I am safe. However we got into the canoe, and proceeded slowly, we were very weak, when thank God, in the afternoon we came to two tents of Chepawyans, who pitied our wretched condition; they gave us broth, but would allow us no meat until the next day: I procured some provisions, a flint and nine rounds of ammunition, and a pair of shoes for each of us on credit, to be paid for when they came to trade, also an old kettle; we now proceeded on our journey with thanks to God, and cheerful hearts. We killed two Swans, and without any accident on the 21st July arrived at Fairford House from whence we commenced our Journey. From this time to the 26th August, our time was spent in fishing and hunting, and with all our exertions we could barely maintain ourselves. During this time seventeen Loons got entangled in the Nets, a few were drowned, but the greater part alive: the Loon is at all times a fierce bird, and all these with beak and claws

[1]. *Ledum grœnlandicum* Œder. [E. A. P.]

fought to the last gasp. I have often taken one, out of the
Net, alive and placed it in the yard, and set the dogs on it,
but it fought so fiercely, screaming all the time, the dogs
would not attack it. They live wholly on fish, which gives
their flesh so strong a taste that few can eat them, especially
if they feed on trout, those that live on Carp, White Fish,
Pickerel and Pike have a better taste, but always bad; they
lay only two, or three eggs, which when boiled are of a yellowish
color, veined with black, and are not eatable. They are most
expert fishers, though seldom fat; and often gorge themselves, [so] that they cannot fly; but they are expert divers,
and have the power of sinking their body so that only their
head is above water, and at will maintaining it; their dive
is generally forty to fifty yards, and but a little below the
surface. On the land he is helpless, can neither walk, nor
fly, but [is] quite at home in the water.

On the 26ᵗʰ August Mʳ Malcolm Ross, with four small
Canoes loaded with Goods arrived from York Factory, each
carrying about six hundred pounds weight. We left this
house and proceeded up the Rein Deer's River to the Lake,
and to near the head of the Rivulet, where was a point of
tolerable Pines, near the middle of the Lake, on the west
bank, which by numerous observations I found to be in
Latitude 57°. 23′ N Longitude 102°. 58′. 35″ West of Greenwich Variation 15 degrees east. We builded Log Huts to pass
the winter, the chimneys were of mud and coarse grass, but
somehow did not carry off the smoke, and the Huts were
wretched with smoke, so that however bad the weather, we
were glad to leave the Huts.[1]

[1] The trading post built by Thompson on the west shore of Reindeer
lake was called by him Bedford House. In it he and Malcolm Ross
spent the winter of 1796–97, one of the coldest winters ever known in western Canada. The exact position of the post has not been determined,
but it cannot have been far from the island which I called Thompson
island in making a survey of the lake in 1892.

CHAPTER IX

WINTER AT REIN DEER LAKE

Build a Trading Post at Rein Deer Lake—Winter at Rein Deer Lake—Intense Cold—Formation of ice in 1795—Aurora—Aurora as souls of the dead—Fishing—Hunting—Moss — Insects — Chepawyan Travelling — Property in Women—History of a quarrel—Immortality—Angling—Origen of the Chepawyan archery.

OUR whole dependence for food was on our set nets, and what little Deer's meat the Chepawyans might bring us. The fishery during the short open season was somewhat successful for white fish, but they were not of the best quality; but when the Lake became frozen over as usual the Fish shifted their ground, and all we could procure was a bare subsistence. Winter soon set in, the most severe I ever experienced; I had for some years been accustomed to keep Meteorological Journals, my Thermometers were from Dolland one of Spirits, and one Quicksilver; each divided to forty two degrees below Zero, being seventy four degrees below freezing point; I had long suspected that in extreme cold, as the Spirits approached the bulb, it required two or three degrees of cold, to make the Thermometer decend one degree; I therefore wrote to Mr Dolland, to make me a large Thermometer divided to upwards of one hundred degrees below zero. He sent me a Thermometer of red colored spirits of wine, divided to 110 degrees below zero, or 142 degrees below the freezing point, (zero is 32 degrees below the freezing point). The month of October

was many degrees below the freezing point, and on the
17ᵗʰ day the snow remained on the ground. · On November
the 10ᵗʰ the Thermometer was 10° below zero; on the 11ᵗʰ
day 27° below Zero, the 12ᵗʰ day 12°, the 13 day 15° degrees;
on the 14ᵗʰ day 25° degrees; on the 15ᵗʰ day 28 degrees below
zero. And this great deep Lake of 230 miles in length, by 80 to
100 miles in width was entirely frozen over. In the course of
the winter, the ice of the Lake became five to six feet thick.
On the following year, the first water seen along shore was on
the 5ᵗʰ day of July. On the 7ᵗʰ day, a gale of wind shook
the ice to pieces, and the whole disappeared, scarce a frag-
ment [remained] on the shore after being frozen over for
7¼ months.

I may here remark that my hard life, obliging me to cut
holes in the ice for angling for fish, at all seasons while the
Lake was frozen over, has led me to notice a curious operation
of nature, the ice of these great Lakes, without any current
in them, is very little thawed on the surface by the action of
mild weather, the little that is softened in the day, the night
makes solid ice, it is the water beneath the ice, that makes
it decay : when the mild season comes, the ice is gradually
worn away by the action of the water; often in making holes
for angling, while the surface appeared solid as [in] winter,
my ice chissel soon went through; on taking up a piece of
about one square foot, the solid ice may be four inches thick.
The rest was what we call candles, that is, icicles of fifteen to
eighteen inches, or more in length, each distinct from the
other, it is thus that nature prepares the ice to be broken up
by a strong gale of wind; In the morning of the 7ᵗʰ July
the Lake had the appearance of winter, in the afternoon [it
was] as clear of ice, as if it had never been frozen over. A
Gale of wind had left nothing but icicles on the shore.

Although during November the cold was intense, yet not
so much so as to prove the Thermometers, 1795 on the
15ᵗʰ December the large Thermometer fell to 42 below

zero, but the other showed only 40 degrees, and that of
Quicksilver fell into the bulb, which was only four fifths
full.   On the morning of the 18ᵗʰ December, by the large
Thermometer it was 56 degrees below zero, the small spirit
Thermometer stood at 41° degrees, and it appeared no degree
of cold could make it descend into the bulb ; the quicksilver in
the bulb appeared to fill only two thirds of the bulb : it may
be remarked that for four days previous to this great degree
of cold, the Thermometer was at 35 degrees, 37, 44 and 46
degrees below zero.   On the 18ᵗʰ December at 8 AM the
Thermometer was $\overline{56}$; at Noon $\overline{44}$; and at 9 PM $\overline{48}$ degrees
below zero.   It was a day of most intense cold, the ice on the
Lake was splitting in all directions, the smoke from the
chimneys fell in lumps to the ground.   These intense colds
gave me frequent opportunities of freezing quicksilver ; I
often attempted to beat it out into thin plates like lead, but
however cautiously I proceeded, the edges were all fractured,
and a few quick blows with the hammer, however light,
would liquefy it.

Hitherto I have said little on the Aurora Borealis of the
northern countries ; at Hudson's Bay they are north westward, and only occasionally brilliant.   I have passed four
winters between the Bay and the Rein Deer's Lake, the more
to the westward, the higher and brighter is this electric fluid,
but always westward ; but at this, the Rein Deer's Lake, as
the winter came on, especially in the months of February
and March, the whole heavens were in a bright glow.   We
seemed to be in the centre of it's action, from the horizon in
every direction from north to south, from east to west, the
Aurora was equally bright, sometimes, indeed often, with a
tremulous motion in immense sheets, slightly tinged with the
colors of the Rainbow, would roll, from horizon to horizon.
Sometimes there would be a stillness of two minutes ; the
Dogs howled with fear, and their brightness was often such
that with only their light I could see to shoot an owl at twenty

yards; in the rapid motions of the Aurora we were all perswaded we heard them, reason told me I did not, but it was cool reason against sense. My men were positive they did hear the rapid motions of the Aurora, this was the eye deceiving the ear; I had my men blindfolded by turns, and then enquired of them, if they heard the rapid motions of the Aurora. They soon became sensible they did not, and yet so powerful was the Illusion of the eye on the ear, that they still believed they heard the Aurora. What is the cause that this place seems to be in the centre of the most vivid brightness and extension of the Aurora : from whence this immense extent of electric fluid, how is it formed, whither does it go. Questions without an answer. I am well acquainted with all the countries to the westward. The farther west the less is this Aurora. At the Mountains it is not seen.

I have said our livelihood depended on fishing and hunting. Part of the fishery was angling for large trout,[1] they are not to be taken but in deep water, from 20 to 40 fathoms, or more, for this fish, hooks are not used; but the Chepawyan method adopted : the first thing done is making one, or more holes in the ice with the ice chissel, which is a small bar of iron of two pounds weight, at one end flat, at the other end a chissel of an inch in width, the greater part of this is inserted in a groove of a strong pole of birch of full six feet in length, the chissel end projecting about five inches; with this, a hole is quickly made in the ice of any dimensions, without the person in the least wetting himself, the axe is never used. A sounding line is now used to ascertain the depth of water, which must not be less than twenty fathoms, as large trout are found only in deep water. The set line is now carefully measured, with a coil of five fathoms neatly made up with a slip knot [it] is attached to the bait, [which] is the half of a white fish, the head part only, as the trout

[1] *Cristivomer namaycush* (Walbaum). [E. A. P.]

always takes the white fish head foremost, a small round stick of birch well dried and hardened by the fire, but not burnt, is slightly attached to the under part of the bait, about six inches in length, the line is fixed about one third below the head of the bait, this is placed as near as possible about six feet above the bottom. The trout takes the bait, the slip knot of five fathoms of line gives way, which enables him to swallow the bait, at the end of which he is brought up with a jerk, which causes the piece of wood to become vertical in his mouth, his jaws are extended and we often find him drowned, a strange death for a fish. In angling for trout, everything is the same, the fish caught alive are better than those drowned, whether by a set line or in a net; the weight of the trout was from twenty five to forty five pounds, I have heard of trout fifty five pounds; they are very rich fish, make a nutritious broth, and pound for pound are equal to good beef. One day as usual, I had pierced the ice with new holes, or cleaned out the old holes with an ice racket, [when] an old Chepawyan Indian came to me, I told him I had five holes in the ice, and for these two days had caught nothing. He shook his head, left me and went about one hundred yards westward of me, we were about five miles from land, he then looked at all the land within sight, shifted his place until all his marks coincided, he then pierched a hole thro' the ice, put down his angling tackle, and in about an hours time brought up a fine trout of full thirty pounds. By one PM he caught another, rather larger, soon after which he gave over, put up his tackle and came to me, I had caught nothing; he asked to see my bait which I showed to him, it was like his, he noticed that it was not greased, he showed his bait which was well greased, and taking out a little bag, a piece of grease with which he greased the bait twice a day; he told me I must do the same. He remarked to me that I came too soon, and staid too late; that the trout took bait only for a while after sunrise to near sunset, but that about noon was the best time; it has always appeared strange to me that a Trout in forty fathoms water, with a covering of full five feet thickness of ice, on a dark cloudy day, should know when the sun rises and sets but so it is. I followed the Chepawyan's advice, and was more successful.

In hunting, we had but little success, and killed only a few Rein Deer. On fine days small herds would go out on the Lake some four miles from land, and lie down for a few hours on the ice as if to cool themselves; one fine cold day Mr Ross and myself killed a Doe, our hands were freezing, we opened her, and put our hands in the blood to warm them, but the heat of the blood was like scalding water which we could not bear. Both of us were accustomed to hunting and knew the heat of the blood of many animals, we were surprised, we examined the stomach, it was full of white moss. I tasted it, and swallowed a little, it was warm in my stomach. I then traced the Deer to where they had been feeding, it was on a white crisp moss in a circular form, of about ten inches diameter, each division distinct, yet close together. I took a small piece, about the size of a nutmeg, chewed it, it had a mild taste. I swallowed it, and it became like a coal of fire in my stomach. I took care never to repeat the experiment : It is by food of this warm nature, that the Animals and Birds of the cold regions are not only enabled to bear the intense cold, but find it warm.

What is the heat imparted to the blood, by each kind of food; from the water melon, and wild rice to the Rein Deer Moss.

This solved to me the excessive heat of the blood of the Rein Deer, on this Lake only I have found this moss. I have tasted all the mosses of Lake Superior and many other Lakes, but have found nothing of the same. Is this moss then peculiar to the northern barren countries of rock and moss, that the food of the Rein Deer and Musk Oxen shall make the temperature of fifty to seventy degrees below the freezing point as the month of April is to our cattle; it appears so.

M[r] Ross and myself several times, when we went a hunting, took a Thermometer with us to ascertain the heat of the blood of the Rein Deer, but it so happened, when we had a Thermometer with us, we killed no Deer, and therefore could not know the heat of the blood. The Stomach, or Paunch, of the Rein Deer is taken out of the animal, the orifice tied up, and then for three days hung in the smoke, but not near the fire. It is now sour, bits of meat and fat are mixed with the contents, it is then boiled, and all those who have eaten of it say it is an agreeable, hearty food.

In the spring of the year, as the snow begins occasionally to thaw, myriads of a small black insect[1] make their appearance, so numerous, that the surface of the snow is black with them, they are about one twentieth of an inch in length, of a compact make, they cover the sides of Lakes, and Rivers; snow shoe paths, and other places; they come with the first thaw of the snow, and disappear with the snow. The question is, from whence are these myriads of insects which are seen on the snow, they cannot come from the ground, penetrate three feet of hard snow, they are never found below the surface of the snow. How do they live, upon what do they live. Upon examining the edges of the ice, as it began to thaw, I saw a great number of insects something like those in the snow, they were rather larger, the head had two feelers, the body increased in size to the end, where it was round. They had two legs, some were dead, others dormant. Those that were fully alive and active, upon my touching them with my finger, made a leap of about an inch into an almost invisible crevice of the ice, and there remained. The native name is Oopinarnartarwewuk, jumping insects. From whence come so suddenly these myriads of insects on the

---

[1] Snow Fleas, *Achorutes*. [E. A. P.]

surface of the snow, and edges of the ice; and in such myriads; and only on the snow and ice, and each has a distinct insect.

My residence on the Rein Deer's Lake which has become the country of the Chepawyans; gave me an insight into the morals and manners of these people which I had not before. I have already noticed the treatment of the Women and every thing that passed this Winter confirmed it; during this season many of them came in to trade; the bank of the Lake to the House, was a low regular slope; seing a Woman carrying a heavy child, and hauling a long, loaded sled; as she came to the bank, I desired one of the Men, who was remarkable for his great strength to assist her, she gave the trace to him: thinking a Woman could not haul any weight worth notice, he carelessly put two fingers to the trace of the Sled, but could not move it; he had at length to employ all his strength to start the Sled, and haul it to the House: the Sled and load weighed about one hundred and sixty pounds: among them was a little girl of about six years of age. She had her sled, and hauled on it, a brass Kettle that held four gallons: The Boys had a light Sled, or carried a few pounds weight, the Men had little else than their Guns; such is the order when removing from place to place during the winter; Those who make use of Canoes during the summer, and they are now almost in general use, place the women in far more easy circumstances, and the Men take their share of paddling the canoes; loading and unloading them; but in fact the Women are considered as the drudges of the Men.

The Women, until they have children appear to be the property of the strongest Man, that has no woman: One day in the latter end of February, a Chepawyan called the Crane and his Wife came to the House, he was well named, tall, thin, and active, he at times hunted for us. His wife was a good looking young Woman, they appeared to love

L

each other but had no children. Six, or seven of us were
sitting in the guard room talking of the weather, the Crane
was smoking his pipe, and his Wife sitting beside him, when
suddenly a Chepawyan entered, equally tall, but powerfully
made. He went directly to the Crane and told him "I am
come for your woman, and I must have her, my woman is
dead, and I must have this woman to do my work and carry
my things"; and suiting the action to the word he twisted his
hand in the hair of her head to drag her away; on this the
Crane started up and seized him by the waist; he let go the
Woman, and in like manner seized the Crane; and a wrestling
match took place which was well maintained by the Crane
for some time; but his adversary was too powerful, and at
length his strength failed, and he was thrown on the floor,
his opponent placing his knee on his breast, with both hands
seized his head and twisted his neck so much, that his face
was almost on his back, and we expected to see it break; in
an instant we made him let go, kicked him out of the house,
with an assurance that if he came back to do the same, we
would send a ball through him; he seemed to think he had
done wrong, upon which we told him that he was welcome
at any time to come and smoke, or trade, but not to quarrel.
After standing a few minutes he called to the Crane; You are
now under the protection of the White Men, in the summer
I shall see you on our lands, and then I shall twist your neck
and take your woman from you; he went away and we saw
no more of him; Their lands, which they claim as their own
country; and to which no other people have a right, are
those eastward of the Rein Deer's and Manito Lakes to
Churchill Factory and northward along the interior of the
sea coast; all other lands they hunt on belonged to the
Nahathaways, who have returned to the Southwestward.
Early in the month of December, past midnight, a Chepawyan
of middle stature, of about twenty five years of age, came to
the house alone, he brought a bundle of Beaver and Marten

skins; he looked about with suspicion; and enquired if any
of the Natives were near the house. We told him, there had
been none for several days; he then traded his furrs for
necessaries, except a few Martens for Beads and Rings. He
told me he had a Wife and two children; and enquired if I
knew a certain Indian. I said I did; " Then when you see
him, tell him we are all well, he is my uncle, and the only
man who is kind to me." After smoking, I offered him a
Bison Robe to sleep on, but he told me he must set off
directly; which he did, having staid only about an hour.
There was something strange about him which excited my
curiousity. About a month afterwards his Uncle came to
the House; I told I had seen his Nephew, and that he had
come alone in the night to trade, and desired me to say they
were all well, and then enquired the reason of his hasty
leaving the House after trading; he smoked for some time;
and then said My Nephew is a man, but he has not been wise,
he is not strong, about five winters ago, a young woman was
given to him, and after a few moons, we camped with some
other tents of Chepawyans, where there was a tall strong
young man who had no woman. He went to my nephew
and demanded him to give up his wife, which he refused to
do, upon which the other took hold of him, threw him on the
ground, and began twisting his neck; we told him to let
him alone and take the woman; she was unwilling to go with
him, upon which he laid hold of her hair to drag her away;
my nephew sprung up, took his gun and shot him dead, and
made the ground red with man's blood, which he ought not
to have done; We all pitched away and left the place:
since which he lives alone and is afraid to meet any tents,
for they take every thing from them, and leave them nothing
but the clothes they have on; he has been twice stripped
of all he had; and therefore keeps away by himself. I told
them that if I had a wife, and any one came to take her away,
I would surely shoot him; Ah, that is the way you White

Men, and our Neighbours the Nahathaways always talk and
do, a Woman cannot be touched but you get hold of guns
and long Knives; What is a woman good for, she cannot
hunt, she is only to work and carry our things, and on no
account whatever ought the ground to be made red with
man's blood. Then the strong men take Women when they
want them; Certainly the strong men have a right to the
Women. And if the Woman has children; That is as the
strong man pleases. So far as the Women are concerned
they are a sett of Brutes. The expression " the ground red
with Man's blood " is used by all the Natives of North
America as very hateful to see; but by the southern Indians,
accustomed to war, it is limited to that of their relations
and tribe; yet it has a meaning I never could comprehend
in the same sense as the Natives use it, for they seem to
attach a mysterious meaning to the expression. In the latter
end of March, this forlorn Native, again came to the House
alone; he had made a good hunt of furrs and traded them in
clothing for himself and family, ammunition and tobacco,
not forgetting beads and other articles for his wife. I enquired of him, if what his uncle had told me was true, he said
it was, that he had been twice pillaged, and that the Women
were worse than the Men; you see I have again come to you
in the night, and before I came into the House, I made sure
there were no Chepawyans, for if I had met any they would
have taken the whole of my hunt from me, and left me with
nothing. I enquired why he did not tent with the Nahathaways who think much of their women, and love brave men.
He was at a loss what to say, or do.

With regard to the immortality of the soul; and the
nature of the other world, the best evidence of their belief
I learned from a woman; her husband had traded with me
two winters. They had a fine boy of six years of age, their
only child; he became ill and died; and according to their
custom she had to mourn for him twelve Moons, crying in

a low voice " She azza, She azza " (my little son) never ceasing while awake, and often bursting into tears.

About three months after, I saw her again, [making] the same cry, the same sorrowful woman, her husband was kind to her ; About six months after this I saw her again, she no longer cried " She azza," and was no longer a sorrowing woman ; I enquired of her the cause of this change. She replied, When my little son went to the other world, there was none to receive him, even his Grandfather is yet alive ; he was friendless, he wandered alone in the pitching track of the tents, (here she shed tears) there was none to take care of him no one to give him a bit of meat. More than two moons ago, his father died, I sorrowed for him, and still sadly regret him, but he is gone to my son, his father will take great care of him. He will no longer wander alone, his father will be always with him, and when I die I shall go to them. Such was the belief that comforted this poor child-less widow, and in which I encouraged her, and telling her that to be happy in the other world, and go to our relations, we must lead good lives here.

These people though subject to great vicissitudes yet suffer less from extreme hunger than the Nahathaways. The latter pride themselves with living by hunting animals, look on fish as an inferior food, and the catching of them beneath a Hunter. The former pride themselves on being expert anglers, and have made it their study ; the great Lakes of their country yield the finest fish, and when the Deer fail they readily take to angling, altho' it affords them no clothing. They are in possession of many secrets of making baits for taking the different kinds of fish ; which they would not impart to me ; but being in their company something was seen. The bait for the Trout, the largest fish of the Lakes, was the head half of a White Fish, well rubbed with Eagles fat, for want of it, other raw fat ; but not greese that had been melted by the fire : The Pike and Pickerel take almost any thing, even a red rag; but the pride of these people is to angle the White Fish, an art known to only a few of the Men; they would not inform me of its composition, the few baits I examined appeared to be all the same, and the castorum of the Beaver worked into a thick paste, was the principal item; around were the fine red feathers of the Woodpecker, a grain of Eagles fat was on the top of the bait, and the hook was well hid in it; the bait had a neat appearance. The art of angling White Fish is to them of importance, a young man offered a gun for the secret and was refused.

These people, the "Dinnae" their native name, though better known to us by the name of Chepawyans; extend in different tribes speaking dialects of the same language, to near the Pacific Ocean, by the way of Fraser's River: I have already mentioned, they claim as their own rightful country, from Churchill Factory, and northward to the arctic sea, their origin by this account of themselves must have been from Greenland. By what means they came to the north eastern part of this conti[nent], is better a subject of discussion in the Appendix than here: If we knew the state of Archery in Greenland, or Iceland it might lead us to something certain on these people; All the Natives of North America, except the "Dinnae" in drawing the Arrow, hold the Bow in a vertical, or upright position, which gives to the arms their full action and force; but the Dinnae, or Chepawyans, hold the Bow in a contrary, or horizontal position, the Arrow is held on the string, by two fingers below and the thumb above and with the Bow string thus drawn to the breast, which does not allow to the Bow two thirds of its force; practice has made them good marksmen, but the arrows are feeble in effect. Do any of the people of Greenland, Iceland, or the northern nations of Europe, or Siberia, handle the Bow in this manner. If so, some inference may be drawn from it. Of the state of the Thermometer, and other peculiarities of the climate they will be found in the Appendix.[1] .

[1] In Thompson's note-books are many pages of meteorological observations taken at various places throughout western Canada ; but in this manuscript as it came to me, there was no appendix, and it is not likely that any was prepared.

CHAPTER X

NORTH WEST COMPANY

*Leave Hudson's Bay Company—Join North West Company—
Instructions to explore the country—Fur Trade—Peter
Pond—West end of Lake Athabasca—Philip Turnor—
Carrying Place of Lake Superior—Brigade—Start on
Survey—Height of Land—Sieux—Rainy Lake—Rainy
River — Massacre — Winipeg River — Winipeg Trading
House—Lake Winipeg.*

THE countries I had explored was under the sanction
of M⟨r⟩ Joseph Colen,[1] the Resident at York Factory
the most enlightened gentleman who had filled that
situation ; by a Letter from him, I was informed, that how-

[1] See note on p. 56. Joseph Colen seems to have been a capable
trader, but his interests were centred in increasing the fur-trade with the
Indians who came to York Factory of their own accord, rather than
following these Indians to their hunting-grounds. As far as we know,
he himself never went inland more than a few miles from the trading
post ; and in spite of the fact that he was being urged by the directors
of the Company in London to have the great unknown spaces to the south
and west of him explored, he was opposed to spending men, money, and
time on such exploration. His orders to Thompson that he should stop
surveying were therefore directly contrary to the wishes of his superiors
in London. It is impossible to avoid the conclusion that his recall in 1798
was due to the fact that he had prevented Thompson from continuing
his explorations, and had forced him out of the Company's service. It is
possible that Thompson may not have known of Colen's true attitude towards his work, and that he may have thought Colen was merely trans-
mitting to him the orders he had received from London ; or possibly the
long time which had elapsed between the date when Thompson left the
Company, and that when he wrote his memoirs, had mellowed his feelings
towards his old chief, and had induced him to write the kindly remarks
here recorded.

ever extensive the countries yet unknown yet he could not sanction any further surveys. My time was up, and I determined to seek that employment from the Company Merchants of Canada, carrying on the Furr Trade, under the name of the North West Company : With two Natives I proceeded to their nearest trading House, under the charge of M[r] Alexander Fraser; and by the usual route of the Canoes arrived at the Great Carrying Place[1] on the north shore of Lake Superior, then the depot of the merchandise from Montreal ; and of the Furrs from the interior countries. The Agents who acted for the Company and were also Partners of the Firm, were the Honorable William McGillvray[2] and

[1] The Grand Portage, or Great Carrying Place, was situated on the north shore of Lake Superior, forty miles south-west of Fort William. For about twenty-five years it was the central depot of the Canadian traders from Montreal who had associated themselves either in the North-West Company or in one of the concerns competing with it. To this place the goods which were to be used in trading with the Indians for their furs were brought from Montreal either in large canoes or in sail-boats ; and the furs which had been collected in the interior country to the west of it, were taken back to Montreal in the same boats. From the shore of Lake Superior the trading goods were carried over a path or trail nine miles in length, past heavy rapids and waterfalls to the banks of Pigeon river, where they were loaded into smaller canoes in charge of resident partners, but manned by Indians or half-breeds, who had brought cargoes of furs from the west and north, and who now took back with them supplies for another year. After the signing of the Treaty of London in 1794, it was found that Grand Portage was in American territory ; therefore, in 1801, the depot was moved to Fort William. Accordingly, it was to Fort William that Thompson brought his furs when he descended the Saskatchewan river from Rocky Mountain House in 1802.

[2] William McGillivray was a Scotsman who, after serving for several years in the employ of the North-West Company in the districts of Red and English rivers, became a partner in the concern by buying Pond's share for the sum of £800 ; and soon became one of its most influential members. In 1814 he was appointed a Legislative Councillor of Lower Canada in recognition of the services rendered by him and the North-West Company during the war with the United States in 1812. With Edward Ellice he represented the North-West Company in the negotiations for a union with the Hudson's Bay Company, and it was largely through his tact and ability that this union was brought about in 1821. His later years were spent in Scotland, where he died about 1825.

Sir Alexander McKenzie,[1] gentlemen of enlarged views; the latter had crossed the Rocky Mountains by the Peace River and was far advanced by Fraser River towards the Pacific Ocean, when want of Provisions and the hostility of the Natives obliged him to return. From the Great Slave he had explored the great River which flowed from it into the Arctic Sea, and which is justly named McKenzie's River.

My arrival enabled these Gentlemen and the other Partners who were present, to learn the true positions of their Trading Houses, in respect to each other; and how situated with regard to the forty ninth degree of Latitude North, as since the year 1792 this parallel of Latitude from the north west corner of the Lake of the Woods to the east foot of the Rocky Mountains, had become the boundary line between the British Dominions and the Territories of the United States: instead of a line due west from the North west corner of the Lake of the Woods to the head of the Mississippe, as designated by the Treaty of 1783.[2] The scource, or head of the Mississippe was then unknown except to the Natives and a very few Furr Traders; and by them, from it's very sinuous course, supposed to be farther north than the northern banks of the Lake of the Woods. And wherever I could mark the line of the 49th parallel of Latitude [I was told] to do so, especially on the Red River. Also, if

---

[1] Mackenzie's name is too well-known to need much comment here. A native of Stornoway on the island of Lewis, he came to Canada in 1779, went to the country west of Lake Superior in 1785, and became a partner in the North-West Company in 1787. In 1789 he descended the Mackenzie river from Lake Athabaska to its mouth, and in 1793 he ascended Peace river to the source of Parsnip river, and thence travelled westward to the Pacific ocean at the mouth of Bella Coola river, being the first white man to cross the North American continent north of Mexico. See George Bryce, *Life of Sir Alexander Mackenzie*, Toronto, 1906 ("The Makers of Canada," vol. viii).

[2] For a full discussion of terms of the treaties affecting the boundary between the United States and Canada, and the awards under these treaties, see James White, "Boundary Disputes and Treaties" (in *Canada and its Provinces*, Toronto, 1913, vol. viii. pp. 751–958).

possible to extend my Surveys to the Missisourie River ;
visit the villages of the ancient agricultural Natives who
dwelt there ; enquire for fossil bones of large animals, and
any monuments, if any, that might throw light on the ancient
state of the unknown countries I had to travel over and
examine. The Agents and Partners all agreed to give orders
to all their Trading Posts, to send Men with me, and every
necessary I required [was] to be at my order.

How very different the liberal and public spirit of this
North West Company of Merchants of Canada ; from the
mean selfish policy of the Hudson's Bay Company styled
Honorable ; and whom, at little expense, might have had
the northern part of this Continent surveyed to the Pacific
Ocean, and greatly extended their Trading Posts ; whatever
they have done, the British Government has obliged them
to do. A short account of the transactions of this Company,
will prove to the public the truth of what I assert, and will
throw some light on the discoveries that from time to time
have been made.

The furr trade was then open to every Person in Canada
who could obtain credit for a canoe load of coarse Merchandise ; and several different Persons engaged in this trade,
besides those Merchants from Scotland who formed the
North West Company : Among the Clerks of this last Company, was a Mr Peter Pond,[1] a native of the city of Boston,

[1] Peter Pond was born in Milford, Connecticut, on January 18, 1740.
When a young man, he went to the Indian country west of Lake Superior.
In 1775 he joined Alexander Henry and the Frobishers on Lake Winnipeg, and with them ascended the Saskatchewan river as far as Cumberland House. In 1778 he reached Athabaska river, and built a trading
post on that stream, forty miles south of Lake Athabaska, which he was
undoubtedly the first white man to visit. Thompson is in error in saying
that Pond's post was on the north side of Lake Athabaska. In the winter
of 1780–81, while at Lake La Ronge, Pond killed his partner Wadin ;
and six years later he killed John Ross, one of the partners of the firm of
Gregory, McLeod, and Company. About 1790 he sold his interest in the
North-West Company and went to the United States, where he spent the
rest of his life. He drew two maps of western Canada, apparently in

United States. He was a person of industrious habits, a good common education, but of a violent temper and unprincipled character; his place was at Fort Chepawyan[1] on the north side of the Athabasca Lake, where he wintered three years. At Lake Superior he procured a Compass, took the courses of the compass through the whole route to his wintering place; and for the distances adopted those of the Canadian canoe men in Leagues, and parts of the same, and sketching off the Lake shores the best he could. In the winters, taking the Depot of Lake Superior as his point of departure, the Latitude and Longitude was known as determined by the French Engineers; he constructed a map of the route followed by the Canoes. It's features were tolerably correct; but by taking the League of the Canoe Men for three geographical miles (I found they averaged only two miles) he increased his Longitude so much as to place the Athabasca Lake, at it's west end near the Pacific Ocean. A copy of

1785 and in 1790 respectively; but the contents of these maps could not have been known before George Charles, who is mentioned below, was sent from London, though the earlier map was known when Philip Turnor was sent to survey Lake Athabaska in 1791. See L. J. Burpee, *The Search for the Western Sea*, Toronto, 1908, pp. 322–349; and Reports of the Canadian Archives for 1889 and 1890, pp. 29–38 and pp. 52–54 respectively.

[1] Fort Chipewyan is at present situated on a rocky point on the north shore, and near the western end, of Lake Athabaska. The first fur-trading post of this name was built on the south side of Lake Athabaska by Roderick Mackenzie in 1788; and it was from here that Alexander Mackenzie set out on his two expeditions to the Arctic and Pacific oceans. But the post was moved over to its present site about the end of the eighteenth century. In 1802 Peter Fidler, of the Hudson's Bay Company, built a trading post beside Fort Chipewyan (or as Thompson called it when he visited it in May, 1804, "Athabasca House"), and named it Nottingham House. Four years later, however, the Hudson's Bay Company abandoned the whole of the Athabaska district to their Canadian rivals, and evacuated Nottingham House. In 1815 they returned to Lake Athabaska, and established a post called Fort Wedderburne on Coal Island, some little distance from the trading store of the North-West Company; but in 1821 the two companies were united, and the site and name of the North-West Company's post were retained. Fort Chipewyan has thus been continuously occupied now for more than a century.

this Map was given to the Agents of the North West Company; whom, in London laid it before Sir Hugh Dalrymple,[1] then in office, whose character stood high as a gentleman of science, and great geographical knowledge, and who comparing the Longitude of the west end of the Athabasca Lake by M[r] Pond's map with the Charts of Captain Cook found the distance to be only one hundred miles; or less, [and] directly conceived that it offered a short route to the coasts of Asia for dispatch and other purposes. To verify this Map, the Colonial Secretary applied to the Hudson Bay Company to send out a Person duly qualified to ascertain the Latitude and Longitude of the west end of the Athabasca Lake. With this request the Company were obliged to appear to comply.

For this purpose in 1785 they sent out a M[r] George Charles[2] aged fifteen years, whom they had made their apprentice for seven years; when he landed at Churchill Factory I saw him, and enquired how he came to undertake this business, he told me he had been about one year in the mathematical school, had three times with a quadrant brought down the Sun to a chalk line on the wall, was declared fully competent, and sent out to go on discovery. Of course nothing could be done. Had this honourable Company intended the position of the west end of the Lake should be known, there were then many Naval Officers on half pay, who would gladly have undertaken the expedition to the Athabasca Lake and settled it's position. What the views of the Company could be for preventing the knowledge required, though often a subject of conversation, none could divine, their charter gave them the Country, and the furr traders of Canada had had Houses there for several years.

Whatever the views of the Company may have been, this trick of sending out a Lad, prevented the Collonial Office

[1] This is an error for Alexander Dalrymple. See note on p. 28.
[2] See note on p. 27.

from obtaining the desired information for five years. The pressing demands of this Office then obliged the Hudson's Bay Company to engage a Gentleman fully competent, a Mr Philip Turnor,[1] one of the compilers of the Nautical Almanac, who, in the year 1790 proceeded to Fort Chepawyan at the west end of the Athabasca Lake, and head of the Great Slave River, where he wintered, and by observations, found the place to be in Latitude . . . Longitude[2] . . . and from this place the following year returned to England ; After this great exertion of the Hudson's Bay Company, they again became dormant to the time of Captain Franklin's survey of the Arctic Coast from the Copper Mine River.[3]

[1] See note on p. 146.

[2] Turnor's latitude and longitude are given by Thompson in his notes as 58° 38′ N., 110° 26½′ W.

[3] In 1819 Captain (afterwards Sir John) Franklin was sent in charge of a party from England to explore the Arctic coast of America, east of the mouth of the Coppermine river. With him were Sir John Richardson, Sir George Back, and Lieutenant Hood as assistants. They went to York Factory on Hudson Bay by ship, and ascended the Hayes and Saskatchewan rivers to Cumberland House by boat before the winter set in. In January, 1820, Franklin and Back proceeded on foot to Fort Chipewyan on Lake Athabaska, while Richardson and Hood followed them in canoes as soon as the rivers were free of ice, and arrived at the fort on July 13. From there the whole party descended the Slave river, crossed Great Slave lake, and ascended Yellowknife river, near the source of which it went into winter quarters, and built houses which Franklin called "Fort Enterprise." In the summer of 1821 the party descended and made a survey of the Coppermine river to its mouth, surveyed the Arctic coast eastward to the mouth of Hood's river, and thence crossed overland to Fort Enterprise, suffering terrible hardships from exposure and starvation, both on the way to, and after their arrival at, the fort, one of the men being driven to such extremities by starvation that he killed Lieutenant Hood. The following year the survivors returned to York Factory, and thence to England. In 1825 it was determined to continue the exploration of the northern coast of America east and west from the mouth of Mackenzie river, and Captain Franklin was again given charge of the expedition. On this occasion he sailed from London to New York. Thence he proceeded to Fort William on Lake Superior, and from there by Lake Winnipeg to the Mackenzie river, and down that stream to the mouth of Great Bear river, which was ascended to Great Bear lake, on the north shore of which Fort Franklin was built. Here the party wintered. In 1826

M' Peter Pond I have mentioned as an unprincipled man
of a violent charac[ter]; he became implicated in the death
of a M' Ross,¹ a furr trader, and afterwards [was] a principal
in the murder of a Mr Wadden,² another furr trader; for
this latter crime he was brought from the Athabasca Lake
to Canada, and sent to Quebec to be tried for the murder
he had committed; but the Law authorities did not consider the jurisdiction of the Court of Quebec to extend into
the territories of the Hudsons Bay Company, and therefore
they could not take cognizance of the crime, and he was set
at liberty; he went to his native city, Boston. This was in
1782. The following year peace was made; the Commissioners on the part of Great Britain were two honest well
meaning gentlemen, but who knew nothing of the geography
of the countries interior of Lake Ontario, and the Maps they
had to guide them were wretched compilations. One of them,
of which I had a fellow Map, was Farren's [Faden's] dated

the party descended the Mackenzie river to its mouth, where it divided,
Franklin and Back going westward along the Arctic coast as far as Point
Beechey, while Richardson and Kendall went eastward along the coast
to the mouth of the Coppermine river, and thence ascended that stream
and crossed country to Fort Franklin, where a second winter was spent.
The following year Franklin and Richardson returned to England by
New York, while Back took the remainder of the party to England by
York Factory.

¹ John Ross was a partner in the firm of Gregory, McLeod, and Company in charge of the Athabaska department, where he was opposed by
Peter Pond of the North-West Company. The two men did not get on
well together, and in an altercation during the winter of 1786–7 Ross was
shot. This murder caused the two opposing firms to unite their interests
under the name of the North-West Company.

² Wadin also fell before Pond. Roderick Mackenzie says that he was
"a Swiss gentleman, of strict probity and known sobriety," who went to
Lake La Ronge in 1779 to engage in the fur trade. In the following year
Pond was sent to the same place to act in conjunction with him. "About
the end of the year 1780, or the beginning of 1781, Mr. Wadin had received Mr. Pond and one of his friends to dinner, and in the course of the
night the former was shot through the lower part of the thigh, when it
was said that he expired from loss of blood" (Alexander Mackenzie,
Voyages, London, 1801, Introduction, p. xvi).

1773, which went as far as Lake Ontario, and to the middle of this Lake, beyond which, the interior countries were represented composed of Rocks and Swamps and laid down as uninhabitable.   Mitchell's Map was the best.   Such Maps gave M[r] Peter Pond who was personally acquainted with those countries every advantage.   A boundary line through the middle of Lake Champlain, and thence due west would have been accepted at that time by the United [States] for it was more than they could justly claim, had a gentleman of abilities been selected on the part of Great Britain, but at that time North America was held in contempt.   To the United States Commissioners M[r] Pond designated a Boundary Line passing through the middle of the S[t] Lawrence to Lake Superior, through that lake and the interior countries to the north west corner of the Lake of the Woods; and thence westward to the head of the Missisourie[1] being twice the area of the Territory the States could justly claim; This exorbitant demand the British Commissioners accepted; and [it] was confirmed by both Nations.   Such was the hand that designated the Boundary Line between the Dominions of Great Britain and the Territories of the United States.   The celebrated Edmund Burke, said, and has left on record, "There is a fatality attending all the measures of the British Ministry on the North American Colonies."   This sad, but just remark has been exemplified in every transaction we have had with the United States on Territory; and in this respect Lord Ashburton was outwitted by M[r] Daniel Webster at the Treaty of Washington, both in New Brunswick, and the interior of Canada.

It may be said, the country thus acquired by the United States is of no importance to England; be it so; then let England make a free gift to the States of what the latter require.   History will place all these transactions in their

---

[1] This is a mistake for the Mississippi.

proper light, and the blockhead treaty of Lord Ashburton [1] will be a subject of ridicule.

The south east end of the Great Carrying, was in a small Bay of Lake Superior, in Latitude 47.58.1 N. Longitude 89.44.20 W of Greenwich. It was then, and had been for several years, the Depot of the Furr Traders; to this place the Canoes from Montreal came, each carrying forty to forty five pieces of merchandise, including spirituous liquors; each piece of the weight of ninety to one hundred pounds; these canoes then were loaded with the packs of furrs, the produce of the winter trade of the interior countries, and returned to Montreal; The Merchandise for the winter trade of the distant trading Posts was here assorted, and made up in pieces each weighing ninety pounds; the Canoes were of a less size, and the load was twenty five pieces, besides the provisions for the voyage and the baggage of the Men: being a weight of about 2900 pounds, to which add five Men, the weight a canoe carries will be 3700 pounds.

These Canoes are formed into what are called Brigades of four to eight Canoes for the different sections of the interior countries. On board of one of these canoes, of a Brigade of four under the charge of Mr Hugh McGillis,[2] I embarked on

---

[1] The Ashburton Treaty between Great Britain and the United States in 1842 defined the boundary line between the possessions of the two countries from New Brunswick and the State of Maine westward as far as the summit of the Rocky Mountains. The subsequent Oregon Treaty signed at Washington in 1846 defined the boundary from the Rocky Mountains westward to the Pacific ocean.

[2] At the time when Thompson joined the North-West Company, Hugh McGillis was one of the senior employees of the company, and was in charge of the Swan river district. When the Company was reorganized in 1802, he became one of the partners, holding two shares, and when the North-West and X Y Companies united in 1804, he was one of those who signed the agreement by attorney. During the winter of 1805–06, when Lieutenant Pike reached the headwaters of the Mississippi, he was in charge of a post at Leech lake. Later, his name appears as one of those officials of the North-West Company taken prisoners by Lord Selkirk at Fort William in 1816.

M

the ninth day of August, in the year 1796, for the survey of the southern sections.

My instruments were, a Sextant of ten inches radius, with Quicksilver and parallel glasses, an excellent Achromatic Telescope; a lesser for common use; drawing instruments, and two Thermometers; all made by Dollond. We proceeded over the Great Carrying Place, the length of which is eight miles and twenty yards in a north west direction to the Pigeon River,[1] which is about three hundred feet above Lake Superior: this was carried over by the Men in five day's hard labor. From this to the Height of Land the distance is thirty eight miles, including twelve carrying places, of five and a half miles of carriage, which makes severe labor for the canoe men: A short distance south eastward of the Height of Land in the crevices of a steep rock, about twenty feet above the water of a small Lake, are a number of Arrows which the Sieux Indians shot from their Bows; the Arrows are small and short. The Chippaways, the Natives say: these Arrows are the voice of the Sieux and tell us, "We have come to war on you, and not finding you, we leave these in the rocks in your country, with which we hoped to have pierced your bodies." This was about the year 1730. These Indians the Sieux Nation[2] are yet a powerful nation, and their

[1] This is a small stream about forty miles in length which flows into the north-western side of Lake Superior. Throughout its length it forms the boundary line between the United States and Canada.

[2] The Sioux are essentially Indians of the great plains and prairies, and have always been among the most powerful of the tribes on the North American continent. They appear to have been centred in the vicinity of the headwaters of the Mississippi river, and to have occasionally extended north-eastward to Lake Winnipeg and Lake of the Woods, and northward to the Saskatchewan river. The division of the Sioux family which is most conspicuous in western Canadian history, consists of the Assiniboin or Stonies, who appear to have separated themselves from the other Sioux tribes some time before the advent of the whites, and to have formed an alliance with the Cree to the north of them, after which they were constantly at war with the Sioux to the south of them. At the present time the total number of Assiniboin in western Canada is about 1,400.

present hunting grounds are between the Mississippe and Missisourie Rivers and [they] now make use of Horses instead of Canoes.

The Height of Land is in Latitude 48 . 6 . 43 N Longitude 90 . 43 . 38 W and Variation six degrees East, and is the dividing ridge of land from which the Streams run southeastward into Lake Superior, and north eastward into Lake Winepeg, and from thence into Hudson's Bay.

The country so far, is at present, of no value to the farmer, time may do something for it as a grazing country, from it's many Brooks and small Lakes of clear water.

The country now declines to the North eastward with many small Streams, which form a fine River. The first place worth notice is the Rainy Lake, a fine body of water of nineteen miles in length, out of which falls the Rainy River by a descent of about ten feet ; close below which is a trading House of the North [West] Company in Latitude 48 . 36 . 58 N Longitude 93 . 19 . 30 W.[1] The distance from the Height of Land is one hundred and seventeen miles the country improving, and in several places good Farms can be made. The Rainy River is a fine stream of water of about 200 yards in breadth, with only one Rapid, at which in the season, many fine Sturgeon are speared by the Natives. The length of the river to the Lake of the Woods is 50½ miles. This is the finest river in this country. The banks present the appearance of a country that can be cultivated but those acquainted with it, think the rock too near the surface. The Lake of the Woods is in length 32¼ miles with many bays, its area may be about 800 square miles, with many islets. The north eastern shores are of granite ; it's western of limestone ; and [it] touches on the great western alluvials.

[1] The post which was on the north bank of the river was known after the union of the North-West and Hudson's Bay Companies as Fort Frances, having been so called after the wife of Sir George Simpson, the Governor of the Hudson's Bay Company.

.   It seems that when the French from Canada first entered
these furr countries, every summer a Priest came to instruct
the Traders and their men in their religious duties, and
preach to them and the Natives in Latin, it being the only
language the Devil does not understand and cannot learn :
He had collected about twenty Men with a few of the Natives
upon a small Island, of rock; and while instructing them, a
large war party of Sieux Indians came on them and began the
work of death; not one escaped; whilst this was going on,
the Priest kept walking backwards and forwards on a level
rock of about fifty yards in length, with his eyes fixed on his
book, without seeming to notice them; at length as he
turned about, one of them sent an arrow through him and
he fell dead.   At this deed the rocky isle trembled and
shook; the Sieux Indians became afraid, and they retired
without stripping the dead, or taking their scalps.   These
Isles, of which there are three, are to this day called " The
Isles of the dead " (Les isles aux Morts) Such was the relation an old Canadian gave me, and which he said he had
learned of the Furr Traders who then resided among those
Indians.

The Lake of the Woods is memorable for being by every
treaty the north western boundary of the Dominions of Great
Britain and the United Territories of the United States.
This Lake may be said to be the most southern Lake of the
Stony Region that has limestone shores at it's west end, the
north and eastern parts like the other Lake, have the shores
and banks of granite, greenstone and clay slate.   This Lake,
by several Falls sends out the River Winepeg (Sea River) in
a north western direction into Lake Winepeg.   It is a bold
deep Stream of about three hundred yards in width, it has
many isles and channels, the whole is of granite formation.
By the course of the River it's length is 125 miles; In this
distance there are thirty two Falls, with as many carrying
places, the total length of which is three miles.   At it's

RAPIDS ON WINNIPEG RIVER, MANITOBA

(*Photograph: J. B. Tyrrell, 1891*)

sortie into Lake Winepeg is a trading House [1] first established by the French and kept up by the North West Company : in Latitude 50.37.46 N Longitude 95.39.34 W Variation nine degrees east. The whole extent of country from Lake Superior to this House can support, comparatively, to the extent of country, but few Natives, who are of the Chippeway Tribe; the country never could have been rich in animals ; and has long been exhausted : the Deer is almost unknown, and but few furr bearing animals remain; the principal support of the Natives is the fish of the Lakes, of which are Sturgeon,[2] White Fish,[3] Pike,[4] Pickerel[5] and Carp,[6] the quality good. The greatest use of the Winepeg House is for a depot of Provisions, which are brought to this place by the canoes and boats from the Bison countries of the Red and Saskatchewan Rivers, and distributed to the canoes and boats for the voyages to the several wintering furr trading Houses. Lake Winepeg[7] (or the Sea) so called by the Natives from it's

[1] This trading post, first known as Fort Maurepas, was founded in 1734 by one of the sons of La Vérendrye on the north side of the Winnipeg river, some little distance above its mouth. When the French left the country the post was abandoned ; but in 1792 Toussaint Lesieur, one of the employees of the North-West Company, built a post, which is now called Fort Alexander, on the south side of the river, and a few miles lower down the stream than the old French fort. Gabriel Franchère, who passed this place in 1814 on his way east from the Columbia river, wrote of it, " This trading post had more the air of a large and well-cultivated farm, than a fur-traders' factory ; a neat and elegant mansion, built on a slight eminence, and surrounded with barns, stables, storehouses, &c., and by fields of barley, peas, oats, and potatoes."

[2] *Acipenser rubicundus* Le Sueur. [E. A. P.]

[3] *Coregonus.* [E. A. P.]

[4] *Esox lucius* Linn. [E. A. P.]

[5] *Stizostedion vitreum* (Mitchill). [E. A. P.]

[6] Suckers, probably *Catostomus catostomus* (Forster), and *Moxostoma lesueuri* (Richardson). [E. A. P.]

[7] Lake Winnipeg is one of the great inland seas of Canada, having a length of 260 miles and a total area of 9,414 square miles. It is thus considerably larger than Lake Ontario, and only 500 square miles less than Lake Erie. It lies in a general south-east and north-west direction, its north-eastern shore being composed of granite and similar plutonic

size, is of the form of a rude Paraelelogram; and it's geological
structure is the same as that of all the Lakes northward and
westward; its eastern shores and banks are of the granitic
order; the north side mostly high banks of earth; the west
side is low, the shores, and the isles wholly of limestone : On
the west side, in it's southern bay, it receives the Red River
distant from the Winepeg House forty two miles. Northward of the same bay [is] the Dauphine River; at its north
west corner the Saskatchewan River, besides other lesser
streams on it's west and east sides, all which enlarge the
Saskatchewan, which flows out at the north east corner of
the Lake in Latitude 53 . 43 . 45 N Longitude 98 . 31 . 0 West.
The length of the west side of this lake from the Winepeg
House to the sortie of the Saskatchewan River into the lake
is 231 miles, N 36 W and it's east side is about 217 miles ;
the north side 45 miles and the south side about the same :
and including its isles, [it] has an area of about 10,080 square
miles. The woods all around this Lake are small, with many
branches, in winter the climate is severe ; and there [are] very
few deer, and other animals ; but the fish are good, and it's
isles in the summer season are covered with the nests of the
common Gull,[1] the eggs of which are nearly as good as those
of our common Fowls ; There are but few natives about this
Lake, and they lead a hard life.

rocks, while on its south-western shores are long low-lying areas of clay
land skirted with beaches of sand, gravel, or boulders, above which occasionally rise cliffs of horizontally stratified limestone. Considering its
great size the lake is shallow. Whitefish of excellent quality and flavour
are particularly abundant in it, and great numbers are caught every year.
The name is an Algonquin one, meaning bad water, and is properly applied by the Indians to Hudson Bay with its salt undrinkable water.
The original Algonquin name is "the Great Lake," and I have not been
able to learn how the name " Bad Water Lake " became applied to it, but
probably it was through an imperfect understanding by the white pioneers
of the information supplied them by the Indians.

[1] *Larus argentatus* Pontoppidan. [E. A. P.]

AUTUMN EVENING ON THE EASTERN SHORE OF LAKE WINNIPEG, MANITOBA

(*Photograph: J. B. Tyrrell, 1890*)

CHAPTER XI

GREAT PLAINS

Great Plains—Low range of hills—Animals of the Hills—Squirrels—Field Mice—Animals of the Plains—Bison—Manner of hunting Bisons—Pounding Bisons—Plains on Fire—Wolves—Red Deer—Jumping Deer—Antelope—Badger—Climate—Mississourie River—Snags—Bow River—Coal—Mammoth.

HITHERTO the Reader has been confined to the sterile Stony Region and the great Valley of the Lakes. My travels will now extend over countries of a very different formation; these are [called] the Great Plains as a general name, and are supposed to be more ancient than the Stony Region and the great Valley of the Lakes.

By a Plain I mean lands bearing grass, but too short for the Scythe; where the grass is long enough for the Scythe, and of which Hay can be made, I name [them] meadows. These Great Plains may be said to commence at the north side of the Gulph of Mexico, and extend northward to the latitude of fifty four degrees; where these plains are bounded by the Forests of the north, which extend unbroken to the arctic Sea. On the east they are bounded by the Mississippe River, and northward of which by the valley of the lakes; and on the west by the Rocky Mountains. The length of these Plains from South to North is 1240 miles; and the breadth from east to west to the foot of the Mountains, from 550 to 800 miles giving an area to the Great Plains of 1,031,500 square miles, in which space the Ozark Hills are included. The perpetual snows and Glaciers of the Mountains, which everywhere border the west side of these Plains, furnish water to form many Rivers; all these south of the latitude of forty nine degrees flow into the Mississippe River, the most northern of which is the Missisourie River. Close northward of the scources of the Missisourie, are the south branches of the Saskatchewan River,[1] which descends to Hudson's Bay. The next great Rivers northward are the Athabasca and Peace Rivers, which with other lesser streams form McKenzie's River, which empties itself into the Arctic Sea. It may be remarked among other great differencies between the Stoney Region and the Great Plains, that all the Rivers of the former Region, or that pass through it, meet with, and also form many Lakes and Falls, while all the Rivers in their courses through the Great Plains, and the northward forest lands, do not form a single Lake. Thus the three great Rivers of North America enter different seas. The Mississippe from Latitude 47.39.15 N Longitude 95.12.45 running about S. by E. into the gulph of Mexico in Latitude . . . Longitude. . . .[2] The Saskatchewan rising in Latitude 51.48.25 N. Longitude 116.45.13 W running NE ward into Hudson's Bay in Latitude 57.6 North Longitude 91.20 W and McKenzie's River, it's great southern branch rising in Latitude 52.20 N Longitude 118.0.0 W running NNE ward into the sea in Latitude . . . Longitude . . .[3]

So different are the courses of these Rivers on the same side of the Rocky Mountains from which they take their rise; and on entering the different seas into which they discharge their waters, they all appear of about equal magni-

[1] The Indian name for this river is Kissiskatchewan, or swift-flowing river, but the fur-traders shortened the word by leaving out the first syllable.

[2] The mouth of the Mississippi is in latitude 29° N., longitude 89° W.

[3] The Mackenzie river discharges its waters into the Arctic sea through many channels, but the mean position of its mouth might be taken as latitude 69° N., and longitude 135° W.

tude. The east side of these Great Plains have a fine appearance, the soil is rich, with many extensive Meadows. A range of fine low Hills sufficiently well wooded, with many springs of fine water and Rivulets, which for small Rivers navigable to Canoes and Boats as the Dauphine, Swan, Mouse, and Stone Indian Rivers, with several Rivulets all flowing through a rich soil. The Hills are the Turtle Hill, the most southern, and not far from the Missisourie River. The next northward are the Hair, the Nut, the Touchwood, the Dauphine, the Eagle, and the Forrest Hills. The west side of these Hills, as seen from the Plains have gentle elevations of about two hundred feet; but as seen from the eastward, present an elevation of five to eight hundred feet above the common level, and have very fine Forrests of well grown trees of Birch,[1] several kinds of Pine,[2] Poplar,[3] Aspin,[4] and small Ash[5] and Oaks.[6] These Hills are the favourite resort of the Moose[7] and the Red Deer,[8] with two or three species of the Antelope.[9] The Black, Brown, and Yellow Bears[10] feed on the Berries, the Nuts and any thing else they can catch; one of them was shot that was guarding part of an Antelope, which he had killed and partly eaten; how this clumsy brute could have caught so fleet an animal as the Antelope was a matter of wonder. The Bears lay up nothing for their subsistence in winter, and are then mostly dormant. As we travelled through the fine forests we were often amazed with

[1] *Betula papyrifera* Marsh. [E. A. P.]

[2] Besides the Banksian Pine, *Pinus divaricata* (Ait.), the spruces are probably included. [E. A. P.]

[3] *Populus balsamifera* Linn. [E. A. P.]

[4] *Populus tremuloides* Michx. [E. A. P.]

[5] *Fraxinus.* [E. A. P.]

[6] *Quercus macrocarpa* Michx. [E. A. P.]

[7] *Alces americanus* (Clinton). [E. A. P.]

[8] *Cervus canadensis* Erxleben. [E. A. P.]

[9] There is only one species, *Antilocapra americana* Ord. Perhaps Thompson here, as elsewhere, includes Deer (*Odocoileus*). [E. A. P.]

[10] The Black Bear, *Ursus americanus* Pallas, and formerly the Grizzly Bear, *Ursus horribilis* Ord. [E. A. P.]

the activity of the Squirrels[1] collecting hazel nuts for their supply in winter, and of which each collects more than a bushel, whereas the Squirrels[2] of the Pine Forests of the north seem to lay up nothing, but are out every day feeding on the cones of the White Pine.[3] The Field Mice[4] are also equally active in laying in store provisions for the winter. The climate is good, the winters about five months, the summers are warm, and autumn has many fine days. The soil is rich and deep, and [there is] much vegetable mould from the annual decay of the leaves of the Forest Trees, and the grass of the Meadows : Civilization will no doubt extend over these low hills ; they are well adapted for raising of cattle ; and when the wolves are destroyed, also for sheep ; and agriculture will succeed to a pastoral life, so far as Markets can be formed in the country, but no further ; for Canada is too distant and difficult of access. The only Port open to them is York Factory on the dismal shores of Hudson's Bay, open four months in the year. And to go to York Factory and return will require all that part of the summer which cannot be spared : but when a civilized population shall cover these countries, means will be found to make it's produce find a Market.

From the gulph of Mexico to the Latitude of 44 degrees north, these Great Plains may be said to be barren for great spaces, even of coarse grass, but the cactus grows in abundance on a soil of sand and rolled gravel ; even the several Rivers that flow through these plains do not seem to fertilise the grounds adjacent to them ; These rivers are too broad in proportion to their depth and in autumn very shallow ; the Mountains are comparatively low and therefore sooner exhausted of their winter snows, and travellers often suffer

[1] Probably Chipmunks, *Eutamias borealis* (Allen).   [E. A. P.]
[2] *Sciurus hudsonicus* Erxleben.   [E. A. P.]
[3] White Spruce, *Picea canadensis* (Mill.).   [E. A. P.]
[4] *Microtus p. drummondi* and other species.   [E. A. P.]

for want of water. But as one advances northward the soil becomes better, and the Missisourie River through its whole length to it's confluence with the Mississippe carries with it lands of deep soil, on which are many Villages of the Natives, who subsist partly by agriculture and partly by hunting. The course of the Missisourie is through an elevated part of these Plains, and it's great body of water has a swift current for about four miles an hour, which makes the ascent of this River in boats very laborious, although there are neither rapids, nor falls : Although the heads of this River give several passages across the Mountains yet from the labor being so great, and also [the being] exposed to attacks from hostile Indians, [it seems] that Steam Vessels are the only proper craft for this River ; and even to these, it's many shoals and sands offer serious impediments, for it's waters are very turbid. From these there arises more vexation than danger ; this latter is incurred every day by what are called Sawyers, Planters, and Snags, names which have been ridiculed without offering better in their stead. But however these things may be laughed at, they are very serious obstacles to the navigation of this River, and also of the Mississippe. They all proceed from trees torn up by the roots, by the freshets from heavy rains, or the melting of the Snow.

The Planter is a tree that has it's head and branches broken, its roots frequently loaded with earth, and some- times stones ; drags the bottom until something stops it, and the roots become firmly fixed in the bottom ; when the water is high and covers them, they are dangerous, but in low water can be seen : The Sawyer is generally a Tree of large dimensions broken about the middle of its length, it's roots are in the mud of the bottom of the River, sufficiently to retain them there ; but not so firmly as to keep the broken tree steady, the strong current bends the tree under as much as the play of the roots will permit, the strain on which causes a reaction, and the tree rises with a spring upwards to

several feet above the water, and with such force as will
damage or destroy any Vessel; but as the rising of these
Sawyers are often seen at some distance, they are avoided:
though I have seen some that being by the current immersed
many feet under water have taken fifteen to twenty minutes
between each appearance. The smaller the Tree the quicker
their work. A Bison Bull in swimming across the River got
on a small one, and remained swimming with all his might,
though still in the same place. When the water becomes
low, many of these Sawyers have very little water and we see
the whole machinery. The Snag is the same as the Planter,
only always under water, so that it is not seen, and cannot
be avoided; several boats have been sunk by them: the
water is so turbid nothing can be seen under it's surface. The
River next northward of the Missisourie is the Bow River,[1] so
named from a species of Yew Tree on its banks, of which
good Bows are made. This is the most southern River of the
British Dominions and the South Branch of the Saskatchewan.

The Bow River flows through the most pleasant of the
Plains, and is the great resort of the Bison and the Red Deer,
and also of the Natives; the soil appears good along it's whole
extent, but for the most part is bare of Woods, and those
that remain are fast diminishing by fire. The soil of the
plains appears to continue increasing in depth, and the same

---

[1] Bow river is the translation of the Cree Indian name Manachaban
Sipi. It is so called on account of the growth of Douglas fir on its banks,
as from this wood, if it could be obtained, bows were made. As here used
the name is applied to the whole length of the south branch of the Saskatchewan river from its source in the Rocky Mountains to its junction
with the north branch at " The Forks." As far as we yet have certain
information, it was first descended in 1800 by four men sent by Thompson
from Rocky Mountain House, and later in the same year it was again
ascended by Belleau, Fidler, and John Wills, to the forks of the Red Deer
and Bow river proper, where Chesterfield House was built by the North-
West, Hudson's Bay, and X Y Companies respectively to secure the trade
with the Blackfeet. The site was occupied by these companies for two
years, and was then abandoned.

through the Forests. In Latitude 56 degrees north, is the Smoke River, the great south branch of the Peace River; by the Gullies and Ravines the earth appears to have a depth of about 300 feet; Those who wish to find a material cause for this apparent increasing depth of earth from south to north; are led to suppose a great flood of water from the gulph of Mexico rushed northwards along the Mountains, denuded all the south parts of it's earth, leaving sand and rounded gravel for a soil; and carried the earth northward, where it has settled in great depth; here is a grand cause with a great effect. But how came the Rivers not to be defaced. The Rivers that roll through this immense unbroken body of land of Plains and Forests, are so beautifully distributed; all their banks so admirably adjusted to the volumes of water, that flow between them, that neither the heaviest rains nor the melting of the Snows of the Mountains inundate the adjacent country. In all seasons, the Indians, the Bisons[1] and Deer,[2] repose on their banks in perfect security. Who ever calmly views the admirable formation and distribution of the Rivers so wonderfully conducted to their several seas; must confess the whole to have been traced by the finger of the Great Supreme Artificer for the most benevolent purposes, both to his creature Man, and the numerous Animals he has made, none of whom can exist without water. Water may be said to be one of the principal elements of life.

Coal appears to be sparingly found in North America; and the beds [are] very far between each other. The only beds of coal that have come to my knowledge, are those which lye near the foot of the Rocky Mountains; the Missisourie is said to have coal, but of this I am not sure. The branches of the Saskatchewan River in the freshets lodge Coal on the sands of the Rivers. On the main River when the water lowers, several bushels of very good Coal can be collected on

[1] *Bison bison* (Linn.). [E. A. P.]
[2] *Odocoileus.* [E. A. P.]

the Sands, and at the Rocky Mountain House,[1] where I passed
two winters and one summer, we found the bank about
100 yards below the House to be of pure coal, and of an
excellent quality. My Blacksmith tried this coal, and at the
first trial it melted the rod of iron, and from the great heat it
gave, he had to use half charcoal; and thought the quality
of the coal superior to any brought from England. This bed
of Coal extends as far as 56 degrees of north Latitude, and
Longitude . . . West. For the Smoke River[2] is so named,
from the volumes of dark smoke sent from the Coal Mines
there on fire, and which have been burning beyond the
memory of the oldest Indian of that River.

From the very numerous remains in Siberia and parts
of Europe of the Elephant, Rhinocerous, and other large
Animals, especially near the Rivers, and in their banks, of
those countries, I was led to expect to find the remains of
those Animals in the Great Plains, and the Rivers that flow
through them : but all my steady researches, and all my
enquiries led to nothing. Over a great extent of these
Plains not a vestige could be found, nor in the banks of the
many Rivers I have examined.[3]

[1] Rocky Mountain House was built by the North-West Company in
1799, under instructions from John McDonald of Garth, who was living
at the time at Fort George. It was situated on the north side of the
North Saskatchewan river, a mile and a quarter above the mouth of
Clearwater river. Thompson spent here the winters of 1800-01 and
1806-07. When I visited the place in 1886, some of the bastions of the
old fort were still standing.

[2] This river, which is one of the large branches of Peace river, is
rightly stated by Thompson to have been named from the seams of coal
which are burning on its banks. It is set on fire by spontaneous com-
bustion caused by the oxidation of iron pyrites, which occurs associated
with the coal.

[3] It is a rather curious circumstance that the occurrence of fossil bones
in western Canada should have been unknown to Thompson and his associates, for while they might not have found them themselves, it would
have been only reasonable to suppose that they would have been told
about them by the Indians. It is true that mastodon bones are very
scarce, there being only one authenticated record of a find of such bones

The fossil bones of the large animals that have been found on this Continent appear to be limited to the United States east of the Allegany Mountains (Hills), and on the west side to the Ohio River, and the countries southward on the east side of the Mississippe and to South America. On the west side of the Mississippe only one large bone has been found, which the Natives reverenced and [which] has given a name to two tribes, the great, and the little, Osage Indians.

This large bone, several years ago, was purchased from the Natives and placed in the museum of Washington City. The Natives when questioned on the fossil bones of the Ohio River, made a fable for an answer. That in old times these Mammoths were numerous; they devoured all other Animals, and did not allow Man to live; at length the Great Spirit became angry. He descended with the Thunder in his hands, and destroyed them all; except the big Bull, the Thunder struck him on the forehead but did not kill him, he bounded away, sprang over the Mississippe River, and ran to the west, where he yet lives. (Note. When on the head waters of the Athabasca River and Mountain defiles to the Columbia River; the Natives, but especially the White and Iroquois Hunters, all declared these places to be the haunt of an enormous Animal who lived on grass, moss and the tender shoots of the willows; nor could all my arguments when there make a single convert to the contrary).

Not a single fossil bone of an Elephant, Rhinocerous, or Mammoth has been found in all Canada nor about any of

on the plains of the west, namely, on Shell river in northern Manitoba. But on the banks of the Red Deer river, as well as on some of the other streams farther south, huge bones of dinosaurs and other gigantic reptilian animals of late Cretaceous age are fairly abundant. In fact this locality is now one of the most famous collecting grounds of these fossil bones in North America. The reason for this ignorance was doubtless that these bones are not found on the banks of the North Saskatchewan river, which was the ordinary line of travel at that time, and that the streams to the south of it, on which they do occur, were practically unknown to the white men.

the Great Lakes, and valley of the [St.] Lawrence, and northward to the Arctic Circle, although almost all these countries
are sufficiently known ; nor has the travels of Captain Franklin
in the Arctic Regions been attended with any success on this
subject.   On the west side of the Rocky Mountains, I passed
six year [1] of discovery, yet not a vestige that these great
Animals once existed in those parts could be found.   We may
therefore conclude, that the great animals of North America
were limited to the east and west sides of the Allegany Hills,
and the east side of the valley of the Mississippe, and no
farther to the northward and westward on this Continent :
and that these were all destroyed by the Deluge, which also
put an end to other races of animals and thus the Great
Creator made the Earth more habitable for his favourite
creature Man.

[1] The years referred to are 1807 to 1812 inclusive.

CHAPTER XII

SWAN RIVER COUNTRY

Cross Lake Winipeg—Dauphine River—Swan River—Swan River House—Set out for Upper House on Stone Indian River—Trading House in charge of M. Belleau—Reach Upper House on Red Deer River—Fearlessness of Plain Deer—Man and the Beaver—Introduction of iron implements by the French—Character of the Beaver—The Dam— Beaver Houses—Burrows—Beaver Hunting—Beaver Dogs —Long Beaver Dam—Tradition of the Beaver—Castorum —Destruction of the Beaver—Journey—Stone Indians.

I HOPE I have now given such a general view of the formation of the Great Plains and their eastern borders as will enable the reader readily to follow me in my travels. One of the principal objects of the North West Company was to ascertain the Courses of the Rivers, the situation of the Lakes, and of their several Trading Houses, which in some parts appeared to be too near each other, and in other parts, too distant.

From the Winepeg House we coasted the Lake with it's shore of limestone, mostly low, but at times forming cliffs to the height of fifty feet to the mouth of the Dauphine River.[1] To this place our straight course has been N 43 W 127 miles. We now proceeded up the Dauphine River, a fine stream of

[1] Dauphin river is now known as the Little Saskatchewan river, and flows from Lake Manitoba into Lake Winnipeg. Thompson omits to mention that he passed through Partridge Crop and St. Martin lakes on the way up the Dauphin river, and that after leaving the head of this river he passed through a long stretch of Lake Manitoba before he reached the Meadow Portage.

N

about thirty yards in width, and an average of three feet in depth. As we advanced the country improved in soil, and also the Forests through which it runs, but the Deer and the Beaver are few. Having proceeded eighty eight miles in a straight course of S 74 W, the River has many turnings in this distance, we came to the Meadow Carrying Place[1] of 2760 yards, which leads from the River to Lake Winepegoos[2] (the little Sea). The Dauphine comes out of this Lake, but it's course is now so circuitous, with shoal Rapids, that the Carrying Place is preferred. We went over this Lake for fifty nine miles to the entrance of the Swan River, a small stream of about fifteen to twenty yards in width, with a depth of about three feet and gentle current, through a fine country, for we are now among the fine low Hills I have already mentioned; the Beaver are now plenty; but the Deer are only beginning to leave the heights of the Hills where they pass the summer.

Having proceeded twelve miles we came to the Swan River House of the North West Company,[3] in Latitude 52.24.5 N Longitude 100.36.52 W Variation 13 East. There were but two families of the Natives, Nahathaway Indians to whom these countries belong : but several Chippewas[4] have lately

[1] Lake Winnipegosis discharges into Lake Manitoba by Waterhen river, a stream which first flows north and then turns and flows a little east of south, almost parallel with its former course. In order to avoid the ascent of this stream it was customary for the canoemen to carry their canoes and cargoes over a low grassy ridge 3,130 yards across, which separated the two lakes. This was known as the Meadow Portage or Carrying Place.

[2] The name of this lake is now regularly spelled Winnipegosis. It is a large narrow body of moderately clear water, with a greatest length of 120 miles, and a total area of 2,000 square miles. The total distance travelled by Thompson through this lake from the Meadow Portage to the mouth of Swan river was 145 miles, and not 59 miles as stated in the text.

[3] For a more exact statement of Thompson's movements at this time, and the position of this house, see p. lxxiii.

[4] The Chippewa, or as they are sometimes called the Ojibways, are one of the great branches of the Algonquin family which was so widely spread

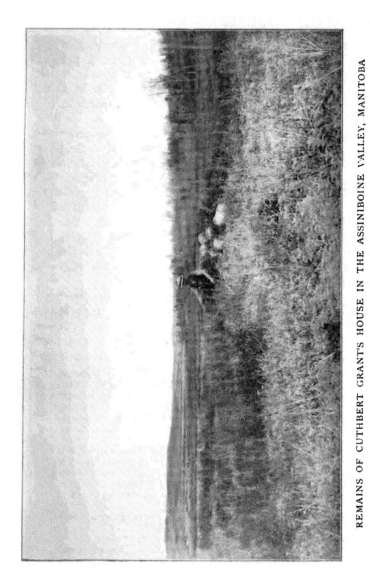

REMAINS OF CUTHBERT GRANT'S HOUSE IN THE ASSINIBOINE VALLEY, MANITOBA

(*Photograph : J. B. Tyrrell, 1890*)

come from the southward where their own countries are exhausted of the Beaver and the Deer. These two families having procured Ammunition and Tobacco went off to inform the others of the arrival of the Canoes. From the Swan River, on the 26th September 1796 [1797] we proceeded with Horses across the country to the Stone Indian River, (on which the North West Company have several trading Houses) to the upper House in charge of M[r] Cuthbert Grant,[1] N 40¼ W 90 miles; this distance was mostly through fine Forests through which our Horses found the ground every where good, except a few wet meadows, in which they did not go ancle deep. My Indian Guide had learned that the Pawnee Indians had been defeated, and altho' by Indians of whom he knew nothing, yet kept bawling the whole day, " We have fought with the Pawnee's and have conquered them." He was a Chippeway. In the evening when we camped, I told him, he was the only Warrior I ever knew, that boasted of conquering a people whom he never saw, nor was likely to see, and that no one would believe him; he replied, We young men, at present, have no opportunities of distinguishing ourselves, the enemies that our fathers warred on are driven across the Missisourie River, far beyond our reach, but I will sing no more.

We now turned to the trading House in charge of M[r] Belleau,[2] situated between the Swan and Stone Indian Rivers,

over Canada from the Rocky Mountains eastward to the Atlantic ocean. The centre of the territory occupied by them was probably about Sault Ste. Marie, at the east end of Lake Superior.

[1] For the position of this post, see p. lxxiii. It appears to have been founded by Peter Grant about 1793, and to have been occupied by Cuthbert Grant afterwards. Cuthbert Grant was the father of the Cuthbert Grant who took so large a part in the Red River troubles in the early part of the nineteenth century. He had been with Peter Pond and Alexander Mackenzie on Lake Athabaska in 1786 and 1789. Masson says that he died in 1799.

[2] Pierre Belleau, the man here referred to, was an old engagé of the North-West Company who was in charge of a number of posts throughout the North-West in the latter part of the eighteenth century. A man of

and as usual observed for Latitude and Longitude, which gave 51° 51′ 9″ N 102°–30″ W the course N. 12 W 30 miles. In this distance the country had much wet ground from the many ponds kept full by Beaver Dams. We returned to Mʳ Grants, and from there journeyed to the Upper House on the Red Deer River,¹ in charge of Mʳ Hugh McGillis, in Latitude 52–59–7 N Longitude 101–32–27 W the course N 10 E 111 Miles, but the Ponds formed by the Beaver, and their Dams which we had to cross lengthened our Road to 150 miles; these sagacious animals were in full possession of the country, but their destruction had already began, and was now in full operation. All the above Trading Houses of the

this name, and probably the same individual, was in charge of the party for the X Y Company which ascended the South Saskatchewan river in the summer of 1800, and founded Chesterfield House at the forks of the Bow and Red Deer rivers.

¹ Thompson's map shows this house to have been on the north bank of the Red Deer river. It was probably opposite the mouth of the Etoimami river, between three and four miles south of Hudson Bay Junction on the Canadian Northern Railway, where the ruins of two old houses were seen in 1889. This post is probably the one referred to as Fort La Biche on Pond's map of 1790, though there it is wrongly placed on the Swan river. In this case, it was doubtless one of the oldest trading posts south of the Saskatchewan river and west of the Manitoba lakes; the only other posts designated on the map being Fort Dauphin on Lake Dauphin, and Fort Epinette on the Assiniboine river. There was also another trading post on the Red Deer river which was known as the Lower Settlement, and was said to be sixty miles below the Upper Settlement. It was situated on the north bank of the river a short distance west of Red Deer lake, on a flat, which, in 1889, was covered with grass and rose bushes or small poplars. Here and there were pits or cellars where potatoes had doubtless been stored during the winter, and it was possible to see that the natural sod had been broken in order to grow potatoes and other vegetables. Just on the bank of the river and almost ready to be carried away by the first flood was a heap of earth and stones representing a chimney of one of the old houses. All remains of the other houses had already been carried away. A little nearer Red Deer lake, and on the south side of the river, were the remains of the chimneys and cellars of four old houses representing the site of a trading post of the Hudson's Bay Company. From one of the heaps of earth and stones, representing all that remained of a chimney of one of the houses, a large poplar tree was then growing.

North West Company from Canada were on the south west
sides of the range of low Hills which border the east side of
the Great Plains and hitherto all my journeys were those of
pleasure : The Moose Deer of these Hills, although always a
very wary animal, yet from their being more numerous, also
from the Forests being more open, were not the same cautious,
timid, animal that it is in the close, dark, Pine Forests of the
north : aided perhaps, by being accustomed to see other
species of Deer and Horses ; but the Stag[1] with his half a
dozen of Does, which he as carefully guards, and is as ready
to fight for, as any Turkish Pacha for his Harem, that is the
pride of these forests and meadows. But when the season of
love is over, as now, his Does leave him, his head droops,
and [he] is no longer the lordly animal that appeared as light
on the ground as a Bird on the wing. On such a variety of
Hill and Plain, of Forests and Meadows I expected to have
found several mineral Springs, which are so frequent in other
countries ; but neither my attention to this object, nor my
enquiries could find one single Spring : all my information
led only to the saline Brooks of the Red River, from some of
which salt is made by boiling the saline water. All those
fine countries are the hunting grounds of the Nahathaway
Indians.

Previous to the discovery of Canada (about 320 years ago,)
this Continent from the Latitude of forty degrees north to
the Arctic Circle, and from the Atlantic to the Pacific Ocean,
may be said to have been in the possession of two distinct
races of Beings, Man and the Beaver. Man was naked and
had to procure clothing from the skins of animals ; his only
arms were a Stake, pointed and hardened in the fire, a Bow
with Arrows, the points hardened with fire, or headed with
stone or bone of the legs of the Deer, a Spear headed in the
same manner, and a club of heavy wood, or made of a rounded
stone of four, or five pounds weight, inclosed in raw hide,

[1] *Cervus canadensis* Erxleben. [E. A. P.]

and by the same bound round a handle of wood of about
two feet in length, bound firm to the Stone.   Such were the
weapons Man had for self defence and with which to procure
his food and clothing.   Against the bones of an Animal his
Arrows and Spear had little effect; the flank of every animal
is open, and thither, into the bowels, the Indian directed
his fatal and unerring Arrows. (Note. Every Hunter is
acquainted with the effects of wounds in the different parts
of an animal; with an arrow in, or a ball through, the bowels,
an animal if pursued will go a long way : but if let alone,
soon becomes as it were sick, lies down on it's belly and there
dies).   Besides his weapons, the Snare was much in use, and
the Spear to assist it for large animals, and by all accounts
the Deer and furr bearing animals were very numerous, and
thus Man was Lord of all the dry land and all that was on it.
The other race was the Beaver, they were safe from every
animal but Man, and the Wolverine.   Every year each pair
having from five to seven young, which they carefully reared,
they become innumerable, and except the Great Lakes, the
waves of which are too turbulent, occupied all the waters of
the northern part of the Continent.   Every River where the
current was moderate and sufficiently deep, the banks at the
water edge were occupied by their houses.   To every small
Lake, and all the Ponds they builded Dams, and enlarged
and deepened them to the height of the dams.   Even to
grounds occasionally overflowed, by heavy rains, they also
made dams, and made them permanent Ponds, and as they
heightened the dams [they] increased the extent and added to
the depth of the water ; Thus all the low lands were in possession of the Beaver, and all the hollows of the higher grounds.
Small Streams were dammed across and Ponds formed; the
dry land with the dominions of Man contracted, every where
he was hemmed in by water without the power of preventing
it : he could not diminish the numbers half so fast as they
multiplied, and their houses were proof against his pointed

stake, and his arrows could seldom pierce their skins. (Note. In my travels, several thousands of the Natives were not half so well armed.) In this state Man and the Beaver had been for many centuries, but the discovery of Canada by the French, and their settlements up the St Lawrence soon placed the Natives far superior to the Beaver.

Without Iron, man is weak, very weak, but armed with Iron, he becomes the Lord of the Earth, no other metal can take it's place. For the furrs which the Natives traded, they procured from the French Axes, Chissels, Knives, Spears and other articles of iron, with which they made good hunts of furr bearing animals and procured woollen clothing. Thus armed the houses of the Beavers were pierced through, the Dams cut through, and the water of the Ponds lowered, or wholly run off, and the houses of the Beaver and their Borrows laid dry, by which means they became an easy prey to the Hunter.

The Beaver[1] is an animal well known; the average weight of a full grown male is about fifty five pounds. his meat is agreeable to most although fat and oily; the tail is a delicacy. They are always in pairs, and work together. their first business is to insure a sufficient depth and extent of water for the winter; and if nature has not done this for them, they make dams to obtain it. If there are more families than one in a piece of water, they all work together, each appearing to labor on a particular part.

The Dam is made of Earth, pieces of wood laid oblique to the direction of the dam. The wood employed is always of Aspin, Poplar or large Willow and Alders; if Pine is used it is through necessity, not by choice; the bottom is well laid, and if small stones are at hand, they make use of them for the bottom of the Dam, the earth is brought between their fore paws and throat, laid down, and by several strokes of the tail made compact: the pieces of wood, are with their

[1] *Castor canadensis* Kuhl. [E. A. P.]

teeth, which are very sharp, and formed like small chissels, cut into the lengths they want, brought to the dam, and worked in, and thus the Dam is raised to the height required. It is a remark of many, that Dams erected by the art of Man are frequently damaged, or wholly carried away by violent freshets, but no power of water has ever carried away a Beaver Dam. Having secured a sufficient depth of water each family builds a separate house, this is in the form of a low dome : from the door way which is a little way in the water, gradually rising to about thirty inches in height and about six feet in diameter; the materials are the same as those of the Dam, and worked in the same manner, only the pieces of wood are much shorter, and if at hand, small flat stones are worked in. And the coating of the first year may be about four to five inches thick and every year an additional coat is added, until it is a foot, or more, in thickness. Grass then grows upon it, and it looks like a little knowl. The next work is to make Burrows of retreat; the first year seldom more than one, or two can be made, and sometimes none; these are carried on, from a few inches below the surface of the water, direct from it, gradually rising, of about a foot in height by twenty inches in breadth, so that a Beaver can turn in them; their length depends on their easiness of digging the ground. The general length is about ten feet, but in good earth they often are of twenty feet, or more. The second and third years the numbers of Burrows are augmented to five or six, and where the Beaver have been a long time, the Ponds, and small Lakes have numerous burrows.

The Indians think the Male and Female are faithful to each other, they bring up their young for the first year with care and protection, until the next spring when the female is about to litter she drives them all away, and some of them, before they can be made to stay away, receive severe cuts on the back from the teeth of the old ones. The young Beavers are very playful, and whimper like children. The Beaver is supposed to attain to the age of fifteen years, some think to twenty years. The Beaver Hunter is often at a loss what to do, and sometimes passes a whole day without coming to a determination; his shortest and surest way, is to stake up the door way of the house, the stakes he carries with him ready for the purpose, but the Beaver are so watchful that his approach is heard and they retire to their burrows. Some prefer, first finding the burrows and closing them up with stakes and cutting off all retreat from the house; whichever method he takes, difficulties and hard labor attends him. To determine the place of the Beavers, for the whole family of seven, or nine, are seldom all found in the house, the Indian is greatly assisted by a peculiar species of small Dog, of a light make, about three feet in height, muzzle sharp, and brown, full black eyes, with a round brown spot above each eye, the body black, the belly of a fawn color, it's scent very keen, and almost unerring. This Dog points out by smelling and scratching, the weakest part of the Beaver House, and the part where they lie; the same in the burrows, which are then doubly staked; the Indian with his Axe and Ice Chissel makes a hole over the place shown by the Dog, the Beaver has changed it's place, to find to which end of the burrow it is gone, a crooked stick is employed until it touches the Beaver; another hole is made, and the Beaver is killed with the Ice Chissel, which has a heavy handle of about seven feet in length. When the dog smells and scratches at two, or three places on the beaver house, it is a mark that there are several in it. The door way being doubly staked, the Indian proceeds to make a hole near the centre of it, to give full range to his ice chissel, and not one escapes, but all [are killed] with hard labor: Such was the manner of killing the Beaver until the introduction of Steel Traps, which baited with Castorum soon brought on the almost total destruction of these numerous and sagacious animals.

From this long digression, I return to my travels in the

·Nut Hill; on a fine afternoon in October, the leaves beginning
to fall with every breeze, a season to me of pleasing melancholy, from the reflections it brings to the mind; my guide
informed me that we would have to pass over a long beaver
Dam; I naturally expected we should have to load our
Horses carefully over it; when we came to it, we found it a
narrow stripe of apparently old solid ground, with short
grass, and wide enough for two horses to walk abreast: we
passed on, the lower side showed a descent of seven feet, and
steep, with a rill of water from beneath it. The side of the
dam next to the water was a gentle slope. To the southward was a sheet of water of about one mile and a half square
of area, surrounded by moderate, low grassy banks, the
Forests mostly of Aspin and Poplar but very numerous
stumps of the trees cut down and partly carried away by the
Beavers. In two places of this Pond were a cluster of Beaver
Houses, like miniature villages. When we had proceeded
over more than half way of the Dam, which was a full mile
in length, we came to an aged Indian, his arms folded across
his breast; with a pensive countenance, looking at the
Beavers swiming in the water, and carrying their winter's
provisions to their houses, his form tall and erect, his hair
almost white, which was almost the only effect that age
appeared to have on him, though we concluded he must be
about eighty years of age, and in this opinion we were afterwards confirmed by the ease and readiness with which he
spoke of times long past. I enquired of him how many
beaver houses there were in the pond before us, he said,
There are now fifty two, we have taken several of their
houses; they are difficult to take, and those we have taken
were by means of the noise of the water on their houses from
a strong wind which enabled us to stake them in, otherwise
they would have retired to their burrows, which are very
many. He invited us to pass the night at his tent which was
close by, the Sun was low, and we accepted the offer.

In the Tent was an old man, almost his equal in age with women and children; we preferred the open air, and made a good fire to which both of the old men came, and after smoking a while conversation came on. As I had always conversed with the Natives as one Indian with another, and been attentive to learn their traditions on the animals on Mankind, and on other matter in ancient times, and the present occasion appeared favorable for this purpose. Setting aside questions and answers which would be tiresome; they said, by ancient tradition of which they did not know the origen the Beavers had been an ancient people, and then lived on the dry land; they were always Beavers, not Men, they were wise and powerful, and neither Man, nor any animal made war on them.

They were well clothed as at present, and as they did not eat meat, they made no use of fire, and did not want it. How long they lived this way we cannot tell, but we must suppose they did not live well, for the Great Spirit became angry with them, and ordered Weesaukejauk to drive them all into the water and there let them live, still to be wise, but without power; to be food and clothing for man, and the prey of other animals, against all which his defence shall be his dams, his house and his burrows: You see how strong he makes his dams, those that we make for fishing wiers are often destroyed by the water, but his always stands. His House is not made of sand, or loose stones, but of strong earth with wood and sometimes small stones; and he makes burrows to escape from his enemies, and he always has his winter stock of provisions secured in good time. When he cuts down a tree, you see how he watches it, and takes care that it shall not fall on him. "But if so wise, for what purpose does the Beaver cut down large trees of which he makes no use whatever." We do not know, perhaps an itching of his teeth and gums.

The old Indian paused, became silent, and then in a low

tone [they] talked with each other; after which he continued his discourse. I have told you that we believe in years long passed away, the Great Spirit was angry with the Beaver, and ordered Weesaukejauk (the Flatterer) to drive them all from the dry land into the water; and they became and continued very numerous; but the Great Spirit has been, and now is, very angry with them and they are now all to be destroyed. About two winters ago Weesaukejauk showed to our brethren, the Nepissings and Algonquins the secret of their destruction; that all of them were infatuated with the love of the Castorum of their own species, and more fond of it than we are of fire water. We are now killing the Beaver without any labor, we are now rich, but [shall] soon be poor, for when the Beaver are destroyed we have nothing to depend on to purchase what we want for our families, strangers now over run our country with their iron traps, and we, and they will soon be poor:

The Indian is not a materialist, nor does he believe in Instinct, a word of civilized man, which accounts for great part of the actions of Mankind, and of all those of animated nature; the Indian believes that every animal has a soul which directs all it's motions, and governs all it's actions; even a tree, he conceives must somehow be animated, though it cannot stir from it's place. Some three years ago (1797) the Indians of Canada and New Brunswick, on seeing the Steel Traps so successful in catching Foxes and other animals, thought of applying it to the Beaver, instead of [using] the awkward traps they made, which often failed; At first they were set in the landing paths of the Beaver, with about four inches of water on them, and a piece of green aspin for a bait, and in this manner more were caught than by the common way; but the beaver paths made their use too limited and their ingenuity was employed to find a bait that would allure the Beaver to the place of the trap; various things and mixtures of ingredients were tried without success;

but chance made some try if the male could not be caught by adding the Castorum of the female; a mixture of this Castorum beat up with the green buds of the aspin was made. A piece of dry willow of about eight inches in length beat and bruised fine, was dipped in the mixture, it was placed at the water edge about a foot from the steel trap, so that the Beaver should pass direct over it and be caught; this bait proved successful, but to the surprise of the Indians, the females were caught as well as the males : The secret of this bait was soon spread, every Indian procured from the Traders four to six steel traps, the weight of one was about six to eight pounds; all labor was now at an end, the Hunter moved about at pleasure with his traps and infallible bait of Castorum. Of the infatuation of this animal for Castorum I saw several instances. A trap was negligently fastened by its small chain to the stake to prevent the Beaver taking away the trap when caught; it slipped, and the Beaver swam away with the trap, and it was looked upon as lost. Two nights after he was taken in a trap with the other trap fast to his thigh. Another time, a Beaver passing over a Trap to get the Castorum, had his hind leg broke, with his teeth he cut his broken leg off, and went away, we concluded he would not come again, but two nights afterwards, he was found fast in a trap. In every case the Castorum is taken away. The stick with this, was always licked, or sucked clean, and seemed to act as a suporific, as they remained more than a day, without coming out of their houses.

The Nepissings, the Algonquins and Iroquois Indians having exhausted their own countries, now spread themselves over these countries, and as they destroyed the Beaver, moved forwards to the northward and westward ; the Natives, the Nahathaways, did not in the least molest them; the Chippaways and other tribes made use of Traps of Steel; and of the Castorum. For several years all these Indians were rich, the Women and Children, as well as the Men, were covered with silver brooches, Ear Rings, Wampum, Beads and other trinkets. Their mantles were of fine scarlet cloth, and all was finery and dress. The Canoes of the Furr Traders were loaded with packs of Beaver, the abundance of the article lowered the London prices. Every intelligent Man saw the poverty that would follow the destruction of the Beaver, but there were no Chiefs to controul it; all was perfect liberty and equality. Four years afterwards (1797) almost the whole of these extensive countries were denuded of Beaver, the Natives became poor, and with difficulty procured the first necessaries of life, and in this state they remain, and probably for ever. A worn out field may be manured, and again made fertile; but the Beaver, once destroyed cannot be replaced: they were the gold coin of the country, with which the necessaries of life were purchased.

It would be worth while for some Gentleman who has nothing to do; to look at the sales by auction; the number of skins by private sale; and otherwise disposed of, to count the number of Beavers that have been killed, and procured from the northern part of this Continent.

We now journeyed to a trading House in charge of Mr Thorburn,[1] in Latitude 50–28–58 N and Longitude 101–45–45

[1] I have never visited the site of this old trading post, but Thompson's survey and observations place it on the bank of the Qu'Appelle river. It was built by a Canadian trader named Robert Grant about the year 1787, and was named by him Fort Esperance. It, or some fort in the immediate vicinity, was continuously occupied thereafter for many years. Its chief trade was with the Assiniboin Indians for buffalo meat. William Thorburn, who was in charge of it at this time, was doubtless the same man who was in charge of a post on the Saskatchewan river when Thompson passed down it in 1794; and in 1797 his name is among the list of partners of the North-West Company as in charge of Red river. From this trading post Thompson travelled south-eastward across the plains towards the mouth of the Souris river, and in his journal he notes that he passed an "old fort," doubtless Mountain à la Bosse, which John McDonnell, writing about 1797, says "has been frequently established and as often abandoned, owing to the oppositions that came into that quarter." It was situated on the south bank of the Assiniboine river, east of the mouth of Gopher Creek, in Sect. 11 or 12, Tp. 10, R. 25, west of

West, in a course S 7 E 68 Miles. Having settled the position of this place, we proceeded down the Stone Indian River to the House in charge of Mr John McDonell,[1] in Latitude 49-40-56 N Longitude 99-27-15 West, on a course S 69 E 131 miles. These distances in a straight line are along the banks of the Stone Indian River, about thirty yards in breadth, but deriving it's water from rains and Snows, is of various depths, according to the seasons; in autumn [it is] always

the Principal Meridian, between two and three miles south of the village of Routledge on the main line of the Canadian Pacific Railway. The situation was a striking one on the point of a level grassy plain which jutted out into the valley at an elevation of 200 feet above the river. The fort would appear to have been enclosed by a stockade 200 by 250 feet on the sides; and within the enclosure were a number of houses for the officers and men.

[1] John McDonnell was a brother of Miles McDonnell, the first Governor of the Red River colony under Lord Selkirk. He became a partner of the North-West Company about 1796, and remained in the North-West until 1815, when he sold out and settled in the township of Hawkesbury, in the province of Quebec, where he died and was buried in the Roman Catholic cemetery. See Masson, *Les Bourgeois de la Compagnie du Nord-Ouest*, vol. i., Quebec, 1889, pp. 267-295.

The trading post which was occupied by McDonnell was situated on the north bank of the Assiniboine (Stone Indian) river, about two miles above the mouth of the Souris or Mouse river, in the north-east quarter of Sect. 19, Tp. 8, R. 16, west of the Principal Meridian, and three miles north of Banting on the south-western branch of the Canadian Pacific Railway. The site was visited by me in 1890, and at that time evidences of the existence of this post could be seen on a grassy prairie about four or five acres in extent, surrounded by a forest of small aspen poplar, near a ford where an old, but well-defined, trail crosses the river. The site of the post was marked by pits and mounds which represented the cellars and chimneys of the houses.

The ruins of another old trading post, possibly one that had belonged to the Hudson's Bay Company, were said to be clearly marked at a place about two miles and a half farther up the stream, and also on its north bank, in Sect. 35, Tp. 8, R. 17. On the south side of the Assiniboine river the remains of two other trading establishments were found in the same year, about half a mile apart. Around these little forts the lines of the palisades, with their bastions and gateways, could readily be traced, and within the stockades were the remains of the cellars and chimneys of a number of houses. Pieces of burnt clay that had evidently been between the logs of which the houses had been built, showed that the houses had been destroyed by fire.

shoal. Its course is on the east side of the great Plains, and
the south west side of the low Hills, from whence it receives
several Brooks, and from the Plains the Calling River and a
few brooks. Its course is very sinuous, this, with it's shoals,
detains the Canoes for the upper trading Houses to late in
the season; From M' Grant's to M' John M°Donell the
distance is in a direct line near two hundred miles which the
windings of the River increases to near six hundred miles.
This River everywhere flows thro' a pleasant country of good
soil, and in time to come will no doubt, be covered with
agricultural population; The Bison, the Moose and the Red
Deer with two species of the Antelope, give to the Nahathaway Indians, an easy subsistence; but in a short time the
only furrs they will have to buy the necessities they want,
and cannot now do without, are the Wolf,[1] Fox,[2] Badger,[3] and
Musk Rat,[4] with the dried meat of the Bison and Deer. The
Stone Indians, a numerous tribe of the Sieux Nation possess
the country southward and westward of this River, to the
Missisourie River, but this latter in common with several
other Tribes. They are friendly to the white people, a fine
looking race of Men and Women, but most noted Horse
thieves of the Horses of other Tribes. It is said of a York-
shire man " Give him a bridle, and he will find a horse";
but these will find both the bridles and the Horses.

We remained with M' John M°Donell twelve days: in
which time I put my journal, surveys and sketches of the
countries that were in black lead into ink; and having sealed
them up directed them to the Agents of the North West
Company.

[1] *Canis nubilus* Say. [E. A. P.]
[2] *Vulpes fulva regalis* Merriam. [E. A. P.]
[3] *Taxidea taxus* (Schreber). [E. A. P.]
[4] *Fiber zibethicus cinnamominus* Hollister. [E. A. P.]

CHAPTER XIII

JOURNEY TO MANDANE VILLAGES

Start for Mandane Villages—Ventures—Cross Stone Indian River—Journal—Warned by Stone Indians to be on our guard against the Sieux—Take great Traverse to Turtle Hills—Ash House—Camp of Stone Indians—Massacre in 1794—Peace in 1802—Storm on the Plains—Men Lost—All day in camp—Buffalo Hunt—Reach Mouse River—Follow Mouse River—Elbow of Mouse River—Sieux Indian war party—Dog Tent Hills—Missisourie Reached.

HAVING made our preparations for a journey to the Mandane Villages on the banks of the Missisourie River; on the 28th November 1797, we set off.[1] Our guide and interpreter, who had resided eight years in their Villages was a Mons.r René Jussomme who fluently spoke the Mandane Language. M.r Hugh M.cCrachan, a good hearted Irishman, who had been often to the Villages, and resided there for weeks and months; and seven french Canadians, a fine, hardy, good humoured sett of Men, fond of full feeding, willing to hunt for it, but more willing to enjoy it: When I have reproved them, for what I thought Gluttony, eating full eight pounds of fresh meat p.r day, they have told me, that, their greatest enjoyment of life was Eating. They are all extremely ignorant, and without the least education, and appear to set no value on it. All these

---

[1] The names of the men who accompanied Thompson on this journey are given by him in his note-books as follows: " René Jussomme, Joseph Boisseau, Hugh McCraken, Alexis Vivier, Pierre Gilbert, Fra.s Perrault, Touss.t Vandril, L.s Jos. Houl, J. B.te Minie." For references to these men, see Coues, *New Light*, p. 301, &c.

o

excepting my servant man, A. Brosseau, who had been a soldier, were free traders on their own account for this journey, each of them on credit from M^r McDonell, took a venture in goods and trinkets to the amount of forty to sixty skins to be paid in furrs, by trading with the natives of the Villages. I was readily supplied with every thing I required which was chiefly ammunition, tobacco and a few trinkets for expenses. For my service I had two Horses. Monsr Jussomme had one, and the men thirty dogs, their own property, each two hauled a flat sled upon which their venture was lashed; these Dogs had all been traded from the Stone Indians, who make great use of them in their encampments. They were all like half dog, half wolf, and always on the watch to devour every thing they could get their teeth on; they did not [do] willing work, and most of them had never hauled a flat sled, but the Canadians soon break them in, by constant flogging, in which they seem to take great delight; when on the march the noise was intolerable, and made me keep two or three miles ahead.

As my journey to the Missisourie is over part of the Great Plains, I shall give it in the form of a journal, this form, however dull, is the only method in my opinion, that can give the reader a clear idea of them. With our three Horses and thirty Dogs with their Sleds, we crossed the Stone River on the ice; the Snow on the ground was three inches in depth. We went about six miles and put up in the woods of the Mouse River,[1] which joins the Stone Indian River about two miles below the House. The dogs unused to hauling going any where, and every where from the Men, who employed themselves all the way in swearing at, and flogging them; until we put up, when the Dogs were un-harnessed, a piece of line tied round the neck of each, and one, or both fore feet were brought through it, to keep them quiet and from straying away. At 8 PM the Thermometer 20 degrees below zero.

[1] Souris river.

November 29th. A westerly breeze, at 7 AM 27 below zero, the Men thought it too cold to proceed.

November 30th. 7 AM 32 being 64 degrees below the freezing point. 9 PM 36 too cold to proceed over the open plains : and certainly an intensity of cold not known on the same parallel of Latitude near the Mountains. Necessity obliged us to hunt the Bison, we killed two Bulls, we could bring only half the meat to the Tent, which satisfied ourselves and the Dogs.

December 1st. A WSW Gale. Thermometer 37 below Zero. We could not proceed but had the good fortune to kill a good Bison Cow which kept us in good humour. The severe cold and high wind made the Tent very smoky, so that, notwithstanding the bad weather, we walked about in the woods the greatest part of the day, and when in the Tent we had to lie down.

December 2nd. At 8 AM Ther 36, at 8 PM 15, the wind WSW. We killed a Bison Cow, which kept the Dogs quiet.

December 3rd. At 8 AM 3, at 8 PM 3 the weather was now mild but a WNW Gale came on with snow and high drift [so] that we could not see a fourth a mile from us. And our journey is over open plains from one patch of Wood to another patch ; for the Mouse River, on which we are camped, has Woods only in places, and many miles distant from each other. And these patches of Wood must be kept in sight to guide over the plains and none of the Men knew the use of the Compass, and did not like to trust it. We could not proceed and the Tent was disagreeable with smoke.

December 4th. 7 AM 4 above Zero WSW gale of Wind. At 9 AM we set off, and went eleven miles to a grove of Oaks,[1] Ash,[2] Elm,[3] Nut[4] Trees, and other hard Woods ; which are

---

[1] *Quercus macrocarpa* Michx. [E. A. P.]
[2] *Fraxinus*. [E. A. P.]
[3] *Ulmus americana* Linn. [E. A. P.]
[4] Probably Hickory, *Hicoria*, species uncertain. [E. A. P.]

always the Woods of this River : At this place we came to
five Tents of Stone Indians, who as usual received us with
kindness ; they did not approve of our journey to the Missisourie : and informed us, that some skirmishes had taken
place between the Mandane and Sieux Indians in which the
latter lost several Men, which they attributed to the Ammunition furnished to the former by the trading parties from the
Stone Indian River, such as ours were ; and that they had
determined to way lay us, and plunder us of all we had, and
also take all our scalps, and [they] warned us to be on our
guarde ; I did not like this news, but the Men paid no attention to it, thinking it proceeded from hatred to the Mandanes.
We then followed the River banks for seven miles, and camped
at 4 PM. The River is about twenty yards wide, at present
the water very low.

December 5ᵗʰ. 7 AM Ther 13 below zero, became mild,
in the afternoon a WSW Gale came on and increased to a
Storm by 6 PM. Monsʳ Jussomme, our Guide, informed us,
that he would now take the great traverse to the Turtle Hill ;
we were early up, and by 7½ AM set off : he led us about
South four miles to a small grove of Aspins on the banks of a
brook thence about six miles to the Turtle Brook from the
Hill ; thence S by W seven miles ; we now came on a rising
ground at 1 PM. but the Turtle Hill was not in sight ; and
all before and around us a boundless plain ; and Monsʳ
Jussomme could not say where we were ; the weather
appeared threatening and preparing for a Storm ; our situation was alarming : and anxiety [was] in the face of every
man, for we did not know to which hand to turn ourselves
for shelter : I mounted my Horse and went to the highest
ground near us, and with my telescope viewed the horizon
all around, but not the least vestige of woods appeared ; but
at due North West from us, where there appeared the tops
of a few Trees like Oaks. They anxiously enquired if I saw
Woods. I told them what I had seen, and that with my old

Soldier I should guide myself by the Compass, and directly proceed as the Woods were far off; McCrachan and a Canadian joined us; the other six conferred among themselves what to do, they had no faith in the Compass on land, and thought best to march in some direction until they could see woods with their own eyes; but had not proceeded half a mile before all followed us, thinking there would be a better chance of safety by being all together. The Gale of Wind came on, and kept increasing. The Snow was four to six inches in depth with a slight crust on it. We held on almost in despair of reaching the Woods; fortunately the Dogs were well broken in, and gave us no trouble. Night came upon us, and we had carefully to keep in file, at times calling to each other to learn that none were missing. At length at 7 PM, thank good Providence, we arrived at the Woods, very much fatigued; walking against the Storm was as laborious as walking knee deep in water. We got up our tent and placed ourselves under shelter. Although we had taken six hours on this last course, yet I found by my Observations we had come only thirteen miles.

December 6th. A heavy westerly gale of wind with mild weather. The Horses and Dogs as well as ourselves were too much fatigued to proceed. Two Bison Bulls were killed, though very tough, kept away hunger and fed the Dogs.

December 7th. At 7 AM Ther 25, only five degrees below the freezing point, a fine mild day. We proceeded five miles up the Mouse River to an old trading House, called "Ash House"[1] from the plenty of those fine Trees; it had to be given up, from it's being too open to the incursions of the Sieux Indians. Two Stone Indians came to us. They said

---

[1] Thompson's survey places this post sixteen and a half miles south and thirty-nine miles west of McDonnell's House, and his latitude is 40° 27' 32" N. It was probably near or opposite the village of Hartney in Manitoba, on the Canadian Northern Railway.

their camp was not far off. Mons͛ Jussomme's Mare and my yellow Horse had both become lame of each one foot, and could proceed no further through the Plains, each of these Horses had one white foot and three black feet; the white foot of each was lame in the same manner, the hair of the white foot was worn away by the hard snow, and a small hole in the flesh also above the hoof. The three black feet had not a hair off them. My other Horse was dark brown with four black feet. As the Horses of this country have no shoes, the colour of the hoof is much regarded; the yellow hoof with white hair is a brittle hoof and soon wears away; for this reason, as much as possible, the Natives take only black hoofed Horses on their War expeditions. As the camp of Stone Indians were going to the house of M͛ John M͛Donell to trade, we delivered the Horses to the care of an old Indian to be taken to the house. Mons͛ Jussomme was now without a Horse and had to purchase Dogs.

December 8ᵗʰ. 7 ᴀᴍ Ther 18 below Zero. A cold day which was employed in hunting, without success. I observed for Latitude and Longitude

December 9ᵗʰ. 7 ᴀᴍ Ther 26 below Zero. We went up the River SW 7¼ miles to eight tents of Stone Indians; who treated us with hospitality, and each of us got a good meal. Learning that we were going to the Missisourie, they warned us to beware of the Sieux Indians, whom they thought would lie in wait for us at the Dog Tent Hills, and [to] keep on our guard against a surprise. We offered a high reward to a young man to guide us to the Mandane Villages, but however tempting the offer, neither himself nor any other would accept the offer. They plainly told us that we might expect to find the Sieux Indians on our road; and they were not on good terms with the Mandanes. We went about three miles and put up in view of the Turtle Hill. We are near the place, where in 1794, fifteen Tents of Stone Indians were destroyed by a large War Party of Sieux Indians, although of the same Nation.[1] From their own accounts, some forty or fifty years ago a feud broke out, and several were killed and wounded on both sides ; about five hundred Tents separated from the main body, and took up their hunting grounds on the Red River and the Plains stretching north westward along the right bank of the Saskatchewan River to within 300 miles of the Mountains, and being in alliance and strict confederacy with the Nahathaways, who accompanied them to war they were powerful, and with their allies, made their brethren the Sieux Nation, feel the Weight of their resentment for several years, until the small pox of 1782 came, which involved them all in one common calamity, and very much reduced the numbers of all parties. The Sieux had lost several of their men, who went to hunt but did not return, and suspicion fell on the Stone Indians and their allies. They determined on revenge, and the destruction of these fifteen Tents was the result. The Sieux afterwards found the loss of their Men was by the Chippaways, their never ceasing enemies, and deeply regretted what they had done ; the old Men made an apology, and proffered peace, which was accepted in 1812, and a reunion took place ; and in this Peace their allies and confederates were included ; and which continues to this day.

December 10th. 7 AM Ther 20 below zero : The hummock of Woods on the Turtle Hill, which was our mark, gave our course by the compass S 30° E. As we had to cross a plain of twenty two miles, and having felt the severe changes of weather, I desired the Men to follow close in file, for they now had faith in the Compass. At 7¼ AM our bit or a caravan set off ; as the Dogs were fresh, we walked at a good pace for some time, a gentle south wind arose ; and kept increasing ; by 10 AM it was a heavy Gale, with high

---

[1] In his original notes, Thompson says that on December 16 they were on the very spot where these fifteen tents of Assiniboin were killed "last year."

drift and dark weather, so much so that I had to keep the
Compass in my hand, for I could not trust to the Wind.
By Noon, it was a perfect Storm, we had no alternative but
to proceed, which we did slowly and with great labor, for
the Storm was ahead, and the snow drift in our faces.   Night
came on, I could no longer see the Compass, and had to trust
to the Wind; the weather became mild with small rain, but
the Storm continued with darkness; some of the foremost
called to lie down where we were, but as it was evident we
were ascending a gentle rising ground, we continued and
soon, thank good Providence, my face struck against some
Oak saplings, and I passed the word that we were in the
Woods, a fire was quickly made, and as it was on an elevated
place it was seen afar off: As yet the only one with me,
was my servant who led the Horse, and we anxiously awaited
the others; they came hardly able to move, one, and then
another, and in something more than half an hour, nine had
arrived; each with Dogs and Sleds, but one Man, and a
Sled with the Dogs were missing; to search for the latter
was useless: but how to find the former, we were at a loss:
and remained so for another half an hour, when we thought
we heard his voice, the Storm was still rageing, we extended
ourselves within call of each other, the most distant man
heard him plainly, went to him, raised him up, and with
assistance brought him to the fire, and we all thanked the
Almighty for our preservation.   He told us he became weak,
fell several times, and at length he could not get up, and
resigned himself to perish in the storm, when by chance
lifting up his head he saw the fire, this gave him courage;
stand he could not but [he] shuffled away on hands and
knees through the snow, bawling with all his might until we
fortunately heard him.   We threw the Tent over some Oak
sapplings and got under shelter from showers of rain, hail
and sleet: At 7¼ PM Ther 36 being four degrees above the
freezing point; by a south wind making in little more than

twelve hours a difference of temperature of fifty six degrees. I had weathered many a hard gale, but this was the most distressing day I had yet seen.

December 11th. At 8 AM Ther 37, being five degrees above the freezing point. A south gale with showers of snow; a mild day, but we were all too tired to proceed. A fine grove of Aspins was within thirty yards, which the darkness prevented us seeing; we removed our Tent to it. The Dogs and Sled missing belonged to Francis Hoole and the value of sixty skins in goods, with all his things were on it, but none would accompany him to look for it, although he offered the half of all that was on it; so much was the chance of the similar distress of yesterday dreaded.

December 12th. Ther 30 two degrees below the freezing point. Wind a SSW gale. We went eight miles along the north side of the Turtle Hill and put up. We were all very hungry, and the Dogs getting weak; we had seriously to attend to hunting; a small herd of Bulls were not far off, and three of us went off to them, the two that were with me were to approach by crawling to them, and if they missed, I was to give chase on horseback, for which I was ready; after an hour spent in approaching them, they both fired, but without effect, the herd started, I gave chase, came up with them and shot a tolerable good Bull; This is the usual manner of hunting the Bison by the Indians of the Plains: This gave us provisions for the present and the Dogs feasted on the offall.

December 13th. At 7 AM Ther 15 below zero, clear weather with a north gale and high drift; we could not proceed, but as usual in clear weather, I observed for Latitude, Longitude and the Variation of the compass. We took the case of Francis Hoole into consideration who had lost his Dogs and all his venture; and each of us agreed to give him goods to the value of two beavers, and haul it for him, which gave him a venture of eighteen skins, and the Irishman

McCrachan, and myself doubled it. For it was out of his power to return alone.

December 14ᵗʰ. At 7 ᴀᴍ Ther 18 below zero. At 8 ᴀᴍ set off, and kept along the Hill to shorten as much as possible the wide Plain we have to cross to the Mouse River. We proceeded in a SE course about seventeen miles; and put up, the day fine, though cold: As this was the last place where Poles to pitch the Tent could be got, we cut the number required of dry Aspin to take with us.

December 15ᵗʰ. At 7 ᴀᴍ Ther 21 below zero. Having no provisions, part of the Men went a hunting, and managed to kill an old Bull, who preferred fighting to running away; after boiling a piece of it for three hours, it was still too tough to be eaten, but by those who have sharp teeth, the tripe of a Bull is the best part of the animal.

December 16ᵗʰ. At 7 ᴀᴍ Ther 19 below zero. We could go no further along the Turtle Hill, and had to cross a wide Plain to a grove of Oaks on the Mouse River; the wind blowing a North Gale with drift, the Men were unwilling to proceed having suffered so much, but as [the] wind was on our backs I persuaded them to follow me, and at 8.20 ᴀᴍ we set [out], and safely arrived at the Grove; our course S by W nineteen miles. On our way we fortunately killed a fat Cow Bison, which was a blessing, for we had not tasted a bit of good meat for many days, and we had nothing else to subsist on. In the evening our conversation turned on the Sieux waylaying us: for we were approaching the Dog Tent Hills, where we were to expect them, and our situation with so many dogs and loaded sleds to take care of, was in a manner defenceless, but we had proceeded too far to return, my hopes lay in the lateness of the season, and the effects the stormy weather must have on a War Party, who frequently take no Tents with them: The last camp of Stone Indians advised us to leave the usual road; cut wood, and haul it with us to make a fire for two nights, and boldly cross to the

Missisourie, which could be done in three days, but this was too much dreaded to be followed. In the evening a very heavy gale came on from the NW^d. We were thankful that we had crossed the Plain, and were well sheltered in a grove of tall Oaks.

December 17th. At 7 AM Ther 22 below zero, at 9 PM Ther 23 below zero. NW Gale with snow drift. Too cold to proceed.

December 18th. At 7 AM Ther 32 below zero. 2 PM 7 below zero, too cold to proceed although a fine clear day. We saw a herd of Cows about a mile from the tent, we crawled to them, and killed three, then went to the tent, harnessed the dogs to bring the meat. While we were busy, a dreadful Storm came on, fortunately an aft wind, had it been a head wind, we could not have reached the Tent.

December 19th. At 7 AM Ther 17 below zero. 9 PM 24 below zero. All day a dreadful Storm from the westward, with high drift. The Sky was as obscure as night, the roaring of the wind was like the waves of the stormy sea on the rocks. It was a terrible day, in the evening the Storm abated. My men attributed these heavy gales of wind and their frequency to the lateness of the season; but this cannot be the cause for no such stormy winds are known to the westward; here are no hills worth notice, all is open to the free passage of the winds from every quarter; for my part I am utterly at a loss, to account for such violent winds on this part of the Plains, and this may account for the few Bison we have seen, and the smallness of the herds, which rarely exceed twenty; whereas to the westward, and near the Mountains the ground is covered with them, and hitherto we have not seen the track of the Deer, and even a Wolf is a rare animal, as for Birds we have seen none: even the long, strong winged Hawks are not known. What can be the cause of these Storms, and the severe cold of this country.

Our Latitude is now 48.9.16 North, Longitude 100.34.12 West, which ought to have a milder climate

December 20th.   At 7 AM $\overline{41}$ below zero.   NNW breeze, though very cold, yet a fine day.   At 9¼ AM we set off, and went up along the Mouse River, about South, thirteen miles, and at 3¼ PM put up close to the River.   The Woods are of Oak, Ash, Elm and some other hard woods, mixed with Poplar and Aspin but no Pines : When the grass is set on fire in the summer, which is too often the case, all the above woods, except the Aspin, have a thick coat of Bark around them, to which the grass does little, or no injury ; but the thin bark of the Aspin however slightly scorched prevents the growth of the Tree, and it becomes dry, and makes the best of fuel, having very little smoke.

December 21st.   A stormy morning with snow to 11 AM then clear and fine.   We could not proceed as Hugh McCrachan was taken ill.   An old Bull was killed for the Dogs.   At 7 PM Ther $\overline{26}$ below zero.

December 22nd.   At 7 AM Ther $\overline{32}$ below zero, NW breeze and clear, keen cold day.   At 8¼ AM we set off, still following up the River, SSW^d for fifteen miles and put up. Where there are Woods along this River ; they are in narrow ledges of forty, to one hundred yards in width.   All the rest are the boundless Plains.

December 23rd.   A cloudy, cold day, with snow until noon, when it became fine and clear.   We set off up along the River SW twelve miles and camped : Three Men went ahead to hunt, they killed four Bulls, no Cows in sight.   We have now plenty to eat, but very tough meat, so much so, we get fairly tired eating before we can get a belly full.   We are now at the Elbow of the Mouse River [1] and can follow it no farther ; as the River now comes from the northwestward

---

[1] The latitude given in Thompson's notes is 48° 9' 15" N.   He must have left the Souris river about the present site of the village of Villard, in McHenry county, in North Dakota.

and is mostly bare of Woods. Although a small Stream of
fifteen yards in breadth, it has every where, like all the
Rivers of the Plains, double banks: the first bank is that
which confines the stream of water, and [is] generally about
ten to twenty feet in height; then on each side is a level
of irregular breadth, generally called Bottom, of thirty to
six hundred yards in breadth, from which rises steep, grassy
sloping banks to the heights of sixty to one hundred feet
which is the common level of the Plain. Large rivers have
often three banks to the level of the Plain. It is in these
Bottoms that the Trees grow, and are sheltered from the
Storms: for on the level of the Plain, it is not possible a
tree can grow but where the Bottoms are wide enough, the
Trees come to perfection: here I measured Oaks of eighteen
feet girth, tall and clean grown, the Elm, Ash, Beach [Birch]
and Bass Wood,[1] with Nut Trees were in full proportion. For
these Bottoms have a rich soil from the overflowing of the
River

December 24th. Wind south, a steady breeze, with low
drift, fine mild weather. At 8¼ AM we set off, and went
ESE ¼ a mile to the heights of the River; and in sight of
the Dog Tent Hill;[2] our course to a Ravine was S 48 W 19
miles; across a plain, the ground was undulating in form,
without any regular vallies; but has many knolls; as we
approached the Hill, we anxiously kept our eyes on it, being
the place the Sieux Indians were to way lay us: About
2 PM I perceived something moving on the ridge of the hill,
and by my Telescope, saw a number of Horsemen riding to
the southward; I made signs to the men to lie down which
they did, after watching their motions for about ten minutes;
I saw plainly they did not see us, and rode descending the
west side of the Hill, and were soon out of sight; thus kind
Providence, by the Storms, and lateness of the season saved

[1] *Tilia americana* (Linn.). [E. A. P.]
[2] Now known as Dog Den Butte.

our lives and property.[1] About a Month after, the Stone Indians informed Mr McDonell, that the above with the want of provisions were the occasion of their leaving the Hill; and they would return. From the eastward, the Dog Tent Hill (by the Stone Indians Sungur Teebe) has the appearance of an irregular bank of about 200 feet above the level of the east Plains, in steep slopes of hard gravelly soil; with nine or ten gullies, or ravines, each has a small spring of water, with a few Oak and Elm Trees in their bottoms; we put up at 4½ PM at the western spring and it's few trees of Oak and Elm. At 7 PM Ther $\overline{15}$ below Zero.

December 26th. 7 AM Ther $\overline{16}$ below zero. Noon Ther $\overline{2}$, at 8 PM 2 above zero. Early a terrible Storm arose from SSW and raged all day; the sound of the wind was like the waves of the sea on a shoal shore. Joseph Houle killed a good Cow but could only bring some of the meat on his back.

December 27th. At 7 AM Ther 5 at noon 20 at 9 PM 25 above zero. The day was clear with a heavy gale from WSW. We could not proceed and had no success in hunting. We cut fire wood to take with us; for we had learned the Mandanes and Pawnees, were hostile to each [other], and a large Village of the latter was but a short distance below the former, and it was to this Village we were journeying; and having very frequently conversed with Messrs Jussomme and McCrachan, on the Roads, the customs and the manners of the several Tribes of Indians of these countries I became acquainted with what we had to expect; in our defenceless state I was determined to avoid any collision with the Natives that were hostile to us. And with the consent of all the Men, took the resolution, to come on the Missisourie River several miles above the lower Mandane Village, and to do this we had a march of two days across the open Plains.

December 28th. At 7 AM Ther 20 above zero. A fine

---

[1] In his notes Thompson says that it was on December 28, after he had left the Dog Tent Hill, that he saw these Indians.

clear mild day, thank God. At 7¼ AM we set off taking firewood and Tent poles with us, and proceeded S 40 W 22
miles and at 4¼ PM, pitched our Tent to pass the night. The
ground we passed over is far from being level, and with six
inches of snow, made tiresome walking; we saw but few
Bisons, and about an hour before we put up, saw ten or
twelve Horsemen far on our left. The night was fine.

December 29th. A very fine mild day. At 7.20 AM we
set off, and seeing the heights of the Missisourie, changed our
course to S 25 W 15 miles, to, and down, the heights of the
River; and at 3¼ PM put up close to the Stream in a fine
bottom of hard wood. The country hilly, and tiresome
walking; we lost much time, partly in viewing the country,
but more so in bringing back the Dogs from running after
the Bisons, of which there were many herds; An old Bull
disdained to run away, but fortunately attacked the Sled,
instead of the Dogs, and would soon have had it in pieces,
had not the Men made him move off, run he would not.
About two miles from the River two Fall Indians came to
us, and killed a good Bull for us: The River is frozen over,
it's width 290 yards but the water is low. The woods the
same as those on the Mouse River, with Poplar, Aspin, and
Birch all of good growth.

December 30th. A northerly gale with cloudy weather.
At 7.40 AM we set off and walked partly on the River ice,
and partly on the Bottoms S 6 E 6 miles to the upper Village
of the Fall Indians: S 27 E 7 miles to the principal Village
of these people. SE 1¼ mile to another Village, thence
S 11 E 2 miles to the fourth Village and S 55 E one mile to
the principal Village of the Mandanes.[1]

Thus from bad weather, we have taken thirty three days

[1] These villages were stretched out for eleven and a half miles along
the banks of the Missouri river, the lowest and largest of them being in
latitude 47° 17′ 22″ N. This would place them between Stanton and
Hancock on the Northern Pacific Railway, in North Dakota. For further
information regarding these villages, see Coues, *New Light*.

to perform a journey of ten days in good weather, but [this] has given me the opportunity of determining the Latitude of six different places ; and the Longitude of three, on the Road to the River. The distance we have gone over is 238 miles.

Three of the Men staid at the Fall Indian[1] Villages ; one with Manoah a frenchman who has long resided with these people ; the rest of us came to the great Village ; and at different houses took up our quarters.

[1] In his notes, Thompson speaks of these people as Willow Indians, though he says that they were commonly called " flying Fall Indians." Later, he evidently confuses them with the Fall or Átsina Indians, who were in league with the Blackfeet.

CHAPTER XIV

MANDANES AND THEIR CUSTOMS

Chippeway War—Meet the " Big White Man "—Five Villages
—Stockades — Form of Houses — Population—Weapons—
Manner of building houses—Furniture—Manoah—Farming
implements—Produce raised—Meals—Character—Law of
Retaliation and compounding by presents—Dress—Appear-
ance—Amusements—Curse of the Mandanes—Annual Cere-
mony among the Mandanes—Language of Fall Indians—
Fall Indians.

THE inhabitants of these Villages, have not been many years on the banks of the Missisourie River : their former residence was on the head waters of the southern branches of the Red River ; and also along it's banks ; where the soil is fertile and easily worked, with their simple tools. Southward of them were the Villages of the Pawnees, with whom they were at peace, except [for] occasional quarrels ; south eastward of them were the Sieux Indians, although numerous, their stone headed arrows could do little injury ; on the north east were the Chippeways in possession of the Forests ; but equally weak until armed with Guns, iron headed arrows and spears : The Chippaways silently collected in the Forests ; and made war on the nearest Village, destroying it with fire, when the greater part of the Men were hunting at some distance, or attacking the Men when hunting ; and thus harassing them when ever they thought proper. The mischief done, they retreated into the forests, where it was too dangerous to search for them. The Chippaways had the policy to harrass and destroy the

Villages nearest to them, leaving the others in security. The people of this Village removed westward from them, and from stream to stream, the Villages in succession, until they gained the banks of the Missisourie; where they have built their Villages and remain in peace from the Chippaways, the open Plains being their defence.

Mons'' Jussome introduced me to a Chief called the "Big White Man"; which well designated him; and told him I was one of the chiefs of the white men, and did not concern myself with trade, which somewhat surprised him, until told that my business, was to see the countries, converse with the Natives, and see how they could be more regularly supplied with Arms, Ammunition and other articles they much wanted: this he said would be very good; as sometimes they were many days without ammunition. Our things were taken in, and to myself and my servant Joseph Boisseau, was shown a bed for each of us. My curiosity was excited by the sight of these Villages containing a native agricultural population; the first I had seen and I hoped to obtain much curious information of the past times of these people; and for this purpose, and to get a ready knowledge of their manners and customs Mess'' Jussomme and M⁰Crachen accompanied me to every Village but the information I obtained fell far short of what I had expected; both of those who accompanied me, were illiterate, without any education, and either did not understand my questions, or the Natives had no answers to give. I shall put together what I saw and what I learned. In company with those I have mentioned; we examined the Villages and counted the houses. The upper Village has thirty one Houses and seven Tents of Fall Indians. The Village next below, is called the Great Village of the above people, it contains eighty two Houses, is situated on the Turtle River, a short distance above it's confluence with the Missisourie. The next Village has fifty two Houses, and is also on the Turtle river; This Village was the residence of

Manoah. A few houses were of Fall Indians, the other Houses were of Mandanes. The fourth Village was on the right bank of the Missisourie, of forty houses of Mandanes. The fifth and last Village contained one hundred and thirteen houses of Mandanes. Except the upper village of the Fall Indians, they were all strongly stockaded with Posts of Wood of ten to twelve inches diameter; about two feet in the ground and ten feet above it, with numerous holes to fire through; they went round the Village, in some places close to the houses; there were two doorways to each of the Stockades, on opposite sides; wide enough to admit a Man on Horseback. I saw no doors, or gates; they are shut up when required, with Logs of wood.

The houses were all of the same architecture; the form of each, and every one was that of a dome, regularly built; the house in which I resided, was one of the largest: the form a circle, probably drawn on the ground by a line from the centre; On this circle was the first tier of boards, a few inches in the ground, and about six feet above it, all inclining inwards; bound together on the top by circular pieces of wood; on the outside of about five inches, and on the inside of about three inches in width; and in these were also inserted the lower end of another set of boards of about five feet in length; and bound together on their tops in the same manner; but inclining inwards at a greater angle than the lower tier; and thus in succession, each tier the boards were shorter, and more inclined inwards, until they were met at the top, by a strong circular piece of wood of about three feet diameter; to which they were fastened; and which served to admit the light, and let out the Smoke: The house in which I lodged was about forty feet in diameter; and the height of the dome about eighteen feet: On the outside it was covered with earth in a dry state to the depth of four or five inches, and made firm and compact. Every house was covered in the same manner. Between each house was a vacant space of fifteen to thirty feet. They appeared to have no order, otherwise than each house occupying a diameter of thirty to forty feet; and a free space around it of an average of twenty feet. On looking down on them, from the upper bank of the River, they appeared like so many large hives clustered together: From what I saw, and the best information I could get, the average population of each house was about ten souls. The houses of the Mandanes had not many children, but it was otherwise with the Fall Indians: the former may be taken at eight soul, and the latter, at ten, to each House. This will give to the Mandanes for 190 houses, a population of 1520 souls; of which they may muster about 220 warriors. The Fall Indians of 128 houses, and seven tents have a population of 1330 souls, of which 190 are warriors; the whole military force of these Villages may be about 400 men fit for war. I have heard their force estimated at 1000 men, but this was for want of calculation.

The native Arms were much the same as those that do not know the use of Iron, Spears and Arrow headed with flint; which they gladly lay aside for iron; they appear to have adopted the Spear as a favorite weapon. It is a handle of about eight feet in length, headed with a flat iron bayonet of nine ten inches in length, sharp pointed, from the point regularly enlarging to four inches in width, both sides sharp edged; the broad end has a handle of iron of about four inches in length, which is inserted in the handle, and bound with small cords; it is a formidable weapon in the hands of a resolute man. Their Guns were few in proportion to the number of Men for they have no supplies, but what are brought to them by small parties of Men, trading on their own account, such as the party with me; we had ten guns, of which the Men traded seven; and parties of Men of the Hudson's Bay Company in the same manner. They had Shields of Bull's hide a safe defence against arrows and the spear, but of no use against balls.

They enquired how we built our houses, as they saw me attentively examining the structure of theirs; when informed; and drawing a rough plan of our Villages, with Streets parallel to each other, and cross Streets at right angles, after looking at it for some time; they shook their heads, and said, In these straight Streets we see no advantage the inhabitants have over their enemies. The whole of their bodies are exposed, and the houses can be set on fire; which our houses cannot be, for the earth cannot burn; our houses being round shelter us except when we fire down on them, and we are high above them; the enemies have never been able to hurt us when we are in our Villages; and it is only when we are absent on large hunting parties that we have suffered; and which we shall not do again. The Sieux Indians have several times on a dark stormy night set fire to the stockade, but this had no effect on the houses. Their manner of building and disposition of the houses, is probably the best, for they build for security, not for convenience. The floor of the house is of earth, level and compact; there is only one door to each house, this is a frame of wood, covered with a parchment Bison skin, of six feet by four feet; so as to admit a horse. To each door was a covered porch of about six feet, made and covered like the door. On entering the door, on the left sits the master of the house and his wife; on a rude kind of sofa; covered with Bison Robes; and before is the fire, in a hollow of a foot in depth; and at one side of the fire is a vase of their pottery, or two, containing pounded maize, which is frequently stirred with a stick, and now and then about a small spoonful of fine ashes put in, to act as salt; and [this] makes good pottage; when they boil meat it is with only water; and the broth is drank. We saw no dried meat of any kind; and their houses are not adapted for curing meat by smoke for although the fire is on one side of the house, and not under the aperture, yet there is not the least appearance of smoke, and the light from the aperture of the dome gave sufficient light within the house. Around the walls, frame bed places were fastened, the bottom three feet from the ground; covered with parchment skins of the Bison, with the hair on except the front, which was open; for a bed, was a Bison robe, soft and comfortable. On the right hand side of the door, were separate Stalls for Horses; every morning the young men take the Horses to grass and watch over them to the evening, when they are brought in, and get a portion of maize : which keeps them in good condition; but in proportion to the population the Horses are few: the Chief with whom I lodged had only three.

They do not require so many Horses as the Indians of the Plains who frequently move from place to place, yet even for the sole purpose of hunting their Horses are too few. We paid a visit to Manoah, a french canadian, who had resided many years with these people; he was a handsome man, with a native woman, fair and graceful, for his wife, they had no children; he was in every respect as a Native. He was an intelligent man, but completely a Frenchman, brave, gay and boastfull; with his gun in one hand, and his spear in the other, he stood erect, and recounted to the Indians about us all his warlike actions, and the battles in which he had borne a part, to all of which, as a matter of course, they assented. From my knowledge of the Indian character, it appeared to me he could not live long, for they utterly dislike a boastful man. I learned that a few years after, coming from a Skirmish, he praised his own courage and conduct and spoke with some contempt of the courage of those with him, which they did not in the least deserve, and for which he was shot. As Manoah was as a Native with them I enquired if they had any traditions of ancient times; he said, he knew of none beyond the days of their great, great Grandfathers, who formerly possessed all the Streams of the Red River, and head of the Mississippe, where the

Wild Rice, and the Deer were plenty, but then the Bison and the Horse were not known to them : On all these streams they had Villages and cultivated the ground as now ; they lived many years this way how many they do not know, at length the Indians of the Woods armed with guns which killed and frightened them, and iron weapons, frequently attacked them, and against these they had no defence ; but were obliged to quit their Villages, and remove from place to place, until they came to the Missisourie River, where our fathers made Villages, and the Indians of the Woods no longer attacked us ; but the lands here are not so good, as the land our fathers left, we have no wild rice, except in a few Ponds, not worth attention. Beyond this tradition, such as it is I could learn nothing. They at present, as perhaps they have always done, subsist mostly on the produce of their agriculture ; and hunt the Bison and Deer,[1] when these animals are near them. They have no other flesh meat ; and the skins of these animals serves for clothing. The grounds they cultivate are the alluvials of the River, called Bottoms. The portion to each family is allotted by a council of old Men, and is always more than they can cultivate, for which they have but few implements. The Hoe and the pointed Stick hardened in the fire are the principal.

They have but few Hoes of iron ; and the Hoe in general use is made of the shoulder blade bone of the Bison or Deer, the latter are preferred ; they are neatly fitted to a handle, and do tolerable well in soft ground.

The produce they raise, is mostly Maize (Indian Corn) of the small red kind, with other varieties all of which come to perfection, with Pumpkins and a variety of small Beans. Melons have been raised to their full size and flavor. Every article seen in their villages were in clean good order, but the want of iron implements limits their industry ; yet they raise, not only enough for themselves, but also for trade with

[1] *Odocoileus hemionus* (Rafinesque). [E. A. P.]

their neighbours. We brought away upwards of 300 pounds weight. In sowing their seed, they have to guard against the flocks of Rooks,[1] which would pick up every grain, and until the grain sprouts, out, parties of Boys and girls during the day are employed to drive them away. During the day they appear to have no regular meals ; but after day set the evening meal is served with meat ; at this meal, several are invited by a tally of wood, which they return, each brings his bowl and rude spoon and knife ; the meat is boiled ; roasting of it would give a disagreeable smell ; which they are carefull to prevent, allowing nothing to be thrown into the fire, and keeping the fireplace very clean. The parties invited were generally from seven to ten men ; women are never of the party, except the Wife of the master of the house, who sometimes joined in their grave, yet cheerful conversation. Loud laughter is seldom heard.

Both sexes have the character of being courteous and kind in their intercourse with each other ; in our rambles through the villages everything was orderly, no scolding, nor loud talking : They look upon stealing as the meanest of vices, and think a Robber a far better man than a Thief. They have no laws for the punishment of crime, everything is left to the injured party, the law of retaliation being in full force. It is this law which makes Murder so much dreaded by them, for vengeance is as likely to fall on the near relations of the murderer, as on himself, and the family of the Relation who may have thus suffered, have now their vengeance to take ; Thus an endless feud arises ; to prevent such blood shed, the murderer, if his life cannot be taken, for he frequently absconds ; the old men attempt to compound for the crime by presents to the injured party, which are always refused, except they know themselves to be too weak to obtain any other redress. If the presents are accepted the price of blood is paid, and the injured party has no longer any right to take

---

[1] Probably the Crow, *Corvus brachyrhynchos* Brehm. [E. A. P.]

the life of the criminal. This law of Retaliation, and compounding by presents for the life of the murderer, when accepted, appears to be the invariable laws with all the Natives of North America.

The dress of the Men is of leather, soft and white. The covering for the body is like a large shirt with sleeves, some wear the Bison leather with the hair on, for winter dress; with a leather belt; the leggins of soft white leather, so long as to pass over the belt; their shoes are made of Bison, with the hair on; and always a Bison Robe. The Women's dress is a shirt of Antelope or Deer leather, which ties over each shoulder, and comes down to the feet, with a belt round the waist short leggins to the knee, and Bison Robe shoes, the sleeves separate, in which they looked well. Both Men and Women are of a stature fully equal to Europeans; and as fair as our french canadians; their eyes of a dark hazel, the hair of dark brown, or black, but not coarse: prominent nose, cheek bones moderate, teeth mouth and chin good; well limbed; the features good, the countenance mild and intelligent; they are a handsome people. Their amusements are gambling after the manner of the Indians of the Plains. They have also their Musicians and dancing Women; In the house of the Chief, in which I staid, every evening, about two or three hours after sunset, about forty or fifty men assembled. They all stood; five or six of them were Musicians, with a drum, tambour, rattle, and rude flutes; The dancing women were twenty four young women of the age of sixteen to twenty-five years. They all came in their common dress; and went into a place set apart for them to dress; and changed to a fine white dress of thin Deer skins, with ornamented belts, which showed their shapes almost as clearly as a silk dress.

They formed two rows of twelve each, and were about three feet apart; The musicians were in front of the Men, and about fourteen feet from the front row of the Women.

When the music struck up, part of the Men sung, and the Women keeping a straight line and respective distance, danced with a light step and slow, graceful motion towards the Musicians, until near to them when the music and singing ceased; the Women retired in regular line, keeping their faces towards the Musicians. A pause of three or four minutes ensued, the music struck up, and the dance renewed in the same manner; and thus in succession for the time of about an hour. Each dance lasted about ten minutes. There was no talking, the utmost decorum was kept; the Men all silently went away; the dancing Women retired to change their dress. They were all courtesans; a sett of handsome tempting women. The Mandanes have many ceremonies, in all of which the women bear a part but my interpreter treated them with contempt; which perhaps they merited.

The curse of the Mandanes is an almost total want of chastity: this, the men with me knew, and I found it was almost their sole motive for their journey hereto: The goods they brought, they sold at 50 to 60 pr cent above what they cost; and reserving enough to pay their debts, and buy some corn; [they] spent the rest on Women. Therefore we could not preach chastity to them, and by experience they informed me that siphylis was common and mild. These people annually, at least once in every summer, have the following detestable ceremony, which lasts three days. The first day both sexes go about within and without the Village, but mostly on the outside, as if in great distress, seeking for persons they cannot find, for a few hours, then sit down and cry as if for sorrow, then retire to their houses. The next day the same is repeated, with apparent greater distress accompanied with low singing. The third day begins with both sexes crying (no tears) and eagerly searching for those they wish to find, but cannot; at length tired with this folly; the sexes separate, and the Men sit down on the ground in one line, with their elbows resting on their knees, and their heads resting on their hands as in sorrow; The Women standing and crying heartily, with dry eyes, form a line opposite the Men; in a few minutes, several Women advance to the Men, each of them takes the Man she chooses by the hand, he rises and goes with her to where she pleases, and they lie down together. And thus until none remain, which finishes this abominable ceremony. No woman can choose her own husband; but the women who love their husbands lead away aged Men. Messrs Jussomme and McCrachan said they had often partaken of the latter part of the third day; and other men said the same. Manoah strongly denied that either himself, or his wife had ever taken part in these rights of the devil.

The white men who have hitherto visited these Villages, have not been examples of chastity; and of course religion is out of the question; and as to the white Men who have no education, and who therefore cannot read, the little religion they ever had is soon forgotten when there is no Church to remind them of it.

Fall Indians who also have Villages, are strictly confederate with the Mandanes, they speak a distinct language; and it is thought no other tribe of Natives speak it: very few of the Mandanes learn it; the former learn the language of the latter, which is a dialect of the Pawnee language. The Fall Indians are now removed far from their original country, which was the Rapids of the Saskatchewan river, northward of the Eagle Hill; A feud arose between them, and their then neighbours, the Nahathaways and the Stone Indians confederates, and [they were] too powerful for them, they then lived wholly in tents, and removed across the Plains to the Missisourie; became confederate with the Mandanes, and from them have learned to build houses, form villages and cultivate the ground; The architecture of their houses is in every respect the same as that of the Mandanes, and their cultivation is the same: Some of them continue to live in

tents and are in friendship with the Chyenne Indians, whose
village was lately destroyed, and now live in tents to the
westward of them. . Another band of these people now dwell
in tents near the head of this River in alliance with the
Peeagans and their allies; The whole tribe of these people
may be estimated at 2200 to 2500 souls. They are not as
fair as the Mandanes; but somewhat taller. Their features,
like those of the plains have a cast of sterness, yet they are
cheerful, very hospitable and friendly to each other, and to
strangers. What has been said of the Mandanes may be said
of them; except in regard to Women. The Fall Indians
exact the strictest chastity of their wives; adultry is punish-
able with death to both parties; though the Woman escapes
this penalty more often than the man: who can only save
his life by absconding which, if the woman does not do, she
suffers a severe beating, and becomes the drudge of the family.
But those living in the Villages I was given to understand have
relaxed this law to the man in favor of a present of a Horse,
and whatever else can be got from him. As they do not
suffer the hardships of the Indians of the Plains, the Men are
nearly equal to the Women in number, and few have more
than two wives, more frequently only one. It always
appeared to me that the Indians of the Plains did not regard
the chastity of their wives as a moral law, but as an unalien-
able right of property to be their wives and the mothers of
their own children; and not to be interfered with by another
Man. The morality of the Indians, may be said to be founded
on it's necessity to the peace and safety of each other, and
although they profess to believe in a Spirit of great power,
and that the wicked are badly treated after death; yet this
seems to have no effect on their passions and desires. The
crimes they hold to be avoided are, theft, treachery and
murder.

Christianity alone by it's holy doctrines and precepts, by
it's promises of a happy immortality, and dreadful punish-

ments to the wicked, can give force to morality. It alone can restrain the passions and desires and guide them to fulfil the intentions of a wise, and benevolent Providence. As the Missisourie River with all it's Villages and population are within the United States, it is to be hoped Missionaries will soon find their way to these Villages, and give them a knowledge of christianity, which they will gladly accept.

CHAPTER XV

RETURN JOURNEY TO McDONELL'S
HOUSE ON MOUSE RIVER

Missisourie River—Start on return journey—Return journey—Reach Trading House in safety—Encounter of Trading Party with the Sieux—Hugh McCrachan—Death of Hugh McCrachan—Route from Stone Indian River House to Villages of the Mandanes.

HAVING made the necessary astronomical observations we prepared to depart; the latitude of the Upper Village (Fall Indians) was found to be 47.25.11 North. Longitude 101.21.5 West of Greenwich. The lower Village (Mandanes) Latitude 47.17.22 North. Long^de 101.14.24 W. Variation of the Compass ten degrees east. In the language of the natives, Missisourie means, "the great troubled, or muddy, River," from the great quantity of sediment it contains. Everywhere this river has bold banks, often steep, and mostly of earth. Above the banks the soil appears hard and dry the bottoms rich and well wooded. From the Mountains to it's confluence with the Mississippe, following it's course is 3560 miles. The whole distance is a continuous River, without meeting, or forming, a single Lake; with very strong current. This River drains a area of 442,239 square miles.

We now set off, our caravan consisted of thirty one Dogs, loaded with furrs of Wolves and Foxes, with meal and corn;

and two Sieux Indian women which the Mandanes had taken
prisoners, and sold to the men, who, when arrived at the
Trading House would sell them to some other Canadians.
My Horse I left with my Host, and bought two stout Dogs
to haul our luggage and provisions. Our march, as usual,
commenced with flogging the Dogs, and swearing at them
in the intervals; my old soldier, who on going out, had only
Horses to take [care] of, and used to reprove them, now he
had Dogs could swear and flog as well as any of them. A
council had been held; as the Articles brought to them was
by no means sufficient to supply their wants, to send a small
party to the Trading House, get a knowledge of the Road,
make sure friends of the Stone Indians and see the stock of
Goods in the Trading Houses; Accordingly a Chief in the
prime of life, called the White Man, with four young men
were selected, and came with us, and also an old man and his
old wife, each of the latter carrying a bag of meal for their
provisions. They said they were anxious to see the Houses of
the White Men before they died; and when told they were
both too weak to perform the journey, they said their hearts
were strong, but by the time they had ascended the heights
of the river they were convinced they were too weak and
returned. Mons' Jussomme and myself spoke to the Chief
of the extreme hazard of such a small party escaping their
enemies; and that if they wished to have a direct trade
with us, they must form a party of at least forty men with
Horses, and come when the Snow was not on the ground;
that even among the Stone Indians, who are friendly, there
were bad men enough, on seeing such a small party, that
would plunder them; and they had all better return. He
said, we do not know the country; we are too few, and I
will return, the young men belong to another Village, and
they will do as they please. After fourteen days on our
return and suffering excessive bad weather, two of the
Mandane young men returned; the other two continued

with us. On the first day of February we came to eight
Tents of Stone Indians, in the same place as [when] we went ;
they treated the two Mandanes with great kindness. We
told them we had returned by the usual route, as the Mandanes assured us there was no danger ; they said we had not
acted wisely, for the good weather will bring the Sieux to
the Dog Tent Hills, you have narrowly escaped, for we are
sure they are now there. We killed very few Bisons and
lived as much on Corn as on Meat.

We continued our Journey and on the third day of
February (1798) we arrived at the Trading House of the
North West Company from whence we set out, thankfull to
the Almighty for our merciful preservation. We have been
absent sixty eight days. The next day Mr Hugh McCrachan
and four men with an assortment of goods for trade set off
for the Mandane Villages, and the two Mandane young men,
to whom Mr McDonell made several presents, which highly
pleased them.

I strongly advised them all not to follow the usual route,
carefully to avoid the Dog Tent Hill, and follow the route
by which we went to the Missisourie, and which the Stone
Indians also strongly advised ; This they all promised to do,
and set off. The weather being fine, Canadian like, who
believe there is no danger until they are involved in it ; they
took the usual route, and at the campment of the Dog Tent
Hills found the Sieux lying in wait for them ; they fell on
them and killed two of the Canadians and one of the Mandanes, and the others would have shared the same fate, had
they not begun quarrelling about the plunder of the goods.
The Mandane got safe to his Village, and Hugh McCrachan
and the two men returned to the House, in a sad worn out
condition, the humanity of some Stone Indians saved their
lives, or they must have perished with hunger. In the
following summer as Mr Hugh McCrachan was on his usual
trading journeys to the Mandanes, he was killed by the

Sieux Indians.[1] Our road from the Village of the Mandanes
to the Stone Indian River House, following from Woods to
Woods for fuel and shelter are to the Dog Tent Hill [which]
is N 28 E 50 miles ; thence to the Elbow of the Mouse River
N 49 E 20 miles ; thence to Turtle Hill south end N 28 E 56
miles, thence along the Hill N 9 W 14 miles ; thence to the
Ash House on the Mouse River N 3 W 24 miles ; thence to
the House of M^r McDonell N 69 E 45 miles. But a straight
line between the two extreme points is N 26 E 188 miles.

The whole of this country may be pastoral, but except in
a few places, cannot become agricultural. Even the fine
Turtle Hill, gently rising, for several miles, with it's Springs
and Brooks of fine Water has very little wood fit for the
Farmer. The principal is Aspin which soon decays : with
small Oaks and Ash. The grass of these plains is so often on
fire, by accident or design, and the bark of the Trees so often
scorched, that their growth is contracted, or they become
dry : and the whole of the great Plains are subject to these
fires during the Summer and Autumn before the Snow lies
on the ground. These great Plains appear to be given by
Providence to the Red Men for ever, as the wilds and sands
of Africa are given to the Arabians.

It may be enquired what can be the cause of the violent
Storms, like Hurricanes which, in a manner desolate this
country, when such Storms are not known to the westward.
No assignable cause is known ; there are no Hills to impede
it's course, or confine it's action. What are called Hills, are
gentle rising grounds, over which the Winds sweep in full
freedom. And the same question may be asked of certain
parts of the Ocean.

My time for full three weeks was employed in calculating

[1] Thompson was probably mistaken in making this statement, for
Hugh McCraken appears to have been alive when Lewis and Clark and
Alexander Henry visited the Mandan villages in 1804 and 1806 re-
spectively.

Q

the astronomical observations made to, and from, the Missi-
sourie River; and making a Map of my survey, which, with
my journal was sealed up, and directed to the Agents of the
North West Company. By a series of observations this Trading
House is in Latitude 49.40.56 North, and Longitude 99.27.15
West. Variation 11 degrees E^t.

CHAPTER XVI

JOURNEY DOWN THE STONE INDIAN
AND UP THE RED RIVER

*Leave McDonell's House—Melting snow—Arrive at Red River
—Chippeway Customs—Ascend the Red River—Prairie
Fires—Salt Brooks—Trading Post Settlements—Cadotte's
House—Baptiste Cadotte—Chippeway Camp—Return to
Cadotte's House.*

ON the 26th day of February (1798) I took leave of
my hospitable friend Mr John McDonell, who
furnished me with everything necessary for my
Journey of survey. With me were three canadians and an
Indian to guide us, and six dogs hauling three Sleds loaded
with Provisions and our baggage. Our Journey was down
the Stone Indian River, sometimes on the Ice of the Stream,
but on account of it's windings, mostly on the North Side;
cutting off the windings as much as possible; In the afternoon
we came to the Manito Hills, they are a low long ridge of sand
knowls, steep on the west side, but less so on the east side;
they have a very little grass in a few places, no snow lies on
them all winter, which is the reason the Natives call them
Manito; or preternatural. Except the Sand Ridge, the
country we have come over is very fine, especially the junction
of the Mouse River which is about 1½ mile below the House:
the woods were of Oak, Ash, Elm, Bass Wood, Poplar,
Aspin and a few Pines having small Plains and Meadows
(short and long grass).[1] In the evening we put up: and as

[1] Their camp this evening (February 26) was at Old Pine Fort, or
Fort Epinette, which Thompson says in his notes had been forsaken

usual had to melt snow to make water to drink and cook our supper. To melt Snow into well tasted water requires some tact. The Kettle is filled with Snow packed hard, it is then hung over the fire, and as it melts it is with a small stick bored full of holes to the bottom to lessen the smoky taste.

several years. It was situated on the north side of the Assiniboine river, in the north-east quarter of Sect. 36, Tp. 8, R. 14, west of the Principal Meridian, about eight miles southward from Carberry Junction on the Canadian Northern Railway. Daniel Harmon in his Journal says that Pine Fort was built in 1785, and abandoned in 1794; and Alexander Henry the younger states that it was abandoned when the fort at the mouth of the Souris was built. It was an important post. John McDonnell describes it as the lowest house of the North-West Company at that time, and says that the Mandans and Gros Ventres came there from the Missouri to trade. He also states that it was abandoned in 1794, because Donald McKay of the Hudson's Bay Company had built a post at the mouth of the Souris river the previous year, and it was necessary to move up beside him. On Peter Pond's map of 1790 there is the note: "Here upon the Branches of the Missury live the Maundiens, who bring to our Factory at Fort Epinitt [Pine Fort], on the Assinipoil River, Indian corn for sale. Our people go to them with loaded horses in twelve days."

When the site was visited by the editor in July, 1890, evidences of the existence of the fort could be distinctly traced, north of the river on a level grassy flat which breaks off towards the stream in a steep-cut bank twenty feet high. To the north the ground rises in several poplar-covered terraces to the main bank of the valley, which is a mile and a half distant, while to the south, across the shallow river, is a low bottom land a mile wide. The position of the old fort had been largely washed away by the river, but the back line, and part of the two end lines of the stockade, could be clearly followed as a trench in which were the butts of spruce posts about four inches in diameter which had been driven into the ground. The north side of the stockade was 56 paces long, while of the east and west ends respectively only lengths of 15 and 13 paces remained, the rest, with the whole of the front, having been washed away by the river. At the north-east corner there had been a bastion 8 feet square, beneath which was an entrance to the enclosure. Just within the eastern end of the enclosure was a pit 3 feet in diameter and 26 inches deep, filled with charred bones and wood. The main feature of the enclosure was a large mound 11 paces in diameter and 2 feet high, with a pit in the middle 6 paces in diameter and 2 feet deep. This doubtless marked the position of a house, some of the timbers of which were still projecting from the bank. At two of the corners piles of stones showed where chimneys had stood. Eight paces west of the enclosure, and just on the edge of the bank, was a large shallow pit.

When it becomes water the taste is disagreeable with smoke, but in this state it readily quenches thirst, and for such is often drank; to clear it of smoke the water is made to boil for a few minutes which clears it of the smoke. Snow is then put in, until it is cold, and the water is well tasted and fit for use. We continued our journey day after day,[1] the Snow increasing every day in depth; and to beat the path for the Dogs and Sleds became very tiresome work; the Snow Shoes sunk six inches every step of the foremost man, our Guide every day became so fatigued I had to relieve him for two or three hours.

On the seventh of March we arrived at it's junction with the Red River in Latitude 49.53.1 N. Longitude 97.0.0 West Variation 9 degrees East.[2] The straight course is N 82 E 112 statute miles; to perform which we walked 169 miles. But the windings of the River is treble the former distance, and more. An Indian compared the devious course of the River to a Spy, who went here and there, and everywhere, to see what was going on in the country. The whole

[1] On March 2, Thompson passed Old Poplar Fort, which was one of the oldest trading posts established by the English traders from Canada on the Assiniboine river. Thompson's notes place it on the north bank of the river about the middle of a straight reach three miles long, and five miles above the Meadow Portage. It was probably in Sect. 6, Tp. 11, R. 7, west of the Principal Meridian. Alexander Henry the younger says that it was abandoned in the autumn of 1781, after it had been attacked by Indians, and three of its defenders had been killed.

Five miles below the site of Poplar House was the south end of the Meadow Portage to Lake Manitoba, just below a willow-covered island in the river. This place, on which the city of Portage la Prairie is now built, is one of the famous places in the history of the western fur trade. It was here that La Vérendrye, having ascended the river until the water became too shallow to allow him to go farther, built, in the autumn of 1738, Fort La Reine, which continued to be one of the chief trading posts of the French in the west until the cession of Canada to Great Britain. After that the place was occupied from time to time by traders of the North-West and Hudson's Bay Companies, until it was finally abandoned by the latter company in 1870.

[2] The correct latitude and longitude of the mouth of the Assiniboine river are 49° 53′ N. and 93° 9′ W.

of this country appeared fit for cultivation, and for raising
cattle. The climate is as mild as Montreal in Canada, which
[is] 4½ degrees south of this River: The Woods as we
descended the River were less in size and height; especially
the Oak. We saw but a few animals, a few Red Deer, and a
chance small herd of Bisons, for those animals avoid deep
snow.

Hitherto we have been on the hunting grounds of the
Nahathaway Indians; who possess this River, and all to the
eastward, and to the northward as far as the latitude of
56 degrees north. The Red River, and all the country
southward and the upper Mississippe, and countries eastward
to, and all, Canada, are the hunting grounds of the Chippaways (or Oojibaways). Part is already occupied by civilized
men, and the greatest part of their territories will in time be
in the hands of those that cultivate the soil. They are a
large, scattered tribe of the primitive Nahathaways, and
speak a close dialect of their language, which they have
softened as they live, comparatively, in a mild climate; their
country is different in soil and it's productions which renders
them less dependent on hunting: The dark extensive forests
of the north, give food, shelter, and comparative security to
the Moose, the Rein Deer, and other wild animals, and
exercise the sagacity and industry of the Hunter. Of all
the Natives, these people are the most superstitious, they may
be accounted the religionists of the North. As they have no
Horses, and only Dogs for winter use and not many of these
to haul their things in winter, they have very few tents of
leather. They are mostly of rush mats neatly made, sometimes of Birch Rind, or Pine Branches, always low, and
seldom comfortable. As soon as mild weather comes on,
they live in Lodges, which are long, in proportion to the
number of families. Strong poles are placed on triangles for
the length required, about six or seven feet high, the front
looks to the south, and is open, the back part is formed of

poles about three feet apart, in a sloping position, resting on the ground, and on the ridge pole, covered with Birch Rind, sometimes rush mats, and pine branches. In summer they all use Canoes and in winter the flat Sled ; in this season the women haul, or carry heavy loads, and the men also take their Share. They are well made for hunting and fatigue, they are more fleshy than their neighbours, and their skin darker. These are the people of whom writers tell so many anecdotes, as they are better known to the Whites than any other tribe ; they are naturally brave, but too much given to revenge : and although they exact fidelity from their wives, rarely punish with death ; the woman is sometimes punished by the husband biting off the fleshy part of the nose ; the Women declare it to be worse than death, as it is the loss of their beauty, and for the rest of life a visible mark of crime and punishment. But this barbarous act, is very rarely inflicted but when the man is drunk.

On the 7th day of March we began the survey of the Red River, and continued to the 14th of March, when we arrived at the Trading House of the North West Company, under the charge of Monsr Charles Chaboiller,[1] who gave us a kind reception. Our journey for the last eight days, has been most wretched traveling : the Snow was full three feet deep ; the ice of the River had much water on it, from the mild weather with small showers of rain, or wet snow.

On the River, the mixture of snow and water which stuck to the Sleds, made it impossible for the Dogs to haul them, and it often required two of us to extricate Sleds with the assistance of the Dogs, and every thing had to be dried in bad weather. To beat the Road was a most laborious work, the ankles and knees were sprained with the weight of wet snow on each Snow Shoe, for the Snow was not on firm ground, but supported by long grass. I had to take his

[1] For an account of Chaboillez, see Elliott Coues, *New Light*, p. 60.

place, and tying a string to the fore bar of each snow shoe, and the other end in my hand, with my gun slung on my back, and thus lifting my snow shoes, marched on; We journeyed on the west side of the River; the whole distance was meadow land, and no other Woods than saplings of Oak, Ash and Alder. From the many charred stumps of Pines it was evident this side of the River was once a Pine Forest. In the more northern parts, where Pine Woods have been destroyed by fire, Aspins, Poplars and Alders have sprung up, and taken the place of the Pines; but along this, the Red River, from the mildness of the climate, and goodness of the soil, Oak, Ash, Alder, and Nut Woods have succeeded the Pines.

This change appears to depend on soil and climate; for in the high northern latitudes, where in many places there is no soil, and the Pines spread their roots over the rocks, Pine grounds, when burned, are succeeded by Pines; for Aspins Poplars and Alders require some soil. Along the Great Plains, there are very many places where large groves of Aspins have been burnt, the charred stumps remaining; and no further production of Trees have taken place, the grass of the Plains covers them: and from this cause the Great Plains are constantly increasing in length and breadth, and the Deer give place to the Bison. But the mercy of Providence has given a productive power to the roots of the grass of the Plains and of the Meadows, on which the fire has no effect. The fire passes in flame and smoke, what was a lovely green is now a deep black; the Rains descend, and this odious colour disappears, and is replaced by a still brighter green; if these grasses had not this wonderful productive power on which fire has no effects, these Great Plains would, many centuries ago, have been without Man, Bird, or Beast.

We crossed several Brooks of salt water, which come from ponds of salt water on the west side of the River, one, or two of these are so strongly impregnated, that good salt is made of the water by boiling; the meat salted with it, is well

preserved, but somewhat corroded. On the 12th we came
to four Lodges of Chippaways, they had killed two poor
Bulls, of which we were glad to get a part, and the next day
two of them came with us, which relieved us from the fatigue
of beating the road. At this trading Post I stayed six days,
making astronomical observations which determined this place
to be in Latitude 48° 58′ 24″ north Longitude 97° 16′ 40″ W
of Greenwich Variation 8½ degrees East. This House is
therefore one minute and thirty six seconds in the United
States; the boundary Line between the British Dominions
and the Territories of the United States being the forty
ninth parallel of north Latitude from the Lake of the Woods
to the east foot of the Rocky Mountains.[1] I pointed out the
Boundary Line to which they must remove; and which
Line, several years after was confirmed by Major Long of
the corps of Engineers, on the part of the United States.
From the junction of the Stone Indian with this, the Red
River, the course is S 11¼ W 65½ statute miles, but to the
Boundary Line 64 miles. The number of Men that now
trade at this house are 95, which at seven souls for each man,
(rather a low average), gives 665 souls. And at the Rainy
River House, which lies in Latitude 48.36.58 N Longitude
93.19.30 W. in a course S 82 E 184 miles. The Chippaways
who trade at this house are 60 men, giving an average of
420 souls: By the extent of their hunting grounds each
family of seven souls, has 150 to 180 square miles of hunting
ground, and yet [they] have very little provisions to spare;
this alone is sufficient to show the ground does not abound in
wild animals. The Beaver has become a very scarce animal;
the soil and climate not requiring the same materials for his
House, become a more easy prey. During the Summer these
Natives subsist on fish, and in Autumn, part of them on wild
rice.

[1] The boundary extended to the watershed range of the Rocky Mountains, and not to the east foot, as is here stated.

The Woods about this House are Oak, Ash, Elm and Nut Woods, the Oaks of fine growth, tall and straight. The largest of these measured ten feet girth at six feet above the ground. In the hollows of the decayed Trees, the Racoons[1] take shelter, they are not found to the northward: they are a fat animal, and like all other animals that feed on Nuts, their fat is oily; without the skin and bowels, the weight of one is about fifteen pounds. They lay up nothing for the winter, and are dormant during the cold weather. The Red River is here 120 yards in width. Eleven miles below this the Reed River from the eastward falls in, it's width is about the same, but not so deep. This part of the River is called Pembina, from a small Stream that comes in. As this River has a rich deep soil and [is] everywhere fit for cultivation, it must become a pastoral and agricultural country, but for want of woods, for buildings and other purposes, must be limited to near the River. The open Plains have no Woods and afford no shelter. Note. Twenty years after this (1798) Several Canadians who had married native women with their families first settled, and they were soon joined by the Servants of the Hudson's Bay Company, who had done the same, with their families. This settlement rapidly increased it's population, and now (1848)[2] numbers about 5000 souls. The great draw back on this fine Settlement is the want of a Market; York Factory in Hudson's Bay, is apparently their Market, but the distance is too great, being N 24 E 606 miles on a straight line, and the devious route they would have to follow cannot be less than 900 miles. In this distance there are many Carrying Places, over which every thing must be carried; such a journey with their products would require the greater part of the short summer of these countries; and leave the Farmer no time for the cultivation of his ground.

[1] *Procyon lotor* (Linn.). [E. A. P.]
[2] The date here inserted is interesting, as it determines the year in which Thompson wrote this portion of his memoirs.

It would be a journey of toil, hard labor and suffering, and night and day devoured by Musketoes and other flies. Hence York Factory cannot be a market for the Red River. The extra produce of this river cannot find a Market at Montreal, the distance is too great, and the obstacles too many, and too laborious to be overcome. Nor can a market be found on the Mississippe, to get to the head of this River is a tedious route with many Carrying Places. In time civilisation will advance to them by this River, but until then the Red River must remain an isolated Settlement.

Here in the Latitude of 49 degrees, the Snow, clear of drift, is three to three and a half feet in depth; and in the Latitude of 58 degrees north the Snow has the same depth; but falls dry as dust, it adheres to nothing, and a cubic foot of well packed snow, when melted, yields only two inches of water. But in the former latitude, a cubic foot of well packed snow when melted, yields from four to five inches of water. Hence the northern Rivers, on the melting of the Snow, are not much affected, the Snow yields but little water, and the frosts of every night check its quantity. But to the southward, the Rivers overflow from the quantity of water contained in the Snow, and the thaw being more steady with greater warmth.

On the 21st March we proceeded on our journey [1] and on the 25th arrived at the trading House of the North West Company under the charge of Monsr Baptiste Cadotte. The Weather was fine, and at night the frost made the Snow firm for several hours of the day. Our journey was along

---

[1] After travelling S. 10° E. ten and a half miles up the west side of Red river, Thompson passed an old house which had formerly been occupied by a trader named Grant. After travelling S. 10° E. thirty-five miles, he reached the trading-post of a trader named Roy or Le Roy, which he places in latitude 48° 23′ 34″ N., five and a half miles south of Salt river. On the morning of March 23, he crossed to the east side of Red river, and went overland to the house of Baptiste Cadotte on the bank of Red Lake river, where the Clearwater river joins it, in latitude 47° 54′ 21″, on the site now occupied by the town of Red Lake Falls.

the Red River; in some places there were fine Ledges of Woods along the River, of moderate width, from thirty to three hundred yards; they were of Oak, Ash, Elm, Bass and other woods. As we ascended, the Aspin became more frequent. The whole a fine rich deep soil. About fifteen to twenty miles westward are the Hair Hills; of gentle rising grounds, with groves of Wood in places. At the east foot of these Hills are the low grounds with Ponds of salt water, and from which several Brooks come into the Red River. The Deer and Bisons are very fond of the grass of these places, which appears to keep them in all seasons in good condition

Mr Baptiste Cadotte[1] was about thirty five years of age. He was the son of a french gentleman by a native woman, and married to a very handsome native woman, also the daughter of a Frenchman: He had been well educated in Lower Canada, and spoke fluently his native Language, with Latin, French and English. I had long wished to meet a well educated native, from whom I could derive sound information for I was well aware that neither myself, nor any other Person I had met with, who was not a Native, were sufficiently masters of the Indian Languages. As the season was advancing to break up the Rivers, and thaw the Snow from off the ground, I enquired if he would advise me to proceed any farther with Dogs and Sleds: he said the season was too far advanced, and my further advance must be in Canoes; my last wintering ground was the Rein Deers Lake[2] in Latitude 57.23 North which Lake was frozen over to the 5th day of July, when it broke up by a gale of wind, and hitherto having been confined to northern climes, I was anxious to see the workings of the climate of 48 degrees north, aided by the

[1] For brief notes on Baptiste Cadotte and his father, see Coues, *New Light*, pp. 929–30.

[2] The previous winter had been spent at Bedford House, on the west side of Reindeer lake, and the weather had been very severe, even for that northern locality.

influence of the great, and warm Valley of the Mississippe, which was near to us. I shall therefore give a few days in the form of a journal.

March 27th. A fine morning. At 6¼ AM we set off and went up along the River thirteen Miles, through Willows, small Birch and Aspins : with a few Oak and Ash in places ; to 2 PM when we came to seven Tents of Chippeways and to Shèshepaskut (Sugar) the principal Chief of the Chippeway Tribe ; he appeared to be about sixty years of age, and yet had the activity and animated countenance of forty. His height was five feet, ten inches. His features round and regular, and his kind behaviour to all around him, and to strangers, concealed the stern, persevering Warrior, under whose conduct the incursions of the Sieux Indians were repressed, and the Village Indians driven to the Missisourie : We stopped at his Tent, as usual we were well received ; he thought the season too much advanced but would send a Guide with us the morrow.

The Snow was thawing and wet, very bad walking. On my Journey to the Missisourie I had two Thermometers ; On my return, on a stormy night, one got broke, and the one remaining I had carefully to keep for my astronomical observations, so that I can only give the weather in general terms.

March 28th. The night was mild, and the Snow still wet. At 5¾ AM the Guide came, and we advanced about four miles, when our Guide took care to break his Snow Shoes, and went back to the Tents, and in the evening the Chief sent me another Guide ; but we had to put up and wait all day. The Chippeways had killed a black Bear,[1] but on coming to our campment, they were so tired with heavy walking, they left the meat with us, until they returned. Three Geese[2] were seen and at 8 PM Lightning, Thunder and Rain came on, the latter during the whole night.

[1] *Ursus americanus* Pallas. [E. A. P.]
[2] *Branta canadensis* (Linn.). [E. A. P.]

March 29th. Rain continued until noon; The Snow was now so mixed with water, that we could not proceed. In the evening Rain came on and continued. Every thing was wet, without a chance of drying our clothes and baggage.

March 30th. Showers of Hail and Sleet. With the Guide went to examine the country before us : which appeared like a Lake, with water. I had therefore to return to Mr Cadotte and wait [for] the Rivers to become clear of ice, which was now too weak to venture upon. Our order of march was each of us carrying upon his back [what] the water could injure, every step, from ancle to the knee in snow water; the Dogs dragging the Sleds floating in the water. Swans, Geese and Ducks were about; but [of] the Eagles and large Hawks which to the northward are the first to arrive, none were seen :

On the 31st. After three hours march, at the rate of one mile an hour; we became too fatigued, laid down our loads, and with one man light we went to the house to get help, bad as the River was, we ventured on it; like desperate men; my companion fell through three times, and I escaped with only once; the water was only three feet deep, and we carried a long light pole in each hand. At 2 PM thank good Providence, we arrived at the house of Mr Cadotte who directly sent off five men to bring every thing to this place. Here a few days has thawed three and a half feet to three feet of heavy snow, which in the Latitide of 57 or 58 degrees north, require five, or six weeks of lingering weather.

CHAPTER XVII

LIFE AT CADOTTE'S HOUSE

Wahbino Dance—Home of Wahbino Singers—End of Wahbino Craze—Man Eater—Weetogo—Sheshepaskut's story of the war with the Chyennes—Suicide of a Sieux woman prisoner—Massacre of Chippeways.

WE had now to wait the River becoming clear of ice, and get a Canoe in order for our voyage. In the mean time I collected some information on the Religion and Ceremonies of these people. I learned that of late a superstition had sprung up, and was now the attention of all the Natives. It appeared the old Songs, Dances, and Ceremonies by frequent repetition had lost all their charms, and religious attention; and were heard and seen with indifference: some novelty was required and called for; and these people are the leaders of the Tribe in superstition and ceremonies. Accordingly two, or three crafty chiefs, contrived to dream (for all comes by Dreams) after having passed some time in a sweating cabin, and singing to the music of the Rattle. They dreamed they saw a powerful Medicine, to which a Manito voice told them to pay great attention and respect, and saw the tambour with the figures on it, and also the Rattle to be used for music in dancing: They also heard the Songs that were to be sung: They were to call it the Wahbino: It was to have two orders; the first only Wahbino the second Keeche Wahbino; and those initiated to bear the name of their order. (fool, or knave) Every thing belonging to the Wahbino was sacred, nothing of it to touch the ground, nor to be touched by a Woman.

Under the guidance of the Wahbino sages, Tambours
were made, the frame circular of eight inches in depth and
eighteen inches diameter, covered with fine parchment; the
frame covered with strange figures in red and black, and to
it were suspended many bits of tin and brass to make a gingling
noise; the Rattle had an ornamented handle; and several
had Wahbino Sticks, flat, about three feet or more in length,
with rude figures carved and painted: The Mania became
so authoritative that every young man had to purchase a
Wahbino Tambour; the price was what they could get
from him: and figured dances were also sold; the Knaves
were in their glory, admired and getting rich on the credulity
of others, but there were several sensible Men among them,
who looked with contempt on the whole of this mumery: it
was harmless, and since there must be some foolery, this was
as harmless as any other. I asked the old Chief, what he
thought of it; he gave me no answer, but looked me full in
the face, as much as to say, how can you ask me such a
question. I was present at the exhibition of a Wahbino
dance: A Keechee Wahbino Man arrived, he soon began to
make a speech to the great power of the Wahbino, and to
dance to his Song. He seated himself on the ground, on
each hand, a few feet from him, sat two men, somewhat in
advance; the Dancers were five young men naked, and
painted, above the waist: I sat down by one of the two
Men; the Wahbino Man began the Song in a bold strong
tone of voice, the Song was pleasing to the ear; the young
Men danced, sometimes slowly, then changed to a quick step
with many wild gestures, sometimes erect, and then, to their
bodies being horizontal: shaking their Tambours, and at
times singing a short chorus. They assumed many attitudes
with ease, and showed a perfect command of their limbs.
With short intervals, this lasted for about an hour. I watched
the countenance of the Indian next to me, he seemed to
regard the whole with sullen indifference; I enquired of him,

"what was the intent and meaning of what I had seen and heard"; With a smile of contempt By what you have seen, and heard; they have made themselves masters of the Squirrels Musk Rats and Racoons, also of the Swans, Geese, Cranes and Ducks : their Manito is weak. "Then all these are to be in abundance." "So they say, but we shall see." "What becomes of the Bison, the Moose and Red Deer. With a look of contempt; Their Manito's are too powerful for the Wahbino. I found that several of the Indians looked on the Wahbino as a jugglery between knaves and fools : yet for full two years it had a surprising influence over the Indians, and too frequently [they] neglected hunting for singing and dancing. About two hours after the exhibition, an Indian arrived with twenty two Beaver Skins to trade necessaries for himself and family, he was a Man in the prime of life. The Knave of a Keeche Wahbino made a speech to him on the powerful effects of the Great Wahbino Song, and which he directly sang to him.

The Song being ended; the Indian presented him eighteen Beaver Skins, reserving only four for himself, for these he traded ammunition and tobacco, and [kept] nothing for his wife and family; and the Knave seemed to think he was but barely paid for his song and ought to have been paid the twenty two Beaver Skins. I enquired of Mʳ Cadotte, if he could interpret to me the Song we had just heard : he replied, that although they spoke in the language of his native tongue, he did not understand a single sentence of the Song, only a chance word, which was of no use.

We both had the same opinion, that they have a kind of a mystical language among themselves, understood only by the initiated, and that the Wahbino Songs, were in this mystical language : that novelty had given it a power, which it would soon lose ; he remarked that almost all the Wahbino singers, were idle Men and poor hunters. This folly spread to a considerable distance, and the Lake of the Woods became

R

it's central place. Several lodges, containing forty or fifty families, living more by fishing than hunting, became enamoured of the Wahbino Song and Dance, and so many dancing together they too often became highly excited and danced too long. One of them made a neat drum for himself; on which he placed strings of particular bones of small animals, as mice, squirrels and frogs, with strings of the bones and claws of small birds: and on beating the drum as the strings of bones changed positions, pretended to tell what was to happen. These Lodges were now encamped at the sortie of the Rainy River into the Lake of the Woods, on a fine, long, sandy Point on the left side of the River: long poles were tied from tree to tree, on which were carefully hung the Wahbino Medicine Bag and Tambour of each Man.

On this Point the North West Canoes camped, when a gale of wind was on the Lake. The Lake was in this state in 1799, when we arrived, and we put up: about 10 AM. At noon by double Altitude I observed for Latitude.

While doing so, an Indian of my acquaintance, came and sat down. When I was done, looking at the parallel glasses and quicksilver, he said, My Wahbino is strong. I knew that his meaning was to say, By what you are doing, you give to yourself great power, my Wahbino can do the same for me. I told him the Great Spirit alone was strong, your Wahbino is like this, taking up a pinch of sand and letting it fall. He then said the Sun is strong; My answer was, the Great Spirit made the Sun, at this he appeared surprised and went away.

The next morning the Gale of Wind continued; the Indian came to me, and said, yesterday you despised my Wahbino, and I have thrown it away.

In the night the Gale had thrown down the Pole to which the Tambour and Medicine Bag was tied; and the Dogs had wetted them; he was indignant, and took the gun to shoot the Dogs, but his good sense prevented him; and looking at his Tambour and Medicine Bag with contempt, exclaimed " If you, the Wahbino had any power, the Dogs would not have treated you as they have done." Other Tambours were in the same condition, the news of this accident spread, the sensible men took advantage of it, and by the following summer nothing more was heard of the Wahbino Medicine.

I called to Mr Cadotte's attention a sad affair that ha'd taken place a few months past on the shores of the Lake of the Woods. About twenty families were together for hunting and fishing. One morning a young man of about twenty two years of age on getting up, said he felt a strong inclination to eat his Sister; as he was a steady young man, and a promising hunter, no notice was taken of this expression; the next morning he said the same and repeated the same several times in the day for a few days. His Parents attempted to reason him out of this horrid inclination; he was silent and gave them no answer; his Sister and her Husband became alarmed, left the place, and went to another Camp. He became aware of it; and then said he must have human flesh to eat, and would have it; in other respects, his behaviour was cool, calm and quiet. His father and relations were much grieved; argument had no effect on him, and he made them no answer to their questions. The Camp became alarmed, for it was doubtful who would be his victim. His Father called the Men to a Council, where the state of the young man was discussed, and their decision was, that an evil Spirit had entered into him, and was in full possession of him to make him become a Man Eater (a Weetego). The father was found fault with for not having called to his assistance a Medicine Man, who by sweating and his Songs to the tambour and rattle might have driven away the evil spirit, before it was too late. Sentence of death was passed on him, which was to be done by his Father. The young man was called, and told to sit down in the middle, there was no fire. which he did, he was then informed of the resolution taken, to which he said " I am willing to die " ; The unhappy Father arose, and placing a cord about his neck strangled him, to which he was quite passive; after about two hours, the body was carried to a large fire, and burned to Ashes, not the least bit of bone remaining. This was carefully done to prevent his soul and the evil spirit which possessed him from returning to this world; and appearing at his grave; which they believe the souls of those who are buried can, and may do, as having a claim to the bones of their bodies. It may be thought the Council acted a cruel part in ordering the father to put his Son to death, when they could have ordered it by the hands of another person. This was done, to prevent the law of retaliation; which had it been done by the hands of any other person, might have been made a pretext of revenge by those who were not the friends of the person who put him to death. Such is the state of Society where there are no positive laws to direct mankind.

From our exploring notes; it appeared to us that this sad evil disposition to become Weetego; or Man Eaters, was wholly confined to the inhabitants of the Forests; no such disposition being known among the Indians of the Plains; and this limited to the Nahathaway and Chippeway Indians, for the numerous Natives under the name of Dinnae (Chepawyans) whose hunting grounds are all the Forests north of the latitude of 56 degrees, have no such horrid disposition among them.

The word Weetego is one of the names of the Evil Spirit and when he gets possession of any Man, (Women are wholly exempt from it) he becomes a Man Eater, and if he succeeds; he no longer keeps company with his relations and friends, but roams all alone through the Forests, a powerful wicked Man, preying upon whom he can, and as such is dreaded by the Natives. Tradition says, such evil Men were more frequent than at present, probably from famine. I have known a few instances of this deplorable turn of mind, and not one instance could plead hunger, much less famine as an excuse, or cause of it. There is yet a dark chapter to be written on this aberration of the human mind on this head.

The Chief, Sheshepaskut, with a few men arrived, with a few Beaver Skins and Provisions; I enquired of him, the cause of his making war on the Chyenne Indians and destroying their Village, and the following is the substance of our conversation. Our people and the Chyenne's for several years had been doubtful friends; but as they had Corn and other Vegetables, which we had not and of which we were fond, and traded with them, we passed over and forgot, many things we did not like; until lately; when we missed our Men who went a hunting, we always said, they have fallen by the hands of our enemies the Sieux Indians. But of late years we became persuaded the Chyennes were the people, as some missing went to hunt where the Sieux never came; We were at a loss what to do; when some of our people went to trade Corn, and while there, saw a Chyenne Hunter bring in a fresh Scalp, which they knew, they said nothing, but came directly to me. A Council was called, at which all the Men who had never returned from hunting were spoken of by their relations; and it was determined the Chyenne Village must be destroyed: As the Geese were now leaving us, and Winter [was] at hand, we defered to make war on them until the next Summer; and in the meantime we sent word to all the men of our tribe to be ready and meet us here when the berries are in flower. Thus the winter passed; and at the time appointed we counted about one hundred and fifty men. We required two hundred, but some of the best hunters could not come, they had to hunt and fish for the families of the warriors that came. We made our War Tent, and our Medicine Men slept in it; their Dreams forbid us to attack them until the Bulls were fat; the Chyenne's would then leave their Village weak to hunt and make provisions. To which we agreed.

The time soon came, and we marched from one piece of Woods to another, mostly in the night until we came to the last great Grove that was near to the Village. Our Scouts were six young men. Two of them went to a small Grove near the Village, and climbing up the tallest Oaks, saw all that passed in the Village and were relieved every morning and evening by other two.

We thus passed six days, our provisions were nearly done, and we did not dare to hunt. Some of our men dreamed we were discovered and left us. On the seventh morning, as we were in council, one of the young men who were on the watch came to us, and gave us notice that the Chyennes had collected their Horses and brought them to the Village. We immediately got ourselves ready and waited for the other young man who was on the Watch; it was near mid day when he came and informed us that a great many men and women had gone off a hunting, and very few remained in the Village. We now marched leisurely to the small Grove of Oaks to give the hunting party time to proceed so far as to be beyond the sound of our Guns. At this Grove we ought to have remained all night and attack the next morning; but our Provisions were done, and if they found the Bisons near; part of them might return; From the Grove to the Village was about a mile of open plain; as we ran over, we were perceived, there were several Horses in the Village on which the young people got, and rode off.

We entered the Village and put every one to death, except three Women; after taking every thing we wanted, we quickly set fire to the Village and with all haste retreated for those that fled at our attack would soon bring back the whole party, and we did not wish to encounter Cavalry in the Plains.

Here the old Chief lighted his pipe, and smoked in a thoughtful manner. Mr Cadotte then took up the narrative. Those left in charge of the village were twelve Men of a certain age, and as there was no time to scalp them in the manner they wished, their heads were cut off, put into bags; with which, and the prisoners, they marched through the Woods to the camp near the Rainy River. Here they recounted their exploits, and prepared for a grand war dance the next day: which accordingly took place. One of the three Women prisoners was a fine steady looking woman with an infant in her arms of eight months, which they in vain tried to take from her. Each time she folded it in her arms with desperate energy, and they allowed her to keep it.

The war circle being made by the Men, their Wives and Children standing behind them, the three prisoners were placed within the war circle; the heads taken were rolled out of the bags on the ground: and preparatory to their being scalped, the whole circle of Men, Women, and Children with tambours rattles and flutes, shouted the War whoop, and danced to the song of Victory. The prisoner Woman with her infant in her arms did not dance, but gently moved away to where the head of her husband was lying, and catching it up, kissed it and placed it to the lips of her infant; it was taken from her and thrown on the ground; a second time she seized it, and did the same; it was again taken from her, and thrown on the ground; a third time she pressed the head of her husband to her heart, to the lips of herself and child; it was taken from her with menace of death: holding up her infant to heaven, she drew a sharp pointed Knife from her bosom, plunged it into her heart; and fell dead on the head of her husband. They buried her, and her infant was taken to, and brought up at, the Rainy River House.

The old Chief still smoking his pipe, said the Great Spirit had made her a Woman, but had given her the heart of a Man.

Our discourse then turned on the Sixty Seven souls, Men Women and Children that two springs ago were destroyed by the Sieux Indians at the Sand Lake of the Mississippe where they were making Sugar; The Chief replied that he did not know what to say to it; it was a bad affair and they longed to revenge it: but they in a manner brought it on themselves. For several years there had been no regular war between us, they had left the Woods, made very little use of Canoes, and having many Horses were living in the Plains and had we waited, would have left the whole of the Woods to us. The Sand Lake was finely wooded with large Maples, which had never been tapped; this tempted our people, they went and made a great deal of Sugar; this did for once, and the Sieux took no notice of it; but when they returned the next spring, this was making that Lake their own, the Sieux did not care for it, but would not allow it to be taken from them. They formed a war party and so completely surprised our people, that not one escaped, and the enmity that was dying away between us is now as bad as ever. While they keep the Plains with their Horses we are not a match for them; for we being foot men, they could get to windward of us, and set fire to the grass; When we marched for the Woods, they would be there before us, dismount, and under cover fire on us. Until we have Horses like them, we must keep to the Woods, and leave the plains to them.

On conversing with these Chippaways they all readily understood me, though frequently I did not understand them, and Mr Cadotte had to interpret between us. He also expressed his surprise that they should understand me, which he did not; they replied, we understand him because he speaks the language of our Fathers, which we have much changed and made better. On comparing the Nouns and Verbs of the primitive language of the Nahathaways with the Chippaway dialect, the greatest change appeared in constantly rejecting the " th " of the former for the " y " of the latter, as for Kether (you) Keyer—for Neether (me) Neeyer—for Weether (thou) Weeyer; and softening a great number of others, rejecting some and substituting others, and giving to the whole a more sonorous sound as best adapted to their oratory. The dialects of the primitive language extend to the Delaware River; and the Delaware Indians speak a dialect of the primitive language.

By astronomical observations this House is in Latitude 47.54.21 N. Longitude 96.19 W Variation 10 degrees East. The course of this River is from the south westward until it is lost in the Plains, the groves are at a considerable distance from each other, by no means sufficient for the regular Farmer, but may become a fine pastoral country, but without a Market, other than the inhabitants of the Red River.

CHAPTER XVIII

DISCOVER THE SCOURCE OF THE MISSISSIPPE

*Another start—Clear Water River—Carrying Place of Red
Lake River—Spearing Fish—Arrive at Turtle Lake—
Birds—Wild Rice—Otter—Turtle Lake.*

THE Rivers becoming clear of ice, a Birch Rind Canoe
of eighteen feet in length, by three feet in breadth
was made ready; and on the ninth day of April
with three Canadians, and a native Woman, the Wife of one
of the Men, and twelve days provisions in dried meat, We
set out to survey the country to the source of the Mississippe
River: We had the choice of two Rivers, that direct from
the Red Lake; the current moderate, but liable to be en-
cumbered with ice from the Lake, or the Clear Water River
of swift current: without any ice; we preferred the latter,
and proceeded slowly up it. This River was fifty five yards
in width by about eight feet in depth, from the melting of
the Snow. But as all these Rivers are fed by Snow and
Rains, in the months of August and September this River's
depth will not exceed one or two feet. Although the
country appears a perfect level the current ran at the rate of
full four miles an hour. The River was too deep, to anchor
our ticklish Canoe, but seeing a piece of Wood on the middle
of the River I left the Canoe and walked as fast as I could,
yet the current carried the wood faster than I walked.

On the eleventh we passed the junction of the Wild Rice
River from the westward, with a body of water equal to half

this River, and we have now less water with more moderate
current.   On the twelfth we arrived at the Carrying Place
which leads to the Red Lake River, having come sixty four
miles up this sinuous River.   The east side, or right bank
had fine Forests, but as we advanced, the Aspin became the
principal growth of the Woods.   The West Bank had patches
of hard wood trees, with much fine meadow which led to
the Plains, the whole a rich deep soil.

The Carrying Place is four miles in length of part marsh
and part good ground to the Bank of the Red Lake River,
in Latitude 48 . 0 . 55 N Longitude 95 . 54 . 28 W.[1]   Variation
10° East.

Our course was now up this River to the Red Lake, a
distance of thirty two miles.   Both banks of this River well
timbered with Oak, Ash and other hard Woods, intermixed
with much Aspin and Poplar.   A rich deep soil, but now from
the melting of the Snow every where covered with water, the
country so level, that only a chance bit of dry bank was to
be seen ; At night we cut down Trees and slept upon them.
As our provisions were dried meat we did not require fire to
cook our supper, and a Canadian never neglects to have
touchwood for his pipe.   By Observations the head of the
River on the banks of the Lake, is in Latitude 47 . 58 . 15 N.
Longitude 95 . 35 . 37 W   The straight course and distance
from M[r] Cadotte's House is, N 82 E 35 miles, to perform
which we have gone over 117 Statute miles and employed
seven long days, setting off at 5 AM and putting up at 7 PM.

At the Lake the kind old Chief, Sheshepaskut with six
Lodges of Chippeways were camped. He gave us three pickerel
and two large pike, a welcome change from dried meat. As
they had no Canoe, and therefore could not spear fish in the
night, they requested the loan of mine, which was lent to
them. The spearing of fish in the night, is a favorite mode

[1] This is the position given in Thompson's notes for the north end of
the portage.

with them, and gives to them a considerable part of their livelihood. The spear handle is a straight pole of ten to twelve feet in length, headed with a barbed iron; A rude narrow basket of iron hoops is fixed to a pole of about six feet in length. A quantity of birch rind is collected and loosely tied in small parcels. When the night comes, the darker the better, two Men and a Boy embark in a Canoe, the one gently and quietly to give motion to the Canoe. The pole and basket is fixed in the Bow under which the Spearman stands, the Birch Rind is set on fire, and burns with a bright light; but only for a short time, the Boy from behind feeds the light, so as to keep a constant blaze. The approach of the flaming light seems to stupify the fish, as they are all speared in a quiesent state. The Lake or River is thus explored for several hours until the Birch Rind is exhausted, and on a calm night a considerable number is thus caught. Those in my canoe, speared three Sturgeon, each weighing about sixty pounds. For a clear water Lake they were very good; for the Sturgeon may be called the Water Hog, and is no where so good and fat as among the alluvials of Rivers. This, the Red Lake is a fine sheet of Water of about thirty miles in length by eight to 10 miles in breadth; the banks rise about twenty to thirty feet, the soil is somewhat sandy and produces Firs of a fine growth, with the other usual woods, and in places, the white Cedar but of short growth. This Lake like several other places, has occasionally a trading House for one Winter only, the country all around, being too poor in furrs to be hunted on a second winter. The Lake being covered with ice, and patches of water, at places we paddled the Canoe, and where the ice was firm, made a rude Sledge on which we placed the Canoe and Baggage, and hauled it over the ice to a patch of water and thus continued for seventeen miles; a laborious work and always wet, the weather frequent showers of Rain and Sleet, and then clear weather. We now came to a

Carrying Place of six miles in length, in a south direction,
over which we carried our Canoe and things.

The Road was through Firs and Aspins, with a few Oaks
and Ash. Near the middle of the Carrying Place the Ground
had many ascents and descents of twenty to forty feet, the
first we have seen since we left the Red River. By 9 PM on
the 23rd of April we had carried all over, and now had to
cross the country to the Turtle Lake,[1] the head of the Mississippe River at which we arrived on the 27th. Our Journey
has been very harassing and fatigueing ; from Pond to Pond
and Brook to Brook with many carrying places, the Ponds,
or small Lakes were some open, others wholly or partly
covered with ice ; the Brooks so winding, that after paddling
an hour we appeared to have made very little, or no advance.

The country everywhere appeared low and level, something like an immense swamp. Everywhere there was much
wild rice,[2] upon which the wild fowl fed, and became very fat
and well tasted ; The Swan was a very rare bird ; and of the
different species of Geese, [there were] only two species of
the Grey Goose ;[3] but the Ducks [were found] in all their
varieties : the Cranes[4] and Bitterns[5] upon their usual food
were equally good ; of the Plover species there were but few,
the Ponds having their low banks covered with long grass.
In some Ponds there were Pelicans[6] and Cormorants,[7] the
former as disgusting as usual. The large spotted Loons[8] were

[1] In Thompson's notes there is this reference to Turtle brook : " This
is the source of the famous Mississippi river in the most direct line. All
the other little sources are reckoned to be subordinate to this, as they are
longer in forming so considerable a stream. The brook that furnishes
water to this lake comes in on the right hand, from the south bay of the
Turtle Lake." The latitude of Turtle lake is given as 47° 38′ 21″ N.

[2] *Zizania aquatica* (Linn.). [E. A. P.]

[3] *Branta canadensis* (Linn.) and *B. c. hutchinsi* (Rich.). [E. A. P.]

[4] *Grus* (perhaps more than one species). [E. A. P.]

[5] *Botaurus lentiginosus* (Montagu). [E. A. P.]

[6] *Pelecanus erythrorhynchos* Gmel. [E. A. P.]

[7] *Phalacrocorax auritus* (Lesson). [E. A. P.]

[8] *Gavia immer* (Brunn.). [E. A. P.]

in every Pond that was open; this wily Bird, as soon as he saw us set up his cry, and was at a loss whether to fly or dive. For the latter the ponds were too shoal and full of rice stalks; and before he could raise his flight he had to beat the water with Wings and Feet before he could raise himself. This exposed them to our shots, and we killed several of them. Their beautiful spotted skins make favorite Caps for the Natives, and two Canoes of Chippaways being in company were thankful to get them. It is very well known that at Churchill Factory in Hudson's Bay in Latitude 58.47.32 N Longitude 94.13.48 West, in the spring wild grey geese are killed with wild Rice in their stomachs; on which they must have fed near the Turtle Lake in Latitude 47.39.15 N Longitude 95.12.45 W, the direct distance between the two places is N 3 E 780 statute miles. Wild Rice, but not in any quantity, so as to feed numerous flocks of Geese, grow in places near the Latitude of 50 degrees north, but even from these few places the distance to Churchill Fort will be about 660 miles. The wild rice grows in great plenty all round the Turtle Lake, allowing this Lake to be their centre. The Ponds, Brooks, Rivulets and small Lakes in which the wild Rice grows in abundance occupies an extent of area of at least six thousand square miles. It is a weak food, those who live for months on it enjoy good health, are moderately active, but very poor in flesh: The Wild Geese, before a Gale of Wind fly at the rate of sixty miles an hour, which at this rate requires thirteen hours from their rice ground to take them to Churchill Fort. (Note. Conversing with Surgeon Howard of Montreal on the great distance the Wild Geese fly without digesting the rice in their stomachs, he related to me an experiment of the late Dr John Hunter on digestion. He had two grey hounds. One morning he fed them both with the same quantity and quality of Meat; the one he tied up, and [it] remained quiet all day; and with the other he hunted all day: about sunset they were both killed. On examining the hound that was tied up, the Meat was wholly digested; but in the stomach of the hound that had hunted all day the meat was but little changed. Thus it appears that animals on a rapid march do not digest their food, or very slowly). These extensive rice grounds are probably the last place where the Wild Fowl that proceed far to the northward (about 1400 miles) to make their nests, and bring up their young, feed for a few days to give them strength for their journey, for the late springs of the northern climes they pass over cannot give them much. In the Brooks and small Lakes were several Otters,[1] of which we killed one; to make the flesh of this animal more palatable, the Natives hang it in the smoke for a couple of days.

For the first time we saw the small brown Eagle, some days we saw at least a dozen of them, but always beyond the reach of our Guns. From M' Cadotte's House on the Red River to this place, the Turtle Lake we have been nineteen days, rising early and putting up late, and yet by my astronomical observations, the course and distance is S 71 E 56 statute miles, in a direct line not quite three miles a day. These circuituous routes deceive the traveller, and induce him to think he is at a much greater distance from a given place than what he actually is. The Turtle Lake, which is the head of the Mississippe River, is four miles in length, by as many in breadth and it's small bays give it the rude form a Turtle.

(Note. By the treaty of 1783 between Great Britain and the United States, the northern boundary of the latter was designated to be a Line due west from the north [west] corner of the Lake of the Woods (in latitude 49.46¾ N) to the head of the Mississippe which was supposed to be still more to the north: This supposition arose from the Fur Traders on ascending the Mississippe which is very sinuous, counting every pipe a League of three miles at the end of which they

[1] *Lutra canadensis* (Schreber). [E. A. P.]

claimed a right to rest and smoke a pipe. By my survey I found these pipes to be the average length of only two miles, and they also threw out of account the windings of the River, and thus placing the Turtle Lake 128 geo. miles too far to the north).[1]

[1] This statement by Thompson has been widely quoted, but is erroneous. The negotiators of the preliminary treaty of peace, November, 1782, had before them a copy of the Mitchell map of North America, published in 1755. The north-west corner of this map contained an "inset" map of the Labrador peninsula and Hudson Bay, doubtless inserted there because, at the date of publication, the geographical information respecting the Red river region was so meagre. The Mississippi river is shown as a large stream where cut off by the inset map, and, to anyone relying solely upon the Mitchell map, it would seem evident that it would extend northward at least as far as the latitude of the north-west angle of the Lake of the Woods. But for this inset map, and errors in the body of the map, our boundary would, almost certainly, have followed the St. Louis river from the present city of Duluth, thence to the headwaters of the Mississippi. Much geographical confusion has been caused by over-estimation of distances, but, as stated above, our territorial losses in this area are not due to this cause. [JAMES WHITE.]

CHAPTER XIX

SCOURCE OF THE MISSISSIPPE TO LAKE SUPERIOR

*Turtle Brook—Red Cedar Lake—Trading Post—Collecting Wild
Rice—Maple Sugar—Rights in Maple Groves—Mississippe
—Lake Winepegoos—Sand Lake River—Ascend Sand Lake
River—Sand Lake Trading Post—Great Swamps—S^t
Louis River—Rapids & Falls—Trading Post—Elevations
—Lake Superior—Copper on Lake Superior—Large Lakes
of North America—Survey of south shore of Lake Superior—
Echo at Ontonoggan River—Arrive at Falls of St Maries—
Meet Sir Alexander Mc Kenzie—Instructions from the North
West Company—Survey of the east and part of the north
shore of Lake Superior.*

TWO canoes of Chippaway Indians came to us on their
way to the Red Cedar Lake; As my Canoe from
coming too often in contact with the ice was Leaky
I embarked with them to the Red Cedar Lake. From the
SW corner of the Turtle Lake a Brook goes out, by the name
of the Turtle Brook of three yards in width by two feet in
depth at 2¼ miles p^r hour, but so very winding, that rather
than follow it we made a Carrying Place of 180 yards, to a
small Lake which sends a Brook into it, and which we followed,
and then continued the main stream following its incredible
windings and turnings through apparently an extensive very
low country of grass and marsh.

There were three Falls, along which we made as many
carrying places, and several rapids over a gravel bottom; As

we proceeded several Brooks came in from each hand, and we entered the Red Cedar Lake[1] in a fine Stream of fifteen yards in width by two feet in depth, and three miles an hour. Proceeding five miles over the Lake we came to the trading house of M[r] John Sayer,[2] a Partner of the North West Company, and in charge of this Department. By my Observations this House is in Latitude 47.27.56 N Longitude 94.47.52 West Variation 6 degrees East. From the north bank of Turtle Lake to this trading house the course and distance S 58 E 25 Miles, but the windings of the River will more than treble this distance. The Stream has a grassy valley in which it holds it's zigzag course; this land is very low. The Woods on each side of the Valley are of Oak, Ash, Elm, Larch, Birch,[3] Pines, Aspins and where a little elevated fine Maple.[4] The soil every where deep and rich with abundance of long grass. The Brooks and Ponds and the Turtle Rivulet almost from side to side full of the Stalks of the Wild Rice, which makes it very laborious to come against the current, as the canoe must keep the middle of the stream against the full force of the current. M[r] Sayer and his Men had passed the whole winter on wild rice and maple sugar, which keeps them alive, but poor in flesh : Being a good shot on the wing I had killed twenty large Ducks more than we wanted, which I gave to him a most welcome present, as they had not tasted meat for a long time. A mess of rice and sugar was equally acceptable to me who had lived wholly on meat; and I tried to live upon it, but the third day was attacked with heart burn and weakness of the stomach, which two meals of meat cured ; but the rice makes good soup. From the remarks I have made in the vicissitudes of my life, I have always found that

---

[1] Now known as Cass lake.

[2] John Sayer was one of the wintering partners who signed the agreement of 1804 consolidating the North-West and X Y Companies. His house at this time was on the north-east side of Cass lake.

[3] *Betula papyrifera* Marsh. [E. A. P.]

[4] *Acer saccharum* Marsh. [E. A. P.]

men leading an active life readily change their food from vegetable to animal without inconvenience, but not from animal to vegetable, the latter often attended with weakness of the bowels.

The wild Rice is fully ripe in the early part of September. The natives lay thin birch rind all over the bottom of the Canoe, a man lightly clothed, or naked places himself in the middle of the Canoe, and with a hand on each side, seizes the stalks and knocks the ears of rice against the inside of the Canoe, into which the rice falls, and thus he continues until the Canoe is full of rice; on coming ashore the Women assist in unloading. A canoe may hold from ten to twelve bushels. He smokes his pipe, sings a Song; and returns to collect another canoe load.

And so plentifull is the rice, an industrious Man may fill his canoe three times in a day. Scaffolds are prepared about six feet from the ground made of small sticks covered with long grass; on this the rice is laid, and gentle clear fires kept underneath by the women, and turned until the rice is fully dried. The quantity collected is no more than the scaffolds can dry, as the rice is better on the stalk than on the ground. The rice when dried is pounded in a mortar made of a piece of hollow oak with a pestle of the same until the husk comes off. It is then put up in bags made of rushes and secured against animals. The Natives collect not only enough for themselves, but also as much as the furr traders will buy from them; Two or three Ponds of water can furnish enough for all that is collected.

In the Spring the Natives employ themselves in making Sugar from the Maple Trees, the process of doing which is well known. The old trees give a stronger sap than the young trees; The Canadians also make a great quantity, which, when the sap is boiled to a proper consistence, they run into moulds where it hardens. But the Indians prefer making it like Muscovado sugar, this is done simply by stirring it quickly about with a small paddle. The Plane Tree[1] also makes a good sugar, the sap is abundant, and the sugar whiter, but not so strong. Both sugars have a taste, which soon becomes agreeable, and as fine white loaf sugar can be made from it as from that of the West Indies. The natives would 'make far more than they do, if they could find a Market.

The men of family that trade at this House are about Sixty, and Mr Sayer, who has been in the Furr Trade many years, is of opinion that seven persons to a family is about a fair average. This will give 420 souls. The Natives here call themselves "Oochepoys"[2] and for some few years have begun to give something like a right of property to each family on the sugar maple groves, and which right continues in the family to the exclusion of others. But as this appropriated space is small in comparison of the whole extent; any, and every person is free to make sugar on the vacant grounds. The appropriation was made by them in a council, in order to give to each family a full extent of ground for making sugar, and to prevent the disputes that would arise where all claim an equal right to the soil and it's productions. And as in the making of sugar, several kettles and many small vessels of wood and birch rind for collecting and boiling the sap are required, which are not wanted for any other purpose, [they] are thus left in safety on their own grounds for future use.

Our Canoe being in very bad order from rough usage among the ice Mr Sayer purchased a good canoe for us for the value of twenty beaver skins in goods and our Canoe. It was my intention to have gone a considerable distance down the River, but Mr Sayer strongly advised [me] to go no further than to Sand Lake River, as beyond we should be in the power of the Sieux Indians. On the third day of May

---

[1] Thompson evidently refers to the Ash-leaved Maple, *Acer negundo* Linn. This tree bears considerable resemblance to the False Plane, *Acer pseudo-platanus* Linn., the "Plane Tree" of Scotland. [E. A. P.]
[2] Another form of the name Ojibway.

we took leave of our kind host; our provisions were wild
rice and maple sugar, with powder and shot for ducks.   One
mile beyond the house we entered the River, now augmented
to twenty six yards in width by three feet in depth, at two
miles an hour.   The valley of the Mississippe lay now clear
before me, it's direction South East; it's appearance was that
of a meadow of long half dried grass without water of about
half a mile in width, or less.   On the left side points of wood
came to the edge of this valley, but not into it, at a mile,
or a mile and a half from each other, the intervals were bays
of hay marsh.   On the right hand the line of Woods was
more regular; Being well experienced in taking levels, the
Valley of the River before us showed a declining plane of full
twenty p^f mile for the first three miles; this would give a
current which no boat could ascend; but this was completely broken down by the innumerable turnings of the
River to every point of the compass.   Seeing a Pole before
us at less than five hundred yards the four hands in the canoe
paddled smartly for thirty five minutes before a current of
2¼ miles an hour to arrive at it, in which time we estimated
we had passed over about three miles of the windings of the
River.   Meeting an Indian in his canoe ascending the River,
he smoked with us, and on my remarking to him the crooked-
ness of the River, he shook his head, and said Snake make this
River.   I thought otherwise, for these windings break the
current and make it navigable.   I have always admired the
formations of the Rivers, as directed by the finger of God
for the most benevolent purposes.

At 7 PM we put up in Lake Winepegoos[1] formed by the
waters of this River.   It's length is seventeen miles, by about
six miles in width, the principal fish is Sturgeon.[2]   The woods
have all day had much Fir, both red and black, the latter very
resinous and much used for torches for night fishing.   The

---

[1] At present known as Lake Winnibigoshish.
[2] *Acipenser rubicundus* Le Sueur.   [E. A. P.]

soil of the Woods is now sandy; with Points of alluvial, on which are Oaks and other hard woods, and the bays have White Cedar,[1] Birch and Larch.[2] On leaving the Lake the valley of the River appeared more level.

On the 4th at noon put ashore to observe for latitude and shortly after the River passing over a fine bottom of gravel, I found the River to be 26 yards wide 2¼ feet deep by 2¼ miles an hour. Nine miles below the Leach River from Leach Lake, southwestward of us comes in, its size appears equal to this River, which it deepens, but does not add to it's breadth. For this day the valley of the River is from half to one mile in width, on each side well wooded with fine Firs.

May 5th. After proceeding two miles saw the first leaves on the Willows; the Maple and other Trees are in full bud, but have no leaves. We came to a Rapid, and a Fall over a smooth Rock of eight feet descent: the whole is thirteen feet perpendicular, with a Carrying Place of 263 yards. Six miles further the Meadow River from the north eastward joins, it's size and water equal to this, the Mississippe, which is now fifty to sixty yards in breadth. We met a Man wounded in the shoulder, in a quarrel with an other Man, his Wife was paddling the Canoe; it appeared jealousy was the cause.

On the 6th May we continued our route: in the course of the day we met an Indian and his Wife. The man had a large fresh scar across his nose, and when smoking with us, asked if he was not still handsome; on arriving at Sand Lake we learned that the evening before, while drinking, another Indian had quarrelled with him, and in a fit of jealousy had bit off his nose and thrown it away, but in the morning finding his nose was missing, he searched for, and found it, the part that remained was still bleeding, on which he stuck the part bitten off, without any thing to keep it; it adhered, and

---

[1] *Thuja occidentalis* Linn. [E. A. P.]
[2] *Larix laricina* (Du Roi). [E. A. P.]

taking a looking glass, [he] exclaimed, " as yet I am not ugly."
I was afterwards informed, the cure became complete, and
only the scar remained. The Swan River from the north
eastward fell in with a bold stream of water. In the afternoon at 5 PM we arrived at the mouth of the Sand Lake
River, a short distance above which I measured the Mississippe
River; 62 yards in width; 12 feet in depth; at 4 yards from
the shore 10 feet, at two yards 8 feet in depth, by full two
miles an hour. The mouth of the Sand Lake River is in
Latitude 46.49.11 N Longitude 93.45.7 W and from the
Red Cedar Lake S 48 E 68 miles.

As the Mississippe is the most magnificent River, and
flows through the finest countries of North America, I shall
endeavour to explain the peculiar formation of its head
waters. From the Turtle to the Red Cedar Lake, the passage
was too much obstructed by ice to allow me to form a correct
idea of it's windings ; but from the latter Lake to the mouth
of the Sand Lake River there was no ice ; From the Red
Cedar Lake to the latter river is 68 miles direct distance ; to
perform which, four hands in a light Canoe paddled forty
three hours and thirteen minutes. Of this direct distance
ten miles were Lake, leaving fifty eight miles of River ; and
allowing three hours and thirteen minutes for passing the
Lake ; forty hours remain. Four hands in a light Canoe
before a current of two, and at times two and a half miles
an hour, will proceed, at least five miles an hour ; and this
rate for forty hours will give a distance of two hundred miles
of the windings of the river for fifty eight miles in a direct
line, being nearly three and a half miles to one mile. Every
mile of these sinuosities of the River, the current turned to
every point of the compass, and it's direct velocity was
diminished, yet continuing to have a steady current measured
at two full miles an hour, must have a descent of full twenty
inches pr mile to maintain this current ; which in two hundred
miles gives a descent or change of level in this distance of

333 feet 4 inches, equal to a change of level of $3\frac{3}{4}$ feet for each mile in a direct line.

Thus the descent from the Turtle to the Red Cedar Lake is $97\frac{1}{4}$ feet, and from this Lake to the Sand Lake River $333\frac{1}{2}$ feet giving a change of level of 431 feet, apparently through a low country. (Note. Lieutenant Lynch of the US Navy in his survey of the River Jordan from the Sea of Tiberias to the Dead Sea says the difference of level of the two seas is something more than one thousand feet. The distance between these seas in the direct line of the River is sixty miles, but the windings of the Jordan increased the distance to two hundred miles which gives a descent of five feet to a mile. They descended it in two boats in safety, passing over twenty seven strong rapids and many lesser to the Dead Sea).

To the intelligent part of mankind, the scources of all the great rivers have always been subjects of curiosity; witness the expeditions undertaken; the sums of money expended, and the sufferings endured to discover the sources of the Nile, the research of ages. Whatever the Nile has been in ancient times in Arts and Arms, the noble valley of the Mississippe bids fair to be, and excluding its pompous, useless, Pyramids and other works; it's anglo saxon population will far exceed the Egyptians in all the arts of civilized life, and in a pure religion. Although these are the predictions of a solitary traveller unknown to the world they will surely be verified (1798).

The course and length of the River Mississippe from it's scource to it's discharge into the Gulf of Mexico in Latitude 29° 0′ North Longitude 89 . 10 West is S 14 E 1344 Miles. This great River including the Missisourie, drains an extent of 981,034 square geographical miles. In common average of low water this River discharges 82,000 cubic feet of water in a second of time; at this rate it anually places in the Gulf of Mexico $17\frac{57}{100}$ cubic miles of fresh water; and including freshets and steady high water a volume equal to 19½ cubic miles.

On the 6th day of May we arrived at the Sand Lake River, up which we turn and bend our course for Lake Superior. Since we left the Red River on the 9th day of April we have not seen the track of a Deer, or the vestige of a Beaver, not a single Aspin marked with it's teeth. The Indians we met all appeared very poor from the animals being almost wholly destroyed in this section of the country; their provisions were of wild rice and sugar; we did not see a single duck in their canoes, ammunition being too scarce; nor did we see a Bow and Arrows with them, weapons which are in constant use among the Nahathaways for killing all kinds of fowl; they were bare footed and poorly dressed.

The Sand Lake River is twenty yards wide, by five feet in depth, at one and a half miles an hour. It's length two miles to the Sand Lake, proceeding more than half a mile we came to a trading house of the North West Company under the charge of Monsr Boiské.[1] Here were the Women and children of about twenty families, the Men were all hunting in the Plains on the west side of the Mississippe to make half dried meat, and procure skins for leather of the Bison but the meat thus split and dried is very coarsely done, and to make it something decent, it has to pass through the hands of the Women. These people can only dress the hide of the Bison into leather; but have not the art of dressing it with the hair on, to make Robes of it, so usefull for cloathing and bedding. As the Men were hunting on what is called the War Grounds, that is, the debatable lands between them and the Sieux Indians, the Women were anxiously waiting their arrival. The night being fine, as usual I was

---

[1] Doubtless the same as Charles Bousquet or Bousquai, who is mentioned by Coues as having been in the Fond du Lac department about this time. Elsewhere Thompson speaks of him as " Mons. Buskay."

observing for the Latitude and Longitude of the place; in the morning an aged Man, no longer able to hunt came to me, and said, I come on the part of the Women, for they want to know where the Men are, are they loaded with meat, and when will they arrive; I requested Monsr Boiské to tell him, that I knew nothing of the matter, and saw only the Moon and Stars. But he took his own view of the question; and told him to tell the Women; the Men are safe, they will be here tomorrow, each has a load of Meat, but it is poor, there is no fat on it; and they must not get drunk again until the Bisons are fat (August), and who ever bites off another man's nose, would be killed by the Sieux in the first battle. Umph, said the old man, while we can get fire water we will drink it. The Women were pleased, and said all the Men were fools that drank fire water. He informed me the Women in general kept themselves sober, and when the men were about to drink they hid all the Arms, and Knives and left them nothing but their teeth and fists to fight with. This gentleman, was of the same opinion with the other Traders, that ardent spirits was a curse to the Natives, it not only occasioned quarrels, but also revived old animosities, that had been forgotten. It kept the Indians poor and was of no use as an article of trade.

He showed me his winter hunt, in value fifty beaver skins. The Minks [1] and Martens [2] were inferior, the Lynxes [3] appeared good, but the furr [was] not so long as in the north. But the Fishers [4] were uncommonly large, the color a rich glossy black brown, and the furr fine: The Beaver's were mostly fall and spring skins, and as each were good in color and furr, but not a single Fox, or Wolf. These animals are almost unknown, there is nothing for them to live on. All

[1] *Lutreola v. letifera* (Hollister). [E. A. P.]
[2] *Martes americana* (Turton). [E. A. P.]
[3] *Lynx canadensis* Kerr. [E. A. P.]
[4] *Martes pennanti* (Erxleben). [E. A. P.]

his furrs came from the Forests between the Mississippe and
Lake Superior.

He had traded 16 Cwt of Maple Sugar from the Natives;
this was packed in baskets of birch rind of 28 to 68 lbs each.
The Sugar appeared clean and well made; that of the Plane
Trees, looked like the East India Sugars, and [was] much the
same in taste : In this article I have always noticed the supply
is greater than the demand. The Men of family that trade
here are about forty two, which at seven souls to each man,
is 294.

We had now to cross the country to gain the River S^t
Louis, and by it descend to Lake Superior. Our Provisions
were four pieces of dried bison meat; four beaver tails and
two quarts of swamp cranberries,[1] they were the largest I had
ever seen, being about the size of a small hazel nut.

This trading house is in Latitude 46.46.30 N Longitude
93.44.17 West Variation 6 degrees East.

On the 7th May went over the Sand Lake of four miles
in length, by about one mile in width to Savannah Brook,
up which we proceeded eight geo. miles of which 1¾ mile is
a large Pond, but the windings lengthen the Brook to thirteen
miles, to a great Swamp of 4½ miles across it in a N 81 E
direction, the latter part of what may be termed bog; over
which we passed by means of a few sticks laid lengthways,
and when we slipped off we sunk to our waists, and with
difficulty regained our footing on the sticks. No Woods grow
on this great Swamp, except scattered pine shrubs of a few
feet in height; yet such as it was, we had to carry our Canoe
and all our things. And all the furrs, provisions, baggage
and Canoes of the Mississippe have to be carried on their
way to the Depot on Lake Superior, and likewise all the
goods for the winter trade. It is a sad piece of work. The
Person in charge of the brigade; crosses it as fast as he can,
leaves the Men to take their own time, who flounce along

---

[1] *Oxycoccus macrocarpus* (Ait.).   [E. A. P.]

with the packs of furrs, or pieces of goods, and "sacre" as often as they please. Heavy Canoes cannot be carried over but at great risque both to the Men and Canoes, and the Company have Canoes at each end. This great Swamp, extended as far as we could see northward and southward, and I could not learn it's termination either way. It appears to be somewhat like a height of land between the Mississippe and the River St Louis, as from it's west side it sends a brook into the former; and from it's east side a brook 'into the latter.

With an extra Man to help us, it took us a long day to get all across it. At the east end I observed for Latitude and Longitude which gave [Latitude] 46.52.3 N Longitude 92.28.42 W Variation 6 degrees east. We now entered a Brook of seven feet wide, three feet deep, by two miles an hour, and descended it for twelve miles, but it's windings will extend it to twenty miles, in which distance it receives one brook from the southward, and two from the northward, which increased it to ten yards wide, seven feet deep by 1¼ miles an hour. We now entered the River St Louis, a bold stream of about one hundred yards in width by eight feet in depth, the current three miles an hour. Having descended the River 4¼ Miles we put up at 7¼ P.M. We have been all day in the Forests that surrounded Lake Superior. The Brook of today has many wind fallen trees across it, which we had to cut away. In several places we saw the marks of beaver for the first time. On examining a Swan[1] we shot, it had thirteen eggs, from the size of a pea to that of a walnut, yet I do not remember ever seeing more than nine young ones with them. The Woods we have passed are a few Oaks of moderate size, some Ash, but the principal part Maple, Plane,[2] White Birch, Poplar and Aspin; on the low grounds, Pine and Larch. Hitherto the width, depth and rate of current of the Brooks

---

[1] *Olor buccinator* (Richardson). [E. A. P.]
[2] Ash-leaved Maple, *Acer negundo* Linn. [E. A. P.]

and Rivers are those of high water from the melting of the snow. But as all of them, even the Red River, depend on the Snow and Rains for their supply of water; in the months of August, September and October they are all shoal. The Men who have navigated these streams for several years are now with me, and they assure me that this river (St Louis) bold and deep as it now is, in the above months has only eighteen inches of depth, running among stones which they are often obliged to turn aside to make a passage for their canoes. In the night we heard a Beaver playing about us, flapping his broad tail on the water, with a noise as loud as the report of a small pistol, which was a novelty to us.

Upon descending the first rapids, and proceeding downwards, the Men were surprised to find the marks on the trees, to which they were accustomed to tie the Canoes at their meals, to be from six to eight feet above the present level of the River This may be accounted for, by our being on this river about a month more early than usual, and the sharp night frosts preventing the melting of the snow on the heights and interiour of Lake Superior. This River has many rapids, on one of which the waves filled the Canoe half full of water; These were succeeded by a Cataract of small low steeps of a full mile in length round a point of rock, across which we made a carrying place of 1576 yards. Four miles further, of almost all rapids; we came to the Long Carrying Place of seven miles in length. On our left the River descends the lower heights by a series of low falls, ending with a steep fall, estimated at 120 feet in height, below which the River flows with a moderate current into Lake Superior.

The surface rock of the country is a slaty sand stone, very good for sharpening knives and axes. Near the mouth of the River is a Trading House of the North West Company under the charge of Monsr Lemoine; his returns were 600 lbs of Furrs with the expectation of trading 400 lbs more 9 kegs of gum from the Pine Trees for the Canoes and 12 Kegs,

each of ten gallons, of Sugar. This House is in Latitude
46.44.33 N Longitude 92.9.45 W Variation 4½ degrees East.
I have only set down my observations made at certain places,
but they are numerous all over the survey, as every clear day
and night, no opportunity was ommitted of taking observations for Latitude, Longitude and Variation to correct the
courses and distances of the survey. The Canoes that descend
the River to the upper end of the Long Carrying Place, are
carefully laid up, and there left, in like manner the Canoes
that come from the Lake are left at the lower end. We
found three large Canoes, and a north Canoe of 28 feet in
length, much broken. This was too large for us, but we had
no choice, we repaired it, and as we had only three men fitted
it up with two oars, which have the force of four paddles, as
we had now to encounter the Winds and waves of Lake
Superior.

The Natives that trade at this House are about thirty
Men of family, and are about 210 souls. In Winter, from the
poverty of the country they can barely live, and a small
stock of sugar is part of their support. Deer[1] are almost unknown, and they are supplied with leather, as with other
necessaries. In the open season their support is by fishing,
for which the spear is much in use. Their canoes are about
fifteen feet in length by three feet in breadth, and flat
bottomed; With a Woman or a Lad to paddle and steer the
canoe, the Indian with his long spear, stands on the gunwales
at the bar behind the bow, and ticklish as the canoe is, and
the Lake almost always somewhat agitated, he preserves his
upright posture, as [if] standing on a rock. On the Lake,
especially in the fore part of the day, a low fog [rises] on the
surface of the water, caused by the coldness of the water
and the higher temperature of the air; which hides the
Canoe; and only the Indian Man, with his poised spear

[1] *Odocoileus v. borealis* (Miller). [E. A. P.]

ready to strike is seen, like a ghost gliding slowly over the water.

I have sometimes amused myself for twenty minutes with the various appearances this low fog gives to these fishermen. As the elevation of the Scource of the Mississippe is a subject of curiousity to all intelligent men, especially to those of the United States, to whom this noble River belongs, I shall continue my estimated calculations to determine its level above that of the Sea in the gulph of Mexico.

From the Mississippe River to the mouth of the Sand Lake River; by this River and the Savannah Brook there is an ascent of 16 ft 3 Inches to the great Morass, which may be taken as level. From the east side of this Morass a Brook descends to the River St Louis, by it's windings of twenty miles, at 12 Inches pr mile is 20 feet, giving to the Mississippe an elevation of 3 feet 9 inches above this part of the River St Louis. The descent of this River to Lake Superior is 34 miles of strong current at 20 inches pr mile, gives 56 feet 8 inches. 11 miles of strong Rapids at 5 feet pr mile, equal to 55 feet of descent. One full mile of low Falls having a Carrying Place; and a descent of twenty feet. One Carrying Place of 7 miles; the Falls 20 feet pr mile equal to 140 feet to which add the last fall of 120 feet in height equal to 260 feet.

Then 21 miles of current at 15 inches pr mile equal to 26 feet 3 inches, giving to the above part of the River St Louis a descent of 417 feet 11 inches to Lake Superior. This Lake, by the levels taken to it's east end is 625 feet above the tide waters of the St Lawrence River. Hence we have from the Sea to Lake Superior an ascent of levels of 625 feet; The ascent to the Morass Brook, of the River St Louis 418 feet; and difference of level of the Mississippe 3 feet 9 Inches, giving a total of 1046 feet 9 inches of this last River above the level of the Sea, at the Mouth of the Sand Lake River; and from hence to the Turtle Lake, by the calculation already made 431 feet; equal to 1478 feet;[1] the elevation of the Turtle Lake, the scource of the Mississippe, above the Sea.

It is tedious to the reader to attend to these calculations and yet to the enquiring mind they are necessary that he may know the ground on which they are based. For the age of guessing is passed away, and the traveller is expected to give his reasons for what he asserts. To take the levels of several hundred miles of Rivers is too expensive, unless there is some great object in view, and all that the public can expect, or obtain, in these almost unknown countries, are the estimates of experienced men.

On Lake Superior a Volume could be written; I have been twice round it, and six times over a great part, each survey correcting the preceding. The last survey of this Lake was under the orders of the Foreign Office for to determine, and settle the Boundary Line, between the Dominions of Great Britain and the Territories of the United States. The Courses were taken by the Compass, and the Distances by Massey's Patent Log, the latter so exact, as to require very little correction. The many astronomical observations made have settled the exact place of the Shores of this great Lake: the Maps of which, with the Boundary Line are in the Foreign Office in London; and also in the Office of the United States at Washington, and are not published.[2] The River S. Louis flows into it's west end; and the discharge of the Lake is at it's south east corner, by the Falls of St Maries, which are in Latitude 46.31.16 North Longitude 84.13.54 W. giving the straight course and distance, S 89 E 383 Miles, it's breadth increases from the west to the east end, to 176 miles. It has two great bays on it's east side, across which are many Islands. The shores of the south side are 671 miles, and

[1] The best information available indicates that Thompson was only 56 feet in error. [JAMES WHITE.]

[2] These maps have since been published in J. B. Moore, *History and Digest of International Arbitrations*, Washington, 1895.

those of the north and east sides 946 miles, being a circuit
of 1617 miles It's area is about 28,090 square miles. It's
level above the Sea is 625 feet.[1] It's depth is as yet unknown,
even near the shores of Pye Island and the head land Thunder
Bay; it has been sounded with 350 fathoms of Line, and no
bottom [found] and this by men experienced in taking sound-
ings. Supposing it's greatest depth to be only 400 fathoms
equal to 2400 feet, it's bottom is 1775 feet below the surface
of the Ocean.[2]

Taking it's area at 28,090 square miles and its average
depth at 200 fathoms, this Lake contains 5930 cubic miles of
fresh water. All summer the water tastes very cold, and in
winter only the bays, and around the Islands are frozen,
which the waves of the frequent gales of wind break up,
and cause much floating ice. In easterly or westerly gales
of wind the roll of it's waves are like those of the sea. When
surveying this Lake in the year 1822 on the north side about
fifty miles eastward of St Louis River, about 1 PM we put
ashore to dine, the day clear and fine and the Lake perfectly
calm : as we were sitting on the Rocks, about a full mile
from us direct out in the Lake suddenly there arose an
ebullition of the water; its appearance was that of a body
of water thrown up from some depth. It was about thirty
yards in length by four feet in height, it's breadth we could
not see, from within this the water was thrown up about
ten feet in very small columns as seen through our glasses.
To the eye it appeared like heavy rain; the Lake became
agitated, the waves rolled on the shore; and we had to secure
the Canoes, this lasted for about half an hour. I took a
sketch of it; when it subsided, the waves still continued;
and we were for three hours unable to proceed. During this
time and the whole day the wind was calm. On the western
part of the south shore, the rock is mostly of Sandstone as

[1] Its elevation is 602 feet.
[2] Its maximum depth is 1,000 feet, nearly 400 feet below mean sea-level.

T

are also the Islands; some of the cliffs are much worn by the waves, and have heaps of debris: the Islands are in the same state. One of them is worn through, and in calm weather a canoe and men can pass with the arch three feet above their heads.

Along the shore, proceeding eastward the limestone appears and continues and seems everywhere to underlay the sandstone. Everywhere the land rises boldly from the Lake shore, and at the distance of about fifteen miles are crowned by the Porcupine hills, lying parallel to the Lake and the elevation of the land appears to be full 2500 feet above the Lake; the whole has the appearance of a continuous Forest, and so far as the eye can judge may be cultivated. The north and east sides of this Lake are very different from the south side; they rise abruptly in rude rounded shaped rock rolling back to the height of 850 to 2000 feet above the Lake; at a distance they appear to be one Forest but a nearer approach shows many a place of bare rock. The whole extent of the 946 miles of this coast is of the granitic order, in all the varieties that quartz, feltspar and mica can form with the materials and offers a fine field for the geologist and mineralogist; but in all this distance were ten Farmers to search for a place where each could have a lot of 200 acres of good land along side of each other I do not think they would find it. In the north east corner of the Lake there is much Basalt, the only place in which I have seen this mineral on the east side of the Mountains. In this corner is Thunder Bay, so named by the Natives from it's frequent occurrence. Off the west point is Pye Island, so named from it's shape, it is of Basalt, part of this Island has perpendicular sides of at least 100 feet in height; close to which, the Lake has been sounded with 350 fathoms of lead line and no bottom [found]; We may conclude the depth of the Lake to be here 400 fathoms, which will give the Basalt walls of the Island 2500 feet in height. The east end of the Bay is Thunder Point, rising

1120 feet above the surface of the water, which has been several times sounded without finding the bottom; giving to the Lake the same depth as at Pye Island. This Basalt Point has a height of 3520 feet; Great part of it is finely fluted, and the edges of their concaves fine and sharp; and the waves of the Lake seem to have no effect on it, though exposed to all their force, indeed the Basalt walls of both places appear as fresh and firm as if Providence had placed them there only a few years ago. From the west end of the Lake by the north and east sides to the Falls of St Maries are thirty one Rivers, of which the St Louis the Mishipacoton and the Neepego, are about 150 yards in width; the others from thirty to sixty yards wide, and twenty eight Brooks. On the south side there are forty Rivers two of these 150 yards in width the others from twenty to seventy yards, and forty one Brooks. All of these Rivers and Brooks are fed by the Rain and snow, and by the evaporation from this great Lake which rests upon the surrounding high Lands, and is not wafted beyond them. From the heights of these lands all the above Streams rush down in a series of Rapids and Falls, with some intervals of moderate current, as they pass over a table land. On the south side the River Ontonoggan (the native name) has from old times been noted for the pieces of pure copper found there, of which the Indians made their weapons before the arrival of the French; and afterwards for the services of the Churches.

Learning from my Men that a short distance up the River there was a large Mass of Copper, we left our canoe and proceeded on foot to it; we found it lying on a beach of limestone at the foot of a high craig of the same; it's shape round, the upper part a low convex, all worn quite smooth by the attrition of water and ice, but now lying dry. We tried to cut a chip from it, but it was too tough for our small axe. (Note. This mass of pure copper has since been taken to Washington at the expense of 5000 dollars, and found to

weigh 3000 lbs by information.) [1] At the extremity of the great
Point called by the Natives Keewewoonanoo (We return)
now shortened to Keewenow, in a small harbour we took
pieces of copper ore. I named it Copperass harbour. Both
at this place, at the above River and a few other places I
learn the people of the United States for these three years
(1848) have worked the Copper Mines with considerable
profit; and have also found much silver.

It is not easy to conceive of the vast quantity of alluvial
of all kinds brought down by seventy one Rivers and sixty
nine Brooks rushing down these high lands, that surround
the Lake, the accumulation of centuries must be very great
yet such is the depth of the Lake, not a single River shows a
point of alluvial worth notice. (Note. In the Province of
Auvergne in France, there appears to have been a Lake of
the size of Lake Superior, the barriers of which appear to have
been broken down by an earthquake, and the Lake emptied.
One alluvial from a River destroyed at the same time, was
computed to be nine hundred feet in height from the bottom
of the Lake. This catastrophe must have happened previous
to the time of Julius Caser, for had it happened in his time,
or since, the Roman historians would have noticed such an
event. Saussave.)

The northern part of North America is noted for it's
numerous and large Lakes far more than [any] other part of
the world. The Great Architect said " Let them be, and
they were " but he has given to his creature the power to

---

[1] This mass of copper, stated on the label to weigh about three tons, is
still in the U.S. National Museum at Washington, D.C. It was observed
by Alexander Henry the elder in 1766, and had then long been known to
the Indians. In 1841 Julius Eldred, having purchased it from the
Chippewa, took it to Detroit, where it was exhibited. In 1843 it was
claimed by the Government and taken to Washington. It remained in
charge of the War Department until 1860, when it was transferred to
the Smithsonian Institution. By an Act of Congress, Eldred was awarded
the sum of $5,664.98 to reimburse him for his expenses in connection
with it. [E. A. P.]

examine his works on our globe; and perhaps learn the order in which he has placed them. If we examine the positions of all these Lakes, their greatest lengths will be found to be about between North and thirty degrees west, and South and thirty degrees east. which are the lines of direction of the east side of the Great Plains, and of the Rocky Mountains: the anomalies to this order are Lakes Michigan, Superior and Athabasca. The west sides of the Lakes are of Limestone and the east sides of Granite. Between these two formations are the great wide chasms, or valleys filled with water, which are the Lakes. And the three above Lakes, although lying west and east, have their south sides of Limestone and their north sides of the granitic order, and their deep waters in their same kind of valley. The few Lakes that lie as it were within the east side of the Great Plains, as Cumberland and the Cedar Lakes are wholly within the Limestone formation, and are comparatively shoal water Lakes.

Having settled by observations the Latitude and Longitude of the trading house of St Louis's River at the west end of Lake Superior; on the 12th of May we proceeded to survey the south side of the Lake. In the afternoon we came to four Lodges of Chipaways. They had just arrived from the interior, having wintered at the west end of the Porcupine Hills and now pass the summer on the borders of the Lake to maintain themselves by fishing. They are about 28 families, and by the usual rule of seven souls to a family their number is 196 persons. My Men thought, for the number of Men, there were more old Women than usual. Although the interior rises high, yet near the Lake the shores are low, with many fine sandy beaches, for setting of nets for fishing; yet the Natives make no use of them, although they see the success of the white men: If a net is given to them, they are too indolent to take care of it, and it soon becomes useless. They prefer the precarious mode of spearing fish, which is practi[ca]ble only in calm, or very moderate weather. The woods seen from the Lake were of white and red Birch,[1] Spruce Pines,[2] Larch and Aspins, all of small growth.

The next day we passed an Island of Sand Stone which the Waves had worn into rude arches, with many caves. The next day we came to three Lodges containing fifteen families, being 105 souls. An American of the States was living with them, and had adopted their way of life in preference to hard labor on a farm. In the afternoon we passed Mons.[r] Michel Cadotte[3] with five men and several Lodges of the natives from their winter quarters, now to live by fishing.

The night and morning of the 15th May was a severe frost. The Land all day very high and bold shores. Having gone eleven miles we came to the Montreal River of 25 yards in width, between banks of rock; near the Lake is a Fall of 30 feet in height. The course of this River is through the Porcupine Hills the lower parts of which are now the coasts of the Lake; Two of my Men had wintered near the head of this River. As the whole length of the River is a series of Falls between steep banks of rock the distance from the Lake to the House was one continued Carrying Place of 130 rests. (A Rest, or Pose, is the distance the cargo of the canoe is carried from place to place and then rest.) In this hilly country a Rest may be from five to six hundred yards, and the 130 rests about forty miles. The men say the distance takes them thirty seven days of carrying to the House. All the trading Houses on the south side of the Lake require many miles of carrying, with some intervals of current to take the cargo of the canoe to the wintering ground. The Men who winter and have to traverse the country in every direction, say the Lakes are few and small, more like beaver ponds than Lakes; and that in very many places sandstone for sharpening

---

[1] *Betula papyrifera* Marsh, and probably the Yellow Birch, *Betula lutea* Michx. [E. A. P.]

[2] Probably White Spruce, *Picea canadensis* (Mill.). [E. A. P.]

[3] This was a brother of Baptiste Cadotte, who was in charge of the trading post on Red Lake river mentioned on p. 252.

knives and axes are to be found. We came to a lodge of five families, they had seen no person for eight Moons, and had all their winters hunt with them, of about 360 pounds of furrs. Further on was a lodge of ten families.

Early on the 17th May we came to the Fair River at the east end of the Porcupine Hills. The interior country has now lower land. The Woods hitherto have much white Cedar,[1] with Birch, Aspin and Pine, with a few Maple[2] and Plane Trees,[3] all of very common growth. An extensive body of ice lying before us, we had to put ashore and pass the day. We set a net but caught only six Carp.[4] The wind having drifted the ice from the shore, early on the 18th we set off and soon came to the Ontonoggan River, where lay the great mass of Copper I have already mentioned. Here was a Mr Cadotte with four Lodges of Indians, he informed us that last summer (1797) a party of Americans had visited the River and proceeded twenty miles up it to the Forks of the River, they had promised the Indians to come this summer (1798) and build a Fort and work the mines, for which the Chippaways were waiting for them, but this promise they did not perform until the year 1845. Mr Cadotte had a few goods remaining and requested a passage with us for himself and goods which we gave him and he embarked with us.

Full twenty five miles North eastward of the Ontonoggan River are high steep rocks of a reddish color, which have the most distant Echo I have ever heard. We stopped a short time to amuse ourselves with it : The Rocks were about 200 feet in height and the place of the Echo appeared about sixty feet above us ; The Echo of the words we spoke, seemed more sharp and clear than our voices and somewhat louder.

---

[1] *Thuja occidentalis* Linn. [E. A. P.]
[2] *Acer saccharum* Marsh. [E. A. P.]
[3] *Acer negundo* Linn. [E. A. P.]
[4] *Catostomus commersonii* (Lacépede). [E. A. P.]

One of the Men, François Babue, who had been many years
in the furr trade of the Lake used to abuse the Echo until
he worked himself into a violent passion; did the same this
time until his expressions becoming too coarse, we moved off,
he swearing, that he thought it very hard he never could
have the last word. The greater part of this day we were in
much danger from the Ice, which lay in the Lake a short
distance from the shore; had it come in we could not have
saved ourselves as the rocks were high and steep. At 7½ PM
we put up on Keewenaw Carrying Place; This is a remarkable place, being an Isthmus of 2000 yards, in a south course
and forms a body of Land in circuit 94 Miles into a Peninsula:
known under the name of Point Keewenaw. The bank is
about twenty feet in height; the first 1100 yards is good
ground; the other 960 yards a perfect swamp. To avoid
going round this Peninsula of high land the people of the
States in time to come will cut a Canal through the Isthmus,
at a small expence, as a Lock is not required.[1] The night
being clear, as usual, I observed for Latitude and Longitude
the former 47.14.27 N. Longitude 88° 38′ 36″ West.

From the Carrying Place is a Brook of 1½ mile to a
small Lake, and then a kind of Lagoon of 24 miles to Lake
Superior. Part of the Lagoon, on one side the Woods
were on fire, the heat and smoke made us lay by for a few
hours. On the 22ⁿᵈ and 24ᵗʰ of May we had heavy rain
with vivid Lightning and loud Thunder. The provisions we
had to live on were hulled Corn, part of a bag of wild rice,
with a few pounds of grease to assist the boiling. It is
customary after supper, to boil corn or rice for the meals of
next day, and in good weather we set off by 4 AM, the Kettles
were taken off the fire in a boiling state and placed in the
Canoe, and two hours afterwards we had a warm breakfast;
If Lightning and Thunder came in the day the Corn became

[1] This prediction has since been fulfilled by the construction of the
Portage Lake canal.

sour and had to be thrown away ; but the rice never soured :
the same thing in the night, when the kettle had corn it was
soured, but if of rice it kept good : the Men assured me that
the Lightning and Thunder had no effect on the wild rice ;
and that in the heats of Summer the Corn soured so frequently, they were half starved ; to boil a Kettle of corn
requires three to four hours. The rice is cooked in half an
hour, but it is very weak food. All the Corn for these voyages
has to be steeped in hot lye of wood ashes to take off the rind
of the grain. On the 28ᵗʰ May we arrived, Thank God at
the Falls of Sᵗ Maries, the discharge of Lake Superior, and
the head of the River Sᵗ Lawrence, which flows into Lake
Huron.

Here I had the pleasure of meeting Sir Alexander
MᶜKenzie the celebrated traveller who was the first to follow
down the great stream of water flowing northward from the
Slave Lake into the Arctic Sea, and which great River bears his
name, and [was] made well known to the public by the journey
of Sir John Franklin. Upon my report to him of the surveys
I had made and the number of astronomical Observations for
Latitude, Longitude and Variation of the Compass, he was
pleased to say I had performed more in ten months than he
expected could be done in two years. The next day the
Honorable William MᶜGillivray arrived. These gentlemen
were the Agents, and principal Partners of the North West
Company : they requested me to continue the survey of the
Lake round the east and north sides to the Grand Portage,
then the Depot of the company. The survey we had finished
was of the south side, from the west, to the east end ; following the shores, the distance is 671 miles, but the direct line
is only 383 miles. We had met with 110 families, and
allowing twenty families not seen, will give 130 families.
Mʳ Cadotte, who has been for many years a Trader in these
parts, thought 125 families to be nearer the number. Allowing these Natives to have possession of hunting ground only

in the distance of 70 miles from the Lake, the extent will be
in the square miles, and this divided by 130 will give to each
family an extent of 206 square miles of hunting ground; yet
with this wide area: the annual average hunt of each family
of all kinds of furrs, from the Bear down to the Musk Rat,[1]
will not exceed sixty to seventy skins in trade; allowing a
Bear skin to be the value of two beavers; and eight to ten
musk Rats to be the value of one beaver. Deer are so scarce
that all they kill does not furnish leather for their wants, and
when the mild seasons come they all descend to Lake Superior
to live by fishing. Calculation is tedious reading, yet without
it we cannot learn the real state of any country. (Note.
Mr Ballantyne of the Hudson's Bay Company has lately
published a work with the title of "Six years residence in
Hudson's Bay," in which speaking of the Bay, he says " the
interior has Myriads of wild animals." The Natives will
thank him to shew them where they are. When he wrote
these words he must have been thinking of Musketoes, and
in this respect he was right.)

The Forests of the Lake are such as has been already
described: I could not learn that any of the Forest Trees
acquired a growth to merit particular notice, except the
white Birch, the Rind of which is very good for canoes, and
of a large size.

On the first day of June we left the Falls of St Maries and
from thence surveyed the east and part of the north shores
of Lake Superior to the 7th day of this month, when late we
arrived at the Grand Portage, then the Depot of the North
West Company, to which the furrs of the interiour country
came, and from whence the merchandise was taken for the
furr trade to about the same time the following year, as
already described. The Falls of St Maries is a rapid of about
three fourths of a mile in length in which it descends eleven

---

[1] *Fiber zibethicus* (Linn.). [E. A. P.]

feet,[1] and then by three channels of easy current descends to
Lake Huron. The carrying place is about a mile in length
of low wet ground, very easy for a canal and locks, and which
at length is about to be completed in this year of 184[8]
The opposite bank of these rapids belong to the United
States, it is steep and above twenty feet in height, and a
canal could not be made but at enormous expence. While waiting [for] the Province of Canada to make a canal on the only
side in which it can be made, these enterprising people made
a deep channel at the foot of their steep bank with a tow path
for their Vessels, but the strength of the current makes the
passage somewhat dangerous. This canal [they] will now do
away with. The mines of copper ore that have been worked
both by the citizens of the United States and the people of
this province now demand a canal which otherwise would
not have [been] made, although the fisheries of Lake Superior
required a canal many years ago, but as yet, only the people
of the States are engaged in these fisheries, although superior
to that of any other which is always the case with deep water.

[1] Eighteen feet ; now increased to about nineteen and a half feet by
the dredging of the St. Mary river below the Sault.

CHAPTER XX

GREAT WESTERN FOREST LANDS

*Western country of Forests and Plains—Inhabitants—Build a
Trading House at Red Deer Lake—Climate—Food during
winter at Red Deer Lake—Porcupines—Beaulieu eats a
porcupine quill [1]—Use of quills—Food of the porcupine—
Intelligence of the porcupine—Stone Indians and Sieux—
Customs—Religion—A Vow—Family Feud—Trading House
at the Fords of the Peace and Smoke Rivers—Iroquois,
Nepissings, and Algonquins brought to the Western Forest
land—Pride of the Iroquois—Encounter of Iroquois and
Willow Indians—Council of Iroquois—Feast of Iroquois—
Dances—Spikanoggan dances—Settlement of the Iroquois—
Theories as to origen of the Indians.*

HITHERTO these travels have extended over a tract
of country on the east parts of North America, which
from it's formation I have called the Stoney Region
(perhaps rocky, would be more appropriate). As already described, it is little else than rocks with innumerable Lakes and
Rivers, and south of 58 degrees north has forests of small Pines,
which increase in size going southward, with Aspin, Poplar
and Birch, but northward of the above latitude the country is
covered with various kinds of moss. Northward of 61 degrees
this region may be said to extend to the Rocky Mountains.
On the latitude 58.40 north this region from Churchill in
Hudsons Bay extend[s] 640 miles to the westward and from
Fort Albany in the same bay, on the parallel of 52 degrees, this

---

[1] There is no reference to this in the manuscript here printed.

region is 660 miles in wi[d]th, including the Lakes on its west side. From Albany southward it's west side embraces the great Lakes Superior and Huron, the north bank of the Ottawa and S‘ Lawrence Rivers to the Gulf, and it's east side is everywhere bounded by the sea. On the whole of this great extent of country containing an area of about . . . square miles, the Deer and other wild animals of the forest are thinly scattered for the comparative extent of the country ; and the native Indians are in the same proportion. The summer is from five to six months, or more properly the open season, with frequent frosts, and heats, but always tormented with Musketoes and other flies. In the winter the snow is deep and the cold intense, in the months of December, January and February the Thermometer is for many days at fifty to seventy degrees below the freezing point. In the open season the Natives and Traders make use of Canoes, and in winter of flat sleds ; for removing from place to place. Such is the country of the north east, or siberian, side of north America.

For Agriculture it offers nothing to the farmer except a few places detached from each other, without a market ; nor can it become a grazing country, the torment of the flies is too great to allow cattle to graze until the cool nights of September ; the sufferings of the Deer must be seen to be believed ; even the timid Moose Deer on some days is so distressed with the flies, as to be careless of life, and the hunters have shot them in this state, and the cloud of flies about them [was] so great, and dense, that they did not dare to go to the animal for several minutes. Such cannot be a grazing country, especially when to this is added, a long cold winter with great depth of snow. We may therefore conclude, that as all kind Providence has fitted the Arabians to live and enjoy his naked hot sandy deserts so the same merciful Being has fitted the Indian to live and enjoy his cold region of forests and deserts of snow. The means for the enjoyment of civilised life is denied to both, and the white man is unfitted to take the place of the indian and the arabian. Modern geologists would consider this Stoney Region to be a formation that had been uncovered and left by the sea, long after the land to its westward, on which I shall now describe.

The climate of this region is best explained by the meteorological tables kept. (To be in a note) that at Bedford House,[1] on the west bank of the Rein's Deer Lake, in Latitude 57° 23′ N. Longitude 102 . 59 west.

		Mean heat		greatest		least heat
October		+26		+54		+15
November	d°	+1.5	d°	+45	d°	−37
December	d°	−18	d°	+30	d°	−56
January	d°	−19	d°	+25	d°	−50
February	d°	−16.7	d°	+15	d°	−49
March	d°	−5	d°	+44	d°	−43
April	d°	+11.5	d°	+40	d°	−30
May 20 days	d°	+24.5	d°	+50	d°	+7

In summer, the Thermometer for a few day in July, the heat was at +80 making the range of heat and cold to be 136 degrees. The Ice in this great Lake was firm to the 6th day of July, when a heavy gale of wind broke it up. Where there is soil in the Pine Forests, the heat of summer thaws it only a few inches.

At the Reed Lake[2] in Latitude 54° 36′ N. [Longitude]

[1] Thompson spent the winter of 1796–97 at this house, just before leaving the service of the Hudson's Bay Company.

[2] Reed lake is on the headwaters of Grass river, on the line of the Hudson Bay Railway from The Pas to Port Nelson. Thompson lived there during the winters of 1794–95 and 1805–06.

100° 37′ West the temperature of the following months was.

October 8 days	Mean	+27	greatest	+38	least heat	+18
November	d°	+18	d°	+34	d°	−15
December	d°	−10	d°	+31	d°	−45
January	d°	−21.3	d°	+11	d°	−47
February	d°	+6	d°	+39	d°	−31
March	d°	+6	d°	+41	d°	−30
April	d°	+31	d°	+63	d°	−7
May 26 days	d°	+43	d°	+73	d°	−19

In the summer, for a few days in July the heat rises to 88 degrees, and except in some few places of thick pine forests, the ground is thawed during the summer.

Leaving the Stoney region and it's Lakes is a great extent of land of very different formation; and extending westward to the foot of the Rocky Mountains; it is almost wholly composed of earth, with few rocks, and only in the northern part has a few Lakes, none of them large; This great body of dry land extends from the gulph of Mexico to beyond the Arctic Circle. From north of the parallel of 52 degrees to the latitude of 72 degrees the whole is a forest of mostly the Pine genus with, in favorable places, Birch, Poplar and Aspin.

Southward of the latitude of 52 degrees are the great plains which extend to the Gulp of Mexico. The breadth of this land is from 550 to about 850 miles. This western country of forests and plains have Animals peculiar to itself; and those that are common to both regions are here larger and in better condition from a somewhat milder climate, and more abundance of food. Of the Natives, there are none sufficiently numerous to be called "a Nation" I have therefore called them "Tribes" though many of them speak languages quite distinct from each other. As the word Tribe may be a small number, speaking the same language, and holding firmly together as one great family. Such are the Rapid Indians,[1] the Sussee[2] and Kootanae[3] Indians, each of these have a very different language, and each so rough and difficult to articulate that the neighbouring people rarely attempt to learn them. Each of these tribes may have a population of 500 to 1000 souls, to speak the language of it's Tribe, and this number is all that do speak the language. The intelligent people of the United States who have paid attention to the north American Indians have always been struck with the numerous radical Languages of the Indians, and from whence they could have come, but all lies in obscurity, and the few theories of learned men on the peopling of this continent are in general so contrary to facts, that they can be regarded only as theory.

On the region of the western forest land, at a fine Lake called the Red Deers Lake,[4] at the head of the small streams

[1] The Rapid Indians, technically known as Atsina, were usually spoken of by travellers in western Canada as Fall Indians or Gros Ventres of the Plains. They were a detached branch of the Arapaho nation, and were of Algonquin stock. On Arrowsmith's map of 1811 they are marked as occupying the upper parts of the country drained by the Red Deer river, which is the northern branch of the South Saskatchewan river.

[2] The Sussee or Sarsi are a tribe of the Athapascan family which has become separated from the rest of the members of the family. At the beginning of the nineteenth century they occupied the country near the headwaters of the North Saskatchewan river, and between that stream and the Athabaska river. At present they are on a reserve near Calgary, Alberta, and in 1911 numbered 205 all told.

[3] The Kutenai Indians form a distinct linguistic stock, occupying the country along the Upper Columbia river from the Upper Columbia lakes to Pend d'Oreille lake. Early in the eighteenth century they occupied the country east of the Rocky Mountains around the headwaters of the Belly river, but they were driven west across the mountains by the Blackfeet as soon as these latter obtained fire-arms from the white traders.

[4] This is Lake La Biche, 105 miles in a direct line north-east of the city of Edmonton, Alberta. Thompson spent at this place the winter of 1798-99.

which feed the Beaver River the southern branch of the Churchill River in October we erected a trading house and passed the winter. Its Latitude 54° 46′ 23″ N Longitude 111° 56′ W. It's climate in

		+		+		−
November	Mean temperature	13.5	greatest	37	least	6
		−		+		−
December	d°	6.5	d°	40	d°	48
		−		+		−
January	d°	5	d°	40	d°	48
		+		+		−
February	d°	9	d°	43	d°	26
		+		+		−
March to the 14th . .	d°	12	d°	44	d°	13

This trading House is 10⅘ Minutes north and 11⅘ degrees west of the Reed Lake on the Stoney region, and so far shows a milder climate. Had the thermometer been continued through the rest of the year, the difference would have been very great, and [it would be clear] that the temperature of April on this dry region is equal to that of May on the Stoney region from the lesser quantity of Snow, and the Sun exerting it's influence on the bare ground in April, which on the latter it does not do to the middle of May. The Lake from our set nets gave us fish of Pike,[1] White Fish,[2] Pickerel[3] and Carp[4] for about one third of our support, and the Hunters furnished the rest, which was almost wholly of the Moose Deer; in five months they gave us forty nine Moose all within twenty miles of the House and a few Bull Bisons,[5] whereas on the Stoney region, it would be a fortunate trading house, that during the winter had the meat

[1] *Esox lucius* Linn. [E. A. P.]

[2] *Coregonus*. Lake La Biche is still famous for the number and quality of its whitefish. [E. A. P.]

[3] *Stizostedion vitreum* (Mitchill). Wall-eyed Pike ; Doré. [E. A. P.]

[4] Both *Catostomus catostomus* (Forster), and *Moxostoma lesueuri* probably occur. [E. A. P.]

[5] *Bison bison* (Linn.). [E. A. P.]

of six Moose Deer[1] brought to it, and even that quantity would rarely happen.

On this region all the animals attain their full size. (Note. A male Beaver,[2] allowed to be full grown and in good condition, measured from the tip of the nose to the insertion of the tail, three feet and half an inch, the tail thirteen inches in length, by seven inches in breadth. Girth round the breast thirty two inches; round the hind quarters thirty six inches. The head five inches in length. Its weight as alive sixty five pounds. A Porcupine[3] from the tip of the nose to the insertion of the tail twenty six inches, the tail ten inches in length, round and closely armed with barbed quills; Girth round the breast twenty inches; the hair of a dark grey, intermixed with which are his well barbed quills which are very slightly fixed in the skin, the quill is white to the barb which is black, and are placed from his shoulders to, and on the tail, the sides and belly have none; they are thickest and longest on the rump. They are from one to two and a half [inches] in length, some few about three inches, and near a quarter of an inch in girth: on the larger quills the barbed part is half an inch in length, containing small circular barbs through its length.

When approached it places it's head under its breast, lies down and presents only it's back and tail, and if an animal attempts to seize him it gives a jerk with it's back, which drives the quills deep into it's mouth, and are held fast by the barbs, and prevents all farther attacks. Confident of their power of defence, they pursue their slow walk, careless of the barking of Dogs, the yelping of Foxes, or other animals. A hungry Fox or Fisher will sometimes try to turn it on it's back but gets it's nose and face so full of quills, as to desist.

[1] *Alces americanus* (Clinton). [E. A. P.]
[2] *Castor canadensis* Kuhl. [E. A. P.]
[3] *Erethizon dorsatum* (Linn.). [E. A. P.]

The natives that traded at this House, were about thirty Nahathaway and the same number of Swampy Ground Stone Indians [1] who still continue to prefer their ancient mode of life to living in the Plains, where the rest of their Tribes are : The languages of both these people are soft and easy to learn and speak, that of the Stone Indians is so agreeable to the ear, it may be called the Italian Language of North America ; and by the Tribes of these people under the name of Sieux extends over the east side of the Plains and down a considerable distance of the upper part of the Mississippe. Their opinions, rites and ceremonies of religion are much the same as the Nahathaways, with whom they are strictly allied. All these people are superior in stature and good looks, to the generality of those of the Stoney Region from a better country and a greater supply of food. They have their Medicine Bags which is generally filled with sweet smelling vegetables, and have the bones of some particular part of the Beaver, Otter, Musk, Rat, Racoon, Bear and Porcupine, mostly of the head, or hind parts, to which they attach a superstitious virtue especially to those of their Poowoggan, the Manito of which they regard as favorable to them.

They all hold the doctrine of the immortality of the Soul, or as they call it, " Life after Death " and their Ideas of the other world is much the same as they have of their present existence, only heightened to constant happiness in social life and success in hunting without fatigue. They all hope to be happy after death, if the Great Spirit finds them to be good ; whether he will do so, does not occupy much of their thoughts in the prime of life, but as age advances is frequently the subject of their conversations for they have much time to spare, and few subjects to engross their attention. They all

---

[1] These are Assiniboin or Stone Indians, who prefer to live in the woods. The Assiniboin are a branch of the Sioux family which broke away from the parent stock, and moved northward towards the Saskatchewan river. See note on p. 326.

agree that the crimes committed is marked on the soul, and thus marked enters the other world ; They believe that those who were placed in the happy state had their Souls clean and white, but none could inform me how the stains on the Soul had been eradicated, this is a doctrine too profound for them, and on which they were utterly at a loss : they feel it and have some ceremonies and sacrifices to obtain it, but in which they place little confidence.

A man who had been guilty of a crime, (I could not learn what it was) enjoined on himself the penance of eating nothing for a whole year, that was not placed in his mouth, and which he steadily kept. He afterwards declared that he would never again make such another vow as the provisions thus placed in his mouth was not enough and badly cooked ; which the Indians said he deserved for placing himself in the power of other people, and in a manner making them his servants.

An Indian named Askeeawawshish (Son of the Earth) between 40 and 50 years of age, and whom I found a good man and respected by the natives when a young man unfortunately became heir to a fued between his family, and that of another family, and each had to retaliate the injuries of times past. One spring on the arrival of the wild geese, when the Indians collect together to enjoy the season, these two families met, the young man of the head of the other family had often said, he would on the first occasion have his revenge ; and sought it of Askeeawawshish, but fell himself in the encounter, some twenty five years before the time I am speaking of. The Indians related this to do away with any impressions I might have against him ; As I understood that he was still continuing his penance for having shed human blood, I was anxious to learn of himself what were his thoughts on this sad subject. His relation was, After the first excitement was over of myself and the family to which I belonged I became melancholy and disheartened, I no longer enjoyed hunting and as both family were nearly

related, the Women said that I ought to go to war and kill a
Snake Indian that he might have a slave to attend him in
the other world. This would please him and make us friends
when we met in the other world. Thus the summer passed
away, and a very hard winter came on, deep snow with heavy
gales of wind with long calms between made hunting so
difficult that we could hardly maintain ourselves ; this made
the old people change my penance for another in which I
was not to leave them, and my penance now is, and from
that time has been, at the first dawn of day to rise take my
rattle and sing to the Great Spirit to make me good and a
skilful hunter, and when I die to blot out the mark of the
red blood on my soul, for I feel perfectly perswaded it will
remain with me as long as I live, and every crime we commit
is in the same state. Such is the confession of every serious
Native, they knew of nothing by which the pardon of sins
can be obtained and although many of us spoke their language
sufficiently fluent for trade and the common business yet we
found ourselves very deficient if we attempted to impress on
them any doctrine of Christianity beyond the unity of God,
his creation and preservation of mankind and of everything
else, to all which they readily assented as consonant to truth
and their own ideas.

On taking the necessaries which they require for the winter
season, and which are mostly on credit ; several of them,
especially of those advanced in life, have made a bargain with
me, that if they should die in the winter I should not demand
the debt due to me, in the other world, and to which I always
agreed. The life of a Hunter is precarious, but a provident
family will make dried provisions for hard times, and let
things be as hard as is sometimes [the case], the Indian sees
none better than himself, and knows he is master of everything he can secure by hunting, or otherwise ; Whereas to
the constant labor of the lower classes of Europe they live in
penury without daring to touch the abundance all around

them. The Natives that live in Villages may profit by the labors of a prudent Missionary, but the wandering Indians that live wholly by hunting, and are rarely more than a few days in [one] place, and in this only by families cannot hope for the labors of a Missionary ; the little they can learn must come from the Traders, and if they cannot learn morality from them, [they] can teach them to leave off the worship and sacrif[ic]ing a dog to the Mauchee Manito (the Devil) and leave off prayers to the inferior Manitoes, and direct all their prayers and thanksgiving to the Great Spirit alone, the Master of Life.

On the more northern part of this great western forest, at the Forks of the Peace and Smoke Rivers, (the principal stream which forms the Mackenzie.) in Latitude 56° 8′ 17″ N. Longitude 117° 13′ 14″ W the temperatures for the year were

	−	+	−	
January	Mean 10	Greatest heat 39	Least 49	Range 88° degrees
	+	+	−	
February	d° 7	d° 41	d° 38	d° 79
	+	+		
March	d° 22.5	d° 57	d° 32	d° 89
	+	+	+	
April	d° 37.6	d° 71	d° 16	d° 55
	+	+	+	
May	d° 64	d° 80	d° 30	d° 50
	+	+	+	
June	d° 64.5	d° 86	d° 44	d° 42
	+	+	+	
July	d° 63	d° 84	d° 46	d° 38
	+	+	+	
August	d° 60	d° 85	d° 38	d° 47
	+	+	+	
September	d° 55	d° 86	d° 21	d° 65
	+	+	+	
October	d° 40	d° 71	d° 19	d° 52
	+	+	−	
November	d° 14.6	d° 41	d° 13	d° 54
	−	+	−	
December	d° 4	d° 19	d° 38	d° 57
	+	+	−	
Mean	35	86	38	124

The trading house at the Forks of the River[1] is about 150 miles eastward of the foot of the Rocky Mountains and its elevation above the level of the sea about 4000 feet.

The whole of the great western forest had very many Beaver, it had few Lakes, but what was better for the Beaver many small brooks, and streams which they dammed up and made Ponds for their houses, and the Natives had thus an anual supply of furrs to trade all they required, and had the furr trade been placed in the hands of one company under the control of govern[ment] might have continued to do so to this time; but from Canada the trade was open to every adventurer, and some of these brought in a great number of Iroquois, Nepissings and Algonquins[2] who with their steel traps had destroyed the Beaver on their own lands in Canada and New Brunswick; The two latter, the men were tall, manly, steady and good hunters, the few women they brought with them were good looking and well behaved and their dress came to the feet and both sexes [were] respected by the Natives. The Iroquois formed about half the number of these immigrants, they considered themselves superior to all other people, especially the white people of Canada, which they carried in their countenances, being accustomed to show themselves off in dances and flourishing their tomahawks before the civilized people of canada, and making speeches on every occasion, which were all admired and praised through politeness to them, gave them a high opinion of themselves: The few women they brought with them were any thing but beauty and their dress was careless with the shirt on the outside and petticoats to only a little below the knees, the toes and feet turned inwards which made them walk like

[1] This post had been built by Sir Alexander Mackenzie in the autumn of 1792, when he was on his way from Lake Athabaska to the Pacific coast.   In it he and his assistant, Alexander McKay, spent the winter of 1792–93.   Thompson was at this post during the winters of 1802–03 and 1803–04.

[2] This influx of eastern Indians occurred about 1798.

ducks, so different from the slender tall forms of the women of the Plains, their easy, graceful walk, and dress touching the ground. Part of these went up the Red Deer River, and about 250 of them came up the Saskatchewan River, in company with the canoes of the Fur Traders to one of the upper Posts called Fort Augustus[1] where the River passes through fine Plains, upon the banks and in the interior country are numerous herds of Bisons and several kinds of Deer,[2] and many Bears[3] of several colours. The Algonquins and Nepissings paid every attention to the advice given to them, and performed the voyage without accident; but the Iroquois treated our warnings with contempt; When advised to be cautious in the hunting of the Bison, especially when wounded; they would laugh and say they killed an ox with the stroke of an axe, and should do the same to the Bisons. The second day in hunting one of them wounded a Bull which ran at him, and although he avoided the full stroke of the head, yet was so much hurt that it was about two months before he was well. The next day as two of them was crossing a low point of wood near the river, they saw a Bull, fired at and wounded him, the Bull rushed on one of them who to escape ran behind an old rotten stump of a tree of about ten feet high, the furious animal came dash against it, threw it down and the man lay beneath it, the Bull also fell on it, and rolled off; The comrade of the poor fellow ran to the river and hailed the canoes; several of the Men came, the Bison was dying, they took the stump away, but the Iroquois was crushed and dead. These two accidents somewhat

[1] See description of this fort on p. 432.

[2] The Mule Deer, *Odocoileus hemionus* (Rafinesque), and rarely the Plains White-tailed Deer, *O. virginianus macrourus* (Rafinesque), still occur; the Elk or Wapiti, *Cervus canadensis* Erxleben, was formerly common. [E. A. P.]

[3] The Black Bear, *Ursus americanus* Pallas, occurs in both the ordinary black and the cinnamon colour phases. Formerly the Grizzly Bear, *Ursus horribilis* Ord, was frequently found. [E. A. P.]

lowered their pride as they found that even their guns could not always protect them.

A few days after, as two of them were hunting (they always went by two) they met a colored Bear,[1] which one of them wounded, the Bear sprung on him, and standing on his hind feet seized the Iroquois hugging him with his fore legs and paws, which broke the bones of both arms above the elbow, and with it's teeth tore the skin of the head from the crown to the forehead, for the poor fellow had drawn his knife to defend himself, but could not use it; fortunately his comrade was near, and putting his gun close to the Bear shot him dead. The poor fellow was a sad figure, none of us were surgeons, but we did the best we could, but for want of proper bandageing his arms were three months in getting well. These accidents happening only to the Iroquois made them superstitious and they concluded that some of the Algonquins had thrown bad medicine on them, and a quarrel would probably have taken place had we not been with them. These accidents were the fault of their mode of hunting, being accustomed to hunt only timid animals, and keeping about one hundred yards from each other, to cover more ground did very well for Deer; but to hunt the animals of the upper countries as the Bison and Bear and which are fierce and dangerous, requires the two hunters to be close to each other, the one reserving his fire in case of the wounded animal being able to attack them; they were faulty in their hunting until experience taught them better.

The native hunt mostly alone, and from the precautions very seldom meet with an accident. On arrival at Fort Augustus all these people had to disperse and go to some place to pass the winter and make their furr hunts. The hills to the southward, at the foot of the mountains were known to have many Beavers, and thither they were disposed to go; but at a kind of council, we pointed out the dangers they

[1] Grizzly Bear, *Ursus horribilis* Ord. [E. A. P.]

would encounter, as it was the country of the powerful tribes
of the Plains who had gained the country by war, and held
it as a conquered country open to the incursions of their
enemies, in which they would probably be destroyed, or at
least plundered; by some of the war parties; and advised
them to go to the forest lands of the north where there were
also many Beaver, the Natives few and peaceable, and where
they could hunt in safety. This advice was directly followed
by the Algonquins and Nepissings, they separated themselves
into small parties and passed the winter in safety and made
good hunts. This advice had a very different effect on the
Iroquois, who determined to send off a large party to examine
the country to the southward and see what the disposition
of the Natives were to them, whom they appeared to
despise. Accordingly part hunted near the Fort while a
party of about seventy five men well armed went off, foolishly
taking their self conceit and arrogance with them. They
soon came to a small camp of Peeagans[1] the owners of the
country, and all their enquiry was where the Beavers were
most plenty as if they were masters of the country. As they
did not understand each other, the whole was by signs, at
which the Indians were tolerably expert. The Peeagans did
not know what to make of them, but let them pass. In this
manner they passed two more small camps to the fourth
which was a larger camp of Willow Indians.[2] Having now
proceeded about eighty miles, they agreed to go no farther
spend a few days and return.

Although the Natives did not much like their behaviour,
they treated them hospitably as usual to strangers. After
smoking and feasting, they performed a dance; and then
sitting down, by signs invited the Willow Indians to a
gambling match, this soon brought on a quarrel, in which

[1] See note on p. 327.
[2] It is most likely that Thompson here refers to the Atsina or Fall
Indians, whose country was on the upper waters of the Red Deer river.

the arrogant gestures of the Iroquois made the other party
seize their arms, and with their guns and Arrows lay dead
twenty five of them; the others fled, leaving their blankets
and a few other things to the Willow Indians, and returned
to Fort Augustus in a sad state. This affair made the Indians
of the Plains look on them with contempt for allowing so many
to be killed like women, without even firing a shot in their
defence, for the Willow Indians were but a few more than the
Iroquois, and mostly armed with Bows and Arrows, which
whatever may be thought by civilized men, is a dreadful
weapon in the hands of a good Archer. The defeated Iroquois
sent word of their misfortune to the parties that were hunting, and alltogether collected about 120 men; Councils were
held and war parties to be formed for revenge, to which the
Nahathaway Indians, (the natives and masters of the country)
were invited, in hopes they would join them; but all to no
purpose, the Nahathaways told them they would not enter
into their quarrel against their old allies, and pointed out to
them that three times their numbers would make no impression on the Indians; they were numerous, good cavalry and
accustomed to war, adding, you, yourselves, may go and take
your revenge, but we do not think any of you will return.
All this lowered their self conceit and arrogance, they saw
plainly the Natives of those countries had no great opinion
of them, and giving up all thought of revenge, as they were
now to separate for the winter agreed to make a feast and
perform all their dances, to which the Nahathaways were
invited; The next day they all appeared in their best dresses;
and the feast took place about noon of the choice pieces of
the Bison and Red Deer;[1] at which as usual, grace was said
and responded to by the guests.

The feast being over the dances began by the Iroquois
and their comrades; after a few common dances, they commenced their favorite dance of the grand Calumet, which

---

[1] *Cervus canadensis* Erxleben. [E. A. P.]

was much admired and praised, and they requested the
Nahathaways to dance their grand Calumet, to which they
replied, they had no smoking dance; this elated the Iroquois
and they began their War dance, from the discovery of the
enemy to the attack and scalping of the dead, and the war
hoop of victory. The Nahathaways praised them. The
Iroquois being now proud of their national dances, requested
the Nahathaways to see their War dance, and intimating
they thought they had none, which was in a manner saying
they were not warriors.

I felt for my old friends and looking round, saw the smile
of contempt on the lips of Spikanoggan (the Gun Case), a
fine, stern warrior of about fifty years of age, with whom I
had been long acquainted, and whom I knew excelled in the
dance. I asked if he intended to take up the challenge, he
said, he had no wish to show himself off in dancing before
these strangers; "You certainly do not wish them to return
to their own country and report of you as so many women.
You Spikanoggan, your eye never pitied, nor your hand ever
spared an enemy, is the fittest man to represent your country
men in the War dance; and show these strangers what you
are. Somewhat nettled, he arose, put on a light war dress,
and with his large dagger in his right hand he began the War
dance, by the Scout, the Spy, the Discovery, the return to
camp, the Council, the silent march to the ambuscade, the
war whoop of attack, the tumult of the battle, the Yells of
doubtful contest and the war whoop of victory; the pursuit,
his breath short and quick the perspiration pouring down on
him his dagger in the fugitive, and the closing war whoop of
the death of his enemy rung through our ears. The varying
passions were strongly marked in his face, and the whole was
performed with enthusiasm. The perfect silence, and all
eyes rivetted on him, showed the admiration of every one,
and for which I rewarded him. The Iroquois seemed lost in
surprise, and after a few minutes said, our dances please our-

selves and also the white people and Indians wherever we go, but your dance is war itself to victory and to death. It was evident they were much mortified and at length one of them remarked that he did not scalp his enemy to which he replied in contempt; "any old woman can scalp a dead man." I was much pleased with the effect this dance had on the Iroquois, it seemed to bring them to their senses, and showed them that the Indians of the interior countries were fully as good Warriors, Hunters, and Dancers, as themselves. They lost all their self conceit and arrogance but became plain well behaved men, left off talking of war, and turned to hunting. Having taken on credit from the Traders their necessaries for the winter, they separated into small parties of two or three, each having about six steel traps for beaver, of light workmanship with strong elastic springs of which the bait is the castorum of the beaver, called the beaver medicine. They chose their hunting grounds to the westward and northward among the forests at the east foot of the Rocky Mountains. None of the Natives formed a favourable opinion of the Iroquois; for their whole number they had only about six women with them, each had a husband; and they could not conceive how men could live without women; they also looked on them as a dirty people for sleeping in their clothes, for the dress that an Iroquois put on in November he will walk and sleep in till the month of April, and longer if it does not wear away, so very contrary to the customs and habits of the Natives.

The learned men of Europe have their theories on the origen of the North American Indians and from whence they came, and from want of information have decided, and set the question at rest, by asserting, they all came direct from the east coast of Asia, a theory so contrary to facts, their own tradition, and all other movements since the furr traders came first among them, particularly of those from Canada. This subject I shall pass over at present, and reserve to the end of my travels.

CHAPTER XXI

SMALL POX AMONG THE INDIANS

Country at the east foot of the Mountains—Cumberland House, the first Trading House of the Hudson's Bay Company— Trading on the Saskatchewan—Abundance of animals— Tribes of the Plains—Description of early days of trading— Buckingham House built—Small pox—Despair of the Indian Camps—Traders distress for want of provisions—How the small pox was caught—Fur of the wolves and dogs who fed on the dead bodies—Disappearance of animals—Trading with the Peeagan Indians—Journey in search of Indians— One Pine—Find a camp of Indians.

IT must now be remembered that what I now relate is of the great body of dry land at the east foot of the Mountains, the northern part of forests and the southern of Plains through which roll the Mississoure and its tributaries, the Bow and Saskatchewan rivers with their many branches.

The Hudson's Bay Company did not extend their settlements into the interior country for several years after Canada, in 1763, was ceded to England. Their first trading house was made by Mr Samuel Hearne in 1774 at the sortie of the Saskatchewan into the Lakes, and was so well situated that it is continued to this day under the name of Cumberland House,[1] its situation has been changed two or three times

[1] Cumberland House is situated on the south side of Pine Island lake, through which the Saskatchewan river now flows on its way from the Forks to Cedar lake and Lake Winnipeg. It is in latitude 53° 56′ 44″ N., longitude 102° 13′ W. It was founded in the autumn of 1774 by Samuel Hearne of the Hudson's Bay Company, who came inland from York Fac-

from wood for fuel and other purposes, having worn too far from the house.

Previous to this the Fur Traders from Canada had extended their Houses a hundred miles beyond up the Saskatchewan, and considerable to the northward on the head waters of the Churchill River. About 1776, the Hudson's Bay Company under Mr Tomison, built a trading house[1] about 120 miles up the first named River. At this time the Nahathaway Indians were very numerous and engrossed to themselves all the Goods brought by the Fur Traders, the Animals of every kind were in abundance. Provisions of all kinds of meat so plentiful, and forced upon the Traders, that all that could be done, was to take a little from each, to give him a little Tobacco, Ammunition to those that had Guns, and Beads, Awls &c to the Women, for they claim a right to the dried Provisions as the Men do to the Furrs.

tory with eight white men and two Indians, and on his return to Hudson Bay in the following year he left it in charge of Mathew Cocking, who in 1772 had made an exploratory trip inland to see where the Canadians were established. On this trip Cocking had learned that the Canadians ascended the Saskatchewan as far as Pine Island lake, and from there they either continued on up ₫he river, or turned northward to Beaver lake and Churchill river. Consequently a house, 38 feet long and 26 feet wide, was built at the parting of the two routes, and it was found to be so favourably situated that the site has been continuously occupied by a trading post ever since. At the time when Cumberland House was built, Frobisher had a post to the north of it on Beaver lake, and Finlay or one of his associates had a post up the Saskatchewan river, but they very soon came down and built beside their rivals, the Hudson's Bay Company.

[1] Hudson House, apparently called after a clerk in the employ of the Hudson's Bay Company named George Hudson. It was situated on the west side of the Saskatchewan river in Sect. 32, Tp. 46, R. 3, west of the Third Meridian. It was 280 miles above Cumberland and 80 miles above the Forks, just about the place where the traveller, in ascending the river, would emerge from the forest and come out on the great plains. After having been occupied for an uncertain number of years this place was abandoned, and another settlement was built twelve or fourteen miles farther down the river, and within the edge of the forest. This latter post is spoken of by Thompson as Lower Hudson House. The position of the upper of the two houses, and the Saskatchewan river below it, is said to have been surveyed by Philip Turnor in 1777 and 1778.

The great Tribes of the Plains were only known by name to the Traders; and the state of the country as described to me by some old furr traders, and particularly by Mitchell Oman,[1] a native of the Orkney Islands, who had been several years in the Hudson Bay service. He was without education, yet of a superior mind to most men, curious and inquisitive, with a very retentive memory Of those times he said, " our situation was by no means pleasant, the Indians were very numerous, and although by far the greater part behaved well, and were kindly to us, yet amongst such a number there will always be bad men, and to protect ourselves from them we had to get a respectable chief to stay with, and assist us in trading, and prevent as much as possible the demands of these Men ; there were two houses from Canada, one was under a M[r] Cole, who by not taking this precaution got into a quarrel and was shot ;[2] The next year we went up the River about 350 miles above Cumberland House and built a trading house which we named Buckingham house,[3] and which was

[1] Mitchell Oman was a native of Stromness, and in 1798–99 was in the employ of the Hudson's Bay Company as a steersman and pilot at £50 a year. As he could not write, necessary accounts were signed by him with his mark. Thompson went up the Saskatchewan with him in 1786, and he appears to have been more or less continually on the river until 1796, when we find him in charge of Cumberland House. In 1799 he went from York Factory to England ; but where he was after that is unknown.

[2] Cole's trading post, called by Alexander Henry the younger Fort Montagne d'Aigle, was situated on a low bottom on the north side of the Saskatchewan river, nine or ten miles below the mouth of Battle river. Cole was a Canadian trader who had spent the winter of 1779–80 at this place. In the spring, just as he and his associates were about to leave with their furs, he gave an Indian some laudanum in a glass of liquor which killed him, and in retaliation he was killed by the other Indians. All the other white men were obliged to abandon everything and escape as best they could down the river. Oman speaks of the occurrence as if he had been there, and as he was an employee of the Hudson's Bay Company, the Company probably had a post beside the others at the time.

[3] The term "the next year" would seem to refer to the autumn of 1780. Thompson quotes Oman as saying that they went up the river 350 miles above Cumberland and built Buckingham House; but Buckingham House of the Hudson's Bay Company, and its neighbour, Fort

situated on the left bank of the River, where it passes thro'
the northern part of the great Plains, which freed us from
being wholly among the Nahathaways and allowed the Indians
of the Plains to trade with us, and the houses from Canada.
But still our situation was critical, and required all our
prudence; The following year, as usual, we went to York
Factory with the furrs, and returned with goods for the
winter trade; we proceeded about 150 miles up the River
to the Eagle Hills, where we saw the first camp and some of
the people sitting on the beach to cool themselves, when we
came to them, to our surprise they had marks of the small
pox, were weak and just recovering, and I could not help
saying, thank heaven we shall now get relief. For none of us
had the least idea of the desolation this dreadful disease had
done, until we went up the bank to the camp and looked into
the tents, in many of which they were all dead, and the
stench was horrid; Those that remained had pitched their
tents about 200 yards from them and were too weak to move
away entirely, which they soon intended to do; they were in

George of the North-West Company, were 550 miles above Cumberland,
or 350 miles above the Forks. The next spring they took their furs down
the river, and in the autumn they had returned up the river as far as the
Eagle Hills, near where Cole was killed, before they met any Indians who
were suffering from smallpox. This must have been in 1781, for it was
in the late summer and autumn of that year that this frightful disease
swept across the plains and reached the Saskatchewan. According to this
statement of Thompson, Buckingham House was first built by Mitchell
Oman in 1780; but if so, it must have been temporarily abandoned
shortly afterwards, perhaps on account of the sacking of York Factory
by the French in 1782. In 1784 the uppermost post of the North-West
Company on the Saskatchewan appears to have been that kept by Edward
Umfreville, sixty miles below the site of Buckingham House, and when
Thompson entered the country of the great plains in 1786 he assisted to
build Manchester House, forty miles below Umfreville's post, and this was
the most western trading post of the Hudson's Bay Company at the time.
. Fort George was built (or rebuilt) by Angus Shaw of the North-West
Company in 1792, and both it and Buckingham House were abandoned
in 1801 in favour of Island Fort, eighteen miles farther up the river. It
was situated on the north side of the river in or near Sect. 19, Tp. 56, R. 5,
west of the Fourth Meridian.

x

such a state of despair and despondence that they could hardly converse with us, a few of them had gained strength to hunt which kept them alive. From what we could learn, three fifths had died under this disease; Our Provisions were nearly out and we had expected to find ten times more than we wanted, instead of which they had not enough for themselves; They informed us, that as far as they knew all the Indians were in the same dreadful state, as themselves, and that we had nothing to expect from them.

We proceeded up the River with heavy hearts, the Bisons were crossing the River in herds, which gave us plenty of provisions for the voyage to our wintering ground.

When we arrived at the House instead of a crowd of Indians to welcome us, all was solitary silence, our hearts failed us. There was no Indian to hunt for us; before the Indians fell sick, a quantity of dried provisions had been collected for the next summers voyage, upon which we had to subsist, until at length two Indians with their families came and hunted for us. These informed us, that the Indians of the forest had beaver robes in their tents some of which were spread over the dead bodies, which we might take, and replace them by a new blanket and that by going to the tents we would render a service to those that were living by furnishing them with tobacco, ammunition, and a few other necessaries and thus the former part of the winter was employed. The bodies lately dead, and not destroyed by the Wolves and Dogs, for both devoured them, we laid logs over them to prevent these animals.

From the best information this disease was caught by the Chipaways (the forest Indians) and the Sieux (of the Plains) about the same time, in the year 1780, by attacking some families of the white people, who had it, and wearing their clothes. They had no idea of the disease and its dreadful nature.

From the Chipaways it extended over all the Indians of

the forest to it's northward extremity, and by the Sieux over
the Indians of the Plains and crossed the Rocky Mountains.
More Men died in proportion than Women and Children, for
unable to bear the heat of the fever they rushed into the
Rivers and Lakes to cool themselves, and the greater part
thus perished. The countries were in a manner depopulated,
the Natives allowed that far more than one half had died,
and from the number of tents which remained, it appeared
that about three fifths had perished; despair and despondency
had to give way to active hunting both for provisions, clothing
and all the necessaries of life; for in their sickness, as usual,
they had offered allmost every thing they had to the Good
Spirit and to the Bad, to preserve their lives, and were in a
manner destitute of everything. All the Wolves[1] and Dogs
that fed on the bodies of those that died of the Small Pox
lost their hair especially on the sides and belly, and even
for six years after many Wolves were found in this condition
and their furr useless. The Dogs were mostly killed.

With the death of the Indians a circumstance took place
which never has, and in all probability, never will be accounted
for. I have already mentioned that before that dreadful
disease appeared among the Indians they were numerous, and
the Bison, Moose, Red, and other Deer more so in proportion
and Provisions of Meat, both dried and fresh in abundance.
Of this all the Traders and Indians were fully sensible, and it
was noted by the Traders and Natives, that at the death of
the latter, and there being thus reduced to a small number,
the numerous herds of Bison and Deer also disappeared both
in the Woods and in the Plains, and the Indians about
Cumberland House declared the same of the Moose, and the
Swans, Geese and Ducks with the Gulls no longer frequented
the Lakes in the same number they used to do; and where
they had abundance of eggs during the early part of the
Summer, they had now to search about to find them. As I

---

[1] *Canis occidentalis* Richardson. [E. A. P.]

was not in the country at this time I can only give the assertion of the Traders and the Natives, who could have no interest in relating this sad state of the country. In the early part of September 1786 I entered these countries and from that time can speak from my own personal knowledge.

In the following October, six men and myself, were fitted out with a small assortment of goods, to find the Peeagan Indians and winter with them : to induce them to hunt for furrs, and make dried Provisions; to get as many as possible to come to the houses to trade, and to trade the furrs of those that would not come.   Each of us had a Horse, and some had two furnished by ourselves.   Our road lay through a fine country with slight undulations of ground, too low to be called Hills, everywhere clothed with fine short grass and hummocks, or islands of wood, almost wholly of Aspin and small, but straight, growth.   About the tenth day we came to the " One Pine."   This had been a fine stately tree of two fathoms girth, growing among a patch of Aspins, and being all alone, without any other pines for more than a hundred miles, had been regarded with superstitious reverence. When the small pox came, a few tents of Peeagans were camping near it, in the distress of this sickness, the master of one of the tents applied his prayers to it, to save the lives of himself and family, burned sweet grass and offered upon its roots, three horses to be at it's service, all he had, the next day the furniture of his horses with his Bow and Quiver of Arrows, and the third morning, having nothing more, a Bowl of Water.   The disease was now on himself and he had to lie down.   Of his large family only himself, one of his wives, and a Boy survived.   As soon as he acquired strength he took his horses, and all his other offerings from the " Pine Tree," then putting his little Axe in his belt, he ascended the Pine Tree to about two thirds of it's height, and there cut it off, out of revenge for not having saved his family; when we passed the branches were withered and the tree going to decay.

For three and twenty days we marched over fine grounds looking for the Indians without seeing any other animals than a chance Bull Bison, from the killing of a few we procured our provisions.

We found a Camp on the south side of the Bow River from its tender grass the favorite haunts of the Bisons, yet this camp had only provisions by daily hunting, and our frequent removals led us over a large tract of country, on which we rarely found the Bisons to be numerous, and various camps with whom we had intelligence were in the same state with the Camp we lived with. It is justly said, that as Mankind decrease, the Beasts of the earth increase, but in this calamity the natives saw all decrease but the Bears. And dried provisions of meat before so abundant that they could not be traded, were now sought as much as furrs. The enquiries of intelligent Traders into this state of the Animals from the Natives were to no purpose. They merely answered, that the Great Spirit having brought this calamity on them, had also taken away the Animals in the same proportion as they were not wanted, and intimating the Bisons and Deer were made and preserved solely for their use ; and if there were no Men there would be no Animals. The Bisons are vagrant, wandering from place to place over the great Plains, but the Moose and other Deer are supposed to keep within a range of ground, which they do not willingly leave, but all were much lessened in number. A few years after I passed over nearly the same grounds and found the Bisons far more numerous.[1]

[1] This statement gives us some idea of the position of the place where Thompson spent the winter with the Piegan in 1787–88, for the only other occasion on which he visited the Bow river was in the autumn of 1800, when he was living at Rocky Mountain House on the Saskatchewan river. On that occasion he explored the country south of the Bow river from the mouth of Highwood river westward to " The Gap " at the foot of the Rocky Mountains, so that we may infer that he also spent his first winter on the plains in this same vicinity.

CHAPTER XXII

PLAIN INDIANS

Plain Indians—Stone Indians—Fall Indians—Sussees—Peeagans —Blood Indians—Blackfeet—Saukamappee's account of former times—War of Peeagans and Snake Indians—Assistance of Nahathaways—Preparations for battle—Story of Saukamappee's life—Small pox caught from Snake Indians by the Peeagans—Treachery of Snake Indians—War Council —Two Indians killed by a grizled bear—Burning the bear —Continue journey — Consultation of Indians — Fifty warriors sent to examine the country—Return of the warriors —Story of encounter with the Snake Indians told by Saukamappee's son—Reproof of young men by Saukamappee.

THE Indians of the Plains are of various Tribes and of several languages which have no affinity with each other.

The Stone Indians[1] are a large tribe of the Sieux Nation, and speak a dialect, differing little from the Sieux tongue, the softest and most pleasing to the ear of all the indian languages. They have always been, and are, in strict alliance with the Nahathaways, and their hunting grounds are on the left bank of the Saskatchewan and eastward and southward

---

[1] The Stone Indians or Assiniboin are a tribe of the Sioux which separated from the parent family before the advent of white men, and went northward and formed an alliance with the Cree. In 1911 there were 1,393 of them in Canada, and in 1904 there were 1,234 in the United States, making a total of 2,627, or nearly 500 less than Thompson's estimate of a century ago.

to the upper part of the Red River, and their number 400
Tents each containing about eight souls, in all 3200.

The Fall Indians,[1] their former residence was on the
Rapids of the Saskatchewan, about 100 miles above Cumberland House; they speak a harsh language, which no other
tribe attempts to learn, in number about 70 tents at ten
souls to each tent. They are a tall well made muscular
people, their countenances manly, but not handsome. Their
Chief was of a bad character, and brought them into so many
quarrels with their allies, they had to leave their country
and wander to the right bank of the Missisourie, to near the
Mandane villages. The Sussees,[2] are about ninety tents and
may number about 650 souls. They are brave and manly,
tall and well limbed, but their faces somewhat flat, and cannot
be called handsome. They speak a very guttural tongue
which no one attempts to learn.

The next of the three tribes of the Peeagan, called
Peeaganakoon, the Blood Indians (Kennekoon) and the Black-
feets (Saxeekoon)[3] these all speak the same tongue, and their
hunting grounds [are] contiguous to each other; these were
formerly on the Bow River, but now [extend] southward to
the Missisourie.

All these Plains, which are now the hunting grounds of
the above Indians, were formerly in full possession of the

[1] The Fall Indians or Atsina, a detached branch of the Arapaho, who
were formerly allies of the Blackfeet. None of them are now living in
Canada. See note on p. 224.

[2] See note on p. 304.

[3] The Piegan, Bloods, and Blackfeet are the three tribal subdivisions
of the Blackfoot or Siksika nation. They belong to the Algonquin linguistic family, which includes the Cree, Chippewa, and many other tribes.
In historic times they have always been inhabitants of the great plains.
In 1911 there were 2,337 in Canada, and in 1909, 2,195 in the United
States, making a total of 4,532. The account given on this and the following pages is one of the most interesting and accurate accounts of this
people that has ever been presented, and the story of the old man Saukamappee carries the history of the Piegan back considerably beyond any
previous authentic record.

Kootanaes,[1] northward; the next the Saleesh[2] and their allies, and the most southern, the Snake Indians[3] and their tribes, now driven across the Mountains. The Peeagan in whose tent I passed the winter was an old man of at least 75 to 80 years of age; his height about six feet, two or three inches, broad shoulders, strong limbed, his hair gray and plentiful, forehead high and nose prominent, his face slightly marked with the small pox, and alltogether his countenance mild, and even, sometimes playfull; although his step was firm and he rode with ease, he no longer hunted, this he left to his sons; his name was Saukamappee (Young Man); his account of former times went back to about 1730 and was as follows.

The Peeagans were always the frontier Tribe, and upon whom the Snake Indians made their attacks, these latter were very numerous, even without their allies; and the Peeagans had to send messengers among us to procure help. Two of them came to the camp of my father, and I was then about his age (pointing to a Lad of about sixteen years) he promised to come and bring some of his people, the Nahathaways with him, for I am myself of that people, and not of those with whom I am. My father brought about twenty warriors with him. There were a few guns amongst us, but very little ammunition, and they were left to hunt for the families; Our weapons was a Lance, mostly pointed with iron, some few of stone, A Bow and a quiver of Arrows; the Bows were of Larch, the length came to the chin; the quiver had about fifty arrows, of which ten had iron points,

[1] See p. 304.

[2] The Saleesh, or Salish, are a linguistic family inhabiting the south-east portion of Vancouver Island, and much of the southern mainland of British Columbia. Those of the interior are divided into the Lillooet, Shuswap, Okinagan, Flatheads, &c. Many of these were encountered by Thompson in his travels west of the Rocky Mountains. In 1909, in both Canada and the United States, the coast Salish numbered 8,474, and those of the interior 10,378, or a total of 18,852.

[3] A name applied to many different bodies of Shoshonean Indians, but most persistently to those of eastern Oregon.

the others were headed with stone. He carried his knife on
his breast and his axe in his belt. Such was my fathers weapons,
and those with him had much the same weapons. I had a
Bow and Arrows and a knife, of which I was very proud.
We came to the Peeagans and their allies. They were camped
in the Plains on the left bank of the River (the north side)
and were a great many. We were feasted, a great War Tent
was made, and a few days passed in speeches, feasting and
dances. A war chief was elected by the chiefs, and we got
ready to march. Our spies had been out and had seen a
large camp of the Snake Indians on the Plains of the Eagle
Hill, and we had to cross the River in canoes, and on rafts,
which we carefully secured for our retreat. When we had
crossed and numbered our men, we were about 350 warriors
(this he showed by counting every finger to be ten, and holding up both hands three times and then one hand) they had
their scouts out, and came to meet us. Both parties made a
great show of their numbers, and I thought that they were
more numerous than ourselves.

After some singing and dancing, they sat down on the
ground, and placed their large shields before them, which
covered them : We did the same, but our shields were not
so many, and some of our shields had to shelter two men.
Theirs were all placed touching each other; their Bows
were not so long as ours, but of better wood, and the back
covered with the sinews of the Bisons which made them very
elastic, and their arrows went a long way and whizzed about
us as balls do from guns. They were all headed with a sharp,
smooth, black stone (flint) which broke when it struck anything. Our iron headed arrows did not go through their
shields, but stuck in them; On both sides several were
wounded, but none lay on the ground; and night put an
end to the battle, without a scalp being taken on either
side, and in those days such was the result, unless one party
was more numerous than the other. The great mischief of

war then, was as now, by attacking and destroying small camps of ten to thirty tents, which are obliged to separate for hunting: I grew to be a man, became a skilfull and fortunate hunter, and my relations procured me a Wife. She was young and handsome and we were fond of each other. We had passed a winter together, when Messengers came from our allies to claim assistance.

By this time the affairs of both parties had much changed; we had more guns and iron headed arrows than before; but our enemies the Snake Indians and their allies had Misstutim (Big Dogs, that is Horses) on which they rode, swift as the Deer, on which they dashed at the Peeagans, and with their stone Pukamoggan knocked them on the head, and they had thus lost several of their best men. This news we did not well comprehend and it alarmed us, for we had no idea of Horses and could not make out what they were. Only three of us went and I should not have gone, had not my wife's relations frequently intimated, that her father's medicine bag would be honored by the scalp of a Snake Indian. When we came to our allies, the great War Tent [was made] with speeches, feasting and dances as before ; and when the War Chief had viewed us all it was found between us and the Stone Indians we had ten guns and each of us about thirty balls, and powder for the war, and we were considered the strength of the battle. After a few days march our scouts brought us word that the enemy was near in a large war party, but had no Horses with them, for at that time they had very few of them. When we came to meet each other, as usual, each displayed their numbers, weapons and shiel[d]s, in all which they were superior to us, except our guns which were not shown, but kept in their leathern cases, and if we had shown [them], they would have taken them for long clubs. For a long time they held us in suspense ; a tall Chief was forming a strong party to make an attack on our centre, and the others to enter into combat with those opposite to them ;

We prepared for the battle the best we could. Those of us
who had guns stood in the front line, and each of us [had]
two balls in his mouth, and a load of powder in his left hand
to reload.

We noticed they had a great many short stone clubs for
close combat, which is a dangerous weapon, and had they
made a bold attack on us, we must have been defeated as
they were more numerous and better armed than we were,
for we could have fired our guns no more than twice; and
were at a loss what to do on the wide plain, and each Chief
encouraged his men to stand firm. Our eyes were all on the
tall Chief and his motions, which appeared to be contrary to
the advice of several old Chiefs, all this time we were about
the strong flight of an arrow from each other. At length the
tall chief retired and they formed their long usual line by
placing their shields on the ground to touch each other, the
shield having a breadth of full three feet or more. We sat
down opposite to them and most of us waited for the night
to make a hasty retreat. The War Chief was close to us,
anxious to see the effect of our guns. The lines were too far
asunder for us to make a sure shot, and we requested him
to close the line to about sixty yards, which was gradually
done, and lying flat on the ground behind the shields, we
watched our opportunity when they drew their bows to shoot
at us, their bodies were then exposed and each of us, as
opportunity offered, fired with deadly aim, and either killed,
or severely wounded, every one we aimed at.

The War Chief was highly pleased, and the Snake Indians
finding so many killed and wounded kept themselves behind
their shields; the War Chief then desired we would spread
ourselves by two's throughout the line, which we did, and our
shots caused consternation and dismay along their whole line.
The battle had begun about Noon, and the Sun was not yet
half down, when we perceived some of them had crawled
away from their shields, and were taking to flight. The War

Chief seeing this went along the line and spoke to every Chief to keep his Men ready for a charge of the whole line of the enemy, of which he would give the signal; this was done by himself stepping in front with his Spear, and calling on them to follow him as he rushed on their line, and in an instant the whole of us followed him, the greater part of the enemy took to flight, but some fought bravely and we lost more than ten killed and many wounded; Part of us pursued, and killed a few, but the chase had soon to be given over, for at the body of every Snake Indian killed, there were five or six of us trying to get his scalp, or part of his clothing, his weapons, or something as a trophy of the battle. As there were only three of us, and seven of our friends, the Stone Indians, we did not interfere, and got nothing.

The next morning the War Chief made a speech, praising their bravery, and telling them to make a large War Tent to commemorate their victory, to which they directly set to work and by noon it was finished.

The War Chief now called on all the other Chiefs to assemble their men and come to the Tent. In a short time they came, all those who had lost relations had their faces blackened; those who killed an enemy, or wished to be thought so, had their faces blackened with red streaks on the face, and those who had no pretensions to the one, or the other, had their faces red with ochre. We did not paint our faces until the War Chief told us to paint our foreheads and eyes black, and the rest of the face of dark red ochre, as having carried guns, and to distinguish us from all the rest. Those who had scalps now came forward with the scalps neatly streched on a round willow with a handle to the frame; they appeared to be more than fifty, and excited loud shouts and the war whoop of victory. When this was over the War Chief told them that if any one had a right to the scalp of an enemy as a war trophy it ought to be us, who with our guns had gained the victory, when from the numbers of our

enemies we were anxious to leave the field of battle; and
that ten scalps must be given to us; this was soon collected,
and he gave to each of us a Scalp. All those whose faces
were blackened for the loss of relations, or friends, now came
forward to claim the other scalps to be held in their hands
for the benefit of their departed relations and friends; this
occasioned a long conversation with those who had the scalps;
at length they came forward to the War Chief, those who had
taken the trophy from the head of the enemy they had killed,
said the Souls of the enemy that each of us has slain, belong
to us, and we have given them to our relations which are in
the other world to be their slaves, and we are contented.
Those who had scalps taken from the enemy that were found
dead under the shields were at a loss what to say, as not one
could declare he had actually slain the enemy whose scalp he
held, and yet wanted to send their Souls to be the slaves of
their departed relations. This caused much discussion; and
the old Chiefs decided it could not be done, and that no one
could send the soul of an enemy to be a slave in the other
world, except the warrior who actually killed him; the scalps
you hold are trophies of the Battle, but they give you no
right to the soul of the enemy from whom it is taken, he
alone who kills an enemy has a right to the soul, and to give
it to be a slave to whom he pleases. This decision did not
please them, but they were obliged to abide by it. The old
Chiefs then turned to us, and praising our conduct in the
battle said, each of you have slain two enemies in battle, if
not more, you will return to your own people, and as you
are young men, consult with the old men to whom you shall
give the souls of those you have slain; until which let them
wander about the other world. The Chiefs wished us to
stay, and promised to each of us a handsome young wife,
and [to] adopt us as their sons, but we told them we were
anxious to see our relations and people, after which, perhaps
we might come back. After all the war ceremonies were

over, we pitched away in large camps with the women and children on the frontier of the Snake Indian country, hunting the Bison and Red Deer which were numerous, and we were anxious to see a horse of which we had heard so much. At last, as the leaves were falling we heard that one was killed by an arrow shot into his belly, but the Snake Indian that rode him, got away; numbers of us went to see him, and we all admired him, he put us in mind of a Stag that had lost his horns; and we did not know what name to give him. But as he was a slave to Man, like the dog, which carried our things; he was named the Big Dog.[1]

We set off for our people, and on the fourth day came to a camp of Stone Indians, the relations of our companions, who received us well and we staid a few day[s]. The Scalps were placed on poles, and the Men and Women danced round them, singing to the sound of Rattles, Tambours and flutes. When night came, one of our party, in a low voice, repeated to the Chief the narrative of the battle, which he in a loud voice walking about the tents, repeated to the whole camp. After which, the Chiefs called those who followed them to a feast, and the battle was always the subject of the conversation and driving the Snake Indians to a great distance. There were now only three of us to proceed, and upon enquiry, [we] learned a camp of our people, the Nahathaways were

[1] We have here, for the first time, a circumstantial account of the use of horses by the Snake Indians west of the Rocky Mountains, and of the first sight of one of these animals by any of the Blackfeet, and the clear inference that the Blackfeet obtained their horses first from the Snake Indians, and not from the Indians to the south of them east of the mountains. Thompson's date of 1730 as the time of the Blackfeet-Snake war, when the Blackfeet obtained their first horses, must be approximately correct, for in 1754, when the same Indians were visited by Anthony Hendry from York Factory, the Blackfeet had very many horses, and their neighbours, the Assiniboin, had a few. Horses had been fairly abundant in America in post-Tertiary times, but like the mammoth and the mastodon had become extinct, and it was not until the middle of the sixteenth century that they were reintroduced on this continent by the Spaniards.

a days journey's from us. and in the evening we came to
them, and all our news had to be told, with the usual songs
and dances; but my mind was wholly bent on making a
grand appearance before my Wife and her Parents, and pre-
senting to her father the scalp I had to ornament his Medicine Bag: and before we came to the camp we had dressed
ourselves, and painted each other's faces to appear to the
best advantage, and were proud of ourselves. On seeing
some of my friends I got away and went to them, and by
enquiries learned that my parents had gone to the low
countries of the Lakes, and that before I was three Moons
away my wife had given herself to another man, and that her
father could not prevent her, and they were all to the northward there to pass the winter.

At this unlooked for news I was quite disheartened; I
said nothing, but my heart was swollen with anger and revenge, and I passed the night scheming mischief. In the
morning my friends reasoned with me upon my vexation
about a worthless woman, and that it was beneath a warrior
anger, there were no want of women to replace her, and a
better wife could be got. Others said, that if I had staid
with my wife instead of running away to kill Snake Indians,
nothing of this would have happened. My anger moderated,
I gave my Scalp to one of my friends to give to my father,
and renouncing my people, I left them, and came to the
Peeagans who gave me a hearty welcome; and upon my
informing them of my intention to remain with them the
great Chief gave me his eldest daughter to be my wife, she
is the sister of the present Chief, and as you see, now an old
woman.

The terror of that battle and of our guns has prevented
any more general battles, and our wars have since been
carried by ambuscade and surprize, of small camps, in which
we have greatly the advantage, from the Guns, arrow shods
of iron, long knives, flat bayonets and axes from the Traders.

While we have these weapons, the Snake Indians have none, but what few they sometimes take from one of our small camps which they have destroyed, and they have no Traders among them. We thus continued to advance through the fine plains to the Stag River [1] when death came over us all, and swept away more than half of us by the Small pox, of which we knew nothing until it brought death among us. We caught it from the Snake Indians.[2] Our Scouts were out for our security, when some returned and informed us of a considerable camp which was too large to attack and something very suspicious about it; from a high knowl they had a good view of the camp, but saw none of the men hunting, or going about; there were a few Horses, but no one came to them, and a herd of Bisons [were] feeding close to the camp with other herds near. This somewhat alarmed us as a stratagem of War; and our Warriors thought this camp had a larger not far off; so that if this camp was attacked which was strong enough to offer a desperate resistance, the other would come to their assistance and overpower us as had been once done by them, and in which we lost many of our men.

The council ordered the Scouts to return and go beyond this camp, and be sure there was no other. In the mean time we advanced our camp; The scouts returned and said no other tents were near, and the camp appeared in the same state as before. Our Scouts had been going too much about their camp and were seen; they expected what would follow, and all those that could walk, as soon as night came on, went away. Next morning at the dawn of day, we attacked the Tents, and with our sharp flat daggers and knives, cut through the tents and entered for the fight; but our war whoop

---

[1] This refers undoubtedly to the Red Deer River, which joins with the Bow River to form the South Saskatchewan.

[2] Here is a definite statement and account of how smallpox was carried from the Snake Indians to the Blackfeet, and doubtless also to their allies, the Cree and Assiniboin.

instantly stopt, our eyes were appalled with terror; there was no one to fight with but the dead and the dying, each a mass of corruption. We did not touch them, but left the tents, and held a council on what was to be done. We all thought the Bad Spirit had made himself master of the camp and destroyed them. It was agreed to take some of the best of the tents, and any other plunder that was clean and good, which we did, and also took away the few Horses they had, and returned to our camp.

The second day after this dreadful disease broke out in our camp, and spread from one tent to another as if the Bad Spirit carried it. We had no belief that one Man could give it to another, any more than a wounded Man could give his wound to another. We did not suffer so much as those that were near the river, into which they rushed and died. We had only a little brook, and about one third of us died, but in some of the other camps there were tents in which every one died. When at length it left us, and we moved about to find our people, it was no longer with the song and the dance; but with tears, shrieks, and howlings of despair for those who would never return to us. War was no longer thought of, and we had enough to do to hunt and make provision for our families, for in our sickness we had consumed all our dried provisions; but the Bisons and Red Deer were also gone, we did not see one half of what was before, whither they had gone we could not tell, we believed the Good Spirit had forsaken us, and allowed the Bad Spirit to become our Master. What little we could spare we offered to the Bad Spirit to let us alone and go to our enemies. To the Good Spirit we offered feathers, branches of trees, and sweet smelling grass. Our hearts were low and dejected, and we shall never be again the same people. To hunt for our families was our sole occupation and kill Beavers, Wolves and Foxes to trade our necessaries; and we thought of War no more, and perhaps would have made peace with them for

they had suffered dreadfully as well as us and had left all this
fine country of the Bow River to us.

We were quiet for about two or three winters, and
although we several times saw their young men on the scout
we took no notice of them, as we all require young men, to
look about the country that our families may sleep in safety
and that we may know where to hunt.   But the snake Indians
are a bad people, even their allies the Saleesh and Kootanaes
cannot trust them, and do not camp with them, no one
believes what they say, and [they] are very treacherous;
every one says they are rightly named Snake People, for their
tongue is forked like that of a Rattle Snake, from which they
have their name.   I think it was about the third falling of
the leaves of the trees, that five of our tents pitched away
to the valleys of the Rocky Mountains, up a branch of this
River (the Bow) to hunt the Big Horn Deer (Mountain
Sheep) as their horns make fine large bowls, and are easily
cleaned; they were to return on the first snow.   All was
quiet and we waited for them until the snow lay on the
ground, when we got alarmed for their safety; and about
thirty warriors set off to seak them.   It was only two days
march, and in the evening they came to the camp, it had
been destroyed by a large party of Snake Indians, who left
their marks, of snakes heads painted black on sticks they had
set up.   The bodies were all there with the Women and
Children, but scalped and partly devoured by the Wolves
and Dogs.

The party on their return related the fate of our people,
and other camps on hearing the news came and joined us.
A War Tent was made and the Chiefs and Warriors assembled,
the red pipes were filled with Tobacco, but before being
lighted an old Chief arose, and beckoning to the Man who
had the fire to keep back, addressed us, saying, I am an old
man, my hair is white and [I] have seen much: formerly
we were healthy and strong and many of us, now we are few

to what we were, and the great sickness may come again.
We were fond of War, even our Women flattered us to war,
and nothing was thought of but scalps for singing and dancing.
Now think of what has happened to us all, by destroying
each other and doing the work of the bad spirit; the Great
Spirit became angry with our making the ground red with
blood : he called to the Bad Spirit to punish and destroy us,
but in doing so not to let one spot of the ground, to be red
with blood, and the Bad Spirit did it as we all know. Now
we must revenge the death of our people and make the
Snake Indians feel the effects of our guns, and other weapons ;
but the young women must all be saved, and if any has a
babe at the breast it must not be taken from her, nor hurt ;
all the Boys and Lads that have no weapons must not be
killed, but brought to our camps, and be adopted amongst
us, to be our people, and make us more numerous and stronger
than we are. Thus the Great Spirit will see that when we
make war we kill only those who are dangerous to us, and
make no more ground red with blood than we can help, and
the Bad Spirit will have no more power on us. Everyone
signified his assent to the old Chief, and since that time, it
has sometimes been acted on, but more with the Women
than the Boys, and while it weakens our enemies makes us
stronger. A red pipe was now lighted and the same old
Chief taking it, gave three whiffs to the Great Spirit praying
him to be kind to them and not forsake them, then three
whiffs to the Sun, the same to the Sky, the Earth and the
four Winds ; the Pipe was passed round, and other pipes
lighted. The War Chief then arose, and said Remember my
friends that while we are smoking the bodies of our friends
and relations are being devoured by wolves and Dogs, and
their Souls are sent by the Snake Indians to be the slaves of
their relations in the other world. We have made no war
on them for more than three summers, and we had hoped to
live quietly until our young men had grown up, for we are

not many as we used to be; but the Snake Indians, that race of liars, whose tongues are like rattle snakes, have already made war on us, and we can no longer be quiet. The country where they now are is but little known to us, and if they did not feel themselves strong they would not have dared to have come so far to destroy our people. We must be courageous and active, but also cautious; and my advice is, that three scout parties, each of about ten warriors with a Chief at their head, take three different directions, and cautiously view the country, and not go too far, for enough of our people are already devoured by wolves and our business is revenge, without loosing our people.

After five days, the scout parties returned without seeing the camp of an enemy, or any fresh traces of them. Our War Chief Kootanae Appe was now distressed, he had expected some camp would have been seen, and he concluded, the Snake Indians had gone to the southward to their allies, to show the scalps they had taken and make their songs and dances for the victory, and in his speech denounced constant war on them until they were· exterminated. Affairs were in this state when we arrived, and the narrative [of the] old man having given us the above information, [he] lighted his pipe; and smoking it out said, the Snake Indians are no match for us; they have no guns and are no match for us, but they have the power to vex us and make us afraid for the small hunting parties that hunt the small deer for dresses and the Big Horn for the same and for Bowls. They keep us always on our guard.

A few days after our arrival, the death cry was given, and the Men all started out of the Tents, and our old tent mate with his gun in his hand. The cry was from a young man who held his Bow and Arrows, and showed one of his thighs torn by a grizled bear, and which had killed two of his companions. The old Man called for his powder horn and shot bag, and seeing the priming of his gun in good order, he set

off with the young man for the Bear, which was at a short
distance. They found him devouring one of the dead. The
moment he saw them he sat up on his hind legs, showing them
his teeth and long clawed paws, in this, his usual position,
to defend his prey, his head is a bad mark, but his breast
offers a direct mark to the heart, through which the old Man
sent his ball and killed him. The two young men who were
destroyed by the Bear, had each, two iron shod Arrows, and
the camp being near, they attacked the bear for his skin and
claws. But unfortunately their arrows stuck in the bones of
his ribs, and only irritated him; he sprung on the first, and
with one of his dreadful fore paws tore out his bowels and three
of his ribs; the second he seized in his paws, and almost
crushed him to death, threw him down, when the third
Indian hearing their cries came to their assistance and sent
an arrow, which only wounded him in the neck, for which
the Bear chased him, and slightly tore one of his thighs.
The first poor fellow was still alive and knew his parents, in
whose arms he expired. The Bear, for the mischief he had
done was condemned to be burnt to ashes, the claws of his
fore paws, very sharp and long, the young man wanted for a
collar but it was not granted; those that burned the Bear
watched until nothing but ashes remained.

The two young men were each wrapped up separately in
Bison robes, laid side by side on the ground, and covered with
logs of wood and stones, in which we assisted. By the advice
of the civil chief in his speeches in the early part of every
night; we pitched southward to about eighty miles beyond
the Bow River. We had a few showers of snow, which soon
melted, the herds of Bisons were sufficient for daily use, but
not enough for dried provisions. However a council was
held, and as they did not intend to go farther south towards
the Snake Indians, but after hunting about where they were
for a Moon, return to the northward to trade their furrs,
whether it would not be adviseable to know if their enemies

were near them or not. After consultation it was agreed to
send out a war chief, with about fifty warriors to examine
the country for a few days journey. The Chief soon collected
his warriors and having examined their arms, and [having
seen] that every one had two pair of shoes, some dried provisions and other necessaries, in the evening the principal
War Chief addressed the Chief at the head of the party;
reminding him that the warriors now accompaning him would
steadily follow him, that they were sent to destroy their
enemies, not to be killed themselves, and made the slaves of
their enemies, that he must be wise and cautious and bring
back the Warriors entrusted to his care. Among them was
the eldest son of the Old Man in whose tent we lived. They
all marched off very quietly, as if for hunting. After they
were gone; the old man said it was not a war party, but one
of those they frequently sent, under guidance of those who
had showed courage and conduct in going to war, for we
cannot afford to lose our people, we are too few, and these
expeditions inure our men to long marches and to suffer
hunger and thirst. At the end of about twenty days they
returned with about thirty five Horses in tolerable condition,
and fifteen fine mules, which they had brought away from a
large camp of Snake Indians. The old Man's son gave him
a long account of the business. On the sixth evening the
scouts ahead came and informed the Chief, that we must be
near a camp, as they had seen horses feeding: night came
on, and we went aside to a wood of cotton and poplar trees
on the edge of a brook, in the morning some of us climbed
the trees and passed the day, but saw nothing. In the night
we went higher up the brook, and as it was shoal, we walked
in it for some distance, to another wood, and there lay down.
Early the next morning, a few of us advanced through the
wood, but we had not gone far, before we heard the women
with their dogs come for wood for fuel. Some of us returned
to the Chief, and the rest watched the women, it was near

midday before they all went away, they had only stone axes and stone clubs to break the wood ; they took only what was dry, and cut none down. Their number showed us the camp must be large, and sometimes some of them came so close to us, that we were afraid of being discovered. The Chief now called us round him, and advised us to be very cautious, as it was plain we were in the vicinity of a large camp, and manage our little provisions, for we must not expect to get any more until we retreated ; if we fire a gun at the Deer it will be heard ; and if we put an arrow in a deer and he gets away, and they see the deer, it will alarm them, and we shall not be able to get away. My intention is to have something to show our people, and when we retreat, take as many horses as we can' with us, to accomplish which, we must have a fair opportunity, and in the mean time be hungry, which we can stand some time, as we have plenty of water to drink. We were getting tired, and our solace was of an evening to look at the horses and mules. At length he said to us to get ready, and pointing to the top of the Mountains, [said] see the blue sky is gone and a heavy storm is there, which will soon reach us ; and so it did : About sunset we proceeded thro' the wood, to the horses, and with the lines we carried, each helping the other, we soon had a horse or a mule to ride on. We wanted to drive some with us, but the Chief would not allow it ; it was yet daylight when we left the wood, and entered the plains, but the Storm of Wind was very strong and on our backs, and at the gallop, or trot, so as not to tire our horses, we continued to midnight, when we came to a brook, with plenty of grass, and let them get a good feed. After which we held on to sun rising, when seeing a fine low ground, we staid the rest of the day, keeping watch until night, when we continued our journey. The storm lasted two days and greatly helped us.

The old Man told his son, who, in his relation had intimated he did not think the Chief very brave ; that it was very fortunate that he was under such a Chief, who had acted so wisely and cautiously; for had he acted otherwise not one of you would have returned, and some young men coming into the tent whom he supposed might have the same opinions as his son, he told them; " that it required no great bravery for a War Party to attack a small camp, which they were sure to master; but that it required great courage and conduct, to be for several days in the face of a large camp undiscovered; and each of you to bring away a horse from the enemy, instead of leaving your own scalps." [1]

[1] This is the end of Saukamapee's story, the chief features of which are the mode of fighting on foot before fire-arms were introduced, the introduction of fire-arms, probably obtained from York Factory on Hudson Bay, the introduction of the horse among the Blackfeet, and the terrible epidemic of smallpox of 1781.

CHAPTER XXIII

PEEAGANS

Land of the Peeagans, Blackfeet and Blood Indians—Manners and Customs of the Peeagan Civil and Military Chiefs— The war chief Kootanaeappi—Appearance of Peeagans— Wear no caps—Thickness of skull—Origen—Apathy— Adornment of the men—Ornaments of the women—Appearance and dress of the women—Dress of men—Marriages— Polygamy—Punishment of adultery—Elopements—Poonokow —Treatment of the Dead—Character—Fear of disgrace— Punishment of children.

THE Peeagans, with the tribes of the Blood, and Blackfeet Indians, who all speak the same language, are the most powerful of the western and northern plains, and by right of conquest have their west boundary to the foot of the Rocky Mountains, southward to the north branches of the Missisourie, eastward for about three hundred miles from the Mountains and northward to the upper part of the Saskatchewan. Other tribes of their allies also at times hunt on part of the above, and a great extent of the Plains, and these great Plains place them under different circumstances, and give them peculiar traits of character from those that hunt in the forests. These latter live a peaceable life, with hard labor, to procure provisions and clothing for their families, in summer they make use of canoes, and in winter haul on sleds all they have, in their frequent removals from place to place. On the other hand the Indians of the Plains make no use of canoes, frequently stay many days in a place, and when they remove have horses and dogs, both in summer and winter to carry their baggage and provisions : they have no hard labor, but have powerful enemies which keep them constantly on the watch and are never secure but in large camps. The manners and customs of all these tribes of the Plains, are much alike, and in giving those of the Peeagans, it may serve for all the others. Being the frontier tribe, they lead a more precarious and watchful life than other tribes, and from their boyhood are taught the use of arms, and to be good warriors, they become martial and more moral than the others, and many of them have a chivalrous bearing, ready for any enterprise. They have a civil and military Chief. The first was called Sakatow, the orator, and [the office] appeared hereditary in his family, as his father had been the civil Chief, and his eldest son was to take his place at his death and occasionally acted for him. The present chief was now about sixty years of age (1800) about five feet ten inches in height, remarkably well made, and in his youth a very handsome man. He was always well dressed, and his insignia of office, was the backs of two fine Otter skins covered with mother of pearl, which from behind his neck hung down his breast to below the belt ; When his son acted for him, he always had this ornament on him. In every council he presided, except one of War. He had couriers which went from camp to camp, and brought the news of how things were, of where the great herds of Bisons were feeding, and of the direction they were taking. The news thus collected, about two or three hours after sun set, walking about the camp, he related in a loud voice, making his comments on it, and giving advice when required. His language was fluent, and he was admired for his eloquence, but not for his principles and his advice could not be depended on, being sometimes too violent, and more likely to produce quarrels than to allay them yet his influence was great.

The War Chief was Kootanae Appe (Kootanae Man)

his stature was six feet six inches, tall and erect, he appeared
to be of Bone and Sinew with no more flesh, than absolutely
required ; his countenance manly, but not stern, his features
prominent, nose somewhat aquiline, his manners kind and
mild ; his word was sacred, he was both loved and respected,
and his people often wished him to take a more active part
in their affairs but he confined himself to War, and the care
of the camp in which he was, which was generally of fifty to
one hundred tents, generally a full day's march nearer to the
Snake Indians than any other camp. It was supposed he
looked on the civil Chief with indifference as a garrulous old
man more fit for talking than any thing else, and they rarely
camped together. Kootanae Appe by his five wives had
twenty two sons and four daughters. His grown up sons
were as tall as himself and the others promised the same.
He was friendly to the White Men, and in his speeches reminded his people of the great benefit of [which] the Traders
were to them, and that it was by their means they had so
many useful articles, and guns for hunting, and to conquer
their enemies. He had acquired his present station and
influence from his conduct in war. He was utterly averse to
small parties, except for horse stealing, which too often brought
great hardships and loss of life. He seldom took the field
with less than two hundred warriors but frequently with
many more ; his policy was to get as many of the allies to
join him as possible, by which all might have a share of the
honour and plunder, and thus avoid those jealousies and
envyings so common amongst the Chiefs. He praised every
Chief that in the least deserved it, but never appeared to
regard fame as worth his notice yet always took care to ·
deserve it, for all his exped[it]ions were successful.

The Peeagans and their allies of the Plains, with us, would
not be counted handsome. From infancy they are exposed
to the weather and have not that softness of expression in
their countenances which is so pleasing, but they are a fine

race of men, tall and muscular, with manly features, and intelligent countenances, the eye large, black and piercing, the nose full and generally straight, the teeth regular and white, the hair long, straight and black; their beards, apparently would be equal to those of white men, did they not continually attempt to eradicate it; for when [they are] grown old and no longer pluck out the hairs they have more beard than could naturally be expected. Their color is something like that of a Spaniard from the south of Spain, and some like that of the French of the south of France, and this comparison is drawn from seeing them when bathing together.

In questioning them of their origen and from whence they formerly came they appear to have no tradition beyond the time of their great granfathers, that they can depend on, and in their idle time, sometimes [this] is the subject of their conversation. They have no tradition that they ever made use of canoes, yet their old men always point out the North East as the place they came from, and their progress has always been to the south west. Since the Traders came to the Saskatchewan River, this has been their course and progress for the distance of four hundred miles from the Eagle Hills to the Mountains near the Missisourie but this rapid advance may be mostly attributed to their being armed with guns and iron weapons. Of their origen, they think themselves and all the animals to be indigenus, and from all times existing as at present.

The Indians are noticed for their apathy, this is more assumed than real; in public he wishes it to appear that nothing can affect him, but in private he feels and expresses himself sensible to every thing that happens to him or to his family. After all his endeavours to attain some object in hunting, or other matters, and cannot do it, he says, the " Great Spirit will have it so," in the same manner as we say " It is the will of Providence." Civilized Men have many things to engage their attention and to take up their time, but the Indian is very different, hunting is his business, not his amusement, and even in this he is limited for want of ammunition hence his whole life is in the enjoyments of his passions, desires and affections contracted within a small circle, and in which it is often intense.

The Men are proud of being noticed and praised as good hunters, warriors, or any other masculine accomplishment, and many of the young men as fine dandies as they can make themselves. I have known some of them to take full an hour to paint their faces with White, Red, Green, Blue and Yellow, or part of these colors, with their looking glasses, and advising one another, how to lay on the different colors in stripes, circles, dots and other fancies; then stand for part of the day in some place of the camp to be admired by the women. When married all this painting is at an end, and if they will paint it [is] only with one color, as red, or yellow ochre.

The country affords no ornaments for the men, but collars of the claws of the fore paws of the Bear. The Women, as usual with all women are fond of ornaments, but the country produces none, except some of the teeth of the deer, which are pierced, strung together, and form bracelets for the wrists and sometimes a fillet of sweet scented grass round the fore head, the rest of their ornaments are from the Traders, as Beads of various colours, Rings, Hawks, Bells, and Thimbles. Scarce any has ear rings, and never any in the nose.

On the first arrival of a stranger in a camp, who has never seen them, he may not find the young women so handsome as he could wish, for there is a line of beauty in women which is somewhat different in every people and nation, but where, if the features are regular, we soon get habituated. These women have in general good features, though hardened by constant exposure to the weather; their dress is of deer skin mostly of the Antelope, white and pliant which is fastened over the shoulders, belted round the waist and descends to their ancles, or to the ground, show them to advantage. The dress of the Men is very simple, a pair of long leggins, which come to the ground and would reach to the breast, are secured by a belt, over which the rest hangs down. Some few wear a shirt of dressed leather, and both sexes wrap a Bison robe round them. Their walk is erect, light and easy, and may be said to be graceful. When on the plains in company with white men, the erect walk of the Indian is shown to great advantage. The Indian with his arms folded in his robe seems to glide over the ground; and the white people seldom in an erect posture, their bodies swayed from right to left, and some with their arms, as if to saw a passage through the air. I have often been vexed at the comparison

The young men seldom marry before they are fully grown, about the age of 22 years or more, and the women about sixteen to eighteen. The older women who are related to them are generally the match makers, and the parties come together without any ceremony. On the marriage of the young men, two of them form a tent until they have families, in which also reside the widowed Mothers and Aunts. Polygamy is allowed and practised, and the Wife more frequently than her husband [is] the cause of it, for when a family comes a single wife can no longer do the duties and labor required unless she, or her husband, have two widowed relations in their tent, and which frequently is not the case; and a second Wife is necessary, for they have to cook, take care of the meat, split and dry it; procure all the wood for fuel, dress the skins into soft leather for robes and clothing; which they have also to make and mend, and other duties which leaves scarce any part of the day to be idle, and in removing from place to place the taking down of the tents and putting them up are all performed by women. Some of the Chiefs have from three to six wives, for until a woman is near fifty years of age, she is sure to find a husband. A young Indian with whom I was acquainted and who was married often said, he would never have more than one wife, he had a small tent, and one of his aunts to help his wife; Nearly two years afterwards passing by where he was, I entered his tent, and [found] his first wife, as usual, sitting beside him, and on the other side three fine women in the prime of life, and as many elderly of the sex, in the back part. When I left the tent, he also came out, and telling me not to laugh at him for what he formerly said of having only one wife and he would explain to me how he had been obliged to take three more. "After I last saw you a friend of mine, whom I regarded and loved as a brother would go to war, he got wounded, returned, and shortly after died, relying on my friendship, when dying he requested his parents to send his two wives to me, where he was sure they would be kindly treated and become my wives. His parents brought them to me, with the dying request of my friend, what could I do but grant the claim of my friend, and make them my wives. Those are the two that sit next the door. The other one was the wife of a cousin who was also a friend of mine, he fell sick and died, and bequeathed his wife to my care. The old women at the back of the tent are their relations. I used to hunt the Antelopes, their skins make the finest leather for clothing, although the meat is not much, yet it is good and sufficient for us; but now I have given that over, and to maintain seven women and myself am obliged to confine myself to hunting the Red Deer and the Bison, which give us plenty of meat, tho' the leather is not so good."

The old Indian (Sarkamappee) whom I have already mentioned, pointed out to me, a curious kind of polygamy. Besides his old wives, on the other side of the tent, sat three young women of about sixteen or eighteen years of age, whom about two months before, had been given to him for wives by their parents; I noticed that he treated them as if they were his daughters; he told me that they were placed with him on trust. "You must know [that] among us are families far more numerous and powerful, than other families and of which some of the relatives make a bad use of their influence, and oppress those that are weak, tho' as brave as themselves. Two of these young women are sisters and the whole three were betrothed to three young men; and would have been given to them, had not three Men of two powerful families who have each already four or five wives, demanded that these young women should be given to them; as their parents are not powerful to prevent this, these three young women have been given to me, and in my tent they will remain until this camp separates, and they go some distance, when they will be given to the young men for whom they are intended; And thus each of them will regard me as their father. He has always been a friend to the weak, and has thereby gained great influence.

Some time after, I met an old Warrior whom I had known for a long time, I spoke to him of what Sarkamappee had told me of the three young women in his tent, and that I had never known such a custom among the Indians of the Woods, and enquired if it was common among those of the plains. He said "it is not common, yet it happens too often; "Had one of those Men who wanted those young women come to Sarkamappee tent, and demanded them, what would he have done." "If any had been fool enough to have done so he would have shot him, as he would a Bear, and as careless of the consequences.

The grown up population of these people appear to be about three men to every five women, and yet the births appear in favour of the boys. The few that are killed in battle will not account for this, and the deficiency may be reckoned to the want of woollen or cotton clothing. Leather does very well in dry weather, but in wet weather, or heavy rains it is very uncomfortable, and as is frequently the case on a march, cannot be dried for a few days; it thus injures the constitution and brings on premature decay. Of this the

Natives appear sensible, for all those that have it in their power, buy woollen clothing.

The Indians of the Plains all punish adultery with death to both parties. This law does not appear to be founded on either religious, or moral, principles, but upon a high right of property as the best gift that Providence has given to them to be their wives and the mothers of their families; and without whom they cannot live. Every year there [are] some runaway matches between the young men and women; these are almost wholly from the hatred of the young women to polygamy. When a fine young woman, proud of herself, finds that instead of being given to her lover, she is to be the fourth, or fifth wife to some Man advanced in years, where she is to be the slave of the family, and bear all the bondage of a wife, without any of it's rights and priviledges, she readily consents to quit the camp with her lover, and go to some other camp at a distance where they have friends. In this case the affair is often made up, and the parents of the young woman are more pleased, than otherwise; yet it sometimes ends fatally. But the most of these elopements are with the young women given to be the third or fourth or fifth wife; in this case the affair is more serious, for it is not the father, but the husband that is wronged, and revenges the injury. If the young couple can escape a few months the affair is sometimes settled by a present of one or two horses; but if the young man is considered a worthless character, which is often the case, his life pays the forfeit of his crime, and if the woman escapes the same fate, her nose is cut off as a mark of infamy, and some of these unfortunate women have been known to prefer death to this disgrace. Yet some cases are very hard.

Poonokow (the Stag) was a son of the War Chief, Kootanae Appee. He was betrothed to a young woman, and only waited until the leather for a tent could be dressed to be a tent for them; during which, upon an insult from the Snake

z

Indians, his father collected his Warriors to revenge it, and
some of his sons accompanied him, among whom was
Poonokow; the expedition was successful and he proudly
returned with two fine horses one of which he intended for
his father in law. During the expedition, by present and
promises the father of another young man obtained her for
his son. A friend went off [to] his fathers camp to inform him
of the disposal of his intended bride, and [to tell him to] think
no more of her, but his love for her was too strong to follow
this advice. With his two horses he went near the camp,
but did not enter it; here his friend parlied with him, whom
he requested to send one of his aunts to him; she came, and
he explained to her how he was dealt with and that he was
determined to have his bride, tho' he should kill the man that
had her. His aunt seeing his resolution, promised to speak to
her and see what she would do, the young woman, as soon as
she was informed of it, went to him, and they both set off
for the Trading House on the Saskatchewan River, a journey
of six days. When near the House, he saw a number of
horses belonging to it, and not wishing to make his appearance on jaded horses, he unsaddled his own, and was putting
the saddles on other two horses, when an Indian who was
guarding them perceiving him and thinking he was stealing
them shot him thro' the belly. He knew the wound was
mortal, but had strength to reach the House, where he lay
down and related what had passed; The next morning
finding himself dying he took his sharp dagger in his hand,
and held it ready to plunge into the heart of the young
woman who had accompanied him and who was sitting beside
him; he said to her, "Am I to go alone; do you really love
me?" She burst into tears, held down her head, but said
nothing. "I see you do not love me and I must go alone,
tell my brother of what has happened and that I die by my
own hand," then with his dagger [he] cut his belly from
side to side, and with a hysteric laugh fell dead. The Traders

buried him. The Peeagan young woman remained two days
and as her fate appeared certain she was advised to go to
some camp of the Blackfeet, but she refused, saying, he told
me to go to his brothers, and to them I must go. And requesting a horse, which was given to her, with provisions,
she went to the camp of the brothers of her deceased lover,
and to them related the sad story; they pitied her, as they
knew the Man to whom she was given would kill her, and
told her so, and enquired what she intended to do. She said
I know what I ought to have done, but my heart was weak,
it is not so now; my life is gone, if I die by the hand of the
man to whom I was given, I shall die a bad death, and in the
other world wander friendless, and no one to take care of
me; your brother loved me, he is in the other world, and
will be kind to me and love me, have pity on me and send me
to him; an arrow thro' her heart laid her dead, for her soul
to rejoin her lover, and they buried her as the widow of their
brother. Whatever may be the idea of some civilized atheists,
the immortality of the soul is the high consolation of all the
rude tribes of North America.

The character of all these people appear[s] to be brave,
steady and deliberate, but on becoming acquainted with them
there is no want of individual character, and almost every
character in civilized society can be traced among them, from
the gravity of a judge to a merry jester, and from open
hearted generosity to the avaricious miser. This last character is more detested by them, than by us, from their precarious manner of life, requiring assistance from each other,
and their general character. Especially in provisions is great
attention [paid] to those that are unfortunate in the chace,
and the tent of a sick man is well supplied. (Note. We had
been hunting the Bison, and every horse was loaded with
meat, even those we rode on; returning we came to a few
Aspins, where everyone made a halt, and from the load of
every horse a small bit was cut and thrown on the decayed

root of a tree, to appease the spirit of a Man who had died there of hunger many years past, and all the conversation until we came to the camp, turned upon such an uncommon death). They have a haughtiness of character, that let their wants be what they will they will not ask assistance from each other, it must be given voluntarily and disgrace they cannot bear, especially in publick. Upon some business I was at one of their camp[s] with five men, in the afternoon as we were about going away, and talking with some twenty men, sitting on our horses, about furrs and provisions an Indian passed us on foot, apparently somewhat irritated at something that had happened in hunting, he had let his horse loose, and his little horse whip was at his wrist; his wife was outside the door of her tent as well as many other women listening to us. When he came to her he said something to her, and struck her gently with his whip; she entered the tent, and in an instant came out, and passed about three yards from him, then facing him, she said to him, you have before all these disgraced me, you shall never do it again; and drawing a sharp pointed Knife she plunged it into her heart, and fell dead. The whole camp seemed to regret her death, and blamed him for it; but not a word [was said] against her suicide, for a blow especially in public, is a high disgrace. She was carefully buried, and what belonged to her, broken or killed. Her husband was fond of her, he sat quietly in his tent all day, but at night went to some distance, and there [would] call upon and lament her. Before her death he was an active and successful hunter, but since then never went a hunting and lived upon any thing that was given him: After he had passed more than two months this way, his friends became alarmed, and represented to him that he was acting more like a woman than a man, and that he must become again the Warrior and the Hunter; and brought to him two young women, the cousins of his former wife, to be his wives; but he never regained his former cheerfulness. The affections of an Indian are deep, for he has nothing to turn them to other things.

The Natives of all these countries are fond of their children, they have faults like other children but are not corrected by being beat. Contempt and ridicule are the correctives employed, these shame them, without breaking their spirit. And as they are all brought up in the open camp, the other children help the punishment. It sometimes happens that Husbands and Wives separate, if they have children the boys are taken by the father, and the Mother brings up the girls, but even in this case the father always retains his rights to them until they are married.

CHAPTER XXIV

PEEAGANS CONTINUED

*Soldiers—Gamblers—Games—Resemblance of Indian language
to European—Religion—Belief in the Immortality of animals
—Passages to the other world—Morals—Medicine Bags—
Red Pipes—Influential men—Dreamers—Treatment of the
old—Numeration—Meals—Horse stealing—Attack on the
Spaniards.*

IN every large camp the Chiefs appoint a number of young
men to keep peace and order in the camp; in proportion to it's size; these are called Soldiers, they are
all young men lately married, or are soon to be married, they
have a Chief, and are armed with a small wooden club.
They have great power and enforce obedience to the Chiefs.

The Hunters having informed the old Men, that the
Bisons were driven to too great a distance for hunting, they
called the Soldiers to see that no person went a hunting until
the herds of Bisons came near of which they would inform
them; The same evening a Chief walked through the camp
informing them that as the Bisons were too far off for hunting
they had given orders to the Soldiers to allow no person to
hunt until farther notice. Such an order is sure to find
some tents ill provided. While we were there, hunting was
forbidden on this account. Two tents which had gambled
away their things, even to their dried provisions, had to steal
a march on the Soldiers under pretence of looking after their
horses; but finding they did not return were watched. In
the evening of the second day, they approached the camp,

with their horses loaded with meat which the Soldiers seized, and the owners quickly gave up; the former distributed the Meat to the tents that had many women and children, and left nothing to the owners; but those that had received the Meat, in the night sent them a portion of it. Not a murmer was heard, every one said they had acted right.

But the great business of the Soldiers is with the Gamblers, for like all people who have too much time on their hands, they are almost to a man, more, or less given to gambling day and night. All these the Soldiers watch with attention, and as soon as they perceive any dispute arise, toss the gambling materials to the right and left, and kick the stakes in the same manner; to which the parties say nothing, but collect everything and begin again; In the day time the game generally played is with a round ring of about three inches diameter, bound round with cloth or leather, and the game is played by two men, each having an arrow in his right hand: one of them rolls the ring over a smooth piece of prepared ground, and when it has rolled a few yards, each following it, gently throw their arrows through it to rest about half way on the ring, which now lies on the ground and according to the position of the arrows, one has gained and the other lost; each of these acts for a party who have an interest in the game; and it sometimes requires two or three hours to decide the game. They have also sometimes horse racing, but not in a regular manner; but bets between individuals upon hunting in running down animal[s], as the Red and Jumping Deer, or the killing of so many Cow Bisons at a single race. Another game is small pieces of wood of different shapes, which are placed in a bowl and then [thrown] up a little way and caught in the bowl, and according as they lay the game is won or lost; if the holder of the bowl has gained, he continues until he has completed twenty, or ten, as the number may be agreed on. He then hands the Bowl to his opponent to try his luck, or if during any part he has

lost, the Bowl is handed to the other, until the first has
gained the number agreed on, who is declared the final winner.
All games are played by either individuals for themselves or
as acting for parties; and I do not know any game where
parties act against parties, it would prove too dangerous,
altho' this is the case with the Indians of the low countries.

The Game to which all the Indians of the Plains are most
addicted, and which they most enjoy is by hiding in one of
the hands, some small flat thing generally the flat tooth of
a Red Deer, and the other party [has] to tell in which hand it
is. It is played by two persons but generally by parties. It
takes place in the early part of the night and continues a few
hours. It is played in a large tent; the opposite parties
sitting on different sides of the tent. In the hind part of the
tent the Umpire sits with the stakes on each side. Both
parties throwing their robes and upper dress off, and sit bare
above the belt, and each having chosen it's lucky man; the
Umpire shows the Red Deers tooth, which is marked to prevent being changed, he hides it in one of his hands, and the
party that guesses the hand in which it is begins the game;
it's lucky man showing he has the tooth, begins a song in
which his companions join him, he in the mean time throwing his arms and hands into every position; the other party
are all quietly watching all his motions. In a few minutes
he extends his arms straight forward with both hands closed,
and about six inches apart, and thus hold them until the
opposite party guess in which hand the tooth is; this is not
always immediately done, but frequently after a short consultation; if they guess wrong, the other winning party
continue with the same gesticulation and song as before;
until a good guess is made and the tooth handed to the lucky
man of the other party, and thus the game is continued until
one of them counts ten, which is game. When the guess is
made in which hand is the tooth, both hands are thrown
open. The Umpire now takes the stakes of the losing party

and places them on the side of the winning party, but keeps them separate. The losing party now hand to the Umpire another stake to regain the one they have lost. Thus the game continues with varied success until they are tired, or one party cannot produce another stake; in this case the losing party either give up the stakes they have lost to the winners, or direct the Umpire to keep [them] for the renewal of the game the next night. However simple this game appears, it causes much excitement and deep attention in the players. The singing, the gesticulation, and the dark flashing eyes as if they would pierce through the body of him that has the tooth, their long hair, and muscular naked bodies, their excited, yet controlled countenances, seen by no other light than a small fire, would form a fine scene for an Artist.

The stakes are Bison Robes, clothing, their tents, horses, and Arms, until they have nothing to cover them but some old robe fit for saddle cloths. Yet they have some things which are never gambled, as all that belongs to their wives and children, and in this the tent is frequently included; and always the Kettle, as it cooks the meat of the children, and the Axe as it cuts wood to warm them. The Dogs and horses of the women are also exempt.

The Languages of this continent on the east and north sides of the Mountains as compared with those of Europe may be classed as resembling in utterance. The Sieux and Stone Indian to the Italian. The Nahathaway and Chipaway with their dialects to the French. The Peeagan with their allies, the Blood and Black feet Indians to the English, and the northern people, the Dinnae, or Chepawyans to the German.

Of the several Tribes that hunt on the great Plains none of them have what we call a creed. Yet there is a general belief in some things, and to directly question them on their religion is of no use, as those that have lived long with them, know very well. Persons who pass through the country often think the answers the Indians give is their real sentiments. The answers are given to please the querist.

The sacred Scriptures to the Christian ; the Koran to the Mahometan give a steady belief to the mind, which is not the case with the Indian, his ideas on what passes in this world is tolerably correct so far as his senses and reason can inform him ; but after death all is wandering conjecture taken up on tradition, dreams and hopes. The young people seldom trouble themselves beyond the present time, but after thirty, their precarious life of hunting and war, the loss of parents, relations and friends with much spare time brings on reflection, and turns their thoughts to futurity. They all appear to acknowledge that there is one great power, always invisible, that is the master of life and to whom every thing belongs, that he is kind and beneficent ; and pleased to see mankind happy, but how far he is pleased to interfere with the concerns of Mankind, they are not agreed ; some think that his providence is continually exerted, that they can have nothing but what he allows to them, founding their arguments on his power and being the master of everything ; but the greater part believe every man to be the master of his own fortune, and that this depends on his own conduct. yet they all allow the Great Spirit to be the master of the seasons, and of the animals with every thing else, that is not under their control. but on all these things their ideas are very vague, and sometimes from their conversation they believe in fatality, which is no part of their belief as grounded on the ever varying visissitude of their lives. Living in the open wide plains, where everything is visible and can be brought within the range of their reason, they are free from the superstitions of the natives of the forests, and seldom address the Great Spirit but on public occasions as on going to War ; and for the herds of Bisons to continue to feed in their country or any epidemic sickness.

They believe there are inferior Beings to the Great Spirit,

under whose orders they act, that have the care of the animals
of the Plains and the Forests; but do not allow them the
power, or reverence, which the Natives of the Forests bestow
on their Manitoes. All the Natives of north America, from
Ocean to Ocean, however unknown to each other, and dis-
similar in language, all believe in the immortality of the
soul, and act on this belief. Although this heavenly belief
has not the high sanction of the holy Redeemer of mankind
who alone has brought life and immortality to light, yet
vague and obscure as it is, it is the mercy of the Almighty to
them. They have no ideas of a judgement in the other world,
with rewards and punishments, but think the other world is
like this we inhabit only far superior to it in the fineness of
the seasons, and the plenty of all kinds of Provisions, which
are readily got, by hunting on fleet horses to catch the Bisons
and Deer, which are always fat. The state of society there
is vague yet somehow the good will be separated from the
bad and be no more troubled by them, that the good will
arrive at a happy country of constantly seeing the Sun, and
the bad wander into darkness from whence they cannot
return. And the darkness will be in proportion to the crimes
they have committed.

Their morals appears to proceed from an inherent sense
of the rights of individuals to their rights of property, whether
given to them, or acquired by industry, or in hunting. All
these belong to the person who is in possession of them;
and which give him a right to defend any attempt to take
them from him. No man is allowed connexion with his
female relations nearer to him than his second cousins, and
by many these are held too near. Two sisters frequently
become the wives of the same husband, and [this] is supposed
to give harmony to their families. Among people who have
no laws, injuries will arise, without any authority to redress
them; this is felt and acknowledged, and most would willingly see a power that could proportion the punishment to

the offence, but to whom shall the power be given, and who would dare to take it, even when offered to him; not One. The Chiefs that are acknowledged as such, have no power beyond their influence, which would immediately cease by any act of authority and they are all careful not to arrogate any superiority over others.

When out on the Plains one of these Chiefs had rendered me several services, for which I had then nothing to pay him. On my return to the house, by the interpreter, I sent him a fine scarlet coat trimmed with orris lace, and a message that as I understood he was going to war, I had sent him this coat as a recompense for his services with some tobacco. But the interpreter, not thinking this homely message sufficiently pompous, on the delivery of the coat, told him I had sent it to him as being a great Chief and to be his dress on going to War as a Chief. He was surprised at such a message; and the next day, by a young man, sent it with the message to the Chief at the next camp, who not liking the tenor of the message, sent both to another camp, and thus it passed to the sixth hand, who being something of a humourist, sent it to a very old chief, who was not expected to live. He kept it, telling the messenger to thank the Trader for sending him such a fine coat to be buried in. Some time after, the Chief to whom I had sent the coat came in to trade and enquired if the message sent with the coat came from me; I told him the message I had sent, and that the coat was a recompense for his services. He was very angry with the interpreter, and told me not to employ him among his people as he was looked on as a pompous fool, and that his lies would cause his death, (which happened two years after;) he then related how the coat and message had been sent forward till it came to the old dying chief; and that the message as delivered by the interpreter had caused much conversation, as I am, as yet, but a young chief. Had the coat with such a message have been sent to the War or civil chief, they would have taken the

Coat, and laughed at the message, but for this I am not old enough. The consequence was, that I had to pay him the value of the coat in other goods. Even the War and Civil Chiefs have no authority beyond the influence of what their good conduct gives to them.

The natives of the forest pride themselves on their Medicine bags, which are generally well stocked with a variety of simples which they gather from the woods and banks of the Lakes and Rivers, and with the virtues of which they are somewhat acquainted. The Indians of the Plains, have none of these, and collect only sweet scented grasses, and the gums that exude from the shrubs that bear berries and a part of these is for giving to their horses to make them long winded in the chase. But these people must also have something to which they can attach somewhat of a supernatural character for religious purposes; and for this purpose they have adopted the Red Pipe, and Pipe Stem, and which seems to have been such from old times; for until the year 1800 they had always raised tobacco in proportion to their wants. When they became acquainted with the tobacco of the U States brought by the traders, which they found to be so superior to their own, that they gradually left off cultivating it and after the above year raised no more. The tobacco they raised had a very hot taste in smoking, and required a great proportion of bears berry weed to be mixed with it. The white people gave it the name of the devil's tobacco. As very few of them can find furrs to trade the quantity of tobacco they require, I enquired of them, why they did not . . .[1]

also for a medicine pipe there are certain ceremonies to be gone through. and a woman is not allowed to touch a medicine pipe; and their long pipe stems are equally sacred These are of three to more than four feet in length, and about three to five inches in girth, and well polished. Each re-

[1] A page of manuscript is here missing.

spectable man has from three to four of these pipes stems,
which are tied together when not in use and hung on a
tree; on removing from place to place the owner slings
them over his back and at the campment again hangs them up.

That equality among the Natives however strictly held,
does not prevent a great part from wishing to distinguish
themselves, in some manner and as there cannot be many
remarkable Warriors and Hunters, a few mix with other
tribes and learn their languages, and become acquainted with
their countries and mode of hunting.   Others turn Dreamers,
and tell what other tribes are doing and intend to do; where
the Bisons and Deer are most plenty; and how the weather
will be; and the boldest Dreamers point out the place of the
camp of their enemies, and what they intend to do   Some
shrewd men, by their dreams procure influence, and become
Chiefs.   And in general dreams are very useful for making
bargains, exchanging and buying horses, making marriages,
and giving advice, which in any other manner would not be
taken,—and dreams also indulges that innate love of mankind
for prying into, and predicting futurity.   If which they have
foretold come to pass they are accounted wise men, and if
it fails, it was only a dream.   Time often hangs heavy on
them, and for this gambling is their greatest relief.

The civilized man from very early youth is accustomed
to hear numbers spoken of from one to one Million; thus
fifty, five hundred, or five thousand, &c. are to him as units,
his mind gives no individuality to each unit that compose
the number be it of what it will.   But the Indian forms his
numbers of individuals, and appears to have no idea of numbers
independent of them.   Perhaps formerly. the uneducated
Shepherds, and Herdsmen obtained their ideas of numbers
in the same manner, and [I] have frequently been told of
Shepherds who could not by numbers count their Sheep in
his flock, but by his own way could quickly tell if there was
one missing.

The Nahathaway Indians count numbers the same manner as we do to the numbers of 100 which they call the great ten; and a thousand, the great, great ten; beyond which they do not pretend to number; and even of this they make no use, and any things, as of birds and animals that would amount to this number, they would express it by a great many. But the Indians of the plains count only by tens, and what is above two tens, they lay small sticks on the ground to show the number of tens they have to count and in describing the herds of Bisons or Deer, they express them by a great, great many, and the space they stand on; for numbers is to them an abstract idea, but space of ground to a certain extent they readily comprehend and the animals it may contain; for they do not appear to extend their faculties beyond what is visible and tangible.

The Peeagan Indians, and their tribes of Blood and Black-feet, being next to the Mountains often send out parties under a young Chief to steal Horses from their enemies to the south and west side of the Mountains, known as the Snake, the Saleesh and the Kootanae Indians. This is allowed to be honourable, especially as it is attended with danger and requires great caution and activity. But the country of the Stone Indians and Sussees are full from four to six hundred miles in the plains, eastward of the Mountans, and too far to look for horses; the Sussees content themselves with rearing horses, but the Stone Indians are always in want of horses which appears to be occasioned by hard usage. They are most noted horse stealers and where ever they appear in small parties, the horses are immediately guarded. They steal horses from other tribes, but frequently at great risque. Those who are near the trading settlements too often steal the horses of other tribes when they come to trade; and also those of the Traders, in doing of which they are very expert. When the Traders leave their stations to proceed with their furrs to the different depots to exchange for goods: the horses of the trading House are sent some few miles under the care of two or three Men well armed, to where there are plenty of good grass, water, and a wood of Poplar and Aspin, the latter to make a smoky fire to relieve the horses from the torment of the Musketoes and horse flies. One summer (I think 1802) a large camp of Stone Indians, had sent some young men to a Blackfoot Camp, who brought away about thirty horses, they were quickly followed to the Stone Indian camp, and about three nights afterwards, the Blackfeet young men took not only the greater part of the horses stolen from them, but collected as many more and drove them all off to their own camp.

This distressed the Stone Indian camp and as they knew the other camps were guarding their horses, they determined to steal horses from the trading Houses. Accordingly six smart young men were selected and sent to the Upper House on the Saskatchewan River,[1] a distance of five or six days journey. When within a few miles of the house they came to about fifty horses guarded by three men whose station was on a low bank that overlooked the place where the horses were feeding, all the mares had, as usual, the fore [feet] tied together with a leather thong to prevent them strolling about and more readily kept together. The Men kept strict watch, only one man slept at a time and in the night two of them walked among the horses well armed. Thus for six days they watched for an opportunity; during which time, with their Arrows they had killed three buck Antelopes.[2] They were now tired of waiting and were determined to try their

[1] Rocky Mountain House.

[2] Although it is probable that in one or two previous instances Thompson refers to the Prong-horned Antelope, *Antilocapra americana* (Ord.), it is certain that in this and in several succeeding instances, he actually refers to deer, usually *Odocoileus hemionus* (Rafinesque), under the name "antelope." I am informed by Mr. J. B. Tyrrell that Thompson's loose use of the word antelope is probably due to a lapse of memory, since in his original notes he used the word *chevreuil*, the name then in common use among the voyageurs for the Mule Deer. [E. A. P.]

fortune; In the afternoon when they perceived the Men
had dined three of them with the skins of the Antelopes and
their horns, disguised themselves to appear like deer, the
other three also, put horns on their heads of which there
were very plenty on the plains; the latter went behind the
horses and there entered among them and untied the feet of
the horses; those with the Antelope skins pretended to feed
as deer, and got among the horses for the same purpose, the
Men were deceived, but remarked it was the first time they
had seen the Antelopes feeding among horses. As soon as
the horses were all untied, the Indians gave a signal to each
other, with the lines bridled the best horses and jumping on
them as they were, horns and all, gave the hunting halloa,
and drove the whole of the horses off at a round gallop. The
men were so surprised that they could scarcely believe what
they saw, and before they could recover themselves to use
their guns, the whole of the horses were far out of shot.

The Stone Indians brought them all to the camp, and
were received with the praises of the men, and the dances of
the women.   Some time after at another trading House, in
the month of July, two of [us] went off to hunt and early
walked off to the Horse tent, on account of the flies, all the
horses were crowded round the smoke of the fires; we
saddled two of the best and rode off a few miles but the flies
were so numerous the horses were frequently for throwing
themselves on the ground to get rid of them, and seeing
nothing, we returned to the Horse tent, where we found the
three men in a violent passion and swearing with all their
might.   On looking at them, one of them . . .[1]
pass part of the summer at one of the trading houses.

In the latter end of August, he took his outfit for the
winter's hunt, and with his two horses carrying his traps and
baggage set off for his winter quarters. A few days after we
were surprised to see him return: he informed us that as he

[1] A page of manuscript is here missing.

2 A

proceeded on his journey the Horses with their load struck a wasp's nest and were severely stung by the wasps, that in running away and rolling themselves on the ground they had lost one of his steel traps and broke another, and spoilt some of his gunpowder, which he wanted to replace, and informed us this was not the first time he had suffered from them. The old man sat very serious smoking his pipe, and shaking his head, said " I can never get my Horses accustomed to the Wasps." When removing their Tents, the Men going before destroy the wasps and nest before the Women and Children come on.

I have already remarked the tribe of the Peeagans have their country along the east foot of the Mountains from the Saskatchewan southward to the Missisourie, and are the frontier people and their enemies on the west side of the Mountains must break through them to make war on their allies, who thus live in security in their rear. This station has given to this Tribe something of a chivalrous character and their war parties carry on their predatory excursions to a distance scarcely credible in search of their enemies, the Snake Indians. In the year 1807,[1] in the early part of September a party of about two hundred and fifty Warriors under the command of Kootana Appe went off to war on the Snake Indians ; they proceeded southward near the east foot of the Mountains and found no natives, they continued further than usual, very unwilling to return without having done something, at length the scouts came in with word that they had seen a long file of Horses and Mules led by Black Men (Spaniards) and not far off. They were soon ready and formed into one line about three feet from each other, for room to handle their Bows and Shiels, having but a few guns ; the ground was a rough undulating plain, and by favor of the ground approached to near the front of the

---

[1] It is apparent from another account by Thompson of this raid that this date should be 1787.

file before they were discovered, when giving the war whoop, and making a rush on the front of the file, the Spaniards all rode off leaving the loaded Horses and Mules to the war party, each of whom endeavoured to make prize of a Horse or Mules. They were loaded with bags containing a great weight of white stone (Silver) which they quickly threw off the animals on the ground; in doing which the saddle girths were cut, except a few, and then [they] rode off. I never could learn the number of the animals, those that came to the camp at which I resided were about thirty horses and a dozen mules, with a few saddles and bridles. The Horses were about fourteen hands high finely shaped, and though very tired yet lively, mostly of a dark brown color, head neat and small, ears short and erect, eyes fine and clear, fine manes and tails with black hoofs. The saddles were larger than our english saddles, the side leather twice as large of thick well tanned leather of a chocolate color with the figures of flowers as if done by a hot iron, the bridles had snaffle bits, heavy and coarse as if made by a blacksmith with only his hammer. The weight and coarseness of these bits had made the Indians throw most of them away.

The place this war party started from is in about 53° 20' N, and the place where they met the Spaniards conveying the silver from the mines is about the latitude of 32 degrees north a distance of 1500 miles in a direct line.

PART II

CHAPTER I

CROSS THE ROCKY MOUNTAINS

Cross the Rocky Mountains by the defiles of the Saskatchewan—
Build new Fort on the Columbia River—Animals—Salmon
—Drying of Salmon by the Indians—New Trading Post
established on McGillivray's River—Raid of the Peeagans
on the Trading Post—Winter in the Mountains—Leave
Trading Post.

I BELIEVE that I have said enough [about the country] on the east side of the Mountains; I shall therefore turn to the west side; I have already related how the Peeagans watched us to prevent our crossing the Mountains and arming the Natives on that side; in which for a time they succeeded, and we abandoned the trading Post near the Mountains [1] in the spring of 1807; the murder of two Peagan Indians by Captain Lewis of the United States, [2] drew the Peagans to the Missisouri to revenge their deaths; and thus gave me an opportunity to cross the Mountains by the defiles of the Saskatchewan River, which led to the head waters of the Columbia River, and we there builded Log Houses, [3] and

[1] This was an outpost from Rocky Mountain House, which appears to have been kept by Jaco Finlay on the Kootenay Plain, near the head-waters of the Saskatchewan river, in the winter of 1806–07, and perhaps also at an earlier date.

[2] This refers to an attack upon Capt. Meriwether Lewis of the Lewis and Clark expedition by the Blackfeet at Marias river, Montana, on July 27, 1806, when Lewis killed a couple of Indians. See Thwaites (ed.), *Original Journals of the Lewis and Clark Expedition*, New York, 1904, vol. v., pp. 223–7. [T. C. E.]

[3] These log houses were "Kootanae House," the first trading post erected by white men, as far as is now known, upon the waters of the Columbia

strongly stockaded it on three sides, the other side resting on the steep bank of the River : the Logs of the House, and the Stockades, Bastions &c were of a peculiar kind of a heavy resinous Fir, of a rough black bark. It was clean grown to about twenty feet, when it threw off a head of long rude branches, with a long narrow leaf for a Fir, which was annually shed, and became from green to a red color. The Stockades were all ball proof, as well as the Logs of the Houses.

At the latter end of Autumn, and through the winter there are plenty of Red Deer,[1] and the Antelope,[2] with a few Mountain Sheep :[3] the Goats[4] with their long silky hair were difficult to hunt from their feeding on the highest parts of the Hills, and the Natives relate that they are wicked, kicking down Stones on them; but during the Summer and early part of Autumn very few Deer[5] were killed, we had very hard times and were obliged to eat several Horses, we found the

river, ante-dating the first erected by an American trader, that of Andrew Henry on the headwaters of the Snake river, by more than three years. Simon Fraser had established trading posts on the Fraser river only the year before. Kootanae House was known to the North-West Company officers east of the mountains as " Old Fort Kootanae," to distinguish it from other posts established on the Kootenay river, south of the 49th parallel of latitude, one near Bonner's Ferry, Idaho, which is noted on Thompson's map, and a later one opposite Jennings, Montana. The chimney bottoms of the post are still to be seen upon Lot 7, Division B of Wilmer District of the Columbia Valley Irrigated Fruit Lands (as platted), about one mile north-west of the town of Athalmer, where the Columbia river leaves Lake Windermere flowing north, and just north of Toby Creek, but a quarter of a mile distant from the mouth of the creek. Thompson, in his survey notes of the Columbia river, says that the " due course " from the post to the junction of Nelson's Rivulet (Toby Creek) and Kootenay Rivulet is " N. 40° E. ½ m. or a little better." According to these survey notes, Thompson first selected a site on what is now Canterbury Point at the north-west corner of Lake Windermere, and completed a warehouse there, but afterwards removed to the site farther north because of lack of easy access to water. [T. C. E.]

[1] *Cervus canadensis* Erxleben. [E. A. P.]
[2] Not *Antilocapra ;* see note on page 368. [E. A. P.]
[3] *Ovis canadensis* Shaw. [E. A. P.]
[4] *Oreamnos montanus* (Ord). [E. A. P.]
[5] Mainly *Odocoileus hemionus* (Rafinesque). [E. A. P.]

RUINS OF KOOTANAE HOUSE, NEAR LAKE WINDERMERE, B.C.

(*Photograph: H. Riess, 1912*)

meat of the tame Horse, better than that of the wild Horse, the fat was not so oily : At length the Salmon [1] made their appearance, and for about three weeks we lived on them. At first they were in tolerable condition, although they had come upwards of twelve hundred miles from the sea, and several weighed twenty five pounds. But as the spawning went on upon a gravel bank a short distance above us, they became poor and not eatable. We preferred Horse meat. As the place where they spawned had shoal swift clear water on it, we often looked at them, the female with her head cleared away the gravel, and made a hole to deposite her spawn in, of perhaps an inch or more in depth, by a foot in length, which done, the male then passed over it several times, when both covered the hole well up with gravel. The Indians affirm, and there is every reason to believe them, that not a single Salmon, of the myriads that come up the River, ever returns to the sea : the shores of the River, after the spawning season, were covered with them, in a lean dying state, yet even in this state, many of the Indians eat them. At some of the Falls of the Columbia, as the Salmon go up, they are speared, and all beyond the wants of the day, are split, and dried in the smoke, for which they have rude sheds, and in their Houses, and often [they] dry enough to trade with other Tribes. When dried by the smoke of Aspin, or other woods of a summer leaf, I have found them good ; but dried by the resinous Wood of the Pine genus, the taste was harsh and unwholesome.

In my new dwelling I remained quiet hunting the wild Horses,[2] fishing, and examining the country ; two Canoes

[1] Probably *Oncorhynchus nerka* (Walbaum). [E. A. P.]

[2] Thompson, in an unpublished manuscript, gives the following account of these horses : " The horses all come from Spanish horses, which have very much multiplied, as every year the mares have a foal. There are several herds of wild horses in places along the mountains, especially on the west side of the mountains ; on the pine hills of Mount Nelson, these have all come from tame horses that have been lost, or wan-

of goods arrived for trade, on Horses, by the defiles of the Saskatchewan River ; half of these goods under the charge of Mr Finan McDonald [1] I sent to make a trading

dered away from tents where sickness prevailed ; they are always fat, with fine coats of hair. For the greatest part of two summers I hunted them, took several of them, and tamed them. Their feeding places were only about two miles from my residence. When I first made my appearance among them, they were in small herds of five to seven, sometimes of mares with a stallion, others were wholly of mares. Upon my approaching them, they appeared at a loss what to do ; they seemed inclined to run away, yet remained. Their nostrils distended, mane erect, and tail straight out, snorting and prancing about in a wild manner. I shot one of them, and they ran off. I went to the horse I had shot and passed my hand over the body to feel its body and condition ; by doing so my hand had a disagreeable smell, which washing my hand for two days with soap barely took away, yet when tamed this did not occur. We now agreed to try and run them down. For this purpose we took two long-winded horses and started a herd of five. They soon left us, but as these hills are covered with short grass, with very little wood, we easily kept them in sight. It was a wild steeple-chase, down hills and up others. After a chase of about four hours they brought us to near the place we started them. Here we left them frightened, tired, and looking wildly about them. The next day we took swift horses, and instead of following them quietly, we dashed at them full speed with a hunting holloa, forcing them to their utmost speed ; the consequence was, two of them fell dead, a fine iron grey stood still ; we alighted and tied his fore feet together and there left him. Following, we came to another horse, tied his feet and left him, we returned to the first horse. I passed my hand over his nostrils, the smell of which was so disagreeable that his nostrils and the skin of his head became contorted, yet when tame, the doing of this appeared agreeable. The next day we went for them on two steady horses, with strong lines, which we tied round his neck, put a bit in his mouth with a short bridle through which the lines passed, untied his feet, brought him to the house, where he was broken to the bit and to the saddle. They lose all their fat and become lean, and it takes about full two months to recover them to a good condition. When in this last state they are made use of to hunt and ride down wild horses, for strange to say, a horse with a good rider will always overtake a horse without a rider, wild or tame."

[1] This is the first mention in the text of this clerk of the North-West Company who accompanied Thompson on his first trip across the mountains, and whose name appears often in the rare and hidden annals of the Columbia river basin during the next nineteen years. He never advanced beyond the grade of clerk, but as such he was the first white man to visit many tribes west of the Rockies. He had been at Rocky Mountain House before Thompson's arrival there on November 29, 1806,

Post [1] at a considerable Lake in M⁰Gillivray's River ; the season was late, and no more could be done ; about the middle of November [2] two Peeagans crossed the Mountains on foot and and remained with him there during the winter. In the spring of 1807, he accompanied Thompson across the Rocky Mountains, and was with him while he was building Kootanae House at the headwaters of the Columbia river. On September 23, he went northward for another load of supplies, but returned with loaded horses on November 7. From that date he remained at or near the fort until June 9, 1808, when Thompson returned from his adventurous trip to Lake Kootenay. That summer he accompanied his chief eastward across the mountains ; and on his return westward he was given a portion of the trading goods, and sent southward down the Kootenay river. He had gone but a short distance down the river when his canoe was frozen in the ice, and he was obliged to return to Kootanae House for horses. With them he continued down to the falls, where he built a warehouse for the goods, and where he and his men spent the winter in two leather tents. During the winter he appears to have sent Boisvert and Boulard on a trip to Pend d'Oreille lake. In the spring of 1809, he crossed the mountains as usual with Thompson, and descended to Fort Augustus. On July 14, he began his return journey, and on September 8 he arrived at Pend d'Oreille lake. Here he spent the winter of 1809–10. When Thompson left that post in the spring, he sent McDonald up to Saleesh House on Clark's Fork ; and here he spent the summer, and probably also part at least of the following winter, varying the monotony of the fur-trader's life by joining the Salish Indians in a battle, fought some time in July, with the Piegan. Early in the year 1811, he appears to have gone with Jaco Finlay to Spokane House, where he was found by Thompson. After the union of the North-West and Hudson's Bay Companies in 1821, McDonald succeeded Donald McKenzie in charge of the Snake country trappers, and had evidently visited that district before. With Peter Skene Ogden in 1825 his name again appears as " avant courier " to the Klamath tribe of southern Oregon near Mount Shasta. Our last record of him is his written request to Dr. McLoughlin at Vancouver, in July, 1826, to be allowed to return across the Rockies, and his departure in September of that year with his family up the river from Kettle Falls. He intermarried with the Kutenai or Spokanes, and tradition connects his blood with some prominent families of Montana to-day. According to Ross Cox, who is our authority as to his personal appearance and characteristics, he was born at Inverness, Scotland. See Ross Cox, *The Columbia River*, London, 1832, vol. i. pp. 164–5. [J. B. T. and T. C. E.]

[1] Thompson's note-books show that McDonald's first trading station among the Kutenai was established in the autumn of 1808 (not 1807), when he built a small log warehouse just above Kootenay Falls.

[2] Thompson's memory of the exact order of occurrences has here failed him somewhat. His note-books show that on August 26, 1807,

came to the House, to see how I was situated; I showed
the strength of the Stockades, and Bastions, and told them
I know you are come as Spies, and intend to destroy us,
but many of you will die before you do so; go back to
your countrymen and tell them so; which they did, and we
remained quiet for the winter; I knew the danger of the
place we were in, but could not help it: As soon as the
Mountains were passable I sent off the Clerk and Men with
the Furrs collected, among which were one hundred of the
Mountain Goat Skins with their long silky hair, of a foot
in length of a white color, tinged at the lower end with a
very light shade of yellow. Some of the ignorant self
sufficient partners of the Company ridiculed such an article
for the London Market; there they went and sold at first
sight for a guinea a skin, and half as much more for another
Lot, but there were no more. These same partners then
wrote to me to procure as many as possible, I returned for
answer, the hunting of the goat was both dangerous and
laborious, and for their ignorant ridicule I would send no
more, and I kept my word.

I had now to prepare for a more serious visit from the
Peagans who had met in council, and it was determined to
send forty men, under a secondary Chief to destroy the
trading Post, and us with it, they came and pitched their
Tents close before the Gate, which was well barred. I had
six men with me, and ten guns, well loaded, the House was
perforated with large augur holes, as well as the Bastions,

while he was building Fort Kootanae, twelve Piegan men and two women
arrived at the fort, having been sent by Kootanae Appee to see what he was
doing. On September 26, twenty-three more Piegan arrived; and these
stayed for a week at the post, making themselves somewhat troublesome,
but there is no mention of a state of siege. On October 30, Thompson
says that two Piegan had left the fort, and that he believed a general
attack on the fort was contemplated; but no such attack was made.
The information received about this time of the destruction of Fort
Augustus on the Saskatchewan river by the Blackfeet would lend strength
to any report of the contemplated hostility of the Piegan.

thus they remained for three weeks without daring to attack us. We had a small stock of dried provisions which we made go as far as possible; they thought to make us suffer for want of water as the bank we were on was about 20 feet high and very steep, but at night, by a strong cord we quietly and gently let down two brass Kettles each holding four Gallons, and drew them up full; which was enough for us: They were at a loss what to do, for Kootanae Appee the War Chief, had publickly told the Chief of this party, (which was formed against his advice) to remember he had Men confided to his care, whom he must bring back, that he was sent to destroy the Enemies not to lose his Men: Finding us always on the watch, they did not think proper to risque their lives, when at the end of three weeks they suddenly decamped; I thought it a ruse de guerre, I afterwards learned that some of them hunting saw some Kootanaes who were also hunting, and as what was done was an act of aggression, something like an act of War; they decamped to cross the mountains to join their own Tribe while all was well with them: the return of this party without success occasioned a strong sensation among the Peeagans. The Civil Chief harangued them, and gave his advice to form a strong war party under Kootanae Appee the War Chief and directly to crush the white Men and the Natives on the west side of the Mountains, before they became well armed, They have always been our slaves (Prisoners) and now they will pretend to equal us; no, we must not suffer this, we must at once crush them. We know them to be desperate Men, and we must destroy them, before they become too powerful for us; the War Chief coolly observed I shall lead the battle according to the will of the Tribe, but we cannot smoke to the Great Spirit for success, as we usually do, it is now about ten winters since we made peace with them, they have tented and hunted with us, and because they have guns and iron headed Arrows, we must break our word of peace with them : We are now called upon to go to war with a people better armed than ourselves ; be it so, let the Warriors get ready ; in ten nights I will call on them. The old, and the intelligent Men, severely blamed the speech of the Civil Chief, they remarked, " the older he gets, the less sense [he possesses]." On the ninth night the War Chief made a short speech, to have each man to take full ten days of dried provisions, for we shall soon leave the country of the Bison, after which we must not fire a shot, or we shall be discovered : On the tenth night he made his final speech, and exhorting the Warriors and their Chiefs to have their Arms in good order, and not forget dried provisions, he named a place; there I shall be the morrow evening, and those who now march with me, there I shall wait for you five nights, and then march to cross the Mountains ; at the end of this time about three hundred Warriors under three Chiefs assembled; and took their route across the Mountains by the Stag River, and by the defiles of another River of the same name, came on the Columbia, about full twenty miles from me; as usual, by another pass of the Mountains, they sent two Men to see the strength of the House; I showed them all round the place, and they staid that night. I plainly saw that a War Party was again formed, to be better conducted than the last ; and I prepared Presents to avert it : the next morning two Kootanae Men arrived, their eyes glared on the Peagans like Tigers, this was most fortunate ; I told them to sit down and smoke which they did ; I then called the two Peagans out, and enquired of them which way they intended to return. They pointed to the northward. I told them to go to Kootanae Appee and his War Party, who were only a days journey from us, and delivering to them the Presents I had made up, to be off directly, as I could not protect them, for you know you are on these lands as Enemies ; the Presents were six feet of Tobacco to the Chief, to be smoked among them, three feet with a fine pipe of red porphyry and an ornamented Pipe Stem; eighteen inches to each of the three Chiefs, and a small piece to each of themselves, and telling them they had no right to be in the Kootanae Country: to haste away; for the Kootanaes would soon be here, and they will fight for their trading Post: In all that regarded the Peeagans I chanced to be right, it was all guess work. Intimately acquainted with the Indians, the Country and the Seasons, I argued and acted on probabilities; I was afterwards informed that the two Peeagans went direct to the camp of the War Party, delivered the Presents and the Message and sat down, upon which the War Chief exclaimed, what can we do with this man, our women cannot mend a pair of shoes, but he sees them, alluding to my Astronomical Observations; then in a thoughful mood he laid the pipe and stem, with the several pieces of Tobacco on the ground, and said, what is to be done with these, if we proceed, nothing of what is before us can be accepted; the eldest of [the] three Chiefs, wistfully eyeing the Tobacco, of which they had none; at length he said, You all know me, who I am, and what I am; I have attacked Tents, my knife could cut through them, and our enemies had no defence against us, and I am ready to do so again, but to go and fight against Logs of Wood, that a Ball cannot go through, and with people we cannot see and with whom we are at peace, is what I am averse to, I go no further. He then cut the end of the Tobacco, filled the red pipe, fitted the stem, and handed it to Kootanae Appee, saying it was not you that brought us here, but the foolish Sakatow (Civil Chief) who, himself never goes to War; they all smoked, took the Tobacco, and returned, very much to the satisfaction of Kootanae Appe my steady friend; thus by the mercy of good Providence I averted this danger; Winter came on, the Snow covered the Mountains, and placed us in safety: The speeches of the Indians on both sides of the Mountains are in plain language, sensible and to the purpose; they sometimes repeat a few sentences two or three times, this is to impress on the hearers the object of the speech; but I never heard a speech in the florid, bombastic style, I have often seen published as spoken to white men, and upon whom it was intended to have an effect. Although through the mercy of Providence we had hitherto escaped, yet I saw the danger of my situation. I therefore in the early part of the next spring took precautions to quit the place.

CHAPTER II

JOURNEY FROM KOOTANAE HOUSE TO RAINY LAKE HOUSE AND RETURN

Journey from Kootanae House—Arrive at the scource of the Columbia River—Animal of the tiger species—Woods— Carrying place at the lower Dalles River—Moss bread— Return journey—Lay up the canoe and proceed on horseback —Deserted by the guide—New guide, the Chief Ugly Head—Hardships of the journey—Bridging a river—Loss of sixty pounds of Beaver furr—Camp at McGillivray's River—Arrive at the scource of the Columbia—Descend the Saskatchewan—Reach Rainy Lake House—Destruction of kegs of Alcohol—Kill two Bison cows—Seepanee—Arrive at the Columbia River—Arrive back at Kootanae House.

BY my journal of 1808 I left the Kootanae House on the 20th of April,[1] proceeded to the Lakes, the scources of the Columbia River, carried everything about two miles across a fine plain to McGillivray's River,[2] on which we embarked, and proceeded down to look for Indians ; where the rocky banks somewhat contracted the Stream, the Water made a hissing noise as if full of small icicles ; on examining the surface, I found it full of small

---

[1] The men who accompanied Thompson on this expedition were Mousseau, Lussier, Beaulieu, and La Camble. Finan McDonald remained at the post.

[2] This is the Kootenay river of to-day. It was named by Thompson "McGillivray's in honour of the family to whom may justly be attributed the knowledge and commerce of the Columbia River." The "Kootanae River" of Thompson's note-books is the Columbia river of to-day. [T. C. E.]

whirlpools of about two inches diameter, all in motion, drifting with the current, and striking against each other, which occasioned the hissing sound. On proceeding to the Lake,[1] where we arrived on the 14th of May; after much loitering along the River looking for Indians, whom at length we found near, and at the Lake; the navigation of the River was very dangerous from violent eddies and whirlpools, which threatened us with sure destruction, and which we escaped by hard paddling, keeping the middle of the River. (Note. M[r] D[d] Ogden[2] of the Hudson's Bay Company relates a most sad instance of the effects of these whirlpools. He was proceeding down the Columbia River to Point Vancouver with eleven men in his Canoe, at the upper Dalles, a name given to where the River is contracted by high steep rocks, he ordered the Canoe ashore, he landed and advised them to carry, they preferred running the Dalles, the path is close along the River without wood, the Canoe entered the Dalles, was caught by a whirlpool, whirled round a few times beyond the power of the Men to extricate it, it approached the centre of the whirlpool, the end of the canoe entered it, and the canoe in a manner became upright, the men clinging to the Bars of the Canoe, and in this manner was drawn into the vortex of the whirlpool and went end foremost down into it; at the foot of this Dalle, not a vestige was seen, but the body of one man much mangled by sharp rocks. The rocks of these Dalles and of many parts of the River are of Basalt Rock, steep sided, of an irregular form, having many sharp Points and small Bays, under the former are strong eddies, and the latter too often [have] whirlpools; which the Canoe must cautiously avoid.)

On the 22nd April altho' in Latitude 50° 10′ N, the Willows and Gooseberry bushes had fine leaves; in hunting we were not successful, but killed an Animal of the Tiger

---

[1] Lake Kootenay.   [2] See note on p. 496.

species.[1] He was three feet in height on the fore leg, from the nose to the insertion of the tail seven feet and a half, the Tail two feet ten inches; very strongly legged with sharp claws, the Back and upper part of the Tail of a Fawn color, the Belly and under part of the Tail and it's tip white, the flesh was white and good, in quantity equal to the Antelope, the Liver was rich, and the two men that eat it, for several hours had a violent head ache, which passed away : The Indians say the habits of this Animal is to lie in covert, and spring upon the back of the Deer, to which he fastens himself by his claws, and directly cuts the back sinew of the neck, the Deer then becomes an easy prey : The Lake I have spoken of, is about three to four miles in width enclosed by ridges of high Mountains, upon which there was much snow. Along the River, in places are very fine woods of Larch,[2] Red Fir,[3] Alder,[4] Plane[5] and other woods : of the Larch, at five and a half feet above the ground I measured one thirteen feet girth and one hundred and fifty feet clean growth, and then a fine head. This is one of many hundreds. I could not help thinking what fine Timber for the Navy [exists] in these forests, without a possibility of being brought to market. The other Woods, fine Red Fir, Pine, Cypress, white Cedar,[6] Poplars, Aspins, Alders, Plane and Willows.

At the lower Dalles[7] we had to carry everything on the right side, up a steep bank of Rock, and among the debris of high Rocks, apparently rude basalt, the slope to the River

[1] Mountain Lion or Puma, *Felis oregonensis hippolestes* Merriam. [E. A. P.]

[2] *Larix occidentalis* Nuttall. [E. A. P.]

[3] Probably *Abies grandis* Lindley. [E. A. P.]

[4] *Alnus*. [E. A. P.]

[5] Probably Dwarf Maple, *Acer glabrum* Torrey. [E. A. P.]

[6] *Thuja plicata*. [E. A. P.]

[7] Kootenay Falls, Lincoln county, Montana, between Libby and Troy on the Great Northern Railway. The " brook " is Falls Creek, just below the falls. Thompson's description is corroborated to the letter by later travellers on this part of the regular Indian trail between Jennings, Mon-

Bank was at a high angle, and our rude path among loose fragments of rock was about three hundred feet above the River, the least slip would have been sure destruction, having carried about one mile, we came to a Brook where we put up for the night. Each trip over this one mile of debris took an hour and a quarter, and cut our shoes to pieces. The banks of the brook were about two hundred feet in height, with a steep slope of debris to descend, with not a grain of sand, or earth, on them, to relieve our crippled feet. From the brook we had one mile to carry to the River, to which we descended by a gap in the Rocks; the River had steep banks of Rocks, and [was] only thirty yards in width; this space was full of violent eddies, which threatened us with destruction and wherever the river contracted the case was always the same, the current was swift, yet to look at the surface the eddies make it appear to move as much backward as forward; where the river is one hundred yards wide and upwards the current is smooth and safe.

In the evening we came upon the remains of an Antelope, on which an Eagle was feeding. We took the remainder, it was much tainted, but as we were hungry, we boiled and eat of it; which made us all sick; had we had time to make charcoal, and boil this with the meat, the taint would have been taken from the meat. The next day we came to ten Lodges of Kootanae and Lake Indians. They had nothing to give us but a few dried Carp and some Moss bread, this is made of a fine black moss, found on the west side of the Mountains attached to the bark of a resinous rough barked Fir and also to the larch. It is about six inches in length, nearly as fine as the hair of the head; it is washed, beaten, and then baked, when it becomes a cake of black bread, of a

tana, and Bonner's Ferry, Idaho. The cañon at the falls is about one mile long, and terminates at a gorge where the trail is compelled to leave the river and picks its way along a dizzy slope of steep bed-rock. [T. C. E.]

KOOTENAY FALLS, MONTANA

slightly bitter taste, but acceptable to the hungry, and in hard times, of great service to the Indians. I never could relish it, it has just nourishment enough to keep a person alive. They informed us that a few days ago, forty seven Peeagans crossed the Mountains and stole thirty five of their Horses, in doing of which, the old Kootanae Chief killed one of them; thus is war continued, for want of the old Men being able to govern the young men.

May 14th. To this date we had the meat of a few small Antelopes, by no means enough to prevent us eating Moss Bread and dried carp, both poor harsh food; for the Carp were of last year's catch and old tasted; the water, from the melting of the snow in the Mountains, had risen upwards of six feet; and overflowed all the extensive fine meadows [1] of this country: We now began our return.[2] The several small camps we came to of Lake Indians all make use of canoes in the open season, made of the bark of the White Pine, or of the Larch, they serve for two seasons but are heavy to carry. The inner side of the bark (that next to the Tree), is the outside of the Canoe, they are all made of one piece, are generally eighteen to twenty feet in length by twenty four to thirty inches on the middle bar, sharp

[1] Known in later years as the Kootenay Bottoms. The Great Northern Railway from Bonner's Ferry, Idaho, north to Lake Kootenay in British Columbia, runs along and through this extensive flat, which is subject to overflow. [T. C. E.]

[2] Thompson now returns upstream to lay up his canoe somewhere near Bonner's Ferry, and to buy horses and proceed overland across this southern loop of the Kootenay river by the same trail as was used by Governor Simpson of the Hudson's Bay Company in 1841. This later became the much used line of travel by miners and pack trains when gold was discovered in the Kootenay district in 1863-64. It followed the bench lands north from Bonner's Ferry, and then turned north-east across "Sarvice Berry Hill" (Thompson's "very hilly country") to the valley of the Moyie river, close to Curzon Junction on the Canadian Pacific Railway; from there it ran along the Moyie river and lakes, across Joseph's Prairie (Cranbrook) to the Kootenay river below Fort Steele. [T. C. E.]

at both ends. We engaged two men with one of these Canoes to guide us over the overflowed meadows, and avoid the current·of the River which we knew to be unnavigable; to effect which we made several short carrying places over strips of land yet dry;   On the sixteenth we met two Canoes from whom we traded twelve singed Musk Rats,[1] and two shoulders of an Antelope: thankful for a change from Moss Bread which gave us all the belly ache.

On the nineteenth of May, learning the country was too much flooded for any of the several tribes of Indians around us, to come to us, I bought Horses, laid up my Canoe as the River was unnavigable to proceed against the current, and proceeded by land over very hilly country; I engaged a Kootanae Indian to guide us, and he, as well as myself endeavoured to procure another man, but none would undertake the journey.

On the twentieth we came to a large Brook, so deep and rapid, the light Horses could not cross it, we had to cut down a large Cedar Tree on it's banks, which fell across it; and became a bridge over which we carried everything; we had to take each Horse separate, and with a strong cord of hide, haul him across, we went up the bank and camped; our Guide went a hunting; in the evening he came to us without success, and we went fasting to sleep, for we were tired. Early next morning he killed a small Antelope, which was a blessing to us. Our guide now deserted us, and went back to the camp, this left us in a sad situation in these Mountains without provisions, or a guide; the melting of the Snow had made every Brook a torrent, and did not allow the usual paths to be taken, we prayed the Almighty to relieve us.

On the twenty second we waited with faint hopes for his return, when at ten AM I sent off two Men to the camp of the Kootanae and Lake Indians to procure another Guide, on their arrival, Ugly Head (so named from his hair curling)

---

[1] *Fiber z. osoyoosensis* Lord. [E. A. P.]

the Lake Indian Chief made a speech, in which he bitterly reproached them for want of a strong heart, and contrasting their cowardly conduct, with ours, who braved every hardship and danger to bring them Arms, Ammunition and all their other wants : calling upon them to find a man, or two, who would be well paid ; but none answered the call : the dangers of the Mountains at this season were too great, and too well known to them, and I was not aware of this until it was too late ; finding no answer given to his call on them, he said while I am alive, the White Men who come to us with goods, shall not perish in the Mountains for want of a Guide and a Hunter. Since your hearts are all weak, I will go with them ; he kept his word, and on the evening of the twenty fourth of May, he came with the two men, and I thanked God, for the anxiety of my situation was great, and was now entirely relieved, for I knew the manly character of the Lake Indian Chief, and justly placed confidence in him.

On the next day our Guide, early went off a hunting, but without success. We set off and came to a large Brook which we named Beaulieu (the name of one of my faithful men) here we had to make a bridge of a large Cedar Tree, and carry everything over, and crossed the Horses by a strong line. About 1½ PM, thank God, we killed an Antelope, and by boiling and roasting on the spit, made a hearty meal, for we were all very hungry ; the rest of the day was through pathless woods over debris of the Mountains to 8 PM, when we had to stop and lie down for want of light to guide us.

On the 26th day we as usual, set off very early, our Guide a hunting without success. We soon came to a deep River with a strong current overflowing the low grounds ; we went up it's rude banks ; our Guide went forward, and at 4½ PM came to us and told us, we can go no further, we must make a Canoe to cross the River,[1] as the Mountains are too steep.

[1] The Moyie river of the present day. The name Moyie is a corruption of the French *mouiller*, to wet, and was given by the trappers owing

Hungry and tired, with heavy hearts we set to work, and got the materials ready to put together the next morning; In the evening our Guide returned, quite undetermined what to do; the sharp Rocks had cut our Horses, they could be traced by their blood; On the 27th our noble Guide told us not to make a Canoe, but try the Mountains higher up the River, we set off over rude rocks and patches of pathless woods, both our Horses and ourselves weak and tired, at length we came to better ground and a path which led to a bold Brook, which our Horses could not cross, and we had to proceed over tolerable ground with small Cypress Woods; late in the afternoon we came to a Family of Lake Indians, of whom we got a bowlfull of small dried Trout, two pounds of dried Meat and four cakes of very clean, well made moss bread, by far the best we had had. We were very hungry, and with a keen appetite devoured the fish, the meat, and a cake of moss bread. Our Guide told us to camp for the night, and he would get information of the way through the Mountains, as usual. In a straight line we have come about ten miles to-day, with the hard work of full twenty miles.

On the 28th we set off very early, but soon came to over-flowed ground, and had to take to the Mountains climbing up the hills and descending them, to the overflowed pathless woods up to our middle in water, we made slow progress, to near Noon, when we stopped to refresh our Horses, our Guide telling us, that for the present we had passed the inundated Ground. We then had a path over tolerable ground to the evening, when we put up at a Lake from which the River comes; having marched fourteen miles in a straight line in nearly as many hours.

On the 29th we had to proceed up along the River to

to the moist conditions which Thompson describes. Thompson else-where calls it McDonald's river, after his clerk Finan McDonald. Governor Simpson of the Hudson's Bay Company called it the Grand Quête, after an Indian chief of that name. The lakes mentioned a little farther on are the Moyie lakes. [T. C. E.]

find a place where we could cross it, the country tolerable, but [covered with] much fallen wood; near noon our Guide killed an Antelope, thank God; upon which we made a hearty meal; we then proceeded and in the evening came to a place where the River was narrow, but the current very strong, we put up, and our Guide killed a Red Deer: which gave us provisions for three days. Early next morning we commenced cutting down large Cedars and Pines to fall across the River and form a Bridge to cross on, but the torrent was so rapid, that every tree we threw across the stream was either broken by the Torrent or swept away: as our last hope, a fine Larch of full twelve feet girth, standing twenty four feet from the bank was cut down, and fell directly across the River, but in falling the middle of the tree bended and was caught by the rapid current, the head was swept from the opposite bank, the butt end of four feet diameter was carried off the ground, as if it had been a Straw; our last hope being gone, and near noon, we desisted, and with our Horses proceeded up the River to the foot of a steep Hill, where the River was divided into five channels, the channel next the opposite bank having most of the water with it's headlong current, and on this side of it a pile of drift wood, which we name an Embarras: The Guide and one of the Men crossed; at the fifth channel swiming their Horses, they then threw down a number of Aspin Trees to form a Bridge to the Embarras, but all were broken, or swept away by the current. I had about three hundred pounds weight of fine Furrs which the water would injure, and I was at a loss what to do, the four channels were easily crossed to the Embarras, upon which we laid everything; we had now no alternative but [to] tie all up in small parcels, as hard as we could, to be hauled across by a Line of Bison hides, which in the water distends and becomes weak; a hempen line contracts in the water and becomes stronger; we thus crossed everything but the large parcel, which was about sixty pounds of Beaver, and the little Baggage of two of the men, the line too much distended broke, and the parcel [was] lost. We crossed swiming our Horses and thus thank kind Providence, crossed and got clear of this terrible River by sun set, and put up. The next day being fine we spread out everything to dry to 11 AM when we set off, and in the evening camped at McGillivray's River, having had a fine country all day. We now raised the bark of a large white Pine, of which to make a Canoe; this work took us a day and a half, when we crossed the River, and held on near it to Skirmish Brook,[1] at 3 PM, the rest of the day was spent in throwing Trees across the Brook for a Bridge but they were swept away. At sun set we felled a large Red Fir of full ten feet girth, this broke, but served our purpose though very hazardous, we all got across and camped at 8 PM.

June 3rd: Early set off and passed two large Brooks, as usual by throwing Bridges of Trees across them. We camped late, and heard distinctly a shot fired about one mile from us. Supposing it to be of Enemies, we passed a rainy night under Arms. The next morning our Guide examined all around for the tracks of Men, or Horses, but found none, he killed an Antelope of which we were in want; we marched to past 5 PM, when thank God, we arrived at the last crossing place of McGillivrays River; here we had to make a Canoe to cross it. On June the 5th by 5 PM we had all crossed to McGillivray's Carrying Place to the scource of the Columbia River. Here we bid adieu to our manly humane Guide, without whose assistance we could never have crossed

---

[1] This is the Wild Horse Creek of to-day, very prominent in mining days, emptying into the Kootenay at Fort Steele. Almost opposite to it, and flowing into the Kootenay river from the west, is his Torrent river, now known as St. Mary's river. The next stream crossed on the way northward, as he followed the east bank of the main stream, was Lussier (now Sheep) river, called after one of his men who had recently lost his baggage in crossing McDonald's river. Two other streams are mentioned by Thompson as flowing into the Kootenay from the east, namely, Bad river, now Bull river, and Stag river, now Elk river. [T. C. E.]

the secondary Mountains, we had come over; he descended
the River for his own Country which he would reach in two
days. The foregoing tedious detail, informs the reader what
travelling is in high hilly countries when the Snow is melting; the same Brooks which cost us so much hard work and
were crossed with danger, in Autumn have very little water;
and [are] almost everywhere fordable, the water not a foot
in depth. We were acquainted with the Kootanae Country
before us, and on the 8th came to Mr Finan McDonald,[1]
and four Men in charge of the Furrs traded in winter, they
have had also hard times, and have been obliged to eat all
the Dogs.

We set off for the Mountain defiles to the Saskatchewan
River, having killed a Horse for food; at the east end of the
defile we had laid up a large Birch Rind Canoe which we
put in good order; the Snow was much melted and the
upper part of the River a torrent of water, we had a Canoe
with three Men and a Chepaway Indian who had followed us
from the Rainy River as Hunter, he sat in the middle of the
Canoe, as ballast; We embarked with the rising Sun, and
merely paddled to give the Canoe steerage way for guidance,
the descent of the River is great in the Mountains and from
them, and [it] foamed against every rock, Snag or root of a
Tree in it's current. Near sun set we came to the Craigs,
which are about fifty feet of steep limestone, at the foot of
which, we put up on the beach, the Canoe unloaded, and
all safe on shore; as usual my share of the work was to light
the fire, while the Men got wood; everything being done
and the Kettle on the fire, I noticed the Indian sitting with

[1] According to his journals, Thompson reached his Kootanae House,
then unoccupied, on June 6, and thence continued down the west bank of
the river on horseback for about a day, when he decided to stop, and built
a canoe of the bark of a pine tree. The next day, just after starting in
his new canoe, he came to where McDonald and his own family were
camped, and they continued down the river together to the place where
they were to begin the crossing of the mountains.

his hands on his knees, and his head resting on his hands, supposing him to be ill, I enquired what was the matter with him. Looking at me he said, I cannot make myself believe, that from where we embarked in the Mountains we have come here in one day; it must be two days, and I have not slept. By my Journals, I found we had come one hundred and thirty two miles; the first part must have been at ten miles p^r hour, as for the last three hours the current was moderate, and we did not advance more than five miles p^r hour.

[We] embarked the Furrs, and with five men set off for the Rainy River House and arrived July 22, where we landed our cargo of Furrs, then made up an assortment of Goods, for two Canoes, each carrying twenty pieces of ninety pounds weight; among which I was obliged to take two Kegs of Alcohol, over ruled by my Partners (Mess^n Don^d McTavish and Jo McDonald [of] Gart[h]) for I had made it a law to myself, that no alcohol should pass the Mountains in my company, and thus be clear of the sad sight of drunkeness, and it's many evils: but these gentlemen insisted upon alcohol being the most profitable article that could be taken for the indian trade. In this I knew they had miscalculated; accordingly when we came to the defiles of the Mountains, I placed the two Kegs of Alcohol on a vicious horse; and by noon the Kegs were empty, and in pieces, the Horse rubbing his load against the Rocks to get rid of it; I wrote to my partners what I had done; and that I would do the same to every Keg of Alcohol, and for the next six years I had charge of the furr trade on the west side of the Mountains, no further attempt was made to introduce spirituous Liquors.

Near the head of the eastern defile, we had the good fortune to kill two Bison Cows; these animals often frequent the gorges of the Mountains for the fresh grass, water, and free[dom] from flies; but are careful not to be shut in by impassable rocks; and on being hunted uniformly make for the open country; yet when found in a narrow place I have seen the Bisons take to the rocky hills and go up steep places where they could barely stand, the Bison is a strong head-long animal. While proceeding up the River,[1] the strong current obliging [the] Men to track up the Canoes, I walked ahead for hunting, on a low point of gravel, I mortally wounded a Doe Red Deer, and as she was dying the Canoes came up, the Men began skinning her, and one man cut off her head, upon this the Deer arose and for half a minute stood on her feet, the Men became frightened, said she was a devil, and would have nothing more to do with her, I cut a piece of meat for my supper, put it in the Canoe, and marched on, when we camped, I expected my piece of meat for supper, but found they had tossed it into the River, and my servant said to the Men, " Does he wish to eat a piece of the devil, if he does, it is not me that will cook it." Instances of this nature are known to the Indians, who call them Seepanee, that is strong of life.

On the 21st we laid up our Canoes for the Winter; the Canoes rest upon their Gunwales, on logs of wood to keep them about one foot from the ground, the timbers are slightly loosened, to prevent the Birch Rind cracking with the frost. Pine Trees, in the form of the roof of a House, with all their branches, are placed over the Canoes to prevent any weight of snow lying on the bottom of the Canoe.

We had now a journey of ten days with horses through the defiles to the Columbia River. We had a Chepaway Indian with us for a hunter who killed a mountain sheep [2] in good condition: On the evening of the 31st October we arrived at the Columbia River; and found the Canoe we had laid up in bad order : In this journey we had plenty of provisions, the Hunter having killed two Goats, from the inside of the male, we had twelve pounds of soft grease; also a Bison Bull

---

[1] The Saskatchewan river.
[2] *Ovis canadensis* Shaw. [E. A. P.]

and two Cows. Having detained Goods for the cargo of the
Canoe, I sent off the Horses up the River with the rest; we
now, as usual, find a great change in the climate, on the east
side, hard frosts and deep snow, here on the west side the
grass is green, even all the leaves are not fallen; and our
poor half starved Horses will now recover their flesh, and
become in good condition, and be free from lameness. I
have noticed that we found the Canoe in bad order; rainy
weather came on and delayed us to the afternoon of the
2nd of November when we had the Canoe repaired, and
embarked the Goods for to winter at the Kootanae House
of last winter, where we arrived on the tenth of November,
and where we shall winter, please God.

CHAPTER III

WINTER AT KOOTANAE HOUSE

Goods sent to trade with the Lake Indians—Birds leave for the South—Mock Sun—Arrival of the birds—Meat Glaciers—Hunting Wild Horses—Measurement of the Rocky Mountains—Scource of Columbia River—Formation of storm clouds—Taking out winter trade of furrs in April—Arrive at Fort Augustus on the Saskatchewan.

AS the season is too late to proceed to the Saleesh Indians; Sent off Horses and Goods to the Lake Indian country :[1] all in safety, as the Snow on the Mountains is too deep for a war party to cross : at McGillivray's River a Canoe took the Goods, and the Horses returned with the Men in charge of them. Since the 10th Inst. (November) the wild Geese have been passing in great numbers to the southward, but too high for a shot, by the very latter end of the Month the Geese and most of the Ducks had left us for the southward but many Swans[2] and some Ducks remained in the two Kootanae Lakes (the scources of the Columbia) these Lakes do not freeze in the winter.

December 22nd. At 8¾ AM the Sun was clear, and the sky clear to the left of the Sun, but to the right a dense atmosphere about twenty degrees from the Sun, it's height about eight degrees, and it's breadth full ten degrees. In this a very bright halo was formed, at times it had the colours of the Rainbow, but of a deeper tint. In the clear sky nothing

---

[1] This was Finan McDonald's party mentioned in note on page 379.
[2] Trumpeter Swan, *Olor buccinator* (Rich.). [E. A. P.]

could be seen; about 9 AM the halo formed a mock sun fully equal in splendor to the real Sun, so that my Men called out there are two Suns, and no doubt a similar appearance caused the supposed appearance of two Suns in Thrace as related by Historians. This remained for about twenty minutes, when the mock Sun, began to lose it's splendor and in half an hour more was not to be seen; I had seen fine bright Halos, but never so perfect a mock Sun.

1809. January 5ᵗʰ. took a wood Canoe and went down to the little Lake, which had upwards of one hundred Ducks about one third of them Stock Ducks,[1] the finest of Ducks. I killed one Stock and three fishing Ducks, the first very good, the latter bad tasted, but the Canadian[s] eat them; after this I frequently killed one of these ducks for a change.

January 11ᵗʰ. Two Swans came, but being disturbed again left us. The Birds about us are, the bald headed Eagle,[2] a small Hawk, the Raven,[3] and Magpies[4] numerous: these with the Raven frequent the edge of the shore ice and make sad havoc among the small fry of fish. There are also some fine Woodpeckers[5] with scarlet heads and a rich plumage. As there was now plenty of shore ice of sufficient thickness, we made a Glacier for frozen meat. This is a square of about twelve feet, the bottom and the sides lined with ice; in this we placed one hundred and sixty Thighs and shoulders of Red Deer, and forty seven Thighs of Antelopes; this is necessary, for as soon as the fine weather comes on, the Deer of all species leave the low lands, and retire for fresh grass and shelter to the vallies of the high Hills. In these meat glaciers, a layer of Meat is laid on the ice, and then a layer of ice, and thus continued: when the warm weather comes on, it is covered with fine branches of the Pine,

[1] Mallard, *Anas platyrhynchos* Linn. [E. A. P.]
[2] *Haliæetus leucocephalus alascanus* Townsend. [E. A. P.]
[3] *Corvus corax principalis* Ridgway. [E. A. P.]
[4] *Pica pica hudsonia* (Sabine). [E. A. P.]
[5] *Phlœotomus pileatus picinus* (Bangs). [E. A. P.]

the ice is found so much thawed that the pieces are joined together, the meat is also thawed, but remains very sound, though [it] has lost it's juice and is dry eating. I have even seen the meat covered with a kind of moss but not in the least tainted.

On the 17th the Kootanae Hunters brought six Red Deer, which I had split and dried for the summer provisions. On the 18th a number of handsome birds[1] made their appearance somewhat larger than a Sparrow, their head, breast and back of a bright brick red, the rest of a blueish colour, the beak short and strong; three foreclaws and one hind claw. I could not learn on what they fed The Kootanaes went a hunting the wild Horses and brought eight near to us, the next day my Men and the Indians set off and had a hard day's chase, but caught none of them. I have often hunted and taken them, it is a wild rough riding business, and requires bold surefooted Horses. For the wild Horses are regardless of danger, they descend the steep sides of Hills with as much readiness as racing over the finest ground, they appear to be more headlong than the Deer. A dull mere pack Horse was missing, with a man I went to look for him, and found him among a dozen wild Horses, when we approached, this dull Horse took to himself all the gestures of the wild Horses, his Nostrils distended, mane erect, and tail straight out; we dashed into the herd and flogged him out; An Indian (half breed) has now eighteen of these wild Horses, which he has caught and tamed; and we also caught three of them.

The whole of the latter part of this month (January) fine mild weather and the Swans frequently arriving. Unfortunately these Indians, like all others, when provisions are plenty, and readily procured; are much addicted to gambling and thus lose several days and nights. The water for the last half of this month has been rising. The month of

[1] Gray-crowned Rosy Finch, *Leucosticts tephrocotis* Swainson. [E. A. P.]

February passed without anything remarkable, the weather variable, mostly mild with slight frosts, many Swans about us, but they keep too far from the shores; we took a few wild Horses. On weighing [we] found the average weight of the thigh of a Red Deer to be thirty-two pound, and the whole of the meat 160 to 170 lbs.

March 10. One of my Men killed a Swan, and I killed another, it was in good condition but not fat, and weighed thirty two and a half pounds. Several flocks of Geese,[1] those we have killed are not fat. For the first time a Swan of the lesser species [2] was killed.

To ascertain the height of the Rocky Mountains above the level of the Ocean had long occupied my attention, but without any satisfaction to myself. I had written to the late Honble W^m McGillivray to buy for me a Mountain Barometer for the measurement of these mountains; he procured for me a Mountain Barometer which he placed in the hands of Mr John McDonald of Gart[h], a Partner, with a promise to take great care of it and deliver it to me in good order, but he tossed it on the loaded Canoes, where it was tossed about, and when he brought it to me at the foot of the Mountains, the case was full of water, and the Barometer broken to pieces. M^r W^m McGillivray bought for me another Barometer, which unfortunately was delivered to the same person, who made the same promises, with the same performance; seeing it was hopeless to procure a Barometer I had to follow the best methods of measurement which circumstances allowed. By a close estimation of the descent of the Columbia River from it's scource to the sea I found it to be 5960 feet (including it's Falls) in 1348 miles, being an average of four feet five inches p^r Mile. Let the descent at the second Kootanae Lake [3]

---

[1] *Branta canadensis* (Linn.). [E. A. P.]
[2] Whistling Swan, *Olor columbianus* (Ord). [E. A. P.]
[3] Lake Windermere of the present day; its elevation is 2,700 feet above sea-level. [T. C. E.]

be 5900 [feet] above the level of the sea; here was one
step gained, and the fine plains on the east side of this Lake
enabled me geometrically to measure the height of the
secondary Mountains; due east of me were a chain of bare
steep Mountains, on which no snow lodged, and destitute
of vegetation; to the west was the rude pyramid of Mount
Nelson [1] (for so I named it); the Base Line was carefully
measured, and the Angles of the heights taken with the
Sextant in an artificial horizon of Quicksilver. By this method
I found the height of Mount Nelson to be 7223 feet above
the level of the Lake, which gave 13,123 feet above the
Pacific Ocean; of the secondary Mountains on the east side,
of one Peak 10,889 feet, and another 10,825 feet above the
level of the sea, but for the primitive Mountains I could not
find a place from which to obtain a measurement and be in
safety; but 5000 feet may safely be added to the height of
Mount Nelson to give the height of the primitive Mountains.
At the greatest elevation of the passage across the Mountains
by the Athabasca River, the point by boiling water gave
11,000 feet, and the peaks of the Mountains are full 7000 feet
above this passage, and the general height may be fairly taken
at 18,000 feet above the Pacific Ocean.[2] Major Long of the
United States Engineers in his topographical Survey, under
the orders of the Executive in the Map of his Survey, places
the ancient Ocean at a level of 6000 feet above the level of
the present sea; and the highest of the Mountains (Latitude 38° North) to be 11,000 feet above the present sea of
the Atlantic, but he has not given us any data for the above

[1] Still known officially as Mount Nelson, but locally as Mount Ham-
mond. Thompson acquired a great admiration for this peak, which is
directly west of his Kootanae House; the entire Selkirk range is called
the Nelson Mountains on his map. The altitude of Mount Nelson by
aneroid barometer is given by A. O. Wheeler (*The Selkirk Mountains*,
Winnipeg, 1902, p. 128) as 12,125 feet. [T. C. E.]

[2] The height of the summit of Athabaska Pass is 6,025 feet, and the
highest peak near the pass is 9,000 feet above sea-level.

assumed levels, on his Map.   Southward of the Latitude of
47° north I am not acquainted with the Rocky Mountains.
At the foot of the above steep bare measured Mountains is
the scource of the Columbia River, it is a Lake[1] of nine Miles
in length by 1⅓ miles in width, it's direction nearly due south
and north, it receives no Water from the east, nor from the
high rolling lands from Mount Nelson on the West, but
appeared wholly supplied by springs in the Lake, it appeared
to have always the same level; and from it's north end it
sends out a Brook which forms a second Lake, from which I
measured the Mountains. This River is perhaps the only
River that is navigable from the sea to it's utmost scource.
On the steep, bare, sides of these Mountains I twice saw the
first formation of the clouds of a Storm. Its first direction
was from the Pacific Ocean, eastward up the valley of the
lower Columbia River, and McGillivray's River, from which
the Hills forced it from east to north; the Sun was shining
on these steep Rocks when the clouds of the Storm entered
about 2000 feet above the level ground; in large revolving
circles, the northern edge of the circle behind cutting
in it's revolution the centre of the circle before it, and
thus circle within circle for nearly twenty miles along these
high Hills until the clouds closed on me, and all was
obscurity: it was a grand sight, and deeply rivetted my
attention.

  April. A month of summer weather, in the very beginning of this month all the birds were laying Eggs. The
Rooks [were] in flocks; the grass green, and the Woods with
young leaves: On the 17th, in two middle sized Canoes,
and a few loaded Horses, began descending the River with
the Furrs and 720 lbs of dried provisions to place them

---

[1] The Upper Columbia lake. Its elevation is practically the same
as that of Lake Windermere, 2,700 feet above the level of the sea. No
stream enters this lake directly from the mountain ranges; its supply
comes by underground channels from the Kootenay river.

beyond the low lands, which will soon be overflowed; as the Snow on the high Hills is fast melting, for although our Latitude is $50\frac{3}{4}$ degrees north yet the climate is as mild as the Latitude of 42 degrees on the east side of the Mountains : and this month was spent in getting the furrs and provisions to a safe place, and making a strong hoard in a steep bank of earth, to place all our lumber and baggage not required : everything was now Summer and the water overflowing the low grounds. We were every day busy with taking the Horses down the River, the Men were too few to manage them, and where the country was rude could only take half of them in a day : In the Canoe I had made a shift to maintain myself and those with me; but the men in charge of the Horses killed three for food, of which only two were eatable; We had now arrived at the Mountain Carrying Place, and had to find, and raise Birch Rind to make a Canoe at the other end, this was a scarce article, plenty of it, but too thin, and it occupied two days to find enough. In the afternoon of June 9th, we left the Columbia River, and entered the defiles of the Mountains, each two men had five loaded Horses in charge, each horse carrying two packs each of seventy five pounds; but as all these defiles have a small River running through them, which is constantly traversing the defile from side to side, it has to be continually crossed; we were too late, the water had risen, and the Horses could not be kept following the Men in charge, so that they often crossed swiming and wetted the Furrs.

On the evening of the 18th, we had passed the defiles, and were on the head waters of the Saskatchewan River, where it is barely navigable with care : here I had my two Canoes of last Autumn, (which had been carefully laid up) brought and put in good order. As the weather was rainy we had to lose time in drying the Furrs ; and it was near noon on the 21st June [when] we got all ready and embarked the Furrs with five men to each Canoe. On the 24th we arrived at Fort Augustus on the Saskatchewan; where everything was put in good order assisted by Mr James Hughes who is in charge of the place. On the 27th of June early, under the care of Parenteau, the Guide [I] sent off the two Canoes for the Rainy River House; there to discharge the Furrs and return with merchandise.

CHAPTER IV

ESTABLISH TRADE RELATIONS WITH
THE SALEESH INDIANS

Start on return journey to the Mountains—Send horses back and embark in canoes—Geology of the defiles of the mountains—Arrive at the Columbia River—Canoes laid up at McGillivray's River—Set off on horses for Saleesh River—Arrive at Saleesh River—Establish a trading post on the Saleesh River—Build a store house—Build a dwelling house—A journey to discover a new crossing place in the mountains—Meet a camp of Indians—Arrive back at Saleesh House—Set off to meet Merchandise from Rainy Lake—Reach McGillivray's River—Return to Saleesh House—Want of food—Finish Houses—Temperature on the west side of Rocky Mountains—Hunting for beaver and birch rind—Mr Coulter killed by the Peeagans—Meet tents of Saleesh Indians—Arrive back at Saleesh camp—Character of country—Morality of Saleesh Indians—Saleesh Indians go to war on the Peeagans—Peeagans defeated.

JULY 14th. Under the charge of Mr Finan McDonald sent a Canoe off for the defiles of the Mountains, it's cargo four pieces of Merchandise: weighing 320 lbs. four, nine gallons kegs of greese (the melted fat of the Bison) and five bags of Pemmican, each of ninety pounds, with five men, a less number could not stem the current. With two men and Horses I went by land, but the woods had been lately burned, the path could not be kept, I therefore sent a Man with the Horses back to Fort Augustus to Mr Hughes, and embarked in the Canoe. The strength of the current obliged us to make constant use of the tow line, in a few places to make a change of labor, we went up with Poles, this is hard work, and puts water in the Canoe. Thus we continued to the 9th day of August, hunting for a livelihood, killing a Bull Bison (there were no Cows) a Red Deer, or a Mountain Sheep. So that we did very well for Provisions: At the east end of the defiles, the banks are of sand Stone, and make excellent grindstones. There is also much petrified wood; from many places of the banks a white silicious water was trickling which petrifies everything it comes on, and forms layers of sandstone, the whole well deserves the attention of the geologist, for nature acts on a great scale : none of the countries have ever been inspected by a regular geologist ; and it is a strange fact that hot springs, so common in Europe, in the great extent of my travels have never been seen by me, nor do the Indians know of any.[1]

Having carefully laid up our Canoe, we went through the defiles with our Horses, and on the 13th of August arrived, thank God, all well at the Columbia River ; here were two Canoes, which we had laid up, and which we now put in order ; and proceeded up the River, and to the head Lake, the scource of the Columbia River, from which there is a good Carrying Place[2] of two miles to M'Gillivray's River, course due South.

We were fortunate enough in hunting to secure provisions and a few tolerably good Salmon were speared in the lower Lake. Late in the afternoon of the 20th we embarked on M'Gillivray's River, and went down it, safely over the Rapids and Falls, to the Road[3] to the Saleesh River, on the

[1] It is remarkable that Thompson did not hear of the hot springs which are situated a few miles from his Kootanae House, near the lower end of Upper Columbia lake.

[2] This is Canal Flat of the present day. [T. C. E.]

[3] Thompson has come from the mouth of Blaeberry Creek on the Columbia by his regular route, up that river to Columbia lake, across the portage, and then down the Kootenay river. He now lays up his

COLUMBIA RIVER, BELOW LAKE WINDERMERE, B.C.

(*Photograph: G. M. Dawson, 1883*)

evening of the 29th instant : As we have now to proceed with Horses only ; laid up the Canoes for the winter ; and arranged everything to be transported by Horses to the Saleesh River. The Latitude of this remarkable place is 48° . 42¾' N. Longitude 116° . 0' . 8" West of Greenwich

On my arrival here, I had sent off M[r] Finan M[c]Donald and a man to follow the road to the Saleesh River, and find the camp of those Indians, to bring Horses and help us through the River. On the 5th of September, sixteen men with twenty five Horses arrived, they brought us lines to tie the loads on the Horses : they appeared a mild intelligent race of men ; in whom confidence could be placed : they lent to us fourteen Horses, which we loaded, and with those we had ; set off ; we went S 15 E 3 Miles to the foot of a high bank,[1] so steep that the Horses often rolled down, at length all got up ; which took us four and a half hours ; we then went five miles to a Brook, and put up ; the Road and Country good, the former often too narrow for our loaded Horses, and we had to cut down many small trees.

Sept[r] 7th we advanced sixteen and a half miles, crossed a large Brook three times from it's windings, the Woods of several kinds of Firs and Pines, with plenty of Cedar, the ground good and level : September 8th. Having gone one Mile we crossed a fine brook of fifteen yards in width ; easy current and deep, but had good fording places : we went on six miles to a Rill, which we followed for near two miles ;

canoes near Bonner's Ferry, Idaho, close to the place where he had landed and met the camp of Indians on May 8 the year before. This trail or " road " crossed the divide between Deep Creek flowing into the Kootenay river, and Pack river flowing into Pend d'Oreille lake, and reached the lake a little east of Sand Point. [T. C. E.]

[1] This very steep hill is fresh in the memories of those who have travelled this trail ; it is about four miles south of Bonner's Ferry, Idaho. The " brook " five miles farther on is Brown's Creek, and the large brook crossed three times is Deep Creek. Pack river is the " fine brook fifteen yards in width " ; and the " rill " is Mud Slough entering Lake Pend d'Oreille. [T. C. E.]

and came to a Lake;[1] here Canoes met us, made of Pine Bark, and the Indians embarked twenty pieces of Goods and Baggage, they advanced SE. about five miles, when the wind obliged them to put ashore; and we also camped; to day we have killed four geese and one crane,[2] all good.

The next day the Canoes set off, but the wind rising we had to take part of the cargo's of the Canoes on the Horses, at 2 PM, thank God, we arrived all well at the Saleesh River; here we were met by fifty four Saleesh Indians; Twenty Three Skeetshoo; and four Kootanae Indians, in all eighty men, and their families; they made us an acceptable present of dried Salmon and other Fish, with Berries, and the meat of an Antelope. The next day with two Indians [I] went to look for a place to build a House for trading; we found a place, but the soil was light, and had no blue clay which is so very necessary for plaistering between the Logs of the House and especially the roofing; as at this time of year, the bark of the Pine Tree cannot be raised to cover the Roof, for want of which, we had an unco[mfo]rtable House. We removed to the place and set up our Tents and a Lodge.[3] On the 11th we made a scaffold to secure the provisions and goods, helved our Tools ready to commence building; our

[1] This is Lake Pend d'Oreille. Here the trail divided, one branch leading westward (of which we shall learn later), and the other eastward to the Flathead country along the line of the present Northern Pacific Railway. Thompson, with some of his party, became the guests of the Indians in their canoes; but the others followed the trail eastward along the shore of the lake, and on September 9 at 2 P.M. they arrived at the mouth of the Saleesh (now Clark's Fork) river. [T. C. E.]

[2] Probably *Grus mexicana* (Müll.). [E. A. P.]

[3] This is Thompson's "Kullyspell House," built on a point extending into Lake Pend d'Oreille between Hope and Clark's Fork stations on the Northern Pacific Railway, and near the mouth of Clark's Fork river. Coues identified it with Hodgkins Point (see *New Light*, p. 673). This trading post was maintained for only a few years, although it was on the direct road between Spokane House and the Flathead Fort. Thompson refers to it in this text as "Saleesh House," but it must not be confused with the house of that name noted on his map, of which we shall learn later. [T. C. E.]

first care was a strong Log building for the Goods and Furrs, and for trading with the Natives. Our arrival rejoiced them very much, for except the four Kootanaes their only arms were a few rude lances, and flint headed Arrows. Good bowmen as they are, these arrow heads broke against the Shield of tough Bison hide, or even against thick leather could do no harm; their only aim was the face: these they were now to exchange for Guns, Ammunition and Iron headed arrows, and thus be on an equality with their enemies, for they were fully their equals in courage: but I informed them, that to procure these advantages they must not pass days and nights in gambling, but be industrious in hunting and working of Beaver and other furrs, all which they promised: some few distant Indians, hearing of our arrival, came with a few furrs, but took only iron work for them; everything else they paid no attention to, even the women preferred an awl or a needle to blue beads, the favorite of the sex for ornament. All those who could procure Guns soon became good shots, which the Peeagan Indians, their enemies in the next battle severely felt; for they are not good shots, except a few; they are accustomed to fire at the Bison on horseback, within a few feet of the animal, it gives them no practice at long shots at small marks. On the contrary, the Indians on the west side of the Mountains are accustomed to fire at the small Antelope at a distance of one hundred and twenty yards, which is a great advantage in battle, where everyone marks out his man.

On the 23rd we had finished the Store House. To make the roof as tight as possible, which was covered with small Logs, we cut long grass and work[ed] it up with mud, and filled up the intervals of the small logs which answered tolerable well for Rain, but the Snow in melting found many a passage; in this manner we also builded our dwelling House; and roofed it, the floors were of split Logs, with the round side downwards, notched so as to lie firm on the Sleepers,

and made smooth with the Adze; our Chimneys were made
of stone and mud rudely worked for about six feet in height
and eighteen inches thick, the rest of layers of grass and
mud worked round strong poles inserted in the stone work,
with cross pieces, and thus carried up to about four feet
above the roof; the fire place is raised a little, and three to
four feet in width by about fifteen inches in depth. The
wood is cut about three feet in length, and placed on the end,
and as it costs nothing but the labor of cutting we are not
sparing of it :

September 27th. In order to examine the Country along
the River below us, with four Horses, one of my Men, by
name Beaulieu and an Indian Lad, set off, my view was to
see if we cannot change our Route to cross the Mountains,
as at present we are too much exposed to the incursions of
the Peeagan Indians; we found the country along the River
of a rich soil well clothed with grass, as low meadows; the
River about three hundred and fifty to four hundred yards
wide, the current moderate, and many Fowl, the most
numerous, was the Brent Goose,[1] the smallest of the species
of wild goose, but equal to the others in flavor and taste.
On the 29th we came to a Fall of the River, the carrying
place only twenty yards. September 30th. As usual went
down along the River, keeping mostly in the Woods: for
firm ground. The Red Fir (from the color of the bark) is of
very fine growth, tall and numbers of eighteen feet girth,
some few were more, with the white Fir and Pine, Birch,
Poplar and Aspin. The Hills distant and not high. At
Noon we came to where the River is much expanded;[2] here

---

[1] *Branta c. hutchinsi* (Rich.). [E. A. P.]

[2] This is about opposite the town of Cusick in the State of Washington.
Thompson followed the north shore of the lake from his Kullyspell House
to the mouth of Pack river (Kootenay Landing), and then continued
westward along the north bank of the Pend d'Oreille lake and river
to the special habitat of the Calispell Indians of to-day. Here the Pend
d'Oreille river and valley widen for a distance of about ten miles.
[T. C. E.]

we saw the Tents of a few Indians, our Indian called to them, they came with a Canoe, and crossed him; he soon returned, and pine bark canoes with six Men, two Women and three Boys came to us. As usual an old Man made a short speech, and made a Present of two cakes of root bread (not moss) twelve pounds of Roots,[1] two dried Salmon, and some boiled Beaver Meat which I paid for in Tobacco; These Roots are about the size of a Nutmeg, they are near the surface, and [are] turned up with a pointed Stick, they are farinaceous, of a pleasant taste, easily masticated, and nutritive, they are found in the small meadows of short grass, in a rich soil, and a short exposure to the Sun dries them sufficiently to keep for years. I have some by me which were dug up in 1811 and are now thirty six years old (1847) and are in good preservation. I showed them to the late Lord Metcalfe who eat two of them, and found them something like bread; but although in good preservation, they, in two years lost their fine aromatic smell. These poor people informed me there were plenty of Beaver about them and the country, but they had nothing but pointed Sticks to work them, not an axe among them. I enquired of the Road before us, they said it was bad for Horses; then how is this River to where it falls into the Columbia, they said it was good, and had only one Fall to that River; I requested them to let me have a Canoe, and one of them to come with us as a guide, to which they readily assented, and tomorrow morning we are to set off down the River. This account of the River below us differs very much from the description of this River by the Lake Indian Chief, whose information I could always depend on, he described the River above where it enters the Columbia to be a series of heavy Falls for one and a half day's march to the smooth water, the sides of the Falls steep basalt rocks.

October 1st. This morning they came with an old useless

[1] Camas, *Quamasia quamash* (Pursh). [E. A. P.]

Canoe, which I refused, and they soon returned with a good canoe. We left the Indian in care of the Horses, until we should return. We descended the River till late in the afternoon, when heavy rain obliged us to put up for the night.[1] The next day we descended the River for three hours. The River had contracted, and the current [was] swift, full near four miles p^r hour. This brought us in sight of a range of high rude Hills covered with Snow, I enquired of our Guide where the River passed, he said, he could not tell, he had never been on the River before; vexed with him, I saw plainly the description of the lower part of this River by the Lake Indian Chief was too true, and we had to turn about, having come about twenty six miles in a WNW course. The same fine Woods near the River with fine Larch. We came to where we had left our Horses, having killed seven Geese and two teal Ducks;[2] the Indians gave us a good Antelope, so that we are rich. And on the evening of the fourth, we found ourselves with fifteen Geese, one Antelope, one Beaver, fifty pounds of dried Salmon, and the same number of Roots:

October 6th. in the afternoon we arrived at the Saleesh House,[3] all well thank God. All along our journey the River had plenty of Swans, Geese, Ducks, Cranes and Plover. We have come seventy five miles, which with twenty six, makes 101 miles that we have examined this fine River, and the country about it, which some day will be under the Plough and the Harrow, and probably by the Natives, who are a very different race of people from those on the east side. These latter seem utterly averse to every kind of manual labour, they will not even make a pipe stem their great favorite, which is the trifling work of a day, and takes them a month;

---

[1] In his borrowed canoe, Thompson proceeded down the Pend d'Oreille river about one full day's journey (" 29 miles," according to his notes). but took two and a half days for his return. He went nearly to the Box Cañon. [T. C. E.]

[2] *Nettion carolinense* (Gmel.). [E. A. P.]

[3] Kullyspell House is meant. See note on p. 410.

those on the west side pride themselves on their industry, and their skill in doing anything, and are as neat in their persons as circumstances will allow, but without Soap, there is no effectual cleanliness; this we know very well, who, too often experience the want of it. Take Soap from the boasted cleanliness of the civilized man, and he will not be as cleanly as the Savage who never knew it's use. During my absence forty four Skeetshoo Indians came to the House, and traded near two hundred pounds weight of Furrs, and three Horses.

October 7th. Having cut the Logs for the House, we began hauling them, to the place for the House.

October 11th. I set off with Horses, two men and a Guide to meet the Canoes from the Rainy Lake with Goods for the Trade of the Natives.[1] We went about ten miles to the top of the River Hills, the first part had very fine woods, the white Cedar was often four to five fathoms girth, clean and tall in proportion, the Larch and Red Fir very fine. On the 20th October we arrived at McGillivray's River, having come about 201 miles over hilly countries, with many small Meadows, and finely wooded with the Red Fir, Larch, Pine, Poplar, Aspin and a few others. Mr James McMillan [2]

[1] For the actual itinerary from October 11 to November 9, see p. xci.

[2] James McMillan is identical with the "A. McMillan" mentioned by Coues in his *New Light*. He was closely associated with Thompson in his work to the west of the mountains. In March, 1808, he made a trip with dogs across the mountains from Fort Augustus to Fort Kootanae, and carried back a load of furs. Later in the same spring he met Thompson at the Kootenay Plain with horses to carry him to Fort Augustus. In the autumn of 1808, he returned with Thompson to the Columbia, and spent the winter with him at Fort Kootanae and with Finan McDonald at the falls of the Kootenay river. In the spring of 1809 he returned across the mountains, but as is stated in the text, he was back at the Kootenay river later in the year. In the spring of 1810, he again accompanied Thompson eastward with the furs; and when later in 1810 Joseph Howse of the Hudson's Bay Company made his first trip across the mountains to the Columbia river, McMillan followed him closely to Flathead lake. During the winter of 1811, he returned to Rocky Mountain House on the Saskatchewan river; and in the summer of the same year, he accompanied John McDonald of Garth

in charge of the Canoes with Goods for the trade, had arrived; here we separated the Goods for the different Posts to trade with the Natives; and with Horses transported the Goods over these hilly countries, very fatigueing to the Horses and ourselves. On the 9th of November, thank God we arrived at the place we had builded a Store,[1] and were now to build a House for ourselves. Four of the Horses were left behind, knocked up with fatigue. We had experienced much bad weather in drizzling rain, and showers of Snow which soon melted, and had to dry everything. We were all of us very hungry, having had but little on the Road: there were some Indians near us, of whom we tried to buy a horse for food, our own were too poor to be eaten, and we fasted, except for a chance Goose or Duck amongst us, until the 14th, when Jaco,[2] a fine half breed arrived and relieved us. From him we traded twenty eight Beaver Tails, forty pounds of Beat Meat, thirty pounds of dried meat, and now, we all, thank God, enjoyed a good meal. We continued to

and J. G. McTavish up the Saskatchewan river and across the mountains by Howse Pass to bring supplies to David Thompson on the Columbia river (see note on p. 539). McMillan appears to have been a very intelligent man; he became a Chief Factor, and remained in the Columbia district until 1829 at least. While he was with the North-West Company, his service was usually at the Flathead and Spokane posts. After the union of the Hudson's Bay and North-West Companies, he was one of the officers who met Governor Simpson at Boat Encampment in the autumn of 1824. He accompanied Simpson to Fort George, and was there placed in command of the expedition sent in November, 1824, to explore the shore-line of Puget Sound and the waters of the Fraser river. In 1827, he built the original Fort Langley on the Fraser river, and he remained in command there until 1828. In 1829, he ascended the Columbia with Governor Simpson (see the latter's *Narrative of a Journey round the World*, London, 1847, vol. i.). He undoubtedly contributed much to the early record of the geography and ethnology of the Spokane, Flathead, and Kootenay districts. [J. B. T. and T. C. E.]

[1] Thompson's note-books show that no building had been done here earlier.

[2] Jacques Raphael Finlay, a half-breed who seems to have already established trade relations with the Flatheads on what is now Jocko Creek, in Missoula county, Montana, to the east of Saleesh House. [T. C. E.]

work at the House, the same day, three Saleesh young Men
came to inform us, that the great Camp of the Saleesh
Indians, with their Allies, were returned from hunting the
Bison, and were two days march from us, had plenty of provisions, and had seen no enemies. So far this was good
news, but it did not relieve us from want until the 24ᵗʰ
when eight Saleesh Men came, from whom I traded three
packs of Furrs (a pack is 90 lbs weight), and thirteen hundred
pounds of dried meat; they were from the great Camp,
which, they said, was moving slowly towards us; hitherto we
had been very unsuccessful in hunting the Antelope, altho'
there were many about us. An Indian remarked to me,
"You have now got provisions for your hungry men for
several days, now we shall kill the Antelope and there will be
want no more this winter," which became true. Amongst
Hunters who depend wholly on the chase, there sometimes
comes a strange turn of mind; they are successful and
everything goes well; a change comes, they either miss, or
wound the Deer, without getting it; they become excited,
and no better success attends them, despondency takes place,
the Manito of the Deer will not allow him to kill them;
the cure for this is a couple of days rest; which strengthens
his mind and body. It is something like the axiom of the
civilised world, that Poverty begets Poverty.

November 30ᵗʰ. We had not finished building our Houses:
this month has been very mild weather, two thirds of it with
a light drizzling rain with a chance shower of Snow, the
Leaves of the Trees are all fallen, and the River clear of ice.
December 3ʳᵈ. At length I was lodged in my House and put
up my Thermometer; the mean cold of the day at 7½ AM,
2 PM and 9 PM +22. December 4ᵗʰ +23. Decʳ 6ᵗʰ +30
Decʳ 8 +19. Ice now drifting in the River, and much ice.
along shore. Decʳ 11ᵗʰ +26, the River clear of ice. Mild
weather returned, Decʳ 17ᵗʰ Mean +37. Decʳ 19ᵗʰ. Thermometer rose to +43. Decʳ 24ᵗʰ, mean temperature +41.

Decr 31st, hitherto this month has been mild weather, with much light drizzling rain; how different from the east side of the Mountains, where the largest Rivers and the Lakes have now thick ice on them: it may be enquired what can be the cause of this great difference of climate on the same parallel of Latitude, it appears equally inexplicable as the great difference of heat on the opposite sides of a Continent. The mean of the Thermometer for the month of December from 7¼ AM to 9 PM +27, the lowest point +13 and the highest +44.

1810 January. This month passed without anything worth notice, although at times the nights and mornings were cold, yet the ducks kept about, the River had drift ice, but not to prevent a canoe crossing: We made a Glacier of shore ice, and placed 1260 lbs of Antelope Meat in it. The Thermometer. the lowest point was −4, the highest +39, the mean heat of the month +23.

February. By weighing we found the average weight of the meat of an Antelope to be fifty nine pounds when fleshy, but when fat to be sixty five pounds. By observations I found the Latitude of this, the Saleesh House,[1] to be 47°. 34′. 35″ north, and it's Longitude 115°. 22′. 51″ West of Greenwich. The range of the Thermometer for the first twenty two days, was, the lowest point − 11, the highest +48, the mean temperature +31, from this date no further attention could be paid to the Thermometer, from my being absent on various duties, the greater part of the Month was spent in looking for Birch Rind to make two Canoes, for the transport of the Furrs, Provisions &c. At the latter end of this month although myself, several others with six Iroquois Indians (who had come this far to trap Beaver) assisted in

---

[1] The site of Saleesh House is well known through Indian tradition as well as by scientific observations. It is near the town of Thompson, in Sanders county, Montana, about one mile south-west of the Northern Pacific Railway siding of Woodlin. [T. C. E.]

looking for Birch Rind fit for large Canoes, we found none;
it is a curious fact that climate has a great influence on the
thickness of the Rind of the Birch Tree. In the mild winters
of this country the Rind is thin, and we had to go to the
tops of the Hills in rocky situations to look for it.

On the evening of the 24th the Indians informed me,
that the Peeagans had attacked a hunting party, killed M[r]
Courter [1] (a trader and Hunter from the U States) and one
Indian, and wounded several others. My Hunter hearing
that two of his brethren were wounded, requested to go, and
see them, which I readily granted, my Guide deserted and
went to a distant camp for safety; but I soon procured
another: On the 26th in the afternoon [we] came to twenty
one Tents of Saleesh Indians, who received us with their
usual kindness; they seemed to think that the imprudence
of M[r] Courter, in going on the War Grounds, with a small
party to hunt the Bison and set traps for the Beaver, which
were numerous, was the cause of his death; and the accidents
to the Indians; during my time the Traders and Hunters
from the United States were most unfortunate, there seemed
to be an infatuation over them, that the Natives of the
Plains were all skulkers in the woods, and never dared shew
themselves on open ground, and they suffered accordingly
being frequently attacked in open ground and killed by the
Peeagans until none remained. From these Indians I traded
about thirty pounds of dried meat, and twenty eight split
and dried Tongues of the Bison. Our Horses being very
tired I staid with them the rest of the day, and enquired for

[1] The nearest approach to this name among American trappers on
the headwaters of the Missouri river at that time is that of John Colter,
a member of the Lewis and Clark expedition, whose remarkable experiences are related in Chittenden, *History of the American Fur Trade*,
ch. x. Colter, however, was not actually killed by the Blackfeet. For
the story of several attacks by the Blackfeet during the winter and spring
of 1810 at the Three Forks of the Missouri, see Chittenden, *op. cit.*, ch. vi.,
and Coues, *New Light*, p. 674, note. [T. C. E.]

Birch Rind, they say, there is plenty of Birch Wood in the Brooks which are in the Hills. And the month ended without any success in Birch Rind for a Canoe.

March 1ˢᵗ. At a camp of Kootanaes, and traded a good Horse for Tobacco and Ammunition; on the 10ᵗʰ while at the Saleesh Camp,[1] an alarm came of the tracks of Peeagans being seen near the Camp, everything was now suspended, scouts went off and came back reporting having seen a body of Cavalry about three miles from us. About one hundred Men now mounted their Horses proud of their Guns and iron headed Arrows to battle with the Enemy; they soon returned, having found these Cavalry to be the Kootanaes under their old Chief who had quitted hunting the Bison, and were returning to their own country; but [it] gave me, as well as the old Men, great pleasure in seeing the alacrity with which they went to seek the enemy, when before, their whole thoughts and exertions were to get away from, and not to meet, their enemies. I now in a small Canoe with two Kullyspell Indians set off for the House, and on the 15ᵗʰ arrived, almost constant bad weather, Rain and showers of Snow. The next day collected the Horses, and on the 17ᵗʰ set off for the Saleesh Camp to bring the Furrs and Provisions to the House. On the 19ᵗʰ at Noon arrived at the Saleesh Camp, Monsʳ Bellaire whom I had left in charge had traded 544 lbs of dried meat of the Bison, much wanted for the voyage in the summer;

March 20ᵗʰ. My men, whom I had left to look for Birch Rind for a Canoe, at length found enough for one large Canoe and have now nearly made it, but the bad weather prevents the inside work. Tied up about 1650 lbs of Furrs, and about 1300 lbs of dried provisions to be taken to the House by the Canoe and by Horses.

March 24ᵗʰ. Numerous flocks of Geese have passed to

---

[1] See Itinerary on p. xci.

the northward as well as Ducks, but the Swans remain here; for how long we cannot say. Most of these Geese from my knowledge of the north eastern country have to proceed to between the parallels of 58 to 62 degrees north and thence to five hundred miles eastward of the Mountains, there to lay their eggs and rear up their young, and late in Autumn with their young return to these mild climates to pass the winter; In a straight line the flight of the Geese from New Orleans is 2700 miles, who thus unerringly guides the wild Geese and Ducks, over this great space, crossing the Rocky Mountains at both seasons, the Indian readily answers, the Manito to whom the Great Spirit has given the care of the Geese and Ducks &c, the civilized world has it's Manito called Instinct an undefinable property of Mind. The Geese and Ducks which remain here are all now paired, repairing, or making their Nests for laying their Eggs. The Swans the same, but this is a most cautious bird, they work at the nest only in the night. I never saw them at it in the day, and they are to be found at some small distance from the nest; even when the female is sitting on the eggs, the male is not near her until his turn comes to take charge of the eggs, which are from three to seven, and so well hidden, they are not found so often as the Eggs of other Fowl.

On the 25th we arrived at the House; the Indians are suffering from Colds, from the almost constant drizzling Rains, and some of us are not much better, but we now plainly, as well as the Indians, see in this climate, the great advantage of woollen over leather clothing, the latter when wet sticks to the skin, and is very uncomfortable, requires time to dry, with caution to keep it to it's shape of clothing. On the contrary the woollen, even when wet, is not uncomfortable, is readily dried and keeps it's shape, which quality they admire. The Indians now fully appreciate the use of woollen clothing, and every one is glad by means of trade, to change his leather dress, for one of the woollen manufacture of England.

March 30ᵗʰ. 6 ᴀᴍ +35, 2 ᴘᴍ +43, 9 ᴘᴍ +32. I have now collected all the Furrs and Provisions safe in the House. On the 31ˢᵗ the Thermometer rose to +46. Thus ended this Month of much travelling by land and by water; the impression of my mind is, from the formation of the country and it's climate, it's extensive Meadows and fine Forests, watered by countless Brooks and Rills of pure water, that it will become the abode of civilized Man, whether Natives or other people; part of it will bear rich crops of grain, the greater part will be pastoral, as it is admirably adapted to the rearing of Cattle and Sheep. (These fine Countries by the capitulation of the Blockhead called Lord Ashburton now belong to the United States.) [1]

The Saleesh Indians were a fine race of moral Indians, the finest I had seen, and set a high value on the chastity of their women; adultery is death to both parties; (Note. in the course of the winter we became well acquainted with these Indians, a camp of them being always near the Post, partly for hunting the Antelope, which was here of a large species, and partly leaving the aged Men and Women in security when they made hunting excursions.) The tribe was under the influence of two Chiefs, the principal we named Cartier, from his resemblance to a Canadian of that name; the other the Orator: both very friendly to us, and of mild manners; and frequently camped near the Fort; or Post, sometime in February; they both as usual, with a few Indians in the evening entered the Hall to smoke, but now with grave faces. I supposed they had heard of

[1] Lord Ashburton had no part in negotiating the Treaty of 1846, which gave these territories to the United States. Thompson wrote to the British Government during the negotiations a number of letters describing his early explorations of this region south of the 49th parallel and its great value. These letters are now on file in the Public Record Office in London.

some chance of war : they soon broke silence, and Cartier mildly said, You know our law is, that a man that seduces a woman must be killed ; I said I have no objection to your law, to what purpose do you tell me this ; the Orator then spoke, my daughter with her mother has always sat quietly in my Tent, until these few days past, when one of your men has been every day, while we are hunting, to my tent with beads and rings to seduce my daughter. Looking round on my men, he said he is not here, (on their entering my servant had gone into my room, I knew it must be him ; the men and myself were every day too much fatigued to think of women.) But wherever he is, we hope you will give him to us that he may die by our law. I told them I had no inclination to screen the Man, but as they were much in want of guns and ammunition for hunting and to protect themselves from their enemies, if they wished me to return with those articles, and various others, they must give me a Man to take his place, otherwise I could not return ; they looked at each other, and said we cannot find a man capable, besides his going among strange people where he may be killed ; very well, then if you kill my man I cannot return to you, but shall stay with the Peeagans, your enemies ; then what is to be done, exclaimed the Orator. I replied, let him live this time, and as you are noted for being a good gelder of Horses ; if this Man ever again enters your Tent, geld him, but let him live ; at this proposition they laughed, and said, well let him live, but so sure as he comes to seduce our women, we shall geld him ; after smoking, they retired in good humour. But my men, all young and in the prime of life, did not at all relish the punishment.

The Saleesh Indians during the winter had traded upwards of twenty guns from me, with several hundreds of iron arrow heads, with which they thought themselves a fair match for the Peeagan Indians in battle on the Plains. In the month of July when the Bison Bulls are getting fat, they formed a camp of about one hundred and fifty men to hunt and make dried Provisions as I had requested them; accompanied by Mr Finan McDonald, Michel Bourdeaux and Bapteste Buché with ammunition tobacco &c to encourage them: they crossed the Mountains by a wide defile of easy passage, eastward of the Saleesh Lake, here they are watched by the Peeagans to prevent them hunting the Bison, and driven back, and could only hunt as it were by stealth; the case was now different, and they were determined to hunt boldly and try a battle with them: they were entering on the grounds, when the scouts, as usual, early each morning sent to view the country came riding at full speed, calling out, " the Enemy is on us;" instantly down went the Tents, and tent poles, which, with the Baggage formed a rude rampart; this was barely done, when a steady charge of cavalry came on them, but the Horses did not break through the rampart, part of pointed poles, each party discharged their arrows, which only wounded a few, none fell; a second, and third charge, was made; but in a weak manner; the battle was now to be of infantry. The Saleesh, about one hundred and fifty Men, took possession of a slightly rising ground about half a mile in front of their Tents, the Peagans, about one hundred and Seventy men drew up and formed a rude line about four hundred yards from them; the Saleesh and the white Men lay quiet on the defensive; the Peeagans, from time to time throughout the day, sent parties of about forty men forward, to dare them to battle; these would often approach to within sixty to eighty yards, insulting them as old women, and dancing in a frantic manner, now springing from the ground as high as they could, then close to the ground, now to the right, and to the left; in all postures; their war coats of leather hanging loose before them; their guns, or bows and arrows, or a lance in their hands; the two former they sometimes discharged at their enemies with little effect : Buché, who was a good shot, said they were harder to hit than a goose on the wing. When these were tired they returned, and a fresh party came forward in like manner, and thus throughout the day, the three men had several shots discharged at them, but their violent gestures prevented a steady aim in return ; the three men were all good shots, and as I have noticed the Indians allow no neutrals, they had to fight in their own defence. Mᶜ Finan McDonald fired forty five shots, killed two men and wounded one, the other two men each fired forty three balls, and each wounded one man ; such were their wild activity, they were an uncertain mark to fire at ; the evening ended the battle ; on the part of the Peeagans, seven killed and thirteen wounded ; on the part of the Saleesh, five killed and nine wounded ; each party took care of their dead and wounded ; no scalps were taken, which the Peeagans accounted a disgrace to them ; the Saleesh set no pride on taking scalps ; This was the first time the Peeagans were in a manner defeated, and they determined to wreck their vengeance on the white men who crossed the mountains to the west side ; and furnished arms and ammunition to their Enemies.

CHAPTER V

JOURNEY FROM SALEESH HOUSE TO
RAINY LAKE HOUSE

*Explore the Spokane River—Return to M*c*Gillivray's River
—Canoes start—David Thompson, James M*c*Millan, and
one man start with sixteen horses—Arrive at carrying
place of Saleesh River—Arrive at M*c*Gillivray's carrying place—Tracks of Peeagans—Cache at carrying place
of the Mountains broken into by a Wolverene—Start
out to meet fresh horses from the East of the Mountains—
Embark on the Saskatchewan—Arrive at the ruins of
Fort Augustus—Proceed on journey of descending the
Saskatchewan—Cumberland House—Pemican—Missasscut
berry—Cedar Lake—Saskatchewan River—Arrive at
Rainy Lake House—Woman conjuress.*

APRIL. Various duties for the Voyage before us, got
the Canoe ready and sent off to the Kullyspel Lake
with Furrs and Provisions, the weather variable, but
very mild. April 9th. 5 AM +38 2 PM +52 9 PM +42
small Rain. April 18th. 5 AM +38 Clear 2 PM +71 hazy.
9 PM +38 calm. Getting all ready to set off the morrow
19th. We left the House to proceed on our Voyage to exchange the Furrs for Goods &c. The 25th part of this day
was passed in observations for Latitude Longitude and Variation of the Compass, of no use to the general reader. The
same on the 26th, when we had the good fortune to kill one
Crane, thirteen Geese and one Duck. April 27th proceeded

on discovery down the Spokane River[1] till 2.25 PM, when
finding the River bounded by high craigs, of contracted
space, with strong rushes of current, small Falls, and Whirlpools, we put ashore to examine the country below us. Of
late a great change had taken place, the remains of the heavy
snows of Winter, which is very deep in these countries, is
everywhere on the ground giving everything a wintry appearance; we landed on the left side which appeared the best,
went up a high steep bank of rocks and earth, and then
through small, close woods, for one mile in deep snow, which
sometimes bore us up, but often [we] sunk in it to our middle;
we were obliged to haul ourselves out by the branches of the
Trees. Having crossed the Carrying Place,[2] we had a steep
bank to go down; from the top I surveyed the country
before me, with the assistance of the Indian; a bold range
of high Mountains covered with snow bounded the left side
of the River, and also formed it's banks in rude craigs: the
right side was of high steep Hills of rock, and ranged away
to a great distance. My Guide who has been here pointed
out the country; about three miles below us was a Fall
that fell over steep Rocks, the height of a large tree (say
80 to 100 feet) but could not be approached in this season,
the Snow was too deep; in the Summer they left the Canoes
a short distance above the Fall, and by hands and feet got
along the steep Rocks to the Fall, beyond which no Indian
had ever gone, except a very few to gather red ochre, which
is of a very fine quality, and in great plenty among the Moun-

[1] This is a mistake for the Pend d'Oreille river. [T. C. E.]
[2] Thompson has descended the Pend d'Oreille (not the Spokane)
river a little farther than before, and is on the edge of Box Cañon above
Metaline (formerly Pend d'Oreille) Falls. He is actually within thirty
miles of the Columbia river, but in a very rough country which even the
Indians avoided in their travel. Later, in 1825, employees of the Hudson's
Bay Company, under the direction of Governor Simpson, explored this
river from where it empties into the Columbia, but soon abandoned any
attempt to navigate it. [T. C. E.]

tains. The road he described as highly dangerous, passable only to light, active, men, and they [are] obliged frequently to go on hands and knees, and thus get up the high steep rocks; which he assured us continued for two and a half days march beyond the great Fall; when they came on the Columbia River. The Spokane River for this distance is a terrible Cataract, bounded on each side by high Craigs, and unnavigable; those who voyage this way make a long carrying place[1] to a small River which runs nearly paralel to the Columbia, and falls into it below the Cataract; this River he said to be too shoal for us. Although so near the Great Falls, he assured us, it would take a whole day to arrive there, including the Carrying Place we were on; this I readily believed, as the Carrying Place alone would require four hours of active men. This range of rude, high, rocky Hills gave me a view of the structure of the country which I had not [had] before. I never to myself, could account for the small quantity of Snow at the west foot of the Mountains along the whole of the Kootanae and Saleesh countries for the length of about 400 miles; these high Hills intercepted all the heavy vapours from the Pacific Ocean, and the great valley between them and the west foot of the mountains have only the light vapours which pass above these Hills; the breadth of this fine valley is irregular, and may be estimated at one hundred miles; the depth of snow on these Hills in Winter must be very great; when we found so much, so late in the season, after such heavy thaws. I now perceived the Columbia River was in a deep valley at the north end of these rude Hills, and it's west side the high rolling lands of Mount Nelson, round which it runs. Attentively surveying the country,

[1] The customary Indian trail to and from the Columbia left the Pend d'Oreille at the Calispell river, crossed the mountains on the westward to the valley of the Colville river, and followed that river (which is not navigable for canoes) to the Columbia just below the Kettle Falls, which Thompson here refers to as the "Cataract," or "Great Falls." The name Ilthkoyape was not yet used by him. [T. C. E.]

BOX CAÑON, PEND D'OREILLE RIVER, WASHINGTON
Thompson descended the river to this point.
(Photograph: Frank Palmer)

and considering all the information I had collected from various Indians, I concluded that we must abandon all thoughts of a passage this way, and return by our old Road, till some future opportunity shall point out a more eligible road, which I much doubt; Near 5 PM began our return and put up at 7½ PM. And I observed for Latitude. Killed one Swan, one Crane, two Geese[1] and found sixteen goose eggs in different nests. The Crane was fat. In many places there is much snow along the beach, and it is deep in the woods. Such is the nature of this region.

May 1st. Came to my Men who are finishing a Canoe, and told them to look for more Birch Rind and white Cedar to make another Canoe; we continued our journey to 9½ PM, the River always from three to five hundred yards wide. Our hunt to-day was one Antelope, three Geese and one Duck. The great depth of snow on this end of the Road, and the weak state of the Horses, put me in mind of a Rivulet which we had to cross on the Carrying Place to McGillivray's River; and by proceeding up it, shorten the distance for the Horses, and avoid the worst part of the deep snow; we found the sortie of the Rivulet,[2] and on the 3rd by proceeding up it we came to the Road; On the 16th with much suffering and hard Labor we got all the Furrs to McGillivray's River, where our Canoes of last year were laid up and which we had to repair, for which purpose all we could procure was nine feet of second rate Birch Rind; May 17th. We got the Canoes repaired, and in the afternoon with forty six packs of Furrs, and eight bags of Pemmecan they went off for the Rocky Mountain defiles. Mr Jas McMillan, one Man and myself with sixteen Horses went by land. On the 20th the Canoes arrived with half Cargo, they crossed us and the

[1] *Branta canadensis* (Linn.). [E. A. P.]
[2] This "rivulet" is now known as Pack river. Thompson's note-books show that he returned to Kullyspell House, and from there started with McMillan for the Rocky Mountains by way of the Kootenay river. [T. C. E.]

Horses to the Saleesh Carrying Place[1] to the Saleesh River; and then returned for the rest of their cargoe of Furrs, with which they arrived. On the 9ᵗʰ June, thank God, we arrived safe at MᶜGillivray's Carrying Place, which leads to the scource of the Columbia River; and crossed all the Horses, they are in poor condition, the grass [being] scant, and bruised in the many rapids we have crossed to this place: we now go direct for the defiles of the Rocky Mountains. When we landed we saw the fresh tracks of Peeagan Scouts, they had this morning broken the branch of an Aspin Tree, and peeled the bark, on examining the tracks, [we] found they had gone up the River to recross the Mountains. Had we been a few hours sooner, we should have had to fight a battle, which, thank God, is thus avoided.

June 16ᵗʰ. Early came to the Carrying Place of the Mountains; Our Hoard strongly built of Pine Logs, and covered with Pine Bark, we found cut through by a Wolverene,[2] whom we killed; he had eaten twenty five pounds of Pemmican, half of a dressed leather Skin, three pairs of Shoes, and cut to pieces seven large Saddles; and broken the Pine Bark covering to pieces: this animal is everywhere a devil for mischief. Left Mᵣ MᶜMillan and four Men in charge of the Furrs, and to wait fresh Horses from the east end of the Defile; We were in hopes of seeing Men and Horses here to cross the Furrs, but suppose the Snow is too deep: but necessity compels me to proceed to the east end of the Defile for fresh Horses; with seven Men and nine Horses, seven out of the sixteen having knocked up and been

[1] Thompson and McMillan have followed the land trail, and the canoes the river, up the Kootenay past Kootenay Falls. The party are now near Jennings, Montana, whence they proceed up the river in the same manner to the portage at Canal Flat, and from there down the Columbia to Blaeberry Creek. Thompson then hurries on across the mountains, and reaches White Mud House, or Terre Blanche, on the Saskatchewan, on June 23; McMillan with the furs follows more slowly, and arrives on July 5. [T. C. E.]

[2] *Gulo luscus* (Linn.). [E. A. P.]

left; on the 18th we crossed the Height of Land, and our jaded Horses got free of the Snow; Early on the 19th came to the Men in charge of the Horses, they were waiting for the Snow to almost disappear. Giving them all the dried Provisions I had, sent them off with all the fresh Horses to M^r McMillan, who is in charge of the Furrs. We went to where the large canoe was laid up, found it very little damaged, repaired it, and with three Men, [and] Pembok a Chippeway Indian; an hour after Noon we embarked on the rapid, sinuous, stream of the head of the great Saskatchewan River; and put up at the lower end of the Kootanae Plains; as we are now in the land of the Bison we hope no more to be in want of Provisions. Pembok went a hunting and killed a Bison Bull of which he brought us about twenty pounds, bull meat is not regarded, it is seldom fat, and always tough.

June 20th. Early we gummed the Canoe, made a Seat for the two men, Boisverd steered the Canoe, and two men paddled, the Indian sat in the middle of the Canoe, and I took the Bow, as the most experienced on rapid Rivers. The melting of the Snow in the Mountains had increased the current to a torrent, on every rock, snag, or root of a tree the water was like a fall, the men paddled merely sufficient to give the Canoe steerage way; we were descending with careless gaiety, when within four inches of the canoe, a large sawyer of 18 inches diameter arose, which gave us a fright that put an end to our cheerfulness, for a blow from such a tree would have dashed the canoe to pieces. A Sawyer, for want of a greek name is a large tree torn from the Banks by the current, and floated down to some place too shoal to allow the Root to pass, here it rests, but the tree itself is in the current below it, it's buoyancy makes it float, but being fast the current buries it, to a certain depth, from which the elasticity and lightness of the wood causes it to rise like the spring of a Bow : again it is buried, and again rises, and thus continues to the great danger of everything that comes in it's way, until the water lowers, and becomes too shoal. I once saw a Bison Bull across a small Sawyer, it had come up and taken him under the Belly, his weight kept it from much play, he was swiming with all his might his fore legs on one side, and his hind legs on the other, and the Sawyer dodging him up and down gave us a hearty laugh; had it been a Deer, we might have relieved him, but the Bison is so savage, that he is never pitied, get into what mischief he will. Our hunt to-day, a Bison Bull, one Red Deer, and wounded a Mountain Sheep, we camped at the foot of the high Craigs of Limestone, to be free of an attack from the Peeagan Indians.

On the evening of the 22nd June, arrived at Fort Augustus,[1]

[1] The reference here is to "old Fort Augustus," situated on the North Saskatchewan river a mile and a half above the mouth of Sturgeon river, in Sect. 15, Tp. 55, R. 22, west of the Fourth Meridian. It was built by Angus Shaw and Duncan McGillivray in 1794, or perhaps the year before, in order to secure the trade of the Blackfeet and Piegan Indians. In 1795, George Sutherland of the Hudson's Bay Company followed the "Canadians," and built a trading post beside them, which he called "Edmonton," probably as a compliment to his clerk, John Prudens, who was a native of Edmonton, near London, England. These two forts formed the most westerly trading establishments on the Saskatchewan river until 1799, when Rocky Mountain House was built two hundred miles farther up the stream ; and they remained the headquarters of the fur-trade of the far west until the summer of 1807, when they were destroyed by the Indians and abandoned. Writing in his note-books on September 25, 1807, Thompson records the destruction of old Fort Augustus as follows : " About 2 or 3 months ago the brother of Old White Swan, a Blackfoot chief, had with his band, a party of Blood Indians, and a few Fall Indians, pillaged Fort Augustus and left the men without even clothing on their backs, but whether they murdered the men or not they do not know, any more than whether they pillaged both forts or only one, but that they were possessed of many guns, much ammunition and tobacco, with various other articles, and finding themselves thus rich, they were gone to war on the Crow Mountain Indians."

New Fort Augustus was built by James Hughes of the North-West Company, and Edmonton by a trader named Rowand of the Hudson's Bay Company, in 1808, at the foot of the high bank within the present city of Edmonton. It was probably this fort at which Thompson stopped on June 27, 1808, when on his way down the Saskatchewan, and which he passed on his way west on September 23 of the same year. It was now in ruins; this is the third year since this Fort has been deserted, it is situated on a high dry bank, as well built as possible with Logs of wood, and now in ruins: it is a strange fact that of all pine log buildings they are in ruins a few months after they cease to be inhabited, however dry the ground and the climate.

We had now full five hundred miles to descend this noble river (Saskatchewan) where it passes through the great Plains, with woods only in places, the very country of the Bison, the Red Deer and the Antelopes. As we descended many herds of the Bison were crossing as the whim took them. They swim well, though slowly, and however troublesome the Flies, they never like the Deer shelter themselves under water, but roll themselves on the ground to get rid of them: It is remarked that all land Animals when killed in the water do float; and all aquatic, as the Beaver, Otter and Musk Rat, do sink in the water when shot, and have to be laid hold of as soon as possible, or they are lost: At this season the Bison Bulls are fatter than the Cows, we preferred them, and when swiming [they] are shot in the head close under the ear, one of them so shot to our surprise sunk like a stone and we had to kill another; thus we held on to where the Forests close on the River, and the Bison is no longer seen, nothing now to amuse us, but myriads of Musketoes and Horse flies to vex us, and allow no rest night nor day.

This turbid River has formed immense alluvials of about two hundred miles in width to the Cedar Lake, through which it passes in several Channels; this very rich soil is much covered with Reeds and rushes, but where the lands have gradually risen and are no longer overflowed, young Forests of Ash, and other Trees cover the ground, and where

certainly here that he stayed from June 24 to July 27, 1809. The new fort was abandoned in the spring of 1810 by both companies; but for how long is not known. It was, however, occupied in 1819, and has been continuously occupied ever since.

this has taken place the Moose Deer have taken possession. On the west side of these alluvials is Cumberland Lake, on the east bank of which is situated Cumberland House in Lat^{de} 53° . 56' . 45" N Longitude 102 . 13 West. This House was the first inland trading post the Hudson's Bay Company made, remarkably well situated for the trade of fine Furrs: it serves as the general Depot for all the dried Provisions made of the meat and fat of the Bison under the name of Pemican, a wholesome, well tasted nutritious food, upon which all persons engaged in the Furr Trade mostly depend for their subsistence during the open season; it is made of the lean and fleshy parts of the Bison dried, smoked, and pounded fine; in this state it is called Beat Meat: the fat of the Bison is of two qualities, called hard and soft; the former is from the inside of the animal, which when melted is called hard fat (properly grease) the latter is made from the large flakes of fat that lie on each side the back bone, covering the ribs, and which is readily separated, and when carefully melted resembles Butter in softness and sweetness. Pimmecan is made up in bags of ninety pounds weight, made of the parchment hide of the Bison with the hair on; the proportion of the Pemmecan when best made for keeping is twenty pounds of soft and the same of hard fat, slowly melted together, and at a low warmth poured on fifty pounds of Beat Meat, well mixed together, and closely packed in a bag of about thirty inches in length, by near twenty inches in breadth, and about four in thickness which makes them flat, the best shape for stowage and carriage. On the great Plains there is a shrub[1] bearing a very sweet berry of a dark blue color, much sought after, great quantities are dried by the Natives; in this state, these berries are as sweet as the best currants, and as much as possible mixed to make Pemmecan; the wood of this shrub, or willow is hard, weighty and flexible, but not elastic, and wherever it can be procured always forms the

---

[1] Service berry, June berry, *Amelanchier alnifolia* Nutt. [E. A. P.]

Arrow of the Indian, the native name is Mis-sars-cut; to which mee-nar is added for the berry; we call it by the native name, but the french who murder every foreign word call the Berry, Poires, and Pim-me-carn; Peemittegar. I have dwelt on the above, as it [is] the staple food of all persons, and affords the most nourishment in the least space and weight, even the gluttonous french canadian that devours eight pounds of fresh meat every day is contented with one and a half pound p^r day: it would be admirable provision for the Army and Navy. It is at Cumberland House all the Pimmecan, and dried provisions of all kinds procured from the great Plains are brought down the Saskatchewan and deposited here, and which forms the supply for the furr Traders going to, and coming from, all the trading Posts; By receiving the turbid waters of the Saskatchewan it has remarkably fine Sturgeon, a fish that requires such water to be in perfection.

The Cedar Lake is fast filling up with alluvial matter, but has yet twenty eight miles of width, which we crossed. This Lake takes it's name from the small Cedar Wood [1] growing on it's banks, and which is not found further north or eastward. The shores of this Lake is of Limestone on both sides; from this Lake there is a descent of five miles of Rapids to Cross Lake, which has a width of three miles, and a length of nine miles in rapids and Falls, is the discharge into Lake Winepeg (Sea Lake) the last two miles is a carrying place; the whole of this is Limestone, and forms it's eastern termination; coasting sixty eight miles of the north end of this Lake, the River again forms, but the whole of the country is now of granitic formation, and continues such to the vicinity of Hudson's Bay; From the Lake Winepeg it proceeds 107 miles forming Lakes in places to the eastern extremity of the granite formation, it now forms a bold, wide rapid River of 177 miles in length to Hudson's Bay, besides it's Rapids has

[1] *Thuja occidentalis* Linn. [E. A. P.]

twenty eight Falls, with 8183 yards of carrying everything at these Falls and the banks of the River; the descent of the River in this last 177 miles is 1580 feet.[1] From where it is first navigable for a Canoe in the Mountains to it's entrance into the Sea it's length is 1725 miles, and this River drains an area of country of 426,529 square miles, the western parts to the Mountains are very fine countries. This was formerly my route from, and to, Hudson's Bay, but our course is along the west side of this large Lake for 194 miles to the sortie of the Winepeg River. The shores of all this distance is of Limestone, and the interior country a fine soil. The area of this Lake is full 14,600 S[quare] Miles.[2] Here is another Depot of Provisions of the Pimmecan and other dried Provisions from the Red, the Swan, and Dauphin Rivers: which flow into this Lake on it's west side. The Winepeg River has its scources on the north side of the heights of Lake Superior, small streams, which find and make, Lakes, and accumulate water, some of considerable size, are the Rainy Lake and Lake of the Woods. This range of country has a great descent, the River as it proceeds from Lake to Lake has many Falls and carrying places. We ascended the River Winepeg 130 miles, carrying over it's 33 falls, 5691 y^{ds} with a descent of 314 feet[3] and a distance of 82 miles, to the Lake of the Woods; over which we went to the Rainy River, and up this fine River, to near the Rainy Lake, where is an old established trading Post and Depot of Merchandize and Provisions of Maize &c. and where, thank God, we arrived safely on the 22nd of July.

Although this whole distance is a granite formation, yet the soil is a rich loam, tending to clay, and yields a good return of Wheat and Barley, of cabbages &c so far as these are sown, which are always in small quantities, as the business of

[1] The length of Nelson river from Lake Winnipeg to Hudson Bay is 435 miles, and the descent in that distance is 712 feet.

[2] The area of Lake Winnipeg is 9,414 square miles.

[3] The descent is 347 feet.

GRAND RAPIDS, SASKATCHEWAN RIVER, MANITOBA

(Photograph: J. B. Tyrrell, 1890)

the country does [not] embrace agriculture, and there are no Mills for making Wheat into flour. The day after my arrival a Lady Conjuress made her appearance. She was well dressed of twenty five years of age, she had her Medicine Bag, and bore in her hands a conjuring stick about 4½ feet in length 1½ inch [wide] at the foot and three inches at the top, by one inch in thickness, one side was painted black, with rude carved figures of Birds Animals and Insects filled with vermillion; the other side was painted red with carved figures in black, she had set herself up for a prophetess, and gradually had gained, by her shrewdness, some influence among the Natives as a dreamer, and expounder of dreams, she recollected me, before I did her, and gave me a haughty look of defiance, as much as to say I am now out of your power. Some six years before this she was living with one of my men as his wife, but became so common that I had to send her to her relations; as all the Indian men are married, a courtesan is neglected by the men and hated by the Women. She had turned Prophetess for a livelihood, and found fools enough to support her: there is scarce a character in civilized society that has not something like it among these rude people.

CHAPTER VI

RETURN JOURNEY TO COLUMBIA BY
DEFILES OF ATHABASCA RIVER

*Leave Rainy Lake House—Canoe party attacked by Peeagans—
Rest of party pursued—Saved by three grizled bears—Find
canoe party safe—Turn to the defiles of the Athabasca River
for safety—Arrive at Athabasca River—Abandon horses—
Build caches—Proceed on snowshoes and with dog sleds—
Build a cache—French Canadians—Enter defiles of Rocky
Mountains supposed by the Indians to be the home of the
Mammoth—Tracks of a large unknown animal—Reach
Secondary Mountains—Reach height of land—The men dis-
couraged—Enormous glacier—Boring holes in the snow—
Begin descent of the west side of the Mountains—Arrive at
the Columbia—Men desert—Remarks on the climate and
country.*

HAVING now made an assortment of goods, wherewith to load four Canoes for the furr trade of the
interior country, we left this Depot; and by the
same route we had come proceeded to the Saskatchewan
River and continued to Cumberland House, where we took
dried Provisions to keep us until we should come to where
the Bisons are; after which we lived by hunting them to
the upper end of the Plains; to where the River passes
through Forests to the Mountains. Here engaged two native
men to hunt for us, the Red Deer and Bisons of the Woods.
The manner of furnishing the Men with Provisions, was by
hunting these animals, and bringing their meat by Horses to

the Canoes a supply for full three days ; when we appointed
a place to meet them with a fresh supply ; thus the Canoes
proceeded to within twenty miles of the east foot of the
Mountains ; [1] we had given them a full supply for three days,
and M[r] William Henry, the two Indians and myself proceeded
to the foot of the Mountains, where we killed three Red
Deer, made a Stage and placed the meat on it in safety to
wait the Canoes.[2] This was on the 13th October 1810, and we
expected the Canoes to arrive late on the 16th or early on
the 17th at latest, but they did not make their appearance ;
our oldest Hunter of about forty years of age as usual rose
very early in the morning and looking at the Stage of Meat,
said to me, I have had bad dreams, this meat will never be
eaten, he then saddled his Horse and rode off. Somewhat
alarmed at his ominous expression and the non arrival of the
canoes, I told M[r] Henry and the Indian to proceed thro' the
Woods down along the River in search of the Canoes, and
see what detained them, with positive orders not to fire a
shot but in self defence ; about eight in the evening they
returned, and related, that a few miles below us they had

---

[1] On his way up the Saskatchewan Thompson had stopped, from September 6 to September 11, at Terre Blanche House, where Alexander Henry was in charge. Along with William Henry, he had set out from there on horseback, and on September 15 had passed White Mud House.

[2] On September 8 the canoes had passed Terre Blanche House, and had thence continued up the river to a place about a day's journey above Rocky Mountain House, where they were stopped by Black Bear, a chief of the Piegan, and ordered to turn back. After some hesitation they returned to Rocky Mountain House, which they reached on September 24. On October 11, however, they again set out up the river, this time in the night. The next morning William Henry arrived with a message from Thompson ; and the following day Alexander Henry went in a canoe to Thompson's camp, which was " on top of a hill 300 feet above the water, where tall pines stood so thickly that I could not see his tent until I came within 10 yards of it." Next day Alexander Henry returned to Rocky Mountain House, and on his arrival there he sent William Henry on horseback to order the Columbia canoes to come back down the river to Thompson. For a fuller account of this stirring episode, see Coues, *New Light*, pp. 640–655.

seen a camp of Peeagans on the bank of the River, that a
short distance below the camp, they had descended the bank
to the River side, and found where the Canoes had been.
They had made a low rampart of Stones to defend themselves,
and there was blood on the stones; they went below this
and fired a shot in hopes of an answer from the Canoes, but
it was not returned: I told them they had acted very
foolishly, that the Peeagans would be on us very early in the
morning, and that we must start at the dawn of day, and
ride for our lives; on this we acted the next morning, and
rode off, leaving the meat: the country we had to pass over
was an open forest, but we had to cross, or ride round so
many fallen trees that active Men on foot could easily keep
up with us; the Peeagans had very early arrived at the Stage
of meat and directly followed the tracks of the Horses, and
would in the evening have come up with us, but providenti-
ally about one in afternoon snow came on which covered our
tracks and retarded them; about an hour after, as they
related, they came on three grizled Bears direct on the track
(they were smelling the tracks of the Horses) they were fully
perswaded that I had placed the Bears there to prevent any
further pursuit; nor could any arguments to the contrary
make them believe otherwise and this belief was a mercy to
us: we rode on through the Woods until it was nearly dark,
when we were obliged to stop; we remained quiet awaiting
our fortune, when finding all quiet, we made a small fire,
and passed the night with some anxiety; my situation pre-
cluded sleep, cut off from my men, uncertain where to find
them, and equally so of the movements of the Indians, I was
at a loss what to do, or which way to proceed; morning came
and I had to determine what course to take, after being
much perplexed whether I should take to the defiles of the
Mountains and see if the Men and Horses were safe that
were left there; or try and find my Men and Canoes. I
determined upon the latter as of the most importance; on

the second day we found them about forty miles below the Indians, at a trading Post lately deserted; here after much consultations, we fully perceived we had no further hopes of passing in safety by the defiles of the Saskatchewan River, and that we must now change our route to the defiles of the Athabasca River which would place us in safety, but would be attended with great inconvenience, fatigue, suffering and privation; but there was no alternative. We therefore directed the Men to proceed through the woods to the defiles of the Mountains and bring down the Horses to take the Goods across the country to the Athabasca River, and on the 28th October they arrived with twenty four Horses and we were now in all twenty four Men; having furnished ourselves with leather Tents and dressed leather for shoes; we loaded our Horses in proportion to their strength from 180 to 240 pounds weight each Horse, and arranged the Men, four to hunt and procure provisions, two Men to clear a path thro' the woods, the other taking care of the Horses, and other duties; with Thomas an Iroquois Indian as Guide; our road lay over the high grounds within about thirty miles of the Mountains; the Woods are mostly of a kind of Cypress, of small clean growth, and not close. With occasional cutting away of few trees we should have made several miles a day, but the forests are so frequently burned and occasions so many windfalls, that the Horses make very slow progress, thus the dense forests are destroyed and meadows formed. We went eight miles in six and a half hours, and put up, without any supper. The country tolerable good with Pine and Aspin Woods.

October 30th. The hunters, thank heaven, killed two cow Bisons and a young grizled Bear. We went six miles and camped, as we had to collect the meat, the ground was wet, the Horses fatigued and heavy loaded.

October 31st. As usual the weather tolerable, we spent three hours clearing a path through the woods, which enabled us to make a march of eleven miles. Our hunt to day was one fat Antelope.[1]

November 1st. A fine cloudy day, Thomas the Guide with two men passed the day examining the country which they found passable, but no success in hunting.

November 2nd. A fine warm day. Having for near three hours cleared a path through the woods, we went ten miles, in this distance we crossed the Pembinaw River of forty yards in width, but shoal; this name is a corruption of Neepin-menan (Summer Berry). Observed for Latitude and Longitude. The Horses in going thro' the wood often deranged their loads, and as they came; the wet ground of to-day, with burnt fallen wood fatigued the Horses, and we camped early. And thus we continued with the usual occurrences and mishaps to the 29th of November, when we came on the Athabasca River; up which we ascended till the afternoon of the 4th of December;[2] here our Guide told me it was of no use at this late season to think of going any further with Horses, and part were sent to the Mountain House, but from this place prepare ourselves with Snow Shoes and Sleds to cross the Mountains: Accordingly the next day we began to make Log Huts to secure the Goods, and Provisions, and shelter ourselves from the cold and bad weather; the Thermometer on our march had descended to − 32 which is 64 degrees below the freezing point, and by means of this intense cold, the marshes and morasses were frozen over,

[1] On the evening of this day, as they were camped on the banks of the Pembina river, two men, Pichette and Coté, arrived with letters and provisions from Alexander Henry at Rocky Mountain House; and the next day Thompson sent back five men and five horses with letters.

[2] The previous day Thomas, the Iroquois, had brought them to an island in Brulé lake, where there was an old hunter's hut or cabin, small, very dirty, without any windows, and with no grass in the vicinity for the horses. They refused to stop at this hut, and moved on to a place five miles north of it, at "a small fountain of water among pines and aspens, with plenty of grass for the horses." Here they remained for the next twenty-five days.

which enabled our Horses to pass over them with safety.
And as yet, we have not more than six inches of snow on the
ground.

Our whole attention for the present was turned to hunting
and securing provisions; having now made Snow Shoes, and
Sleds, on the 30ᵗʰ day of December [1] we commenced our
journey to cross the Mountains and proceeded up the Athabasca River, sometimes on it's shoals and ice, and at times
through the woods of it's banks. The soil was sandy and a
Gale of Wind drifted it to lie on the low branched pines, of
wretched growth, for Snow does not lie on Sand Hills; On
the 31ˢᵗ December we proceeded but slowly and I had to
reduce the weight of the Loads of the Dogs to less than two
thirds, and make a Log Hoard to secure what we left. This,
the work of two hours the men took five hours to finish,
during which time they cooked twice a four gallon Kettle
full of Meat, which they devoured, although they had had a
hearty breakfast, in fact a french Canadian has the appetite
of a Wolf, and glories in it; each man requires eight pounds
of meat pʳ day, or more; upon my reproaching some of them
with their gluttony, the reply I got was, "What pleasure
have we in Life but eating." A French Canadian if left to
himself, and living on what his Master has, will rise very early
make a hearty meal, smoke his pipe, and lie down to sleep,
and he will do little else through the day: to enumerate
the large animals that had been killed, and I may say devoured
by my men would not be credible to a man of a regular life,

---

[1] It was on December 29 that Thompson left William Henry with the
horses, and set out with dogs and sleds to make the final dash across the
Rocky Mountains to the Columbia river. " I gave the men their loads
for the sleds," he says in his note-books, " each sled that has 2 Dogs—
B. D'Eau, Coté, Luscier and L'Amoureux have 120 lbs and necessaries for
the journey, and Vallade, Battoche, Pareil and Du Nord each 1 Dog and
sled, have 70 lbs per sled. 4 horses loaded with meat, having 208 lbs of
Pemican, 35 lbs of Grease and 60 lbs of flour also accompany us to ease
the dogs under the care of Villiard and Vaudette. Thomas the Iroquois
for guide and Baptiste for hunter."

yet these same hardy canadians, as future years proved to me, could live upon as little as any other person. In their own houses in Canada a few ounces of Pork, with plenty of coarse bread and Potatoes is sufficient for the day, and [they are] contented. Yet the same Men when with me on government surveys, where the allowance was one pound of mess Pork (the best) one and a half pound of good fresh Biscuit and half a pound of pease, did not find it too much, and the evening of each day left nothing. Thus ended the year.

1811. January 1ˢᵗ. The Thermometer –22. Our Hunters were fortunate in killing two young Bulls, and a Mountain Sheep; we marched all day to 4¾ PM when we camped, placing the branches of the Pine under us, and a few small branchy Trees to windward, this was all our protection from the bitter cold.

January 2ⁿᵈ. Ther – 20. Collected the meat of the hunt of yesterday, and staid all day roughly splitting and drying what we could to take with us, as [of] meat in this state, the weight is much lessened but not the nourishment. I now lessened the Dog Sleds to eight, the men had beaten two of them to be useless; a Canadian never seems to be better pleased than, [when] swearing at, and flogging his Dogs. It is quite his amusement, careless of consequences.

Jany 3ʳᵈ. Arrangements for the journey.

Jany 4ᵗʰ. As usual the Men early up cooking a plentiful breakfast, they are stimulated to this by the sight of the snowy Mountains before us, and are determined to put themselves in a good condition for fasting, with which the passage of the Mountains threaten them.

Jany 5ᵗʰ. Thermometer – 26 very cold. Having secured the goods and provisions we could not take with us, by 11 AM set off with eight Sleds, to each two dogs, with goods and Provisions to cross the Mountains, and three Horses to assist us as far as the depth of the Snow will permit. We are now entering the defiles of the Rocky Mountains by the Athabasca

River, the woods of Pine are stunted, full of branches to the ground, and the Aspin, Willow &c not much better : strange to say, here is a strong belief that the haunt of the Mammoth, is about this defile, I questioned several, none could positively say, they had seen him, but their belief I found firm and not to be shaken. I remarked to them, that such an enormous heavy Animal must leave indelible marks of his feet, and his feeding. This they all acknowledged, and that they had never seen any marks of him, and therefore could show me none. All I could say did not shake their belief in his existence.

January 6ᵗʰ. We came to the last grass for the Horses in Marshes and along small Ponds, where a herd of Bisons had lately been feeding ; and here we left the Horses poor and tired, and notwithstanding the bitter cold, [they] lived through the winter, yet they have only a clothing of close hair, short and without any furr.

January 7ᵗʰ. Continuing our journey in the afternoon we came on the track of a large animal, the snow about six inches deep on the ice ; I measured it ; four large toes each of four inches in length to each a short claw ; the ball of the foot sunk three inches lower than the toes, the hinder part of the foot did not mark well, the length fourteen inches, by eight inches in breadth, walking from north to south, and having passed about six hours. We were in no humour to follow him : the Men and Indians would have it to be a young mammoth and I held it to be the track of a large old grizled Bear ; yet the shortness of the nails, the ball of the foot, and it's great size was not that of a Bear, otherwise that of a very large old Bear, his claws worn away ; this the Indians would not allow. Saw several tracks of Moose Deer. 9 PM Ther − 4.

Janu[ar]y 8ᵗʰ. A fine day. We are now following the Brooks in the open defiles of the secondary Mountains ; when we can no longer follow it, the road is to cross a point of high land, very fatigueing, and come on another Brook, and thus in succession ; these secondary Mountains appear to be about

2 to 3000 feet above their base, with patches of dwarf pines, and much snow; we marched ten miles today; and as we advance we feel the mild weather from the Pacific Ocean. This morning at 7 AM Ther +6 at 9 PM +22. One of my men named Du Nord beat a dog to death, he is what we call a "flash" man, a showy fellow before the women but a coward in heart, and would willingly desert if he had courage to go alone; very glutinous and requires full ten pounds of meat each day. And as I am constantly ahead [I] cannot prevent his dog flogging and beating: We saw no tracks of Animals.

January 9ᵗʰ. Ther +32. SE wind and snowed all day which made hauling very bad. We could proceed only about four miles, this partly up a brook and then over a steep high point with dwarf pines. We had to take only half a load and return for the rest. The snow is full seven feet deep, tho' firm and wet, yet the Dogs often sunk in it, but our snow shoes did [not] sink more than three inches; and the weather so mild that the snow is dropping from the trees, and everything wet; here the Men finished the last of the fresh and half dried Meat, which I find to be eight pounds for each man pʳ day. Ther +22.

January 10ᵗʰ. Ther +16. A day of Snow and southerly Gale of wind, the afternoon fine, the view now before us was an ascent of deep snow, in all appearance to the height of land between the Atlantic and Pacific Oceans, it was to me a most exhilarating sight, but to my uneducated men a dreadful sight, they had no scientific object in view, their feelings were of the place they were; our guide Thomas told us, that although we could barely find wood to make a fire, we must now provide wood to pass the following night on the height of the defile we were in, and which we had to follow; my men were the most hardy that could be picked out of a hundred brave hardy Men, but the scene of desolation before us was dreadful, and I knew it, a heavy gale of wind

much more a mountain storm would have buried us beneath
it, but thank God the weather was fine, we had to cut wood
such as it was, and each took a little on his sled, yet such
was the despondency of the Men, aided by the coward Du
Nord, sitting down at every half mile, that when night came,
we had only wood to make a bottom, and on this to lay
wherewith to make a small fire, which soon burnt out and in
this exposed situation we passed the rest of a long night
without fire, and part of my men had strong feelings of personal insecurity, on our right about one third of a mile from
us lay an enormous Glacier, the eastern face of which quite
steep, of about two thousand feet in height, was of a clean
fine green color, which I much admired but whatever was
the appearance, my opinion was, that the whole was not
solid ice, but formed on rocks from rills of water frozen in
their course; westward of this steep face, we could see the
glacier with it's fine green color and it's patches of snow in
a gentle slope for about two miles; eastward of this glacier
and near to us, was a high steep wall of rock, at the foot of
this, with a fine south exposure had grown a little Forest of
Pines of about five hundred yards in length by one hundred
in breadth, by some avalanche they had all been cut clean off
as with a scythe, not one of these trees appeared an inch
higher than the others. My men were not at their ease, yet
when night came they admired the brilliancy of the Stars,
and as one of them said, he thought he could almost touch
them with his hand: as usual, when the fire was made I set
off to examine the country before us, and found we had now
to descend the west side of the Mountains; I returned and
found part of my Men with a Pole of twenty feet in length
boring the Snow to find the bottom; I told them while we
had good Snow Shoes it was no matter to us whether the
Snow was ten or one hundred feet deep. On looking into the
hole they had bored, I was surprised to see the color of the sides
of a beautiful blue; the surface was of a very light color,

but as it descended the color became more deep, and at the lowest point was of a blue, almost black. The altitude of this place above the level of the Ocean, by the point of boiling water is computed to be eleven thousand feet (Sir George Simpson).[1] Many reflections came on my mind; a new world was in a manner before me, and my object was to be at the Pacific Ocean before the month of August,[2] how were we to find Provisions, and how many Men would remain with me, for they were dispirited, amidst various thoughts I fell asleep on my bed of Snow.

Early next morning we began our descent, here we soon found ourselves not only with a change of climate, but more so of Forest Trees, we had not gone half a mile before we came to fine tall clean grown Pines of eighteen feet girth. The descent was so steep that the Dogs could not guide the Sleds, and often came across the Trees with some force, the Dogs on one side and the Sled on the other, which gave us some trouble to disentangle them; after a hurried day's march down the mountain we came, on a Brook and camped on the Snow, it being too deep to clear away.

January 11th. The weather bad, though mild, we continued our descent, but steep only in two places, and at length came on a tolerable level country; and camped at the junction of two brooks; here Thomas came to us, he had, thank Heaven, killed two Buck Moose Deer, very much wanted; I gave the Men some Pemmecan for supper, and limited the quantity, part of them grumbled, although they are sure that early the morrow they will have two large deer to eat; in the last thirty six hours they have devoured fifty six pounds of pemmecan, being one fourth of all we have: we have come about 9 miles.

[1] The altitude is 6,025 feet.
[2] This is the only statement of Thompson's as yet discovered with regard to the date on which he expected to reach the mouth of the Columbia river. It argues against any extreme haste on his part to forestall the Astor party. [T. C. E.]

January 12[th]. A day of Snow, all we could do was to bring the meat of the two deer, split and partly dry the fleshy parts.

Jan[ua]ry 13[th]. Ther +14. Sent the Men to collect and bring forward the Goods left on the Way; which they brought except five pounds of Ball, which being in a leather bag was carried away by a Wolverene.

Thus we continued day after day to march a few miles,[1] as the Snow was too wet and too deep to allow the dogs to make any progress; on the 26th we put up on the banks of the Columbia River, my Men had become so disheartened, sitting down every half mile, and perfectly lost at all they saw around them so utterly different from the east side of the Mountains, four of them deserted to return back; and I was not sorry to be rid of them, as for more than a month past they had been very useless, in short they became an incumbrance on me, and the other men were equally so to be rid of them; having now taken up my residence for the rest of the winter I may make my remarks on the countries and the climates we have passed.

On the east side the snow is light and about two feet in depth: on the west side which is open to the winds from the Pacific Ocean and the distance short the snow loads the Mountains and the low lands northward of about 150 miles below the head of the Columbia River, (southward of which there

---

[1] On January 18, Thompson reached a point within a mile of the Columbia river. From January 19 to January 23, he continued southward along the bank of this river; but in this time he advanced in all only about twelve miles. Some of his men refused to go with him farther, and in consequence he "determined to return to the junction of the rivers Flatheart and Canoe river, with the Kootanae River, and then wait for men, goods, provisions, &c., and build canoes for the journey." On January 26 they reached Canoe river, where, says Thompson in his notes, "Du Nord, Bapt. Le Tendre and Bapt. D'Eau deserted. Em Luscier returned ill and Pareil and Coté I sent with letters to Mr. Wm. Henry and to bring more goods. Vallade and L'Amoureux stay here with me. I wrote letters on boards to Mr. Wm. Henry and to the partners."

2 F

is a wide valley with very little or no snow.) On the east side the Climate is severe. December 24, 1810. 7 AM – 32, 9 PM – 22. December 25th 7 AM Ther – 30 9 PM – 22 December 26th 7 AM – 34 9 PM – 24 : this is a sample of many bitter days. On the west side of the Mountains, January 17th 7 AM +30 only two degrees below the freezing point 9 AM +34 Jany 18th 7 AM +35 9 PM +34 the 19th 7 AM +36 9 PM +36, steady rain, showing a difference of climate in these cold months of upwards of sixty degrees in favor of the west side ; these days are chosen as being the last remarks on the state of the Thermometer on the east side, and the first, and nearest in point of time on the west side.

The east side of the Mountains is formed of long slopes, very few in this defile that are steep ; but the west side is more abrupt, and has many places that require steady sure footed Horses, to descend it's banks in the open season : one is tempted to enquire what may be the volume of water contained in the immense quantities of snow brought to, and lodged on, the Mountains, from the Pacific Ocean, and how from an Ocean of salt water the immense evaporation constantly going on is pure fresh water ; these are mysterious operations on a scale so vast that the human mind is lost in the contemplation.

CHAPTER VII

JOURNEY FROM CANOE RIVER TO
ILTHKOYAPE FALLS

*Residence at junction of two rivers with the Columbia—Trees of
enormous growth—Build a hut—Send letters but men cannot
proceed through the snow—Make a canoe from cedar wood—
Prepare for voyage—Start off into Saleesh country—Meet
Nepissing and Iroquois Indians—Continue journey—
Columbia River—M'Gillivray's River—Meet Kootanae
Indians at Saleesh River—Abandon canoes—Saleesh River
swollen into a dangerous stream—Country inundated—
Arrive at Spokane River—War habits of Kullyspel Indians
—Continue Journey—Arrive at Spokane House—War party
of Kullyspel and Shawpatin Indians—Break up war party
—Arrive at Ilthkoyape Falls.*

OUR residence was near the junction of two Rivers from
the Mountains with the Columbia :[1] the upper
Stream which forms the defile by which we came to
the Columbia, I named the Flat Heart, from the Men being
dispirited ; it had nothing particular. The other was the
Canoe River ; which ran through a bold rude valley, of a
steady descent, which gave to this River a very rapid descent
without any falls : yet such was the steady slope of it's current

---

[1] This was the famous " Boat Encampment " of later times, the
rendezvous for travel across the Rocky Mountains by the Athabaska
Pass. Thompson's " Flat Heart " river is now Wood river. It is clear
from this text that both the Athabaska Pass and the Canoe river region
had been visited earlier than this by the guide, Thomas the Iroquois, and
by other Nipissing and Iroquois Indians ; but Thompson was the first white
man to cross it. [T. C. E.]

that by close examination I estimated it's change of level to be full three feet in each one hundred and twenty feet, it's breadth thirty yards, the water clear over a bed of pebbles and small stones, Moose Deer and Beaver were plentiful and the mildness of the climate, and large supply of water induced many of them to build slight houses, or to live on the banks of the River and it's many Brooks; these two streams, at the foot of the hills have formed a wide alluvial, on which are forest Trees of enormous size; the white Cedars were from fifteen to thirty six feet girth; clean grown and tall in proportion, numbers were of the largest size, and in walking round them they appeared to have six or eight sides. The pines were from eighteen to forty two feet in girth, measured at ten feet above the ground, which the snow enabled us to do. They were finely formed, and rose full two hundred feet without a branch, and threw off very luxuriant heads; the white Birch was also a stately Tree, tall and erect, but none above fifteen feet girth and these were few; what appeared remarkable these gigantic Trees did not intermix with each other. The Birch was distinct from the others, neither Pine nor cedar grew among them; next to the Birch was the Cedar, with scarce a Pine amongst them, and then the Pine Forest with very few Cedars; these Forests did not extend beyond these alluvials; on the east side of the Mountains the Trees were small, a stunted growth with branches to the ground; there we were Men, but on the west side we were pigmies; in such forests what could we do with Axes of two pounds weight. We sought for Elm and Ash as congenial to the soil, but found none.

On the 27th January we set to work to clear away the Snow to the depth of three feet almost as firm as Ice, and with Boards split from the Cedar Trees made a Hut of about twelve feet square in which we were tolerably comfortable; our great anxiety was to procure provisions; on visiting the ground between the River and the Mountains not a track was seen, but on the long descents of Mount Nelson [1] we found Moose Deer, each was, as it were shut up in a pound formed of hard snow, from which they could not move, it was formed of a rude circle among Willows and young Aspins; and [they] were thus shot on the spot, all those we killed were fleshy but none fat, but we were most thankful for this plentiful supply. On examining the head of the Moose, the brain was found to lie wholly between the lower part of the eyes and the upper gristle of the nose; in a narrow cavity the brain of a three year old Doe Moose, measured half a pint, full measure, and I estimated the brain to be the one, seven hundred[th] part of the full weight of the deer, the nostrils seemed to communicate direct with the brain, and as this Deer always feeds in thickets, that allow no range of sight, Providence has admirably formed his sense of hearing and smell for self preservation.

From the mildness of the climate we had hopes of finding part of the banks of the River with very little snow, but we found the snow deep, and very firm, the River open and only a chance bridge of ice and snow across it; as in all appearance we had to stay about three months we agreed to build a Hut and make it a shelter from the weather which we effected by the twelfth of February; and were thus protected from the many showers of wet snow and rain, and enabled to dry our clothes.

On the 17th two men [2] whom I had sent across the Mountains returned with two sled loads of Goods and dried provisions, and a Nahathaway Indian, by name the "Yellow Bird" to hunt for us; our hunting grounds are the Canoe River and it's branches, the Snow is much wasted, and in this fine valley the Moose Deer can move freely about.

---

[1] Thompson refers to the whole Selkirk range as Mount Nelson. He is here at the northern end of the range. [T. C. E.]

[2] Thompson gives in his notes the names of three men, besides the Indian, namely, Pareil, Coté, and Villiard.

On the 19ᵗʰ a day of heavy snow which again is three feet in depth, and so wet that we cannot use our Snow Shoes. The snow on the trees pouring down like heavy rain.

On the 22ⁿᵈ at 7 AM Ther +32 at 2 PM +42 at 9 PM +31 Wind SSW. The Thermometer is placed in a box on the north side of a large tree, five feet above the Snow, if another was placed forty, or more feet above the Snow, clear of it's effects, I have no doubt the Thermometer would be full five degrees higher, as the Snow on the higher part of the Trees thaws quicker than that on the lower branches. Sent two Men with Letters to cross the Mountains, the netting of the fore, and hind, parts of the Snow Shoes are cut out, and only the middle remains which is quite enough in the present state of the Snow.

On the first day of March, the Men I sent with Letters to cross the Mountains returned, having found the Snow too deep and wet; the Hunter has found several places where the Wolves[1] have destroyed the Moose Deer, where shut up in the deep snow. A bald headed Eagle,[2] a Rook,[3] and many small Birds about us. Having now examined the White Birch[4] in every quarter, for Birch Rind wherewith to make a Canoe for our voyage to the Pacific Ocean, without finding any even thick enough to make a dish; such is the influence of a mild climate on the rind of the Birch Tree. We had to turn our thoughts to some other material, and Cedar wood being the lightest and most pliable for a Canoe, we split out thin boards of Cedar wood of about six inches in breadth and builded a Canoe of twenty five feet in length by fifty inches in breadth, of the same form of a common Canoe, using cedar boards instead of Birch Rind, which proved to be equally light and much stronger than Birch Rind, the greatest

[1] *Canis occidentalis* Richardson. [E. A. P.]
[2] *Haliætus leucocephalus alascanus* Townsend. [E. A. P.]
[3] Probably Western Crow, *Corvus b. hesperis* (Ridgway). [E. A. P.]
[4] Probably *Betula fontinalis* Sargent. [E. A. P.]

difficulty we had was sewing the boards to each round the timbers. As we had no nails we had to make use of the fine Roots of the Pine which we split;

On the 16th April we had finished the Canoe[1] and got all ready for our voyage. We have killed seventeen Moose Deer but a part of the meat was lost in not being able to bring it to the Hut, and some being killed among steep rocks from whence we could not get the meat; all the Skins were useless, there being no woman to dress them so that all the Provisions we had procured for the voyage was only 220 pounds weight. Although a very great quantity of snow had thawed, yet the many heavy showers of Snow kept it to the same depth, and the River had still the same appearance as when we first saw it in January; the River about two hundred yards in width running clear, with steep banks of snow on each [side] of about three and a half feet; which had a most dreary appearance; Our voyage to the Sea was to proceed down the River, but having only three men, (Pierre Pareille, Joseph Coté, and René Valade) being the only Men that had the courage to risque the chances of the Voyage, we were too weak to make our way through the numerous Indians we had to pass; so few men would be a temptation to some of them to take from us what little we had; while twice this number well armed would command respect; in order to augment my number of men I had to proceed up the River and to the Saleesh Country to where I knew I should find the free Hunters, and engage some of them to accompany me, this gave us a long journey of hardship and much suffering, but by the mercy of good Providence ensured the success of the voyage.

On the 17th April we embarked our Provisions and Baggage with our Snow Shoes, and proceeded up the River.[2] We found

---

[1] The canoe was clinker-built, twenty-five feet long, forty-two inches wide, and sharp at both ends; the boards were not nailed, but sewn together.

[2] After having spent three months in the deep snow on the banks

the Current very strong with many pieces of Rapids, which we ascended with the Pole and tracking Line, seven of these Rapids were so strong that two of us had to walk in the water with the Canoe, while the other two Men on snow shoes tracked it up by a line; at sunset we found a few bare stone in the mouth of a Brook on which we sat down all night, having come nine miles.

On the 18th, cold and benumbed we set off, but the Rapids were so strong we advanced only five miles and camped on the Snow, but made a fire on large logs of cedar.

April 19th. We proceeded five miles of strong rapids, in places we had to carry the cargo, such as it was, to where the River expanded to a small Lake which was frozen over,[1] and we had to camp, we anxiously wished to clear away the snow to the ground; but found it five and a half feet deep, and were obliged to put up with a fire on logs and sit on the snow.

On the 26th we had hauled and carried the Canoe and Baggage to the River, where having come seven miles, we camped on the snow; during this time we had killed two Swans,[2] the female had twelve small eggs, yet I have never found more than five eggs in their Nests, nor have I seen more than seven young ones with them.

On the 27th having gone five miles, we found the River with too much ice to allow us to proceed,[3] and we had to wait with patience on our beds of snow for the ice to clear away; hitherto the Forests were of the ordinary size of three

of the Columbia river, the little party set off up the river to the country where they were known, and could depend on getting assistance in both their trading and exploring enterprises. They had with them three pieces of goods and 235 lbs. of provisions.

[1] This was Kinbasket lake. As the ice was still firm on it, they were delayed from April 19 to April 26, and were at last obliged to make sleds and haul their boat over the ice to the open water of the river above the lake.

[2] Trumpeter Swan, *Olor buccinator* (Richardson). [E. A. P.]

[3] Here they were again held up by the ice for six days.

to twelve feet girth, of Cedar, Pines, Birch, Aspins, Alders and Willows; hunting procured a few Geese and Ducks, but not sufficient to maintain us, and we had to take some of our dried provisions.

On the third of May we proceeded a short distance, and on the fourth met a Canoe with two Nepissing Indians (their country is near Montreal in Canada) and the next day the Grand Nepissing and three Iroquois Indians, they are all on their way to the Valley of the Canoe River to trap Beaver, and hunt Moose Deer; three of these I engaged to assist in the Canoes and hunt for my Men, and by them wrote to M[r] William Henry who is in charge of the Men and Goods; and engaged Charles a fine, steady Iroquois to accompany us as Bowsman, being an excellent Canoe Man; We passed a large Valley bearing N 70° E. having a fine navigable River [1] for twenty miles, being the junction of three branches; we camped as usual on the snow, our legs and feet benumbed walking the Canoe up a strong Rapids, and when on shore with wet feet and shoes walking on Snow Shoes. The Grand Nepissing tells me that for these three years past he has killed, one year at the little Lake below us two hundred Beavers, at a place above five hundred Beavers, and at the Canoe River five hundred Beavers, without any other labor than setting his steel traps with the Castorum of the Beaver, as before described, such is the infatuation of this Animal for Castorum.

May 7th. As we proceeded the country became more open, the Rapids not so frequent nor so strong, we killed one Swan, three Geese and a Teal Duck but since we left our Hut have not seen the track of a Deer or any other Animal.

May 8th. We had many strong Rapids and in the evening came to a Hut we had built on the banks of this River,[2] at the sortie of the defiles of the Mountains by the Saskatchewan River, the distance between them being one hundred and

---

[1] Probably Bush river.   [2] Blaeberry Creek.

twenty miles, this was our usual route from the east side to the west side of the Mountains : there are now many fowl but we killed only one Goose.

May 9th. Proceeding up the River at length we had the pleasure of camping on ground clear of snow, but the Mountains have all the appearance of winter, and we are not likely to have much more snow, as Mount Nelson now shelters us from the heavy Snow Showers of the Pacific Ocean ; saw with pleasure the tracks of two Red Deer.

On the 14th we came to the head of the Columbia River 268 miles from our winter Hut. I could never pass this singular place without admiring it's situation, and romantic bold scenery which I have already described ; other Rivers have their scources so ramified in Rills and Brooks that it is not easy to determine the parent stream, this is not the case with Columbia River, near the foot of a steep secondary mountain, surrounded by a fine grassy Plain, lies it's scource, in a fine Lake of about eleven square miles of area, from which issues it's wild rapid Stream, yet navigable to the sea, it's descent is great. By a close estimation it's head is 5960 feet [1] above the level of the Pacific Ocean, it's length 1348 miles, and it drains an area of Country of 319,083 square miles, it's descent is an average of four feet six inches p^r mile, including it's Falls, except the lower part of the River, every inch may be said to be of rapid current. From the head Lake to McGillivray's River is a carrying place of two miles over a level plain,[2] this River comes from the centre of the primitive

[1] The correct elevation is 2,700 feet.
[2] This is now known as Canal Flat, but was called by Thompson " McGillivray's Portage "—that is, portage to McGillivray's river. Here Thompson met two Indians who had just come from the Tobacco Plains, where they had left most of the Kutenai and all the freemen going to the Salish country. " They tell me," he says in his notes, " the H. B. are in the lake, just arrived from their winter quarters." This, the only mention Thompson makes of the Hudson's Bay people in his notes of this year, refers to Joseph Howse and his men, who had spent the winter near Flathead lake, about where Kalispell, Montana, now stands.

Mountains with a rapid stream throughout it's whole course it is a deep volume of water of about 150 yards in breadth. (Note. May 9th Kootanae Lake; there are many Cormorants,[1] we killed one, they are very fishy tasted and their eggs almost as bad as those of a Loon; it's eyes a fine bright green the eye ball a deep black, the eye lids and about them a light light blue, the head and neck of a glossy black, with a bunch of feathers on each side of the back of the head.) We descended this River for about two hundred and forty miles to a Path that leads to the Saleesh River. In this distance the scenery is very varied; well wooded banks, rude steep rocks, fine Meadows for several miles, then closing to sixty yards of Basalt Rocks, again expending to 350 yards; the current always strong and frequently dangerous from eddies and whirlpools, yet only one carrying place at a dangerous Dalle, of three fourths of a mile; we procured only one Red Deer by hunting, and both the Columbia and this River [afford] no fish, the current is too rapid, and the shores and bottom too hard;

On the 19th in the morning we came to the path[2] that leads to the Saleesh River, here was fortunately a Tent of Kootanae Indians who informed us the great camp has moved from this place only three days ago, and that we should find them on our road; I directly sent off two men[3] to follow after them and procure Horses to carry the Goods we had to the Saleesh River; as we could proceed no farther by water, we laid up our Canoe in safety for future use, and arranged everything to be taken by Horses; in the afternoon of the next day, the two men returned with four Kootanae Indians and seven Horses; with their furniture of saddles,

---

[1] *Phalacrocorax auritus* (Lesson). [E. A. P.]

[2] This was near what is now the site of Jennings, Montana. From here they portaged south across country to the Clark's Fork river, somewhere above Thompson's Falls; there they built another canoe, and descended that river. [T. C. E.]

[3] Charles and Pareil.

lines and saddle cloth of the Bison hides, we went two miles
and put up at sun set: the next day, having gone five
miles we came to the camp of the Kootanaes, and traded five
Horses with their furniture and twenty dressed leather skins
of the Red Deer; for shoes and clothing, which was mostly
paid for in Tobacco and Ammunition: Ignace an Iroquois
Indian was in this Camp. I engaged him as Steersman for
the voyage before us, with a Kootanae as Guide and Hunter
we proceeded, and on the 27th came to the Saleesh River, a
distance of seventy four miles across the country; and as
usual had several bold Brooks to cross, over which we had to
fell large trees for Bridges, and carry every things, with
mishaps incident to such narrow bridges; at the last of
the[m] Ignace carrying two rolls of Tobacco, preferred wading
across the Brook to passing on a single tree, when almost
across he stumbled; the rolls of Tobacco fell (each seventy
pounds) and were swept away by the torrent; we had to
make a small raft and search for them, fortunately the River
was very high and stopped the current, here we found them,
and carried them back. Our Hunter had killed only three
antelopes [1] and those amongst Craigs [so] that we got but little
of the meat and we had to kill two Horses for food, and then
a fine Mare. We went to the Saleesh House in hopes of
seeing M[r] Finan M[c]Donald, and those with him, but saw
neither him nor a Letter. We had now to build a Canoe
and proceed down this River to the Path that leads to the
Columbia River; we had to look for white Cedar; which
having found, we split out Boards, but the fire having injured
the bark, the wood was brittle and could not be bent to the
required shape and we had to look for a tree uninjured by
fire; of which we made our Canoe, and finished it on the
5th of June, on the banks of a small River, where the Indians
had a Weir for fish; on all the Streams that come from, or
form Lake, there are Weirs at which the Natives catch

[1] Probably *Odocoileus hemionus* (Rafinesque). [E. A. P.]

Mullets, gray Carp,[1] and small Trout; the gray Carp is a
tolerable good [fish], much like the red Carp of Canada;
but all the Streams that have no Lake are without fish:
having killed a fifth Horse to take with us, we embarked and
were soon in the Saleesh River; but how very different from
what it was in the Autumn of 1809. Then it had a gentle
current of 350 to 500 yards in width in places bordered by
fine Forests, in other places by rich Meadows of considerable
extent, with plenty of Swans, Geese, Ducks and Plover; all
the time we have been here the water has been rising at the
rate of two feet each day, the River now presented a great
width agitated by eddies and whirlpools, it's apparent height
above the level of Autumn was about thirty feet, rushing
through the woods in a fearful manner, every Island was a
dangerous Fall, and [had a] strong eddy at the lower end;
we saw the risque before us, but we were all experienced
men and kept the waves of the middle of the River, one place
appeared so formidable that we put ashore, and carried everything for two and a half hours: we continued under the
mercy of the Almighty and at sunset put up; each of us
thankful for our preservation; as the morrow did not promise
anything better, and necessity urged us on, my poor fellows,
before laying down said their prayers, crossed themselves, and
promised a Mass to be said for each, by the first Priest they
should see.

The Country was inundated to the foot of the Hills, and
to the Hills all the Antelopes had retired, so that we could
procure nothing by hunting and had to live on Horse Meat:
and meeting with a Tent of Indians we traded an old Horse
for meat to live on. On the 8th June we arrived at the
Long Carrying Place that leads across the country to the
Ilthkoyape Falls of the Columbia River by way of the Spokane
River. A small camp of Kullyspell Indians being near I hired
two of them to go to the Spokane House on this River, and

---

[1] Suckers, probably species of *Catostomus*. [E. A. P.]

inform Mr Finan McDonald who is there to come to us and bring Horses to convey our Goods and Baggage to his place; in the meantime I conversed with these Indians on their forms and proceedings on going to War. As I saw some of them with white earth on their heads, which is the first step; I found them in all this to differ very little from the Indians on the east side of the Mountains; those who attempt to get up a War Party, begin quietly to put white earth on their heads, upon doing of which each morning and evening they pretend to cry for a short time, naming their Relations and friends who have fallen in battle; if the Tribe is inclined to war, this number will augment, until they find themselves strong enough to make the Chief call a council: if the Tribe is not inclined to war; after a few days the white earth is no longer made use of. When the Chief calls a council, which is generally composed of all the steady Men from about twenty five years and upwards, the affair is coolly discussed, and the subject is mostly of their Men who have been slain by their enemies, and too often with their wives and children, with encroachments on their hunting grounds; or a desire to enlarge them: if War is resolved on, the first step is to send two Men who can speak well, to the next friendly Tribe, to discourse with the Chief and the old Men on the subject, in which care is taken not to mention the resolution taken, but the discourse to be on the injuries they have received; and that if they wish to revenge them their Tribe will be confederate with them. If this offer is approved, the Chief calls a Council. And if it is not approved by the Tribe, although as a Tribe they take no part in it, yet as many Warriors as please may march to the assistance of the War Tribe, and thus all the friendly Tribes are solicited, and those who do not declare for the War Tribe send many Warriors to assist them. The Tribes that join form but one Council, and elect a leading Chief of tried conduct and experience; the intended expedition is now calmly dis-

cussed; the number of their men and their leaders, of their
Guns and Ammunition and iron headed Arrows and Spears;
if this is not satisfactory, the change is made to Horse stealing,
but if otherwise, the line of March is now determined; and
they proceed; there is one peculiarity with these Natives
which is but seldom done with the Indians on the east side
of the Mountains, a Vow to shed blood before they return,
which often places them at a loss how to act; if they find no
enemies, which sometimes happens, as blood must be shed
when they commence their return, the Chiefs hold a Council,
when some friendless young man is killed; or a small part of
his scalp is cut away, but if there is no person with them on
whom this may be safely done, two of the principal Chiefs
cut their arms to make the blood flow, with which they
mark a Tree to apprise their enemies how far they have
been in search of them, with strange figures denoting defiance.
Since the introduction of fire arms, their battles are decided
more by their effects, than the number of Men; a very old
Indian told me, when a young man he made a heavy war
club, with which he felt himself confident of victory, they
formed a very large party against the Peeagans, and hoped
for success, when for the first time their enemies had two
Guns and every shot killed a Man, we could not stand this,
and thought they brought bad spirits with [them], we all
fled and hid ourselves in the Mountains, we were not allowed
to remain quiet, and constant war parties now harassed us,
destroyed the Men, Women and Children of our Camps and
took away our Horses and Mules, for we had no defence
until you crossed the Mountains and brought us fire arms,
now we no longer hide ourselves but have regained much of
our country, hunt the Bisons for food and clothing, and have
good leather Tents.

June 12th. Mr Finan McDonald and the Men arrived
with thirteen Horses to carry all we have to the Columbia
River.

June 13ᵗʰ. We came to seven tents of Kullyspel Indians,[1] as the Antelopes have all gone to the high hills, the Natives are obliged to make wiers for fish, mostly Mullets and gray Carp and thus wait the arrival of the Salmon from the Sea now daily expected; they gave us a few Carp, very acceptable as our Horse meat is done;

On the evening of the 14ᵗʰ we arrived at the Spokane House[2] on the River of that name, where I left a small assort-

[1] This was on the " Skeetshoo River House rivulet," the Little Spokane river of to-day. [T. C. E.]

[2] Spokane House was built in 1810 or 1811 by Finan McDonald or Jaco Finlay, at the junction of the Spokane and Little Spokane rivers, ten miles north-west of the city of Spokane, State of Washington. From this text and his map, it is clear that Thompson intended the name Skeetshoo to apply to the lake (Cœur d'Alène) and river flowing from it as far as this junction, and the name Spokane to apply to the stream into which it emptied; see entry of July 3, *infra*. The peninsula at this confluence is a beautiful, protected flat, triangular in shape, and was always a favourite gathering-place for the Indians to catch and dry fish. Alexander Henry first recorded the name Spokane, and described this river, and the Spokane and Simpoil Indians as residing upon it (see Coues, *New Light*, pp. 711–12). A local Indian name for the river is Sen-a-hom-a-na, meaning "river of salmon trout." Henry cites Speh-kun-ne as the Salish or Flathead word meaning both "sun " and "moon," a fact which affords some earlier authority for the usually accepted meaning of that word, namely, "children of the sun" (see Ross Cox, *Adventures*, p. 104); but there is reason to believe that Spokane was merely the Indian name for this peninsula, or fishing-place. Alexander Henry, never having been across the Rocky Mountains himself at the time, must have taken his very complete data from David Thompson, or from clerks of the Company.

Spokane House became the principal distributing and wintering point of the North-West Company for the Upper Columbia, Kootenay, and Flathead trade, and was continued by their successors, the Hudson's Bay Company, until April, 1826, when it was formally abandoned in favour of the new establishment at Kettle Falls (Fort Colvile), built under orders from Governor Simpson. In August, 1812, the Pacific Fur Company under the leadership of John Clarke, from Astoria, built a rival house or fort upon this peninsula, but this became the property of the North-West Company by their purchase at Astoria in October, 1813. All goods for Spokane House were transported at first from Fort William on Lake Superior across the Rocky Mountains, and later from Astoria or Fort George in batteaux up the Columbia river to the mouth of the Spokane, and thence across country on horses about sixty miles, the

ment of Goods to continue the trade; there were forty Tents of Spokane Indians, with Jaco, a half breed, as Clerk. We remained here two days; I observed for Latitude 47°. 47′. 4″ N. Longitude 117°. 27′. 11″ W. Variation 21 degrees East. On conversing with the Natives I learned they were preparing to form a large War Party, in company with the Kullyspel and Shawpatin Indians, against the Teekanoggin Indians,[1] a defenceless Tribe to the southwestward of us; I was very sorry to find that all I could say, or preach to them against warring on defenceless Natives was of no avail. Proud of their Guns and iron shod arrows, they were anxious to try these arms in battle. As I could not break up the War Party, which was at some distance from me, my endeavour was to change it's direction; accordingly I made up a small present of Tobacco and Vermillion for each of the Chiefs, which I sent by two respectable Spokane Indians, with a Speech, reminding them of the defenceless state in which three winters ago I found them, hiding themselves from their enemies, living on roots and fish, in the same state in which the poor Teekanoggans now were, and whom I should soon visit and let them have guns and iron heads for their arrows, that if they were the brave men they pretended to be, they would go against the Peeagans, and their allies who had destroyed very many of them : this had the effect of about fifty warriors marching to the assistance of

Spokane river being entirely unnavigable. For interesting accounts of Spokane House consult Ross Cox, Alexander Ross, Gabriel Franchère, and Washington Irving. David Douglas, botanist from London, in his journal on May 9, 1826, writes: " I set out across the mountains [from Kettle Falls] for the abandoned establishment at Spokane, distant about one hundred and ten miles. My object was to see Mr. Jaques Raphael Finley, a Canadian Sauteur, now resident here." This was Thompson's " Jaco Finlay." The old chimney bottoms of Spokane House are still visible (1912). [T. C. E.]

[1] The Okinagan Indians. This name has always perplexed white men. Thompson in his notes spells it Oachenawawgan, and on his map Ookenawkane. [T. C. E.]

the Saleesh and Kootanae Indians who were encamped against the Peeagans and their allies, and the others went to the Columbia for the Salmon fishery.

June 18th. Our path as usual lay across several Brooks,[1] with the labor of making bridges of trees over those we could not ford, and I noticed a great change in the soil which hitherto has been a light sandy loam, today a fine vegetable mould on a rich clayey loam very fit for agriculture. On the afternoon of the 19th June, thank God, we arrived safe at the Ilthkoyape Falls [2] of the Columbia River;

[1] Thompson travelled the regular Indian trail north through the valley of the Cólville river to Kettle Falls. [T. C. E.]

[2] Kettle Falls of to-day, one of the most beautiful and romantic points on the Columbia river. The falls are double, a few hundred yards apart, not high, but magnificent in the sweep and swirl of the water. They are forty-one miles south of the Canadian boundary, and practically half-way from the source to the mouth of the river. The portage around the falls was on the east bank; and the spot where Thompson probably camped and built his canoe was on the Bushnell Flat, one mile below the falls on the east bank. Ilthkoyape is strictly a Thompsonian designation; it is used by no one else except Daniel Harmon, and by him only in quoting a letter from David Thompson. Ross Cox, Alexander Ross, and Gabriel Franchère called the falls La Chaudière, because of the boiling appearance of the water. The meaning of the name Ilthkoyape has been satisfactorily explained by Mr. Jacob A. Meyers, who lives near Kettle Falls. It is derived from *Ilth-kape*, the Salish word for "kettle" (a basket vessel of woven osiers, roots, and hard-twisted cords), and *Hoy-ape*, the Salish word for "trap" or "net" (see the Salish vocabulary in Coues, *New Light*, pp. 714–15); and it was used to describe the place where the Indians fished with the kettle or basket net. The Indians living on the upper Okanagan river still use a word that sounds like *Ilkopt* or *Ilkohopit* when speaking of the Kettle river or the Kettle Falls. On the early maps of Arrowsmith the name Sayalpee is found immediately above the falls. [T. C. E.]

ILTHKOYAPE OR KETTLE FALLS, COLUMBIA RIVER, WASHINGTON

(Photograph : Frederick Wheeler)

CHAPTER VIII

ILTHKOYAPE INDIANS [1]

Village of Ilthkoyape Indians—Appearance—Habits of salmon fishing—Search for cedar to make a canoe—Precautions necessary in salmon fishing—Habits of the salmon—Canoe finished.

HERE for the country, was a considerable Village of the Natives who have given their name to these Falls; which are about ten feet of descent in a steep slope, in places broken; This Village is built of long sheds of about twenty feet in breadth by from thirty to sixty feet in length, they were built of boards which somehow they had contrived to split from large Cedars drifted down the River, partly covered with the same and with Mats, so as to withstand the Rain; each Shed had many cross poles for smoke drying the Salmon as they have no salt; the number of Men were about . . . so that we count the population at . . . Souls; the Sheds were clean and comfortable, and their persons would have been clean, but they had no soap, and could wash with only simple water; The Men were of common size with tolerable good features, straight, well limbed for activity, their eyes of a mild cast, black and inclining to a deep hazel; their hair long, lightly black, and not coarse, the Women had no beauty to spare, and wanted the agile step of those that dwell in tents.

The arrival of the Salmon throughout this River is hailed

[1] There was no tribe of Indians known as the Ilthkoyapes. Father De Smet in 1843 called them the Shuyelphis; but the fur-traders called them the Chaudières. [T. C. E.]

with Dances and many ceremonies which I was five days too
late to see; and therefore cannot say what they are; but
deep attention is paid by them to what they believe will
keep the Salmon about them; for this purpose the Beach of
the River is kept very clean, no part whatever of the Salmon
is allowed to touch the River after it is brought on shore, the
scales the bowels &c are all cleaned on the land a few yards
from the River, for experience has taught them the delicate
perceptions of this fish, even a Dog going in the edge of the
water, the Salmon dash down the Current, and any part of
one of them being thrown into the water, they do not return
until the next day, especially if blood has been washed; in
spearing of them, if the fish is loose on the Spear and gets
away, the fishing is done for that day. The spearing of the
Salmon at the Fall was committed for [to] one Man for the
public good, of course the supply was scant until the fish
became sufficiently numerous to use the Seine Net. The
third day we were here, the Spearman in going to the Fall
with his Spear came close to the bleached skull of a Dog,
this polluted his Spear; he returned to his shed, informed
them of the accident, and to prevent the fish going away he
must purify himself and his Spear, this was done by boiling
the bark of the red Thorn, the steam of which on himself
and the head of his spear began the process. When the heat
had moderated, his face and hands and the Spear were washed
with it and by noon he was ready and proceeded to the
Fall. On our arrival the Chief presented us with a roasted
Salmon and some Roots, but what was this small supply to
nine hungry men, and as we found the Village had no provisions to spare we had to kill a Horse for provisions, this
was a meat I never could relish, but my Canadians had strong
stomachs, and a fat Horse appeared to be as much relished
as a Deer.

At this Village were Natives from several of the surrounding Tribes, as a kind of general rendezvous for News, Trade

and settling disputes, in which these Villages acted as
Arbitrators as they never join any war party. Anxious to
acquire a knowledge of the Country, it's soil, forests and
animals I spent a day conversing with them; and learned
that this Village was the highest up the River, that no Indians
hunted more than a few miles above them, that all the rest
of this River to it's scource, except a few Kootanaes had no
natives on it, such was the effects of the harassing incursions
of the Peeagans and their allies. The country to the northward was sandy with much rock on the surface which, by their
description seemed to be Trap Rock; the Trees few and
scattered, and these of dwarf Pines and Cedars; there were
no animals until Winter set in when the Antelopes come down
to the low grounds. This accounts for their being poorly
clothed; they have but few Horses, and their Canoes are
half of the hollow trunk of drift Cedar or Pine, reduced by
fire to the thickness and length they require, patched up at
both ends; of the country below us they could give no
farther information than to the next Village.

Our great object was to procure information where good
clean Cedar and White Birch could be found, as the Country
appeared to have none of either, for two days some of the
Natives with my men, in different directions examined the
country for materials to make a Canoe, but found none; and
I was at a loss what to do. On our Road to this place we had
seen a hummuck of Cedar, it appeared of bad growth, full of
Branches, and the Fire had passed; and it was seven miles
from the River, but as a last hope necessity again compelled
us to examine it, and by dint of searching we found materials
for a Canoe, by pieces from different trees; which we hauled
to the River and constructed a Canoe.

I looked upon a part of the precautions of the Natives as
so much superstition, yet I found they were not so; one of
my men, after picking the bone of a Horse about 10 AM
carelessly threw it into the River, instantly the Salmon near

us dashed down the current and did not return until the afternoon; an Indian dived, and in a few minutes brought it up, but the fishery was over for several hours : the greatest number speared in one day was only eleven, their weight from fifteen to thirty pounds ; they were finely formed, but not fat though well tasted ; from the Pacific Ocean to this place is about 740 miles. The River at these Falls is about 300 yards wide, and from the immense numbers that ascended these Falls from Sun rise to it's setting might have employed at least thirty spearmen, and why only one was employed I never could learn ; Both sides of the River are bordered with Hills of four or five degrees of altitude, and I remarked the leaping of the Fish up the Falls was regulated by the appearance of the Sun on these Hills, and not by it's actual rising and setting.

It is a firm belief of the Natives of this River, that of the myriads of Salmon that annually leave the salt water Ocean and enter fresh water Rivers, not one ever returns alive to the sea ; they all proceed to their respective spawning places, accomplish this, and soon after (a few weeks) die of exhaustion ; that such is the case of those who come to, and beyond these Falls there can be no doubt, as after the spawning season the shores are covered with them, besides all that are carried away by the stream. It does not appear that they take any nourishment after they leave the sea as their stomachs are always empty, probably from finding in fresh water no nourishment suitable to them ; it is affirmed that no Salmon spawns twice ; if so, at what age does a Salmon acquire the power of spawning, the life and habits of this fish has something curious ; some of them are spawned above a thousand miles from the sea, in fresh water, in which they are nourished ; and continue to be so to the sea ; here a change takes place and they now find their support in salt water ; until they acquire the power of spawning, when they enter fresh water Rivers which now has no food adapted to them, ascend to the very place where they became alive, there deposit their spawn, and die on their way to the sea. Whatever the history and the habits of the Salmon may be, they form the principal support of all the Natives of this River, from season to season. The Dogs that with impunity eat all other fish in a raw state, die from eating Salmon in this state, which may also be the case with other carnivorous animals, as we never saw any feeding on them; but when cooked the Dogs eat with safety.

On the second of July we finished our Canoe, during this time we had only one Salmon each day, and we had to live on horse meat. On the 29th June a Canadian and two Indians arrived, they bring the melancholy news of the death of the Wife and Child of the former; and of Francois Dejarlaiz, his Wife and four Children, all drowned in one of the Dalles of the Saleesh River, with the loss of all their property: this is another instance of the difference of the navigation of the Rivers on the west and east sides of the Mountains. On the latter the Rapids are plainly seen, and the Falls give distant warning by their heavy sound; but the Dalles of the Rivers on the west side as they pass through the Basalt Ridge make no noise, the narrow channel between their steep walls has a treacherous smoothness which lulls suspicion until the swift current hurries the Canoe on the fatal whirlpool, and eddies from which there is no retreat.

CHAPTER IX

JOURNEY TO THE PACIFIC FROM ILTHKOYAPE FALLS

Start on voyage to the Pacific Ocean—Companions—Pass Spokane River—Visit from Simpoil chiefs and their people—Home of Simpoil Indians—Appearance—Religion—Leave Simpoil Indians—Trade with the Inspaelis Tribe—Appearance— Language — Life — Country — Dances — Religion— Leave Inspaelis Tribe and come to village of Smeatbhowe Tribe— Sinkowarsin Tribe—Continue journey—Shawpatin Indians —Skaemena Tribe.

HAVING prepared ourselves, and everything about us as well as circumstances permitted, and half a Horse for our support, we got ready for our voyage to the Pacific Ocean. The River before us [was] wholly unknown to us, and all information only a day's journey of Rapids direct before us : by Observations I found the Latitude of these, the Ilthkoyape Falls to be 48°. 38'. 7" N Longitude 117°. 48'. 49" west, and the Variation 20 degrees East.[1] The names of my men were Michel Bourdeaux, Pierre Pareil, Joseph Coté, Michel Boulard, Francois Gregoire ; with Charles and Ignace, two good Iroquois Indians, and two Simpoil natives for Interpreters. We placed the Horses in care of the Chief of the Village.

After praying the Almighty to protect and prosper us on

[1] Kettle Falls is in latitude 48° 36' N., longitude 118° 13' W. Its elevation is 1,250 feet above sea-level. [T. C. E.]

THOMPSON OR RICKEY RAPIDS, COLUMBIA RIVER, WASHINGTON,
FIVE MILES BELOW KETTLE FALLS

(*Photograph: Frank Palmer*)

our voyage to the Ocean,[1] early on the third of July we embarked and descended the River for near seventy miles, and in the evening came to the Village of the Simpoil Indians. In the above distance we had several strong Rapids [2] which required all our skill and activity, at one of which we had to carry everything for near three fourths of a mile, the water is high in the River, the current very strong with many small whirlpools and eddies, but not dangerous. At fifty six miles we passed the junction of the Spokane River, which comes from the southeastward by a long series of unnavigable Falls; the whole of this day the country has a pleasing appearance, in places thinly wooded, but the greater part meadows of short grass, very fine for sheep. The grounds high and dry; above and below the Spokane River the banks were often of perpendicular Rock of trap and basalt of a black gray color, in places reddish, these banks had a curious appearance to the height of about three hundred and fifty feet, they retired from the River by a perpendicular step of twenty to thirty feet, then a level table of ten to twenty feet, from which rose another steep step, and level table to the top of the bank. The width of the River may be estimated at about five hundred yards, deep, and a rapid current.

---

[1] In his note-book, Thompson describes the object of his voyage as follows: "We set off on a voyage down the Columbia River to explore this river in order to open out a passage for the interior trade with the Pacific Ocean." [T. C. E.]

[2] The first rapids of the day were seven miles below the falls. "Last ¼ mile very strong, dangerous rapids. Run it close on the right," says Thompson in his note-book. These rapids were marked Thompson Rapids on the Arrowsmith maps (1830–50), which were drawn from information supplied by the Hudson's Bay Company. But they were often described as the Grand Rapids, and now they are known as Rickey Rapids. Thus has passed away the only bit of nomenclature on the main course of the Columbia river given in honour of its first explorer. Other rapids passed during the day were Turtle Rapids at 36 miles, Black Island Rapids at 50 miles, Spokane Rapids at 65 miles, and Hell Gate (forming a complete letter S) at 86 miles. At this last the party was compelled to carry " full ¼ of this the major part of the cargo, and run the canoe with the rest close to the left bank." [T. C. E.]

Having pitched our tents,[1] by my two Simpoil Natives I
sent for the Chiefs of the Village to come and smoke, they
came, and the Men followed in single file, and all sat down
round the tent; the Chief made a short speech, saying he
was glad to see us, and then made a present of two half dried
Salmon, and about half a bushel of Roots of two kinds, the
one called Kamass[2] a white root, of a slight bitter taste which
becomes a favorite, and is agreeable to the stomach; the
other is a kind of small onion, which is dug out of the ground
near the surface in a soft rich soil of loam, then washed and
baked in a smothered heat, when from white, they become a
rich dark brown and very sweet, they are nourishing, but
eaten too freely with moss bread are apt to loosen the bowels,
and these two served for the rough bread and cheese of the
country. I have already remarked that this bread is made
from the long black moss, like hair that grows on the red
Fir Trees. Four pipes were now lighted and the smoking
enjoyed as a feast. The Chief made a long speech in a loud
singing voice, and each sentence [was] responded to by the
others by Oy Oy : the Speech being ended and interpreted
to us, was thanks for our arrival, and hoping we would bring
to them Guns, Ammunition, Axes, Knives, Awls, and not to
forget Steels and Flints with many other articles, they were
able and willing to hunt, and would be able to pay for everything they wanted, but at present they had only their hands
to procure food and clothing, and much more to the same
purpose, all too true. I then explained to them my object
to know how this River was to the sea, and if good, very
large Canoes with Goods of all kinds would arrive, by which
they would be supplied with Clothing and all they wanted
if they were industrious hunters. The two Simpoil Indians
were now called upon to tell them all the News they had

[1] This camp was ninety miles from Ilthkoyape, and three-quarters of
a mile up the San Poil river.
[2] *Quamasia quamash* (Pursh). [E. A. P.]

COLUMBIA RIVER, ABOVE THE MOUTH OF SPOKANE RIVER, WASHINGTON

(Photograph: Frank Palmer)

collected; at the end of every three, or four, sentences, they
stopped and the Chief repeated the same aloud, so that all
could hear, and he was answered by Oy Oy. We noticed
that the News, whether good or bad, was pronounced in the
same tone of voice. Smoking for the present being over,
permission was asked for the Women to come and see us,
which being accorded they soon came with their children,
and made us a present of Roots and Berries; and sat down
around the Men. Smoking commenced for a short time,
each Man took three hearty whiffs at the calumets passed,
but the Women were allowed only one whiff which they made
a long whiff.

The Chief now proposed they should all dance, to this
we assented; the Men formed two slightly curved lines with
the women close behind them; they had no instruments
and the only music was the song of a man painted Red and
Black, his hair stuck full of Feathers. His voice was strong
and good, but had few notes; during the song which lasted
about eight minutes, the dancers moved very slowly forward
with an easy motion, and without changing their position
danced back to the place they had left. At the end of the
song each person sat down in the place where the song left
them : the Chief made a speech of about two minutes; the
Song commenced and the dance, and in this manner continued
for about an hour when they ended and they retired to their
Lodges, and left us to our repose, which we much wanted :

The next day to acquire a knowledge of the country, I
remained until near Noon; the information was, the country
around them was much the same as that we had passed, to
the foot of the Hills; whither all the Deer[1] had gone for
green grass and water; that they were not willingly confined
to the banks of the River, but would follow the Deer, if they
had Guns, or if their arrows were shod with iron; in the

---

[1] In this paragraph the words Deer and Antelope appear to be used
interchangeably, Deer (*Odocoileus*) being referred to. [E. A. P.]

hills the ground was too uneven to surround the Antelope, and in winter when they come to the low grounds, and we surround them, the heads of our arrows break when they strike against a bone and they escape; I found that all these Natives in their unarmed state had the same way of hunting the Deer, by surrounding them. For this purpose the least number required is thirty active Men and Lads, but the more the better; they scatter themselves early in the morning, and as much as possible guide the Antelopes to the level plain agreed upon; the rude circle is gradually lessened in a gentle manner so as not to alarm them; and the Deer meeting each other seems to give them confidence, until the signal is given; when the weapons are flint headed arrows, which more frequently wound than kill, the Deer soon break through the circle of Men and escape; and the same from the noise of the Gun; but the iron headed arrows carry silent certain death to the tender Antelope: the number thus encircled are from twenty to sixty; out of which the flint headed arrow kill but few, but the iron shod arrow more than half of the number. This is the only method by which they procure clothing: their Lodges are made of light poles covered with matts made of rushes, sufficient for this season, but a poor defence against the weather of winter; their wood for the fire and all other purposes is procured from the Trees drifted down the River in freshets, and left on the shore, and when too long they burn through the Log, or Pole to the desired length; and their whole time is taken up in expedients for self preservation.

This is the only village of this tribe, their language is the same as the Saleesh Indians, they are full sixty Men of families, and the number of souls about 420. They are of middle size, their features good, and would be better if they had more nourishment; for want of which they are slightly made, can bear fatigue but not steady labor; the Women and Children were treated with kind attention, and under all their wants they were cheerful and contented, and I hope we shall soon be able to supply their wants; for at present two thirds of their food is roots and berries, the few Salmon they get is from a Wier across a Brook of fifteen yards wide, they are small and poor, they did not know the use of the Net or Seine. Of their Religion I had no time to learn much. They seemed to acknowledge a Great Spirit who dwelled in the clouds to be the master of everything, and when they died their Souls went to him; the Sun, Moon and Stars were all divinities, but the Sun above all; and that he made the Lightning, Thunder and Rain. Their worship was in dancing, and the last dance they gave me was for a safe voyage and return to them.

At noon we left this poor but friendly people, and proceeded down the River for six hours, the first four hours the country was bold high grassy hills, which at length came on the River in steep banks, with isolated rocks, and steep cliffs all having a ruinous appearance, the ravines were many, steep, narrow and rocky, the descent of the Rains had not left a grain of earth, these cliffs contracted the width of the River, the waves ran high with many whirlpools and eddies, in one place the Steersman who was standing to guide the Canoe lost his balance and fell out of the Canoe, but we recovered him, we carried along part of a dangerous rapid; at 6 PM we tried to find a place to pitch our cotton tents, but after an hour's search, we had to sit on the rocks and leave the Canoe in the water.[1] To stem this current is impossible, and although the River is very high, yet some three years past, by the Trees lodged among the Rocks, the water must have been twelve feet higher than at present.

July 5th. A rainy morning, having broken two of our paddles from drift wood we split out four paddles and made

[1] This was at the head of the Kalichen Falls or Rapids, afterwards known as "Rapide d'Ignace," and now known as the Box Cañon or Okanogan Dalles, fifty-one miles from where he started at noon. [T. C. E.]

two for present use; and then embarked, in a short distance
we came to a heavy Rapid, the high waves of which obliged
us to put ashore, and carry everything full two miles; while
we were doing this a Chief with about sixty men, their women
and Children came to, and helped, us over the Carrying
Place. This being done, the Chief for himself and his people
made a present of five Horses, five good Salmon well roasted,
a bushel of arrow wood berries which are sweet, wholesome
and nourishing; about two bushels of various roots, some of
which I had not seen before, and the dried meat of four
small, very fat, animals, which I took to be Marmots;[1] the
two latter with the five Horses I requested the Chief to take
in charge until we returned; for what we kept I paid three
feet of tobacco; fourteen plain and stone rings, eighteen
hawks bells, six feet of a string of blue beads, nine feet of
gartering, four papers of vermillion, four awls and six buttons,
which they thankfully accepted; such is the barter of these
countries with the Natives; heavy rain obliged us to pass
the day here.

This tribe is called Inspaelis, as they procure the Salmon
from the River, and not from a Weir on a Brook, the Salmon
are larger and in good condition, and from their clothing the
Deer are more plentifull than with the Simpoils, they are a
finer people, several of the Men were six feet in height; the
face rather oval, the eyes black, the nose straight and
prominent, the cheek bones moderate, teeth and mouth good,
the chin round, on the whole their appearance is manly,
mild, open and friendly. The men were ornamented with a
few shells, the women more profusely, in their ears, round
the neck, and hanging to their girdles; the tint of the skin
was not so dark as that of a Spaniard, some of the Women
daubed their faces with red ochre. Their Language is a
dialect of the Saleesh; my canadian interpreter (Michel
Bourdeaux) could not understand them, altho' they under-

---

[1] *Marmota flaviventer* (Aud. and Bach.). [E. A. P.]

stood him; my two Simpoils now became our interpreters, by whom I learned they have sufficient Deer in winter for their support and clothing if they were better armed; they have good blankets made of Bear, of Musk Rat,[1] or the black tailed Antelope,[2] which are cut into narrow stripes, and neatly interwoven. Each blanket was of one of these animals, and not mixed.

They described their country as high, dry and hilly, with short grass, the rock showing itself in many places, with but few trees, and those of Fir, stunted and scattered; such a country appears fit for only sheep, deer, and horses; but has many Brooks of clear water: their manner of hunting is the same as alredy described.

After smoking some time, they prepared to give us a Dance, that we might have a safe voyage to the sea and in like manner return to them. The Chief made a short prayer, after which the dance commenced of the Men and Women, each separate, to the music of their singing, which was pleasingly plaintive, their voices full and clear and not too loud; each line of Men and Women had a clear space of three or four feet, within which they danced; at first the step was slow, and the singing the same, but both gradually increased, the step of the dance very quick as if pursuing, or being pursued. This lasted for about eight minutes, when a pause of two minutes took place; a prayer was made, and the dance and singing repeated twice: the whole was strictly a religious ceremony, every face was grave and serious, almost to sadness; the prayers of the Chief was accompanied with holding up his hands to heaven, and so far as I have seen the people on the west side of the Mountains, their Religion appears simple and rational, without sacrifices or superstition, and offer a most extensive and hopeful field for the labors of Missionaries to bring them to the knowledge of the heavenly

[1] *Fiber z. osoyoosensis* Lord. [E. A. P.]
[2] *Odocoileus hemionus* (Rafinesque). [E. A. P.]

Redeemer of Mankind. They went to their Lodges, and sent us a Salmon for which I paid six inches of tobacco. The rapid of this carrying place is in several ridges, rushing down a descent of full thirty feet ; and the Salmon ascended to these.

July 6ᵗʰ. A rainy morning ; early several Men with a few Women came and smoked a while, the Women had bracelets of Shells and fillets of the same round the head. At 6⅓ ᴀᴍ we embarked and in less than four hours [1] came to a Tribe and Village called Smeathhowe ; as usual we put ashore, and I sent the Simpoils to invite them to come and smoke with us. They found them consulting what they should make a present of, for the stranger must have a present made to him or them. My reason for putting ashore and smoking with the Natives, is to make friends with them, against my return, for in descending the current of a large River, we might pass on without much attention to them ; but in returning against the current, our progress will be slow and close along the shore, and consequently very much in their power ; whereas staying a few hours, and smoking with them, while explaining to them the object of my voyage makes them friendly to us. The Men, Women and Children now came dancing, and singing a mild, plaintive song to which they kept time, when close to us, they twice said Oy Oy and sat down around us ; one of them directed the Women

---

[1] Thompson makes here no mention of the Okanagan river, which he passed during these four hours, but in his notes he says, " Last course fine view and see the high woody mountains of the Oachenawawgan River." This view must have been at the upper end of Columbia Bar, about four miles above the mouth of the river, and indicates that the high water allowed them to cut across the bar and save several miles, passing the mouth of the river a full mile away. It was here that David Stuart and his party of the Pacific Fur Company established Fort Okanagan the following September. Thompson next stops at the famous salmon fishery at the mouth of the Methow river with the Indians of that neighbourhood. Upon leaving these Indians he portages around the Methow Rapids just below. [T. C. E.]

COLUMBIA RIVER, ABOVE THE MOUTH OF OKANAGAN RIVER

and Children to sit near the Men; the pipes were lighted, and they all smoked with avidity the men taking from three to six whiffs, some swallowing the smoke, but the Women were allowed only one whiff. They now gave us three well roasted Salmon, and half a bushel of Arrow Wood Berries,[1] very acceptable to us, for which I paid them. I learned that from the time of the arrival of the Salmon, all the fish that are taken for a certain time must be roasted, not boiled; the Chiefs then assemble, and after some ceremonies, the Salmon are allowed to be boiled, or cooked for the rest of the season, as the people choose. The appearance of this tribe is the same as the last, except the Women being more profusely ornated with shells: their knowledge of the River extended no farther than to the next village, where we would learn the state of the River beyond them. At Noon we left them and soon came to a bold Rapid of two miles in length, the waves being too high for our Canoe we had to carry, the Chief and four young men came with horses and helped us to the foot of the Rapid for which I gave them eight inches of Tobacco, which was thankfully accepted; this carrying place took us to 2¾ PM. We then descended a strong current for full three and a half hours, and camped on the left for the first time, the right being steep rocks.[2] The country and banks of the river high, bold hills, very rude; with steep cliffs; we could have passed hours in viewing the wild scenery, but these romantic cliffs always indicated danger to us from the stream being contracted and forming whirlpools, very disagreeable companions on a River: on a Cliff we saw a

[1] *Amelanchier alnifolia* Nuttall. [E. A. P.]
[2] Thompson's observation this evening placed him in latitude 47° 32' N., just above the mouth of the Wenatchee river in Douglas county, State of Washington, and not far below the Entiatqua Rapids. During the day he had travelled nearly seventy miles through a rugged part of the river, with rapid current. He was now on the stretch of river travelled two months later by Alexander Ross on his way to Okanagan with Stuart, and described by him in his *Oregon Settlers*. [T. C. E.]

2 H

Mountain Sheep[1] looking down on us, which we longed to eat, but [he] could not be approached. We had to kill two Rattle Snakes[2] that would not get out of our way.

July 7th. Having descended ten miles, we saw several Men on horseback proceeding to the westward, two of them rode to the River side, we went to, and smoked with them, and each of us held on our ways. I learned that they were sent from a Village to apprise them of our coming. Having continued for four miles, we came to two long Lodges of the same structure as those we have passed, sufficiently well covered with rush matts; one of these Lodges was two hundred and forty feet in length; the other sixty feet in length; each by thirty feet in breadth; all these measurements are by stepping the lengths at three feet each step. By their account the name of this tribe is Sinkowarsin;[3] they are about one hundred and twenty families, and from the Women and Children must be about eight hundred Souls: the Language is still a dialect of the Saleesh, but my Simpoil Interpreters find several words they did not understand; when we passed, and put ashore below them, they were all dancing in their Lodges, to the sound of their songs, for hitherto we have not seen a musical instrument even of the most rude kind along this River. We sent to them to come and smoke, five steady looking men came, sat down near us and smoked, but although many of the Natives we had passed viewed us with some suspicion, as at a loss what to make of us, these Men much more so, nor could their countenances conceal that they did not know what to make of us;

---

[1] *Ovis canadensis californiana* Douglas. [E. A. P.]

[2] *Crotalus confluentus lucifer* Baird and Girard. [E. A. P.]

[3] These were Pisquosh Indians, now known as Wenatchees, belonging to the Salish family and speaking the same language as the San Poil, Nespalem, Okinagan, and Methow tribes. They were at the fishery at Cabinet Rapids. According to his notes, Thompson had observed "high rocky mountains to the south-west," the Wenatchee Mountains, and had portaged at a rapid with a "rude rock in one end," the Rock Island Rapids with Bishop's Rock at the end. [T. C. E.]

all the other Villagers had been apprised of us by some who
had smoked with us, these had only heard of us by report ;
except what they learned from the two horsemen ; no speech,
as usual, was made, and the Simpoil Indians who accompanied
us, explained to them all they saw with us, after smoking a
few pipes, I requested all the other men to come, which they
did, but in an irregular manner, and it was twenty minutes
before they could be made to sit down.   Smoking commenced,
and they offered us a small present of Roots and Berries,
their attention was strongly fixed on our persons, especially
on those who had let their beards grow ; on our dresses which
were wholly of woollen or cotton, their clothing being of
leather.   On our Guns, Axes Knives and making of a fire,
to which last they paid great attention, they appeared delighted with the use of the Axe in cutting and splitting of
the drift wood ; I now explained to them by the interpreters
the object of my voyage down the River, that it was to procure for them articles and clothing such as they saw with us,
besides many other things, equally wanted by them.   All this
passed in conversation with one and another, there was no
Chief to speak to them ; a fine looking man came and sat
close to me with strong curiosity in his face ; after eyeing me
all over, he felt my feet and legs to be sure that I was something like themselves, but did not appear sure that I was so,
a very old Man now came to thank me for visiting them, and
that he had the pleasure of smoking good tobacco before he
died ; at length being satisfied that we came as friends, and
[with] the intention of doing them good, they brought to us
two Salmon, for which I paid them ; they then lifted up
their arms and hands towards the skies praying for our safety
and to return to them : their appearance was much the same
as those we had passed, but having more nourishment their
persons were more full in form, and many of the men were
handsome, with a manly look, the Women I could not call
any beautiful, but many were pretty, good looking with mild

features, the children well formed and playful, and respect with kind attention to each other pervaded the whole; tho' at present poor in provisions, they were all in good health, and except the infirmities of old age, we have not seen a sick person, partly from using much vegetable food, and partly from a fine dry temperate climate.

They describe their country to the southward to be being high dry and barren, without animals; to the northward the lands are good with Antelopes, Mountain Sheep (Big Horn)[1] and Goats,[2] of which their clothing is made, and of the fine long wool of the latter they make good rude blankets. They had also a few Bison Robes which they must have traded from other Tribes; all these things allowed them to be better clothed than any tribe we had yet seen. We saw no weapons of war with them, and like all the other Tribes they may be said to be unarmed: and like them also they were all as cleanly as people can be without the use of Soap, an article not half so much valued in civilized life as it ought to be. What would become of the Belle and the Beau without it. And also all linen, and cotton; I have often known the want of it, and had to use fine blue clay as a substitute.

As we were about to leave this people with their prayers for our safety, a fine looking man came to us and requested a passage in our Canoe for himself and Wife, to a tribe below us of which he was a Chief. He remarked to us that the Simpoil Indians could not interpret for us much farther down the River, as the Natives spoke a different language, which both himself and his Wife well understood, and that he would then become our Interpreter, glad of the offer we gave them a passage with their little baggage. After descending seven miles we put ashore to boil Salmon, for while with the Indians our whole time is occupied in talking and smoking with them, and keeping guard on all that is passing, for with

[1] *Ovis canadensis californiana* Douglas. [E. A. P.]
[2] *Oreamnos montanus* (Ord). [E. A. P.]

people to whom we are utterly unknown, a trifling accident might produce serious effects.   Here was a place for a winter campment, it was of the form of a long Lodge, the earth a dry light soil excavated to the depth of one foot, clean and level, the floor of earth, over which the Lodge is erected. Having descended the current for twenty one miles we camped for the night.[1] To this distance the Banks of the River have become much lower, but all the bays opposite the Points of the River have steep banks of trap rock, about forty to fifty feet, the points are of fine meadow, and when the water subsides to it's usual level must be extensive : the current more moderate, yet has many whirlpools. On the whole this day the River and country has a more pleasing appearance than usual, but without woods, except a few scattered dwarf red Fir.

July 8th.   Having proceeded seven miles we came to a village of Sixty Two families,[2] the rapid current drove us half a mile below the village before we could land ; the Chief, a middle aged, manly looking man on Horseback now rode down to examine us, he appeared very much agitated, the foam coming out of his mouth ; wheeling his horse backwards and forwards, and calling aloud, who are you, what are you. Our custom was to leave one, or two, men in the Canoe to keep it afloat, the rest of us drew up near the shore, about three feet from each other all well armed, myself in the front apparently unarmed ; this Chief sometimes appeared to make a dash at us, we then presented our guns and he wheeled his horse ; in about a quarter of an hour he became

[1] This camp was near the mouth of Crab Creek and the head of Priest Rapids, where the town of Beverley is situated to-day. Thompson and his men suffered here from high wind and mosquitoes during the night ; and rigged up a mast and sail the next morning. This is the southern limit for Indians of the Salish family. [T. C. E.]

[2] These Indians, called Skummooin in Thompson's notes, are Shahaptins from the Kimooenim (Snake) river, a name which puzzled Lewis and Clark in 1805–06. The active, white-haired man is mentioned by Alexander Ross the following month, but higher up the stream. [T. C. E.]

composed, my native interpreter, who stood with us now spoke to him in a manly manner telling him who we were, and what we came for, to which he listened with attention, then called out oy, oy. He was now joined by a well made, short, stout old man, his hair quite white, he was on foot and came with a message. We invited him to come with his people and smoke, upon which he set off on a gallop, the old man on foot keeping near him. Having repeated to the people what we had said and to come forward and smoke, he returned at the same pace, the old man keeping close to him. To our admiration, he was naked and barefooted, and we could not help saying to each other, which of us at his age will be equally active. The Man came and smoking commenced, a present of four Salmon, and two [fish] of a small species, with berries were made, of the latter we took only part. By the interpreter I told them what I had to say, the Chief repeated the words in a loud voice, which was repeated by a man in a louder voice. The women now came forwards, singing and dancing which they continued all the time the men were smoking : The Men were well formed, but not handsome, tho' their features were regular, they were poorly clothed ; and the women equally so, two of them were naked, but not abashed ; they all had shells in their nostrils some had fillets round the head and bracelets of shells round the wrists, or arms, but want of clothing made them appear to disadvantage. These people are altogether distinct from those we have seen, and are of the Shawpatin, or as it is sometimes pronounced, Sararpatin nation, of which there are several tribes, and speak a Language peculiar to themselves, it appeared soft, with many vowels, and easy of pronunciation; it is the native tongue of the Interpreter. These people, as well as those of the last Village, are making use of the Seine Net, which is well made from wild Hemp, which grows on the rich low grounds. The net appeared about full six feet in breadth by about thirty fathoms in length; it was trimmed and worked in the manner we use it, which gave them a supply for the day, and a few to dry. But fish however plenty can never compensate the want of Deer, Sheep, and Goats for clothing, and frequently a change of food.

We left these people and proceeded forty miles to 5¾ PM when seeing a large camp[1] before us we put ashore; four Horsemen came to us, and having smoked I told them to invite the Men to come and smoke, they came and sat down in an orderly manner, the pipes went round, and the often repeated speech was made of my going to the Sea, to procure all the Articles they were so much in want of, and return to them, and for which they must be industrious hunters in the winter season, and procure furrs for payment; all this was readily promised, they said somewhere near their campment would be a good place for us to make a Lodge and trade with them, as the large River close below them led to a fine country and skirted the distant Mountains we saw; that they had a very mild winter, the depth of Snow they showed was about eight inches, they had sometimes more but [it] soon melted away. They represented to us, that they had plenty of Deer, two of the species very small,[2] with small Trout and other Fish for the winter, with dried Salmon; all the above in long detail was repeated by three Chiefs, after each other, in a loud voice : they made us a present of four Salmon, for the first time fat, and gave a little oil on the kettle when

[1] This was one mile below Pasco, Franklin county, State of Washington, where the Northern Pacific Railway crosses the Columbia and Snake rivers. The Indians of this encampment were the Sokulks, who had entertained Lewis and Clark in October, 1805. The name Skaemena, applied by Thompson, is not noted by other travellers, but presumably refers to the Eyakema (Yakima) River Indians. The Shahaptin and Yakima families often met here. [T. C. E.]

[2] These small deer are the Columbian Black-tailed Deer, *Odocoileus columbianus* (Richardson), later described from the mouth of the Columbia river ; and the Coast White-tailed Deer, *Odocoileus virginianus leucurus* (Douglas), described from the Falls of the Willamette. [E. A. P.]

boiled, they had neither roots nor berries ; while the Salmon season continues they live wholly by the Seine Net.

The name of this Tribe is Skaemena, they are Shawpatins, and number one hundred and fifty families, and are not less than about one thousand souls. They were all tolerably well dressed, many of the women had not a shell in their nostril ; and [were] less ornamented than those we have seen. They were healthy, and as clean as people can be without Soap. The Men were generally above the middle size, rather tall, well made for activity, their features good, mild yet manly ; many of the women would pass for handsome if better dressed, they were decent, modest and well behaved. And both sexes kind and attentive to each other, and to their children, most of the latter were poorly clothed, or naked. After giving a dance for a safe voyage, at 9 PM they left us and we passed a quiet night.

CHAPTER X

JOURNEY TO THE PACIFIC CONTINUED

Meet chief of all the Shawpatin Tribes—Proceed on journey and meet several families—Mount Hood—Meet Indians engaged in seining Salmon—Character of country and incidents of travel—Interpreter leaves the party—Honesty of the natives —Description of the country—Arrive at two villages and camp near the Wawthlarlar—People of the villages— Salmon—Continue journey—Reach the Pacific Ocean— Visit Astoria—Finish the work of completely surveying northern part of North America from sea to sea.

JULY 9th.[1] having gone half a mile we came to the junction of the Shawpatin River with the Columbia, the water is high in both, the former is about five hundred yards in width, strong current and turbid water, the natives say, when the water is low it is a series of rapids ; close below the confluence the Columbia is between eight and nine hundred in width. In the distance of three miles we passed twenty families seineing of Salmon, at two miles

[1] Thompson's notes for the day begin as follows : " July 9th, Tuesday. At 6.10 A.M. set off.   Course S. 80° E., ¼ mile to the junction of the Shawpatin with this the Columbia.   Here I erected a small pole, with a half sheet of paper well tied about it, with these words on it :   Know hereby that this country is claimed by Great Britain as part of its Territories, and that the N.W. Company of Merchants from Canada, finding the Factory for this people inconvenient for them, do hereby intend to erect a factory at this place for the commerce of the country around. D. Thompson."   His idea clearly was to provide against being driven from this place, and the country around the lower portion of the Columbia river, as he and his partners had been driven from Grand Portage on Lake Superior, and from the State of Minnesota.

lower down we came to about twenty families, with whom was the Chief[1] of all the Shawpatin Tribes ; he received us in manners superior to all the other Chiefs ; he appeared about forty years of age, say six feet in height of a mild manly countenance good features and every way a handsome man, clean and well dressed ; we found him an intelligent friendly man, he made no speeches, but discoursed with us as man with man ; I found my Interpreter to be a person much noticed by him ; he had several active men about him who acted as Couriers to the other Tribes ; others as soldiers without arms, while we were there two old Chiefs made their appearance, upon which he sent some of them about one hundred yards to meet them ; upon explaining to him the object of our voyage, he entered into all our views in a thoughtful manner, pointing out to us their helpless state, and that under their present circumstances they could never hope to be better, for we must continue in the state of our fathers, and our children will be the same, unless you white men will bring us Arms, Arrow shods of iron, axes, knives and many other things which you have and which we very much want ; we informed him that we had armed all the Natives, particularly the Saleesh and Kootanaes and that as soon as possible we should do the same to all his people, that the way we brought the Goods at present obliged us to cross high Mountains, and through hostile people, that we now sought a short safe way, by which all the Articles they wanted would come in safety. He requested we would make a

[1] Chief Yellepit, of the Walla Walla tribe, which occupied both sides of the Columbia for thirty miles below Snake river, as well as the country about the Walla Walla river. Thompson says in his notes that " he had an American medal of 1801, Thomas Jefferson, and a small flag of that nation." The medal was given him by Lewis and Clark, who describe him as a " bold, handsome Indian, with a dignified countenance, about 35 years of age, about 5 feet 8 inches high and well-proportioned " (see Thwaites, *Original Journals of the Lewis and Clark Expedition*, New York, 1905, vol iii. p. 134). Alexander Ross also mentions him, under the name Allowcatt. [T. C. E.]

Lodge for trading at the junction of the Rivers and many of the Natives would readily find their way to that place; he viewed all we had with great attention, but the women were most delighted with the Kettles, the Axe, the Awl, and the Needle; and I remarked in all their Speeches, they never mentioned Tobacco, or woollen clothing as necessaries although highly desired, yet they were pleased when anything was paid for, to see blue beads, Rings and other trifles for the women form part of the payment. This Chief whom with his small party had come here to have space for fishing, had separated themselves from the others, were actively employed in cleaning, splitting and preserving the Salmon by smoke, using all the precautions which I have already noticed; he made a present of two good Salmon, for which I paid him five feet of Tobacco: he remarked to me, that they were obliged to be very industrious during the Salmon season, as it was the principal dependance throughout the year; for their only way of hunting the Deer was by surrounding them, which seldom gave all of them meat enough;

Hitherto the country has lowered much, and along the River when the water is low there must be much fine meadow, but on the upper banks, and to the foot of the Hills the land is too dry, the grass short and not tender, a hard soil with the trap rock in places, how far it is fit for the plough I cannot say, the climate is very fine and even. In this month of July the heat of the day is always tempered by the westerly winds which rise about 10 AM. and gradually increase to a Gale at 10 PM; then abate, and by 2 or 3 AM [there is] a fine calm and heavy dew, but at times the Gale continued all night; I remarked to the Chief the utter want of Forest Trees, nothing to be seen but a chance dwarf Fir, and their whole dependence was on drift wood, that in other countries there were Forests of various Trees which would require more than one Moon to cross them. He said that they had no Forests, that it was only in the countries of the

Saleesh tribes he had seen Forests of one or two day's journey; that it was more than three winters since he had been there, that the south part of that country belonged to them, of late they had left it on account of the hostility of the Snake Indians of the Straw Tent Tribe, but if armed, they would again possess that country, from which, even from here, we are not far; for in one day's march we come to the Mountains [1] which there, are low; the next day we cross them, and the third day are where we hunt the Bisons, for which we have plenty of good Horses; but they had no bison clothing among them. Through the whole of these Tribes I have seen no weapons of war, rarely a Bow and Arrows, and those fit only for small Deer; not a single stone axe, and small sharp stones for knives without handles, they certainly have no turn for mechanics, an Esquimaux with their means would soon have stone tools and Kettles to hold water and boil their fish and meat; whereas all these Tribes do not appear to have anything better than a weak small basket of Rushes for these necessary purposes. Most of the musical instruments of the eastern Natives are made of parchment, or raw hide dried as the tambour, drum and rattle; and even allowing the skins of animals to be too valuable for such purposes, yet the hoofs of the small deer might be made into an agreeable Rattle as with the Indians on the east side of the Mountains; the whole of their Music is their own voices which costs neither time nor labor.

We embarked and proceeded thirty two miles down the River, and passed about eighty families in small straggling Lodges; at one of which of ten families we put ashore to smoke with them, but they were terrified at our appearance. My men stayed on the beach, and I went forward a few paces unarmed, and sat down with a pipe and stem in my hand;

---

[1] The mountains here referred to are the Blue Mountains of eastern Oregon; and the country where buffalo still ranged was the southern Idaho country along the courses of the Upper Snake river. [T. C. E.]

they sent forward two very old Men, who lying flat on the ground in the most pitiful manner; crawling slowly, frequently lifted their heads a little as if imploring mercy; my Native Interpreter would not speak to them, and all the signs I could make gave them no confidence; close behind the men three women crawled on their knees; lifting up their hands to me as if supplicating for their lives; the men were naked and the women nearly the same, the whole, a scene of wretched destitution, it was too painful, they did not smoke with us, I gave to each of the men two inches of Tobacco, and left them. They appeared as if outcasts from the others; all those we have passed today appeared idle, we saw none of them employed with the Seine, when I spoke to the Interpreter when we camped to learn the state of these people, he gave me no answer, and both himself and his Wife did not wish to be spoken to about them.

In the afternoon, when the River ran to the WSW a high Mountain, isolated, of a conical form, a mass of pure Snow without the appearance of rock, appeared, which I took to be Mount Hood, and which it was; from the lower part of the River this Mountain is in full view, and with a powerful achromatic Telescope I examined it; when clear, the Snow always appeared as fresh fallen, it stands south of the Columbia River, near the shores of the Pacific Ocean, and from six thousand feet and upwards [is] one immense mass of pure snow; what is below the limit of perpetual Snow, appears to be continually renewed by fresh falls of Snow, its many Streamlets form Rivers, one of which the Wilarmet, a noble River through a fine country falls into the Columbia River.[1]

July 10ᵗʰ. A fine morning. Having gone twenty one miles, we came to eighty two families, they were well arranged for the Salmon fishery, their Seine Net was about eight feet in width with strong poles at each end and good lines, and

[1] Thompson's camping-place this night was not far from Castle Rock, Oregon. [T. C. E.]

about fifty fathoms in length; they had also dipping Nets
with strong hoops, and about five feet in depth. Their Canoes,
as usual with all the Tribes, [were] made of the hollow Trees
drifted down the River : I measured one of them thirty six feet
in length, by three feet in width ; We staid about an hour
with them smoking and talking, but they had no information
to give us : proceeding seven miles we put ashore at two
Lodges containing eighty families ; with whom we staid two
hours ; after smoking had commenced they made us a present
of three Salmon, for which I paid two feet of tobacco. They
then gave us a Dance to their singing, superior to any dance,
and the Song more varied in the notes, to which the dancers
kept time with an easy graceful step, for which all the
Natives are remarkable, the youth of each sex formed a
separate curved line, the elderly people behind them, the
dancing and singing were regulated by an old Chief, and
ended by a short prayer for safe return. On enquiring why
they always preferred the curved, to the straight, line in
dancing, the answer was, that the curved line gave them the
pleasure of seeing each other, and that every one behaved
well, which a straight line did not allow ; in none of their
dances that I have seen do they intermix with each other,
but each person keeps steady to the first place : slowly
dancing a few steps forward, and backwards without any
change of the body. At the end of each dance, which may
last a few minutes, they sat down, in doing so, both sexes
with an easy motion sunk to the ground, none of us could do
the same, we were too stiff. After leaving these friendly
people we went to two men who were seining Salmon, and
bought two fish. Shortly after 6 PM we put up, very much
fatigued with a heavy gale of head wind which drifted the
sand like dust.[1]

[1] This camp was, as nearly as can be determined, on the north bank
of the river opposite the John Day river and below what are now known
as the Indian Rapids. It was here that Thompson first heard from the
Indians " news of the American ship's arrival." [T. C. E.]

From information, and from what we have seen the country though much lowered, is still high dry country, covered with short grass, now faded for want of rain, the banks of the river are all of this kind of grassy ground, gently sloping from the interior, which is an undulating plain to the foot of the distant hills. And the soil everywhere appears poor and sandy, it may do for sheep, but what we see is not fit for any other animal. And we never see an animal of any kind; the few Trees are as usual stunted red Fir, the only Tree that will grow on these dry grounds, and the Natives wholly depend on the drift wood for all purposes. The Night being clear I observed for Latitude and Longitude; of which I make a constant practice, to correct the survey of the River and to give a true geographical position to every part, though of no importance to the general reader; and therefore not noticed.

July 11th. A fine morning, having proceeded three miles we came to a Village of sixty three families, with whom we staid smoking for near an hour; and went on our way, over many strong Rapids, some of them required all our skill to avoid being upset, or sunk by the waves; we passed two Villages but could not put ashore; At 2 PM we came to a Village of about three hundred families.[1] We put ashore close below them; they gave us a very rude irregular dance to discordant singing; several respectable Men, came and tried to keep order, which they barely maintained, we saw no person who appeared to act as a Chief, no speeches were made, and as my stock of Tobacco was diminishing every

---

[1] Having passed through the dangerous John Day Rapids and Hell Gate Rapids, and portaging over the "Great Falls" at Celilo, Thompson camped on the south bank of the river at the head of the upper Dalles (Ten Mile Rapids), at the Indian village of Echeloots (Klickitats), where is situated another great salmon fishery of the Columbia, rivalling that of Kettle Falls above. The Indians of this village were the first Thompson had met belonging to the Chinookan family; and here his Shahaptin interpreter left him, and returned to the village at Celilo, where Thompson found him on the return journey. [T. C. E.]

day, I allowed smoking to only the respectable men; they
were all poorly clothed, and the women more so than the
Men, and this sex in decency, modesty, and cleanliness, fell
short of the upper country women : like all the Natives along
this River their living was the Salmon fishery with the Seine
and Dipping nets. Had they been clean and well dressed,
both Sexes would have had a good personal appearance ;
they informed me they had heard of white people from the
sea, and warned us all to beware of the Dalles and Falls which
were close below us ; the soil was light and like what we had
passed : At night the old Men with some trouble got them
all to retire to their lodges, and after smoking a few pipes
left us to pass a quiet night.

July 12ᵗʰ. We were now at the head of the Dalles, to
which there is a carrying place of a full mile. I have already
mentioned the Dalles of the Saleesh and Spokane Rivers;
these Dalles were of the same formation, steep high walls of
Basalt Rock, with sudden sharp breaks in them, which were
at right angles to the direction of the wall of the River, these
breaks formed rude bays, under each point was a violent
eddy, and each bay a powerful, dangerous, whirlpool ; these
walls of Rock contract the River from eight hundred to one
thousand yards in width to sixty yards, or less : imagination
can hardly form an idea of the working of this immense body
of water under such a compression, raging and hissing, as if
alive. (some twenty two years after I passed in 1811, Mʳ
Peter Ogden[1] one of the Partners of the Hudson's Bay Com-

---

[1] Peter Skene Ogden, born in Quebec in 1794, was the youngest son
of Isaac Ogden, a U.E. Loyalist of Lower Canada who was for many
years a Justice of the King's Bench at Montreal. He entered the service
of the North-West Company in 1811 at Isle à la Crosse, was transferred
to the Columbia district in 1818, and remained there until his death at
Oregon City in 1854. Next to Dr. John McLoughlin, he was the most
prominent officer of the Hudson's Bay Company in the district. For a
sketch of his life, see *Quarterly of the Oregon Historical Society*, vol. xi.
Ogden visited Montreal and Lachine on vacation in 1844, and he may have
then met Thompson and told him the incident here recorded. [T. C. E.]

pany on his way to Fort Vancouver came to these Dalles in a Canoe with eleven men; Mr Ogden put ashore and walked down, he advised the Men to carry the Canoe with the Baggage over the carrying place, the road of which is near the bank; the water being low, they preferred running the Dalles, they had not gone far, when to avoid the ridge of waves, which they ought to have kept, they took the apparent smooth water, were drawn into a whirlpool, which wheeled them round into it's Vortex, the Canoe with the Men clinging to it, went down end foremost, and [they] were all drowned: at the foot of the Dalles search was made for their bodies, but only one Man was found, his body much mangled by the Rocks). Last evening when the old Men quitted us, they promised to send us Men and Horses to take everything over the carrying place, but after waiting for them some time, we set to work and crossed everything over a tolerable good path to a small sandy bay; here we had the pleasure of seeing many grey colored Seals,[1] they were apparently in chase of the Salmon, we fired several shots at them to no purpose. About one mile more of Rapids, of which we carried two hundred yards, finished the Falls and Rapids of this River:[2] the Country in appearance has improved, the grass somewhat green, and a few Trees in places, my Interpreter with his Wife left us at the great village, but his own people are higher up the River. I paid him as well as I could for his services, which were of great service to us. but he said he would accompany us to the sea, if he understood the language of the Natives. He was a fine steady manly character, cheerful often smiling but never laughing; he once remarked to me, when he saw my men laughing heartily, that Men ought not to laugh, it was allowed only to Women.

[1] Probably *Phoca richardi* Gray. [E. A. P.]

[2] Thompson's description of the famous Dalles or troughs of the Columbia is brief, but accurate and realistic. When the water is very low, steamboats have been successfully run down through these Dalles, but at great risk. [T. C. E.]

As a change is now to take place, I may remark in justice to the Natives we have passed, that however numerous and poor, not a single insult or aggression was attempted; everything we had was highly valuable to them, yet not a single article was stolen from us; they never offered us women, as is too much the custom of the Indians on the east side of the mountains; everything and every part of their conduct, was with decency and good order; they all appeared anxious to possess every article they saw with us, but by fair barter. And no doubt, a few years hence will find them cultivating the ground, and under the instruction of Missionaries.

Having proceeded sixteen miles, we saw the first Ash Trees [1] with Willow and Aspin a most agreeable change from bare banks and monotonous plains; continuing nine miles we saw two Mountains to the westward, each isolated and heavily capped with Snow; on each side of the River high hills are seen, their summits covered with Snow. Both sides of the River have woods of Aspin, Cedar, Ash, and Willow, but none of fine growth, they are full of branches: having descended forty miles, the greatest part fine steady current, we came to a Village of Houses built of Logs; the people of which are called Wawthlarlar; [2] on the left bank is a Village of Log Houses, the people of which are named Weeyarkeek. At the desire of the Chief of the Wawthlarlar we camped near his Village at 5 PM and bought two good Salmon. These people are a distinct race from those above the Dalles, they are not so tall, but strongly built, brawny, fat people, the

[1] Thompson is now on the stretch of river just below Lyle, Klickitat county, State of Washington. It is on the south side of the river just above this point that the ash and oak trees begin. [T. C. E.]

[2] These Indians were called by Lewis and Clark the Wahclellahs; and those on the south side, the Yehhuhs. Thompson is now at the head of the Cascades, the "Great Shoots" of Lewis and Clark, and the fallen "Bridge of the Gods" of Indian tradition. According to the text, he camped on the north side of the river, but his notes indicate that he camped on the south side just above the site of Cascade Locks, Oregon. [T. C. E.]

face round, the eye black, or hazel, the hair brown, that of the Women and Children light brown, the cheek bones not too high, the Nose full and rather flat, the mouth rather large, the lips thick, the teeth good and the neck short; except a few of both sexes who were clothed, they were all naked, the female sex had scarcely a trace of the decency and modesty of the upper country women. Some of them offered their favors, but they were so devoid of temptation, that not one pretended to understand them; what a change in a few miles.

The Chief came and invited me to his House, which was near to us, it was well and strongly built of Logs, the inside clean and well arranged, separate bed places fastened to the walls, and raised about three feet above the floor, which was of earth, and clean; a number of small poles were fixed in the upper part on which were hanging as many Salmon, drying and smoking as could be placed, for the Salmon are fat and good on their first arrival, they were now losing much of their good condition; the Salmon that enter the Columbia River are of five species as pointed out to me by the Natives, the smallest are about five pounds in weight; and the largest from fifty to fifty five pounds weight; the Natives say, that no two species enters the same stream to spawn, and that each species enters a separate River for that purpose; one of the smaller species was named quinze sous, which amused the fancy of my men, it being the name of a small silver coin. I staid about an hour in the House, he kept talking to me, pointing out the arrangements of his house, and making use of as many English words as he had learned from the ships when trading with them, some of them not the best. The fire place was on the left hand side of the door, for which some earth had been taken away to keep the wood steady on the fire; there was no aperture for the smoke, in order to give the Salmon the full benefit of it. The fireplace was surrounded with rush Mats, the whole appeared comfortable to naked people, but to me was intolerably close and warm, I was glad to breathe fresh air, and get to my Men. The last five, or six, Villages we have passed, as well as these people appear to live wholly on Salmon, without Berries, Roots, or any other vegetable, yet all appeared healthy, and no cutaneous disorders were perceived. For the first time since we entered this River we had the pleasure of cutting standing Trees for fuel; the drift wood was good, but so much sand adhered to it as blunted the edges of our axes, and to sharpen them we had only a file; for the last two miles, there has been sufficient woods along the River side; I was anxious to learn the state of the River below us, but could learn only by signs that there were Falls and Carrying places.

July 13th. We staid till 9¼ AM but could not procure a Guide for the Rapids and Falls.[1] We proceeded three miles of which we carried one mile of a steep Rapid; we continued our course and camped at 8¼ PM. We passed several Houses on each side of the River, they all appeared constructed as I have already described; at one of them we put ashore and traded a few half dried Salmon; and a Native in his canoe came to us and gave us a Salmon, we camped a short distance above Point Vancouver, from which place to the Sea the River has been surveyed by Lieut Broughton R.N. and well described by him.

July 14th. We continued our journey, amused with the Seals playing in the River; on the 15th near noon we arrived at Tongue Point,[2] which at right angles stretches it[s] steep rocky shores across the River for a full half a mile, and brought us to a full view of the Pacific Ocean; which to me was a

[1] Thompson made short work of these famous rapids, 'the Cascades of the Columbia. His portage was on the north side of the river, and he must have re-embarked in very swift water. His camp for the night was nearly opposite Cape Horn. [T. C. E.]

[2] So named by Lieutenant Broughton in 1792 because of its peculiar appearance. [T. C. E.]

great pleasure, but my Men seemed disappointed; they had been accustomed to the boundless horizon of the great Lakes of Canada, and their high rolling waves; from the Ocean they expected a more boundless view, a something beyond the power of their senses which they could not describe; and my informing them, that directly opposite to us, at the distance of five thousand miles was the Empire of Japan added nothing to their Ideas, but a Map would. The waves being too high for us to double the Point we went close to the River bank where there is a narrow isthmus, of one hundred yards, and carried across it;[1] from thence near two miles to the fur trading Post of M^r J J Astor of the City of New York; which was four low Log Huts, the far famed Fort Astoria of the United States; the place was in charge of Messrs McDougall and Stuart who had been Clerks of the North West Company; and by whom we were politely received.[2] They had been here but a few months, and arriving after a long voyage round Cape Horn, in the rainy season without sufficient shelter from Tents, had suffered

---

[1] Franchère's description of the arrival of Thompson and his men throws a touch of colour on the scene: " Toward midday we saw a large canoe with a flag displayed at her stern, rounding the point which we called Tongue Point. The flag she bore was the British, and her crew was composed of eight Canadian boatmen or voyageurs. A well-dressed man, who appeared to be the commander, was the first to leap ashore" (Franchère, *Narrative*, p. 120). [T. C. E.]

[2] Fort Astoria was on the south bank of the river, in latitude 46° 11′ N., longitude 123° 52′ W., according to present-day observations. The building of it had begun on April 12, 1811, when the partners of the Pacific Fur Company had begun to land their stores from the *Tonquin*, and to prepare a place for a trading post. The site, however, had been chosen a few days before. The post was in command of Duncan McDougall and David Stuart; for biographical sketches of these men, see Coues, *New Light*, p. 759 and p. 783 respectively. For comparative accounts of Thompson's visit, see Franchère and Alexander Ross, both of whom were present; Washington Irving, who drew from the original journals kept at the fort; and Ross Cox, who arrived later. Astoria passed into the hands of the North-West Company by purchase in October, 1813. [T. C. E.]

from Ague and low Fever, from which most of them had recovered.

This place was about seven miles from the sea, and too much exposed to the undulations of the waves; the quality of their goods for trade very low, but good enough for the beggarly Natives about them, of the same race I have described, and with few exceptions, [they] appeared a race of worthless, idle, impudent Knaves, without anything to barter, yet begging everything they saw. They were all accustomed to trade with the Ships, mostly of the United States, and had learned a great part of the worst words of their language. The next day in my Canoe with my Men I went to Cape Disappointment,[1] which terminates the course of this River, and remained until the tide came in; at ebb tide we noticed the current of the river riding in waves over the surface to the sea for about four miles; on all the shores of this Ocean, the agitation of the sea is constantly breaking against the rocky shore with high surges, and my men now allowed the great volume of water forming these high surges to be far superior to those of any Lake.

Thus I have fully completed the survey of this part of North America from sea to sea, and by almost innumerable astronomical Observations have determined the positions of the Mountains, Lakes and Rivers, and other remarkable places on the northern part of this Continent; the Maps of all of which have been drawn, and laid down in geographical position, being now the work of twenty seven years.

[1] This well-defined headland is at the mouth of the Columbia at the north side, and ten miles from Astoria as the crow flies. It was observed several times by Spanish navigators earlier, but it was named Cape Disappointment in 1788 by Captain John Meares, because he was unable to discover and enter a river supposed to empty there. [T. C. E.]

CHAPTER XI

DESCRIPTION OF THE COURSE OF
COLUMBIA RIVER

*Description of the Columbia throughout its course—Descent—
Snow Birds—Trees—Chief of the Chinooks, Komkomle
—Chinook cradles—Klatsup Tribe—Slaves—War canoe—
Best navigable water found on the north shore of rivers
flowing east.*

I MAY now give some general description of this River
From its scource in Latitude 50°. 12'. 6" N Longitude
115°. 39'. 30" West to Cape Disappointment in
Lat^de 46 . 18 . 10 N 123 . 43 . 6 West the distance in a straight
line is about S 64 W 630 statute miles; it's scource is
5960 feet above the level of the tide waters of the Pacific
Ocean, including it's Falls and many strong Rapids some of
them of thirty feet descent in two miles; did the River
descend in a straight line, it would be at a change of level
of 9 feet, 5¼ inches p^r mile.[1] Such a change of level could
not be ascended, but Providence in this country of Hills and
Mountains has formed a bold vally through which it holds
it's course, between Mount Nelson and the Rocky Mountains,
and which gives it a length of 1348 miles, making an average
change of level of four feet five inches p^r mile, and [it] is
ascended with toil and hard labor. In the winter season
there is very little snow on the ground for near 770 miles

---

[1] Thompson is singularly in error as to the fall of the Columbia from
its source to its mouth. Its source in Upper Columbia lake is 2,700 feet
above sea-level; and as its length is 1,400 miles, it has a fall of about two
feet a mile. [T. C. E.]

from the sea, and [this] does not lie long; but for the next 400 miles the snow comes on the ground early in December, becomes three to four feet in depth of very compact snow and does not dissolve until the latter end of April; the next 180 miles to the head of the River is almost without snow during winter; throughout the whole of the River the climate is mild and the upper Lakes are open, and have many Swans and Ducks during the winter, of the former there is a large species of which I killed several, weighing from thirty two to thirty five pounds; the inside fat filled a common dinner plate.

The geese are all birds of passage and do not return till the middle of March, at which time the Rooks and a variety of small Birds make their appearance. Of the anomalies of this River not the least curious are it's Woods and Forests: I have already described the Forest of gigantic Trees, at the junction of the Canoe with this River, more remarkable for the size of it's Pines and Cedars than it's extent, which may be about six square miles. Above which there are no forests, only patches of woods, and single Trees, mostly of Fir with some Aspins; below the Forest of the Canoe River, the Columbia has very common woods, to the Ilthkoyape Falls, 740 miles from the sea; in this distance down to Point Vancouver, the banks of the River and the interior country are bare of Woods, except for a chance straggling Tree of Fir. From the last named place to the Sea, there are Woods. They cannot be called Forests, but of common growth; the largest Oak[1] measured only eighteen feet girth, with about thirty feet of clean timber, the rest was in branches. On Tongue Point a pine at ten feet above the ground, clean grown, measured forty eight feet girth, and it's length in proportion; another Pine, thrown down by the wind, measured one hundred and seventy three feet in length, here it was broken off by the steep rock bank on which it fell, and

[1] *Quercus garryana* Hooker. [E. A. P.]

at this length was three feet in diameter without a branch ; close behind Astoria I measured a very tall Pine forty two feet girth : the Raspberry stalk measured eighteen to twenty one feet in height, and the size of a man's arm ; the Raspberries were rather larger than common, of a sweet insipid taste, without the least acid.

On the east side of Cape Disappointment is a Bay, part of which is called Gray's Bay ;[1] in which is situated the village of the Chinooks, whose Chief was the noted Komkomle,[2] a friend of the white men, and who by influence and example kept order as much as possible ; he was a strong well made man, his hair short of a dark brown and was naked except a short kilt around his waist to the middle of the thigh ; his wife was a handsome Woman, rosy cheeks, and large hazel

[1] The bay immediately at the mouth of the river protected by Cape Disappointment is Baker's Bay, so named in honour of Captain Baker of the trading brig *Jenny* found lying there by Lieutenant Broughton when he arrived in October, 1792. About ten miles further east on the north shore was the Chinook village of Chief Comcomly, and about ten miles beyond that are the bay and river named in honour of Captain Robert Gray, who anchored there in May, 1792. Thompson's reference is to the entire north side of the river opposite Astoria. [T. C. E.]

[2] No visitor at the mouth of the Columbia failed to mention Comcomly. Lewis and Clark found him upon the beach when they arrived in November, 1805 ; and so did the crew of the *Tonquin* in April, 1811. All the authorities tell interesting tales as to his authority and conduct. Washington Irving dubbed him "the one-eyed potentate." On March 5, 1814, Comcomly attended a dinner given in his honour on board the *Pedlar*, "clothed with a red coat, New Brunswick Regiment 104th, a Chinese hat, white shirt, cravat, trousers, cotton stockings, and a pair of fine shoes, and two guns were fired on the occasion" (Coues, *New Light*, p. 850). Commander Charles Wilkes found his grave behind Astoria in 1841, and has left us a picture of it (*United States Exploring Expedition*, vol. iv. p. 321). Comcomly's daughters intermarried with the fur-traders ; and one of his grandsons, Ranald MacDonald, born at Fort George in February, 1824, was educated in Upper Canada, served as bank clerk in Ontario, ran away to sea from New York, was cast away on the shores of Japan, and, as one of the first foreigners allowed upon that island, assisted in opening the way for communication between Japan and the rest of the world, but ended his days and was buried near Kettle Falls on the Columbia. [T. C. E.]

eyes, and being well dressed with ornaments of beads and shells, had a fine appearance, both were in the prime of life; she had a fine boy of about nine months old, in their kind of cradle, a flat board at the head of which a narrow board projected, under which was a soft but firm compress against which the head of the child was firmly placed so as to flatten the skull, and throw the brain backwards, leaving the forehead only about an inch in height above the eye brows; all the infants I saw were not treated this way, only those families that aspired to some distinction; another Tribe to the northward, on the contrary, apply a thin board to each side of the head, and thereby compress the forehead to be as high as possible above the eyebrows, and form a long narrow face: the latter appeared like so many Don-Quixote's with a melancholy cast of the countenance; the broad faces of the former, had either an air of ferocity, or a broad grin, both sufficiently distorted to be the ideal of ugliness. A short time before my arrival, the Gentlemen of Astoria informed [me] the Chief Komkomle had met a War Party in their war canoes, and after a long conference had induced them to retire to their Village; when he saw them advancing he left his Village in a small Canoe with three Slaves, and proceeded towards them, then going ashore, he called to them, and they came to him, he squatted down on the ground and made a long speech to them which pacified them; this war party of about a dozen of large Canoes was to revenge an insult one of their young men had received at Komkomle's Village, from another young man in a quarrel at gambling; such, or the affair of a Woman is the cause of their feuds, which too often terminate in loss of life.

In a Bay near the sea, on the left side of the River is the Village of the Klatsups, of the same race as the opposite Village; and as far as I could see Komkomle appeared to act as their Chief, at all conferences squatting down on the ground, an attitude very different from that of the Chiefs of

the interior country, who always stand erect when they address
their people, or strangers.   Almost the whole of the people
of this Village were naked except a rude kilt round the waist,
the few women that were dressed looked much better than
those who were naked ; from what I could see and learn of
them they are very sensual people.   They had a few Sea
Otters[1] on which they set a high value, more than they were
worth, and although Astoria had been settled a few months,
yet they had been unable to settle any steady rate of barter,
either for furrs or provisions, every Sturgeon, or Salmon had
to be again valued in barter ; a great part of this fault lay
in the very low quality of the goods, especially the cotton
goods, and all their Tobacco was in leaf and of the lowest
price.   The Natives were displeased with several of their
articles.

These people had many Slaves, all that I could learn of
them was, that they were prisoners taken in their marauding
expeditions along the sea shore, most of them youths when
taken ; they appeared as well off as their masters, except
their paddling the Canoes, and hauling the Seine Net, in all
which their masters took a share of the labor.   For their
war expeditions they have Canoes well arranged for this purpose, made of Trees drifted down the River ; these Canoes
were all of Pine, some of them fifty feet in length, by four
to five feet in breadth ; they had fashioned them to be high
at the stern but much more so forward ; which was decked
about ten feet, and rose sloping to the height of full three
feet above the rest of the Canoe, the extreme end of which
is flat, with a width sufficient for two men to stand on ; on
this deck, the warriors stand for attack, or defence, each
armed with one, or two, long spears.   Their defensive armour
is made of well dressed buck Moose Skins which are well tied
over the shoulders, and hang loose before them, and in this
manner are well calculated to deaden the force of the arrow,

------

[1] *Latax lutris* (Linn.).   [E. A. P.]

or the thrust of the Spear : with both of these weapons they
are dextrous, and have courage to use them ; I saw no fire
arms among them, which appears the Ships seldom trade
with the natives, and which, for want of a regular supply of
ammunition they do not value, the case will now be otherwise.

My surveys for fifteen years on the east side of the Mountains forced on my attention, the deepest channel,[1] and the
most navigable part of the Rivers, which I was frequently
ascending and descending ; all the great Streams northward
of the Missisourie take their rise in the Mountains and flow
northeastward, either into Hudsons Bay, or the Artic Sea :
these are the Saskatchewan and it's great branches into the
former ; the Athabasca and Peace River with their tributaries
into the latter sea. Besides the above many Rivers descend
to Hudson's Bay, from the interior numerous Lakes, all their
courses are north of east ; in all these numerous Rivers, the
best channel and the best navigable water is constantly on
the left side, or as it may be truly called, the north side of
the River ;[2] it is along this side the Canoes and Boats always
ascend, and very rarely on the right or south side, and this
only for a short distance ; even this is caused by the above

[1] Until about 1880 the ships' channel from the Columbia Bar entered
Baker's Bay, and then followed the north bank up the river, very seldom
favouring the south bank. The ships of the fur-traders came to anchor
opposite Astoria, four miles away, and all goods were landed in small
boats. It was this arrangement that led to the drowning of Alexander
Henry and Donald McTavish while crossing the river to the *Isaac Todd*
on May 22, 1814. The introduction of irrigation in cultivation of the
land and the cutting down of the timber has caused so much silt to enter
the river that bars and islands have been formed, and the ships' channel
has been changed to the south bank from Gray's Bay to the Cape.
[T. C. E.]

[2] The sun shines more directly and with greater force on the northern
sides of the valleys ; consequently these sides are dry, and the dry or
soft rock breaks down more rapidly. The southern sides of the valleys,
being less directly influenced by the rays of the sun, are moister, and
more thickly covered with vegetation ; consequently neither the water
falling as rain, nor that flowing in the streams, cuts down the southern
bank as quickly as it does the northern one.

Law which detains the greatest volume of water on the north shore, for it is in this deep water the drift Trees with their Roots loaded with earth, and often Stones; float down, and some chance one is stopped along the bank, or on some inequality of the bottom; sand and gravel collect around it, and thus it becomes a shoal, perhaps an Islet: this tendency of the deep water to the north shore of Rivers that have an easterly direction is so universal, and invariable that it may be classed [as] the Law of Rivers flowing eastward. But of rivers whose general course is south to north or from north to south, as the Mississippe, there was no such law acting on the waters of the River, the only steady difference noticed was, the deepest water [was] more frequently on the east side than on the west side. As I was acquainted with no large River that ran from east to west, I was at a loss to know how far this Law would be found in Rivers flowing in that direction; this opportunity the Columbia River afforded me, as well as its branches; and on my passage up it, from the Sea to the Mountains, our ascent of the Current and Rapids as well as the Carrying Places to the Falls, were wholly on the north side of the River. I have often thought what could be the cause of this invariable Law, but all my reasonings on this fact has only led to inefficient theories, and if not accounted for by some more learned man, must be placed with the unknown cause, which, on the same parallel of Latitude, gives to the west side of the Continents a much warmer Climate and finer countries than the east side. Perhaps the attention of some of the curious in these matters may be directed to see how far this Law guides the waters of the great Rivers in their neighbourhood; both in the United States, and in other parts of the world. The Lakes have generally, the deepest water and the highest and steepest banks of the east side.

CHAPTER XII

FROM ASTORIA TO SPOKANE HOUSE

Preparations for return journey—Leave Astoria—Hostility of the Natives—A prophetess—Attack by the natives—Arrive in the country of friendly Indians—More trouble with Indians —Basalt rocks—Island sacred to the dead—Mussel Rapid— Rattle snakes—Fang teeth of the rattle snakes—Collecting poison from the rattle snakes—Rattle snake's enemy—Uses of the rattle snakes—Reach junction of the Shawpatin River —Camp with Shawpatin Tribe—Pay the Interpreter and leave the Shawpatin Camp—Abandon canoes and proceed on horseback—Natives along the Columbia River—Arrive at Spokane House.

HAVING procured a few Articles to assist me in buying provisions, for which I gave my note, and having found the Latitude of Astoria to be 46° . 13' . 56" North, the Longitude 123° . 36' . 16" West of Greenwich, and the Variation 20 degrees East ; we prepared for our return up the River. With M[r] M[c]Dougall I exchanged a Man, by the name of Michel Boulard,[1] well versed in Indian affairs, but weak for the hard labor of ascending the River, for a powerful well made Sandwich Islander, (whom we named Coxe,[2] from his resemblance to a seaman of that name ;) he

---

[1] Boulard had been with Thompson for several years, and his name appears at many places in his journals.

[2] Alexander Ross says this exchange of men did not take place until July 31, farther up the river, and that "Cox was looked upon by Mr. Thompson as a prodigy of wit and humour." Cox seems to have been back at Astoria again in April, 1814 (see Coues, *New Light*, p. 868). [T. C. E.]

spoke some english, and was anxious to acquire our language, and would act as Interpreter on our Ship from England to this River.

On the 22nd July, in company with M[r] David Stuart[1] and three small wood Canoes, with eight Men, with an assortment of Goods for trade with the Natives, we left Astoria with a prayer to all merciful Providence to grant us a safe journey; with the exception of Coxe, my men were as before two Iroquois Indians, four Canadians, with Coxe, seven Men. We were all eight well armed, each man had a Gun and a long knife, except Coxe, who had one of my Pistols, of Mortimer's make of eighteen inches barrel, carrying a ball of eighteen to the pound: for I remembered the menacing looks of many of the Natives. On the contrary M[r] David Stuart and his Men were in a manner unarmed, and the Natives who were all well armed viewed them with a kind of contempt.

We proceeded on our journey, and on the 25th came to a party of the Natives seineing of Salmon, each haul they caught about ten, they gave us surly looks, and nothing we could offer, would induce them to let us have a single fish: We camped a short distance below Point Vancouver; the River has much subsided, yet the water is still high and the fine low points and meadows inundated. The next morning one of my [men] shot an Antelope; it was fleshy, but not fat, it appeared to be of a species I had not noticed, finely formed, it's measure was, from the nose to the insertion of the tail, five feet five inches, the length of the tail fourteen inches, the height at the fore leg, three feet, three and a half inches; at the hind leg, three feet six inches, round the

---

[1] David Stuart and his party were bound for the interior to establish a trading post, the location of which had not been decided upon. Thompson accompanied them, but has little to say of them. In the light of his narrative, however, it is now possible to estimate better the accuracy of the various annalists at Astoria, Franchère, Ross Cox, and Alexander Ross, the last of whom was with the Stuart party as clerk. [T. C. E.]

breast three feet four inches ; the back of a fawn color, the throat, breast and belly, were white : the Horns had each three branches, and [were] eight inches from tip to tip, the meat was well tasted.[1]

On the 27th a blind Chief in his Canoe with two Slaves to work it, came and smoked with us, he was the only person I had seen thus afflicted.   Some time after two Canoes came to us, they had scowling looks.   M[r] Stuart requested them to bring us some Salmon, which they promised, but they did not keep their word : the surly looks of those we passed to-day led us to suspect an attack on us ; we continued our voyage with all the exertion we could make against a strong current, to get past this people as fast as possible ; when we camped, we kept our Canoes in the water ready for self defence.

July 28th.   A fine morning ; to my surprise, very early, apparently a young man, well dressed in leather, carrying a Bow and Quiver of Arrows, with his Wife, a young woman in good clothing, came to my tent door and requested me to give them my protection ;[2] somewhat at a loss what answer to give, on looking at them, in the Man I recognised the Woman who three years ago was the wife of Boisverd, a canadian and my servant ; her conduct then was so loose that I had then requested him to send her away to her friends, but the Kootanaes were also displeased with her ; she left them, and found her way from Tribe to Tribe to the Sea.

---

[1] This was apparently a specimen of the Coast White-tailed Deer, *Odocoileus v. leucurus* (Douglas).   [E. A. P.]

[2] This throws new light on the " two strangers " who had arrived at Astoria from the interior on June 15, 1811, carrying a letter addressed to " Mr. John Stuart, Fort Estacatadene, New Caledonia "—a letter which had been given them by Finan McDonald to get them out of the Spokane country (see the accounts of them given by Gabriel Franchère and Alexander Ross).   Thompson had seen them at Astoria, but does not mention them until they seek his protection at the rapids.   An account of the career and death of a woman who is probably identical with the one here referred to will be found in Sir John Franklin's *Narrative of a Second Expedition to the Shores of the Polar Sea*, London, 1828, pp. 305–06.   [J. B. T. and T. C. E.]

She became a prophetess, declared her sex changed, that she was now a Man, dressed, and armed herself as such, and also took a young woman to Wife, of whom she pretended to be very jealous : when with the Chinooks, as a prophetess, she predicted diseases to them, which made some of them threaten her life, and she found it necessary for her safety to endeavour to return to her own country at the head of this River.

Having proceeded half a mile up a Rapid, we came to four men who were waiting for us, they had seven Salmon, the whole of which they gave us as a present ; I was surprized at this generosity and change of behaviour, as we were all very hungry, at the head of the Rapid we put ashore, and boiled them ; while this was doing, the four men addressed me ; saying, when you passed going down to the sea, we were all strong in life, and your return to us finds us strong to live, but what is this we hear, casting their eyes with a stern look on her, is it true that the white men, (looking at Mᵣ Stuart and his Men) have brought with them the Small Pox to destroy us ; and also two men of enormous size, who are on their way to us, overturning the Ground, and burying all the Villages and Lodges underneath it : is this true and are we all soon to die. I told them not to be alarmed, for the white Men who had arrived had not brought the Small Pox, and the Natives were strong to live, and every evening were dancing and singing ; and pointing to the skies, said, you ought to know that the Great Spirit is the only Master of the ground, and such as it was in the day of your grandfathers it is now, and will continue the same for your grandsons : At all which they appeared much pleased, and thanked me for the good words I had told them ; but I saw plainly, that if the man woman had not been sitting behind us they would have plunged a dagger in her. This day till 2¾ PM we had to ascend heavy rapids, with several carrying places, which we soon managed, but Mᵣ Stuarts log Canoes could not be carried, they had to be dragged over the rough

2 K

rocky paths of every carrying place, besides the labour of
getting them up the banks which took much time and delay,
but I could not think of leaving them exposed to the villainy
of the Natives. Mʳ Stuart had to hire the Natives, who were
collecting around us, to help his Men to get the log Canoes
over the Carrying Places. About 10 AM, they demanded
payment; and would give no more help until paid; at least
three times the number demanded that had helped to carry
the goods and drag the canoes. Mʳ Stuart hesitated who to
pay, but Dagger in hand they were ready to enforce their
demands, and he had to distribute leaf Tobacco, to ten times
the value of their services; it appeared to us, they were
determined to pick a quarrel for the sake of plunder. Every
man was armed with what we called the double Dagger, it
is composed of two blades, each of six to eight inches in length,
and about a full inch in width, each blade sharp pointed with
two sharp edges; each blade was fixed in a handle of wood,
in a right line with each other, the handle being between
both blades, it is a most formidable weapon, and cannot
without great danger be wrested from the holder; several of
them took a pleasure with a whet stone sharpening each edge
to flourish their daggers close to our faces, one fellow several
times came this way to me; as if meditating a blow, I drew
a Pistol and flourished it around his breast, and I saw no more
of him. There were several respectable looking men who did
not approve of their wild behaviour, and at times spoke a
few words to them, which seemed to have some effect.

We had yet the great Rapid and Dalles¹ to ascend, and
the Natives appeared to afford no more help, and keep Mʳ
Stuart where he was at the foot of the Rapid; we both of
us saw our danger, and that we must go on as fast as possible

¹ The Cascades of the Columbia, which Thompson had descended on
July 13. For an account by another eye-witness of the events that follow,
see Alexander Ross, *Oregon Settlers*, pp. 109–11. Franchère, Ross Cox,
and Washington Irving also describe the episode. [T. C. E.]

to get clear of these people : We expressed our surprise that
we who had come so far should meet such hard treatment ;
that we came to supply their wants, and not to kill, or be
killed, and if they continued to threaten our lives, they must
not expect to see us again ; upon this they called to the
young men, to go and assist Mr Stuart up the rapids and
over the carrying places, which they willingly and readily did ;
but there was a large party that rendered no assistance ; we
soon ascended the Rapids with the line, and carried over the
worst places to the head of the Dalles, where we put our Canoe
in the water, and in it placed our baggage ready to set off.
This we had done sooner than the natives expected, and we
were waiting to learn how Mr Stuart was getting forward :
our place was on a level rock of basalt which formed the rim
of the River, and nearly on a level with it, so that we could
not be surrounded. As this was the last place where we
could be attacked at a disadvantage in position, I was anxious
to see what these people would do ; our arms were in good
order and each of us in his place ; about fifteen yards from
us, running parallel with the River, was a bank of gravel,
about twenty feet in height, steep, except opposite to us,
where it was broken into a slope. This bank formed the edge
of a plain, we were scarcely ready before a number of them,
came over the plain to the sloping part of the bank, each
armed with a double Dagger, a Bow and three Quivers of
Arrows, they formed three rows on the slope, from the top
to half down the bank, the Arrows were all poisoned, as we
afterwards learned ; each man had one arrow to the bow,
and three more in the hand that held the Bow ; their bringing
so many Quivers of Arrows was meant to intimidate us ; the
notch of the arrow was on the bow string but not drawn, I
directed my men, who formed a line of three feet from each
other, to direct a steady aim at the most respectable men,
and not vary their aim ; on casting my eye on Coxe, the
Sandwich Islander, he had marked out his man with his

large Pistol, which he held as steady as if it had been in a Vice, my orders were, as soon as they drew the arrow to fire on them, but not before; in this anxious posture we stood opposed to each other for full fifteen minutes, (it seemed a long half hour) when the upper rank began to break up, and in a few minutes the whole of them retired, to our great satisfaction; for a single shower of arrows would have laid us all dead; we heartily thanked God.

Mr Stuart soon after came, and by hard exertion we got everything he had over except one Canoe, we then went about half a mile, and camped late, very thankful that we were once more together. On talking over the events of the day, we hardly knew what to make of these people; they appeared a mixture of kindness and treachery; willingly rendering every service required, and performing well what they undertook, but demanding exorbitant prices for their services, and dagger in hand ready to enforce their demands, fortunately they were contented with Tobacco of a cheap quality. They steal all they can lay their hands on, and nothing can be got from them which they have stolen; we noticed, that the party which came on the bank of gravel to attack us, were all men of from thirty to fifty years of age, and were from near the sea; as my party were well armed and [had] little to do but take care of ourselves, we were marked to be the first to fall, Mr Stuart and party would then be easy work: still there were some few kind men among them, and more than one man came close to us with his dagger, and in a mild voice warned us of our danger, and to be courageous; and two men in a canoe told us, a large party were determined to kill us, and to keep a good watch, which we did all night, but none came near to us.

July 29th. Very early brought the canoe that was left behind; we loaded and at day light set off; fortunately for us the ground for upwards of five miles was inundated, two canoes with each two men came up to, and followed us, keeping close behind us, these called aloud, and were answered by a Party on shore keeping on the edge of the overflowed grounds; and thus following us, and calling to each other for the five miles, at the end of this distance was a Point of Pine Woods, with dry banks, very fit for an attack as the current obliged us to keep close to the shore, so far as the water would allow us, the calling to each other became more frequent, which also plainly shewed us where they were; when within three hundred yards of the Point to their disappointment, we sheered off from the shore, and crossed the River, which here is a thousand yards in width, and thus set ourselves free from these Scoundrels.

Their determination was to kill and plunder us, but they were equally determined that not one of them should be killed in so doing; there was no Chief among them, each man appeared to be his own leader; whatever conduct in canoes they may have as warriors I do not know, but on land they were bungling blockheads. Thankful to the Almighty for his kind protection of us, we proceeded about one mile and put ashore to boil Salmon, glad that we should now proceed in peace. After proceeding a few miles, we recrossed the River and soon after camped, enjoying the hopes of meeting with our former friendly Indians. Soon after a Canoe with four Men came, and passed the night with us. They are going to the Shawpatin's to trade Horses. They informed us of what I have already related, and that the instigators were Natives near the Sea. As usual we had to pick up pieces of drift wood to make our fire.

July 30th. We came to a Lodge of Shawpatin Indians with whom we smoked, and thanked God we were once more with friendly Natives in whom we could place confidence. We have passed much Oak, but have not seen any of a fine growth.

July 31st. The first five miles the River had banks of Basalt, mostly in rude pillars and columns, close behind which, and

in places attached were ruinous like walls of the same; some
of the columns were entire for forty feet, these were generally
fluted; others in a dilapidated state, the fracture always
horizontal, in blocks of one to three feet, the color was a
greyish black, the whole had a ruinous appearance, they were
the facings of sterile, sandy plains, with short, scanty dry
grass, on which a sheep could hardly live. Near 9 AM we came
to the Upper Dalles,[1] above which is a long heavy Rapid; to
avoid these unnavigable places, there is a carrying place on
the left side of five miles. We sent the Indian Interpreter
to the Village at the head of the Rapids to assist us over;
and bring us some Salmon, at 1 PM several of the Natives
came with Horses and brought us some Salmon, and in three
hours time we got all across; and some time after the canoes
also; as we were getting everything in order for the morrow,
one came and informed us, that some of the Chiefs with
their men were coming to seize our Arms, and keep them, we
directly got ready for the defensive; and soon saw a straggling
party coming towards us: when near us and seeing us ready
to defend ourselves, they made a halt, after some sharp
words on each side, they retired; we had to keep watch all
night it was very stormy and drifting the sand; they kept
walking about, and with all our watching they stole from us
fifteen feet of the line for tracking the Canoe up the current.
These people are part of those of the large Village that
behaved so rudely as we passed on our road to the Sea. I
have already remarked that the Dalles of all the Rivers on the

[1] After no very strenuous or exceptional experiences on the "middle
river," Thompson reached the "Big Eddy" at the foot of the Dalles,
four miles above the present city of the Dalles. Stuart, leaving his
party behind, accompanied Thompson during the day in order to learn
the portage, but returned at night. The portage around the Dalles
is about seven miles long, and very tedious, on account of the
sand; it is on the south side of the river, where a government canal
and locks are now (1912) being constructed. The famous Indian village
of Wishram described by Washington Irving was situated on both sides
of the river along and above this portage. [T. C. E.]

west side of the Mountains are formed of Basalt; these last, which we call the great or upper Dalles, had the Natives been more peacably inclined, I intended to have passed a few hours in examining them, but what I did see led me to believe that the imagination may have full play to form to itself the ruins of buildings, temples, fortifications, tables, dykes, and many other things in great variety; I am aware that geologists give an igneous origen to basalt; this is a theory I could never bring myself to believe; what is of igneous origen must have been in a fluid state, and could never have cooled down in isolated fluted columns, and many other forms that have sharp edges; there is not the least vestige of volcanic action, no hot springs are known, nor salts of any kind; I have calmly examined Basalt Rocks over many hundred square miles, and every where they have the same indestructable appearance, neither heat nor frost, weather, or water seem to act upon them, what is broken, or shivered, does not decay, nor form rounded debris. Every where they present the same sterile, barren rock, alike deny-ing sustenance to man, or beast.

August 1st. We had some difficulty to get the Inter-preter [1] to embark, which having done we set off, thankful to Heaven for having passed the last of these troublesome people; a short distance above the Village we came to an Isle, which was held sacred to their dead. There were many sheds under which the dead bodies were placed, all which I wished to examine, but my Interpreter begged of me not to do it, as the relations of the dead would be very angry; we passed about one hundred and seventy men in several parties, into which they have now divided themselves, for to have full space for seineing Salmon, upon which they are all employed; as all these were friendly we stopped a short time and smoked with them. Having proceeded twenty six miles, the banks of the river the same barren basalt, and the plains much the

[1] Thompson set out from the head of the Upper Dalles. [T. C. E.]

same, we camped at 7 PM, and with searching about found bits of wood enough to boil the Kettle.[1]

August 2nd. Early set off, and proceeded twenty six miles; in this distance we passed one hundred and fifty five men, with their families, they were all employed with the Seine, and with success; in the early part of the day, measured a Salmon four feet, four inches in length; and it's girth two feet four inches, this is of the largest species; but not the largest I have seen: the banks of the same material, but much higher; the first bank about one hundred feet broken into several steeps; then about eight hundred feet, in rude like walls, retiring behind each other, and rising with narrow table bits of rough grass, the country on each side rude and hilly without woods for several miles, and destitute of Deer, or the wild Sheep of the Mountains.

August 2nd.[2] Having advanced a full mile we came to a Rapid, which from the very many shells, we named the Muscle Rapid; these shells are very frequently found on the beach, as well as on the rapids, but always empty; on the shoals in the River, the Natives find them alive, but do not consider them good to eat, and only hunger obliges them to use them for food, and yet I could not learn the eating of them is attended with any bad effects other than they are very weak and watery food without nourishment. It is with some regret we proceed past several parties of the Natives, they are all glad to smoke with us, and eager to learn the news; every trifle seemed to be of some importance to them, and the story of the Woman that carried a Bow and Arrows and had a Wife, was to them a romance to which they

[1] The camping-place at night was some distance below the mouth of the John Day river. The Hell Gate and John Day Rapids were difficult to ascend with the line. [T. C. E.]

[2] This day's travel included several strong rapids, and took the party only about as far as Roosevelt on the north bank, or Arlington on the south bank. The rapids where mussels were observed were probably those now known as Indian Rapids near Squally Hook. [T. C. E.]

paid great attention and my Interpreter took pleasure in relating it.

August the 3rd and 4th.[1] The appearance of the country much better; the banks of moderate height with low points of good meadow land; the interior country though still bare of Woods is level without hills, the grass good and very fit for Sheep. That hateful reptile the Black Rattle Snake continues to be very numerous. What they feed on I cannot imagine, small birds there are none, and the track of a Mouse in the sand is not seen, yet when killed their inside is full of fat. His visage is of a dirty black, as broad as it is long, high cheek bones, and eyes starting out of their sockets like those of a crab, the very face of the devil; of all Snakes they are supposed to be the most poisonous, and we dread them accordingly. On going ashore our custom always is, to throw part of our paddles on the grassy ground, and although we think we can see everything on the short, scanty grass, yet by doing so we are almost sure to start one of these Snakes that we did not see. Every morning we rose very early, while the Dew was falling and tied up our bedding as hard as we could, these were two Blankets, or one with a Bison Robe; and when we put up for the night, did not untie them until we lay down, by which time they were all withdrawn into their holes in the sand, for they always avoid Dew and Rain; they are fond of getting on anything soft and warm. One evening, seeing a convenient place, and a little wood we put up rather early, and one of the Men undid his blankets and laid down, the fish was soon boiled and we called him to supper, he sat up, but did not dare to move, a Rattle Snake had crept in his blanket and was

[1] On August 3, Thompson got beyond the high hills into the lower country, and appears to have camped near Cayote station in Oregon. On August 4, he lined up the Umatilla Rapids, where he complained of rattlesnakes (which still exist in some abundance in that neighbourhood), and camped near either Juniper on the south bank, or Tomar on the north bank. [T. C. E.]

now half erect, within six inches of his face threatening to bite him, he looked the very image of despair. We were utterly at a loss how to relieve him, but seeing several of us approaching he set off and left us. When any animal comes near him, he retires about ten feet, then places himself on the defensive, with one third of his length on the ground. The rest of the body is erect, with his head forward ready to dart; his teeth is clean and white; in the lower jaw are two curved fang teeth of about one fourth of an inch in length; each of these has a fine groove in the inside, and a bag of poison at it's root, of a black color, containing a quantity equal to a drop of Spirits, these fang teeth are moveable, and lie flat in his mouth, until he is to seize his prey, or defend himself. They are then erected, and when he bites, the fang teeth presses on the bag of poison which rushes through the groove into the wound, and the animal is poisoned; these teeth are loose in the socket, and readily drawn out by his biting a bit of soft leather; or cloth.

The Hunters assured me that a full grown snake biting in a fleshy part, unless instantly cut out, and well sucked, is fatal in three or four minutes. I saw a Hunter who had been slightly bitten in the calf of the Leg, the part was quickly cut out and sucked, he had no other injury than a stiff leg, with very little sensation in it, he said it was like a leg of Wood, but did not prevent him from hunting; At the tail of each is a rattle, which he sometimes uses to warn animals that he is ready for mischief; it is said he adds a rattle every year but this is a fable, for of the many that are killed, the greatest number of rattles I have seen was thirteen, and this number is rare; I have heard of fifteen rattles, but snakes having this number must be very scarce. We sometimes cut willows of about six feet in length, get round a large one, and flog him, the length he darts to bite is only fifteen to eighteen inches, so that we were safe; in this case the Snake coils himself round a willow, keeps darting his head with a quick motion, and the rattle moving with great quickness and making a surprising noise. Mice and small birds appear to be it's food, a single bite is given, and he coils to wait it's effect, when dead the victim is smoothed and softened with the saliva, and then swallowed head foremost, the fang teeth lying flat in his mouth. The only Natives that use poisoned weapons, are the scoundrels that possess this River from it's mouth up to the first Falls; to collect the poison, aged Widows are employed, in each hand they have a small forked stick of about five feet in length, and with these the head and tail of the Snake is pinned fast down to the ground; then with a rude pair of pincers the fang teeth are gently extracted so as to bring the bladders of poison with them; these bladders are carefully placed in a muscle shell brought for this purpose, the Snake is then let loose, and is accounted harmless; the aged Women thus proceed until a sufficient quantity is collected, and then placed in one muscle shell; the arrow shods, whether of iron, or flint being well fixed to the arrow shaft, for about half an inch in length, is dipped in the poison and carefully set to dry, when dry it has the appearance of dark brown varnish; when fresh the scratch of an arrow thus poisoned is fatal. The late Mr Alexander Stuart in a skirmish with the Natives near the sea in an attempt to plunder him, was wounded in the shoulder with one of these arrows, five years after it had been dipped in the poison, and which to appearance was worn off; yet it affected his health, and was supposed to have hastened his death. There are four species of the Rattle Snake, three of them are common in some parts of Upper Canada, all of them have very short rattles and if taken in time their bites can be cured; but the black Rattle Snake is found on the upper part of the Missisourie, and along the Columbia River, on the warm sandy soils of these Rivers, where they are too numerous. When near the Missisourie, I remember starting a bull bison, headlong he ran over some sand knowls, where a number of these reptiles were basking in the sun, they bit him with good will, he ran on kicking and flinging up his hind feet, but did not fall as far as I could see him. These Snakes have always much fat in their insides, which is of a fine white color, which the Hunters say possesses a peculiar quality; when they are fatigued and the joints stiff, by this fat being rubbed round the knees and ankles they become supple, and free from stiffness; one of them related that being very tired he made a free use of it, which weakened his joints for two days [so] that he could hardly stand, and never more made use of it; the opinion of the Hunters were that the use of it brought on a weakness of the Knee and Ankle. The Rattle Snake fears no animal but the Hog. This voracious brute is it's master: as soon as the Hog sees a Snake, with a peculiar grunt he sets off full speed. The snake exerts itself to get away, but the Hog soon comes up with it, and directly placing one of his fore feet on, about the middle of the Snake holds it fast, in an instant he bites off the tail about near two inches above the Rattle, which he throws away and seizing the bitten end in his mouth devours it, the snake writhing in agonies, holding itself straight from the Hog to get away, not once turning to revenge itself, when within about two inches of the head, the Hog drops the rest with the head. What can be the cause of this powerful antipathy which is far stronger than the love of life, to which even the dreadful venomous Rattle Snake yields it's life, without the slightest defence; in this respect the Indians justly look on the Hog as a Manito. I have never yet seen the doctrine of antipathies explained, yet it's action and effects are strangely powerful. The civilized world is well acquainted with the superstitions on Vipers, of which it may be said, there is no end. The Indians, and also the white Hunters have their superstitions; and every part of a venomous Snake has its use, or certain properties; and there is one that I have more than once seen tried and each time [it] produced its

effect. This is the Rattle of the Snake; those who have seen
the rattle, or a good drawing of it, know it is in shape like a
thin oblong clean skin bladder, each slightly connected with
each other, in each of the small circular hard substance about
the size of the head of a large pin; when a Woman is in hard
labor, and her situation doubtful, one or two of the rattles
is bruised very fine, mixed with a little water and given to
the woman, which very soon relieves her : among the Indians
I remember five cases and each successful; and they informed
me they never adminerster it, but in cases of necessity : how it
is supposed to act I could never learn. The skin is used to
cover the sinew part of the Bows which are strengthened
with sinews, each bow requires two skins, as only the widest
part can be made use of : the flesh is some times eaten, and
is said to be in taste like an eel : it's poison I have already
noticed, I do not know of any experiments made on it, or
any use to which it is applied, except the poisoning of
weapons; it's antipathy to the Hog so well known has induced the Hunters to procure the large teeth of full grown
Hogs; form a band of them, which is tied close below the
knee, and sometimes another at the ankle, of each leg. This
is held to be full security against all kinds of venomous snakes;
and so far as is known, no person thus fortified has ever been
bitten by a snake. On this part of the continent venomous
Snakes are not known northward of the fiftieth parallel of
Latitude.

August 4th and 5th. Two fine days, we proceeded sixty
miles, strong current and Rapids; for the whole of this distance the sides of the River are of Basalt Rock, in all it's
wildest forms, a fine field for the imagination to play in, and
form structures from a Castle to a Table. Parts are in pillars
much shattered, other parts show fluted columns, like those
of an organ; rising above each other, and retiring to the
height of three hundred and fifty to four hundred feet, on
the top of which are sandy plains as already described. The

Columbia is here nine hundred yards in width with a powerful current, and if a River of it's simple action could force a passage through Rocks, in how many places may it be said this River has done it. Yet every intelligent man must confess that the headlong current of this River has nowhere opened a passage, but everywhere adapts its width and depth to the vallies and chasms (the Dalles) of this basalt formation : which has been opened by the Deity. We were now at the junction of the Shawpatin River with the Columbia (by the United States named Lewis and Clarke's River) a distance of three hundred and thirty four miles from the sea : From the above place to the Ilthkoyape Falls, is four hundred and three miles, the whole of this distance we knew by experience to be little else than a series of heavy rapids from their descent, which would occasion us heavy work and much carrying, even if we could ascend the River, which appeared very doubtful; for altho' the water had lowered about ten feet, yet it was still high and the low points overflowed. We had passed one hundred and twenty Men at their occupation of seineing Salmon, and were now at Lodges containing two hundred Men with their families, they were all of the Shawpatin tribe, and this place their principal village,[1] they are a fine race of Men and Women and with their children very cleanly in their persons, and we no longer had to see naked females, many were well clothed, all of them decently with leather, and in cleanly order, it was a pleasure to see them. We camped with them, and as usual [they] entertained us

---

[1] These are the Sokulks once more, really Nez Percés. Alexander Ross supplements the narrative here with an interesting note : " On the 14th, early in the morning, what did we see triumphantly waving in the air, at the confluence of the two great branches, but a British flag, hoisted in the middle of the Indian camp, planted there by Mr. Thompson as he passed, with a written paper laying claim to the country north of the forks, as British territory " (*Oregon Settlers*, p. 128). Ross says that these Indians called Thompson " Koo-Koo-Sint," which appears to be a corruption of the Salish word for " star," and probably meant " the Star Man." [T. C. E.]

with singing and dancing for an hour ; here I traded a Horse for my Indian Interpreter, and otherwise paid him for his services, and he remained with his people. We smoked and talked until late. They were pleased with the account of the exertions we were making to supply them with the many articles they want, and the hopes of a Vessel with goods coming by sea next year : but that at present I must proceed to the Mountains for Goods : all these natives have the good sense to see that to assist me is to forward their own interests. The junction of this River with the Columbia is in Latitude 46°. 12'. 15" N Longitude 119°. 31'. 33" West Variation 18 degrees East.

August 6th. We left this friendly Village with hearty wishes for our safe return, and ascended a strong current to Noon on the 8th.[1] The water was high, the tops of the Willows just above water : the width of the River between four and five hundred yards, the land moderately high, the banks sloping, but all sandy, sterile, with coarse hard grass in round tufts, equally bare of Birds and Deer as the lands we have passed. We were now at the Road which led to the Spokane River, having come fifty six miles up this River ; we had smoked at four small Villages of whom we procured Salmon of the lesser species, of about three to five pounds weight, they were well tasted and in good condition, but to cook them we were still dependent on drift wood, for these sterile grounds produce no Trees. At the Road was a Village of fifty Men with their families ; they were anxiously waiting our arrival, they had sung and made speeches until they were hoarse, and danced till they were tired : we sat down and smoked ; told the news, and then informed them that I had

[1] They had now left the Columbia, and had begun the ascent of the Snake river. Thompson had decided to return to Spokane House overland, instead of by the slow river route against the current, and had sent a messenger to Jaco Finlay for horses. Meanwhile, he continued in his canoe up the Snake river to the crossing of the main trail leading northward. [T. C. E.]

to go to the Mountains northeastward of us, and the course
of this River being southward, I could proceed no farther in
my canoe; that my Men would require horses to carry our
things on our intended journey, for which I would pay them
on my return from the Mountains; to all that I said they
listened, at times saying Oy Oy we hear you; they retired
and shortly after made me a present of eight Horses and a
War Garment of thick Moose leather such as I have already
described : but saddles and other furniture, they had none to
spare us : and we had to make use of our clothes for these
purposes.

On the 9th we laid up the Canoe for future use,[1] it was
very leaky as there being no Trees we could procure no
Gum for the seams; while we were doing this the old Men
came to us, and after smoking, said, the Chiefs and the Men
below us are good people, but whatever they give they expect
will be paid, but this is not to make a Present, which is a
gift without payment such as we have made to you; this
was all very good, but I knew they could not afford to make
Presents, and gave to each Person who brought me a Horse,
for the value of ten beaver skins in goods, payable at any of
the trading Posts, which being explained to them, they were
much pleased, though they could not comprehend how a bit
of paper could contain the price of a Horse. Having finished
a series of Observations I found the Latitude of this place to
be 46° . 36' . 13" N Longitude 118° . 49' . 51" west, and the
Variation 19 degrees East. In the afternoon we left this
place, and also on the 10th, went north eastward twenty

---

[1] This was at the mouth of the Palouse river ("Drewyer's River" of
Lewis and Clark), otherwise styled by the fur-traders Pavion, Pavilion, or
Flag river. It was another established camping-place for the Nez Percés.
Later it became Lyons Ferry, the crossing-place for all travel between the
Walla Walla and Kootenay and Colville and Spokane districts, and the
crossing of the first military road surveyed by the United States Government between the Columbia and the Missouri. Thompson did not wait
for the horses which Jaco Finlay was to send, but negotiated a horse trade
against a note in hand. [T. C. E.]

eight miles, we crossed several Brooks, and at length, thank heaven, got clear of the sterile, sandy ground with wretched grass, of the basalt formation which in this distance often shows itself above ground with many sharp splinters which cut the feet of the Horses; in taking my leave of the Basalt Rocks, I may safely say, that, although I have paid attention everywhere, to find some traces of an igneous origen, yet I have not found any, no ashes, no scoriæ, and every spring of water cold. For my part I have no belief in its supposed origen, but believe that as the Deity has created all the other various rocks, so he has likewise created the several hundred square miles of Basalt Rocks of the Columbia River and adjacent countries. In geographical position it appears to lie about midway between the Mountains and the Ocean, and in a direction nearly parallel to the Mountains. In the great deserts of this formation nothing is heard but the hissing of the Snakes, nothing seen but a chance Eagle like a speck in the sky, swiftly winging his way to a better country: but these countries are free from the most intolerable of all plagues, the Musketoes, Sand and Horse Flies; they are not found in arid, and very dry countries. The number of Natives along the banks of the Columbia River may be esti-mated at 13,615 souls, reckoning each family to average seven souls; This estimation is not above the population; the manner in which this estimation was made was by counting the number of married men that smoked with us, and also that danced, for we remarked that all the Men of every village, or lodge came to enjoy smoking Tobacco; they speak of Tobacco as their Friend, especially in distress, as it soothes and softens their hardships. Their subsistence appears to be about ten months on fresh and dried Salmon, and two months on berries, roots, and a few Antelopes; those on the upper part of the River, once a year cross the Mountains to hunt the Bison, and thus furnish themselves with dried Provisions and Bison Robes for clothing, during which they are too

2 L

frequently attacked by the Peeagans and their Allies; their Horses stolen and some of themselves killed and wounded, but as soon as these Natives are armed, this warfare will cease.

On the 11th we had a complete change of soil, a fine light loam, with Brooks and Pond[s] of Water, bushes of willows first made their appearance with a number of small birds, some few singing, a few ducks were seen, then hummocks of Aspins; the grass green and tender on which our Horses fed with avidity; but saw no Deer. Having gone about forty miles, we arrived, thank God, at the trading Post on the Spokane River.[1] Provisions having fallen short and our Guide assuring us we should see no Deer, nor Indians to supply us, we had to shoot a Horse for a supply.

[1] Spokane House, ninety miles from Snake River as the crow flies. Jaco Finlay had gone to meet them, but returned by evening. [T. C. E.]

CHAPTER XIII

JOURNEYS AROUND SPOKANE HOUSE

Arrive at Ilthkoyape Falls—Build a canoe—Ascend the Canoe River—Valley of the Canoe River—Arrival of the party with supplies—Return to the mouth of the Canoe River—Supplies sent to the Trading Posts of the Interior—Cross to the East side of the Mountains—Home of the Mammoth—Reach head waters of the Athabasca River—Arrive at Columbia River—Set out for Ilthkoyape Falls—Reach Ilthkoyape House, Spokane House and Saleesh House—Peeagans in search of trading party—Arrival of Messrs John George McTavish and James McMillan with supplies—Winter at Saleesh House—Seek a place of greater security for a Trading Post—Return to the House.

AT the House we remained till the 17th, the Salmon caught here were few, and poor. Several Indians of the Kullyspell and Skeetshoo tribes came to see us, but finding we had not brought a supply of goods, they returned; my Canadian Interpreter spoke their language fluently, and for hours they would sit listening to all he related; frequently asking questions of explanation, they could not well comprehend how the Salmon could live in the Lake of Bad Water, as they called the Ocean; but since he had seen them come from that Lake they believed him: like all the Natives of these countries, their greatest enjoyment seemed to be, to sit smoking and listening to news. On our passage up, however busy the Natives were in fishing, they always gladly left their Nets to smoke and learn our adventures.

Being informed that we were now on our way to the Mountains for a supply of Goods for trade, they said they would take courage, and as soon as the furr of the animals became good they would apply themselves to hunting. This trading Post is in Latitude 47 . 47 . 4 N, Longitude 117 . 27 . 11 west. Variation 19 degrees East.

Leaving this trading Post, to meet the Men and Goods, which are expected from the east side of the Mountains we had to proceed to the Columbia River, to the Ilthkoyape Falls there to build a Canoe, and ascend the River; on the 28th we arrived, having come sixty eight miles, over a fine country of open Woods and Meadows with Ponds and Brooks of Water;[1] all fit for cultivation and for cattle. We were well received, and with these people were a number of Ookanawgan Indians and eight Men of the Spokane tribe : they gave us a dance, accompanied with singing, regulated by the old Men, each party seemed to wish to outvie each other in the easy motions and graceful attitudes of the dance, in which some of them made use of their Arms, gently waving them, keeping time to the tune of the Song, which was plaintive, and the Dance alternately advancing and retiring. We were obliged to go about seven miles for Cedar Wood, and very little of it good for our purpose, and it was the second day of September that we finished the Canoe and were ready to continue our journey. During this time we were visited by parties from several tribes, all anxious to learn the news, and when they may hope for my return with goods for to supply their wants, especially Guns, Axes, and Knives; but they had no Provisions to trade with us but a few pounds of dried Salmon, and we had to subsist on Horse meat, which I could never relish, and contrived to maintain myself by shooting

---

[1] This was the same road as Thompson had followed on June 18–19 of this same year. [T. C. E.]

SITE OF SPOKANE HOUSE, EIGHT MILES NORTH-WEST OF THE
CITY OF SPOKANE, WASHINGTON

(Photograph: T. C. Elliott, 1913)

a few Ducks and Pheasants; for the Antelopes were only beginning to leave the hills, and I had no ammunition to spare.

Cartier the head Chief of the Saleesh Indians, with about twenty men of his tribe also came, these people are the frontier tribe. I strongly requested him to collect his tribe with their allies, the Kootanaes, Spokane, and Skeetshoo Indians who were not far off. He replied, You are well aware when you go to hunt the Bison, we also prepare for war with the Peeagans and their allies; if we had ammunition we should already have been there, for the Cow Bisons are now all fat, but we cannot go with empty Guns: we do not fear War, but we wish to meet our Enemies well armed; all this I knew to be true and reasonable, and reserving only a few loads of ammunition I gave him the rest, with a Note to M[r] Finan M[c]Donald who was at the Post on the lower part of the Saleesh River,[1] to supply them with all he could spare. They set off, with a promise to meet me with Provisions at the upper Saleesh House in two Moons hence. When we had been six days here, a quarrel arose among the people of this Village, in which one man was killed, and several of them wounded. I wished to see the manner in which they treated the dead: but could not well do it, as my Interpreter heard them whispering to each other, anxious to know which party I should support, and any attention, though from mere curiosity, would be construed as favorable to the party of which he was, all of which I most carefully avoided; but my Interpreter by pretending to be looking for some trifle to trade, saw all that passed; the body was . . .[2]

[1] This was doubtless Kullyspell House. Finan McDonald was probably in charge of this post; but at this time he, with four men and two Indians, was on a trip up the Columbia river from Ilthkoyape Falls. He went up the river as far as the present town of Revelstoke, and returned to the falls on August 27, where Thompson was at that time.

[2] Two pages of manuscript are here wanting. In the index prepared by Thompson, the contents of these pages are given as " The Dead. Columbia. Strong current. Columbia. Coxe. Ice." For the itinerary, see pp. xciv–xcvi.

·meaning ; he [Coxe] had lived wholly on an Island, and knew
.it's extent, but had no idea beyond it, as we proceeded up
the River, and passed the great Branches, the stream became
lessened, and not so wide, as he did not know from what
cause, every day he expected to get to the end of it ; as we
approached the cold increased, and the first shower of snow,
he was for some time catching in his hand, and before he
could satisfy his curiousity it was melted : the next morning
thin ice was formed, which he closely examined in his hand,
but like the Snow it also melted into water, and he was
puzzled how the Snow and ice could become water, but the
great Mountains soon settled his mind, where all became
familiar to him.

On examining every where to find a Letter, or some marks
from some of my people, whom I expected here, nor from my
Iroquois I hung up a letter for the latter, as I conceived the
Men with Goods had passed by the Canoe River, which was
near the Road of the Defile, and proceeded up it's strong
current in a valley of the Mountains in a direction of N 42° W
for forty eight miles, the work of three and a half days, with
seven men in a light canoe ; which was thirty one working
hours, being at the rate of one and a half mile pʳ hour, and
this wholly by Poles shod with iron ; the paddle was no use
in this very rapid current ; we often estimated it's descent
in many places to be three feet in forty yards.   Such velocity
of water has always a bottom of Rock, or large gravel.   This
River was about thirty yards in width and two feet in depth ;
the canoe drew only four inches of water ; the Poles can be
used only in shallow water, and in four feet do not advance
much ; those for a canoe are about eight feet in length and
can ascend a very strong current.   The descent for these forty
eight miles cannot be less than ten feet pʳ Mile,[1] or four

[1] The actual descent of the Canoe river is about five feet to the mile.
Thompson, though accurate in his horizontal distances, often over-esti-
mated his vertical distances.

hundred and eighty feet. Every person is acquainted with the change of velocity in streams swollen by heavy rains or the melting of snow. I have dwelt longer on this subject than I intended, from the many works I have seen limiting the navigation of Streams to those that do not exceed a velocity of four miles p^r hour, and a descent of twenty inches p^r mile; this is all right for the heavy craft of Europe, and for deep Rivers; it may seem strange, yet it is strictly true, that the streams from the great Mountains, in their vallies are navigable to light vessels, and have few, or no Falls, while all those that rise in hilly countries have many Falls which have to be passed by carrying places. Of such are all the Rivers that fall into the great Lakes of Canada. The valley of this River with it's stream diminished to a Brook is computed by the Hunters to be near one hundred miles in length, with a breadth never exceeding one mile; the Moose Deer and Beaver have been, and are yet so abundant throughout this Valley, that the Hunters call it the "sack of Provisions"; the paths of the former, from the low Hills on one side crossing to the other side are five to six feet in width and worn a foot deep in the ground; almost all our Meat, while in this quarter, came from this River.

The Beaver were very numerous; and were yet plentiful; the grand Nepissing informed me that in this River he had taken by traps eight hundred and fifty Beavers and should pass his winter in the Valley with two Iroquois his companions. But another year of trapping will in a manner exterminate them, such is the infatuation of this animal for it's castorum: The great difference of climate, and also the formation of the country has changed in part, the habits of this animal, the mildness of the former does not oblige them to build houses; and the country has few Lakes, and those banked with rock; the very unequal heights of water in the Rivers could not be provided against, for except their houses were built for the lowest state of the water, they would often be dry, and if for this state of the water, they would often be several feet under water ; the Beaver therefore seeks the little shelter he wants in the banks, the roots of trees, and other chance places, and prepares very little aspin young trees for winter food, and thus like other animals adapts itself to the climate of it's residence.

As we were sitting round our camp fire, at a loss whether to proceed, or to return, for a North West course did not lead across the Mountains, the season was fast advancing, thank kind Providence two Men in a small canoe came up to us.   They informed us that the day after I hung up the Letter they had arrived with the Goods on Horses from across the Mountains and were there waiting orders under the charge of Mᵣ William Henry ; this good news was joyfully received, and early the next morning we were in our canoes, and in a few hours ran down the forty eight miles we had ascended, and came to the Men and Goods ; after a glad meeting, we found they were making a canoe of very bad Birch Rind which could never be made water tight ; the men left the work, and split out thin boards of white cedar wood, of which a canoe was made ; in the meantime the canoe we had was loaded with the goods, and nine men,[1] and sent down the Columbia to the Ilthkoyape Falls to the care of Mᵣ Finan McDonald for the supply of the lower posts on McGillivray's, the Saleesh and Spokane Rivers.

We had to cross to the east side of the Mountains for the rest of the goods and Provisions,[2] the snow so deep at the height of land, that with difficulty the Horses got through it ; and in one place they had to pass the night up to their

---

[1] These men were Hamelin, Mousseau, l'Amoureux, Vaudette, Bereis, Méthode, Canada, L. Paquin, and Michel Kinville, who was in charge.

[2] Having sent off one loaded canoe, they turned eastward, and on September 29, started to cross the mountains for the remainder of their trading goods. On October 4, they arrived at William Henry's camp on the east side of the mountains, where two Indians arrived with a letter from John McDonald of Garth, asking them to meet him at the Kootenay

bellies in snow, and the next morning were so discouraged it was some time before we could get them to a steady walk : but on the 13th of October all was completed and the Horses sent back to winter on the east side of the Mountains. The Thermometer was at +22 and ice forming, and the water in the River lowering ; and we had yet several hundred miles to pass to the most distant Post.

I now recur to what I have already noticed in the early part of last winter, when proceeding up the Athabasca River to cross the Mountains, in company with . . . Men and four hunters, on one of the channels of the River we came to the track of a large animal, which measured fourteen inches in length by eight inches in breadth by a tape line. As the snow was about six inches in depth the track was well defined, and we could see it for a full one hundred yards from us, this animal was proceeding from north to south. We did not attempt to follow it, we had no time for it, and the Hunters, eager as they are to follow and shoot every animal made no attempt to follow this beast, for what could the balls of our fowling guns do against such an animal. Report from old times had made the head branches of this River, and the Mountains in the vicinity the abode of one, or more, very large animals, to which I never appeared to give credence ; for these reports appeared to arise from that fondness for the marvellous so common to mankind ; but the sight of the track of that large beast staggered me, and I often thought of it, yet never could bring myself to believe such an animal existed, but thought it might be the track of some monster Bear.

On the sixth of October we camped in the passes of the Mountains, the Hunters there pointed out to me a low Mountain apparently close to us, and said that on the top of

Plain on the Saskatchewan river, as he was on his way west with supplies for them. The late date of the receipt of the letter, however, made it impossible for them to comply with his request ; see note on p. 539. Henry's camp was a short distance below the mouth of the Miette river at the head of which is Yellowhead Pass.

that eminence, there was a Lake of several miles around
which was deep moss, with much coarse grass in places, and
rushes; that these animals fed there, they were sure from
the great quantity of moss torn up, with grass and rushes;
the hunters all agreed this animal was not carnivorous, but
fed on moss, and vegetables. Yet they all agree that not
one of them had ever seen the animal; I told them that I
thought curiosity alone ought to have prompted them to get
a sight of one of them; they replied, that they were curious
enough to see them, but at a distance, the search for him,
might bring them so near that they could not get away; I
had known these men for years, and could always depend on
their word, they had no interest to deceive themselves, or
other persons. The circumstantial evidence of the existence
of this animal is sufficient, but notwithstanding the many
months the Hunters have traversed this extent of country in
all directions, and this animal having never been seen, there
is no direct evidence of it's existence. Yet when I think of
all I have seen and heard, if put on my oath, I could neither
assert, nor deny, it's existence; for many hundreds of miles
of the Rocky Mountains are yet unknown, and through the
defiles by which we pass, distant one hundred and twenty
miles from each other, we hasten our march as much as
possible.

October 7ᵗʰ. We came to a scaffold of meat which the
hunters had made. Three of us leading horses very carelessly
approached it; but quickly wheeled about, as we saw it in
possession of a large Bear,[1] who showed us his paws and teeth
in proof that he was the lawful owner, but not liking the
Horses he walked off, and we quietly took what he had left.
This day the hunters were fortunate in killing two cow Bisons[2]
and four Mountain Sheep,[3] all in good condition; we marched

---

[1] Doubtless a Grizzly Bear, *Ursus horribilis* Ord. [E. A. P.]
[2] *Bison bison* (Linn.). [E. A. P.]
[3] *Ovis canadensis* Shaw. [E. A. P.]

only eight miles and camped to split and dry the meat by smoke: we continued with much bad weather, hunting for our livelihood till the 13th, on which day we arrived at the Columbia River; the next day I sent Men with the Horses to the east side of the Mountains, where the Horses are to pass the winter, the grass there is scant but there is not much snow, whereas the snow here in the winter is very deep, and the country too rude to allow the Horses to pass to where there is less snow and plenty of grass. We waited here to the 21st October in hopes of seeing the Canoe[1] come down the River as I had received a Letter informing me that such would be the case, during this time the weather became severe, ice formed all along the shores of the Rivers, the Thermometer fell to Zero, and we had near three hundred miles of this River to descend to meet the Horses at the Ilthkoyape Falls, we found ourselves obliged to leave this place, and having hung up a Letter, on the 21st we embarked and proceeded down the River, the snow on the shores was two feet in depth, and deeper in the woods. In the afternoon on one of the dry shoals of the River we came to a herd of eight Rein Deer,[2] they were not shy, and we shot a good Doe, and might have killed two, or three more. The hunters often mentioned to me that they had seen Rein Deer, but I doubted if they were of the same species that is found around Hudson's Bay and the interior country; upon examination I found no difference: the question is from whence do they come, as they are not known in any part of these countries except in the vicinity of the Canoe River, by the head of which they probably have a pass to the east side of the Mountains.

[1] These were the canoes which were being brought by John McDonald of Garth, J. G. McTavish, and James McMillan across the mountains by the old route at the head of the Saskatchewan river. They turned southward, however, up the Columbia river, and McDonald wintered at old Kootanae House, while McTavish and McMillan met Thompson later at Saleesh House.

[2] *Rangifer montanus* Seton-Thompson. [E. A. P.]

On the 24th we passed the two Narrows, called Dalles,[1] below the second, the River expanded, with slack current, all which for near half a mile was covered with snow, mixed with water, through which we had to force our way with the Poles, but it became so compact, that we had to carry the last three hundred yards. It was cold work, the snow on the shore being full two feet deep; an Indian and his family came to us, he had been working Beaver, when the Snow became too deep; we enquired if the Snow was more than usual, he said he did not know, as he had never left the Village at this season, but now many of them would leave it to hunt furrs, to trade with us. The next day we had to carry four hundred yards on account of the snow covering the River; we came to some families who had fresh Salmon, but they were very poor, necessity made them eatable: all this day the Snow as we descended the River became less, and on the 27th there was none on the shores, and very little in the woods, flocks of Geese were about us and a few Ducks, to us all most agreeable.

On the 30th we arrived all safe thank kind Providence at the Ilthkoyape Falls, and found the Village wholly deserted, they had separated for hunting, to procure clothing of leather. We had expected to meet Men and Horses to convey the goods across the country to the trading Posts, but seeing no person, the next day we went off on foot for the Spokane house, and on the third of November we arrived,[2] very tired having seen nothing worth notice; and having procured Horses we proceeded for the place we had left and on the

[1] The upper of these is Death Rapids, dangerous of passage at all times of the year, and on several occasions fatally so. The lower is the Little Dalles, just above Revelstoke; and the expansion of the river is the beginning of the Arrow lakes. [T. C. E.]

[2] As soon as Thompson arrived at Spokane House, he sent off a letter to Finan McDonald, who appears to have been at Kullyspell House, to keep watch on the Kootenay river for the canoes which were being brought by John McDonald of Garth,

sixth arrived at the Columbia. In all our late journeys we found a great difference in travelling to what we had in the spring of the year, then the Brooks were swollen every one a torrent dangerous to pass; now every Brook we could ford with safety; the water low, and no overflowed ground.

On the evening of the 13th we arrived at the Saleesh River,[1] Geese and Ducks were about, the weather mild like April, the grass green, and everything as pleasing as this month could present: The two Men I had sent to the Lake Indians to inform them of my arrival, returned and said they found them all gambling, and doing nothing else, and left them at the same; upon which I sent them word that if they wished to procure Guns, Kettles, and other articles they must hunt and procure furrs and dry provisions, or they would get nothing, it had the desired effect; and we proceeded by land up this fine River. We arrived at the Saleesh House,[2] which we found in a ruinous state, here we learned our steady enemies the Peeagans had sent a War Party to intercept us, thinking we must pass by the head of the River; they had come on a Tent of Kootanae Indians, and disregarding the Peace between them had put every one to death; such

[1] The distance from Spokane House to the north end of the " Skeetshoo Road " was about seventy-five miles. The trail ran eastward, just north of the city of Spokane, to Rathdrum, then north by Spirit lake to Hoodoo lake and to the Pend d'Oreille river about opposite Laclede station on the Great Northern Railway. This road was used by Ross Cox on the famous race-horse Le Bleu in the spring of 1813, when he made the distance in about eight hours (see *Adventures*, pp. 216–17). [T. C. E.]

[2] Saleesh House was situated near the south-eastern end of Thompson's Prairie in Sanders county, Montana. The river valley for nearly twenty miles to the south-east is quite narrow; and just above the mouth of Thompson river, where the hills close in abruptly, there is a cliff of shell rock known to the Indians as Bad Rock. About twelve miles farther up, the valley widens into another prairie known to the later fur-traders as the Horse Plains, but now designated by the railway station called Plains. The battle-ground to which Thompson refers was on these Horse Plains. [T. C. E.]

is the peace they make : and meeting three of the Iroquois hunters, stripped them naked and robbed them of all they had. The House was situated in a small bay of the river, close to us was a spur of the hills which came on the River in a cliff of about sixty feet in height, beyond which to the south eastward the country opened out to a great extent of fine meadow ground, the scene of many a battle ; the Saleesh Indians with their allies, when hard pressed, always made for this rock as their natural defence, and which had always proved a shield to them, and [they] shewed us, the bones of their enemies slain at different times in attempting to force this pass ; to me it appeared easy to become master of it, to proceed farther up the River was to be still more exposed.

On the 24th we were agreeably surprised by the appearance of Messrs John George McTavish [1] and James McMillan in company with fifteen men, and ten horses carrying about twelve hundred pounds weight of merchandize for trading furrs.[2] As the season was late an assortment of Goods to load six Horses was made up and Mr Finan McDonald having fortunately found the Saleesh Indians about twenty five miles higher up the River, had traded a large canoe load of dried Provisions, and now also arrived, which enabled Mr John

[1] John George McTavish was the partner of the North-West Company who negotiated the purchase of the Pacific Fur Company with McDougall at Astoria in the autumn of 1813. He now arrived by way of the " Kootanae Road," and established his headquarters at Spokane House. He remained upon Columbian waters until at least 1814 ; he was one of the large party that set off up the river from Fort George on April 4, 1814 (see Coues, *New Light*, p. 873). [T. C. E.]

[2] According to Thompson's notes, these men arrived about 11 A.M. on November 25, having left John McDonald of Garth at Kootanae House on October 16. This was the party that had been sent from Rainy Lake House to bring goods and supplies to Thompson when it was learned that he would not arrive with his consignment of furs that summer. McTavish left for the lower " settlement " on November 27, while McMillan and Finan McDonald stayed with Thompson at Saleesh House.

THOMPSON'S PRAIRIE, MONTANA, ON WHICH SALEESH HOUSE
WAS SITUATED

(Photograph: T. C. Elliott)

G. M{cTavish and the Men with the Horses and Goods to
proceed to the lower settlement on this River, there to
winter and trade with the Natives. The season, though late
continuing mild and open, M{r Finan M{cDonald with an
assortment of Goods went up the River to trade provisions,
and he returned with all they could spare ; all the dried
provisions are of Bison meat, and must be carefully kept for
the voyage of next summer ; so that for the winter we
depend for subsistence on the Antelopes ; they are in sufficient
numbers, but the hunting is precarious. When the ground is
soft with rain in the open Cypress Woods they are easily
approached, but sometimes the ground is white with snow
and a slight frost, the tread of the Hunter is heard, and
approach is almost impossible, but when several hunters are
out, the Antelopes in running from one Hunter come in the
way of another, and are shot : We continued repairing, in
some cases rebuilding our Houses, and by the 16{th December
we were all under shelter, and strange to say, the Roofs kept
out the rain, but the melting of a smart shower of snow
dropped through in many places.

On the twentieth the Antelopes [1] became numerous. They
all came from the lower part of the River, the Snow having
become too deep on the Basalt Hills on the south side of the
Columbia, through which M{cGillivray's, the Saleesh and
Spokane Rivers pass in Falls and Cataracts : these Hills as I
have already noticed intercept the winds from the Pacific
Ocean, and receive all the Snow, which obliges all the Animals
to go to the eastward, where there is very little snow ; and
which makes these countries the favorite resort of the Indians
and the Deer during winter. As we were all anxious to find
a place of greater security for a trading post,[2] on the afternoon
of the 20{th, with an Indian and one Man with three Horses

---

[1] Deer, probably mostly *Odocoileus hemionus*. [E. A. P.]
[2] In his notes Thompson says that it was "in order to remove ourselves further from the Peagans."

we set off to examine the south branch of this River,[1] the
confluence of which is a few miles above the House; when
we had gone about four miles we came to the three Tents,
in one of which was a fine old Indian whom we had named
" le bon Vieux," smoking with him, we explained the object
of our journey; looking at our Horses he told us they were
too poor for the country of the south Branch, which was
hilly and required strong Horses, and sent a young man to
bring three of his Horses, which he lent us for the journey;
sending ours to feed and rest; In the afternoon of the next
day we came to a few Tents, the Men were all away hunting
the Deer by surrounding them, in the evening they arrived
with eight deer, they would have killed a few more if they
had more Men, as they were only twenty two Men and Lads,
whereas thirty Men are required for this mode of hunting;
and although they have several fine active young women,
they are never employed in hunting, but restricted to what
are considered feminine duties. Having examined the country
for full thirty miles; we found the River to be about eighty
to one hundred and fifty yards in width about three feet
deep, and a strong current, flowing thro' a hilly country,
clothed with good short grass and open woods of Cypress
and Firs, with Aspins in the low ground, and from the top
of a Hill the country to the south eastward, from whence
the River came, appeared the same and hilly lands, and from
what we saw, the Hills came boldly on the River and left no
space of low ground; and on the twenty fourth we returned
to the House. The weather was so mild the Deer were
approaching the Hills. Swans, Geese and Ducks were in the
River; and we had to send Men and a Canoe to the great
Camp for Deer, they brought eighteen Antelopes, which

[1] About thirty miles south-east of the site of Saleesh House, the
Flathead and Missoula rivers join together and form the present Clark's
Fork of the Columbia; the south branch to which Thompson here refers
is the Missoula river, or as it is now officially known, the Clark's Fork
river. [T. C. E.]

were most welcome. And the rest of the Month was spent
in hunting, and building a large Canoe of Cedar Wood;
and thus the year closed thank God, with our being all well,
notwithstanding much exposure to the weather and frequent
want of food. The lowest point of the Thermometer was
+0 on the 17th day.

CHAPTER XIV

FROM SALEESH HOUSE TO MONTREAL

Council of peace between Peeagans and Saleesh Indians—Council among the Saleesh Indians and their allies—War between Saleesh Indians and the Peeagans—Canadian Trappers—Saleesh Lake—Peeagans attack Fort on the Missisourie—Sketches of the Rocky Mountains—Start out for Lake Superior—Horse and kettle stolen by an Indian—Arrive at carrying place across the Mountains—Height of land—Reach Mr William Henry's Post on the Athabasca—Arrive at Slave River—Arrive at Isle à la Crosse—Arrive at Cumberland—Arrive at Fort William—Danger of the rest of the journey on account of the war between Great Britain and the United States—Arrive safe at Montreal.

THE Peeagans and their allies, for these two years past, had been anxiously watching the progress of the tribes on the west side of the Mountains in procuring Arms and Ammunition, and their boldness in hunting the Bison on part of their old lands. The Peeagans were the frontier and most powerful tribe and covered their allies from many [an] attack; they were safe, and no retaliation could be made on them, the Peeagans bore the brunt of the war. Deeply sensible of this, five respectable Men had approached the camp on horseback and called to the Saleesh for five old Men to meet them, as they wished for Peace: this was accorded, and on meeting, the Peeagans briefly explained to them, that their people had held a great council, and were desirous of making peace with them and their allies, upon which they were invited to the camp, a Tent provided for them, into which they entered, their Horses were taken to pasture, the best of provisions set before them, and smoking in common pipes took place; in the meantime the Saleesh held a private council, in which they agreed to return the answer, that they would willingly make a sure peace, if it could be depended on, but the affair was of too much consequence for them to decide and they must take the sense of their allies, at the same time remarking that they saw none of their allies with them. The Peeagans replied our Allies do more harm to us than to you, for on pretence of making an inroad on you, they often steal our Horses. And after some conversation an answer was to be given at the end of the time of one Moon. The evening passed away in amicable enquiries after the wounded and the missing, particularly the Women and children; the Saleesh spoke to them that the white men had told them, that it was a disgrace to them to kill Women and Children, and if War should continue they would make prisoners of them, but not destroy them. The next morning their horses were brought, some dried Provisions given them and they returned. After some consultation, messengers were sent to the different tribes accustomed to hunt the Bison in company with the Saleesh, requesting them to send some of their Chiefs to the Council to be held near the House of the White Men, to consider whether they would be for Peace, or continue the War. From every tribe several of the most respectable Men came, and were now assembled; of the Shawpatins only two came, but they were remarkably fine, tall, good looking, well dressed Men, they said their tribe was hunting near their enemies and could spare no more, and that they came with the mouth of their people. We were invited to attend; with Michel the Interpreter and two men, we took our place; Michel informed us that from the expressions he heard he expected a severe contest of opinions; The Saleesh Chief spoke first, briefly reminding them for what purpose they were assembled, to allow the aged Men to speak first, and each tribe to speak truly the mouth of their people. He then sat down in his place, next to the old men, the smoking continued for a few minutes in silence, when an old Spokane throwing aside his robe showed a breast well marked with scars, and in a tone of bitterness, said, So our enemies have proposed peace, how often have they done so, and whenever we trusted to their mouths, we separated into small parties for hunting the Bison, and in this situation they were sure to attack us, and destroy the Women and children, who is there among us that has not cut off his hair several times, and mourned over our relations and friends, their [flesh] devoured, and their bones gnawed, by Wolves and Dogs. A state of peace has always been a time of anxiety, we were willing to trust and sure to be deceived ; who is there among us all that believes them ; then waving his hand over the old men, [he] continued, we were foremost in the battle ; but now we can only defend the Tents with the Women and Children. Do as you please, I now sleep all night, but if you make peace I shall sleep in the day, and watch all night. Several of the old men followed, in much the same feeling of insecurity, yet wishing for peace, if it could be depended on ; for they were now too old for active warfare ; several from the other Tribes all made speeches and spoke freely, yet calmly of the line of conduct to be followed by them, then the Saleesh Orator in his usual flowery, declamatory language, which seemed to make no impression : after some conversation, the Saleesh Chief rose up, and made a long, and animated speech, following the harangues of each Tribe, and concluded by saying, you all know we are the frontier tribe, the enemies must break thro' or elude us, before they can attack you, it is our Horses they steal, and our Men that are slain in battle far more than any other people, as a proof of the truth of what I say, we have now twenty Tents of Women who have

no husbands, with their children, whose fathers are in the
land of Spirits, and as many tents of aged Women whose
Sons have fallen in battle; the different speakers have all
noticed the arrival of the White Men among us for these
three years bringing us Gun, Ammunition and shods of iron
for the heads of our arrows. Before their arrival we were
pitiful and could not defend ourselves, we are as well armed
as our enemies, and our last battle has obliged them to give
up to us great part of our lands for hunting the Bison. Now
we do not fear to war with them, but it is a hard life to be
constantly watching, and the lives of our Women and Children
liable to be destroyed; to prevent this harassed state of life
I am very willing to make peace, but who are we to make
peace with. It is the Peeagans only to offer us peace, none
of their allies were with them, and peace with the Peeagans
will not prevent their allies from making war with us. We
wished for Peace, but we do not see how we can obtain it.
Let us hear what the Chief of the White Men says, he is well
acquainted with all the people on the other side of the
Mountains, his mouth is straight, he will tell us who they
are, and what can be our hopes of peace. My reply was,
You are all of the belief that the Great Spirit has made the
ground to look green, and hates to see it red with the blood
of Men and war is the cause of the ground being red : the
enemies you have against you are the three tribes of the
Peeagans, they have all the same mouth, the next to them
are the people of the Rapids, they are on the Missisourie,
eastward of those named are the Susseekoon, they are not
many, and no one learns their speech, then the Assinikoon,
they are very numerous, and speak well; over all these
people the Peeagans have no control, and cannot prevent
their making war on you, so that your making peace with
the tribe which proposes peace to you, will not ensure your
being in safety from the other tribes for they do not offer
to make peace with you ; my advice is, that you do not make

peace with only one Tribe, and leave yourselves exposed to
the inroads of all the others, and let your Answer [be] that
you claim by ancient rights the freedom of hunting the
Bison, that you will not make War upon any of them but shall
always be ready to defend yourselves; the Chief said my
advice was good; but the Men in the prime of life, remarked,
that if they promised never to make inroads on them, this
would place the Tents of their Wives and Children in safety,
and leave the Men to war on whom they pleased, as their
Tents would be safe; we are now as well armed as they are;
while we had no Guns, nor iron heads for our arrows, we had
to yield to them, and were called cowards. We must therefore show ourselves on their lands, as they have been seen
on our grounds, and for which purpose we are ready. Silence
ensued for a few minutes; when the Chief again took up his
speech. You have all heard what has been said, and from
the Chief of the White Men we know the names and numbers
of our enemies; and learn there can be no hopes of peace.
It has been truly said, our enemies have often been seen on
our lands and have left their marks in blood, we are not now
as we were then, and those that are for war, shall have a fair
field to show themselves in, for in the summer at the time
the Bull Bisons become fat, we shall then not only hunt
upon the lands we claim, but extend our hunting on the
lands of the Peeagans, which will be sure to bring on a battle
between us, and you may all prepare yourselves for that time,
and our answer to the Peeagans shall be, " that as we are now,
such we will remain." They all signified their assent by
repeated Oy Oy Oy, and after smoking they quietly went to
their Tents. The next day Messengers were sent to their
allies, to notify them of what had passed, and that war must
be prepared for. The next day the Chief, the Orator and
some old Men, came to the House and discoursed a long
time; their opinions were not all the same, but all came to
the same conclusion, that they could not make a peace that

would place them in safety and give them the freedom of hunting in small parties; you see the hearts of our men are sore. We have suffered so much from those on the east side of the Mountains that we must now show ourselves to be men, and make ourselves respected, we shall muster strong, but although the Shawpatins are many and good Warriors, they cannot send many men to our assistance, as they are the frontier tribe on the south, and next to them is the great tribe of the Snake Indians of the Straw Tents, who are their enemies. We advised them to be cautious, saying you cannot afford to lose many men, and you have already about forty Tents of Widows and aged Women to maintain. Time passed on. August came, when the Bull Bisons are fat. The Chief kept his word, and at the appointed time a strong party was formed, and marched to the hunting of the Bison. With these people when they went on the Bison grounds two or three men were sent to assist the Chief in encourageing them to make dried provisions, and do what they could to prevent gambling, in which they lose much time, the two Men now sent were Michel Bourdeaux the Interpreter, and Michel Kinville who also spoke the language, they were the sole survivors of about three hundred and fifty free hunters [1] almost all of them of french origen; the hunting was carried on with cautious boldness into the lands of their enemies, this insult brought on a battle; the Saleesh and their allies had chosen their ground, on a grassy ridge with sloping ground behind it. Horses were not brought into action, but only used to watch each others motions; the ground chosen gave the Saleesh a clear view of their enemies, and concealed their own numbers. The action was on the green plains, no Woods were near; the Peeagans and their allies cautiously

---

[1] This number must be taken as approximate, and applicable to free-hunters of either Algonquin, Iroquois, or mixed blood that had been killed by the Piegan or Blackfeet during Thompson's acquaintance with the tribe. [T. C. E.]

advanced to the attack, their object being to ascertain the strength of their enemies before they ventured a general attack, for this purpose they made slight attacks on one part of the line, holding the rest in check, but no more force was employed against them than necessary, thus most of the day passed. At length in the afternoon, a determination was taken to make a bold attack and try their numbers. Every preparation being made, they formed a single line of about three feet from each other, and advanced singing and dancing, the Saleesh saw the time was come to bring their whole force into line, but they did not quit their vantage ground ; they also sung and danced their wild war dance ; the Peeagans advanced to within about one hundred and fifty yards, the song and the dance ceased, the wild war yell was given, and the rush forward ; it was gallantly met, several were slain on each side, and three times as many wounded, and with difficulty the Peeagans carried off their dead and wounded and they accounted themselves defeated : In the assault both Michel Bourdeaux and Michel Kinville were shot dead. They were the last of those free hunters. I deeply regretted them. I found them brave faithful and intelligent. The combatan[t]s were about three hundred and fifty on each side, the loss in killed and wounded made them withdraw to where they could hunt in safety. War in the open plains between the Natives is very different from War in the woods ; in the former they act as a body in concert in all their movements, in the Woods it is almost Man to Man.

Christmas and New Years days came and passed. We could not honour them, the occupations of every day demanded our attentions ; and time passed on, employed in hunting for a livelihood. On the 15th January the ground was entirely bare of snow even on part of the Hills, and the rest of the month had many rainy days ; Swans were numerous, and many flocks of Geese with a few Ducks.

In February with an Indian and a Man I examined the

country to the south eastward,[1] it was hilly, with sufficient woods of Aspin Cypress and some Pines and Firs with Cedar in places, having several Brooks of good water will become a fine country for raising Sheep, Cattle and Horses. A few days afterwards we made an excursion to the Saleesh Lake, and beyond it, the Lake is a fine sheet of water of about twenty miles in length by three to four miles in width; the haunt in all seasons of aquatic fowl, the country around especially to the eastward and southward for many miles very fine, and will become a rich agricultural country, for which its mild climate is very favorable; on the fine grounds many battles have been fought, the bones of the slain mark the places. These meadows are admirably adapted for hunting the Antelope by surrounding them, but this mode is not attempted with the Red Deer, they are too bold to be encircled, though frequently driven over high steep banks; it was from about the Lake most of our winter provisions came. At the end of the month several Indians of a Tribe we had [not] yet seen came to trade, they informed us, that near the time of one Moon past the Meadow Indians (the Peeagans and their Allies) had attacked a Fort built at the head of the south branch of the Missisourie River; the account they gave was that a number of free hunters[2] had come up the Missisourie River to trap Beaver and proceed to the Snake Indian country, but that tempted by hunting the Bison, and making dried provisions they had built a Fort on the above River, and had been successful in trapping Beaver and hunting; they had extended their hunting excursions beyond the bounds of prudence, and their shots had been heard by the Indians of the Plains, these

---

[1] For Thompson's travels this winter, see itinerary.

[2] The identity of this party of American trappers cannot be ascertained. Andrew Henry and his party were on the Upper Missouri that winter, after spending the winter of 1810–11 on the headwaters of the Snake river. Other traders came up from Lisa's Fort at the mouth of the Big Horn river in eastern Montana. The southern branch of the Missouri would naturally be taken to be the Yellowstone. [T. C. E.]

ever watchful people ever alive to what is passing soon found by their scouts, that a strong house was built on their lands ; they had for several years been hostile to the Trappers who destroyed the Beaver on their lands and had shot several of them, for the loss of the Beaver deprived them of the means of supplying by trade their wants ; they formed a strong party and approached the fort, they first made themselves masters of the port holes of the bastions, and then cut down two of the Stockades, but was prevented from entering by a heavy fire from the house, the battle continued for some time and the Meadow Indians retired ; my informant said he had lately been there, and found [entry to] the House through the door and the windows marked by many round balls, and the Stockades with very many rifle balls ; these Men had ten killed whom they buried in a pit which they filled with stones and set a single Cross on it ; they then retreated to the camp of the Snake Indians, where they arrived in a famished state. He knew nothing of their wounded ; nor the loss of the Meadow Indians, they had taken [them] away to the perogues, four of them he described as long and about five feet in width, in which the Indians descended the River.   All these free Hunters come infatuated with the idea that the Indians are cowards, and that they themselves are the bravest of men, for which they have dearly paid.

For these four years I have occasionally sketched off various parts of the bold, lofty scenery of the Rocky Mountains about twenty different views, part on each side of the Mountains, and also Mount Nelson, which stands alone in native grandeur, I believe the only drawings that have been made of these Mountains, but North America being an obscure part of the world, especially the interior of Canada they would not pay a lithographic publication ; By the 13th March the season, apparently was sufficiently advanced to hope that we should have a safe voyage to Lake Superior, there to exchange the Furrs for Merchandize ; and praying good Providence to protect us, we embarked, and went down the Saleesh River to the carrying place road, to the Columbia River, over this Road the cargoes of the canoes were transported by Horses :[1] on the 30th early we perceived a small Kettle and one of our best horses had been stolen by a young man ; the same day we came to three Tents, and to the Men related what had happened, remarking to them, this was the first theft we had known among them ; they appeared much hurt at a theft being committed by any of their people, and said he had acted very badly, the Horse and Kettle were not their property and they could not take them from him, but would show us his Tent ; in the evening we camped, and two Men came to us and staid all night. Early in the morning I sent two Men with the two Indians who guided the Men to the Tent but did nothing more, the Men made him give up the Horse and the Kettle, and gave him a few kicks to disgrace him ; the Natives who heard of this theft thought it a disgrace to the tribe but never thought they had a right to punish it, that belonged to the injured person, or party.

Up to the 22nd of April[2] we had been employed in carrying all the Furrs, Provisions and Baggage to the Ilthkoyape Falls of the Columbia River, and building two Canoes of Cedar boards, and two of Birch Rind, which with the two

[1] That is, they went by canoes all the way from Thompson's Prairie down Clark's Fork and across Pend d'Oreille lake and down Pend d'Oreille river to the Skeetshoo Road ; then by horses to Kettle Falls by way of Spokane House. [T. C. E.]

[2] In his note-books at this point, Thompson gives the record of a rough survey of a route from Ilthkoyape Falls up Ilthkoyape Brook (Kettle river), across to Osoyoos lake, up the river, through Okanagan lake, across country to the Shewap (Shooswap) river, and down this river to the Shewap village, in latitude 51° 67' N., longitude 119° 48' W. There is no statement as to who made the survey ; but as Thompson obtained the survey of the Fraser river from John Stuart it is probable that this survey was also made by Stuart, doubtless in 1813, when he was on his way from Harmon's Post on Stuart's lake to join J. G. McTavish on the Columbia river. Evidence of this survey may be seen on Thompson's map.

Canoes left here, placed six Canoes at our service. On the 22nd two of the Canoes were loaded with twenty five packs, two with twenty packs, each and two with sixteen packs, in all one hundred and twenty two packs, each weighing ninety pounds; and each canoe three hundred pounds of dried provisions, with five men to each Canoe, to proceed up the Columbia River to the carrying place leading across the Mountains. We had hoped that we should find the shores of the River clear of Snow, but on the 28th, we found the snow six inches in depth, and the next day, the snow increased to four feet in depth, and so solid that we sank only about four to six inches when walking on it, and although the weather was mild, yet such a depth of snow was disheartening, for after a hard day's work, we had to lie down on the snow, our feet and legs, benumbed by leading the canoes up the rapids; but there was no help we had to march on. On the fifth of May we arrived at the Mountain Carrying Place;[1] a light Canoe and five men had come down the River to help us, here I left the Canoes to dry the Packs of Furrs and get everything in good order to cross the Mountains so soon as the Snow permitted; having made for ourselves Bears Paws, which are rough made snow shoes round at each end, with three hunters [I] set off to cross the Mountains to the east side. These hunters informed me, that although the Columbia River had no Beaver, yet all the Brooks and Streams that flowed into the River had many Beavers. On the 8th at noon we gained the height of land, having with great labor ascended the hills which were under deep snow, mixed with icicles from the dropings of the Trees, which made very severe walking; a short distance after we began our ascent we crossed a Brook where the Beavers had been walking on

---

[1] This was Boat Encampment, the western end of the trail across Athabaska Pass. Thompson thus opened in person the trade route up the Columbia river and across the Rocky Mountains with a large shipment of furs for the Montreal market. [T. C. E.]

the snow, one of them had been surprised and destroyed by a Wolverene. On the east side we had made a hoard of Meat, on which we depended for a supply but found it broken up, and the Meat destroyed by a large grizled Bear, and we had to march on without provisions. The mild weather causes heavy avalanches of Snow in the Mountains, which, thank Good Providence we escaped. At the height of land, where we camped in January last year and where my Men expressed their fears of an avalanche coming on them, and which then appeared to me not likely to happen from the direction I supposed they would take, we found an avalanche had taken place, and the spot on which we then camped was covered with an avalanche, which had here spent its force, in heaps of snow in wild forms round which we walked. On the 11th May, early the Men sent forward arrived with three Horses which relieved us of carrying our baggage, and the same day [we] arrived at the House of Mr William Henry, who had everything in good order.

We now set to work to get a Canoe ready, making paddles, poles and [collecting] Gum for the Voyage, but having no provisions and sick of horse meat, sent off the Hunters, who brought four sheep, an animal peculiar to these Mountains, and by the Americans named Big Horn. This was enough for our present supply, and being now on the lands of the Bison and Red Deer, we trusted to our Guns for a future supply : agreements were made with the Hunters to supply the people with meat at the rate of the value of three beaver skins for a Bison or Red Deer in such articles as they wanted. On the 13th we embarked on our voyage to Fort William on Lake Superior ; on the 20th we arrived at the sortie of the Slave River into this, the Athabasca River ; having come before a strong current 340 miles ; the lower we proceed the more the country is just clearing from winter, a few willows budding, tolerable days, but keen frosty nights ; we were much delayed by the floating ice in the River, and as usual lost time in taking Observations for Latitude, Longitude and the Variation of the Needle whenever the weather permitted; continuing our voyage by the early part of June we had shot many Swans, Geese and Ducks. On examining them, very few had eggs in them ready to lay, whereas on the west side of the Mountains all these Fowl had their nests made, and were sitting on their eggs in the very early part of March; which proves that in every respect, the climate on the west side of the Mountains is full three months in advance of the climate on the east side.[1] On the fourth of June we put ashore to hunt and killed two Bison Bulls. I have already remarked that all the Bisons that take to the Woods, become much larger than those of the plains, these were so, their horns from tip to tip measured two feet, and on the curve twenty eight inches, and when fat [they] must weigh at least two thousand pounds.[2]

On the evening of June 6th we arrived at the old trading Post of Isle a la Crosse, famous for it's fine White Fish, which is a Fish peculiar to the northern Lakes of this Continent; only part of this Lake was open; from the Beaver River a short distance, of this part the ice on the shore was three feet thick, the weather cold to shivering; one of my poor fellows remarked, that we had been travelling from the beginning of March to part of June, and were more deeply in winter than when we began the Voyage. The great difference in

[1] This statement is much exaggerated. As a matter of fact there is very little difference in the time of nesting on the east and west side of the mountains. [E. A. P.]

[2] A northern race of the bison has been separated as a sub-species under the name *Bison bison athabascæ* Rhoads, the type being taken from the country immediately south of Great Slave lake, where herds aggregating a few hundreds still exist. Before northern specimens had been examined by mammalogists, the animal had been extirpated over most of its former habitat, so that the exact limits of range of the northern race will never be known. In view of Thompson's intimate acquaintance with the bison of the plains, his statement that the two here killed were of the woodland form is thus of distinct scientific value. The locality was on Beaver river, in latitude 54° 18′ N., longitude 109° W. [E. A. P.]

climate struck me very forcibly; especially on the future cultivation of these countries; yet this very place, a few days after the ice has left the Lake has a fine warm summer; Barley, Oats, and sometimes Wheat come to maturity, and good gardens of all the common vegetables; for the Lake moderates the frosts and cold of Autumn: Between fifty and sixty small Canoes of Chepawyans were here. These people have worked their way from the rocky regions of the cold North, southerly to this place. This present race have learned to build small Canoes of Birch Rind, and almost every way imitate their neighbours the Nahathaway Indians; who are also progressing to the southward. We waited three days for the ice to break up and give us a free passage, which took place late on the ninth; and early on the tenth, in company with nine loaded Canoes each carrying twenty five packs of Furrs, each weighing ninety pounds. On the thirteenth we went among some low grassy islets in hope of finding eggs, the nests were mostly made, but as yet no eggs laid. On the evening of the seventeenth we had the first Musketoes, the intolerable plague and curse of all the countries on the east side of the Mountains, and on the evening of the next day, thank Good Providence we arrived safe at Cumberland House. From hence to Lake Superior has been already described. On the twelfth of July we arrived at Fort William, the trading depot of the North West Company. Here we had a respite in some manner from the torment of Musketoes and Midges: much as I suffered, the Men suffered still more, they had to bear them and work hard, and at night got no sound sleep; smoke was of no avail against them, they could bear more than we could. On the fifteenth a vessel arrived with the news that War had been declared by the United States, against Great Britain and we were warned to be on our guard; this made us all look very serious, for the whole returns of the Company were yet here, getting ready to be sent to Montreal; everything was expedited every exertion made to get the Furrs sent off, in which we were well seconded by the Men, who alarmed at the chance of being made prisoners, and thus deprived of seeing their families and enjoying their wages were most anxious to arrive at Montreal : we had only a short distance to dread being captured, being the Falls of St Maries and the Straits to Lake Huron, once in this Lake we held ourselves to be safe, by passing to, and down, the Ottawa River; in which thank good Providence we succeeded, and by the middle of August with the Men and Furrs we were safe in Montreal.

LIST OF WORKS CITED

BALLANTYNE, ROBERT M.

"Hudson's Bay, or Every-day Life in the Wilds of North America, during Six Years' Residence in the Territories of the Honourable Hudson's Bay Company." Edinburgh, 1848. Pp. x, 328.

BIGSBY, JOHN J.

"The Shoe and Canoe, or Pictures of Travel in the Canadas." Two vols. London, 1850. Pp. xv, 352 ; viii, 346.

BRYCE, GEORGE.

"Mackenzie, Selkirk, Simpson." (Makers of Canada Series.) Toronto, 1910. Pp. 305.

BURPEE, LAWRENCE J.

"The Search for the Western Sea: the Story of the Exploration of North-Western America." Toronto [1908]. Pp. lx, 651.

CHITTENDEN, HIRAM MARTIN.

"The American Fur Trade of the Far West: a History of the Pioneer Trading Posts and Early Fur Companies of the Missouri Valley and the Rocky Mountains, and of the Overland Commerce with Santa Fe." Three vols. New York, 1902. Pp. xxv, 1029.

COOK, JAMES.

"A Voyage to the Pacific Ocean undertaken by the command of His Majesty for making Discoveries in the Northern Hemisphere, performed under the direction of Captains Cook, Clerke, and Gore in His Majesty's ships the *Resolution* and *Discovery*, in the years 1776, 1777, 1778, 1779, and 1780." Three vols. London, 1784. Pp. xcvi, 421 ; 548 ; 564.

COUES, ELLIOTT (Ed.).

"New Light on the Early History of the Greater Northwest: The Manuscript Journals of Alexander Henry, Fur Trader of the North-West Company, and of David Thompson, Official Geographer and Explorer of the same Company, 1799–1814." Three vols. New York, 1897. Pp. xxviii, 1027.

2 N

Cox, Ross.

"The Columbia River; or Scenes and Adventures during a Residence of Six Years on the Western Side of the Rocky Mountains, among Various Tribes of Indians hitherto unknown, together with a Journey Across the American Continent." Two vols. London, 1832. Pp. xx, 233; vi, 350.

Day, Elsie.

"An Old Westminster Endowment." (*Journal of Education*, September, 1885, pp. 1–14.)

Elliott, T. C.

"Peter Skene Ogden, Fur Trader." (*Quarterly of the Oregon Historical Society*, vol. xi, pp. 229–278.)

Franchère, Gabriel.

"Narrative of a Voyage to the Northwest Coast of America in the Years 1811, 1812, 1813, and 1814; or, The First American Settlement on the Pacific." Translated and edited by J. V. Huntington. New York, Redfield, 1854. Pp. 376.

Franklin, Sir John.

"Narrative of a Second Expedition to the Shores of the Polar Sea, in the years 1825, 1826, and 1827, with Appendix." London, 1828. Pp. xxiv, 319; clvii.

Harmon, Daniel Williams.

"A Journal of Voyages and Travels in the Interiour of North America, between the 47th and 58th Degrees of North Latitude, extending from Montreal nearly to the Pacific Ocean." Andover, 1820. Pp. xxiii, 432.

Hearne, Samuel.

"A Journey from Prince of Wales's Fort in Hudson's Bay to the Northern Ocean in the years 1769, 1770, 1771, and 1772." London, 1795. Pp. xliv, 458.

Palliser, John.

"The Journals, Detailed Reports, and Observations relative to the Exploration, by Captain Palliser, of that portion of British North America which in latitude lies between the British Boundary Line and the height of land or watershed of the Northern or Frozen Ocean respectively, and in longitude, between the Western Shore of Lake Superior and the Pacific Ocean during the years 1857, 1858, 1859, and 1860." London, 1863. Pp. 325.

IRVING, WASHINGTON.

"Astoria; or, Enterprise beyond the Rocky Mountains." London, 1839. Pp. 440.

LINDSEY, CHARLES.

"An Investigation of the Unsettled Boundaries of Ontario." Toronto, 1873. Pp. 250.

MACKENZIE, ALEXANDER.

"Voyages from Montreal on the River St. Lawrence, through the Continent of North America, to the Frozen and Pacific Oceans, in the years 1789 and 1793. With a Preliminary Account of the Rise, Progress, and Present State of the Fur Trade of that Country." London, 1801. Pp. cxxxii, 412.

MASSON, L. R.

"Les Bourgeois de la Compagnie du Nord-Ouest: Récits de voyages, lettres, et rapports inédits relatifs au Nord-Ouest canadien, publié avec un esquisse historique et des annotations." Première série. Québec, 1889. Pp. ix, 413. Deuxième série. Québec, 1890. Pp. vi, 499.

MOORE, JOHN BASSETT.

"History and Digest of the International Arbitrations to which the United States has been a party, together with Appendices containing the Treaties relating to such Arbitrations, and Historical and Legal Notes on other International Arbitrations, ancient and modern." Six vols. Washington, 1898. Pp. xcviii, 5240; maps.

ROSS, ALEXANDER.

"Adventures of the First Settlers on the Oregon or Columbia River; being a Narrative of the Expedition fitted out by John Jacob Astor to establish the 'Pacific Fur Company,' with an account of some Indian tribes on the coast of the Pacific." London, 1849. Pp. xvi, 352.

SIMPSON, SIR GEORGE.

"Narrative of a Journey Round the World, during the years 1841 and 1842." Two vols. London, 1847. Pp. xi, 438; vii, 469.

THWAITES, REUBEN GOLD (Ed.).

"Original Journals of the Lewis and Clark Expedition, 1804–1806, printed from the Original Manuscripts in the Library of the American Philosophical Society, and by direction of its Committee on Historical

Documents, together with manuscript material of Lewis and Clark from other sources, including Note-books, Letters, Maps, &c., and the Journals of Charles Floyd and Joseph Whitehouse; now for the first time published in full and exactly as written. With Introduction, Notes, and Index." Seven vols. and atlas. New York, 1904–1905. Pp. xciii, 374; ix, 386; x, 363; x, 372; ix, 395; x, 280; xiii, 534.

TYRRELL, J. B. (Ed.).

"A Journey from Prince of Wales's Fort in Hudson's Bay to the Northern Ocean, in the years 1769, 1770, 1771, and 1772." By Samuel Hearne. New edition, with Introduction, Notes, and Illustrations. Toronto: The Champlain Society, 1911. Pp. xv, 437.

TYRRELL, J. B.

"Brief Narrative of the Journeys of David Thompson." (*Proceedings of the Canadian Institute*, Toronto, 3rd sect., vol. vi, 1887–88, pp. 135–160.)

TYRRELL, J. B.

"Report on the Dubawnt, Kazan, and Ferguson Rivers, and the North-West Coast of Hudson Bay, and on Two Overland Routes from Hudson Bay to Lake Winnipeg." (*Annual Report of the Geological Survey of Canada*, vol. ix, 1895, Part F, pp. 128.)

UMFREVILLE, EDWARD.

"The Present State of Hudson's Bay. Containing a full Description of that Settlement, and the Adjacent Country; and likewise of the Fur Trade, with Hints for its Improvement, &c. &c. To which are added Remarks and Observations made in the Inland Parts, during a residence of near four years; a specimen of five Indian languages; and a Journal of a Journey from Montreal to New York." London, 1790. Pp. vii, 230.

WHEELER, A. O.

"The Selkirk Mountains: a Guide for Mountain Pilgrims and Climbers." Winnipeg, 1912. Pp. 196.

WHITE, JAMES.

"Boundary Disputes and Treaties." (*Canada and its Provinces*, edited by Adam Shortt and Arthur G. Doughty, Toronto, 1914, vol. viii, pp. 751–958.)

WHITE, JAMES (Ed.).

"Handbook of the Indians of Canada, published as an Appendix to the Tenth Report of the Geographic Board of Canada; reprinted by permission of Mr. F. W. Hodge, Ethnologist-in-Charge, from ' Handbook of American Indians North of Mexico,' published as Bulletin 30, Bureau of American Ethnology, and edited by Frederick William Hodge ; reprinted under the direction of James White, F.R.G.S., Secretary, Commission of Conservation." Ottawa, 1913. Pp. x, 632.

WILKES, CHARLES.

" Narrative of the United States Exploring Expedition, during the years 1838, 1839, 1840, 1841, 1842." Five vols. New York, 1856. Pp. lx, 434 ; xv, 476 ; xv, 438 ; xvi, 539 ; xv, 558.

INDEX

Abies balsamea, 115
—— *grandis*, 387
Abitibi, Lake, 146, 147
Acer glabrum, 387
—— *negundo*, 276, 284, 295
—— *pseudo-platanus*, 276
—— *saccharum*, 274, 275–6, 295
Achorutes, 160
Acipenser rubicundus, 60, 181, 277
Acton House, 88
Acworth, Abram, xxiv
Adams, Thomas, xxv
Albany Factory, 8
Albany river, 8, 146, 147
Alces americanus, 76, 95–7, 185, 306
Alder. *See Alnus*
Alexandria, lxxiv
Algonquin Indians, 79, 194, 311, 312
Allowcatt. *See* Yellepit
Alnus, 387
Alopex lagopus innuitus, 41, 49
Amelanchier alnifolia, 59, 434, 481
Amisk lake, lxxvii
Anas platyrhynchos, 31, 400
Annel, Magnus, lxviii
Antelope. *See Antilocapra americana*
Antilocapra americana, 185, 368
Apistawahshish, 126
Ap-Thomas, name of, xxiii
Aquila chrysætos, 61
Arapaho nation of Indians, 304, 327
Arctostaphylos uva-ursi, 58, 145
Arrow lakes, the, liii, xcv, 540
Arrowhead, xcv
Arrowsmith, maps of, lxii–lxiii, 466
Ash. *See Fraxinus*
Ash House, lxxiv, 213, 241
Ashburton, *Lord*, 176–7
—— Treaty, the, 177
Askeeawawshish, 308
Aspin. *See Populus tremuloides*

Assiniboin (Stone) Indians, xxxi, xciv, 178, 206, 208, 212, 214, 218, 235, 239, 240, 245, 307, 326, 334, 361, 367, 368
Assiniboine (Stone Indian) river, xliv, lxxiii, lxxiv, lxxv, 185, 195, 207, 210, 243, 249
Astor, J. J., 501
Astoria. *See* Fort Astoria
Astur atricapillus, 46, 50
Athabaska expedition, the, xxxvi–xli
—— House, lxxxiii. *See also* Fort Chipewyan
—— Lake, xxxiii, xxxiv, xxxvi, xxxvii, xl, xli, lxxi, lxxxiii, 28, 56, 133, 134, 138, 140, 146–8, 172, 174, 293
—— Pass, xciii, xcviii, 403, 441, 444–9, 556
—— river, xxix, xxxiv, xlv, lii, liii, lxxix, lxxxii, lxxxiii, xciii, xcvi, xcviii, 171, 184, 442, 443, 508, 557
Athalmer, site of, 376
Athapapuskow lake, lxix, lxxxiv, lxxxv
—— river, lxxxv
Athapascan family of Indians, 304
Atsina. *See* Rapid Indians
Aurora borealis, 51, 156–7

Babue, François, 296
Back, *Sir* George, 28, 174–5
Badger. *See Taxidea taxus*
Baker's Bay, 505
Balæna mysticetus, 19
Baldwin, a "Canadian trader," lxvii
Ballantyne, R. M., 28, 109, 298
Ballenden, John, xxvii
Barren Grounds, the, 140–1
Basalt, 290–1, 386, 519, 529
Basswood. *See Tilia americana*
Battleford, site of, lxviii
Battoche, 443

567

Colville river, 466
Comcomly, *Chief*, 505–6
Connelly, xlviii
Cook, *Captain* James, lviii–lix ;
   cited, bdx
—— William, xxix, xxxvii, xxxix,
   lxii, 99
Copper, 291–2
Copperass harbour, 292
Coppermine river, xxvi, lviii, lix, 174
Coregonus, 60, 111, 181, 305
Cormorant. *See Phalacrocorax au-
   ritus*
Corvus brachyrhynchos, 61, 232
—— —— *hesperis*, 454
—— —— *corax principalis*, 49, 113, 400
Coté, Joseph, 442, 443, 449, 453, 472
Coues, Elliott, cited, lxxxix, 281,
   505
Cox, Ross, 501, 541 ; cited, 379
Coxe (" Sandwich islander "), 510–
   11, 533–4
Crab Creek, 485
Cranberry. *See Oxycoccus* and *Vac-
   cinium vitisidæa*
—— lake, xlvii, xlviii, lxx, lxxxiv,
   lxxxv
—— Portage, lxix, lxxxiv, lxxxv
Crane. *See Grus americana* and *G.
   canadensis*
Cree (Nahathaway) Indians, xxxi,
   8, 78–94, 129, 130, 131, 165, 178,
   205, 208, 235, 246, 260, 264, 315–
   17, 319, 326, 361, 367, 559
—— river, 144
Cristivomer namaycush, 41, 43, 59,
   157
Crooked river, lxx
Cross lake, 435
—— Portage, lxvii, 117
Crossbeak. *See Loxia*
Crotalus confluentus lucifer, 482,
   521–5
Crow. *See Corvus*
Crowberry. *See Empetrum nigrum*
Cumberland House, xxviii, xxxi,
   xxxii, xxxiii, xxxv–xxxix, xlviii,
   lxi, lxv, lxvi, lxvii, lxix, lxxi,
   lxxvii, lxxxiv, lxxxv, lxxxvi,
   lxxxix, xcii, xcviii, 53, 146, 147,
   318–19, 434, 438, 559
—— lake, 53, 293, 434
Curlew. *See Numenius borealis* and
   N. hudsonicus
Currant. *See Ribes hudsonianum,
   R. oxyacanthoides,* and *R. rubrum*

Curzon Junction, site of, 389
Cusick, site of, xciv, 412
Cuthbert Grant's House, lxxiii–
   lxxiv, 195

DALLES des Morts, the, liii, xcv–
   xcvi, 540
Dalrymple, Alexander, 28, 173
Dauphin hills, 185
—— lake, lxxii
—— river, lxxii, 182, 185, 193, 436
Davy, Andrew, 118
Day, *Miss* Elsie, xxiv
Dead Sea, the, 281
Death Rapids. *See* Dalles des
   Morts
D'Eau, Baptiste, 443, 449
Deer. *See Odocoileus* and *Cervus
   canadensis*
—— lake, xl
—— Park, site of, xcv
Deers river, xlii
Dejarlaiz, François, 471
Delaware Indians, 79, 265
Delphinapterus catodon, 14, 19, 23–4
Deluge, account of the, 88
Dinnae Indians. *See* Chipewyan
   Indians
Dog Den Butte. *See* Dog Tent Hills
—— lake, lxxxiv
—— river, lxxxiv
—— Tent Hills, 214, 218, 221, 222,
   240, 241
Douglas, David, cited, 465
Duck. *See Anas platyrhynchos,
   Clangula canadensis americana,*
   and *Nettion carolinense*
—— lake, lxviii
—— Portage, lxvii, lxx, 78
—— —— House, lxxi
Duluth, site of, xliv, 272
Du Nord, 443, 446, 449
Dupleix, Louis, xlvii
Dymond, Joseph, 9

EAGLE. *See Aquila chrysætos* and
   Haliæetus leucocephalus alascanus
—— hills, 185, 321
Ectopistes migratorius, 61
Edmonton, xc, 432
Elbow lake, lxx
—— river, lxx
Eldred, Julius, 292
Elk. *See Cervus canadensis*
Ellice, Edward, 169
Elm. *See Ulmus americana*

INDEX

Henry, Andrew, 376, 553
—— William, xcii, 439, 443, 457, 536, 557
Henry's House, xcvi
Hickory. *See Hicoria*
Hicoria, 211
Highwood river. *See* Spitchee river
Hill river, xxxviii
Hipberry. *See Rosa acicularis*
Hodges (Hudson's Bay Company surgeon), 26
Holland, contraband trade with, 7
Holy lake, lxvi
Hood, *Lieutenant*, 174
Hoodoo lake, 541
Hood's river, 174
Horse Plains, the, 541–2
—— Shoe House, lxxxiii
Horses, 179, 214, 330, 334, 367–70, 377–8, 401
Houle (Hoole), Louis Joseph (Francis), 209, 222
Howard, *Surgeon*, 271
Howse, Joseph, l–li, lxxxvi, xc, 415, 458
—— Pass, l, lxxxvi, 416
Hudson Bay, xxvi, xlii, lviii, lxv, lxvi, lxvii; description of, 8, 29; life at a trading post on, 30–54; country about, 56
—— —— Railway, 55, 117
—— George, 319
—— Strait, 8, 39
Hudson's Bay Company, Thompson apprenticed to, xxiv–xxv, 3; competes with North-West Company for trade with Muskrat country, xxxiv–xxxix, 133–4; Thompson leaves service of, xli, lxxi, 169; gets credit for Thompson's map, lxii; policy of, 142, 171, 173–4; builds first inland posts, 318–19; is amalgamated with North-West Company, lxiii, 106; crosses Rocky Mountains, l–li; employs surgeons, 26; sends out three ships a year to Hudson Bay, 27
Hudson's House, Lower, xxviii–xxix, xxx, lxv, lxix, 319
—— Upper, xxxiv, lxix, lxxxviii, 319
Huggemowequan, 97
Hughes, James, xlv, lxxix, lxxxi, cx, 406, 432
Hungry Hall, lxix

Hunter, *Dr.* John, 270
Huron, Lake, liv, xcviii, 560
Hutchins, Thomas, xxv, 147

IDAHO, state of, xlix, lviii, lxxxvii
Ignace (Iroquois guide), 460, 472
Ilthkoyape Brook. *See* Kettle river
—— Falls. *See* Kettle Falls.
—— Indians, 467
Indian lake, xlvii, xlviii, lxxxv, 28
—— Rapids, 494, 520
Indians. *See* names of tribes and nations
Inspaelis, 478–80
Iroquois Indians, 205, 311–17, 457, 535
Irving, Washington, lxii, 501; cited, 505
Isaac Todd, the, 508
Isaac's House, lxix
Island Fort, 321
Isle à la Crosse, xlv, lxxviii, xcviii, 28, 558
—— —— lake, lxxviii, lxxix
Itasca lake, lxxvi
Ithenootosequan lake. *See* Elbow lake

JAMES Bay, 8
Jarvis, E., 147
Jay, Canada. *See Perisoreus canadensis*
Jefferson (second in command at Churchill), 11, 26
Jennings, John, xxvii
—— site of, 376, 430, 459
Jérémie, cited, lxvii
Jocko Creek, xcvii, 416
John Day Rapids, 495, 520
—— river, 494, 520
Jordan river, 280
Joseph's Prairie, 389
Jumbo Hill, xcvii
Juniper. *See Juniperus sabina*
Juniperus sabina, 58
Jussomme, René, 209, 210, 212, 222, 226, 235, 239

KABINAKAGAMI lake, 147
—— river, 147
Kalichen Falls, 476
Kalispell, site of, li, 458
Kaministikwia, xlviii
—— river, lxxxii, lxxxiv
Kayaks, 16, 21
Kazan river, 16, 131

2 O

THE END

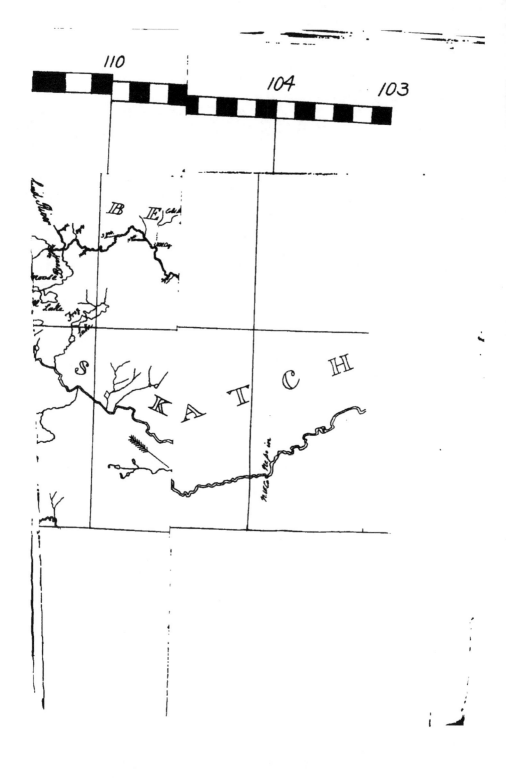

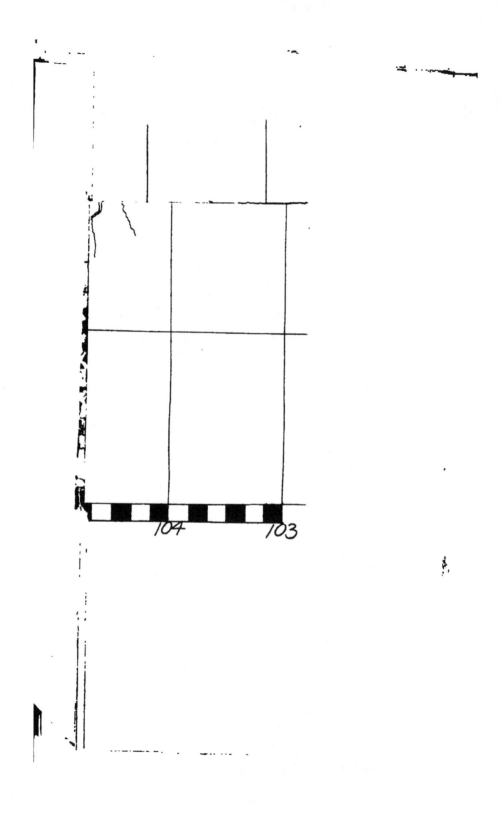

104   103

CPSIA information can be obtained
at www.ICGtesting.com
Printed in the USA
LVHW051748170520
655861LV00004B/177

9 781375 641623